HIS INVENTION
SO FERTILE

By the same author

His Invention So Fertile

A Life of Christopher Wren

Adrian Tinniswood

OXFORD
UNIVERSITY PRESS
2001

OXFORD
UNIVERSITY PRESS

Oxford   New York

Athens   Auckland   Bangkok   Bogotá   Buenos Aires   Cape Town
Chennai   Dar es Salaam   Delhi   Florence   Hong Kong   Istanbul   Karachi
Kolkata   Kuala Lumpur   Madrid   Melbourne   Mexico City   Mumbai   Nairobi
Paris   São Paulo   Shanghai   Singapore   Taipei   Tokyo   Toronto   Warsaw

and associated companies in
Berlin   Ibadan

Copyright © 2001 by Adrian Tinniswood

Published by Oxford University Press, Inc.,
198 Madison Avenue, New York, New York 10016

Oxford is a registered trademark of Oxford University Press

All rights reserved. No part of this publication
may be reproduced, stored in a retrieval system, or transmitted,
in any form or by any means, electronic, mechanical,
photocopying, recording, or otherwise, without the prior
permission of Oxford University Press.

Library of Congress Cataloging-in-Publication Data is available
ISBN 0-19-514989-0

1 3 5 7 9 8 6 4 2

Printed in the United States of America
on acid-free paper

For my brother

And besides his peculiar eminency as an architect, so extensive was his learning and knowledge in all the polite arts, but especially the mathematics; his invention so fertile, and his discoveries so numerous and useful; that he will always be esteemed a benefactor to mankind, and an ornament to the age, in which he lived.

John Ward, 'Christopher Wren',
The Lives of the Professors of Gresham College (1740)

Contents

List of Illustrations

Plates

Text Figures

The author and publishers would like to express their thanks to all the libraries and individuals who have helped with these illustrations; especially to the staff of the Codrington Library at All Souls, the Guildhall in London and Westminster City Archives, Christine Woollett at the Royal Society and Geoffrey Fisher at the Courtauld Institute's Conway Library, and A. F. Kersting. Acknowledgement for the reproduction of photographs or originals is gratefully made to the Ashmolean Museum, Oxford (1); the President and Council of the Royal Society (3, 4, 5, 6, 7, 9); A. F. Kersting (8, 25, 26, 27, 28, 30, 37); the Warden and Fellows of All Souls (12, 20, 22, 23, 29, 31, 32, 46); the Guildhall Library, Corporation of London (13, 14); the Courtauld Institute of Art (19, 21); Westminster City Archives (35); the Trustees of Sir John Soane's Museum (38); Pitkin Unichrome (41, 44); the *Daily Mail* (45); Kerry Downes (*1, 2*); Faber & Faber, from Eduard Sekler's *Wren and His Place in European Architecture* (*3*); the Controller of Her Majesty's Stationery Office, for Crown Copyright material (*4, 5*); Penguin Books, from Sir John Summerson's *Architecture in Britain 1530–1830* (*6*). While every effort has been made to trace the owners of copyright material reproduced herein, the publishers would like to apologize for any omissions and will be pleased to incorporate missing acknowledgements in any future editions.

Foreword

I have known and enjoyed Christopher Wren's architecture for nearly three decades. And how could it be otherwise for anyone with even a passing acquaintance with that architecture? Who could stand beneath the dome of St Paul's, or gaze across the Thames at Greenwich Hospital, or hear divine service in St James Piccadilly, and remain unmoved by the experience?

I was dimly aware, of course, that Wren had been a professor of astronomy before he turned to architecture. But, frankly, it seemed of little consequence. Buildings were his life and his legacy, and the fact that the genius who built Trinity College Library and transformed Hampton Court Palace also lectured on the heavens was a matter of indifference to me. Then, six years ago, I began to think more seriously about the circuitous path he took to become Britain's most eminent architect. Sir John Summerson famously said that if Wren had died at thirty, he would still have been 'a figure of some importance in English scientific thought, but without the word "architecture" occurring once in his biographies'. Over the course of time my hesitant interest in Wren as a figure of some importance in English scientific thought has grown into an obsession with a man who, I have no doubt whatsoever, helped to change the course of European cultural history – and not only by creating the greatest buildings that Britain has ever seen.

That obsession led me into unfamiliar and magical territory. I learned about the paths of comets and the internal organs of spaniels. I became familiar with brilliant men who, until I started my research, were little more than names to me: Hooke and Boyle, Wilkins and Neile, Evelyn and Petty and Scarburgh. And my respect for Wren's achievements deepened into a passionate commitment to the man himself. Some biographers come to hate their subjects; others patronize them. I can honestly say that I am still in awe of mine – still astounded at the power of his intellect, still amazed at the extent of his achievements. Here was a man who made ground-breaking discoveries in optics, astronomy, anatomy, mathematics; a man who combined his scientific interests with an architectural career spanning six reigns and nearly six decades; the arbiter of architectural taste to generations of designers and courtiers. As Hugh Chesterman's poem puts it:

> Clever men like Christopher Wren
> Only occur just now and then.
> No one expects in perpetuity
> Architects of his ingenuity;
> No, never a cleverer dipped his pen
> Than clever Sir Christopher – Christopher Wren.

But cleverness is not a virtue that the British value particularly highly; even Chesterman's funny, affectionate verse carries a suggestion of uneasiness at clever Sir Christopher. For some reason, we feel a need to look behind the brilliant façade for the 'real' man, as though the intellect is a mask and the emotions are somehow more compelling than the life of the mind. At first, I was guilty of this myself, but as I hunted in vain for that spurious reality, I eventually realized that in order to understand his life's work, we need to appreciate that Wren's work *was* his life. It defined him then, just as it defines him now; and nothing else seemed to matter to him. I like to think that, after all these years, I finally understand Christopher Wren. But I still don't know him. And I doubt that even his most intimate friends could claim that they did.

Many people have helped in the writing of this book. A special debt of thanks is due to Tricia Lankester, without whose constant encouragement and support I doubt that I would have completed it. Tricia read each chapter of the manuscript as it was finished; took me to task whenever my writing showed signs of losing its way (which was often); and offered comments and suggestions that were sometimes welcome, always right and invariably helpful.

I would also like to record my thanks to the following: my agent, Felicity Bryan, whose faith in me will, I hope for both our sakes, be amply rewarded; Dr Fran Burstall, who shared his considerable knowledge of the mathematical sciences in general, and geometry in particular; Howard Colvin, who was good enough to spend time with me discussing his unrivalled insights into seventeenth-century English architecture; Dan Franklin and Tristan Jones at Jonathan Cape, who between them managed to bring order to chaos; Rob Harper, who not only looked after the health of our cats, but also managed to explain the finer points of canine anatomy in all its awful detail; Olivia Lankester, whose efforts in the archives of the Royal Society deserve a greater reward than they received; Harold Lansdowne, whose ability to bring London and its past to life has been so instructive and so inspiring; Dr Katherine Ponganis, who instructed me in the basics of astronomy and cosmology; David Thwaites, a good friend whose continued interest in my work — at a time when he had much more serious matters to occupy his mind — helped me to make sense of my thoughts about Wren; and Margaret Willes, whose kindness in reading through the final manuscript and correcting so many errors and infelicities has earned her my eternal gratitude. Needless to say, any mistakes that remain are all my own work.

Without exception, the staff at the many libraries and other repositories of learning which I have haunted, pale-faced and wide-eyed, during the writing of *His Invention So Fertile* have been quite wonderful. Their patience has been astonishing. In particular, I would like to thank staff at the Bodleian Library; the British Library; Bristol University Library; the London Library; and the Royal Society. I would also like to register my respect for the guides and volunteers who work so hard to safeguard Wren's buildings, and to make our experience of them so enjoyable; without their efforts, Wren's legacy would be diminished.

The most cursory glance will reveal how much I owe to the twenty volumes of the Wren Society — with all its faults it is still to my mind not only a marvellous resource, but the greatest single homage ever paid to a British architect. I would also like to offer a homage of my own to those scholars, past and present, who have done so much to foster Wren studies; and in particular to J. M. Bennett, Professor Kerry Downes, Sir John Summerson and Margaret Whinney.

Last, but certainly not least, I would like to thank Helen, who bought me a telescope and helped me to see.

Bath, April 2001

Introduction

*T*he spaniel whined.

Wide awake, it lay on its side, writhing against the cords which tied it to the table, the hands which held it down. But it wasn't the cords or the rough, determined hands that made the animal struggle and yelp. It was the searing pain in its gut – a pain caused by a small, sharp-eyed man in his middle twenties who was carefully removing its spleen.

The operation was quite straightforward. After clipping away the dog's fur and marking the incision point with ink, the man carefully cut through the muscles and the peritoneum with a sharp blade like a sow-gelder's knife. While his assistant pushed down hard on the spaniel's abdomen, he thrust two fingers into the wound, pulled out the spleen, tied off the blood vessels with strong thread and cut them. The ends of the vessels and the wound itself were smeared with an astringent made up of plantain mixed with egg-white and oil of St John's wort, and the wound was sutured, leaving room for matter to escape. Finally, the incision was covered with a large plaster and the spaniel, now in deep shock, was wrapped in a cloth and laid on a bed of straw to recover.

Post-operative care would involve letting a few ounces of blood from the animal's left hind leg six hours later, and, the following day, checking for clotted blood in the abdomen. If there was any evidence of this, one assistant would hold the dog in his arms or suspend it over a table so that the incision faced downwards, while a second squirted half a pint of barley water, honey of roses and sugar into the wound until the red gouts had been washed out.

Christopher Wren was pleased. Canine splenectomy was a new and difficult operation, and he was getting quite good at it. But then the young don was good at everything he did. His reputation already extended far beyond his college of All Souls. Far beyond Oxford, in fact. People in London talked of him as 'that miracle of a youth'. He was praised in print as a boy who had 'enriched astronomy, gnomics, statics and mechanics with brilliant inventions',[1] Great things were expected of him in the sciences. And indeed, he lived up to those expectations— even if he did not always live up to his own.

I

The Beauty of Holiness

*C*hristopher Wren once told his friend, the antiquary and folklorist John Aubrey, that he was born in his father's parsonage house at East Knoyle in Wiltshire on Thursday 20 October 1631. He was wrong on both counts.

He was actually born in a tiny stone cottage down in the village: his parents had moved there temporarily after fire damaged their rectory. And the year of his birth was 1632, not 1631. This in itself was a common enough slip for the time. The antiquary Anthony Wood also replied to an enquiry from Aubrey (who was trying to compile an astrological collection): 'My nativity I cannot yet retrieve; but by talking with an ancient servant of my father's I find I was born on the 17 of December, but the year when I am not certain: 'twas possibly about 1647.'[1] But the error caused confusion among Wren scholars for centuries, and the natal waters were muddied by two more points. A Christopher Wren really *was* born at East Knoyle in 1631 – he was the architect's brother, who according to their father was 'born, baptised and dead in the same hour'.[2] (It was common practice in an age of high infant mortality to reuse forenames – the family also christened two daughters Elizabeth, for example.) And, as well as recording the baptism of this first Christopher, the East Knoyle parish registers contain an entry on 10 November 1631 for the christening of 'Christopher sonne of Christopher Dtr in Divinitie et rector'. This was the result of a simple mistake. The first volume of parish registers begins in 1538 and continues for nearly a hundred years, yet it is all in the same hand. It was obviously copied out at some point, and along the way the copyist missed a year, so that all subsequent entries, including that of Christopher's baptism, are one year out.

3

Wren had nine sisters and a second brother, stillborn in 1638. Only six girls survived into adolescence: Mary (born 1624); Katherine (born 1626); Susan (born 1627); the second Elizabeth (born 1633); Anne (born 1634); and Rachel (born 1636). Five were still alive in the early 1650s, when their father, Christopher Wren senior, wrote down a list of his children's birthdays; Elizabeth, he recorded, had died of consumption in 1649.

If an informed outsider had been asked to predict young Christopher's future as his mother went into labour that evening in October 1632, they would have said without hesitation that if the child was a boy, he was bound to enter the Church.

At the time, his father was forty-three and a rising figure in the Anglican establishment. That rise had begun at the beginning of the seventeenth century when, as pupils at the Merchant Taylors' School in London, he and his older brother Matthew attracted the attention of Lancelot Andrewes, the Dean of Westminster and an old boy of the school. As a result of his patronage, Matthew went to Pembroke Hall, Cambridge,★ where the Dean was also Master. Andrewes became Bishop of Ely in 1609; Matthew became his chaplain six years later, to follow this in 1621 with an appointment as chaplain to Charles, Prince of Wales and future King of England.

Christopher Wren senior had a less spectacular but equally trouble-free start to his career. After St John's College, Oxford and ordination he was appointed chaplain to Andrewes, now Bishop of Winchester, in succession to Matthew. The Bishop presented him in 1620 to the living of Fonthill Bishop in Wiltshire, where he met Mary, the only child and heiress of a local landowner, Robert Cox. They were married in 1623, when Wren was thirty-four and his bride was twenty; in the same year Andrewes made him rector of the neighbouring parish, East Knoyle.

Andrewes died in 1626, but by this time Matthew Wren was manoeuvring into a position in which he would be well able to further his brother's ecclesiastical career. Their connection with the Bishop of Winchester had brought both Wrens into contact with that faction of the Anglican Church which saw radical Protestantism and Puritan piety as a direct threat not only to the Church, but to the stability of the monarchy itself. Bishops such as Andrewes, William Laud (then at St David's) and Richard Neile (Durham) thought that James I was far too tolerant of Puritanism, while the King's inept attempt to marry his son

---

★Pembroke Hall became Pembroke College in 1856.

and heir Prince Charles to the Spanish Infanta in 1623 threatened to drive the more militantly anti-Catholic churchgoers into the Puritan camp.

An indication of the circles in which Matthew Wren was moving can be found in his own account of a meeting held late in 1623, a few months after the Prince had been packed off to Spain for the abortive attempt to win the Infanta's hand. As Charles's chaplain, Matthew was ordered by King James to accompany him, partly to see that Charles was not seduced by the Papists and partly to make sure that the Prince's other travelling companion, the wild Duke of Buckingham, didn't cause a diplomatic incident. The party returned that October without disgracing themselves unduly – but also without the Infanta. Shortly afterwards, Matthew was called at short notice to a clandestine meeting with Bishop Andrewes at Winchester House on the Thames. There, he recalled later, 'I found the Steward at the water-gate, waiting to let me in . . . I asked where his Lordship was? He answered, "In his great gallery" (a place where I knew his Lordship scarce came once in a year) and thither I going, the door was locked; but upon my lifting the latch, my Lord of St David's opened the door, and letting me in, locked it again.'[3]

Once inside, Matthew found himself confronted by not one, but three bishops – Andrewes, Laud and Neile. They immediately began to interrogate him about the Prince of Wales:

'We must know of you [said Neile], what your thoughts are concerning your master the Prince. You have now been his servant above two years, and you were with him in Spain; we know he respects you well; and we know you are no fool, but can observe how things are like to go.'

'What things, my Lord?' quoth I.

'In brief,' said he, 'how the Prince's heart stands to the Church of England, that when God brings him to the Crown, we may know what to hope for.'

Matthew answered that as far as he could tell, Charles was sound: 'I know my master's learning is not equal to his father's; yet, I know his judgement to be very right; and as for . . . upholding the doctrine and discipline, and the right estate of the Church, I have more confidence of him, than of his father, in whom they say (better than I can) is so much inconstancy.'

As far as this went, Matthew's assessment proved correct. 'The neglect of punishing Puritans breeds Papists,' declared Charles; and within months of his succession to the throne in 1625 he had promised the Archbishopric of Canterbury to Laud on the death of the Calvinist George Abbot.

Laud had to wait eight years to step into Abbot's shoes, although as the King's right-hand man after Buckingham's assassination in 1628 he wasted no time in punishing Puritans and promoting absolutist values in church and state. In the meantime, Matthew Wren was making steady progress up the ecclesiastical ladder. In 1626 he was elected Master of Peterhouse, where he was a Fellow; in 1628 the King appointed him Dean of Windsor and Registrar of the Order of the Garter; and in 1634, the year after Laud became Archbishop, he was made Bishop of Hereford. The following year he was moved to Norwich, and that March his brother Christopher succeeded him as Dean of Windsor, keeping the living of East Knoyle and adding that of Great Haseley in Oxfordshire to it soon after his appointment to the Deanery.

The two brothers now found themselves at the heart of a battle that was splitting the Church of England in the 1630s. In essence, that battle was both an ideological struggle between the forces of conservatism, as represented by Archbishop Laud and his followers, and the progressive Puritans who sought to democratize the institutions of the Church and wrest power from the establishment; and a theological dispute in which a predominantly Calvinist clergy and educated laity reacted to the challenge of Charles I's bishops, who rejected predestination and argued for divine grace freely available through the sacraments.

The practical consequences for the Anglican liturgy were profound, and can still be seen today in parish churches all over England. For Laudians like the Wren brothers, a church was not simply a meeting place where sermons were preached and business transacted. It was 'the place where our Lord God most holy doth inhabit', as Robert Skinner declared in a sermon preached before the King in 1634; 'his proper mansion or dwelling house'.[4] Any object within it was 'holy in relation to the holy use whereto it is assigned'. This meant everything – the bread, the oil, the chalice, even the cloth bags that were used to bring communion bread into the church.

Holiest of all was the altar. It was no longer acceptable to regard it, as the Puritans did, as simply a wooden table which stood in the middle of the chancel (usually on an east–west axis), to be dragged out into the nave for parish meetings or school lessons; it was, in Laud's words, 'the greatest place of God's residence upon earth . . . yea, greater than the pulpit'.[5] The Puritans must be made to honour it, and to conform, outwardly at least, to the rituals of respect that accompanied the new movement. 'We are now well nigh fallen into an hatred of the true worship,' declared Matthew Wren, 'and into contempt of all things divine and holy.'[6]

So in the face of bitter opposition from a broad spectrum of radical Protestants, Laud and his followers sought to impose their particular brand of Anglicanism on clergy and laity. In Norwich, Matthew Wren made sure that preaching licences went to ritualists and opponents of Nonconformity; at Winchester, Bishop Walter Curle suspended recalcitrant clergy and encouraged reverence in divine service, 'so God may be worshipped not only in holiness, but in the beauty of holiness'; and, with a few exceptions, episcopal appointments and promotions all went to anti-Calvinists.[7] The Laudian faction was also close to the monarch. Unlike his father, who had been careful to keep both camps happy, Charles I chose only ritualists and anti-Calvinists as his clerical intimates, from privy councillors to clerks of the closet and royal almoners.

It was against this background that in many dioceses the emphasis of Anglican worship shifted from the Word of Christ, as exemplified by the sermon, to the Body of Christ represented by the celebration of Holy Communion at the altar. The Puritans' predilection for receiving Communion as they sat in their pews was actively discouraged: now they were required to kneel before an altar placed firmly against the east wall of the chancel. And that chancel was in all probability newly railed – partly, as one bishop put it in 1638, 'to keep out dogs from going in and profaning that holy place, from pissing against it or worse', but also to accentuate the sense of separateness from the main body of the church. Many of the High Church radicals saw the architecture of a church building as a metaphor for the spiritual life, with its progress from baptism in the font (which stood at the west end of the church), through nave and instruction, to chancel and the holy mystery of the Eucharist:

> Some are unworthy to come within the doors of the church and therefore are to stand without. Some are fit to be received in, to be baptised; some to be instructed in the grounds of religion and to repair with the rest of the congregation. All which is done in the nave and body of the church. And as men profit in knowledge and a working

faith, to discern the Lord's body, they are admitted into a higher room, where the sacrament of the body and blood of Jesus Christ is to be administered at the holy table in the chancel, which divideth it from the rest of the church.[8]

Dean Wren was determined to put Laudian principles into practice at his own church of St Mary's at East Knoyle. In 1639, when Inigo Jones was modernizing the medieval cathedral of St Paul's, Charles I and his bishops were battling with the Scottish Covenanters and Christopher was six or seven years old, he commissioned the complete redecoration of the church chancel in a style which must have seemed to his neighbours and parishioners a startlingly direct ideological statement.

The result is still dramatic today, when much of his work has been defaced or over-restored. The dark, undistinguished nave, full of Victorian stained glass and florid memorials to long-dead local dignitaries, suddenly gives way to a bright, white chancel alive with plaster figures. Angels climb ladders up to heaven. Jacob dreams his dream of God beneath them. Abraham makes ready to sacrifice his son Isaac. The mutilated remains of an Ascension scene decorate the chancel arch, with Apostles and angels gazing up at a blank space where Christ once hovered in the clouds, until Roundhead soldiers removed him as a Popish icon. Strapwork panels around the walls are filled with urgent texts exhorting the congregation to ponder on the holy nature of the building in which they worshipped: 'Dread is this place. This is noe other but the howse of God and the gate of heaven'; 'My howse shalbe called the howse of prayer to all nations'. And in a corner there is the kneeling figure of the Dean himself, dressed in the robes of a Stuart clergyman and holding up his arms as he is divinely inspired by the dove of the Holy Ghost.

Dean Wren's new chancel was much more than mere decoration. In the Laudian scheme of things it was a fit and proper setting for the high point of Christian worship, and the texts and images which covered its walls were coded declarations of support for a particular and controversial brand of Anglicanism. It was also a particularly personal statement of faith, in that the Dean designed it himself. Years later, in May 1647, Robert Brockway of Frome St Quintin in Dorset, who had carried out the work, explained its genesis:

[The Doctor] did invent and make a model or draught thereof in paper, which he gave to this examinant and caused him to make it, viz, the picture of the Ascension, with the twelve Apostles, and Christ ascending in the clouds . . . Further, on each side of the window there was set up the picture of Jacob's dream and his sacrifice [in fact, a depiction of Abraham and Isaac]; clouds above; Jacob sleeping below, and a ladder let down to the earth. On the one side of the window, angels holding crowns of laurel in their hands, ascended, and on the other side of the window they descended; and underneath were these words written, 'Let prayers ascend that grace may descend.'

Brockway also testified that Dr Wren paid for the work himself, 'and used to come every day to overlook it, and give directions therein'.[9]

I say 'testified', because Brockway was giving evidence before a Parliamentary Commission at Longford Castle, where Dr Wren stood accused of 'heretical practices'. In the eight years that passed between the decoration of the chancel and Brockway's statement to the Commission, the power struggle between High and Low Church had spilled over into war between Charles I and his Parliament. In December 1640, Parliament impeached Archbishop Laud on the grounds of treason and sent him to the Tower. Charged with 'endeavouring to subvert the laws, to overthrow the Protestant religion, and to act as an enemy to Parliament', he was found guilty and beheaded on 10 January 1645.

Christopher Wren's uncle Matthew, who was by now Bishop of Ely, fared little better. He was accused by Parliament in 1641 of 'setting up of idolatry and superstition in divers places and acting the same in his own person', and on 5 July a committee of the House of Commons met to consider nine charges, including 'causing the communion-table to be placed altar-wise, and to be railed in; and kneeling, and consecrating the bread and wine, at the west side of the communion-table, with his back towards the people, and bowing to, or before the same'; and 'causing all the pews or seats to be so contrived, as that the people must of necessity kneel with their faces towards the east'.[10] The debate that followed resulted in a call for the King to dismiss the Bishop as unfit to hold any church office: nothing came of it until the Civil War broke out, but within days of Charles I raising his standard at Nottingham on 22 August 1642, Parliamentary troops broke into Matthew Wren's London house and carted him off to the Tower of London. He languished there, untried and unconvicted of any offence, for eighteen years.

The Wren family's fall from grace didn't end with Matthew's imprisonment, although after Archbishop Laud's impeachment and

Bishop Wren's troubles the Dean took hasty steps to avoid confrontation. In the early 1640s, with the plaster on the walls of his new chancel scarcely dry, he wrote from Windsor to his East Knoyle churchwarden, Randall Dominick. If anyone had taken offence from the new images, he said, Dominick had full authority to pull them down. Nothing happened, so perhaps the parishioners either subscribed to Wren's brand of Anglicanism or didn't dare to complain. Or then again, perhaps they simply didn't care.

When war broke out in 1642, Windsor Castle was held for Parliament. At first the Governor, Colonel Venn, did nothing to bother Dr Wren, who was allowed to remain in his medieval Deanery tucked away behind the soaring buttresses of St George's Chapel. But, convinced that this wouldn't last, the Dean buried the jewel-encrusted George and Garter of Gustavus Adolphus, the most precious of the Order of the Garter's possessions, underneath the floor of his Treasury. His fears were well-founded. In October 1642 a Captain Fogg turned up at the door of the Deanery, claiming to hold a warrant from the King and demanding the keys to the Treasury. If the Dean and prebends wouldn't give them up, he said, he would pull the chapel down about their ears. Either by accident or by design, the keyholders were away from Windsor at the time, so a smith was called and the doors prised open with iron bars. The Parliamentarians took all the plate they could find, together with all the Order's records and register-books. They also ransacked the Chapel Royal. And just for good measure, they sacked the Deanery itself. Books, furniture, pictures and plate were all carried away; the only items Dr Wren managed to recover were a harpsichord, which was finally returned to him six years later, and three of the Order's register-books, which he kept with him until his death in 1658, handing them on to his son to return at the Restoration. The troops missed the concealed George and Garter, but they were found three years later and sold by order of Parliament.

The Wrens decided that the Deanery at Windsor was not a safe place to be – quite understandably, in the circumstances. Mary Wren was pregnant with their eleventh and last child (Frances, who was born in April 1643 and died eight months later); and so the family decamped to the relative safety of East Knoyle. At least in Wiltshire 'gentlemen of ancient families and estates [were] for the most part well-affected to the King', even if 'people of an inferior degree . . . were fast friends to the Parliament'.[11] There is an unauthenticated story that they spent some time in the Royalist stronghold of Bristol between the summer of 1643, when Charles's nephew Prince Rupert, the 'Mad Cavalier', took the city for the King, and September 1645, when he surrendered it to the Parliamentarian general, Thomas Fairfax.

During a Parliamentarian sweep through south Wiltshire in 1644, Sir Edward Hungerford extracted £25 from Christopher Williams and Henry Marshman, rents due to the Dean as part of the East Knoyle parsonage. A few months later, when the Parliamentarian forces were safely under siege in Wardour Castle, Dean Wren set out with a troop of the King's Horse to collect his overdue rents – including those of Williams and Marshman, whom he forced to pay a second time.

Despite this dubious act of profiteering, the Dean went out of his way to help the Royalists. In the spring of 1645 a troop of the King's men was routed by Cromwell at Devizes, twenty miles north, and remnants were trying to escape from the Parliamentary forces by running south. One night an East Knoyle alehouse keeper named George Styles was woken by the arrival of a large company of Royalist soldiers – accompanied by Dean Wren. Styles's wife found a bed for Wren and one of the commanders: 'and in the morning as they lay in bed, the Doctor spake these words to his friend, "Sir, all is well, there is no danger, for I left word with my wife that if there were, she should send word." '[12]

Given his Royalist sympathies and his Laudian connections, it was inevitable that Dean Wren should lose his living at East Knoyle – and the £230 a year that went with it – in the wave of purges that occurred after Charles I's defeat at the Battle of Naseby in 1645. And the inevitable happened, in spite of a letter from the Committee of Lords and Commons for Sequestrations to the Wiltshire Committee hearing his case, pleading that he was 'a Person far from meriting the Doom of Sequestracion' and asking the Committee to look upon him with 'favourable inclinations'.[13] (The Dean had obviously not lost all of the powerful friends he had made in the 1630s.) But the letter carried little weight beside the plaster figures at St Mary's, which were still there to bear mute witness to his Laudian loyalties – 'suspicious pictures in the Chancell', as one parishioner described them in a deposition to the Committee.[14] In 1646 he was deprived of his position in favour of William Clifford, a Puritan preacher from Gloucester who disdained the suspicious pictures and 'preacheth constantly twice everye Lords daye'.[15]

Dean Wren seems to have lost his Great Haseley living at around the same time and, according to local tradition, the family stayed on in East Knoyle for another couple of years after his ejection from St Mary's. He tried to make a living as a schoolmaster, but he was growing old –

he turned sixty in 1649 – and eventually he gave up all hope of re-establishing himself in the village which had been his home on and off for twenty-five years. So the Wrens abandoned East Knoyle for another rectory in another country parish. This time the village was Bletchingdon, seven miles north of Oxford, and the rectory belonged to William Holder, who in 1643 had married the Dean's third daughter, Susan.

Bletchingdon had seen its fair share of action during the war. Charles I's troops arrived in July 1643, and during the skirmishes that took place in the area the following October, the fields and cottages round about were littered with dead and dying men in their hundreds. The manor house, which had been rebuilt in the 1630s by the new lord of the manor, a London merchant's son named Thomas Coghill, was commandeered by the Royalists, who fortified it and installed a garrison of 200, only to surrender without a fight as soon as Cromwell appeared at the gates in the spring of 1644. The Royalist commander, a Colonel Windebank, was subsequently court-martialled and shot for his faint-heartedness. But by the end of the 1640s things had quietened down and, after all the recent turmoil in their own lives, Bletchingdon's quiet ordinariness must have seemed like heaven to the Wrens.

Holder's church, St Giles, was medieval, although its chancel had been restored and beautified in 1634 by his predecessor, Christopher Potter, the devoutly Laudian Provost of Queen's College, Oxford. There was an ale-house – the Angel and Crown – and Coghill's 'Greate House', which stood a quarter of a mile from the village centre. Most of the population, which numbered only around 160, lived either on outlying farms or in the straggling rows of stone-roofed cottages which lined two sides of a triangular green. The third side was formed by the park walls of Coghill's mansion; and the rectory that Susan and William shared with the Dean and the Wren children was on a little lane between the green and St Giles, which stood within the park and was reached via a muddy footpath. The family's new home was a substantial stone-built house, bigger than most in the village, with a living hall, a parlour and a buttery on the ground floor, bedchambers above them, and a single-storey group of domestic offices, including kitchen, larder and dairy, at the rear.

Susan Holder, who ran the Bletchingdon household, is the only woman in Sir Christopher Wren's life to earn more than a passing reference in the letters and journals of the time. His other sisters are noted only for their marriages or the dates of their deaths, or both, or neither. His mother Mary remains a frustratingly shadowy character: never even mentioned in the boy's letters, she was still alive in 1645, when her husband was sleeping in an East Knoyle bed with a Royalist commander while she kept an eye open for Parliamentarian soldiers. After that she simply disappears from view. (The move to Susan's home in Bletchingdon may have been prompted by her death, and the Dean's subsequent need for help in raising the family.) And although Christopher married twice, neither wife made any impact on his public and professional life; nor, for that matter, on his private life, in spite of their bearing him four children between them. Both wives died young, so he was either single or widowed for all but nine of his ninety-one years.

Susan, on the other hand, earned the respect of her peers, although Wren himself never refers to her. John Aubrey had a soft spot for her, writing that she was 'not lesse to be admired, in her sex and station, than her brother Sir Christopher', and adding with all the unconscious chauvinism of his age that 'her excellences doe not inflate her', something 'which is rare to be found in a woman'.[16] She had a gift for healing, and after the Restoration, when her husband was a Sub-Dean of the Chapel Royal and the couple were part of the royal household, she achieved a certain fame when she managed to cure a wound on Charles II's hand which had defeated the best efforts of his personal physicians, 'to the great griefe of all the Surgeons, who envy and hate her'.[17]

One would like to know more about Susan Holder and her relationship with her adolescent brother, six years her junior. The same is true of another woman – or girl, rather – who figures vaguely in his life at Bletchingdon. Sir Thomas Coghill's daughter, Faith, was four years younger than Wren, and the two young people would have seen each other regularly at Sunday service in the little church and mixed socially at the Holders' rectory and the Coghills' home. Perhaps Faith played with Wren's younger sisters, Anne and Rachel; perhaps he spent time with her three brothers. Pure speculation, of course, and supremely unimportant in the normal run of things. But the relationship gains greater significance and a certain romance from the fact that two decades later, Wren and Faith Coghill were married.

2

I Will Perform as Much as I Am Able

hroughout the worst period of his father's trials and tribulations, the mid-1640s, Christopher Wren spent much of his time away at school in London. In *Parentalia,* the collection of family memoirs which is still a core source for Wren studies, his own son records that he was 'of tender health', and that his constitution 'was naturally rather delicate than strong, especially in his Youth, which seemed consumptive'.[1] As a result, until he was nine he was taught at home by his father and a domestic tutor, the Reverend William Shepheard. ('Home' at that time was the Deanery at Windsor, although the family still spent extended periods at East Knoyle.) Then in about 1641 the boy went as a boarder to Westminster School, a natural choice for any child of Wren's background: it was run by the notorious disciplinarian Richard Busby, a firm believer in King and corporal punishment. During the war Busby managed to combine these two interests by birching any boys who showed signs of deviating towards the Parliamentary cause, although since he thrashed any boy at the least provocation, one wonders whether Royalist children really had any preferential treatment. His enthusiasm for the King was such that John Owen, Dean of Christ Church, told Oliver Cromwell that 'it would never be well with the nation till Westminster School was suppressed'. Much the same sentiments, although from a different perspective, were expressed by one of Wren's contemporaries at Westminster, Richard South, later to become one of the Restoration court's most popular preachers. South said that 'Westminster School was so untaintedly loyal that he could truly and knowingly own that in the very worst of times he and his companions were really King's scholars as well as called so'.[2]

Other contemporaries included John Dryden and John Locke. There is something satisfying about the picture of these four boys, who would make their names as architect, Anglican divine, poet and philosopher, working together at their Latin and Greek primers (written, incidentally, by Busby himself and sold to his pupils as a profitable sideline). The headmaster had also translated Euclid into Latin, so although it was unusual for mathematics to figure in school syllabuses of the day, Busby's entrepreneurialism extended to the teaching of geometry.

The earliest of Wren's writings to survive dates from these early school-days. It is a Latin letter to his father from Westminster and endorsed across the bottom in Dean Wren's hand, 'Written in his tenth year':

Reverend Father:

There is a common saying among the ancients which I remember to have had from your mouth: that there is no equivalent which can be given back to parents. For their cares and perpetual labours concerning their children are the evidence of immeasurable love. Now these precepts so often repeated, which have compelled my soul to all that is highest in man and to virtue, have superseded in me all other affections. What in me lies I will perform as much as I am able, lest these gifts should have been bestowed on an ungrateful soul. May the good God Almighty be with me in my undertakings and make good to thee all thou most desirest in the tenderness of thy fatherly love. Thus prays thy son, most devoted to thee in all obedience.[3]

Given the date of this precocious exercise in filial devotion – probably the autumn of 1642, and possibly to mark Christopher's tenth birthday in October of that year – it would be nice to think of it as a childish message of support for the increasingly beleaguered Dean. But that is being sentimental. The letter is more likely just a Latin exercise by a rather bright young boy who is eager to show off to his father.

Perhaps because he was still quite a sickly child, perhaps because of the change in family circumstances, Wren left Westminster in 1646, when he was still only thirteen. Already he had seen his father go from eminent divine to humiliated and disgraced ex-parson. He had seen his uncle, one of the most prominent churchmen in England, thrown into the Tower of London and left to rot. And, of course, he had seen the religious and political belief-systems that had informed the whole of his childhood ridiculed and discredited and dismantled. What effects did these things have on him at the time?

We don't know. We don't know if he was proud or pious or just plain bored as he sat with his sisters in the rector's family pew at East Knoyle and watched his father stand at the candle-lit altar elevating the Host, or if he had any inkling that the angels and Old Testament figures which hovered over the chancel walls were an expression of pro-Catholic sentiment that was tantamount to treason. We don't know if he cried when he was told how soldiers had ransacked his father's Deanery, or when he heard that his uncle had been sent to the Tower.

It is a little easier to guess at the long-term consequences of Wren's childhood experiences. A career in the Church was no longer an option. The hopes in that direction that the Dean must have had for his son vanished with Matthew's imprisonment. More interestingly, the collapse of Laudianism may account for Christopher's lack of religious zeal in adulthood. He became a conventional and reasonably orthodox Anglican, but apart from his son's statement that at the end of his life in the 1720s he spent his time in 'Meditations and Researches in holy Writ', there is little to show that religion was particularly important to him. Did the treatment meted out to his father and uncle teach Wren the fragility of political life? The importance of being on the winning side, whichever side that happened to be? The idea that it was better to abstain from political controversy altogether, that he should keep his mind 'invincibly armed against all the enchantments of Enthusiasm', as a colleague was to put it years later?

I think it did. Like any of us, he was angry and frustrated at times, pleased with himself when things went well and exasperated with others when they didn't. But he was also a supreme pragmatist, well able to switch allegiance if it was in his interest to do so. His son's summary of his character in *Parentalia*, written soon after his death in 1723, suggests that the events of his childhood had taught Wren the dangers of extremism: 'He was happily endued with such an Evenness of Temper, a steady Tranquillity of Mind, and christian Fortitude, that no injurious Incidents, or Inquietudes of human Life, could ever ruffle or discompose; and was in Practice a Stoick.'[4] It is also tempting to think that having had his world turned upside down politically, spiritually and personally in the 1640s, he saw in the scientific studies that would occupy half his life a means of placing that world on a systematic and rational footing.

But if Christopher Wren's father failed to fire him with enthusiasm for his own fierce brand of Laudianism (or chose not to), there was another side to the Dean's character which would have a much more profound influence on the boy's development.

In 1740 Wren's son wrote that, 'My Grandfather was a Learned Man, skillful in all the Branches of Mathematicks.' Wren himself told Aubrey years later that the Dean, rather than his official tutors, had taught him arithmetic; and in 1647 he mentioned to his father in passing the ideas 'which I owe to you in Organics or Mechanics'.[5]

Although we don't know the specifics, we do know that the Dean's interests extended well beyond the Church. While at Windsor he began a short historical account of which Knights of the Garter had given what towards the furnishing of the altar in St George's, and some years before that we find him musing on numerology: 'All the numeral Letters in the Latin tongue [i.e., MDCLXVI] can make up but 1666, so that when the odd 666, are completed in the Years of Christ, it may bode some ominous Matter, and perhaps the last End.'[6] (And he was right, of course, about the ominous matter, if not the last end – although ironically the Fire of London was to be a blessing in disguise for his son.) In 1639, while rector of Great Haseley, he made notes on coats of arms in the church there, and recorded with interest how he had 'digged out of a heap of rubbish' a statue of a medieval knight that 'makes it appear he was (not two Inches lower than) seven Foot high'. He owned a copy of *The Elements of Architecture* (1624), Henry Wotton's 'methodical direction how to censure fabrics', and in the margins he noted down his thoughts on building, design – even gardening, in which he anticipated William Kent by a century: 'I invented the Serpentine; a Form admirably conveying the Current [of a river] in circular, and yet contrary Motions, upon one and the same Level, with Walks and Retirements between, to the Advantage of all Purposes, either of Gardenings, Plantings, or Banquetings, or airy Delights, and the multiplying of infinite Fish in a little Compass of Ground, without any Sense of their being restrained.'[7]

The Dean was also intrigued by curiosities of nature. He left an account of an oak tree in the New Forest which burst into leaf every Christmas, twigs from which he had personally handed out to 'great Persons of both Sexes in Court, and to others, ecclesiastical Persons'. And in later life, when he was living at Bletchingdon with his daughter and son-in-law, he showed a lively interest in astronomy. This was partly professional, to be sure – 'either, God, or Copernicus speaking

Contradictions, cannot both speake Truth', he noted in the margins of Thomas Browne's *Pseudodoxia epidemica* (1646) – but it was more wide-ranging than one might expect. For example, his marginalia show that he was pretty well acquainted with the works of most of the major astronomers of the past hundred years, including Gassendi, Tycho Brahe, Galileo and Kepler.

This all makes the Dean sound like a Trollopian cleric, dabbling in antiquarian fieldwork and shaky 'science', spending his declining years in the Bletchingdon parsonage writing letters to *Notes and Queries* and contributing esoteric and unreadable articles to the *Barsetshire Archaeological Magazine*. If he had lived in Victorian England, that might have been true. But the gap between Bletchingdon and Barchester involved a great deal more than just two hundred years; Dr Wren was a virtuoso, standing at the beginning of a great amateur tradition rather than at the end.

The virtuoso is first mentioned in England by Henry Peacham in the 1634 edition of *The Compleat Gentleman,* a handbook of appropriate behaviour for the country gentleman. Discussing classical antiquities, Peacham says that, 'The possession of such rarities, by reason of their deadly costliness, doth properly belong to Princes, or rather to princely minds ... Such as are skilled in them, are by the Italians termed *Virtuosi*.'[8] Ten years later, during a stay in Paris, John Evelyn wrote in his diary that 'We went ... to visit Mons Perishot, one of the greatest virtuosos in France, for his collection of pictures, achates, medals, and flowers, especially tulips & anemones.'[9] These early references make the virtuoso out to be little more than a collector; and certainly collecting formed an important part of his activities. But the nature of the objects in a virtuoso's cabinet of curiosities ranged astonishingly widely, from the beautiful and precious through the informative and educational to the downright odd, like the petrified hedgehog which Evelyn admired in Signor Rugini's collection in Venice in 1645, or the sea-horse teeth, electric eels and embalmed child that formed part of the cabinet of curiosities in Sir Walter Cope's London house at the beginning of the century.

The virtuoso might be interested in anything or everything, and his studies might encompass science, history, the arts – almost any field of learning, in fact, from alchemy to zoology. The potential breadth of his interests is suggested by the pastimes which Robert Burton offered as an antidote to ennui in *The Anatomy of Melancholy* (1621): paintings, statues, jewels, coins and antiquities; heraldry and coats of arms; natural history;

chemistry, astronomy, geometry, algebra, 'the Mathematicks'; and mechanical inventions such as fireworks, waterworks, cranes and pulleys.

This is quite a list, and it reflects the all-embracing and undiscriminating nature of so much early seventeenth-century scholarship. Not that all virtuosi were particularly scholarly. Some were; others saw a pleasant and entertaining way to occupy their copious leisure time in the study of the stars or the practice of mathematics, the collecting of precious gems or the invention of mechanical toys. And others still were attracted by the enhanced social status that could be obtained by the possession of rare and strange objects: a cabinet of curiosities or an ability to perform spectacular chemical experiments not only conferred popular celebrity, but also gave the virtuoso the opportunity to meet and mix with his social superiors, breaking down strict class barriers as kings and princes made the pilgrimage to his house. The mixture of motives was summed up as early as 1605 in Francis Bacon's *Advancement of Learning*:

> Men have entered into a desire of learning and knowledge, sometimes upon a natural curiosity and inquisitive appetite; sometimes to entertain their minds with variety and delight; sometimes for ornament and reputation; . . . as if there were sought in knowledge a couch, whereupon to rest a searching and restless spirit; or a terrace, for a wandering and variable mind to walk up and down with a fair prospect; or a tower of state, for a proud mind to raise itself upon.[10]

Bacon is here criticizing those who 'seldom sincerely give a true account of their gift of reason, to the benefit and use of men';[11] and a characteristic of the virtuoso is the pursuit of knowledge for its own sake, in spite of the warnings of Bacon and others. Back in 1574, Hubert Lanquet had advised the young Philip Sidney that, 'You were quite right to learn the elements of astronomy, but I do not advise you to proceed far in the science, because it is very difficult, and not likely to be of much use to you. I know not whether it is wise to apply your mind to geometry . . . I consider it absurd to learn the rudiments of many sciences simply for display and not for use.' But in the sixty-odd years that lie between this letter and Christopher Wren's schooldays, attitudes had changed quite radically. The syllabus at Busby's Westminster might focus firmly on the classics, as it did at every school; but natural philosophy, history and the arts were now accepted as part of a gentleman's cultural baggage – not for 'the benefit and use of men' necessarily (although this might be a pleasant by-product), but as ends in themselves. Even in 1622, when Dean Wren was still an unmarried vicar at Fonthill, the first edition of Peacham's *Compleat Gentleman* declared, 'How sweet a thing it is to converse with the wisest of all Ages by History; to have insight into the most pleasing and admirable Sciences of the Mathematiques, Poetry, Picture, Heraldry, &c.'[12]

The detailed evidence for Dean Wren's scientific interests is scanty, consisting of merely the notes, fragments and marginalia mentioned above. We know little more about the other formative influence of Wren's childhood – his brother-in-law, William Holder. Aubrey, who knew Holder personally, described him as 'a handsome, gracefull person, and of a delicate constitution, and of an even and smooth temper'. More significantly, he said that Holder was 'very helpfull' in Wren's education, that he looked after him 'as if he had been his owne Child', and that he 'gave him his first Instructions in Geometrie and Arithmetique'[13] – a claim supported by Wren's son, who tells us that 'in the Principles of Mathematicks, upon the early Appearance of an uncommon Genius, [his father] was initiated by Dr William Holder'.[14]

Christopher Wren wasn't Holder's only pupil. In 1659, while still rector of Bletchingdon, he taught the son of a Parliamentarian soldier, a deaf–mute named Alexander Popham, to speak. This led in 1669 to his *Elements of Speech: an essay of inquiry into the natural production of letters; with an appendix concerning persons deaf and dumb*, and in the following year to a heated dispute with John Wallis (a friend of Wren's at Oxford in the 1650s and, according to Aubrey, 'a most ill-natured man, an egregious liar and backbiter, a flatterer and fawner')[15] who claimed the credit for teaching Popham. At the age of seventy-eight Holder published *A Discourse concerning Time*, and several writers have seen in this a re-worked version of his lessons with Wren.[16] True or not, Holder's assertion in the *Discourse* that 'I doe not intend to fall upon nice, Philosophical Disquisitions about the Nature of Time . . . but upon the Use of it'[17] fits in with Wren's practical bent. And one of Wren's earliest scientific interests was the science of sundials: we know from Aubrey that as a teenager he made 'severall curious Dialls, with his owne handes' in the grounds of the parsonage at Bletchingdon, and *Parentalia* mentions a reflecting dial on the ceiling of a room, complete with figures representing Astronomy and Geometry.[18]

Of course we don't know how good Wren was at dialling, as the seventeenth century called the theory and practice of sundials. No examples of his work in this field have survived, unless one accepts his conjectural authorship of the seventeenth-century dial that graces the wall of the library at All Souls, the college of which he was elected a Fellow in 1653. But such things certainly were not children's toys – the sundial was the most reliable means of telling time in the seventeenth century, as it was in the eighteenth, when people were still setting their watches and clocks by dials. There was an established body of literature, from Thomas Fale's *Horologiographia*, the first English-language work on the subject, which appeared in 1593 and offered instruction and delight 'not onely for Students of the Arts Mathematicall, but also for divers Artificers, Architects, Surveyours of buildings, free-Masons, Saylors, and others',[19] to the works of advanced mathematicians like William Oughtred (1575–1660), whose double horizontal dial, which simultaneously showed the hour and the position of the sun in terms of date, declination, altitude and azimuth, caused Pepys's friends such envy: 'Up betimes, and studying of my double horizontal diall . . . Dean Honiwood comes to me, who dotes mightily upon it, and I think I must give it him.'[20] And Wren wasn't alone in beginning an eminent scientific career by designing sundials: like him, the young Isaac Newton also experimented with reflecting dials, a rather spectacular form in which a mirror is placed on a south-facing windowsill so that the sun's rays reflect on to a ceiling which has been calibrated to show the hours. In fact, from late Elizabethan times onwards an interest in the geometry of dialling was an established first step for aspiring mathematicians.

While still a schoolboy, Wren also designed an instrument for describing lines corresponding to the hours of the day on a dial. Nor was dialling the only outlet for his early scientific interests: at the age of thirteen, he invented and dedicated to his father an instrument which he called a *panorganum astronomicum* (probably a set of pasteboard wheels and circles which showed the phases of the moon and the movements of the sun and the stars); also an unspecified 'pneumatick engine'.[21] The inspiration for such devices is much more likely to have come from Dean Wren and William Holder than from the curriculum at Westminster.

It would still be a mistake to over-estimate the significance of the influence of Holder and the Dean on Wren's subsequent development. Neither were scientists or true experimental philosophers in the sense that Wren himself was to become. Nor could they be – until Wren's generation, there *were* no scientists in the sense that we understand the word today. Even so, we can't ignore their interest in subjects like mechanics, mathematics and astronomy – subjects that were largely disregarded by the orthodox school curriculum. Wren may have had 'an uncommon Genius' for system and science. But what if his father and brother-in-law hadn't cared? What if they hadn't provided suitable role-models for a young adolescent whose natural bent was for science rather than religion or the arts?

A third early role-model, and in many ways the most influential, was the Royalist physician Charles Scarburgh, a friend and contemporary of William Holder at Cambridge. Scarburgh was an academic rather than a virtuoso, although his interests ranged wide. As a Fellow of Caius College in the early 1640s, he studied medicine and anatomy, collected books on navigation, astronomy, architecture and fortification, and taught classes in mathematics. His Royalist sympathies led him to leave Cambridge when it was occupied by Parliamentarian forces early in the war, and enlist in the army of Charles I at Oxford, where William Harvey, the King's physician, was Warden of Merton. There Scarburgh joined a small but influential group of scientists of which Harvey, whose seminal work on the circulation of the blood had established his reputation as a leading figure in European medicine, was the head. The older man took the younger, 'in whose conversation he much delighted',[22] under his wing: he persuaded him to leave the army and 'took him to him and made him lie in his chamber, and said to him, Prithee leave off thy gunning, and stay here; I will bring thee into practice'.[23] Harvey proved as good as his word, obtaining an MD for Scarburgh before leaving for London when Oxford fell to Parliament in June 1646. Scarburgh followed him to the capital soon afterwards and set up as a physician.

At this point Christopher Wren was introduced to the doctor – as a patient. In about 1647 he contracted a serious illness: he may have been showing symptoms of the apparent consumption referred to by his son in *Parentalia*. Dean Wren took him out of school and, perhaps on the recommendation of William Holder, sent him to Charles Scarburgh for treatment.

We don't know anything about that treatment, although if it was anything like the advice that the doctor gave to one of Charles II's mistresses three decades later, it must have been based on sound common sense: consulted by the Duchess of Portsmouth about her weight problem, Scarburgh simply said, 'Eat less, use more exercise, take physic, or be sick.'[24] But the boy was convinced that the doctor had saved him from death, writing that he had Scarburgh to thank 'for life itself which, when suffering from recent sickness, I received from him as from the Hand of God'.[25] He remained at the doctor's London home to convalesce for several months at least and possibly for a year or more, during which time the doctor–patient relationship grew into something more like that between a teacher and his pupil. Writing to Dean Wren from Scarburgh's house in 1647, the teenager told his father that, 'I am greatly enjoying the society of the famous physician who is most kind to me; so gracious and unassuming is he as not to disdain to submit those mathematical studies in which he has so distinguished himself to what I will not call my judgement but rather my taste, so that he even lends a patient ear to my opinions and often defers to my poor reasonings.'[26]

The reference to 'mathematical studies' points to Scarburgh's continued interest in scientific matters above and beyond the theory and practice of medicine. Never quite at the cutting edge of seventeenth-century science, he hovered on the sidelines, but his interest in natural philosophy – and his circle of scholarly friends – went far beyond those of Holder and Dean Wren. His portrait, which hangs at the Royal College of Physicians, shows a thin-faced, rather self-conscious man with long, delicate fingers, surrounded by the signs of his scientific pursuits. The most prominent – appropriately for one of the most eminent medical men of the Restoration, the man who as the King's physician cared for Charles II in his last illness – is an anatomical textbook, which lies open on a table beside a prism (optics) and a globe (navigation and astronomy). In the background, Rome, a city that Scarburgh never visited, represents architecture. It is surely no coincidence that as Wren grew up, he came to share every one of these interests.

Within a short time of Scarburgh's arrival in London he had not only established a fashionable and profitable practice, but had gathered round him a group of men whose ideological and scientific interests mirrored his own. According to his near-contemporary, Walter Pope, he 'lived magnificently, his table being always accessible to all learned men, but more particularly to the distressed Royalists, and yet more particularly to the scholars ejected out of either of the universities for adhering to the King's cause'.[27] These scholars are not named, but would certainly have included William Harvey and Seth Ward, a clerical friend from Scarburgh's Cambridge days who combined a staunch anti-Puritanism with an active interest in mathematics and astronomy. Scarburgh also belonged to a small group of experimental philosophers which met weekly to discuss 'physick, anatomy, geometry, astronomy, navigation, staticks, magneticks, chymicks, mechanicks and natural experiments'.[28]

The backgrounds of its members were as varied as the issues investigated. Five were qualified medical men – Scarburgh himself, Francis Glisson, Jonathan Goddard, George Ent and Christopher Merrett – although their interests ranged far beyond medicine. Others, such as John Wallis, John Wilkins and Samuel Foster, a professor of astronomy in whose lodgings at Gresham College the group met during term-time, were primarily mathematicians. Nor were they all Royalists. Foster, Goddard and Wilkins had been active in the cause of Parliament; Wallis had put his mathematical skills to use as a code-breaker for Cromwell during the war; and Glisson had a brother who was Physician-General in the New Model Army. Small wonder that they agreed to keep off 'matters of theology and state affairs'.[29]

What united the group was a commitment to a Baconian conception of the right way to arrive at knowledge. In his *Great Instauration* Francis Bacon had argued for the rejection of traditional Aristotelian learning, which had for centuries been at the heart of scientific pursuits. He suggested that instead of using unproven hypotheses to test the validity of empirical observations, one should *begin* with those observations:

> There are and can exist but two ways of investigating and discovering truth. The one hurries on rapidly from the senses and particulars to the most general axioms; and from them as principles and their supposed indisputable truth derives and discovers the intermediate axioms. This is the way now in use. The other constructs its axioms from the senses and particulars, by ascending continually and gradually, till it finally arrives at the most general axioms, which is the true but unattempted way.[30]

This emphasis on experiment as a way of testing hypotheses, which was to inform almost the whole of seventeenth-century science, may not seem particularly remarkable today. But to Scarburgh's generation, which had been raised on a mixture of bizarre folk-myths and outmoded classical authorities, it was an earth-shattering and liberating development. There was still a popular belief in the existence of centaurs, unicorns and giants; commentators could uphold in all seriousness the notion that serpents were generated from the brains of the dead, that the chameleon lived on air and the ostrich ate iron, that the elixir of youth was a reality and that basilisks hatched from eggs laid by cocks.[31] In medicine, most people still believed in the four humours (blood, phlegm, yellow bile and black bile) and the ebb and flow of blood, because the second-century physician Galen had said that this was how the body worked – even though, as far as we know, he never dissected an adult human. It was Scarburgh's friend Harvey, with his call for 'ocular inspection [of] Nature her selfe', who had shown that blood circulated round the body, with all the implications that had for humoral pathology. In astronomy, Copernicus's *De Revolutionibus* (1543) had contradicted Aristotle and Ptolemy by proposing that the earth moved round the sun. Yet even in the seventeenth century this was still being hotly debated across Europe. Giordano Bruno had been burned at the stake in 1600 for maintaining that there were other worlds besides ours. Galileo, whose *Dialogues Concerning the Two Chief World Systems, Ptolemaic and Copernican* appeared in the year of Wren's birth, had been hauled before the Inquisition as a result in 1633. And Wren's own father could not bring himself to admit that Copernicus was right (and Aristotle, Ptolemy and the Church wrong), preferring instead to believe the theories of the Danish astronomer Tycho Brahe, who held that although the other planets revolved around the sun, the sun still turned about a fixed earth.

According to Bacon, Aristotle 'corrupted natural philosophy by logic . . . being everywhere more anxious as to definitions in teaching, and the accuracy of the wording of his propositions, than the internal truth of things'. Established knowledge was not knowledge at all, but a series of axioms which had never been questioned. Better by far to look for oneself, to collect data and check facts and only then to proceed to a theory; this was a 'more perfect use of reasoning in the investigation of things'.[32]

Wren's introduction to this new and exciting milieu, where learning involved ocular inspection of Nature herself rather than the interpretation of texts which had been gathering dust and errors for centuries, had a tremendous impact on the youth. The mathematical studies that he refers to in his letter to his father aren't described in any detail, although we can guess at them – and understand the active role Scarburgh played in his scientific education – by his account in the same letter of how he passed his time at the doctor's house. With a naïve adolescent arrogance which gives the lie to his remarks about how Scarburgh occasionally deferred 'to my poor reasonings', he mentions that 'the other day I wrote a treatise on trigonometry which sums up as I think, by a new method and in a few brief rules, the whole theory of spherical trigonometry'. He engraved the details on a brass disc the size of a coin, a feat that so delighted Scarburgh that he insisted on having a disc of his own. The boy also impressed the doctor with his design for a weather-clock that recorded fluctuations in wind speed and temperature through the night (an idea he would return to several times in later life) and the doctor asked him to have it constructed in brass at his expense.

Wren was also allowed to browse through Scarburgh's library of scientific works, later described by Evelyn as 'the very best collection, especially of mathematical books, that was I believe in Europe'.[33] It included his copy of William Oughtred's *Clavis Mathematicae*. Scarburgh was a great admirer of Oughtred, whose achievements stretched far beyond the double horizontal sundial mentioned earlier. The *Clavis* was a seminal work on algebra: Scarburgh had used it as a textbook while teaching mathematics at Cambridge, and had sought Oughtred out at his home in Albury, Surrey, to debate some of its finer points. Obviously aware of Wren's interest in sundials, Scarburgh suggested that it might be a good move for the boy to translate one of Oughtred's early tracts on dialling into Latin, thereby making it accessible to an international readership: 'The doctor promises, I may both gain an old man's favour, and at the same time win that of all those students of mathematics who acknowledge Oughtred as their father and teacher.'[34]

Wren certainly gained an old man's favour. When the treatise on dialling was published, as an appendix to a 1652 Latin edition of the *Clavis*, Oughtred presented Wren with an inscribed copy, and described him in the preface as 'a youth generally admired for his talents, who, when not yet sixteen years old, enriched astronomy, gnomics, statics and mechanics, with brilliant inventions, and from that time has continued to enrich them, and in truth is one from whom I can, not vainly, look for great things'.[35] But Scarburgh's influence on Wren amounted to much more than advice on how to curry favour with the grand old man of Stuart mathematics. He fostered the boy's interest in maths: there is a touch of hero-worship in Wren's declaration, in the letter to Oughtred which accompanied his translation, that it was to Scarburgh's 'kindness and liberality of mind that I am indebted . . . for any little skill that I can boast in mathematics'. He also encouraged Wren to take an interest in anatomy and, quite possibly, architecture, during the period when the boy was lodging with him and later, throughout the 1650s and 1660s. The two men were still good friends in the 1670s when both were leaders in their respective fields, Wren as Surveyor-General of the King's Works and Scarburgh as Physician to the Royal Household and a leading member of the Royal College of Physicians.

Most importantly of all, Scarburgh introduced Wren to a circle in which science was not just a virtuoso's plaything but a valid scholarly activity. The astronomers and anatomists and mathematicians that Scarburgh knew were filled with an intense excitement at the possibilities opened up by experimental philosophy – the whole universe lay waiting to be explored and explained. While still only fourteen or fifteen, the boy must have sat at the doctor's table, listening to and disputing with men who talked of Kepler and Galileo; who had worked with Harvey (one of whom *was* Harvey, come to that); men who held that the earth moved in an elliptical orbit round the sun and that blood circulated round the body. Such men weren't content to accept the old scholastic 'truths' which had been taken for granted for centuries without being tested. They followed Francis Bacon, who had said that 'it is works we are in pursuit of, not speculations'. They were striking out on a voyage of discovery; and while still only a teenager, Wren found himself one of their number.

Wren went up to Wadham College, Oxford – which was then scarcely forty years old – as a gentleman commoner, some time in the academic year 1649/50. Oxford, rather than Cambridge, was the obvious choice for the Laudian Dean's only son. On a practical level, the family had recently settled at the Holders' Bletchingdon parsonage, and this was just seven miles to the north of the city. The Dean could keep an eye on his son's progress, and Holder, who knew people among the teaching staff, could be 'a kind and necessary friend' to the young student.

Moreover, while Cambridge had been purged of the King's men quite early on in the Civil War, Oxford, by comparison, had retained an affection for both Royalism and Laudianism. For some four years from 1642 it had been the headquarters of the court: Charles I had used Christ Church as his own lodgings and Merton as the Queen's, and the city had held out against Cromwell until 1646. And Archbishop Laud himself had been the university's Chancellor, introducing ritualism and ornament into its chapels and, through the Laudian Statutes which he prompted the university authorities to adopt in 1636, ensuring a bias in favour of a conservative High Church Anglicanism in matters of religion and an equally conservative Aristotelianism in natural philosophy and the arts.

Even so, by 1649 this was all in the past, albeit the recent past. The political climate in the city had changed overnight when the soldiers of the New Model Army marched in and 'thrust themselves into the pulpits, purposely by their rascally doctrine to obtain either proselytes, or draw off from their loyal principles and orthodox religion the scholars and inhabitants'.[36] And the fact that Oxford had identified itself so strongly with the losing side in the war had inevitable repercussions. They came most dramatically during a series of Parliamentary Visitations between 1647 and 1649, described by a Royalist priest in the following verses:

> Whilst out of town, strange news alarmed
> My ears, which sounded oddly,
> That Oxford was to be reformed
> By Dunces known as Godly.
>
> Ent'ring the City to inspect
> These blessed Regulators,
> There only found a meagre sect
> Of formal, ugly creatures.[37]

These formal, ugly creatures expelled between 300 and 400 members of the university and sacked all but three heads of colleges, replacing them with men more sympathetic to Puritanism and the Parliamentary cause. One of this new wave was John Wilkins, who in April 1648 was made Warden of Wadham College, in place of the Royalist John Pitt. Wilkins' presence at Oxford may well have been the most important reason why Dean Wren decided to send his son there: he had a reputation for being liberal and tolerant, with 'nothing of Bigotry, Unmannerliness, or Censoriousness, which then were in the Zenith, amongst some of the Heads, and Fellows of Colleges in Oxford'.[38] For this reason many country gentlemen, 'but especially those then stiled Cavaliers and Malignants, for adhering to the King and the Church', decided to send their sons to Wadham.[39] Dean Wren fell squarely into that category. It may also be significant that Wilkins was not only a divine, but a man with well-known scientific interests. By the time he arrived at the Warden's Lodge at Wadham, his published work already included three popular (and self-explanatory) titles: *The Discovery of a World in the Moone, or a Discourse tending to prove that 'tis probable there may be another Habitable World in that Planet* (1638); *A Discourse concerning a new Planet, tending to prove that 'tis probable our Earth is one of the Planets* (1640); and *Mathematical Magick, or the Wonders that may be performed by Mechanical Geometry* (1648). This last was dedicated to Charles Louis, nephew of Charles I and dispossessed Elector Palatine, whose chaplain Wilkins was.

The new Warden had met both the Dean and his son when Charles Louis lodged at the Deanery at Windsor in the late 1630s or early 1640s, 'for retirement, and benefit of the air'[40] – yet another reason for Dean Wren's choice of Wadham as a suitable college for Christopher. A rough draft of a letter from Wren to the Elector Palatine, apparently intended to accompany the details of three unspecified inventions relating to agriculture, printing and microscopy, and dating from some time in the 1650s, refers to 'that devotion towards your Highness, which I conceived while yet a child, when you was [sic] pleased to honour my father's house by your presence for some weeks'. In the same draft Wren intimates that Wilkins has suggested he write to the Elector, and describes himself as 'a most addicted client' of the Warden.[41]

When Wren arrived at Wadham aged seventeen – the most common age of matriculation, although around one in eight students was fifteen or younger – the university was slowly returning to normal after the war, leaving only the high preponderance of veterans among students, academics and domestic staff, and the scores of maimed ex-soldiers who begged for alms at the college gates and in the quadrangles, as reminders of past troubles. Oxford was still theoretically entrenched in the medieval scholastic tradition, and, ostensibly at least, there was little opportunity for the study of contemporary cultural developments. Undergraduates in the faculty of Arts had to spend four years 'in the study of Arts and in diligent attendance, according to the exigence of the statutes, upon the public lectures within the University'. This meant grammar, rhetoric, logic, moral philosophy, geometry and Greek, with a heavy emphasis throughout on Aristotle and commentaries on Aristotle. In petitioning for his degree, a student stated that his qualifications would 'suffice for his admission to lecture on every book of Aristotle's logic'.[42] Lectures, which were in Latin, lasted a civilized forty-five minutes, and students were fined for non-attendance. Conversation at dinner and supper was also in Latin. Tutors directed students' studies, read with them each morning and pointed them in the direction of the right texts: Keckerman and Robert Sanderson on logic; Cicero, Pliny, Caesar and Livy for rhetoric and history; the Greek Testament; Franciscus Pavonius's *Summa Ethicae* for moral philosophy. A master's degree meant another three years of Aristotle together with Greek, Hebrew, classical history, natural philosophy, geometry and astronomy. The few texts in the curriculum whose authors hadn't been dead for centuries were commentaries. And they were commentaries on those same long-dead authors.

In practice, though, things weren't quite as straightforward as this. Some gentleman commoners, who tended to come from the higher social groups, opted out of the formal disputations and public exercises by which their academic progress was judged, and many didn't bother to take a degree at all: their parents considered that a couple of years of study was quite enough education to fit them for their station in life. (Fewer than half the students admitted to Oxford in the seventeenth century actually got as far as graduating.) For those who took their studies seriously, and also wanted to find out about more modern developments, the opportunities were there, in spite of the conservative nature of the official curriculum. The individual colleges specified their own programmes of learning, and tutors had some freedom to direct their students towards more up-to-date work. (Students working towards their master's degrees were in any case left to pursue their studies independently.) There were also chairs in geometry and astronomy, both founded in 1619 by Sir Henry Savile, Warden of Merton College, in an attempt to offer a more forward-looking approach to the sciences. For example, although the university statutes stipulated that the 'professor of Geometry must understand that it is his proper province publicly to expound the thirteen books of Euclid's Elements, the Conics of Apollonius, and all the books of Archimedes', he was required to teach and expound 'arithmetic of all kinds, both speculative and practical; land-surveying or practical geometry; canonics of music, and mechanics'. He was also given a free choice of the texts he chose to lecture on; instructed to hold arithmetic classes at his lodgings once a week, 'without any formality, and in the vulgar tongue if he thinks fit'; and told to take his students out into the fields every now and then to give them lessons in 'the practice of geometry'.[43]

The Savilian Professor of Astronomy was also given a reasonably free hand. He had to explain Ptolemy, just as the Professor of Geometry had to work through Euclid, but he was also instructed to discuss the discoveries of Copernicus and other more modern writers. In addition it was his business to explain and teach 'the whole science of optics, gnomonics, geography, and the rules of navigation in so far as they are dependent on mathematics'.[44] And he was forbidden to mention astrology.

Although Oxford was by no means as reactionary and conservative in the early 1650s as some historians have asserted – both Harvey and Galileo were taught, for instance, and Aristotle was routinely criticized – formal classical learning formed the basis of all undergraduate study. As a gentleman commoner Wren enjoyed certain privileges – comfortable lodgings and meals at high table, for example. But he still had to attend lectures in Latin at the Schools in rhetoric, grammar, dialectic and moral philosophy; he still had to respond and oppose at formal disputations. None of these tasks seems to have presented him with much difficulty, but while they instilled in him a sound knowledge of the classics, they certainly didn't imbue him with respect for classical authority or formal book-learning: in later life he was in no doubt that 'the Mathematical Wits of this Age have excelled the Ancients (who pierc'd but to the Bark and Outside of Things)';[45] and long after the Restoration Aubrey commented that Wren was no great reader.

There was play as well as work, of course. Wren probably took part in games of bowls, boating, tennis, fives and archery – all undergraduate pastimes which were officially encouraged, so long as they didn't encroach on morning studies. The university authorities (and anxious parents) were rather less enthusiastic about winter evenings being whiled away on backgammon, billiards, dice and cards, but these were popular all the same – as, no doubt, were more traditional student activities. Upwards of 300 ale-houses in the city served a population of around 10,000; the number of prostitutes and women of easy virtue who were happy to entertain young students was considerably greater.*

It is hard to picture the pathologically earnest young Wren – small, delicate, accustomed to the company of older men and desperate to excel academically – drinking himself sick in the Mitre or whoring in the High; hard even to think of him indulging in those comparatively harmless sartorial excesses which the university's Puritan reformers condemned as passionately as brothels and ale-houses, such as the powdering of hair, the fashion for boots and spurs and the wearing of brightly coloured ribbons on hats and breeches. It is much easier to imagine him responding with pleasure to the fiercely competitive atmosphere which gradually re-emerged at Oxford as the disruptions caused by war and military occupation gave way to the day-to-day business of education. By temperament and inclination he was perfectly suited to the very public displays of erudition – the daily conversations in Latin, the disputations and oral exercises and examinations, delivered

---

*Seventeenth-century Oxford was notorious for its 'drunkennesse, swearinge, and other debauched courses'. In the 1680s the Nonconformist Samuel Wesley went to see for himself what 'a perfect Sodom and Gomorrah' it was and, shocked and appalled, swiftly enrolled as an undergraduate.

in front of critical and well-informed audiences – which made up the daily life of a student in Cromwellian Oxford.

We know little of how Wren spent his days away from his books. But two events in his undergraduate life, both a far cry from hard living, strong liquor and flamboyance, are of particular interest – and as with so much of his early career, they raise more questions than they answer. The first is referred to in one of his letters to the Dean, undated but written during 'my Easter holydays', perhaps in 1650. It describes a stay with a friend (a fellow student?) at a country house. Neither the friend's family nor the house is mentioned by name:

> The noble mansion (not indeed unworthy to be a palace for a prince in dimensions, in the symmetry of the fabric or in the splendour of the appointments) stands almost on the topmost brow of a hill. Delightful gardens surround it, furnished with innumerable walks, some laid down with gravel, some with swelling turf, nor are pools lacking, nor groves of trees . . . there is moreover a park adjoining, both pleasant and spacious. Out of doors one might call it a terrestrial paradise; within, heaven itself . . .[46]

As an architectural description this is commonplace stuff – a proper appreciation of size, symmetry, splendour and setting was hardly revolutionary among educated gentry in the mid-seventeenth century. But as the earliest surviving reference to building in Wren's writings, it does at least show that the future architect of St Paul's took an interest in design at a point when scientific pursuits were uppermost in his mind. Moreover, the letter goes on to give a rare glimpse into his personal attitudes to religion at this stage in his life:

> Why indeed should I not call so charming a spot heaven? A spot in which the piety and devotion of another age, put to flight by the impiety and crime of ours, have found sanctuary, in which the virtues are all not merely observed but cherished . . . in which holy mothers and maids singing divine songs, offering the pure incense of their prayers, reading, meditating and conversing of holy things, spend almost all day in the company of God and his angels.[47]

His hosts, whoever they were, obviously didn't belong to the Puritan wing of the Anglican Church; the reference to 'the piety and devotion of another age' suggests that they may even have been Roman

Catholics.★ The idea that an eighteen-year-old boy with an eighteen-year-old's raging hormones should *enjoy* spending his Easter vacation in a household where the mother and sisters of his friend devoted most of their waking hours to religion says a great deal about Wren's earnestness. Or more accurately, I suppose, it says a great deal about what he wanted his father to know about how he spent his holidays.

We know of the other event in Wren's life as an undergraduate from some Latin verse which he contributed, along with other students, to a 1651 pamphlet called *News from the Dead, or a true and exact narration of the miraculous Deliverance of Anne Greene.* In December 1650 a hapless servant called Anne Greene was hanged in Oxford Castle for murdering her bastard child. Executed criminals were much sought-after by doctors, and after Anne had been cut down she was put in a coffin and taken to a private house to await dissection. When the coffin was opened, the crowd that had gathered to witness the spectacle – dissections were very public affairs – saw that she was breathing, and one bystander tried to put a stop to that by stamping on her chest. At this point the anatomists arrived and managed to resuscitate her; and five days later she was well enough to go home, 'taking with her the coffin wherein she lay, as a trophy of this her wonderful preservation'.[48†] One can get some idea of the tone of the undergraduate verse that accompanied the account of this miracle from a single example:

> Thus 'tis more easy to recall the dead
> Than to restore a once-lost maidenhead.[49]

★Romantically inclined nineteenth-century biographers suggested that the house was the Coghills' mansion at Bletchingdon and that one of the maids who sang divine songs was Wren's future wife, Faith Coghill. A nice idea.
†Anthony Wood, who described the event, mentions a similar occurrence eight years later. This time the victim – another servant-girl hanged for killing her baby – wasn't so lucky. The town bailiffs heard that she had been rescuscitated and lynched her.

3

The Theory and Practice of Physick

*A*round 1656, by which time he was a professional academic and a Fellow of All Souls, Wren's interest in anatomy led him to carry out a series of canine splenectomies. These gruesome vivisections enjoyed quite a vogue during the last years of the Commonwealth, when an unknown number of luckless dogs had their spleens whipped out by, among others, Charles Scarburgh; the Royalist physician George Thomson; and the surgeon William Day, from whom 'ye same spleen and ye dog was stole . . . and brought up to London and there dissected'. Robert Boyle asked 'that dexterous Dissector' Dr Jolive to remove the spleen from Boyle's own setter – Jolive gave it to him to hold in his hand while he severed the connecting tissue. Surprisingly, a number of the patients actually survived; in the early 1660s the Oxford apothecary Stephen Toone kept a dog 'which they call "Spleen" because his spleen is taken out'.[1] One of George Thomson's patients lived for more than two years, and Boyle's setter also survived 'as sportive and wanton as before', until he too was stolen.

The possibility of a spleenless existence was at the heart of these experiments. Traditional medical practice, derived in the main from the second-century Greek authority, Galen, had relied on maintaining a correct balance of the four humours: blood, which was produced by the heart; phlegm, which came from the brain; yellow bile (choler), which was secreted by the liver; and black bile (melancholy), from the spleen. A predominance of one or other of the humours caused mental and physiological changes – melancholia, for example, or a choleric disposition. Humoral pathology, and Galen's accompanying belief that all parts of the body had been perfectly designed for a purpose, had come under increasingly critical scrutiny during the sixteenth century, although it was still possible for a doctor to be imprisoned for casting doubt on any aspect of Galen's writings. In the seventeenth, the appearance in 1628 of William Harvey's great work on the circulation of the blood, *De Motu Cordis*, seemed to contradict Galenic teaching, which asserted that blood ebbed and flowed from the liver to all parts of the body, distributing the humours uniformly; in addition, 'natural spirits' supplied by the liver were supplemented in the heart by 'vital spirits' from the air.

The situation by the 1650s was in fact much more confused than the preceding account implies, with some physicians still accepting Galenic humoral pathology, others rejecting it entirely and others still attempting rather desperately to reconcile it with the implications of Harvey's theories. Convinced Harveians, like Charles Scarburgh (and, we must presume, Wren himself), took more than the circulation of the blood from Harvey – they took his method, which was to look and see how the body functioned, rather than accepting the word of ancient authorities. Hence the spate of canine splenectomies: if a creature could lose its spleen and survive, where did that leave accepted Galenic theory and the four humours?

Wren's interest in the debate – at a practical level, at least – probably has its origins in his relationship with Charles Scarburgh. In addition to his other qualities Scarburgh was a skilled anatomist, and his prowess was publicly acknowledged in 1656 when the Royal College of Physicians appointed him Lumleian lecturer in succession to his friend Harvey. George Thomson, who claimed to have been 'the first who made this Experimental Dissection [i.e., canine splenectomy] to a purpose',[2] later accused Scarburgh of having stolen the experiment from him; whether or not the accusation was justified, it suggests that Scarburgh was practising splenectomy at around the same time as Wren. Given the previous close relationship between the two, it seems likely that the older man at least inspired the younger to try the experiment, even if he didn't show him how to do it. Certainly someone must have been instructing Wren in surgical procedures: after all, the successful removal of a body part is not something one just does. A sound knowledge of anatomy is required in the first place, simply in order to *find* the spleen. So is a steady hand – and one well-used to wielding the knife, considering that the wretched spaniel was not exactly a willing accomplice to the operation.

In fact, Wren's medical interests during the 1650s extended beyond the removal of spleens. His other major foray into medical research also involved experimenting on live dogs – with even less happy results for the animals, but more profound consequences for the history of medicine. Like the canine splenectomies, his pioneering work on intravenous injection was an indirect result of Harvey's *De Motu Cordis*, which had raised more questions than it had answered. If blood circulated quickly around the body, then presumably the effects of a scorpion's sting or a viper's bite were caused by the injection of fluid poison into the bloodstream, which carried it to other parts of the system as effectively as if it had been ingested (as opposed to traditional explanations, which centred on the corruption of animal spirits caused by the biter's bad attitude). During discussions with John Wilkins and Robert Boyle, in which the latter was speculating on the application of poisons, Wren said he thought he could formulate a method to introduce liquid poison into the bloodstream. Boyle quickly produced a large dog and Wren proved as good as his word, as he wrote to William Petty, an old Oxford associate from the early 1650s, in an undated letter, *c.* 1656–8:

> Shall I trouble you with what we doe in Anatomy? . . . the most considerable [Experiment] I have made of late is this. I have injected Wine and Ale in a liveing Dog into the Mass of Blood by a Veine, in good Quantities, till I have made him extremely drunk, but soon after he Pisseth it out: with 2 ounces of Infusion of Crocus Metall [*crocus metallorum*, an emetic]: thus injected, the Dog immediately fell a Vomitting, & so vomited till he died. It will be too long to tell you the Effects of Opium, Scammony, & other things that I have tried in this way: I am now in further pursuit of the Experiment, which I take to be of great concernment, and what will give great light both to the Theory and Practice of Physick.[3]

Some years later Robert Boyle described these experiments in more detail, recalling how in the presence of various Oxford physicians and virtuosi, the dog's paws were tied securely to the four corners of a table and an incision made over 'the larger Vessels' – probably the lateral saphenous vein – in the poor creature's hind leg.[4] Wren applied a ligature and placed a half-inch by quarter-inch pierced brass plate he had devised over the vein, using thread attached to four tiny holes in the corners of the plate. He then used a lancet to slit the vein through the aperture in the plate, the purpose of which was to prevent the vein from 'starting aside' (i.e., slipping out of position); amidst the resulting gush of blood he inserted a narrow pipe into the animal's leg and injected a warm solution of opium in white wine.

Once released from the table, the dog began to stagger around as 'by the circular motion of [the blood, the opium was] carried to the Brain, and other Parts of the Body'. With a less than adequate sense of the ground-breaking seriousness of the occasion, everyone present immediately began to offer bets that it was going to die. They lost, however, because Boyle, who was anxious to keep his dog 'for further Observation', had him whipped up and down the garden until he came to his senses. The dog survived to grow fat and famous, although Boyle's observation of his health was cut short when, after further experiments, he was stolen. Perhaps Wren's experiment was carried out on the same luckless setter whose spleen was removed by Dr Jolive.

As usually happened with scientific experiments which yielded swift and dramatic results, intravenous injection soon became something of a party trick. Wren later performed it on another dog for the Marquess of Dorchester, and also experimented with different substances, as he recounted in his letter to Petty. Boyle suggested — with a chillingly dispassionate curiosity — that substances might be injected into human bodies, 'especially those of Malefactors'; and he later recalled that a few months after the initial experiments, 'a foreign Ambassador, a very curious person', told how he had attempted to have *crocus metallorum* injected into one of his servants, 'an inferior Domestic . . . that deserved to have been hanged'. The attempt was abandoned when the fellow fainted. The experiment was repeated fairly frequently with animals, however: in 1664, for example, Pepys saw Dr Timothy Clarke, an early member of the Royal Society who had been shown how to perform the injection by Wren, bungle 'an experiment of killing a dog by letting opium into his hind leg'.[5] Clarke and his assistant couldn't find the lateral saphenous vein.

As far as we know, Wren wasn't directly involved in this later 'research', not necessarily because he was averse to turning tricks in public, but because by the 1660s his interests lay elsewhere. His initial series of experiments at Oxford, however, were publicized beyond his immediate circle: first by Boyle in his *Usefulness of Natural Philosophy* (1663) and then by the Royal Society. By the end of 1664 the experiment was known in Breslau and Hamburg.[6] It led directly to the first attempts at the transfusion of blood, on the principle that if intravenous injection could introduce poisons into the system of a healthy creature, it could also introduce health-giving substances – such as good blood to replace bad. Richard Lower, a contemporary of Wren's at both Westminster School and Oxford (he went up to Christ Church the same year Wren went to Wadham) transfused blood from one dog to another in 1665, and two years later he transfused nine or ten ounces of sheep's blood into a human being, a 'poor and debauched man . . . cracked a little in his head'.[7] Astonishingly, the patient survived – probably because the amount of blood which actually reached him was much less than was claimed. Experiments gradually petered out after the French surgeon Jean-Baptiste Denis, who independently of Lower had been busy swapping blood between sheep and horses, goats and dogs, and calves, lambs and people, narrowly escaped prosecution when he finally managed to kill a human subject in 1668.

One might imagine from all this that Wren had opted for medicine as a career, proof of Walter Charleton's 1657 observation that 'our late warrs and schisms having almost wholly discouraged men from the study of theologie, and brought the civil law into contempt, the major part of young schollers in our universities addict themselves to physick'.[8] But his addictions ranged much wider than physick. *Parentalia* has a lengthy catalogue of 'New Theories, Inventions, Experiments, and Mechanick Improvements' developed by Wren during the 1650s and exhibited to the Wadham group. It shows that his interests encompassed not only anatomy, but astronomy and lens-grinding, ciphers, fortifications and military engines, a double-writing instrument, a 'Strainer of the Breath, to make the same Air serve in Respiration', an invention 'to weave many Ribbons at once with only turning a Wheel', a cheap method of embroidering bed-hangings, whale-fishing, water-pumps and 'Ways of submarine Navigation', a weather-clock and weather-wheel, new musical instruments, 'a Speaking Organ, articulating Sounds', new surveying techniques, and 'diverse Improvements in the Art of Husbandry' – to name but a few.[9]

Again the obvious question is, why? What was a young Oxford don doing dabbling in textile manufacture and whale-fishing, meteorology, music and military matters? The answer lies, partly at least, in the company he was keeping. Even as a child, Wren was temperamentally inclined towards practical problem-solving, and the encouragement he received from his father the Dean, his brother-in-law William Holder and especially his early mentor Charles Scarburgh did much to foster his curiosity. His formal academic training may have pushed him further in the direction of experimental philosophy, although this is less likely. But his great good fortune lay in being up at Oxford – with his interests and his formidable intellect – at a time when an older generation of like-minded individuals were gathering there. He had duly obtained his BA in 1651, which was slightly irregular, since he was still a good two years short of the four-year residency requirements necessary for a degree, but by no means uncommon: in the aftermath of the war and the subsequent ejections of dons, the university regulations were still being interpreted quite generously.[10] The BA was followed by an MA in 1653, and in the same year he was elected to a fellowship at All Souls College. This marked the real beginning of Wren's career as an academic, providing him with an income, a congenial home for as long as he liked and remarkably little in the way of duties and obligations. All Souls was altogether more prestigious than Wadham: founded in 1438 by Archbishop Henry Chichele and Henry VI, it was essentially a research institute, with a warden, forty fellows and no students at all. All Souls fellowships were sought-after commodities: in the years immediately after the war they were doled out to ex-soldiers and the sons of regicides, men who were owed favours by Parliament. They also exchanged hands for money, sometimes for huge sums – an illegal practice which the Warden, a mild-mannered reformer named John Palmer, tried unsuccessfully to stamp out.

While All Souls provided Wren with a stable base in Oxford, much more important for his subsequent career was the fact that within a short time of arriving at university he had become part of an 'experimental philosophical club' founded in the autumn of 1649 by William Petty, an ambitious Parliamentarian physician with a passionate commitment to Baconian principles. Petty, who was one of the doctors who had managed to raise Anne Greene from the dead in 1650 (the other was Thomas Willis, a Royalist soldier who had stayed on in Oxford to study medicine after the city fell to Cromwell in 1646), was a Fellow of Brasenose who deputed at dissections for Thomas Clayton, the Regius Professor of Medicine, because the latter 'could not endure the sight of a bloody body'.[11] As with any such group, the club's membership fluctuated: between 1649 and the end of the 1650s some fifty names were associated with it at one time or another, but at its height it had twenty-five or thirty members, of whom some were much more active than others. They met initially in Petty's rooms at Buckley Hall in the High Street, over a shop belonging to John Clarke, Harvey's old apothecary – a convenient arrangement, since Clarke could provide instruments and chemicals for their experiments. It was in Petty's lodgings that the fortunate Anne Greene was resurrected.

The club was in some senses a continuation of the London gathering Wren had come into contact with during his stay at Charles Scarburgh's house, including several members of the original circle who, like John Wilkins, had benefited from the Parliamentary Visitations of 1647–9. John Wallis, for example, had arrived at Oxford with Wilkins in 1649, being appointed Savilian Professor of Geometry. Seth Ward, another of the London group of the 1640s, was made Savilian Professor of Astronomy in 1650 after the incumbent Edward Greaves had been ejected by the Visitation – and this in spite of Ward's staunchly Royalist background. The appointment was largely due to some swift political footwork on the part of Scarburgh and William Holder. And in 1651 Jonathan Goddard, another friend of Scarburgh's and yet another of the experimental philosophers who had met in London in the mid-1640s, was appointed Warden of Merton College, a reward for his services as Physician-in-Chief to Cromwell's army during campaigns in Scotland and Ireland.

All of these men were high achievers and committed Baconian experimentalists, sharing Petty's view that he 'never knew any man who had once tasted the sweetnes of experimentall knowledge that ever afterward lusted after the vaporous garlick and onions of phantasmaticall seeming philosophy'.[12] Indeed, Aubrey was later to claim, not altogether accurately, that 'till about the year 1649, when experimental philosophy was first cultivated by a club at Oxford, it was held a strange presumption for a man to attempt an innovation in learning'. And all belonged to the generation before Wren's: when he graduated BA in 1651 at the age of eighteen, Ward and Goddard were both about thirty-four, Wallis thirty-five and Wilkins, described by Aubrey as the 'principal reviver of experimental philosophy', thirty-seven. Willis was thirty and Petty twenty-eight. Along with the twenty or so other regular members they were, in fact, the pioneers of a scientific revolution, men that were 'daily conversant in the works of nature, that doe dilligently observe, compare and apply them, and produce wonderfull artifices by so doing'.[13] And they welcomed the undergraduate Wren to their meetings as an equal. In 1650, for example, John Wallis wrote admiringly to a friend that 'besides divers other fine inventions and contrivances, [Wren] hath found out a way to measure the moistnesse and dryness of the air exactly'[14] – a reference, perhaps, to improvements that the student was making to the weather-clock he had devised while staying with Scarburgh.

Notwithstanding his earlier contacts with several of the leading members of the Oxford group at Scarburgh's house, the fact that Wren was accepted by them at all says a great deal for his ability to ingratiate himself with his elders; that they welcomed and respected such a young man says even more for his scientific skills. However, initially at least, he gained much more from them than they did from him. Dean Wren and William Holder may have encouraged his appetite for natural philosophy; Charles Scarburgh may have nurtured it. But the experimental philosophical club of Oxford stimulated that appetite, feeding it with new ideas, new outlets and new opportunities and, in the process, turning a precocious teenager into one of the leading figures in seventeenth-century science.

In late 1651 or early 1652 William Petty left Oxford for Ireland as physician to Cromwell's army and remained there for much of the 1650s, undertaking a survey of the country, allocating confiscated lands to military and civilian personnel – and accruing a considerable fortune in the process.* With Petty's departure the club moved the venue of its Thursday afternoon meetings to Wadham College, where it met in John Wilkins' lodgings. Its aims, which were set out by Seth Ward in February 1652, soon after the move, were nothing if not ambitious: as well as equipping a laboratory and an observatory, and constantly making chemical experiments, the 'Greate Clubb' agreed collectively to examine and index all the books 'of our public library' with a view to 'gather together such things as are already discovered . . . then to have a collection of those wch are still inquirenda and according to our opportunityes to make inquisitive experiments'. The objective was that 'out of a sufficient number of such experiments, the way of nature in workeing may be discovered'.[15]

We don't know how far the Greate Clubb succeeded in its aims. As with any loose informal gathering of volunteers, members tended to move on, lose interest or promise contributions on the spur of the moment which were hopelessly unrealistic. We do know, however, that for most of the 1650s Wren's researches were carried out in collaboration with fellow members of the Oxford group, in which Wadham men predominated.† Not all were professional academics: Wren's cousins

---

*Besides his government pay and the 'commission' he received on the sale of Irish lands, Petty took around £400 a year from the private medical practice he set up in Dublin. Sixteen years later Thomas Willis's medical practice was earning him the highest income in the whole of Oxford. No wonder Wren later wished he had gone in for medicine.

†Of the fifty men associated with the Oxford group at this period, twelve were from Wadham. The college that contributed the second-highest number was Christ Church, with five.

Matthew and Thomas (the sons of Uncle Matthew), for example, were private residents hanging around on the periphery of university life but unable to enrol because of their straitened circumstances, caused by their father's prolonged imprisonment in the Tower. The brilliant, pious, effete and neurotic Robert Boyle, who took lodgings next door to the Three Tuns on the High in the autumn of 1654, was another private resident. Boyle, a younger son of the Earl of Cork, quickly became an important member of the group; as we have seen, Wren's experiments with splenectomy and intravenous injection were carried out at Boyle's prompting and with his cooperation.

Wren was also closely involved with both professional and amateur astronomers. There was Sir Paul Neile, a well-known virtuoso on the fringe of the group who was 'famous for his optic glasses',[16] and with whom Wren observed the heavens through the former's 35-foot telescope during visits to his country house in the village of White Waltham, a few miles south-west of Maidenhead; John Wallis, with whom he saw the solar eclipse of 1654; and Seth Ward, who built an observatory over the entrance tower at Wadham which was equipped by Neile with telescopes of 6, 12 and 22 feet. This observatory was regularly used by Wren during the mid-1650s.

But Wren's most important collaborator was the Warden of Wadham, who took the young man under his wing, introduced him to the right people and did all he could to encourage his scientific interests. 'Lustie, strong-growne, well sett, and broad-shouldered', John Wilkins was an immensely powerful figure in Commonwealth Oxford, and a good man to have as a mentor. He had been Warden of Wadham since 1648, of course, but in 1652 Oliver Cromwell – who was by then Chancellor of the university – appointed him, as one of a committee of five, to carry out the Chancellor's duties. Of the other four, three at least had close personal links with Cromwell: Jonathan Goddard had been his physician; John Owen, Dean of Christ Church, was his chaplain on the Irish and Scottish campaigns; and Peter French was his brother-in-law and one of the official preachers to his Council. The fifth was Thomas Goodwin, President of Magdalen. Wilkins was a regular visitor to the Protector's lodgings in Whitehall and in 1656 became one of the family when he married Peter French's widow, Robina. A measure of his influence is seen by the fact that when Cromwell's son Richard was elected as Chancellor in the summer of 1657, it was Wilkins who escorted him at his installation.

Like Cromwell, Wilkins was essentially a conservative in politics. He used his power wisely, advocating religious toleration – much to the disgust of his more radical Puritan colleagues – and fighting hard to preserve Oxford's traditional independence whenever it seemed threatened by government interference. Even John Evelyn, who was no friend to the Commonwealth, was impressed, describing Wilkins as 'a most obliging person, who ... tooke great pains to preserve the Universities from the ignorant sacrilegious Commanders and Souldiers, who would faine have demolish'd all places and persons that pretended to learning'.[17] The Warden also fostered the new philosophy at Oxford and played a leading role in the activities of the Clubb. He gave £200 towards the erecting of a 'College for Experiments et Mechanicks at Oxford, over the Schooles or in the long gallery, where all the models of Inv[entive] Arts etc are to be reserved' (which sadly came to nothing);[18] and it was he who who urged Robert Boyle to settle in Oxford, saying that the latter would be 'the means to quicken and direct us in our enquiries'. He turned the Warden's garden over to experiments in horticulture and the improvement of fruit trees and flowering plants. Even the non-academic staff at Wadham were appointed on the strength of their scientific connections and skills: the manciple, Christopher Brookes, was the son-in-law of William Oughtred and ran a successful instrument-making business at the college; and the cook's daughter was married to the mathematician John Collins.

A vivid glimpse into Wilkins' lodgings and the activities in which he and Wren were engaged comes from Evelyn, who visited Oxford in July of 1654. Two days after being entertained at a concert at All Souls, where he met 'that miracle of a youth Mr Christopher Wren, nephew of the Bishop of Ely' he was invited to dine with Wilkins, who

> shew'd me the transparent apiaries, which he had built like castles and palaces, and so order'd them one upon another as to take the hony without destroying the bees. These were adorn'd with a variety of dials, little statues, vanes, &c ... He had also contriv'd an hollow statue which gave a voice and utter'd words, by a long conceal'd pipe that went to its mouth, whilst one speaks through it at a good distance. He had above in his lodgings and gallery variety of shadows, dyals, perspectives, and many other artificial, mathematical, and magical curiosities, a way-wiser, a thermometer, a monstrous magnet, conic and other sections, a ballance on a demi-circle, most of them of his owne and that prodigious young scholar Mr Chr Wren, who presented me with a piece of white marble, which he

had stain'd with a lively red very deepe, as beautiful as if it had ben natural.[19]

Much of Wren's scientific work in the early 1650s can be traced to his association with Wilkins. In the catalogue of 'New Theories, Inventions, Experiments, and Mechanick Improvements' mentioned above, for instance, the reference to 'Ways of submarine Navigation' (whatever they were) has its origin in a discussion in Wilkins' *Mathematical Magick* of 1648 about 'the Possibility of framing an Ark for Submarine Navigations'.[20] So does Wren's attempt to devise a 'Strainer of the Breath, to make the same Air serve in Respiration': as Wilkins had pointed out, 'the greatest difficulty of all' in underwater travel was 'how the air may be supplied for respiration'.[21] The 'Speaking Organ, articulating Sounds' was probably the talking statue that Evelyn was shown, or a variation on it; the improvements in husbandry were almost certainly carried out with Wilkins and in Wilkins' college garden; the ciphers that, according to *Parentalia*, Wren worked on at Oxford may well be related to a pet project of Wilkins' for a universal language which would enable scientists of different countries to communicate more easily.

One can see that it is often hard to establish the 'prodigious young scholar's' individual contribution to particular inventions and theories – a fact which is scarcely surprising, given the intensely collaborative nature of scientific activity within the Oxford group and the fragmentary nature of the documentary evidence for Wren's work during this period of his career. However, one invention that he laid unequivocal claim to, and which caused quite a stir at the time – even being brought to the attention of Cromwell himself – was the double-writing instrument mentioned in the *Parentalia* catalogue. One of the earliest products of his time at Oxford, this seems to have been developed in the early 1650s: in an undated letter, possibly addressed to Wilkins, Wren describes how three years previously his invention was shown to 'the then great, now greatest Person in the Nation'.[22] (Wren's choice of phrase is interesting considering his political background but not, perhaps, surprising if his correspondent was indeed John Wilkins.) Cromwell became Protector under the Instrument of Government in December 1653, which would date the device to some time between the end of 1650 and the establishment of the Protectorate.

The double-writing instrument was, as its name implies, a sort of pantograph that via a system of hinged bars enabled its user to write two copies of a document simultaneously. As Wren proudly put it, 'to copy out in every Punctilio the exact Resemblance, or rather the very Identity of the two Copies, as if one should fancy such a Piece of Magick as should make the same Thing really two; or with drunken Eyes should see the same Thing double, is what might be thought almost impossible for the Hand of Man.'[23] At different stages of its development he showed the device to members of the Oxford group, including Wilkins, of course, who encouraged him to perfect it. In another undated letter to an unknown correspondent, variously identified as Wilkins and Wren's cousin Matthew, he enclosed a drawing of the instrument and talked of how pleased he was with its simplicity:

> I now send you a Twin of the Like Production to officiate in its place [he had apparently already sent a design for an earlier version of the instrument]; and something it would say to you too, concerning its Parent, its Birth & Original: for It fears when the meaness of its Birth is discover'd, it may be slighted: the misapprehending World measures the Excellence of things by their Rarity, or Difficulty of Framing, not by the Concinnity and apt Disposal of Parts to attain their End by a right Line as it were & the Simplest way. Any New Invention in Mechanicks perform'd by an Operose way of divers unessential though well compacted Parts, shall be admired together with the Artist, meerly for the Variety of the Motions and the Difficulty of Performance; comes a more judicious Hand and with a far smaller number of Peeces, & those perhaps of more trivial Materials, but compos'd with more Brain & less ostentation, frames the same thing in a little Volume, & such a one I shall call a Master . . .[24]

Wren intended at the time to publish his design, but soon lost interest, referring to it as 'a cast-off Toy'. Some years later, however, he heard that his double-writing instrument had been plagiarized and was being hawked about London 'by several, as a Production of their own'.[25] This struck a nerve: he was already sensitive to a story doing the rounds that William Petty had been first with the invention. (Petty had in fact announced a double-writing instrument as early as 1648, but had still not perfected it – in 1654 Samuel Hartlib recorded that, 'Those that know the way which Mr Wren doth use, say [Petty's] art of double writing is not worth a rush.'[26] He didn't care if the invention was put to commercial use by others, but was anxious lest this should somehow provide ammunition for those who advocated Petty's prior claim: 'tho' I care not for having a Successor in Invention, yet it behoves me to vindicate myself from the Aspersion of having a Predecessor'.[27] He accordingly asserted his right to the device.

This episode speaks volumes about the complicated nature of Wren's personality as he reached adulthood. His lack of interest in exploiting his inventions and his ready willingness to pass on his ideas to others would remain defining characteristics: after a visit to All Souls in 1663, for example, the Frenchman Balthazar de Monconys described him as 'one of the most courteous and most open men that I have found in England';[28] and throughout the 1660s, '70s and '80s the appearance of a new theory or a new instrument was repeatedly greeted by his friends' assertions that Wren had thought of it or invented it years before but hadn't bothered to publish it – something which the proud theorists and inventors in question must have found deeply irritating. There was the occasional tantrum, of course – he was only human. Aubrey recalled how on one occasion, which sheds a different light on his apparent unworldliness, he presented a machine for weaving 'seven pair or nine paire of stockings at once' to the silk stocking weavers' guild in London, and asked £400 for it. When they refused his price, he lost his temper and smashed the machine to pieces before their eyes.[29] But by and large, he was astonishingly free with his ideas. However, as the exchanges over the double-writing instrument show, while he may have been quite unworldly in one respect, and remarkably uninterested in publishing the results of his work, he was not prepared to lose the credit for them when they did emerge into the light of day. The good opinion of his peers mattered terribly to him, as it would throughout his life.

A more intriguing point concerns Wren's early enthusiasm for the 'apt Disposal of Parts' and 'the Simplest way'. To 21st-century eyes, the fact that the man who would become the leading architect of the English Baroque should call for less ostentation seems curious; simplicity and a lack of ostentation are hardly the qualities that spring to mind as one stands beneath the dome of St Paul's, or wanders through the state apartments at Hampton Court.

Even more so than many of his collaborators in the Oxford group, Wren pursued an amazingly wide range of scientific interests. To the modern reader, accustomed to a high degree of specialization within disciplines, his approach seems almost dilettantish, and he can easily come across as 'a skilled dabbler, an amateur . . . [whose] sheer diversity of interest prevented him from attaining the heights which his ability allowed'.[30] How, we ask, can we possibly take Wren's scientific career seriously, when we see him making a glass-walled beehive or a talking statue one minute, and inventing his double-writing instrument or digging around in a spaniel's insides the next? But this is now and that was then. His contemporaries in the scientific community saw nothing blameworthy at all, marvelling at the breadth of his achievement rather than bemoaning the dilution of his talent or casting a sceptical eye on the catholicity of his interests. As far as we can tell, they concurred wholeheartedly with Evelyn's opinion of Wren as 'a miracle of a youth'; they too felt a tremendous sense of excitement in the process of discovery, an exhilaration at the thought that everything could be known, everything could be explained and ordered.

All the same, Wren *did* begin to specialize in one particular field of study as the 1650s wore on, although never to the exclusion of his other interests. He needed a career; and the discipline he chose was one in which excitement was particularly intense – astronomy.

It is no exaggeration to say that although Copernicus may have turned the universe inside out in the sixteenth century, the real revolution in the *practice* of astronomy occurred in the seventeenth. During a stay in Venice in May 1609, Galileo Galilei, then a professor of mathematics at Padua, heard a rumour of a Dutch invention 'by the aid of which visible objects, although at a great distance from the eye of the observer, were seen distinctly as if near'.[31] Back in Padua, he set about making his own telescopes (he had made four by January 1610, the last and most powerful of which had a magnification of × 30); and when he trained them on the heavens, he was astonished by what he saw. The moon's surface was not smooth, as the Greeks had thought, but covered in mountains and valleys; Jupiter was a round disc, with four moons of its own; and most startling of all, he found a vast number of stars which, invisible as they were to the naked eye, no one had seen before. 'Upon whatever part of [the Milky Way] you direct the telescope,' he wrote, 'straightway a vast crowd of stars presents itself to view; many of them are tolerably large and extremely bright, but the number of small ones is quite beyond determination.'[32] Initial reactions to his discoveries were mixed: traditional Aristotelians, for example, refused point-blank to believe it was possible to see anything in the heavens not mentioned by Aristotle, while governments decided the stars could be left to themselves, seizing instead on the military potential of the telescope. But the ability to observe the previously unobservable opened up new worlds – quite literally – to professional astronomers and virtuosi alike, transforming astronomy and offering an ambitious experimental philosopher unrivalled opportunities for research and wonder, as the English diplomat Sir Henry Wotton was quick to appreciate. In March 1610 Wotton, then James I's ambassador in Venice, despatched home a copy of Galileo's *Sidereus Nuncius* with a covering letter:

> I send herewith unto his Majesty the strangest piece of news (as I may justly call it) that he hath ever yet received from any part of the world; which is the annexed book (come abroad this very day) of the Mathematical Professor at Padua, who by the help of an optical instrument (which both enlargeth and approximateth the object) . . . hath discovered four new planets rolling about the sphere of Jupiter, besides many other unknown fixed stars; likewise the true cause of the *Via Lactea,* so long searched; and lastly that the moon is not spherical, but endued with many prominences, and, which is of all the strangest, illuminated with the solar light by reflection from the body of the earth, as he seemeth to say. So as upon the whole subject he hath first overthrown all former astronomy . . .[33]

By the 1650s the telescope was an established and essential instrument in every astronomer's armoury, but the sense of excitement persisted. Wren himself wrote that 'the incomparable Galileo, who was the first to direct a telescope to the sky . . . so overcame yielding nature, that all celestial mysteries were at once disclosed to him'. As Henry Oldenburg, a Bremen-born private tutor and a member of the Oxford group, put it: 'If any thing is able to conduct our reasoning about ye Celestiall bodies, it is the perfecting of Telescopes. By improving ym we may by their means make navigations as well into ye Heavens and discover new Countries there, as Columbus did by ships in America.'[34]

Wren's interest in astronomy dated back to his childhood and the pasteboard *panorganum astronomicum* he had presented to his father at the age of thirteen. As an undergraduate, he may well have attended Seth Ward's astronomy lectures, at which students were taught about the constellations and the meaning of concepts such as meridian, longitude and latitude, equinoxes and ecliptic, given basic instruction in observational techniques and, where appropriate, asked to consider the various hypotheses on stellar and planetary motion. (Until the construction of Ward's observatory at Wadham in 1652, an upper room in the Schools' tower was used for instruction.) As a Fellow at All Souls,

Wren's interest continued to grow; as previously mentioned, he and Wallis observed a solar eclipse together in 1654; and during the summer of the following year he was collaborating with Wilkins on the construction of an eighty-foot telescope 'to see at once the whole moon'.[35]

Lunar observation was the area of astronomy where the development of the telescope had had the most immediate impact. The moon offered a large image and was easy to locate in the sky – important considerations when one recalls that the telescopes of the day generally produced faint images, had a small field of view and, in the case of larger, more powerful instruments, were often supported on decidedly wobbly gantries and pulleys. The moon was also visible for long periods at predictable regular intervals. And it was spectacular. With the naked eye, men had been able to make out only irregular patches. Now, its craters, mountains and large dark areas fired the imagination. ('Like a tarte that my cooke made me last weeke,' said the amateur astronomer William Lower, when he first looked at the moon through a telescope at the beginning of the century.[36]) As a result, the advent of the telescope had led to a spate of attempts to map the moon. Michel Florent van Langren, court astronomer to Philip IV of Spain, published one of the first in 1645, with three hundred prominent features given the names of saints, biblical characters and members of Philip's court. Two years later the *Selenographia* of Johannes Hevelius of Danzig appeared, with a new set of names derived from analogies with terrestrial geography, such as Mount Sinai, the Carpathian Mountains, the Isle of Sicily and various oceans, seas and lakes. Hevelius's map was the most accurate to date, although the fact that it was taken from eye-observation rather than using any through-the-lens measuring device meant that a number of errors crept in. His naming system failed to gain wide acceptance, though; legend has it that after his death in 1687, the original copper plate of the map was melted down and turned into a teapot. It was superseded in 1651 by the lunar map of the Italian Jesuit Giovanni Riccioli, which mixed rather fanciful labels for larger features – the Oceanus Procellarum or 'Ocean of Storms', the Terra Sanitatis ('Land of Health'), the Mare Tranquillitatis ('Sea of Tranquillity') – with craters named after astronomers and other well-known historical figures. Riccioli gave himself a large crater; but as a devout anti-Copernican, he dropped Copernicus into the Ocean of Storms and allocated a small and insignificant crater to Galileo.

As with so much else, Wren's interest in mapping the moon was probably due to the influence of John Wilkins. He would have read Wilkins' 1638 *Discovery of a World in the Moone*, which argued that the moon was habitable, with 'an Atmospheara, or an orbe of gross vaporous aire' (and in which, incidentally, Wilkins agreed with Kepler that 'as soon as the Art of Flying is found out', a colony will be 'transplanted into that other World').[37]

The more immediate stimulus, however, was Wren's reading of the *Selenographia* of Hevelius, a copy of which had been placed in the Oxford library in 1650; quite simply, he thought he could do better. In September 1655, around the time of his and Wilkins' attempts to build the 80-foot telescope (which don't seem to have gone beyond a 24-foot instrument), he was telling friends that he was planning a new selenographia, 'which will be far more accurate than that of Hevelius, doing all by rule and demonstration which hath been hitherto done by guesses', and he spoke of an 'Exercit[atio] de Libratione Lunae far more accurate than that of Hevelius'.[38] (The moon's libration is the apparent wobble which causes areas at the edge of the disc to appear and disappear and allows slightly more than 59 per cent of its surface to be seen from the earth.) Soon afterwards he was writing to William Petty that he and his fellows in the Oxford group 'not only draw Pictures of the Moon, as Hevelius has done, but Survey her & give exact maps of her, & discover exactly her various Inclinations, and herein Hevelius's Errors'.[39]

Such a detailed lunar survey involved accurate measurements and the best possible optics. As regards the latter, Wren went back to the source, dissecting a horse's eye to discover 'what ye diameters of ye severall spheres of ye Humors were, and what ye proportions of ye distances of ye Centers of every sphericall sup[er]ficies was upon ye Axis of ye Eye'; and constructing a model of the eye 'with the Humours truely & dioptically made'.[40] We don't know the outcome of this, though the conflation of anatomy and astronomy shows the practical value of the seventeenth century's refusal to compartmentalize different scientific disciplines. But Wren learned that a lens with a back surface which was a hyperboloid would be an improvement on current spherical lenses; and in the course of his research he made the important mathematical discovery (important for those who care about such things, at least) that the hyperboloid of revolution is a ruled surface.

Wren's solution to the other problem in lunar surveying, the difficulty in making precise measurements of features seen through the telescope, was to make use of a moving-wire eyepiece micrometer. This had been developed in the early 1640s (but not published) by the English astronomer William Gascoigne, who rather charmingly hit on the idea when a spider spun its web in his telescope. Gascoigne's invention, which involved two parallel finely-ground pieces of metal which were moved in the focal plane of the object glass by means of a screw attached to a graduated disc, was probably passed on to his friend William Oughtred, from him to Charles Scarburgh and Seth Ward, and thence to Wren; Gascoigne himself had died in 1644 on Marston Moor, aged just twenty-four. Wren improved on the device, which was fairly crude: at around the time of his work on lunar topography, he referred to the fact that he and his collaborators had made the telescope 'an Astronomical Instrument, to observe to Seconds'; and some years later his friend Thomas Sprat recalled that Wren had 'invented many Ways to make astronomical Observations more accurate and easy', including the addition of reticles and screws to telescopes, 'for taking small Distances, and apparent Diameters to seconds'.[41] With its aid, he mapped the moon and other celestial objects (he also used it to make an accurate map of the Pleiades); and by the beginning of the 1660s he had translated the results of his survey into an exquisite ten-inch lunar globe, made of painted and contoured pasteboard.

He was particularly proud of this globe. Soon after the Restoration he had it mounted on a pedestal of lignum vitae and presented to the King, who was delighted with the model and flattered by the inscription: 'To Charles II, King of Great Britain, France, and Scotland, for the expansion of whose Dominions since no one Globe can suffice, Christopher Wren dedicates another in this Lunar Sphere'. Charles placed it in his private cabinet at Whitehall and showed it off to visitors at every opportunity. It occupies a prominent position in the early eighteenth-century portrait of Wren that hangs in the Sheldonian Theatre, along with the other monuments to a lifetime's achievement – a telescope, a celestial globe, a plan of St Paul's Cathedral, an engraving of the Sheldonian and a view of the City churches.

4

The Natural Simplicity of the Contrivance

*W*ren's life wasn't confined to Wadham and All Souls. He went down to observe the heavens at Sir Paul Neile's house at White Waltham; he spent long periods with his father and the Holders (and perhaps Faith Coghill) at Bletchingdon rectory; and he seems to have travelled pretty frequently between Oxford and London. It isn't clear where he lodged or what took him to the capital in these years: when one considers that the 57-mile journey involved an extremely hard day's ride on horseback, or two even harder days by coach, he must have had good reasons.* Perhaps his uncle was chief among them: poor Matthew Wren was still in the Tower of London, where he had languished ever since his arrest in 1642.

The young man also visited various well-known virtuosi in London. In 1652, for example, Wilkins took him to see the astrologer, alchemist and antiquary Elias Ashmole, who was just beginning to catalogue the Tradescant collection of natural and ethnological rarities at Lambeth. (Three years later, Dean Wren in his capacity as ex-Registrar of the Garter was to help Ashmole with the latter's most famous work, his *Institutions, Laws and Ceremonies of the Most Noble Order of the Garter,* eventually published in 1672.) And at the beginning of March 1653 Wren called on the well-known intellectual Samuel Hartlib, who already knew him by reputation, at least – as far back as 1650 John Wallis

---

*It was more usual for the journey to take two days, even on horseback. Walter Pope noted with some amazement that Seth Ward used to ride between London and Oxford in a single day, 'upon a high-mettled, dancing, I might say, a run-away Mare' (*Life of Seth, Lord Bishop of Salisbury* [1697], 54).

had written, as we saw earlier, to say that the young undergraduate, 'besides divers other fine inventions and contrivances, hath found out a way to measure the moistnesse and dryness of the air exactly'.[1] Now Hartlib took the opportunity to quiz Wren about a story he had heard the previous week, that the young man was in the midst of negotiations over an invention 'to facilitate the carriages of [wagons], which may be worth to the public above £10,000; he is offered £1000, but demands £1000 more'.[2] Wren denied he had invented any such thing, but the incident is an indication of the way in which rumours about his scientific prowess were beginning to circulate outside Oxford.

Hartlib continued both to see and to correspond with Wren. In February 1655 they were discussing the 'transparent apiaries' which Wilkins had shown to Evelyn in the Wadham garden, and later that year Hartlib's *Reformed Common-Wealth of Bees* included Wren's account of how to make the glass-walled beehives. Then in May 1656 Hartlib heard another story about Wren, when Boyle wrote to report that the don from All Souls was to succeed Daniel Whistler as Professor of Geometry at Gresham College in London. This time the rumour was very nearly true.

Gresham College was an institution with an eminent reputation, especially in the sciences. It had been founded in 1597 under the terms of the will of Sir Thomas Gresham, a wealthy Elizabethan merchant whose claim to fame was the building of London's main commercial centre, the Royal Exchange in Cornhill. In a surprisingly enlightened move, Sir Thomas left his town house, a sprawling courtyard mansion which lay between Bishopsgate Street and Broad Street, as a sort of adult education centre for the capital. In return for £50 a year and free lodgings in the college, professors of divinity, law, physic, rhetoric, music, geometry and astronomy gave open weekly lectures to the citizens of London in the great hall behind the main block. In sharp contrast to teaching methods at Oxford and Cambridge, these lectures – which were to be delivered in both Latin and English – emphasized practice rather than theory. The Professor of Physic, for example, was required to begin with 'physiologie, then pathologie, and lastly therapeutice; whereby the body of the said art may be better imprinted by good method in the studious auditors, rather than be disjoined and delivered out of order by exposition of some part of Galen or Hippocrates'. And besides discoursing on planetary theory, the Professor of Astronomy was to instruct students in 'the use of the astrolabe and the staff, and other common instruments for the capacity of mariners'.[3]

The chairs in geometry and astronomy were the first to be established in England, and during the first three decades of the seventeenth century Gresham College developed a considerable reputation as a centre for research in the mathematical sciences, attracting men of the stature of Henry Briggs (Professor of Geometry from 1597 to 1620, who was described by William Oughtred as 'the English Archimedes';[4] and Edmund Gunter (Professor of Astronomy, 1619–26), whom Aubrey claimed was 'the first that brought Mathematicall Instruments to perfection'. His *Booke of the Quadrant, Sector and Crosse-staffe* 'did open men's understandings and made young men in love with that Studie. Before, the Mathematicall Sciences were lock't-up in the Greeke and Latin tongues; and so lay untoucht, kept safe in some Libraries.'[5] Both men had strong Puritan sympathies and particular interests in navigation and shipping; and several of their successors shared both their Puritanism and their research interests – notably the astronomy professors Henry Gellibrand, a staunch Calvinist who fell foul of Laud in the 1630s, and Samuel Foster, a 'zealous nonconformist'[6] who replaced him, only to be ejected in favour of a Royalist the following year. (He was allowed to take up his chair again in 1641, and remained at Gresham until 1652.) A close collaboration grew up with the instrument-makers, naval architects and artisans at the dockyards over in Deptford, which turned the college into a prominent centre for applied mathematics and navigation.

During the 1630s and 1640s, however, Gresham's reputation declined from the peak it had reached under Briggs and Gunter. Far from being at the leading edge of technological advance, complaints were made that the professors were failing even to fulfil their less than arduous teaching duties, either paying deputies to read for them or not bothering to lecture at all. The Professor of Divinity, Richard Holdsworth, spent most of his time at Cambridge, where he was also Master of Emmanuel; the Professor of Law, Thomas Eden, had to resign his chair in 1640 because of 'several other imployments . . . interfering with his attendance at Gresham';[7] and the Professor of Geometry, John Greaves, went off to explore the Middle East in 1633 and didn't come back for seven years. (He was eventually sacked 'on account of his long absence, and his neglect of his lecture'.[8]) There was something of a renaissance in the mid-1640s, when Samuel Foster hosted meetings of like-minded virtuosi in his lodgings at the college – the meetings which Charles

Scarburgh had attended, along with John Wallis, John Wilkins, Jonathan Goddard and others. But there was still a feeling among Baconians, at least, that something had gone wrong with Gresham. A proposal for reform, probably written by William Petty in 1649, suggested that the chairs of divinity, law and rhetoric should be done away with altogether: they were no longer of any use to the citizens of London, and the information provided by their lectures could just as easily be obtained from books or, in the case of divinity, from the hundreds of sermons preached every day 'in ordinary Meeting houses and places about this Citty'. The remaining four subjects, being practical in nature, needed 'personal professors' whose teaching should be directed towards experiment and utility. The Professor of Physic, for instance, ought to lecture on the preparation of medicines, and employ himself about 'Anatomicall Operations upon the dead Bodies of severall Animalls and in making Experiments concerning the Use of the parts, the motion of the Blood, &c upon living Brutes'. The Professor of Geometry didn't need to bother teaching basic arithmetic, because that was taught in every school; instead, he should devote himself to the practice of measuring, surveying and fortification. The Professor of Astronomy, whose brief was in many ways the most ambitious,

> may at convenient tymes teach Men to know and finde out all the most knowne and remarkable stars and planets, and how to observe their motions distances eclypses &c and [to] make use of those phenomena or observations either to the examining correcting or new forming of Theories and Systems of the World. Hee may also treate of Dialling, Navigation & Geography, and shew the practise of whatsoever [is] practicall in them.[9]

And to replace the redundant professorships of divinity, law and rhetoric, Petty advocated the setting up of several new chairs, whose holders would teach Londoners about magnetism, optics, material technology, armaments and a whole variety of trades, from ship-building to metal-founding.

Petty's proposals to provide the college with a new, almost exclusively scientific focus came to nothing. (Gresham's original seven professor-ships are still in existence today, together with an eighth, a chair of commerce which was instituted in 1985.) But his ideas suggest that even in 1649, about the time that Wren entered Wadham as a gentleman commoner, the experimental philosophical club at Oxford was thinking about the institutionalization of science. Informal groups of virtuosi, such as those which met at Foster's lodgings, or Wilkins', or Petty's, were fine as far as they went; but they didn't go far enough. They had no status beyond their immediate circle. The idea of commandeering a small existing institution – and one, moreover, which already had a distinguished pedigree in the field of scientific research – was much more attractive. In 1651 William Petty became the somewhat unlikely Professor of Music at the college, although his duties in Ireland meant that he was rarely there. In 1652 a second member of the Oxford group, Laurence Rooke, was elected Professor of Astronomy at Gresham; three years later Jonathan Goddard became Professor of Physic 'through the favour and power of Cromwell';[10] and in August 1657 Christopher Wren took up a vacant chair there. To suggest that there was a deliberate conspiracy by Oxford fifth-columnists to infiltrate Gresham is putting it rather too strongly. But the fact remains that in the space of six years, four of the seven professorships, including all three of the scientific chairs, belonged to members of the Oxford group. The rest were occupied by pretty uninspiring types. John Bond, a committed Parliamentarian but otherwise undistinguished, was Professor of Law. Richard Hunt, a complete nonentity, held the chair of Rhetoric. And Thomas Horton, who had Divinity, so to speak, had married in 1651 and spent most of the decade trying to argue his way out of losing his post: the college statutes stipulated that 'none shall be chossen to reade any of the said lectures, so longe as he shall be married, nor be suffered to reade any of the said lectures after that he shalbe married'.[11]

The circumstances of Wren's own appointment at Gresham are something of a mystery. The vacant chair was in geometry, the result of Daniel Whistler's decision to renounce the life of the mind and marry. But in a curious game of musical chairs, Laurence Rooke, whose main interests lay in astronomy, moved sideways to take Whistler's place and the young Wren stepped into Rooke's job. An eighteenth-century source suggests a charmingly simple reason for the exchange. Rooke preferred the Professor of Geometry's lodgings, because they were more suitable for the gatherings of virtuosi who met in his rooms after his lectures, but also because they were much quieter than the Astronomy Professor's lodgings which gave on to busy Broad Street. *And* they had a balcony overlooking the south-east corner of the main quadrangle.

Be that as it may, John Wilkins seems to have been the prime mover in Wren's appointment. Around the time of Wilkins' marriage to

Cromwell's widowed sister★ and soon after Whistler had announced his intention to give up the college cloister for the pleasures of the flesh, Cromwell wrote to the authorities at Gresham saying that 'we desire you suspend [the election of a new Professor of Geometry, which was actually scheduled for that afternoon] for some time, till We shall have an opportunity to speak with some of you in order to that business'.[12] It was only a couple of weeks later that Boyle was telling Hartlib that Wren had got the job. The evidence for Wilkins' involvement may be circumstantial, but it is fairly compelling.

Wren took up the chair of astronomy at Gresham in the summer of 1657, the heir to a great if slightly tarnished tradition. The inaugural address he gave in the reading hall at the college on 7 August began conventionally enough, with the expected self-deprecatory noises. He spoke of his 'slender Abilities' and his 'juvenile Blushes' at being faced with such a distinguished audience, and claimed (of course) that he would never have dreamed of taking up the chair of astronomy if it hadn't been for the urgings of 'the great Ornaments of Learning and our Nation, whom to obey is with me sacred'.[13] But once these pleasantries were out of the way, he launched into an excited tribute to experimental philosophy in general, and the new astronomy in particular. 'We have no barren Age,' he declared, comparing his contemporaries with the astronomers of the past, to the detriment of the latter. 'How much the Mathematical Wits of this Age have excell'd the Ancients, (who pierc'd but to the Bark and Outside of Things) in handling particular Disquisitions of Nature, in clearing up History, and fixing Chronology.'

Wren went on to describe how astronomy could shed light on problems in other fields of study. In theology, for instance, the miracle recounted in 2 Kings 20:11, when God caused the shadow on the sundial of Ahaz to move backwards ten degrees, might be explained by the appearance of a parhelion (a luminous spot in the sky caused by the refraction of sunlight through 'nitrous Vapours' – ice crystals, in fact). As if aware that he was venturing into dangerous territory, he hastily added that explaining a biblical miracle need not diminish it – the rainbow was just such an example. Then, in a display of sophistry worthy of a Jesuit, he told his audience that astronomy could show how it was that Christ was buried on a Friday night, rose again before dawn on the following Sunday, and yet spent three days and three nights in the tomb. When a

★A connection which enabled him to avoid Whistler's choice, since although the Warden of Wadham was also supposed to be a bachelor, Cromwell stepped in with a special dispensation which allowed him to keep his place.

day and two nights pass in Judaea, he said, a night and two days pass in the 'contrary Hemisphere'. And that adds up to three days and three nights – QED.

Medicine could also learn from astronomy. Wren had nothing but contempt for the 'ungrounded Fancies of that Sort of astrological Medicasters, who . . . intitle one Planet or other to every Herb, or Drug'; astrology 'cannot but be thought extremely unreasonable and ridiculous' to those who sought truth in experiment and demonstrable hypotheses. But the way in which Hippocrates and the ancients had categorised disease under season and climate had a lot to be said for it; changes in the weather clearly caused changes in animal physiology, as his own experiments had shown. If medical men and astronomers cared to relate these physiological changes to the occurrence of epidemical disease, a new science was waiting for them, 'a true Astrology . . . which would be of admirable Use to Physick'.

Astronomy had also played a crucial part in geography, leading to the discovery of our own world. The stars 'undertook to guide the creeping Ships of the Ancients'; the stars, assisted by the compass, helped Columbus to discover America, Vasco da Gama to reach the Indies by sea, and 'Circumnavigators of our Nation' to show that the earth was round.

From here, Wren proceeded to catalogue for his audience the contributions of astronomers who, in little more than a century, had transformed human understanding of the universe. Copernicus, by suggesting that the earth moved round the sun, had liberated philosophy from 'the Tyranny of the Greek and Roman Monarchies'. (A curious phrase – was it perhaps an oblique reference to Cromwell, a repayment of the debt Wren owed to the Protector? Assuming Wren's father was in the audience, we can almost hear the old Royalist snort.) William Gilbert was 'the sole Inventor of Magneticks' and 'the Father of the new Philosophy', the man who showed Descartes the way to truth. Galileo was praised for 'perfecting the great Invention of Telescopes', which allowed men to test the hypotheses of Copernicus and Gilbert; and Kepler, for compiling another new science, dioptrics, and for inventing the elliptical hypothesis, the idea that planetary orbits are elliptical rather than circular.

These assessments, not quite as platitudinous as they appear today, represent a clear statement of faith in the new astronomy. True, there were few among the experimental philosophers in the audience who would have taken issue with Wren's pantheon. Wilkins had long ago argued that nothing in Scripture was incompatible with the idea that the sun is 'the Centre of this World'; and in 1654 Seth Ward asserted that 'there is not one man here [i.e., in Oxford], who is so farre astronomicall, as to be able to calculate an eclipse, who hath not received the Copernican system . . . either as an opinion, or at leastwise, as the most intelligible, and most convenient hypothesis'.[14] In the year of Wren's oration, Christiaan Huygens pronounced from The Hague that only those of slow wits and a superstitious veneration of human authority could fail to accept the 'divinely invented system' of Copernicus – and most English scientists agreed with him. But heliocentrism was still far from being undisputed. Sporadic resistance to Copernicus continued in Britain, largely on theological grounds. Some scholars, like Sir Henry Savile at the beginning of the century, simply refused to choose between the competing systems. Savile said he didn't care which was true: 'Is it not all one . . . sitting at dinner, whether my table be brought to me, or I goe to my table, so I eat my meat?'[15] – sentiments which were echoed in the 1670s by the Royalist divine Robert South: 'What am I benefitted, whether the sun moves about the earth, or whether the sun is in the centre of the world?. . . The day begins no sooner, nor stays any longer with Ptolemy than with Copernicus.'[16] Others clung tenaciously to the Ptolemaic system or, like Wren's own father, preferred Tycho Brahe's compromise explanation that while the other planets did indeed revolve around the sun, the sun moved round the earth. Dean Wren was not alone: the Tychonic system was still being taught at the University of Leyden as late as 1680.[17] In 1634 the Scottish clergyman Alexander Ross published a violent attack on the Copernican hypothesis; and nearly forty years later John Owen, the fierce Puritan divine who had been Cromwell's chaplain – and, incidentally, one of the committee which ran Oxford University in the early 1650s, along with Wilkins and Goddard – dismissed heliocentrism as incompatible with Holy Scripture. University teachers could still be sacked for advocating Copernicanism in Germany and Sweden; and in most of Catholic Europe there was of course much more, and much more sustained, opposition to the new philosophy. The position of the Catholic Church, which had been set out in an edict of 1616, was that the idea of a stationary sun was 'foolish and absurd, philosophically and formally heretical'; to hold that the earth moved either through the heavens or on its own axis was 'erroneous in faith'. It wasn't until 1757 that Pope Benedict XIV revoked that edict.

So if Copernicanism was accepted as a given by Wren and his friends, there were still plenty who disagreed with them. Of the other icons of modern astronomy that Wren singled out for special praise, William Gilbert, whose *De Magnete* (1600) offered an explanation as to why celestial bodies moved in some relation to one another once the solid Ptolemaic spheres which held them in place had been removed (it was magnetism, or an analogous force), was an Englishman, and as such his ideas were particularly revered by the Oxford group. Galileo's contribution was self-evident and beyond dispute. As far as Kepler's elliptical hypothesis was concerned, the situation was more complicated. Wren's contemporaries tended to agree that planetary orbits were elliptical; but they didn't know why, they couldn't calculate them, and some of them didn't think it really mattered that much. Samuel Foster, for example, wrote rather disarmingly that while 'Kepler makes the Orbits of the Planets to be ellipses, which is the better way', he preferred to 'make them perfect Circles, which is the easier way'.[18] Early on in his four-year tenure at Gresham, Wren gave a series of lectures on Kepler, whose published writings he studied in some depth. In 1658 he also became deeply involved in the pure mathematics of Kepler's second law of planetary motion, which implied that planets moved more quickly around the sun, as one focus of the ellipse, than they did around the empty focus. He published a solution to Kepler's problem the following year.[19] Opinions differ as to its value – one recent historian dismissed it as 'garbled' and 'scarcely comprehensible', while others see it as showing an understanding of Kepler which was exceptionally rare for the time[20] – but it served to enhance his growing reputation both in England and abroad.

To return to the Gresham address. Finally (or almost finally – Wren's speech actually ended with a homage to Gresham College and Wren's predecessors in the chair of astronomy, and an elegant if rather contrived tribute to London in which the sun, the moon and the five planets bestowed their different blessings on the city), the new professor talked with evident excitement about the difference that these discoveries had made. What would the ancients have made of an age in which men could 'stretch out their Eyes, as Snails do, and extend them to fifty Feet in length; by which means, they should be able to discover Two thousand Times as many Stars as we can'? They would have exchanged their lives for a few clear nights with a telescope, and the chance to see the four moons of Jupiter; to study the way Mars, Venus and Mercury waxed and waned; to view Saturn, 'a very Proteus, changing more admirably than our Moon, by the various Turnings, and Inumbrations of his several Bodies'; and – a clear reference to Wren's lunar survey – to explore the moon itself, 'discovering the Heighths and Shape of the Mountains, and Depths of round and uniform Vallies, the Shadows of the Mountains, the Figure of the Shores, describing Pictures of her, with more Accurateness, than we can our own Globe'.

The Gresham address is far and away the most comprehensive and detailed account we have of Wren's thinking on science in the 1650s, or indeed, at any time in his life. We must constantly remind ourselves that it comes from a young man of only twenty-four, so learned, witty, confident and passionate is it, showing both a scholarly understanding of recent developments in astronomy and the sheer, naked joy Wren felt at the new worlds that were opening up as a result. Above all, the speech suggests that if Oxford, and the extra-curricular activities of the Oxford group, had taught him well, he was repaying that debt with interest.

The reference in the address to Saturn as 'a very Proteus' gives a clue to one of Wren's major areas of astronomical research in the late 1650s. At the time of the Gresham inaugural, he had been studying Saturn for about three years, although other members of the Oxford group had been making systematic observations of the planet since 1649. The cause of this interest, which was shared by astronomers all over Europe, dates back to July 1610, when Galileo first turned his telescope on Saturn and found, to his astonishment, that he was looking at a central globe flanked by two smaller spheres. Two years later he was even more surprised to see that the small spheres had vanished. 'Are the two lesser stars consumed after the manner of solar spots?' he asked: 'Has Saturn, perhaps, devoured his own children?'[21] The children reappeared again, only to be replaced in 1616 by a pair of 'half ellipses with two dark little triangles'.[22]

Galileo was of course seeing the changing shape of Saturn's rings, first at a narrow angle to the earth, then edgewise on, and finally wider open. Imperfections in his telescope's lens distorted the image. Although he didn't attempt to explain what he saw, other astronomers came up with some ingenious hypotheses: Saturn was oval with a huge crater or black spot at each end; it had sickle-shaped handles attached; there were really four satellites, two dark ones close to the planet and two bright ones further away; a torrid zone exhaled gases, and when these gases were fairly dense, they reflected sunlight at their edges, while at maximum density they caused the planet to appear elongated.[23]

None of these theories was particularly satisfactory, and astronomers continued to search for an explanation which fitted more closely with the observable facts. In England, one of the topics discussed by the group that met in London in the mid-1640s was 'the Oval shape of Saturn';[24] and when Wren went up to Oxford in 1649/50, Sir Paul Neile and William Balle, another member of the 'Greate Clubb', were already engaged in making detailed observations of the planet and its mysterious disappearing appendages. He joined the two men in their investigations by 1654, as his interest in astronomy began to grow, and he responded to the problem in a practical way – as he usually did – by making a model of Saturn in wax the following year. A true description of Saturn alone 'were enough for the Life of one Astronomer', he said in his inaugural address; and, as his remarks in the same speech about the turnings of the planet's 'several Bodies' suggest, in the summer of 1657 he was still quite a long way from a solution to the problem.

But early one morning that December, while he was observing Saturn through Neile's telescope at White Waltham – at a stage in the planet's orbit when the rings were plainly visible from the earth – he had the idea that its 'arms' didn't actually change at all; they 'kept their length'. This led him to suggest that Saturn was 'exactly spherical' and that the reason for its apparent changes of shape was the existence of an 'elliptical corona, which, touching the globe at two points equidistant from the poles, represents the shape of handles';[25] a thin elongated ring, in other words, joined to Saturn in two places around its equator. This vaporous corona, a few miles thick, 'like a cloud, drinks in the splendour of the sun, and in turn gives back a visible glimmering brilliance. Therefore (if the harsh star, so far removed from the shining focus of the universe can give out any vital breath), indeed the inhabitants of Saturn have a very delightful spectacle of the corona.'[26]

As theories went, this was a pretty good one, a major advance on recent speculation. It conformed closely to recorded observations and explained convincingly and correctly why Saturn appeared at times 'unarmed' – having no real thickness, the corona is invisible when it is edgewise on to the earth – and, again correctly, why its appendages altered their shape as the planet rotated on its axis and pursued its orbit round the sun. Perhaps more interestingly, the subsequent history of Wren's hypothesis helps to explain why his scientific reputation – so high among his contemporaries – was all but eclipsed by his later career as an architect.

He lectured on Saturn's corona at Gresham and, after experimenting with two pasteboard models to demonstrate its movements, made a more elaborate model in copper, which in May 1658 was placed on top of the gantry supporting a 35-foot telescope that Neile had donated to the college. And that summer his thoughts turned to publication: he prepared a rough draft of a paper 'Concerning the Body of Saturn and its Phases' [*De Corpore Saturni . . .*], which at this stage he showed to Laurence Rooke, but to no one else.

Early the following year he found out about a rival hypothesis being put forward by the Dutch scientist Christiaan Huygens, who was suggesting that Saturn was surrounded by a symmetrical uniform ring.★ As soon as he heard this, Wren felt less excited about his own theory: 'I confess I was so fond of the neatness of [Huygens' theory],' he recalled two years later, '& the Natural Simplicity of the contrivance agreeing soe well with the physicall causes of the heavenly bodies, that I loved the Invention beyond my owne.'[27] Wren's choice of words is important here. He didn't actually *reject* his original idea about the elliptical corona – indeed, in the same letter he went on to say he supposed that 'future observations will never be able to determine which is the trewest' – but, in an echo of his justification of his double-writing instrument, he preferred Huygens' hypothesis because of its neatness, its 'Natural Simplicity'.

There the matter might have ended, except that at a meeting of the recently-formed Royal Society on 4 September 1661, when both Wren and Neile were present, Sir Kenelm Digby read a letter he had just received from a French mathematician, Bernard Frenicle de Bessy, outlining a theory about Saturn's rings which was remarkably close to Wren's. Neile sprang up and declared that Wren had already formulated a similar idea three years previously; and the Society, ever conscious of precedence and prior claims in such matters (especially when they offered a chance to show the superiority of English scientists over their French counterparts), asked a reluctant Wren to 'deliver a copy of his observations and hypothesis of Saturn to the amanuensis to be transmitted . . . to Monsieur Frenicle'.[28]

Wren complied to the extent that four weeks later he sent the manuscript of *De Corpore Saturni* to Neile, with a rambling and apologetic covering letter in which he begged Neile to keep the paper in his own hands and to restore it to him. He added rather petulantly that he really ought to have turned down the Society's request,

★Huygens had first published his ring-hypothesis, disguised in an anagram, in March 1656. He didn't give a complete explanation until the publication of his *Systema Saturnium* of July 1659, but the idea was circulating in Paris by Easter 1658, and Huygens told it to John Wallis (who presumably passed it on to Wren) in January of the following year.

considering that many of those present at the meeting had 'been at the trouble to heare the Astronomy Reader at Gresham give fuller discourses on the same subject, which he thought was publication enough'.[29] Neile completely ignored his wishes – from the best of motives, no doubt – and copies of the paper were duly sent off both to Paris and to Huygens at The Hague. Several members of the Royal Society, including Boyle and Abraham Hill, also had copies taken for their own use at the same time.

There are several possible explanations for Wren's self-effacing behaviour over *De Corpore*. One, sometimes put forward by historians still imbued with quaint notions of an altruistic scientific community in search of truth rather than reputation, is that he didn't really care about being given credit for his discoveries. This is hardly sustainable in the light of the way he squirmed over the Society's request – his letter to Neile smacks of embarrassment rather than modesty or nonchalance. A more convincing interpretation is that he believed (correctly, of course, as it turned out) that Huygens was right about Saturn's rings; and while he was not quite prepared to admit this to his friends, or even to himself, he felt it better to let the whole matter drop – until Neile's well-meaning remarks at the Royal Society meeting in September 1661 and the resulting peer pressure forced him to dig out his draft of *De Corpore*. He hated being wrong. But even more, he hated being seen to be wrong.

London, the city that was now Wren's home, had a population around thirty times greater than that of Oxford. Over the previous hundred years the second-largest conurbation in Christendom (only Paris was bigger) had steadily spread beyond the densely-packed residential courts and alleys of the Square Mile, until around 300,000 people – nigh on one in seventeen of the entire population of England – were living either within the City's walls or in the sprawling suburbs which extended beyond it. To the west, the fashionable area between the old City and Westminster was being settled by the wealthy, who congregated close to the seat of government in the Palace of Whitehall – then a rambling, incoherent collection of Tudor buildings whose only concession to modernity was the Palladian Banqueting House which Inigo Jones had built in 1619–22, and which formed such an elegant backdrop to the inelegant decapitation of Charles I in January 1649. Jones's brand of classicism could also be seen in the buildings surrounding Covent Garden Piazza, laid out by the 4th Earl of Bedford in the 1630s, and in the west front and portico of St Paul's Cathedral, completed in 1642.

Houses for prosperous traders and artisans of the middling sort were appearing in increasing numbers to the north of the city walls, with ribbon development creeping up to Shoreditch and towards Hackney, and more tightly packed housing towards Clerkenwell and around Moorfields, although there was open pasture beyond, and windmills still ground corn at Finsbury Fields. To the east of the Tower, the shipyards and their related trades meant the proliferation of less salubrious residential areas along the Thames at Wapping and Shadwell.

As with most seventeenth-century capitals, London's houses were a polyglot mix of old and new, brick, stone and timber, pretentious palaces and squalid slums. Outside the city walls, for example, Essex House and Somerset House, the great Renaissance mansion built for the Protector Somerset between 1547 and 1552, still stretched from the Strand down to the Thames to either side of Arundel House, a hopelessly irregular rabbit warren of medieval and Tudor buildings. But closer to the heart of the City there were acres of labyrinthine alleys and courts, punctuated by medieval churches – nearly a hundred of them – and occasional public buildings such as Gresham's Royal Exchange, the New Exchange on the Strand, the medieval Guildhall and, of course, Gresham College itself.

Whenever Wren emerged from the main entrance of Gresham College on to Bishopsgate Street, he would have found himself on one of the few paved streets in the City. Most, like the back entrance from his lodgings on to Broad Street, were cobbled canyons in which steeply projecting jettied upper storeys all but blocked out the sun. As one of the main north-south thoroughfares, Bishopsgate Street would have been crowded with carts and horses, and incredibly noisy with the clatter of wheels and hooves and the shouts of traders and street-vendors. The air was generally heavy with the smog caused by tens of thousands of domestic fires: in 1661 John Evelyn bemoaned the fact that 'this glorious and ancient city should wrap her stately head in clouds of smoke and sulphur', and one can't help but wonder just how much of the heavens could be seen through the Neile telescope lately erected at Gresham.[30] If Wren turned left out of the college, a moment's walk – and like most men of his class, he usually *did* walk, although hackneys and sedan chairs were available – would bring him to the medieval and recently repaired Bishopsgate itself. From here he sometimes left the City proper to stroll up past Bethlehem Hospital, where polite society went to be entertained by the antics of the lunatics, to Moorfields, where a dozen or so like-minded 'Mathematicall friends', including Sir Paul Neile, Charles Scarburgh and fellow Greshamites Laurence Rooke and Jonathan Goddard, were wont to gather for an afternoon's conversation.[31] A right turn out of the college would take him across the junction of Cornhill and Leadenhall Street to the houses and shops on London Bridge – still the only bridge over the Thames, and still adorned with the rotting heads of traitors, as it had been for centuries. He may have passed his time talking to friends and ogling the women in the shops at the Royal Exchange, although if his leisure habits in later life are anything to go by, the moment he left the confines of his college he probably made for one of the coffee- or chocolate-houses which had sprung up in the 1650s. When Wren arrived at Gresham, a Frenchman had just opened a house selling 'an excellent West India drink called chocolate' round the corner in Queen's Head Alley, while in Bartholomew Lane, behind the Exchange, another new business was advertising 'the drink called Coffee (which is a very wholsom and Physical drink) having many excellent vertues, closes the Orifice of the Stomack, fortifies the heat within, helpeth Digestion, quickneth the Spirits, maketh the heart lightsom, is good against Eye-sores, Coughs, or Colds, Rhumes, Comsumptions [sic], Head-ach, Dropsie, Gout, Scurvy, King's Evil, and many others'.[32]

Wren's lecturing duties at Gresham certainly weren't of the sort to bring on a 'Head-ach', although the contents of the renowned college cellars may have done. During term-time, which occupied fewer than twenty weeks of the year, each professor was required to give a single hour-long lecture twice a week: in Latin at eight in the morning on a stipulated day; and again at two in the afternoon of the same day in English. The timetable ran as follows: divinity on Mondays; law on Tuesdays; astronomy on Wednesdays; geometry on Thursdays, rhetoric on Fridays; and physic and music on Saturdays. There were plenty of familiar faces in the city: his cousin Matthew was there, and Thomas Sprat, a friend from Wadham. Apart from Rooke, Goddard and, on the rare occasions when he showed up, William Petty, Wren met regularly with Charles Scarburgh, who was giving lectures in the public theatre at Surgeon's Hall over by St Giles Cripplegate – where, incidentally, the doctor used as teaching aids some pasteboard models 'of all the Muscles of a human Body, as they naturally arise in Dissection', said to have been made by Wren. Wilkins, who moved to Cambridge as Master of Trinity in 1659, was often in town. And there were always the dutiful visits to be made to poor uncle Matthew.

He was also making new friends, and on one occasion at least, this led directly to an unhappy encounter with his imprisoned uncle. Presumably through the influence of Wilkins, he became friendly with John Claypole, the Protector's son-in-law (he was married to Cromwell's favourite daughter, Elizabeth) and a man who 'being a lover of mathematicks, had conceiv'd a great esteem for him, and took all occasions to cultivate his friendship, and to court his conversation, particularly by frequent invitations to his house, and table'.[33] On one of these occasions, while Wren and Claypole were eating, Cromwell walked in, sat down at the table and joined in the meal. After a while, he looked at Wren and said, 'Your uncle has been long confin'd in the Tower.' Wren agreed in characteristically non-committal fashion, replying, 'He has so, Sir, but bears his afflictions with great patience and resignation'; to which Cromwell simply said, 'He may come out if he will.'

Wren couldn't believe it. He asked Cromwell's permission to take the good news to his uncle in person and then, as soon as the meal was over, rushed to the Tower. But when he arrived, Matthew was less than impressed, and put his nephew firmly in his place. It wasn't the first time he had been offered his freedom, he said. But if it meant acknowledging that he owed his release to Cromwell, and submitting to his 'detestable tyranny', he would rather stay where he was. And so he did. He continued taking his exercise on the leads of the roof of the Tower, scribbling endless and tedious annotations in his Bible and composing vitriolic sermons on the iniquities of Scottish Presbyterianism and its impact on the Anglican episcopacy. One would give a great deal to know what else was said about the propriety of Wren's socializing with Cromwell, and what went through the crestfallen young man's mind as he left his uncle in the Tower that day.

Matthew's stubborn high principles meant the postponement of his liberation; he was finally released from captivity in March 1660, two months before Charles II's return, and restored to his bishopric soon after. His brother, Wren's father, didn't live to see the Restoration. On 29 May 1658, exactly two years to the day before his King finally marched in triumph down the Strand to reclaim his throne, the Dean died at William Holder's rectory in Bletchingdon, where he was buried beneath the chancel; he was sixty-eight. Just over three months later, the chief architect of his misfortunes followed him to the grave: on 3 September 1658, Oliver Cromwell unexpectedly died of pneumonia, four weeks after Elizabeth Claypole's death from cancer. The following

May his son and successor Richard, unable to hold together opposing interest groups within Parliament and the military, was forced to abdicate by an army cabal; political tensions increased dramatically. A nationwide Royalist rising planned for that August took place only in Cheshire, and was efficiently put down by the radical republican commander John Lambert; and in October Lambert's troops occupied London and expelled the Rump Parliament from Westminster. 'Now no Government in the Nation,' wrote Evelyn in his diary. 'All in confusion; no Magistrate either own'd or pretended but the Souldiers, and they not agreed. God Almighty have mercy on and settle us!'[34]

Among the public buildings occupied by Lambert's troops was Gresham College. Wren, who still kept up his fellowship at All Souls, was in Oxford, and asked his cousin Matthew to find out if he was expected to lecture when the new term began on 24 October. Matthew wrote back telling him not to bother; apart from Jonathan Goddard, there were no professors in residence. In fact, when Matthew tried to get into the building, his way was barred by a soldier brandishing a gun who told him that no one was allowed in to lectures, 'the college being reform'd into a Garrison'.[35] He prudently advised his cousin that it would not be amiss for him to write a 'short and civil' letter to the college authorities, apologizing for his absence and making it clear that it was due solely to 'this publick Interruption and Exclusion from your Chamber'. At around the same time Thomas Sprat provided the exiled professor with a rather wittier picture of Gresham under military occupation. 'This day I went to visit Gresham-college,' he wrote to Wren, 'but found the Place in such a nasty Condition, so defil'd, and the Smells so infernal, that if you should now come to make Use of your Tube [i.e., the Neile telescope], it would be like Dives looking out of Hell into Heaven.'[36] He confirmed that Goddard was the sole professor left at the college, explaining that the latter could only bear the stench of the soldiers because he had 'prepar'd his Nose for Camp Perfumes, by his Voyage into Scotland [as physician to Cromwell's army in 1651], and had ... such excellent Restoratives in his Cellar'; and concluded by hoping that Wren would make good use of his enforced leisure by publishing the lectures he was unable to give in person.

Wren returned to Gresham the following year, after General Monck's forces had marched unopposed into the capital in February, setting in train the events which led to the Declaration of Breda and Charles II's landing at Dover on 25 May. With the Restoration, wrote William Petty, England now had 'a Philosophicall and Mathematico-Mechanical

King, one that cared not for the vulgar exercise of the Body'.[37] As events turned out this was unduly optimistic, both as to Charles's commitment to the new science and to his indifference to vulgar exercise – an activity in which he excelled. But for all his many faults, he was to prove a good friend to Christopher Wren.

5

The Key That Opens Treasures

*A*t three o'clock in the afternoon of Wednesday 28 November 1660, Wren finished his weekly lecture and, still wearing his hood and gown, walked out of the Gresham reading hall, across the college's outer courtyard and into Laurence Rooke's lodgings.

He was joined by eleven others who had come to hear his lecture. Most were old friends from his Oxford days. Besides Rooke, John Wilkins was there. So were Jonathan Goddard and William Petty (the other two Gresham scientists), Robert Boyle, Sir Paul Neile, William Balle and four more recent acquaintances: Abraham Hill, a wealthy City merchant with a republican background; William, Viscount Brouncker, the son of one of Charles I's courtiers; Alexander Bruce, brother of the Earl of Kincardine, who had returned to London that June after several years in Bremen and The Hague; and Sir Robert Moray, a professional soldier and diplomat who had recently taken up lodgings in the Palace of Whitehall after years in exile on the Continent. Of the four new faces only Brouncker, a distinguished amateur mathematician, was a prominent figure in the scientific world, although the others had more than a passing interest in natural philosophy. Moray, for instance (who at fifty-two was the oldest man present), had kept up a chemical laboratory during a stay in Maastricht in the late 1650s. 'I have had 7 stills going these 2 days with one fire,' he once wrote to Bruce, who was a fellow Scot and a good friend. 'I be sitting at the cheek of a furnace [that] will gar your eyn reel when you see it'.[1]

In itself, the gathering that took place in Rooke's apartment that dark November afternoon was nothing out of the ordinary. The group, or various permutations of it, had been meeting regularly since Lambert's troops had vacated Gresham in 1659, and possibly since around the time that Wren took up his chair at the college in the summer of 1657; and its numbers had been swelled by the restoration of the monarchy in May 1660. Exiled Royalists like Moray and Bruce were back in England for the first time in years; others, such as Brouncker and Neile (who regained his pre-war position as Usher of the Privy Chamber in the King's household), were in London looking for preferment and reward for their loyalty from the new regime. And ardent Cromwellians like Wilkins, who lost his post as Master of Trinity College Cambridge, Goddard, who was ejected from the Wardenship of Merton in July 1660, and Petty, whose career in government came to an abrupt halt, were in the capital with time on their hands. Although the 'Greate Clubb' of which such great things had been expected continued to meet in Oxford – now not at Wadham but in Boyle's lodgings on the High – its heart was at Gresham.

What makes 28 November 1660 a milestone in the history of science is the fact that it marked the beginning of what became the Royal Society. In the course of the group's conversation that day, the discussion turned to the idea of giving their gatherings a more formal structure. 'Something was offered about a design of founding a Colledge for the Promoting of Physico-Mathematicall Experimentall Learning . . . & according to the Manner in other Countreys, where there were voluntary associations of men into Academies for the advancement of various parts of learning, so they might do something answerable here for the promoting of Experimentall Philosophy'.[2] Whoever proposed the idea, the others responded enthusiastically, and the upshot was that by the end of the afternoon the twelve men had agreed to continue meeting every Wednesday at three, either in Rooke's chambers at Gresham or, out of term-time, at Balle's rooms in the Temple. They would defray expenses by each paying ten shillings up front and one shilling a week, whether they attended or not. And they appointed Wilkins as Chairman, Balle as Treasurer and William Croone – a medical man who the previous year had rather oddly been given the chair in rhetoric at Gresham – as 'Register' or secretary. (Even more oddly, Croone wasn't even there at the time.) Those present drew up a list of forty interested parties judged willing and fit to be admitted to their company. It comprised most of the usual suspects, including Seth Ward, John Wallis, Charles Scarburgh and Thomas Willis.[3] And so the Royal Society was born.★

A vast body of literature has grown up around the origins of the Royal Society, and various claims have been made for its true progenitors, with the Wadham group and the gatherings at Gresham in the mid-1640s leading the field. Questions of priority seem to matter just as much to historians of science as they do to scientists. The Society's grand-parentage is clear enough, at least. In the posthumously published *New Atlantis* (1627), an unfinished fantasy in which a party of lost travellers come upon a utopian island in the South Seas, Francis Bacon described Solomon's House, an order or society of wise men who devised new experiments of their own, and sought out those published in books and conducted in foreign countries. The order boasted extensive chemical laboratories, astronomical observatories, pharmaceutical and medical facilities, 'a mathematical-house, where are represented all instruments, as well of geometry as astronomy', gardens, and a repository containing 'patterns and samples of all manner of the more rare and excellent inventions'. Research was carried out in optics, microscopy, magnetics, even genetic engineering; and the Fellows of Solomon's House worked together to discover 'the knowledge of causes, and secret motions of things; and the enlarging of the bounds of human empire, to the effecting of all things possible'.[4]

The idea of creating a permanent research institute of the sort envisaged by Bacon in *The New Atlantis*, which would both bring together the sum of human knowledge and add to it by systematic and coordinated experiment, had been floating around for years. In the 1640s and 1650s Samuel Hartlib vigorously promoted the notion of a national, state-sanctioned Agency for the Advancement of Universal Learning, intended 'for the makeing some further progresse & Advance-ment in a usefull improvement of Experiments, to the more cleare elucidation as well of things Naturall as Artificiall'; his friend, the Puritan clergyman John Beale, advocated a 'Colledge of Noble Mechaniques & Ingenious Artificers'; and in 1659 Evelyn proposed to Boyle a design for a well-equipped residential college outside London, where a small group of philosophically inclined gentlemen could retire to pursue their studies away from the political upheavals that were sweeping the country. (Evelyn's name, incidentally, was on the shortlist of prospective

★But not the name, which came with the incorporation of the Society under the terms of its first royal charter, granted by Charles II and passed on 15 July 1662.

members drawn up at the Society's inaugural meeting.) One recalls, too, the hopes Seth Ward had expressed in 1652 that members of the 'Greate Clubb' would trawl through all the books in the Oxford library to 'gather together such things as are already discovered' and establish what was still to be done by experiment; and John Wilkins' abortive attempt the following year to set up a 'College for Experiments et Mechanicks at Oxford . . . where all the models of Inv[entive] Arts etc are to be reserved'.

It may well have been Wilkins who was the moving force behind the founding of the Royal Society. His earlier scheme was still alive in May 1657, when John Evelyn mentioned in a letter to Boyle 'that Mathematico-Chymico-Mechanical School designed by our noble friend Dr Wilkinson [a slip of Evelyn's pen]', describing it as 'another Solomon's house'.[5] But the new society, which embodied a structured approach to experimental philosophy hitherto unknown in England, represents a coming together of long-held personal ambitions on the part of several of its members – for regular scholarly discourse with like-minded friends, for the public legitimization of the new philosophy, for personal recognition and, not least, for a permanent institutionalized framework in the more stable society promised by the restoration of the monarchy.

In spite of being in at the birth of the Royal Society, Wren's own role in its early meetings is complicated and in many ways peripheral. Although he was still, at twenty-eight, one of the junior members of the company, the others immediately looked to him for contributions. At the second meeting of the group on 5 December (when Moray brought welcome news from court that the King 'had been acquainted with the design of the meeting, and well approved of it'), he was asked to bring in his 'pendulum experiment' and appointed to an ad hoc committee along with Brouncker, Boyle, Moray and Petty, to prepare 'some questions, in order to the tryal of the quicksilver experiment upon Tenerife'[6] – a reference to plans for observing the behaviour of a mercury barometer at the top of the 12,000-foot-high Pica de Tenerife. The following week Wren was one of six men appointed to discuss alternative venues for meetings. (In fact the Society was to remain at Gresham for fifty years, apart from a gap from 1666 to 1673 when the college was commandeered by the Lord Mayor in the aftermath of the Fire of London.) The week after *that*, he and Petty were asked to 'consider the philosophy of shipping, and to bring in their thoughts about it'.[7]

As the Society groped its way towards a stable institutional structure, Wren had every chance to play an active part. That structure was given shape under the terms of the royal charters of 1662 and 1663: Lord Brouncker was named as President, William Balle as Treasurer, and there were to be two Secretaries – John Wilkins and the emigré Henry Oldenburg. (As it turned out, Oldenburg performed the duties of Secretary, while Wilkins acted more as a research director.) The election of Fellows was formalized and a 21-man decision-making body, the Council, was created, consisting of the 4 officers and 17 other Fellows. Ten members of the Council were to be replaced by ballot on 30 November each year, an event which, although it was actually two days after the date of the inaugural meeting in Rooke's lodgings, soon became known as the anniversary elections.

Wren was nominated to the first Council. When the Society heard that the King intended to pay a visit in 1663, it was to Wren that the others turned for ideas for suitably impressive experiments. When eight groups were set up in 1664 'for the consideration of several subjects belonging to the cognizance of the Society', Wren was appointed to three of them: the Astronomical and Optical Committee; the Mechanical Committee, whose wide-ranging brief was 'to consider and improve all mechanical inventions'; and the Committee charged with the even more daunting task of 'collecting all the phaenomena of nature hitherto observed, and all experiments made and recorded'.[8]

But important though the Royal Society must have been to Wren, he made a limited contribution to its proceedings during the early 1660s. He left the Council when its second royal charter was passed nine months after the first, played little part in committee work and, while other members of the Society were in a frenzy of excitement over Charles II's projected visit (which never in fact materialized), sent Brouncker a depressingly perceptive account of why the enterprise was doomed from the start. Chemical experiments would be dirty and tedious, anatomical demonstrations 'sordid and noisome', mathematical proofs and the display of astronomical instruments frankly incomprehensible to the uninitiated. Agricultural and industrial machinery needed 'letters and references', and more time than a royal visit allowed; 'scenographical, catoptrical, and dioptical tricks' required more skill in the execution than the Society's resources would permit; architectural designs were no use without an actual building, or at least an insight into the great works of antiquity. Surprise and spectacle were what was needed, but not conjuring tricks which would devalue the work of the Society. To 'produce knacks only . . . will scarce become the gravity of the occasion'; yet, at the same time, 'the key, that opens treasures is often plain and rusty; but unless it be gilt, the key alone will make no shew at court'.[9] He went on to offer some more positive ideas – a circular barometer, an artificial eye, a compass suspended in water and resting on springs so that it could be used in a carriage and thus allow the King to 'sail [i.e., navigate] by land'[10] – but the tone of his letter is hurried, almost impatient.

There is a simple explanation for his lack of involvement. In the spring of 1661, only a few months after the founding meeting at Gresham, he left the college to take Seth Ward's place as Savilian Professor of Astronomy at Oxford.

Whether or not the restoration of the monarchy was good for the nation is debatable, but there is no doubt it was good for Wren. To counterbalance his close association with Wilkins, whose links with Cromwell made him *persona non grata* in government circles, he boasted a strong Royalist pedigree and, more importantly, he now had friends with considerable influence at court. The most important was uncle Matthew, who had finally been liberated from the Tower in March 1660 and reinstated as Bishop of Ely when Charles II returned two months later. (The Bishop had lost none of his High Church ardour. He promptly set about purging his diocese of disaffected ministers with 'a Zeal that was apt to carry him beyond the Bounds of the Law', and took steps to ensure the restoration of the Laudian liturgical setting, demanding, for example, that every church should have 'a decent rail of wood (or some other comely enclosure covered with cloth or silk) placed handsomely above those steps before the holy table'.[11]) Wren was also still close to Charles Scarburgh, one of the delegation sent over to The Hague to bring the King home, and Sir Paul Neile, now a member of the royal household with lodgings in the Palace of Whitehall. Neile in particular lost no time in recommending Wren for preferment and, when Seth Ward – who despite his own Royalist background had no friends powerful enough to mitigate his collaboration with the Commonwealth – was ejected from Oxford, Wren stepped into his place.* He was appointed Savilian Professor of Astronomy on 5 February 1661, resigning from Gresham in March and taking up his new chair on 15 May. He took his doctorate later that year.

---

*The eclipse of Seth Ward and John Wilkins was only temporary. Both men turned to careers in the Church. Ward became Bishop of Exeter in 1662, and of Salisbury five years later. Wilkins' rehabilitation took a little longer, but through the patronage of the Duke of Buckingham he was made Bishop of Chester in November 1668.

The Savilian chair was a tremendously important advance in Wren's career. In the absence of an official Astronomer Royal – John Flamsteed was the first, and he wasn't appointed until 1675 – it was the most prestigious astronomy post in the country, and at twenty-eight Wren was effectively at the top of his profession. But of course it meant new responsibilities – and living in Oxford, at least during term-time. And Oxford was a place where pre-war values were reasserting themselves, even more strongly than they were in the capital. Within months of the Restoration the university had returned exultantly to its pre-Commonwealth Laudianism: in Christ Church Cathedral, the statutory offices and daily services were sung rather than spoken, the communion-table was placed altar-wise beneath a rich canopy of state; the practice of genuflecting to the east was reintroduced; and surplices, derided by Puritans as the 'rags of popery', were worn once more.

Although Richard Baylie, Archbishop Laud's nephew, was now Vice-Chancellor of the university, the real force behind this re-establishment of the Laudian liturgy was John Fell, described by Anthony Wood as 'the most zealous man of his time for the Church of England, and none that I yet know of did go beyond him in the performance of the rules belonging thereto'.[12] Fell, an immensely powerful figure in Restoration Oxford, was the new Dean of Christ Church and the son of Samuel Fell, an earlier Dean of Christ Church and the Royalist Vice-Chancellor of the university who had been deposed and imprisoned during the Puritan purge of 1647–8.* The brother-in-law of Thomas Willis, John Fell had held semi-clandestine services for Royalist students and ejected dons in Willis's lodgings on Merton Street during the 1650s. Wren had been a regular member of the congregation, and this obviously stood him in good stead. But his links with Fell, like the rest of his High Church connections, also placed him in a difficult position. Fell was 'no admirer' of the Royal Society.[13] Not only did he see it as a threat to the reputation of the university but, like many of the senior Laudian clergy now back in power, he mistrusted experimental philosophy and its proponents as a threat to religion and authority. In the climate of Restoration Oxford, Wren had to moderate his enthusiasm for the advancement of learning or risk alienating a party which offered the opportunity for more tangible advancement. So perhaps there are underlying political reasons behind

---

*Mrs Fell had refused to leave the Deanery in spite of her husband's dismissal; she was carried into the quad, still sitting in her chair, by Roundhead troops.

Wren's disengagement from the Royal Society. The brutal truth is that High Church divines did a great deal more to further his subsequent career than his friends at Gresham.

Wren continued to attend meetings when he could (usually during vacations), but one senses in the Society's London-based members a growing sense of frustration at his absence and his apparent lack of commitment. Take just a few examples. On 15 January 1662 the Society asked Wren, William Balle and Laurence Rooke to examine unspecified observations which had been communicated by Edward Montagu, Earl of Sandwich, during a voyage to Portugal and Tangier. In August Wren was once more asked to consider the Earl's observations; and again at the beginning of September, when he told them that it 'required more time than he could yet obtain from his other employments'. The following April he was asked yet again to tell the Society what he had concluded, after which they gave up. A similar pattern of events – or non-events – followed an experiment in which Wren tried to incubate chickens' eggs using the heat from a lamp. He was requested in April 1663 to provide Robert Hooke, the Society's Curator of Experiments, with the details. When Hooke was asked at the following week's meeting if they had arrived, he covered for Wren (who was an old friend from Oxford in the 1650s), saying that 'he had received it in good part; and that the doctor had promised to communicate the rest to him'. The doctor didn't; and two months later the Society was reminding him yet again. Likewise, following the death of Laurence Rooke in June 1662, Wren was asked on 9 July to continue the former's work observing the moons of Jupiter. He was asked again in September. And again in February.[14]

The longest-running saga of all concerns the famous lunar globe. Early in 1661, and presumably as a way of keeping his name before the King, Wren presented Charles with drawings of various insects, including a flea and a louse, made with the help of a microscope – a branch of optics in which he had been interested since the early 1650s. The drawings must have created quite an impression, since soon afterwards the Society decided that an effective way of currying royal favour might be for Wren to make some more – and to finish off his model of the moon and present that to the King, as well. The idea was put to Charles, who approved it, and accordingly Sir Robert Moray and Sir Paul Neile wrote to Wren to tell him of the royal command, saying 'how much our whole Society is rejoiced, that his Majesty has a just Esteem of your Parts', and dangling a further carrot in front of him: 'we expect you will signify to us your Readiness to comply with his Majesty's pleasure; and you may be sure we will improve it as much to your Honour and Advantage, as is possible . . .'[15]

Wren politely declined the opportunity to produce a second set of microscopical drawings for the royal collection, but by the middle of August he had completed the globe, and a few weeks later he presented it to the King – in person, bypassing the Royal Society altogether. Henry Oldenburg, the Society's Secretary, described it rather wistfully to Christiaan Huygens in a letter of 7 September, saying that Wren had given it to Charles 'without showing it to the company', that as a result he had 'not yet been so fortunate as to see it', but that he had been told 'it is a globe which so accurately represents the Moon that on it are visible all the Moon's inequalities, heights, depths, seas, rivers, islands, continents, etc, exactly as Mr Wren saw all these things with the telescope during one whole lunation; thus this artificial globe presents, according to its various positions with respect to the Sun, all the different parts of the Moon, exactly as they appear in the heavens.'[16]

Oldenburg also told Huygens that Wren had been ordered to make another globe, a little larger, which would be kept in the Society's repository at Gresham. If Wren had – either intentionally or inadvertently – deprived the Society of some of the reflected glory, then at least they would have their own model of the moon.

Nothing happened. Weeks passed. Then months. Then years. And still no globe. Eventually in September 1664, after Hevelius had written to ask about the famous globe★ and the letter had been read out at a meeting at which he was present, Wren was 'desired to defer no longer the making of a larger telescopical moon for the Society'.[17] No doubt a little embarrassed, he immediately promised they should have it the very next time he came up to London. The other members clearly knew by now how hard it was to get him to do something he didn't want to do, and said that if he would choose a suitable globe to work on, the Society's Treasurer would pay for it. Two months later Oldenburg was writing back to Hevelius with the by now very old news that the original was in the King's cabinet, but that 'our own Society has ordered that very ingenious man to make another of the same kind, but greater in size and still more perfect'. He ended by

★Hevelius was particularly interested because he was under the impression that the model was based on his own *Selenographia*. He didn't realize that Wren had originally embarked on the project because the *Selenographia* contained so many mistakes.

saying, 'I will tell you later, God willing, of his success in this'.[18] Nothing more was heard about the globe.

The Frenchman Samuel Sorbière, who was introduced to the Royal Society by Sir Robert Moray during his visit to England in the summer of 1663, wrote a pleasantly ordinary account of the Wednesday afternoon gatherings at Gresham. Meetings took place in a large wainscoted chamber, he said, where two tiers of bare wooden benches, one slightly higher than the other, were arranged before a table in front of the fire. Seven or eight chairs upholstered in green cloth were ranged around the table; they remained unoccupied on the occasions when Sorbière was present, leading him to suggest they were reserved 'for Persons of Great Quality'.[19] Brouncker, as President, sat at the table in the room's only armchair, with the Secretary on his left, taking minutes. All the other members took their places on the forms 'as they think fit, and without any Ceremony; and if any one comes in after the Society is fixed, no Body stirs, but he takes a Place presently where he can find it, so that no Interruption may be given to him that speaks'. Members stood to address the chair bare-headed, until Brouncker signalled for them to replace their hats; and everyone was civil, respectful and polite. No one was ever interrupted, and if anyone dared whisper to his neighbour, 'the least Sign from the President causes a sudden stop, tho' they have not told their Mind out'.[20]

Sorbière was elected to the Society during his visit, although members soon had cause to rue their actions. His account of their proceedings was included in his *Relation d'un Voyage en Angleterre*, which was published in 1664. The book caused a deal of patriotic indignation: the English were outraged by his patronizing attitude to the Anglican Church, his low opinion of the current state of English literature, his insolent tone. (He dared to suggest that as a race they were haughty towards strangers, and took unreasonable offence when boys chased after him in the street calling him a 'French dog'.) Anxious to distance the Society from such sentiments, Thomas Sprat (Fellow of the Royal Society, 1663) composed an open letter to his old friend Wren in which he responded to Sorbière's narrative at great length. Quite apart from the slurs on the nation's honour, he – and, one presumes, Wren and the other members – were irritated that the Frenchman didn't devote more ink to recording their achievements and ideals, and less to the arrangements of the furniture: 'Can you, Sir, indure to read all this Stuff with any Patience? . . . Is not this a shameful Sign of his Weakness, that he has insisted so long on such mean Circumstances, while he was describing a Subject that might have yielded him so much Noble Matter for his Pen?'[21] Most historians of science would agree with Sprat – and they're right, of course. It is the evolution of a stable institutional structure for experimental science which makes the Royal Society so important in the history of European culture; the individual contributions to the advancement of human knowledge made by Wren and Boyle and Hooke and the rest that changed the world. It doesn't add much to know those contributions were made, that institutional structure developed, by men who flinched like schoolboys when Brouncker caught them whispering to each other. But for me, that information doesn't trivialize the achievements; it only makes them more manageable. I feel absurdly reassured to know that history was made in those prosaic classroom surroundings – that an austere, diffident, slightly effeminate Robert Boyle discoursed there on the nature of air, and a crooked, pop-eyed, curly-haired Robert Hooke displayed his spring-balance watch and reported back on the experiments which led to the law named after him, that the extension of an elastic body under stress is proportional to the stress. I want to believe that Christopher Wren squirmed with embarrassment on a hard wooden bench while Paul Neile held his hat in his hand and made extravagant claims for his friend's theory about Saturn's rings, or that he sat red-faced when Brouncker or Oldenburg reminded him yet again of his promises about his lunar globe. I want my heroes to be people, not ideas.

Colleagues in the Royal Society, who were just as eager that their new assembly should be validated in the eyes of the world as they were to push the frontiers of knowledge in the right direction, may have found Wren exasperatingly evasive when it came to following through on his ideas; but the aura of promise, of an awesome intellect which had neither achieved its full potential nor gained rightful recognition, continued to cling to him as it had in the 1650s. And his friends took every opportunity to ensure he gained the credit that he seemed so reluctant to take for himself. Robert Hooke, for example, who began as a casual collaborator in the early days of the Royal Society and became one of his closest friends, was always quick to acknowledge his debt. Hooke's great work on experimental microscopy, *Micrographia* (1665), discharges his obligation to Wren's earlier insect drawings with a glowing encomium: 'I must affirm, that, since the time of Archimedes, there scarce ever met in one man, in so great a perfection,

1. Bust of Sir Christopher Wren by Edward Pierce, *c.* 1673.

2. Christopher Wren, Dean of Windsor.

3. John Wilkins,
Warden of Wadham College, Oxford.

4. John Evelyn.

5. Robert Boyle.

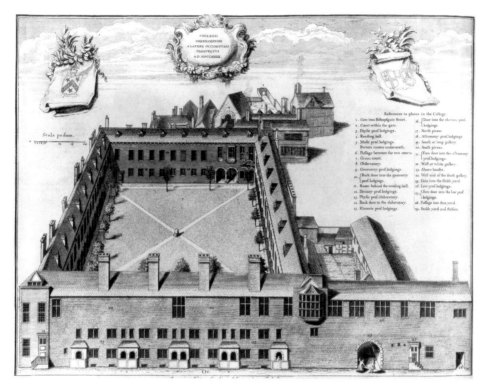

6. Gresham College, London.
The door leading to Wren's lodgings is in the bottom left corner; the reading hall where he lectured is the tall building with the steep gable beyond the quadrangle.

7. The frontispiece to Thomas Sprat's *History of the Royal Society* (1667), designed by John Evelyn and engraved by Wenceslaus Hollar.

8. Pembroke College Chapel, Cambridge.

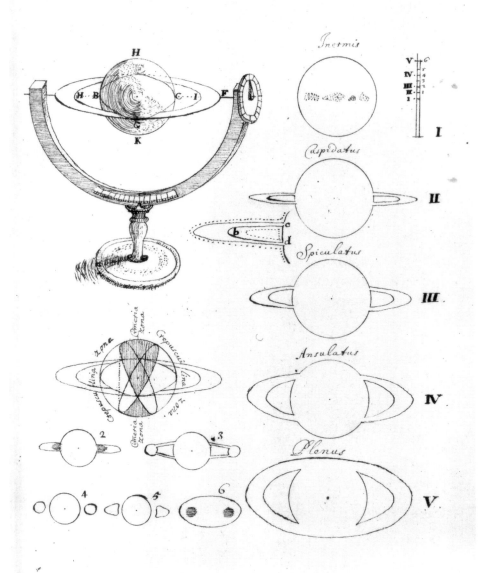

9. Wren's model of Saturn, with his sketches showing how it might explain the changing appearance of the planet.

FACING PAGE
(*Above*) 10. The south front of the Sheldonian Theatre, Oxford, engraved by David Loggan in 1675.
(*Below*) 11. The Custom House, London – Wren's first commission as Surveyor-General of the King's Works.

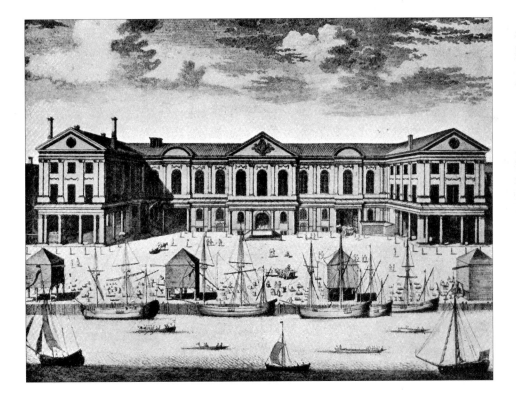

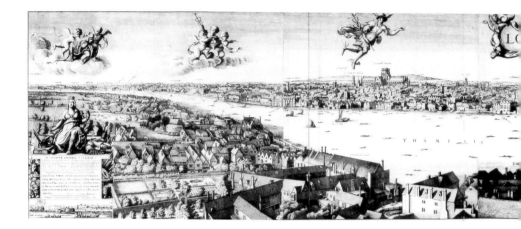

12. St Paul's Cathedral: Wren's pre-Fire design.

13. Wenceslaus Hollar's panorama of London before the Great Fire.

14. Old St Paul's in ruins, drawn by Thomas Wyck, *c.* 1673.

Madm:

The Artificer having never before mett with a drowned watch; like an ignorant physician has been soe long about the cure, that he hath made me very unquiet that your comands should be soe long deferred, how-ever I have sent the Watch at last, & envie the felicity of it, that it should be soe neer your side; & soe often enjoy your Eye, & be consulted by you how your time shall passe while you employ your hand in your excelent workes. But have a care of it, for I have put such a Spell into it; that every Beating of the Ballance will tell you, 'tis the pulse of my Heart which labours as much to serve you and more trewly then the Watch; for the Watch I beleeve will sometimes lye, & sometimes perhaps be idle & unwilling to goe, having receiued soe much injury by being drenched in that briny bath, that I dispair it should ever be a trew servant to you more: But as for me (unlesse you drown me too in my teares) you may be confident I shall never cease to be

June 14th.

> Your most affectionate
> humble Servant
>
> Chr: Wren

I have put the Watch in a Box that
it might take noe harme, & wrapt it
about with a litle Leather, & that it might
not jog, I was fain to fill up the corners
either with a few shavings or wast paper.

15. Letter from Wren to Faith Coghill, his future wife.

such a Mechanical Hand, and so Philosophical a Mind'.[22] Even when Wren's researches were carried on in collaborative networks – as they often were – his collaborators made sure that his role was publicized. During his early years in the Savilian chair, for instance, he worked closely with Thomas Willis, whose own Laudian loyalties and Royalist connections had earned him Oxford's Sedleian Professorship of Natural Philosophy at the Restoration. He went along to Willis' dissections, discussed the results with him, and contributed in a more practical manner by illustrating Willis' pioneering work on the structure of the human brain, the *Cerebri Anatome*, published in 1664. Like Hooke, Willis paid tribute to Wren in print, declaring in his preface that 'Dr Wren was pleased out of his singular humanity, wherewith he abounds, to delineate with his own most skilful hands many Figures of the Brain and Skull'.[23]

Wren continued to pursue his medical interests in the 1660s. In collaboration with Willis, Robert Boyle and Richard Lower, he developed a theory of muscular action and speculated on the constituent parts of air. However, he didn't neglect his primary area of research: John Evelyn, who hunted down Boyle late one afternoon during a visit to Oxford in October 1664, found him with John Wallis and 'that incomparable genius' Wren in the Schools' tower, once again the university's main observatory now that Wilkins and Seth Ward had left Wadham, and the place where Wren made most of his observations. The trio were busy trying to view Mercury's transit of the sun – unsuccessfully, as it turned out, because the sun dropped below the horizon just as the transit began.

Towards the end of his *Observations* on Sorbière's book, Thomas Sprat broke off from demolishing the Frenchman's underestimation of English culture to address Wren directly with a prophecy: 'You must give me leave, Sir, to presage, that to you your Country is to owe very much of its Ornament, as well as Experimental Knowledge, its Reputation, and indeed all the Living and Beneficial Arts, the Enlargement of their Bounds.' He went further in his 1667 *History of the Royal Society,* a passionate piece of propagandist polemic for experimental philosophy which, in stressing the collaborative and institutional nature of the Society, assiduously forbore to single out individuals – with one exception:

I must break this Law, in the particular case of Dr Christopher Wren . . . For in turning over the Registers of the Society, I perceiv'd that many excellent things, whose first Invention ought to be ascrib'd to him, were casually omitted. This moves me . . . to give this separate Account of his endeavours, in promoting the Design of the Royal Society, in the small time wherein he has had the opportunity of attending it.[24]

Sprat offered his readers a formidable list of what he saw as Wren's major scientific achievements: work on refraction and the theory of motion; plans for a history of the seasons; accurate optical measurement; his ideas on the rings of Saturn; the lunar globe and celestial mapping; magnetism and navigation; microscopy, anatomy and intravenous injection.

This is a short account of the Principal Discoveries which Dr Wren has presented or suggested to this Assembly. I know very well, that some of them he did only start and design; and that they have been since carry'd on to perfection, by the Industry of other hands. I purpose not to rob them of their share in the honour. Yet it is but reasonable, that the original Invention should be ascribed to the true Author, rather than the Finishers. Nor do I fear that this will be thought too much, which I have said concerning him. For there is a peculiar reverence due to so much excellence cover'd with so much modesty. And it is not Flattery but honesty, to give him his just praise; who is so far from usurping the fame of other men, that he endeavours with all care to conceal his own.[25]

Sprat's eulogy brings us face to face once again with the problem which lies at the core of Wren's scientific career – his refusal to follow through with his ideas, his apparent lack of concern with credit and reputation. This seems to me more puzzling than the transition from astronomer to architect, which is traditionally seen as the big issue in Wren's eventful life. The image of an unworldly young seeker after knowledge, self-effacing to the point of extinction and endeavouring with all care to conceal his achievements – and massive achievements they were, at that – is attractive; but it sits uneasily with Wren the ambitious professor, making ruthless use of his family connections, dining out with Cromwell one minute and rushing to curry favour with King Charles the next. In the context of seventeenth-century social and political mores, there is nothing unusual in the way he used his influence; everybody did it. The difficulty lies in reconciling his striving for success and status with his reluctance – one might almost say his inability – to capitalize on his inventions and discoveries. Is the truth simply that, as John Summerson suggested in his 1953 biography, Wren found it all too easy, that 'he had a contempt for his own easy mastery of every known branch of scientific thought'?[26]

At first sight, the idea that he just didn't care seems odd. From the little we know of Wren's personality at the time, the Professor of Astronomy comes across as a cold, monastically austere character, dedicating himself to the life of the mind with a frightening singleness of purpose. Even those who considered themselves his friends valued him for his intellect, not his warmth or his compassion; his real friends were ideas. Yet there is a restlessness about him which can't simply be attributed to the conventionally catholic interests of the seventeenth-century virtuoso – a hunger, almost, as he pursued first one thing, then another and another, switching between disciplines, hunting for answers, chewing over problems and spitting out solutions. And then moving on. The breadth of Wren's knowledge is beyond doubt; the personal fulfilment it brought him is open to question. And how strange to know so much, and care so little.

All of which makes us eager for a voyeuristic glimpse into Wren's private life in the early 1660s. He may or may not have kept in touch with Faith Coghill, who still lived with her (now widowed) mother in Bletchingdon. But he was still a bachelor, while most of his friends and colleagues – Wilkins, Wallis, Scarburgh, Evelyn, Willis – were married men with married lives. Moray was a widower; Petty would not marry until 1667 – although he had already fathered an illegitimate daughter, who later became a well-known actress at the Duke's Playhouse. One can't help wondering who, if anyone, Wren slept with. It is hard to imagine him cruising the dark alleys of Oxford for paid sex, or copulating with whores in the bushes of Lincoln's Inn Fields and St James's Park.

The only reference we have to any hint of a sexual relationship at this time is fleeting and enigmatic – a 1663 letter from Thomas Sprat, his old Oxford friend and the only man familiar enough to call him 'Kit Wren' to his face. (In typical seventeenth-century fashion, 'Doctor Wren' was usual from even his closest friends.) Discussing the art of conversation, Sprat declares that women are the best speakers: 'I could give you two undeniable Instances, in your *Laura* (as I think you call her) and her who was once my *Clelia*; the one speaks with a great Freedom and Spirit, and Abundance of excellent Words; the other talks less, but with as much

Sweetness and Nature.'[27] Sprat talks as if 'Laura' were Wren's mistress and thus, in the context of the time, a woman of easy virtue; although given the Petrarchan overtones, she could just have easily been Faith Coghill, a totally respectable object of unrequited desire. We don't know. With the exception of the Sprat letter, all the evidence points to Wren as a remote, rather cerebral character who, at least until he married Faith in 1669, focused his pent-up energy on pushing back the frontiers of knowledge.

That may be true. However, we need to bear in mind the example of another of Wren's close friends. Robert Hooke was also a bachelor-academic, who lived an apparently monastic and entirely cerebral existence in his lodgings at Gresham, without a care in the world for physical and emotional gratification. Except that Hooke kept a diary which, when it was finally published in the 1930s, cast a radically different light on his private life. This quiet, earnest, withdrawn man regularly had sex with a succession of servant-girls at Gresham – Nell Young, Doll Lord, Betty Orchard. A typical entry in the diary reads, 'Played with Nell – 𝓧. Hurt small of Back.'[28] (𝓧 was Hooke's private symbol for orgasm.) He regularly had sex with his teenage niece and ward, Grace Hooke. ('Grace 𝓧, paid me 1sh', is the enigmatic entry for 16 January 1677.[29]) And he regularly masturbated alone, unless his meticulous recording of every occasion on which he reached orgasm didn't run to naming a partner. Of course, Hooke's experience hardly demonstrates that Christopher Wren had an equally eventful home life. What it *does* demonstrate is the danger of assuming that public virtue implies an absence of private passions.

Publicly, Wren held that ideas were useless unless they had a practical application – a theme which the Royal Society returned to again and again during its early years, as it tried to counter criticism that its activities were pointless and its aspirations laughable. Referring to experiments in microscopy, James Harrington wrote that the Society was good at two things, 'a diminishing of a commonwealth and the multiplying of a louse'; in 1664 Pepys remarked on William Petty's discomfiture during an audience with Charles II, when Petty's 'Philosophicall and Mathematico-Mechanical King' hooted with laughter at Gresham 'for spending time only in weighing of ayre, and doing nothing else since they sat'. By 1664 Evelyn was railing in print against people who, 'led away and perverted by the noise of a few Ignorant and Comical Buffoons whose Malevolence or Impertinences intitle them to nothing that is truly Great and Venerable . . . [are] asking, "What have the Society done?"' Those who ridiculed the Society could do more damage than its more earnest critics, said Thomas Sprat: 'We ought to have a great dread of the power of these terrible men . . . [who] may do it more injury than all the arguments of our severe and frowning and dogmatical adversaries.'[30]

In an authoritative and rigorously argued address to the Royal Society in January 1662, Wren emphasized the pre-eminence of utility in the Society's activities. Apart from the pleasure that accrues 'from the Converse and Communication of every one's Thoughts', its role was twofold: to benefit mankind, and to perfect something 'for which Posterity may be really obliged to us'.[31] Making a useful contribution *and* gaining public recognition for that contribution, two ideas which – ironically, considering his track record to date – would inform the whole of Wren's later career – were paramount. And as far as he was concerned, there were three ways to achieve these goals: by advancing knowledge; by showing the way to economic gain; and by improving the health of mankind. There was no need to worry about the first, he said. So long as members continued with their experiments, the theories would come naturally. The same could be said of the second. Plans for improvements in navigation, and a 'history of trades' – a scheme to draw up an encyclopaedia of industrial processes and craft practices which had long been cherished by several members, including Evelyn and Petty – were bound to lead to profit. In any case, as he sensibly pointed out, 'there can hardly be any Thing propos'd worth our Consideration, that will not itself, or some Corollary from it, be reduceable to this Head'.

One might imagine that Wren's third area, the health of humanity, could be left to the physicians, of whom the Society boasted more than its fair share.* A decent laboratory at Gresham, more chemical research and more frequent dissections would all be helpful, he said. But – and here he came to the crux of his speech – there was a more ambitious collaborative enterprise, perfectly suited to the workings of the Society, which would oblige posterity more than anything else he could think of. 'The History of Seasons is this excellent Work I would recommend to you, desir'd by all modern Philosophers, though no Body hath had yet the Patience to pursue it.'

---

*In the following year's list of 115 members, no fewer than 22 were medical men, making them by far the largest professional group. They included Wren's old mentor Charles Scarburgh, who was elected to the Society on 16 January 1661 (on the same day as Wren's brother-in-law William Holder).

This was a field of study which was particularly dear to Wren's heart. He proposed that the Society should produce 'a History of Things depending upon Alteration of the Air and Seasons' – an account, in other words, of how the weather and the seasons impacted on the physiological effects of wine, coffee and tobacco, on the state of agriculture, on the reproductive habits of fish, insects and reptiles, on the incidence of epidemics and the death-rate in London. This would necessarily have to be combined with an accurate record of changes in wind speed and direction, humidity, temperature, rainfall, and meteorological oddities such as parhelia, falling stars, and 'unusual Colours and Shapes of Clouds'.

A good idea. The problem was, how could one record the information systematically? When he was a teenager staying with Charles Scarburgh, Wren had devised a recording weather-clock with a revolving cylinder, and he returned to this invention once more, telling the meeting that he could provide them with a solution:

> I might seem to promise too much, should I say, an Engine may be fram'd, which if you visit your Chamber but one half Hour of the Day, shall tell you how many Changes of Wind have been in your absence ... Neither shall the Thermometer need a constant Observance, for after the same Method may that be made to be its own Register ... Many other things I might suggest of this Nature, which if the Design be once begun, I shall most willingly submit, upon Occasion, to the Judgment of the Society.[32]

Wren's hints generated considerable interest among the other members, and over the following weeks he brought in a scheme for a weather-cock (presumably a version of the wind-recording instrument he had devised fifteen years earlier); read a paper on the weather-glass, an open tube that registered the effects of both temperature and air pressure; and demonstrated an idea for a self-emptying rain-gauge. Nothing more was heard of the scheme until June 1663, when Balthazar de Monconys, a Frenchman who visited London while accompanying the young Duc de Chevreuse on a grand tour of Europe, was shown a clock-operated temperature-, wind- and rain-gauge made by 'M Renes' – the first known automated meteorograph.

The subsequent development of Wren's device is rather complicated. In the September following Monconys' visit, when the Royal Society was racking its brains to think of suitably marvellous inventions to set before the King on his projected tour of inspection, John Wilkins 'put the company in mind to improve their former consideration of making an history of the weather', and Wren was written to in Oxford to send them details of the 'weather-engine' he had proposed the previous year.[33] In December 1663, after the usual prevarications and reminders, it arrived: a description of a device for measuring wind direction and temperature, operated by a rack and pinion attached to the movement of a clock and making use of two pencils which moved continuously on a revolving drum (for the temperature) and a disc which was turned by a weather-vane. The idea was dropped again, only to be resurrected once more in 1670. But having come up with the basic idea, Wren characteristically left it to others – specifically Robert Hooke, as the Society's Curator of Experiments – to perfect the invention. Hooke was still valiantly working on it in the 1680s, and by this point it is impossible to tell exactly which of the two men was responsible for what. Although various members occasionally reported on weather conditions, the Royal Society made no systematic 'history of the seasons' during Wren's lifetime.

The starting point for the various incarnations of the weather-engine had been a proposed investigation into the nation's health, a conflation of Wren's interests in medicine, physics and – since meteorology fell within the sphere of astronomy – his own chosen profession, all of which he brought together for an eminently practical purpose. His other great passion during the early 1660s – and indeed, for most of his life – showed a similarly practical bent (and, one might add, a similar drive to come up with a solution to an apparently insoluble problem).

The quest for longitude was a dream shared by every mathematical practitioner in Europe. Demonstrating and improving the art of navigation, which largely depended on taking accurate readings from the sun and stars once a vessel was out of sight of land, had always been a fundamental part of academic astronomy: the Gresham professors were instructed to include in their lectures 'the use of the astrolabe and the staff, and other common instruments for the capacity of mariners'; and the Oxford University Statutes required Savilian professors 'to explain and teach . . . the rules of navigation in so far as they are dependent on mathematics'.[34] The pressure to develop more efficient sea-travel grew dramatically in the wake of the great voyages of discovery of the previous century, and this was nowhere more marked than in Britain, whose economy depended on foreign trade, and whose trade depended entirely on its shipping. The potential for financial gain on long-distance routes was enormous – a pound of pepper bought for 2½d in Madras or

Bombay, for example, sold in London for 1s 8d, a gross profit margin of 700% – but so were the risks, and anything which increased a vessel's chances of reaching its home port with its cargo intact was to be welcomed by both merchants and the state.

Several of Wren's predecessors at Gresham and Oxford – notably Gunter, Briggs and Gellibrand – had made important contributions in the field of navigation in the early part of the century, directed chiefly towards simplifying the formidably complicated arithmetical calcu-lations which mariners were called on to make during a voyage. But a method of accurate position-finding continued to elude their best efforts. To determine any given position on the earth's surface, two coordinates are needed: parallels of latitude, which indicate angular distance north or south of the Equator as measured from the earth's centre; and meridians of longitude, which show angular distance east or west of a selected prime meridian, a notional line circling the globe and passing through the two Poles. (The Canaries, the Azores and the west coast of Africa were all favourites in Wren's day – the current meridian at Greenwich wasn't internationally recognized until 1884.) If a navigator knew exactly where his ship was in relation to both the Equator and this north–south meridian, then he could transfer that knowledge to a map or chart and plot his position, like using the x-axis and the y-axis on a two-dimensional graph.

With the help of a quadrant, an astrolabe or a cross-staff, a seventeenth-century navigator could find the altitude of the sun at its zenith or – on a cloudless night in the northern hemisphere – the pole-star and, armed with this information and a formidable set of tables, could establish his vessel's latitude with reasonable accuracy. But neither the sun nor the stars showed how far east or west of a designated prime meridian it lay. Ocean-going mariners had to depend on their experience of currents and prevailing winds, and wildly inaccurate methods of measuring a ship's speed – and thus their distance from their point of departure. By the time they had been out of sight of land for more than a few days, they had little idea of their position. As the mathematician Thomas Digges put it in 1576, navigators 'can neither truly give the place or situation of any Coast, Harbour, Road or Town, nor yet in sailing discern how the place they sail unto beareth from them, or how far it is distant'.[35] They had to strike sail each night for fear that they would founder on rocks which were charted, since they didn't know where they were on their charts. When 'contrary and adverse tempests' blew them off course, they had no idea how to get back to their intended route. When they set out on any ocean-going voyage, they could only hope to God and their compass that they arrived somewhere – anywhere – that was reasonably close to their intended destination.

At the Restoration, Gresham College was still a centre for research into navigational methods. Rooke and Petty were both enthusiasts, as was Brouncker, whose appointment as Commissioner for the Navy in 1664 gave him a professional interest. An anonymous ballad, probably composed around the time that the Royal Society was founded, expressed high hopes for the future:

> The Colledge will the whole world measure,
> Which most impossible conclude,
> And Navigation make a pleasure
> By fynding out the Longitude.
> Every Tarpaulin shall then with ease
> Sayle any ship to the Antipodes.[36]

Not surprisingly, Wren was also preoccupied with longitude, 'than which,' as he said in his inaugural Gresham oration, 'Industry hath hardly left any Thing more glorious to be aim'd at in Art'.[37] Surviving references are tantalizingly vague, however. *Parentalia* lists among his 'philosophical Tracts, Manuscripts and printed', papers with titles such as 'Of the Longitude' and 'To find the Velocity of a Ship in sailing'. In the 1650s he also began collecting notes and ideas for a much more substantial illustrated discourse, which set out the history of the problem and gave some possible solutions, and he continued to return to it until 1720, three years before his death. In the preface to the work, apparently written in 1658 and quoted by his son in an early draft of *Parentalia*, he says that, 'After the Labours of so many Witts as good as frustrate, 'twill seem a great Presumption to think it fesable [to find longitude at sea]: our greatest incouragement is that the World hath yet gone the wrong way to work. 'Tis not from Astronomy nor Magneticismes, but from more obvious Principles we must receive this Magnale Artis.'[38]

The reference to 'obvious Principles' may mean that while he was still at Gresham Wren was thinking about a mechanical way of measuring a ship's speed. Sixty-six years later Parliament set up a Board of Longitude and offered a prize of £20,000 to anyone who could come up with a method of determining longitude to within half a degree on a voyage from Great Britain to the West Indies. This was a powerful incentive, especially to an old man who was by now obsessively worried about money and recognition. So Wren wrote to Isaac Newton, then President of the Royal Society, enclosing a sealed paper containing coded descriptions of 'three distinct Instruments, proper (as I conceive) for Discovering the Longitude at Sea'.★ All three are rather obscure, even when the cipher is decoded. But one, 'Pipe screwe moving wheels from beake', suggests a mechanism mounted on the prow or 'beake' of a vessel to measure the flow of water and translate this into knots via a system of cogs and screws – a method which was doomed to failure, since it couldn't distinguish between a ship's movement through the sea and the action of the current.[39]

Wren also investigated the most obvious mechanical principle of all, the development of an accurate marine chronometer. Since the earth rotates through a full 360 degrees during each 24-hour period, it followed that it rotates through 15 degrees every hour. By comparing the time at the prime meridian with the time on board ship (which could be ascertained by watching the sun reach its zenith and calling that noon, local time), a navigator could easily work out his vessel's east–west position. So, for example, if a ship set sail from the Canary Islands and found that at midday it was two hours behind Canary Islands time, a navigator knew for sure that his longitude was thirty degrees west. That was the theory, anyway. But existing timepieces just weren't that accurate – they could lose or gain up to fifteen minutes each day. To take a rather extreme example, after three weeks at an average of three knots, a vessel out from the coast of Portugese West Africa on a course due west along the Equator would be in the middle of the Atlantic. But a navigator foolhardy enough to depend on a chronometer for checking his longitude – and no navigator in his right mind would do so – might find that on paper his ship was either somewhere in the Indian Ocean or in the Pacific, a thousand miles west of the Galapagos Islands. Even an error of *one minute* a day could place a vessel more than 350 miles away from its true position after three weeks at sea.

The many attempts to improve the accuracy of timepieces during the seventeenth century – Christiaan Huygens' pendulum clock and the spiral balance spring over which both Huygens and Robert Hooke claimed priority, to name but a few – were all conducted with a view to

★Ciphers were a generally accepted method of ensuring priority. If a scientist had a solution to a problem or hypothesis, but was as yet unable or unwilling to demonstrate it, he might publish the idea in code. No one else could steal it, and at a later date he would be able to establish that he had been the first to come up with it.

producing a reliable marine chronometer for measuring longitude. And all failed. It wasn't until 1773 that John Harrison won the Board of Longitude's prize with his famous series of timekeepers. Wren's second coded message, even more cryptic than the first, said 'Watch magnetic balance wound in vacuo'. It isn't altogether clear exactly what this refers to, but it seems to hark back to 1662, and a passing interest in timepieces. At a Royal Society meeting that February he proposed graphite as a better lubricant than oil 'for preserving the pivots of the wheels of watches or clocks from grating or wearing out',[40] and went on to suggest an experiment of placing a watch in Boyle's vacuum pump in order to see how it worked in the absence of air. Neither idea aroused much enthusiasm – members were much more interested in putting pigeons, snakes, even their own arms into the vacuum – but in the context of the time, the notion of testing or improving the workings of a timepiece implies that Wren, like his friend Hooke, was exploring a horological solution to the great problem. He also experimented with furnaces which maintained constant temperature, with a view to 'keeping the motion of Watches equal, in order to Longitudes and Astronomical uses'.[41]

Wren also looked to 'Magneticismes' for a reliable way of determining longitude. Since the end of the fifteenth century, when Portugese pilots had tried to make use of the fact that the difference between true north and magnetic north varied from place to place, navigators, instrument-makers and mathematicians had looked for accurate ways of measuring magnetic variation with a view to establishing a vessel's east–west position on the globe. Henry Gellibrand's demonstration in the 1630s that the variation also changed through time complicated things considerably; but this doesn't seem to have deterred Wren. In 1657 he had high hopes of the 'Observation of the Mutation of the magnetical Variation', confessing that while it was as yet crude, it could turn out to be of 'so great Use . . . to the Navigator, that thereby we may attain the Knowledge of *Longitudes*'.[42] The following year he designed a forty-inch needle 'by which I hope to discover the Annual Motion of Variation & Anomalies in it', and this in turn led to a paper, now lost, which was called 'To observe the Variations of the magnetical Needle'.[43]

Considering that he was eager to investigate any and every avenue in his quest for longitude, it is surprising that astronomical observation doesn't seem to have played a larger part in Wren's thinking – especially since most seventeenth-century astronomers, from Galileo to Newton, were convinced that the only answer was to keep watching the skies. Galileo's response to the sight of Jupiter's four major moons in 1610 had been to view them as a potential celestial chronometer. If one could produce tables that predicted in advance the precise times at which each moon was eclipsed by the planet, a navigator could make an observation through a telescope, compare the local time of the eclipse with his printed ephemerides, and calculate his longitude using the 15°=1 hour rule – just as if he had a perfectly accurate clock set to prime-meridian time. The predictions weren't the big problem here: as with all astronomical methods of determining longitude, the difficulty lay in making timed observations of the moons on a rolling sea with a big, flimsy telescope and poor optics. (There were also cloudy skies to contend with, and the fact that Jupiter and its moons disappeared from the sky for months at a time.) Galileo devised a rather bizarre piece of headgear to get round the instability problem, a bronze mask with a telescope fixed to one eye, leaving the other eye free to locate the planet. He hawked the idea around the courts of Europe in the hope of winning the cash prizes offered for a solution to the problem of longitude, but no government was convinced.

Nevertheless, throughout the seventeenth century astronomers and navigators continued to take an interest in the possibilities of planetary, lunar and stellar observations. Laurence Rooke's research on the moons of Jupiter – the research which the Royal Society repeatedly begged Wren to take up after Rooke's death in 1662 – was certainly connected with longitude. So were the unspecified observations off Portugal mentioned above, which the Earl of Sandwich reported to the Society in the same year, and which Wren also failed to comment on, pleading that he didn't have the time.

There *are* scattered indications that Wren viewed the heavens as a key to the problem of longitude. At some time before 1663 he devised a 'double-telescope', a pair of telescopes joined together with a hinge and connected at the eyepiece end by a graduated rule, so that two observers could direct the instrument simultaneously on different celestial objects and find the angle between them – a way of establishing the relative positions of planets and fixed stars, perhaps with a view to using their movements as timekeepers, like Jupiter's moons. And the third coded description in the sealed paper he gave to Newton in 1714 reads, 'Fix head hippes handes poise tube on eye'.[44] This sounds like a development of Galileo's telescopic mask, a frame or clamp which would keep the observer steady aboard ship while he took his readings from the stars.

Of course Wren may have been absorbed in astronomical solutions to longitude for much of his life: it would be strange if he hadn't been. But we just don't know. His reluctance to publish his findings, his haphazard approach to research, the loss of most of his scientific papers,* his voracious appetite for every sort of scientific problem, and the natural preoccupation of subsequent generations with his career in architecture – all obscure the truth about so many of his activities in his late twenties and early thirties. We have to rely on a handful of surviving letters, on passing references in the letters of others, on respectful (but often exasperated) entries in the Royal Society's minutes, on the lists of inventions and discoveries in *Parentalia* which promise so much and explain so little. What we know of Wren's attempts to find an answer to the problem of longitude suggests a driven man, confident enough to switch between different disciplines in pursuit of a result, and incapable of admitting failure. What we don't know could fill another book.

---

*When John Ward looked through sixty years' worth of Wren's papers, while researching his *Lives of the Professors of Gresham College* (1740), he noted that 'Sir Christopher had his thoughts very early upon [longitude], and always kept it in his view afterwards'. The papers, which consisted of 'divers methods proposed by Sir Christopher for that end, with draughts of several instruments proper for the purpose', have long since disappeared (Ward, *Lives*, 109).

6

An Ingenious Gentleman

The year 1661 was a significant one for Wren, and not only because of his appointment to the Savilian Professorship of Astronomy. Just months after he took up his post at Oxford he received what on the face of it seems a bizarre invitation – to direct the building of new harbour defences at Tangier. Under the terms of Charles II's marriage contract with Catherine of Braganza, her father, John IV of Portugal, agreed to hand over £800,000 in cash together with the Portugese territories of Bombay and Tangier. The royal wedding didn't take place until May 1662, but preparations for the handover of territory had begun the previous autumn and Tangier, which provided Britain with a longed-for base in the Mediterranean, was a particularly welcome prize. (Or so it seemed at the time – the Crown abandoned it in 1683, after Parliament expressed a reluctance to continue funding the garrison, on the grounds that it was badly managed and a hotbed of Popery.) On 6 September the Earl of Peterborough was appointed Chief Governor, and on 30 January a fleet under Lord Sandwich arrived to deposit Peterborough and a small army of soldiers and engineers in Tangier, and formally take possession from the Portugese.

One of the first steps towards establishing a British presence was the building of a harbour, a mole and a series of fortifications to protect the city from the Moors, who were in a state of perpetual war with the Portugese and who were unlikely to view the British any more kindly. While preparations for the expedition were at an early stage, the King offered the job to Wren.

Wren went up to London for some preliminary discussions about the scheme, and also to consult over plans for repairing the decrepit medieval fabric of St Paul's Cathedral. In an undated letter probably written in the autumn of 1661, Thomas Sprat warned him that Richard Baylie, the Vice-Chancellor of Oxford University, was demanding to know why the Astronomy Professor had absented himself without leave during term-time. Sprat had tried to cover for him, he said, protesting that the King had commanded his presence in London to consult over the Tangier project and 'the rebuilding of St Paul's'; but Baylie 'took it very ill, [that] you had not all this while given him any Account what hinder'd you from the Discharge of your Office'.[1]

In the event, Wren was not enthralled at the prospect of a long and unpleasant sea voyage followed by an even longer, even more unpleasant stay in a sweltering war zone. So he turned down the King's offer, diplomatically pleading ill health – in spite of the fact that the position came with some powerful inducements. Cousin Matthew, who was now secretary to the Lord Chancellor, the Earl of Clarendon, wrote to say that if his kinsman would accept, a leave of absence from Oxford would be arranged (and Baylie placated, presumably); there would be an ample salary; and, most remarkably of all, Wren would be granted the reversion of the office of Surveyor-General of the King's Works. This meant that on the death of the present Surveyor-General, Sir John Denham, he would automatically be appointed to the single most prestigious architectural post in Britain, with a huge staff, a healthy salary of over £380 a year plus expenses, and overall responsibility for all the royal residences, from sprawling Tudor palaces like Whitehall, Greenwich and Hampton Court to the King's hunting lodge at Lyndhurst, deep in the heart of the New Forest.[2]

How and why should a newly appointed young professor of astronomy with no track record as a surveyor have been asked, out of the blue, to leave Oxford and work as a military engineer on a major project which was of enormous importance to British interests? For that matter, why should his advice have been sought on the repair of St Paul's? The Tangier offer came at around the same time that Wren had a royal audience to present his lunar globe to the King; perhaps Charles, who was quite capable of making important appointments on an arbitrary whim, thought a survey of Tangier would be child's play to anyone who could make an accurate survey of the moon. On the other hand, maybe the impetus came from Matthew Wren, who felt he would do his cousin a favour by putting him forward to Chancellor Clarendon as the right man for the job. *Parentalia* suggests the invitation came because Wren was already 'esteemed one of the best Geometricians in Europe',[3] and certainly the use of mathematicians in military fortification was not unusual. Jonas Moore, who was given the Tangier job after Wren had turned it down, was well known as a mathematician; but as the Surveyor of the Fen Drainage System in 1649 and the designer of a citadel for London under Cromwell he also had extensive practical experience. (He was knighted for his work at Tangier in 1663, and made Surveyor-General of the Ordnance.) Perhaps Wren also had experience of the business of fortification, more than we know. There are some tantalizing references in the *Parentalia* list of Wren's 'Theories, Inventions, Experiments, and Mechanick Improvements' shown to the Oxford group in the 1650s. They include schemes 'to build in the Sea, Forts, Moles, &c', 'Inventions for better making and fortifying Havens, for clearing Sands, and to sound at Sea', and 'New Designs tending to Strength, Convenience, and Beauty in Building'.[4] *Parentalia*'s dates aren't always reliable, however, and in the absence of any corroborating evidence we have no way of knowing whether the entries refer to youthful schemes which have since been lost, or to preliminary work that Wren put in on the Tangier project. But coupled with the Tangier offer and Sprat's reference to St Paul's, they suggest that by 1661 Wren was already known to be taking an active interest in the business of building.

This leads on to the other intriguing point about the affair, the promise of the reversion of Sir John Denham's post at the King's Works. When Denham died eight years later Wren did indeed get the Surveyor-Generalship, of course – he hung on to it for close on fifty years – so it is tempting to see in the offer an early recognition of his potential as an architectural genius. But in Restoration England, technical expertise was no prerequisite for a senior post in the King's service. Faced with a horde of Royalists queuing up to remind their sovereign of all they had suffered in his cause during the Commonwealth, Charles II was quick to appreciate that doling out government sinecures was a cheap and easy way of repaying loyalty. (And the granting of reversions – rights of succession to a post on the death or retirement of an incumbent – was even cheaper and easier.) So in the weeks after Charles's return to England, the office of Sergeant Painter of the King's Works went to Sir Robert Howard, a Cavalier earl's son who had no experience of painting but who pocketed the £10 annual salary as a modest but agreeable addition to his already large income. That of Paymaster went to Hugh May, along with a rather less modest £189 2s 10d – not because of his accounting skills but for the sake of his faithful service to the exiled court at The Hague in the 1650s.★ And the top job was given to the cavalier poet Denham, who happily drew £382 5s 8d a year but designed scarcely a single building. Described by Anthony Wood as 'a slow, dreaming young man, and more addicted to gaming than study', and by John Evelyn as 'a better poet than architect', he is chiefly remembered today (when he is remembered at all) for his poem *Cooper's Hill*. Denham had been imprisoned after unsuccessfully defending Farnham Castle for the King in 1642, and on his release he played a minor but significant role in Royalist intrigues – fund-raising in Scotland, spying in a desultory fashion and regularly carrying coded despatches between France and Holland. In 1660, like many of his fellow Royalists, he travelled post-haste to Breda, where he reminded the King of his faithful service and recalled that eleven years before Charles had promised him the office of Surveyor-General if he were ever to be restored to the throne. The incumbent, a plumber named John Embree, was summarily ejected; and on 13 June, only two weeks after the King's triumphant return to London, Denham's patent was confirmed. (Much to the dismay of the obvious choice for the job, Inigo Jones's pupil John Webb, who wrote a desperate and unsuccessful petition begging that 'His Majestie may please to grant some other place more proper for Mr Denham's abilityes and confirm unto Mr Webb the Surveyor's place wherein he hath consumed 30 years study'.)[5]

So we needn't read too much into the fact that Wren's name was mentioned in connection with the Surveyor-Generalship at such an early date. In itself it implies neither architectural ambition nor recognition of architectural talent, simply an acknowledgement of his family's political pedigree and a desire on the part of the Crown to lure someone loyal and at least halfway qualified to a desolate spot on the shores of north Africa. No doubt he felt flattered, although not flattered enough to pack his bags and head off for Tangier. But in the end, the hindsight which lends significance to every passing reference to building in the career of England's greatest architect resolves itself into little more than the plain fact that while he was in his twenties Wren was well connected and included architecture among his other interests. He was still first and foremost a professional scientist. Like William Petty, who told his wife that 'I do elude my melancholy sometimes by contriving

★May's appointment turned out to be a great success. Not only was he a more than competent administrator, he quickly developed into one of the most gifted architects of his generation.

many noble palaces on paper',[6] he was a paper architect who read his Serlio and his Alberti and his Vignola and amused himself and others with his scribblings.

But in Restoration England, busy reinventing itself as a sophisticated centre of culture, paper architects were well placed to turn their scribblings into stone. In the words of Sir Roger Pratt, one of the first Caroline amateurs to carve out a reputation for himself as a practising architect, 'there is no doubt but that the most beautiful buildings of these times are chiefly to be seen in Italy and France'. And while Pratt's declaration that 'Architecture here [i.e., in England] has not received those advantages which it has in other parts, it continuing almost still as rude here as it was at the very first', is more questionable, it was certainly true that after the death of Inigo Jones in 1652, the English building trades did not have the theoretical knowledge to cope with the classical design vocabulary demanded by Royalist patrons, many of whom had experienced European trends at first hand during their years of exile.★ The deficit was supplied by unqualified but educated dilettantes, the sort of 'ingenious gentleman', to quote Pratt one more time, 'who has seen much of that kind abroad and been somewhat versed in the best authors of Architecture: viz Palladio, Scamozzi, Serlio, etc'; and whose designs 'though but roughly drawn . . . will generally fall out better than one which shall be given you by a home-bred Architect for want of his better experience'.[7]

So among Wren's immediate circle in the Royal Society, ingenious gentlemen of the likes of John Wallis, John Evelyn, William Petty and Robert Hooke all took to dabbling in architecture. Wallis, as Savilian Professor of Geometry, lectured occasionally on the subject. The proposal for a monastic college of natural philosophers that Evelyn sent to Boyle in 1659 was accompanied by a plan and elevation showing a double-pile pavilion of five bays with a broad broken pediment, evidence of his self-imposed exile in Italy during the war; five years later, when his translation of Fréart de Chambray's *Parallèle de l'architecture antique et de la moderne* was published, we find him helping Hugh May to design a chapel for the Earl of Clarendon at Cornbury in Oxfordshire and talking Charles II through an unrealized scheme for a new Palace of Whitehall. Hooke took to architecture a little later, but to greater effect: having produced a plan for a new City of London after the fire of 1666

★There were exceptions in the building trades, of course, the most capable of whom was John Webb.

(along with Wren, Evelyn and others) he went on to design or remodel more than twenty buildings, including the new Bethlehem Hospital in Moorfields and Montagu House, Bloomsbury. He was also one of the surveyors for the rebuilding of London – 'by which he hath gott a great Estate', according to Aubrey – and he collaborated with Wren on the rebuilding of the City churches. Petty's architectural career is much vaguer. Although among the noble palaces he contrived on paper was a project for a grandiose £20,000 reconstruction of Dublin Castle after a fire there in 1684, it was never carried out. He designed two garden pavilions for his town house in St George's Lane, Dublin, in 1677, and also built a fortified country residence for himself (and it certainly needed to be fortified, considering his carpetbagging treatment of the Irish) on his Killowen estate in County Kerry. William Winde, another Royal Society member and sometime friend of Wren, was a minor courtier, an even more minor mathematician, and a professional soldier, who began in the early 1660s by working on Hamstead Marshall in Berkshire and Ashdown House in Oxfordshire for his godfather, the 1st Earl of Craven, and went on to advise on the design of several influential country houses, including Cliveden in Buckinghamshire (1674–7) and Belton House, Lincolnshire (1685–8).

We shouldn't over-estimate the actual architectural input of these men. It was usually limited to providing rough drafts, often no more than sketch plans and quite crude elevations, which were then worked up on site by mason-contractors and other craftsmen. Where Wren had the edge was in his knowledge of the mathematical sciences. Like the author of an anonymous *Essay on the Usefulness of Mathematical Learning* at the end of the century, he understood that architecture owed '[its] being to Mathematicks, as laying the foundation of [its] Theory'; and that 'he that would invent, must be skilled in numbers'.[8] Given his connections, his interests and his academic grounding, we shouldn't be too surprised to find that the Professor of Astronomy would be given the opportunity to design a building.

And so he was, three years into the Restoration. Wren's first known foray into architecture came about through family patronage. Soon after being reinstated as Bishop of Ely, his uncle Matthew offered to fund a replacement for the modest fourteenth-century chapel at Pembroke Hall, Cambridge, where he had been an undergraduate more than half a century before. The new chapel was to be a public act of thanksgiving, not only for the Bishop's safe deliverance (although he certainly intended it as a personal monument) but also for the restoration of the monarchy and the episcopacy. For reasons we can only guess at – Wren's developing interest in architecture, Matthew's desire for an architect who was sympathetic to his own views of an appropriate setting for the Anglican liturgy, the family ties and inexperience that meant the younger man would do as he was told – he invited his nephew to design the new building.

Wren's scheme for the chapel was probably drawn up either in the winter of 1662/3 or early the following spring; it had been passed by the Bishop (who was presumably consulted closely over the design) and the college authorities by 13 May 1663, when the Master, Dr Frank, 'did in the name of Bishop Wren and in the Presence of divers Heads of Colleges . . . and of the Dean, Arch-deacon, and many of the Prebendaries of Ely lay the first Stone of the Foundation of the new Chapel of Pembroke-Hall'.[9] Frank signed the contract for the brickwork three days later, and the shell was more or less complete by January 1665, when his successor, Robert Mapletoft, agreed the contract for the wainscoting, seating and woodcarving with Cornelius Austin, whom Wren later employed at Emmanuel Chapel and Trinity Library. That summer Wren was organizing the transport of black and white marble paving from London to Cambridge via the port of King's Lynn, noting that insurance would cost a shilling in the pound, or 2s 6d 'if there be warr wth the Hollander'.[10] And the new building was consecrated by the aged but still fiercely Laudian Bishop on 21 September 1665 – St Matthew's Day. The total cost, reckoned at £3658 1s 5d, leaves us in no doubt that in spite of his trials and tribulations during the Interregnum, Bishop Matthew had managed to acquire – or regain – a sizeable personal fortune. He also gave Pembroke a manor he had purchased in 1662 (Hardwick, a few miles west of Cambridge) to ensure there would be revenue for the upkeep of the monument he had chosen as his resting place. He died at his residence in Holborn on 24 April 1667, and was taken 'by the Heralds, with all decent Pomp and Ceremony; and deposited in a Stone Coffin in a Vault under his own Chapel'.[11]

Pembroke Chapel was the first thoroughly classical building to appear in either Oxford or Cambridge and, in spite of some bookish features, it shows a surprising sureness of touch for someone with no experience of architecture. Some of this must have come from the craftsmen and contractors who put flesh on the bare bones of the plans and elevations that Wren provided; and some, possibly, from Bishop Matthew, who as Master of Peterhouse in the 1620s had supervised the building of that college's chapel just across the road from Pembroke. (Although if this was the case, the Bishop's architectural tastes had certainly moved a long way from the ultra-conservative Tudor-Gothic of Peterhouse.) But if we should be wary of claiming too big a share for Wren in his first building, we should not underestimate his achievement. Quite sensibly, his chapel was structurally unambitious, nothing more than a rectangular four-bay box. An entrance on the north side led into an outer chapel, and from there through a screen into the main body of the building, with the sanctuary distinguished only by a Venetian window and a pedimented reredos. (A chancel was added during George Gilbert Scott junior's remodelling in the 1880s, when the chapel was extended eastward by one bay.) The public face of the building is at the west end, looking out onto Trumpington Street. It simultaneously proclaims the chapel's presence to the world and holds the world at bay, since the actual entrance is within the college precincts. Wren's treatment is based on a classical temple façade which derives from engravings in the *Architettura* of Sebastiano Serlio, an influential Renaissance textbook which had appeared in an English edition in 1611. It contrives to raise expectations of what lies within while at the same time subverting ideas of what a temple should be: the pediment is there and, in the four Corinthian pilasters, the suggestion of both a portico and a triumphal arch. But there is no door – just a high arched window flanked by niches and, where one would expect the door to be, a blind moulded panel.

In addition to his drawings for the chapel, which unfortunately haven't survived, Wren caused a wooden model to be made – which has, albeit in a rather battered state. The purpose of this was both to give his uncle and the Pembroke Fellows an idea of the finished product, and to act as a guide for the builders. In his professional life as a scientist he was familiar with the value of three-dimensional models in exploring and explaining the solution to a problem. Witness his pasteboard and copper representations of Saturn and its rings, for example, or the lunar globe that caused such a stir at the Royal Society. But we needn't read too much into the Pembroke model. Such things were common practice in the seventeenth-century building world, and plenty of Wren's contemporaries recognized that they helped craftsmen on site to see how their different contributions fitted together – *and* that they could sell a design to anxious patrons more effectively than a set of presentation drawings. But, when coupled with the fact that he was to rely heavily on the use of models throughout his architectural career, its existence suggests that his experience of their value in science was readily transferred to architecture.

The history of Wren's second commission, the Sheldonian Theatre in Oxford, is better documented than Pembroke Chapel – and its quality is much more debatable. Even Wren's defenders have felt rather negative about the building, describing it as 'not . . . overwhelmingly impressive', and saying it shows that Wren was 'not yet very competent in his handling of detail' or 'not yet capable of handling a large architectural composition with assurance'. Detractors have taken a less hesitant line – 'an eclectic confusion, cobbled together by an experimental engineer'.[12]

So what went wrong?

Wren owed the opportunity to design the Sheldonian to another Laudian bishop. Gilbert Sheldon had been the Royalist Warden of his old college, All Souls, until he was ejected during the Parliamentary Visitation of 1648; after that he took himself off to the estate of the arch-Royalist Sir Robert Shirley at Staunton Harold in Leicestershire. There he established himself as one of the leaders of the High Church in exile and, in the words of the inscription over the church that Shirley built in the grounds of his house in 1653, did 'ye best things in ye worst times, And hoped them in the most callamitous'. His loyalty was rewarded: he was reinstated as Warden of All Souls in 1659, appointed Bishop of London the following year and, when William Juxon died in the summer of 1663, succeeded him as Archbishop of Canterbury. As the High Church party reasserted itself in Oxford, Dean Fell resurrected an idea which had been cherished by Laud when he was Chancellor of the University in the 1630s – the removal of the wholly secular and often rowdy degree ceremonies from their traditional venue, the university church of St Mary the Virgin on the High, to a more appropriate setting. The notion that 'sacrifice is made equally to God and Apollo' in a place where homage was due to God and God alone was as repugnant to Fell and his colleagues as it had been to Laud. They approached Sheldon, as an obvious and prestigious sympathizer, for a donation to launch an appeal for the necessary funds; and he promptly stumped up £1000.

Wren's involvement in the scheme for the 'New Theatre', as it was originally to be called, probably pre-dates Sheldon's. It may be due to Dean Fell, who acted as accountant to the project, determined the function of the building and, following his promotion to Vice-Chancellor in 1666, had a controlling interest in the whole business. On

16 April 1663, a month after the university had begun negotiations with the city authorities for a site on Canditch (the forerunner of Broad Street) and more than a year before it wrote to thank Sheldon for his donation, Oldenburg was telling John Evelyn that, 'Dr Wren hath brought to town ye modell of a Theater, to be built for ye Oxonian Acts, and for Playes also: wch ye King seeing this very morning, commended highly, and so did all others, yt are severe Judges of such matters. He is desired to shew it on Wednesday next to ye Society, to have their approbation likewise.'[13] He did that very thing, although not until a fortnight later – the King's approbation mattered rather more to Wren than that of the Society – and it caused quite a stir. He was asked to write down 'a scheme and description of the whole frame of it, to remain as a memorial among the archives of the society' (characteristically he didn't, or if he did, it hasn't survived); and soon afterwards members were spreading the news of Wren's new theatre, 'to be used . . . for conferring degrees, dissection of bodies, and acting of plays'.[14]

Nothing is known of this first design except that it proved too ambitious, for financial rather than technical reasons: the plans to include facilities for staging plays and dissecting bodies were jettisoned when Wren 'was obliged to put a Stop to the bolder Strokes of his Pencil, and confine the Expence within the Limits of a private Purse'.[15] The purse was Sheldon's: potential sponsors had met the news of his initial donation with a deafening silence, and in September 1665, when work was already in progress, he had to be persuaded to fund the whole project himself, a decision which would eventually cost him a massive £14,470. But even as built, the Theatre was quite unlike anything Oxford – or England – had ever seen. There was no precedent in England for the sort of academic assembly hall that the university required, and for inspiration Wren went once again to Serlio – or more precisely, to Serlio's engravings of the Theatre of Marcellus in Rome, built in the first century BC.

This was rather a clever idea. The ruined Theatre was well known to seventeenth-century cognoscenti – Evelyn, who went over it in November 1644, declared that 'the architecture from what remaines appeares to be inferior to none'.[16] By using it as his model, Wren made a visual break with the past and clearly distanced the new building and its function from religious worship in the Gothic surroundings of St Mary's, taking for Apollo what was due to him and leaving God out of it entirely. And besides making the right cultural references to antiquity and classical authority, a building constructed on a D-shaped plan – like the Theatre of Marcellus, with its stepped tiers of seats and clear sightlines – was admirably suited to fulfil the New Theatre's brief. However, there was one big problem. Like any Roman theatre, the original had no roof, and spectators relied on temporary awnings for shelter from the weather. The climate in Oxford obviously called for something more permanent; but no timbers were long enough to roof the proposed 70-foot span. The obvious solutions, Gothic vaulting or the introduction of load-bearing columns, would destroy the effect of an ancient Roman theatre and, in the case of the latter, would also interrupt the sightlines.

So Wren turned for help to his fellow Savilian professor, John Wallis. Since the 1640s Wallis had been experimenting with, and occasionally lecturing on, a 'geometrical flat floor', a grid of overlapping timbers which in theory could span a space much greater than the length of the longest member. He had demonstrated a small-scale model of the floor at Wadham in the early 1650s and presented another to Charles II in 1660; and the idea was still attracting attention in 1663, when he showed it to Sorbière, who confessed himself 'mightily pleased' with it.[17] Wren adapted the concept behind Wallis's floor for his new theatre, creating a series of trusses which were built up from shorter sections and held in place by their own weight, with help from judiciously placed iron bolts and plates. The roof design was hailed by contemporaries as a marvel of engineering: in 1677, eight years after the Sheldonian was completed, Robert Plot singled it out for special praise in his *Natural History of Oxfordshire*, saying it was 'perhaps not to be parallel'd in the *World*'.[18] He was right: it was so efficient that for nearly a century the University Press stored its books in the roof-space, and for many years it was the largest unsupported floor in existence. When the Sheldonian was examined in 1720, after rumours that it was in need of repair, the surveyors found that although the ceiling had sagged slightly owing to the weight of books, 'the whole Fabrick of the said Theatre is, in our Opinion, like to remain and continue in such good Repair and Condition, for one hundred or two hundred Years yet to come'.[19]

A broad flat ceiling, however ingenious its construction, was not enough to maintain the illusion that the assembled worthies were in a Roman theatre. They needed to look up and see the heavens, even though the lowering skies above Oxford were safely hidden from view. And so they could. As the building neared completion in 1669, a marvellous piece of allegorical *trompe-l'oeil* was created by Robert

Streater, Robert Howard's successor as the King's Sergeant Painter. 'A very civil little man, and lame,' said Pepys, when he was taken to the artist's Whitehall studio to see the paintings in progress; he found Wren in attendance to supervise the work, and the consensus was that Streater's designs would outshine Rubens' work at the Banqueting House. (Privately, Pepys disagreed: 'I do not fully think so. But they will certainly be very noble.'[20] Eighteen years later James II was less diplomatic, remarking when he saw them *in situ* that it was a pity they hadn't been done by the current court painter, the Italian Antonio Verrio.) Streater developed Wren's Roman theatre theme by creating a scene in thirty-two panels, in which putti roll back awnings to reveal the sky – where the clouds part to show a victorious Truth descending in glory to enlighten the Arts and the Sciences, and to cast out from the university the figures of Envy, Rapine and 'brutish, scoffing Ignorance', who is 'endeavoring to vilifie and contemn what she understands not'.[21] Personifications of the mathematical sciences are there – Astronomy with her celestial globe, Geography, Arithmetic, Optics with her telescope, Geometry and Architecture. So too are the medical sciences, and Logic and Law. And over the Vice-Chancellor's throne floats Theology, pointing to the stone tablets of Mosaic Law with her iron rod and appealing to Truth for assistance. Although we may not want to go so far as one contemporary, who declared that 'Future ages must confess they owe/To Streater more than Michelangelo', the result is undeniably impressive, the message unequivocal.[22]

Before we think about what that unequivocal message actually is, we should perhaps ask why the Sheldonian has had such a luke-warm reception from twentieth-century critics. What flaws there are lie on the outside, and they are probably the result of Sheldon's refusal to pay for an elaborate exterior, Wren's inability to find an adequate external expression for a building which was wholly conditioned by the functionality of its interior space and, more interestingly, his refusal to bend the knee to classical authority in the way that our experience of eighteenth-century architecture has conditioned us to believe is right. It is hard to disentangle the three. He was no slave to classical precedent: internally, for instance, he turned the absence of a stage at the flattened south end of the theatre into a virtue, by placing the Vice-Chancellor's throne in the centre of the northern horseshoe – thus making the Vice-Chancellor both the focus of attention and an integral part of the assembly, and putting the 'hub' into 'hubris' in a thoroughly Baroque fashion. But the Theatre of Marcellus's curving D-shaped plan, which is retained internally, gives way on the exterior of the Sheldonian to an awkward straight-sided polygon – cheaper, certainly, but a lot less elegant. There are no pilasters to link the rest of the building with the entrance façade that closes the D; another economy, perhaps, but a regrettable one. And the entrance façade itself is an unconventional affair, in which the upper storey rises dramatically (and awkwardly) through a massive broken pediment that spans the whole width of the building.

The Sheldonian certainly has its faults. But to dismiss it as the work of an untrained amateur architect, or even to see it as little more than a harbinger of greater things to come, is simply wrong. As far as conservative Restoration Oxford was concerned, its classical references, its structural ingenuity, its ability both to break with recent history and to conjure up a more distant, more authoritative and more respectable past, made the Sheldonian little short of revolutionary.

The funding problems meant that progress on the building of the Sheldonian was initially slow. The foundation stone was not laid until 26 July 1664, well over a year after Wren had exhibited his model. But as work went on, Wren embarked on a second architectural project in Oxford. His 'client', Ralph Bathurst, was an old friend who had also been active in Wilkins' experimental philosophical club in the early 1650s, when he lectured on embriology and foetal nutrition and took his MD. Now he was President of Trinity College, and in June 1665 he approached Wren to design a new quadrangle in the college gardens. Wren argued against it, saying 'it be much the worst situation for the chambers, and the beauty of the College, and of the particular pile of buildings', but he acknowledged with his customary pragmatism that benefactors were more likely to stump up the money for a grandiose-sounding 'quadrangle' than for a single block.[23] In the event, he did design a single block – a plain, rather pedestrian affair of two storeys with a hipped roof. It was finished in 1668.

The Sheldonian Theatre was finally inaugurated on Friday 9 July 1669. In 'a fabrick comparable to any of this kind of former ages, and doubtless exceeding any of the present', John Fell took his place at a chair and desk covered with brocade and cloth of gold. Beneath Streater's allegory of Truth putting Ignorance to flight, heads of colleges, doctors and alumni assembled to hear the Register read out Sheldon's grant of the building to the university 'for their scolastic exercises upon these solemn occasions'. Evelyn, who had gone up to Oxford for the ceremony, recorded how speeches praised Wren, 'the ingenious architect', and Sheldon, who was absent (and who never in fact visited his Theatre in any official capacity).

> This ended, after loud musiq from the corridor above, where an organ was plac'd, there follow'd divers panegyric speeches both in prose and verse . . . mingled with excellent musiq, vocal and instrumental, to entertain the ladies and the rest of the company. A speech was then made in praise of academical learning. This lasted from 11 in the morning till 7 at night, which was concluded with ringing of bells and universal joy and feasting.[24]

Except that joy was not quite universal. The centrepiece of the celebrations was a long speech by Robert South, the University Orator, and Evelyn noted with some irritation that the 'ill natur'd man' made 'some malicious and indecent reflections on the Royal Society, as underminers of the University, which was very foolish and untrue, as well as unseasonable'. John Wallis, who was also there, was furious. The first part of South's oration, he wrote to Boyle, 'consisted of satyrical invectives against Cromwell, fanaticks, the Royal Society, and new philosophy; the next, of encomiasticks, in praise of the archbishop, the theatre, the Vice-Chancellor, the architect, and the painter; the last, of execrations against fanaticks, conventicles, comprehension, and new philosophy . . .'[25] Wren must also have felt a little uncomfortable.* Lavish public praise for what was only his third completed building was obviously welcome and, in the summer of 1669, timely, since only a few months previously he had succeeded Sir John Denham as Surveyor-General of the King's Works. But any warm glow of pride was tempered by an attack which lumped him and his friends in the Royal Society together with religious extremists and political hate-figures like Cromwell, and this in the presence of some of the nation's most distinguished academics. With hindsight, it almost seems as if the establishment was calling on him to make a choice – in a building whose iconography and pioneering construction methods have come to be seen as a tangible demonstration of the power of experimental philosophy and the triumph of truth over ignorance.

But as usual, hindsight plays us false. In 1669 the Sheldonian was not

---

*If he was there. It would be odd if he hadn't been, although contemporary sources make no mention of his presence. However, he would certainly have had the contents of the speech reported to him.

the celebration of radical new ideas that it came to be for later generations, but an uncompromising declaration of faith in ancient authority and a return to familiar, more stable values; a statement of the new science subjugated to the old order. The ideological programme behind it was Fell's: unbending Theology's iron rod and tablets of stone took precedence over telescopes and celestial globes; the engineering marvels of Wren's ceiling were hidden behind more than painted canvas panels. If we see Robert South's oration as an unwitting invitation to Wren to choose between architecture and science, then we make a distinction which he would have found meaningless. But if on the other hand the choice was between the respect of established hierarchies and institutions, and a place in the vanguard of the new philosophy, then I think Wren had already chosen. By the time he reached his late thirties, he wanted success, he wanted power – things which only the establishment could offer.

At the end of 1664 reports began to circulate among members of the Royal Society about the appearance of a comet in the south-eastern skies. On 15 December Robert Hooke wrote from Gresham to Boyle in Oxford, saying that although he hadn't yet seen it – because of cloud and the polluted London skies – the blazing star was reported to have 'a very long tail extended toward the north west, some say about ten yards long, some about two'.[26] At a Royal Society meeting at Gresham that Wren attended six days later, Moray announced he had viewed the blazing star from his observatory at Whitehall on 17 December. Members also heard accounts from the Earl of Sandwich, who had caught sight of it while on board ship at Spithead, and two of the Society's correspondents in Ireland, who sent word that it could be seen from Dublin. Everyone present was urged to make their own observations of the comet's progress, and to communicate them to the Society.

The arrival of a comet always caused excitement and consternation. Such 'Blazeing Starrs', to quote astrologer John Gadbury's *De cometis* (1665), 'Threaten the World with Famine, Plague, & Warrs:/To Princes, Death: to Kingdoms, many Crosses:/To all Estates, inevitable Losses!'[27] Aristotle, who had argued that comets were hot, dry gases exhaled from the surface of the earth, ignited by the heat of the sun and whirled around the celestial sphere until they were consumed, believed that they heralded drought, earthquakes, tidal waves and storms. Most early societies went beyond meteorological phenomena and regarded them as harbingers of doom, believing, like the first-century poet Marcus Manilius, that they 'presage civil discord and strife between kin'.[28] Luther thought they were signs of divine wrath, perhaps even of the Second Coming; and one of his followers, Andreas Celichius, adapted Aristotelian teaching to suggest in the year after the appearance of the great comet of 1577 that 'the thick smoke of human sins, rising every day, every hour, every moment . . . [became] gradually so thick as to form a comet, with curled and plaited tresses, which at last is kindled by the hot and fiery anger of the Supreme Heavenly Judge'. Although a contemporary, Andreas Dudith, came back with the entirely logical rejoinder that 'if comets were caused by the sins of mortals, they would never be absent from the sky', theologians, astrologers and popular writers continued to see them as signs of impending calamity or, more rarely, divine providence.

Exactly which, depended on whose side you were on. The comet of 1618–19 presaged the fall of the house of Stuart, according to the Parliamentarian astrologer William Lilly, writing during the Civil War. (It also foretold the death of Anne of Denmark and the devastation of the Thirty Years' War.) The daytime star or comet which appeared at the birth of Charles II in 1630, on the other hand, showed that he was to be 'the most Mighty Monarch in the Universe', said Edward Matthew; but then he was writing in the months following Charles's restoration. The Welsh prophet Arise Evans went further, declaring in 1664 that the celestial apparition was the same comet that had been seen at Christ's nativity, and that it meant England would go to war with the Dutch and suffer a dreadful plague before the conversion of the Jews and the coming of Christ, who would reign side by side with Charles. He got the first two right, at least.

Comets sometimes took a more direct hand in human events. A Parliamentarian pamphlet of 1642 described an incident at Totnes in Devon, in which a Royalist soldier named Ralph Ashley attempted to rape a young Puritan virgin: 'At that instant, a fearefull Comet appeared, to the terrour and amazment of all the Country thereabouts. Likewise declaring how he persisting in his damnable attemt, was struck with a flaming Sword, which issued from the Comet, so that he dyed a fearefull example to all his fellow Cavaliers.'[29]

The scientific community tended to take a more restrained view of the causal nature of comets. It was quite possible that a comet might have some *physical* impact on the earth – at the end of the seventeenth century Edmund Halley suggested that it was a close approach by a comet which affected the tides and thus caused the biblical Flood – but its role as harbinger or catalyst of social and political upheaval was another matter.

Wren's general attitude towards popular folklore was ambivalent. For example, he was a believer in sympathetic magic, recounting to a Royal Society meeting in 1663 how he had experimented on a servant who had cut her finger by rubbing a rag over the girl's wound, covering the dressing with powdered sulphate and tucking it in her bosom. When her finger was cured, Wren took the rag from her and heated it at the fire while she was sweeping the next room; she screamed in pain and threw down her broom, and on examination her finger was found to be inflamed. He cooled the rag, and within a day or two her finger returned to normal. Boyle, who was present at the Gresham meeting, immediately volunteered to repeat the experiment on a dog. Wren himself made a related trial years later: in 1677 he told friends at the Crown Tavern in Threadneedle Street how he had just cured his second wife's thrush by hanging a bag of live boglice round her neck.

At other times, he adopted a much more critical stance, as he did during a stay at a Wiltshire country house, the talk of the country because of a ghostly knocking on the wainscot. He duly heard the Devil drumming on the wall; but simply noted how strange it was that the phenomenon occurred only when a particular maidservant was in the room next door.

However, like many professional scientists of his time,* Wren had nothing but contempt for the idea that ordinary events in the heavens like planetary conjunctions and the movements of the constellations had some causal connection with human affairs, dismissing astrology out of hand as 'unreasonable and ridiculous'.[30] Extraordinary and apparently haphazard apparitions like comets may or may not signify divine wrath or divine benevolence: what was certain was that 'Experiment and Reason is the only Way of prophesying natural Events'.[31] Since 1577, when Tycho Brahe had shown that comets were astronomical rather than meteorological phenomena, attention had steadily shifted towards establishing their paths through the skies. Did they shoot out from the sun and eventually fall back into it in an elliptical arc, due to the sun's sweeping magnetic force, as the Puritan astronomer Jeremiah Horrox

---

*There were some notable exceptions. Wren's early mentor William Oughtred, for instance, regularly cast horoscopes, confessing with disarming candour that he 'was not satisfied how it came about that one might foretell by the Starres, but so it was that it fell out true' (*Aubrey's Brief Lives*, ed. Oliver Lawson-Dick [1992 edn.], 223).

had proposed in the 1630s? Or did they enter the solar system in a straight line, make a slight swerve round the sun and head off out into space? Like most of his colleagues, Wren believed the latter; but since the earth was both revolving on its own axis and orbiting the sun, it was extremely difficult to work out a given cometary path. The appearance of the Great Comet of 1664 was a chance to determine that path, both by observation and by collating the observations of others. It was another problem in search of a solution.

He worked closely on that problem with Robert Hooke, who, having already figured more than once in these pages, deserves a fuller introduction than he has received so far. Hooke was weird. Brilliantly inventive, absurdly hypochondriacal, suspicious to the point of paranoia, sexually frustrated − except on the occasions when those frustrations were relieved by his maidservants, his adolescent niece or his own hand − he was one of Wren's closest scientific, and later architectural, collaborators. He was also a distant kinsman: one of Wren's sisters, either Katherine or Rachel, was married to John Hooke, a relative of Robert who succeeded William Holder as rector of Bletchingdon in 1662. Hooke's early life had striking parallels with Wren's. Born in 1635 at Freshwater on the Isle of Wight, he too was a sickly child, and his father − also a clergyman − educated him at home, where he amused himself making sundials, clocks and mechanical toys. At the age of thirteen, he also went to Westminster School and then, in 1653, to Oxford − Christ Church rather than Wadham, but he soon became a member of John Wilkins' circle, gaining a reputation in the Oxford group for designing ingenious experiments. This led to a spell assisting Thomas Willis and Robert Boyle with their chemical researches; and then in 1662 to his appointment (on Boyle's recommendation) as the Royal Society's first Curator of Experiments, where his job was 'to furnish the Society every day they meete with three or four considerable experiments'.[32] He was elected an FRS in 1663 and appointed Professor of Geometry at Gresham College two years later.

Hooke's contributions to science were ultimately much more significant than Wren's. He invented the balance spring for watches and the marine barometer, anticipated Newton's theory of gravity and first pointed out the real nature of combustion. Schoolchildren still hear his name in physics lessons today, when they are taught Hooke's Law, that in elastic bodies stress is proportional to strain. But in the 1660s, Hooke's relationship with Wren consisted largely of picking up the ball whenever his friend dropped it. Physically, the pair made quite an odd couple. Wren was handsome with a confident, patrician air about him, curly, shoulder-length hair and piercingly perceptive eyes. Hooke was crooked, pale and chinless with a large head, 'his eie full and popping, and not quick'; his hair was very long, neglected and lank, and it flopped over his face.[33] Emotionally, if not intellectually, Hooke was the junior partner in the friendship, deferring to Wren's judgement and defending him fiercely whenever questions of priority in discoveries and inventions arose. Yet there was, to quote Aubrey, 'a wonderful consimility of phansey' between the pair.

The Great Comet was a case in point. Although Hooke also took a keen interest in it – and with more accuracy, believed that it moved in a closed path, and that it would eventually reappear – all the observations which came in to the Royal Society were initially referred to Wren, the most illustrious astronomer in the group. At a meeting at Gresham on 1 February 1665, he came up with a theory to locate the comet's rectilinear path through the heavens. With that he lost interest, and the society asked Hooke to take over the project, as he had with Wren's scheme for incubating chickens' eggs, with Wren's microscopic drawings, with Wren's weather-engine.

Then, in the last days of March 1665, a second comet appeared. (In fact it was probably the first, which had rounded the sun and was now passing the earth on its return journey out of the solar system.) Wren's interest was immediately rekindled, and he wrote to Sir Robert Moray asking that the Royal Society should once more send him all their observations, and that Hooke should be requested to return his papers on the first comet. In the light of his own sighting of the 'second' comet on 7 April, he seems to have revised his ideas:

> Though this last appearance were brighter & more silver coloured then ever the first was, yet as long as I see it in the same path & Retrograde when the other should be retrograde, I have some suspicions it may be the same. Is it thus, or else doe comets kindle one an other, or propagate by a kind of Generation?[34]

Hooke duly returned Wren's observations and diagrams, having first asked the Royal Society's amanuensis to make copies. The two men exchanged letters during April and May. Wren believed he had come up with 'the trew Hypothesis' about the comet's path, and wanted Hooke to come up to Oxford to compare notes, 'though I dare not importune you to it, for I know you are full of employment for the Society wch you almost wholly preserve together by your own constant paines'.[35] For his part, Hooke hesitantly proposed a circular path for the comet, although he deferred to the other's reputation and judgement. 'I weary you with my Conjectures,' he wrote to Wren on 4 May, 'and I doubt not but that before this, you have perfected the Theory of Comets, so as to be able to predict much more certainly what we are to expect of these Comets for the future; whereof if at your Leisure you will please to afford me a Word or two, you will much oblige me.'[36]

Any moves Wren made towards perfecting his theory are lost, and it was left once more to Hooke to pursue the ideas the two men had discussed. Those discussions continued sporadically for the rest of their lives. When another comet appeared in April 1677, for example, Hooke rushed to tell Wren about it, and the pair went for a stroll in St James's Park, talking about the ideas they had had in the 1660s and what light this new apparition might shed on them. But in the spring of 1665 Wren's long passion for astronomy, though not exactly on the wane, was competing with his developing architectural interests. The one provided him with reputation, respect, a reasonable income and a congenial lifestyle; the other offered fulfilment and a wider fame. For a time, the two could exist side by side. But only for a time.

7

The Most Esteem'd Fabricks of Paris

*T*he comets that held Wren's attention in the winter of 1664 and the spring of 1665 provoked fear rather than curiosity in the population at large, which could not have cared less about hypotheses or rectilinear paths. The two blazing stars were clearly harbingers of doom, and astrologers predicted that their arrival, coupled with a conjunction of Mars and Saturn the previous November, meant war, pestilence and famine. Reports reaching England from Vienna early in January 1665 told of how the first comet had been accompanied by 'the appearance of a Coffin, which causes great anxiety of thought amongst the people'.[1] Ghostly apparitions were seen in the heavens; gunshots and cannon fire were heard; and even those who adhered to the new philosophy grew uneasy. The physician George Thomson, later to inspire reverent awe for his courage in carrying out a pioneering post-mortem on a plague victim, was convinced by 'long observation' and 'sad experience' that 'comets, or blazing stars, do portend some evil to come upon mortals'.[2]

Uncannily enough, these fears were justified. When the hard winter of 1664/5 eased in April, cases of bubonic plague began to appear in St Giles-in-the-Field and other outlying London parishes. This was not so unusual – five plague victims had died in London the previous year, and twelve the year before that. But by the first week of June – and it was a hot June – the pestilence was spreading, and 112 deaths were reported. In the last week of June the bills of mortality proclaimed that the weekly death-toll had trebled, by the middle of July it had increased tenfold. Nearly 100,000 Londoners would die before it finally began to subside in the cold of the following winter. Red chalk crosses began to appear on nailed and padlocked doors all over the city, together with the pathetic plea, 'Lord have mercy upon us'. An anonymous poet wrote of how 'Ladyes, who wore black patches out of pride, Now weare them their plague sores to hide'. As pest-houses were quickly built to accommodate the sick and dying, and communal pits dug to accommodate the dead, the same poet lamented that:

> Into the vallies are the bodyes throwne
> Vallyes no more but now dead mountains grown.
> Thick grass and moss begins to growe
> Out of the Putrified corps and now
> The Cattell did the men devoure
> As greedily as men did them before.[3]

A day of prayer and fasting was appointed for Wednesday 12 July; five days previously Charles II and the Duke of York had fled Whitehall for Syon House in Isleworth, staying there for only two days before moving further away from the city, to Hampton Court Palace. The Royal Society broke up in disarray on 28 June. Oldenburg, who attributed the 'pestilential infection' to the wrath of God, hoping that 'when we have purged our foul sins this horrible evil will cease', stayed put in London.[4] So did Viscount Brouncker, who was sick, and a handful of other active members. But most dispersed either to Oxford or to the cleaner air of the countryside around London. 'Almost the whole of our Society is now scattered throughout Britain,' Oldenburg told Hevelius at the beginning of August. Robert Boyle had gone back to Oxford towards the end of May. Sir Robert Moray accompanied the King to Hampton Court. Hooke fled Gresham College about a fortnight after the discontinuance of the Society's meetings, going first to Nonsuch and then on to Lord Berkeley's country house at Durdans near Epsom, where he was joined by John Wilkins and William Petty. On 4 August Evelyn found the trio happily engaged in 'contriving chariots, new rigging for ships, a wheel for one to run races in, and other mechanical inventions'.[5]

Wren travelled rather further than Epsom or Hampton Court. Around the middle of July he left for Paris on his first and only excursion outside England, not returning to these shores until the end of February or the beginning of March 1666. Given the circumstances, it wouldn't be all that surprising to find that the main aim of his trip was to seek refuge from the plague. And no doubt the rocketing mortality rates in

London sent him on his way with renewed zeal, although in fact Oxford, where he still spent most of his time, was to enjoy almost complete immunity throughout the plague year. The court moved there for safety in September; Charles II took up residence at Christ Church and deposited Catherine of Braganza at Merton where, with a breathtaking lack of tact, he also lodged his very pregnant mistress Lady Castlemaine.* When Parliament assembled at Oxford on 9 October, the Lords gathered in the Astronomy School where Wren normally gave his lectures.

But frightening though the pestilence may have been, Wren's Paris trip had been planned months before it took hold. He told Sir John Denham at the end of March 1665 that he intended to spend the summer in Paris; Denham passed on the information to Evelyn, who offered Wren 'some addresses to friends of mine there, that shall exceedingly cherish you'.[6] Who Evelyn's friends were, we don't know, although during stays in France in the 1640s and early 1650s he had made the acquaintance of several well-known virtuosi. Denham, incidentally, had also spent time in Paris during the Commonwealth, when he was in attendance on Henrietta Maria, Charles I's queen. He didn't mix much in the intellectual circles that Evelyn frequented – he seems to have spent most of his time gambling and drinking – but he came into regular contact with the Queen's confidant, Henry Jermyn, who by 1665 was Earl of St Albans, English ambassador at the court of Louis XIV and, according to persistent but false rumours, Henrietta Maria's husband. It was perhaps Denham who provided an introduction to the Earl. According to *Parentalia*, Jermyn 'us'd [Wren] with all Kindness and Indulgence imaginable' during the visit.[7]

The usual practice for cross-channel travellers in the mid-seventeenth century was to board a Thames wherry in London and sail down to Gravesend, then to hire post-horses to Rochester, Sittingbourne and Canterbury before finally arriving at Dover a day or two later to take the packet-boat for Calais. It was possible to take ship at Gravesend and sail direct to Calais, a route which the philosopher John Locke followed when he travelled to France ten years after Wren. But Locke was more intrepid than most: even the short Dover–Calais crossing, a mere twenty-five miles, could easily take sixteen unpleasant and frightening

---

*Anthony Wood noted with a certain satisfaction in the following January that a paper was pinned to Lady Castlemaine's door at Merton. It read: 'The reason why she is not ducked/'Cause by Caesar she is fucked.'

hours if, as frequently happened, seas were stormy, winds were unfavourable, or the unwelcome attentions of Dunkirk-based privateers forced the captain to change his course and run.

Once they arrived on French soil, sick, tired and thanking God for their safe passage, most English visitors spent the night recuperating in Calais. The next day they would set about hiring horses and guides, and banding together with fellow travellers for the dangerous journey ahead. Certain areas, such as the forests south of Montreuil, were notorious for footpads and robbers who lay in ambush among the trees and ditches, and travellers were advised to draw their swords as they approached such trouble-spots. French highwaymen were reckoned to kill their victims routinely, a practice which, according to the anonymous and chauvinistic author of *A New Journey to France* (1715), 'shews their Barbarity . . . in Comparison with our generous English Highway-men, who seldom or never kill, unless resistance is made'.[8] But even an armed band could do little against the other species of robber who preyed on travellers – the tax officers at the internal customs barriers between provinces, who scandalized the English by searching luggage that had already been searched at Calais and demanding additional duty on goods.

The roads in France were generally rather better than those in England, especially on major routes; some were even paved, which was more than could be said for most English highways. But the 150-mile journey, down the coast to Boulogne, then south through Abbeville to Amiens or Beauvais, and finally into Paris, could still take nearly a week, with inns along the way varying from more than adequate – 'a good supper . . . clean sheets of the country and a pretty girle to lay them on' – to frankly appalling: 'ill meat and worse cookery' and a bed garrisoned with '6 legd creature[s] to defend it against the next comers'.[9]

So at the end of a journey that lasted perhaps ten days Wren, the earnest academic whose world for the past sixteen years had comprised the urbane and familiar pleasures of Oxford and London, would finally have found himself in a city which was famous throughout Europe – for its stench, its traffic jams and its lousy shops. 'The nastiest lane in London, is Frankincense and Juniper, to the sweetest street in this City,' wrote the Laudian cleric Peter Heylyn. John Evelyn recalled that the place smelled 'as if sulphur were mingled with the mud'.[10] The streets were frequently gridlocked: 'Sometimes one shall meet with a stop half a mile long of those Coaches, Carts, and Horses, that can move neither forward nor backward by reason of some sudden encounter of others coming a crosse-way; so that oftentimes it will be an hour or two before they can dis-intangle.'[11] And as for the tradesmen, traveller after traveller in the seventeenth century comments on the crude designs of the painted signs that marked out their shops – nothing compared to the elaborate boards which hung over the streets of London, showing Adam and Eve with the apple (for greengrocers) or unicorns' horns and dragons (for apothecaries) – and the poverty of both choice and quality of the goods inside. 'You shall scarcely see any but seems rather to be a Cobler's hole than of any trade, and pittifull signs to set them forth,' said Major Richard Ferrier, who visited the city in 1687. 'Pedlars with shops' was Heylyn's verdict: 'Two severall ranks of shops in Cheapside can shew more plate, and more variety of Mercery wares, good and rich, than three parts of Paris.'[12]

It makes you wonder why Wren bothered.

Of course there were other sights, other attractions which out-weighed the chaos, the squalor and the discomfort.★ Paris in the 1660s was the city of Molière, Racine and Corneille; of Mansart and Le Vau and Le Brun; of glittering entertainments like the famous three-day Fête of the Enchanted Island which Louis XIV held at Versailles in May 1664, and which still had all Europe talking about its pageants, tableaux and fireworks. But if Wren hadn't come to Paris to shop, he hadn't come to party, either, or to watch a Molière comedy. Why, just at this point in his career, did he decide to make such an arduous and dangerous journey? Why did he forsake the comparative comfort of his Oxford lodgings while the finishing touches were still being put to his uncle's chapel at Pembroke, and Gilbert Sheldon's Theatre was in the middle of its first full building season?

With hindsight, the obvious answer is to study French architecture. Wren's reputation as a designer of buildings was already established, at least among his fellow dons at Oxford and the members of the Royal Society: Evelyn, for example, in his April letter offering introductions in France, also begged Wren to accept his translation of Fréart de Chambray's *Parallèle de l'architecture antique et de la moderne*, 'not as a recompense of your many favours to me, much less a thing in the least assistant to you (who are Yrself a Master), but as a toaken of my respect, as the Booke itself is of the affection I have to an Art which you so hapily

---

★At one point during Wren's stay in Paris that discomfort turned into something more serious: he came down with a kidney infection. A doctor recommended bleeding, but he rejected the advice and, after dreaming that 'a Woman in a romantick Habit' fed him dates from a palm-tree, relied instead on a diet of dates. Rather surprisingly, this cured him.

cultivate.'[13] However, of the prominent gentlemen-amateurs who were dabbling in architecture during the early years of the Restoration, Wren was alone in never having travelled abroad. Roger Pratt, Hugh May, William Winde, Evelyn, the untalented Surveyor-General Denham, had all had the chance to see European architecture either during the Civil War or in the 1650s. Even John Webb, the only established professional architect among them, and a man who having trained under Inigo Jones might not have felt the need to broaden his horizons by foreign travel, visited France for a time in the summer of 1656. All these men could speak with confidence of the buildings they had seen in Italy, France and the Low Countries, and did, often at great length. Wren thus found himself having to defer to their greater knowledge – an experience he was neither used to nor happy with.

It scarcely needs saying that every practising architect, even an amateur – especially an amateur – operates within a tradition, a complex framework of influences, cultural references and personal experiences. For an architect working in England in the early 1660s, that framework was quite restricted. A number of English editions of architectural classics had appeared in recent years: Joseph Moxon's *Vignola* (1655), for example; Godfrey Richards' translation of Palladio's *First Book of Architecture* (1663); and Evelyn's translation of Fréart's *Parallèle de l'architecture*. And Wren had access to foreign editions of Palladio, Scamozzi, Alberti and, as we have seen in his designs for Pembroke Chapel and the Sheldonian, Serlio's *Architettura*. But valuable though they were in forming taste, engravings were no substitute for the real thing; and as far as actual buildings were concerned, English architecture after the Restoration lagged a long way behind the European main-stream. With a few notable exceptions, such as the Corinthian portico which Jones had slapped on to the west end of St Paul's Cathedral in 1633–42, the monumental classicism which was such a feature of post-Renaissance Italy was hard to find in England. The two universities still tended to cling to Tudor-Gothic as tenaciously as their teaching staff clung to Aristotle. Charles I, who in happier circumstances might have been a great patron of innovative architecture, had been first too hard up to commission major royal buildings, and then too preoccupied with hanging on to his throne; while the Church of England, another potential patron of public architecture, had its own share of troubles to distract its attention from large-scale building works. When Continental influence did show itself, it was usually in the simple and restrained Dutch classicism of the smaller country house, or in imperfectly understood details taken from imported pattern-books. While Borromini and Bernini were deliberately distorting classical forms to create the Baroque dynamic in Rome, English artisans were distorting them because they didn't know any better.

The situation in France was quite different. Since the sixteenth century, when François I had imported Italian artists of the calibre of Leonardo, Vignola, Serlio, Primaticcio and Cellini, French architecture and design had been much more closely linked to the ideals of the Italian Renaissance. True, in 1665 what we regard as the landmark buildings of Louis XIV's long reign – Louis Le Vau's Collège des Quatres Nations, the east wing of the Louvre, triumphal arches like the Porte Saint-Denis and the Porte Saint-Martin, piazzas such as Jules Hardouin-Mansart's Place des Victoires and, above all, that pre-eminent Baroque expression of absolutism, the Palace of Versailles – were all either incomplete or still to come. It would be another twenty years or so before the rest of Europe, including Louis' political enemies, would seek to match the magnificence of his reign by emulating the grandeur of his buildings. But at the time of Wren's visit, French architecture was nevertheless much more advanced than its English counterpart, both in its confident handling of a classical vocabulary and in its determination to adapt classicism in the service of a national style. Of the three great French classicists of the seventeenth century, Jacques Lemercier had died in 1654, François Mansart was in his sixties (he would die the following year), and Le Vau was fifty-three, with his best work behind him. Wren could thus walk the streets of Paris and pass by any number of buildings that would hold their own with – indeed, outshine – the isolated and often hesitant examples of classicism he could see in London, Oxford and Cambridge. Neither Pembroke Chapel nor the Sheldonian, both still incomplete when he left England, were any match for great churches like Lemercier's Sorbonne (1635) and Mansart's Sainte Marie de la Visitation (1632–3), or private houses such as Le Vau's Hôtel Lambert (1640) and Antoine Le Pautre's Hôtel de Beauvais (1652–5).

Just as influential as the buildings themselves was the ideological agenda which was beginning to emerge under the influence of Jean-Baptiste Colbert, the King's chief minister. In 1663 Colbert reorganized Cardinal Mazarin's Academy of Painting and Sculpture, ensuring in the process that it operated as an arm of the state. At about the same time he turned the old Gobelin tapestry factory into a workshop which produced all the royal furnishings, from hangings to chairs to mosaics and marbles. And in the following year, 1664, he became Superintendent of the King's Buildings. Colbert thus had control over all the key positions in relation to the arts in France. And he bent them to one aim, and one aim only – the glorification of the monarch and the greater prestige of France, which to him were one and the same thing. The result was the emergence of an amazing uniformity of style in architecture – something which Wren, with his passion for system and order, found particularly attractive.

But before we get too carried away with the opportunities Wren's Paris trip afforded him for the study of architecture, we need to appreciate that the current state of French building design was only part of the reason for his visit, and perhaps not the most important part, at that.

Like its architecture, the scientific reputation of France in the 1660s was riding high, much higher than that of England, although it relied heavily on the work of the previous generation: Pierre Gassendi, whose redefinition of Epicurean atomic theory posed a serious threat to established Aristotelianism; the mathematician and physicist Blaise Pascal; and Marin Mersenne, the legendary friar whose salon at the convent of l'Annonciade near the Palais Royale had attracted an array of stars to make the Royal Society green with envy – van Helmont, Galileo, Pascal, Fermat. And of course there was Descartes himself, who towered above them all in the seventeenth-century scientific pantheon, with his call for clear and distinct ideas, and his insistence on the supremacy of reason.

Wren couldn't hope to meet such icons – they were all dead – but he could at least talk with the heirs to the tradition of philosophical enquiry that they had established in France. More specifically, he was eager to discuss astronomy and other matters with men whose work was known to him. The *savants* that he mixed with in Paris were an intriguing bunch, with interests as varied as his own. They included Melchisédech Thévenot, a topographer and patron of the sciences who kept a laboratory of sorts in Paris and organized experiments and observations in his country house out at Issy, a few miles south of Paris. There was the Intendant Général des Fortifications, Pierre Petit, who had collaborated with Pascal in the 1640s, and whose collection of telescopes was one of the best in Paris. His *Dissertation sur la nature des comètes*, which appeared in 1665, was widely praised; Wren took home a copy to present to the Royal Society, which made Petit a Fellow in 1667. He was described by one contemporary as 'a passable physicist among the best' and less charitably by another (Christiaan Huygens) as 'a comical fellow, who thinks he knows everything, without ever wishing to admit he can learn anything from anybody'.[14] A third member of the group was Henri Justel, a Huguenot who kept up a diligent correspondence with philosophers all over Europe and who wrote to Oldenburg in January 1666 that he was seeing Wren 'practically every day'.[15] After a regular exchange of political and scientific gossip with Oldenburg which lasted up to the latter's death in 1677, Justel fled to England during a spate of religious persecutions in 1681, where he too was made an FRS and appointed Keeper of Charles II's library at the Palace of St James's.

The fourth member of Wren's Parisian circle of virtuosi, and perhaps the most interesting, was Adrien Auzout, a physicist, mathematician and astronomer whose name constantly crops up in accounts of scientific discussions in Paris during the 1650s and 1660s. Born in Rouen in 1622, the son of a minor government official, Auzout seems to have spent the early part of his life in estate management in the provinces before moving to Paris, where he began to focus on optics and astronomical observation. He is chiefly remembered today for his part in developing the telescopic sight and the micrometer for accurately measuring the size of an observed image. Like Wren, he had made systematic observations of the comets of 1664 and 1665, publishing his results in his *Ephémérides du Comète* and presenting a copy to the Royal Society. At the moment when Wren arrived in Paris, Auzout was involved in two scholarly disputes, in which he conducted himself with admirable good manners and restraint. The first was with Robert Hooke, and related to a remark made by the latter in his *Micrographia* about the possibility of constructing a lens-grinding machine. As well as casting doubt on its feasibility, Auzout took Hooke to task for publishing his idea on the basis of a simple theory, 'without having tried it in great or small',[16] a criticism that must have rankled with the Society, which prided itself on the primacy of practice over theory. The second debate was with Hevelius, whom Auzout accused of making a mistake in his observations of the second comet. In both disputes, Oldenburg acted as a sort of go-between and arbiter; as a result, Wren was familiar with the Frenchman's work before he went to Paris, just as Auzout was familiar with Wren's – he wrote to Oldenburg on 11 July to say how glad he was that 'your learned Mr Wren' would soon be in Paris.

Another factor which must have made Auzout a congenial companion during Wren's stay was their shared interest in architecture; Martin Lister, who was in Paris several times in the 1660s, later recalled that 'Monsieur Auzout was very Curious and Understanding in Architecture', and that he had 'studied Vitruvius more than 40 years together'.[17] This interest in antiquity's greatest architectural theorist may have been Auzout's undoing. Although he was elected to the new Académie des Sciences in 1666 (unlike Petit, Justel and Thévenot), he was forced out two years later after publicly and tactlessly finding three hundred errors in a translation of Vitruvius's *De Architectura* by Claude Perrault, who had just been chosen by Louis XIV to work on new proposals for remodelling the Louvre. Auzout spent most of the rest of his life in Rome, although he made a short visit to Justel in England in 1682, when he attended the Royal Society (which had made him a member in May 1666, two months after Wren had particularly commended him). He was so enamoured of the ale at Magdalen College that he begged Justel to obtain the recipe for him.

Wren must have welcomed the chance to discuss the latest scientific developments with such men; after all, they were engaged in serious research in fields that – in the case of Petit and Auzout, at least – coincided with his own. Just how those discussions were conducted is another matter. Wren had no French, as far as we know; Auzout had a little English, and Thévenot rather more (he translated the writings of several English travellers into his own language). Much of the discourse would have been in Latin, still the lingua franca of educated Europe, although the French were much more advanced than the English in making use of their own language, even in the staid scholastic environment of the lecture hall. Sir Thomas Browne's eldest son, Edward, who studied medicine in Paris in the autumn of 1664 and again, after visits to several Italian universities, in the summer of 1665 (when he spent some time exploring the French countryside in Wren's company), was disappointed to find that he couldn't understand the lectures he attended 'by reason [the lecturer] used the French tongue so much'.[18] Even when Latin *was* used, the difference in accent proved a problem, and English travellers often complained that they couldn't understand their Continental colleagues: the Scots law student John Lauder, who also arrived in Paris in 1665, found that 'the accent the French gives the Latin is so different from ours that sometymes we would not have understood some of them . . . nor some of them us'.[19]★

★The exasperation was mutual. After his visit to England in 1663, Samuel Sorbière complained that the English 'speak *Latin* with such an Accent and Way of Pronunciation, that they are as hard to be understood, as if they spoke their own Language' (Samuel Sorbière, *A Voyage to England* [1709], 38).

As interesting as what Wren could learn from his French hosts is what *they* wanted from *him*. For some time Auzout, Petit and Thévenot had been active members of a group which met each week in the town house of a wealthy patron, Henri-Louis Habert de Montmor, in the rue Sainte-Avoye north of the Quays. The Montmor Academy was formally constituted in 1657 and existed for a stormy seven years which were characterized by an entertaining degree of in-fighting and unscholarly conduct. Discourses on the nature of gout and 'whether the mathematical point really exists' led to frayed tempers and furious arguments, and one speaker was actually hissed by the assembled *savants* as he gave his ideas about the generation of the chick in the egg. The root of the conflict lay in the different approaches taken by the talkers – those who favoured the old scholastic methods of dispute and rhetoric – and the experimentalists: the neo-Baconians who believed, in the words of one (hostile) member of the Academy, that 'there was no need to argue on any matter before some trial of it had been made, which would furnish basis enough for sound discourse without other philosophising'.[20] Auzout, Petit and Thévenot belonged to the latter party, and when the Montmor Academy broke up acrimoniously in June 1664, they regrouped at Thévenot's house, working towards the establishment of a society of experimental philosophers under the patronage of Louis XIV with permanent premises and decent facilities. In the dedication to his *Ephémérides du Comète*, Auzout pleaded with the King to provide an observatory and telescopes: 'It is a question, Sire, of Your Majesty's own fame, and of the reputation of France, and that is what makes us hope that your Majesty will command some place for making all sorts of celestial observations, and cause it to be furnished with all the instruments necessary for this end.' And six months or so before Wren's arrival in Paris, Auzout, Petit and Thévenot had circulated to ex-Montmorians and others a draft programme for a new *Compagnie des Sciences et des Arts*, which mirrored the aims of the Royal Society. It would 'strive to disabuse the Human Race of all the Vulgar Errors which have so long passed as truths, for want of the necessary experiments being made to test them and discover their falseness'; and would seek 'perfection of the sciences and the arts, and . . . search in general for everything which can bring utility or convenience to the human race, and especially to France'.[21]

The parallels with the Royal Society are obvious. One can't escape the conclusion that for the virtuosi of the embryonic *Compagnie*, the arrival in Paris of a noted experimentalist and founder-member of the

Royal Society – just at the moment when they were struggling for official recognition – was a major event. 'I fear that he will not find our Company in very good shape,' Auzout told Oldenburg when he heard of Wren's impending visit, 'but if he sees nothing very splendid here, at least we shall learn much from him.'[22]

So they talked to Wren of the Royal Society and the importance of royal patronage. Auzout and Petit discussed the 'Cometicall Observations' which Wren had brought with him, and which Auzout was delighted to find coincided with his own. The latter talked through his dispute with Hooke, which as the summer wore on was becoming increasingly involved, with Hooke asserting that it was theoretically possible to build a telescope big enough to see small animals on the moon, and the Frenchman denying it. Auzout also consulted with Wren over experiments he was trying, using different liquids inserted between two glasses to increase the focal length of a lens.

Of course, the *savants* did more than discuss: they were eager to show their distinguished guest the scientific sights of Paris, just as he was eager to see them. Wren was taken to the workshops of various instrument-makers, and shown Pascal's famous calculating engine, a marvellous device which used a series of gears and dials to add and subtract numbers up to 999,999. He went out to Issy, where Thévenot's telescopes were kept. He must have enjoyed the attention shown to him as a distinguished visitor at the noted salon of the Abbé Bourdelot, who presided over another of the informal groups which flourished in Paris after the collapse of the Montmor Academy; although he noted only that 'Abbé Burdelo keeps an academy at his house for philosophy every Monday afternoon'[23] and confided to Justel that he wished that they made experiments instead of simply talking. At Bourdelot's he heard the assembly discuss a deaf mute who could dance in time to music, and saw the Queen of Poland's physician give a discourse on a curious hair condition which, he said, afflicted only Poles and Cossacks. (This was *plica polonica*, a rather nasty disease in which filth and the presence of parasites causes the hair to become matted together – although why Poles and Cossacks should have more headlice than anyone else is hard to understand.) And, mindful of his interest in architecture, the group also took Wren to meet the celebrity that everyone in Paris was talking about in the summer of 1665. They took him to see Bernini.

With hindsight, this meeting is one of the most momentous in the history of seventeenth-century architecture – the man destined to be England's greatest exponent of the Baroque in a face-to-face encounter with the most famous Baroque architect in Europe. Bernini had arrived in Paris from Rome on Tuesday 2 June, four or five weeks before Wren. We get some indication of the impact of his visit from the fact that less than three weeks after his arrival, Wren was making lighthearted references to it in a letter to Ralph Bathurst, the same letter in which he discussed the new quadrangle at Trinity. Arguing for the idea of a single block of lodgings, he told Bathurst that he would refer the matter 'to Mons Mansard, or Signor Bernini, both of which I shall see at Paris within this fortnight'.[24] We don't need to take this too seriously: the tone of the letter suggests that Wren is speaking with his tongue in his cheek. But clearly, Bernini's presence in Paris was already a talking-point in England.

Gian Lorenzo Bernini had been summoned to France by Louis XIV to complete the east wing of the Louvre. The reconstruction of the palace had proceeded in fits and starts for more than a century, ever since François I had demolished the medieval keep and Pierre Lescot had begun a scheme for four huge ranges completely enclosing a square court. By the early 1660s, the west wing, the south wing facing the Seine and part of the north wing had been built. But the King wasn't satisfied with designs submitted by French architects for the east façade, and Colbert, in his new role as Superintendent of the King's Buildings, was instructed to ask Pope Alexander VII for the loan of his artistic director. Sculptor, architect, painter, poet and papal Rome's undisputed arbiter of taste, Bernini was widely acknowledged by contemporaries as the greatest artist of the century. Over a period spanning more than forty years, from the daring and dynamic baldacchino he designed to stand under Michelangelo's dome at St Peter's in 1624 to the colossal colonnaded piazza in front of the basilica, which was nearing completion in 1665, Bernini showed that he, more than any other man alive, knew how to do the grand architectural gesture. And a grand gesture was just what the Sun King wanted to complete the Louvre, no matter what it cost. When the two men met at St Germain on 4 June, it was clear that they were made for each other. 'Let no one speak to me of anything small,' declared Bernini, to which Louis replied, 'I see that this is indeed the man as I imagined him,' before uttering those magic words which every architect dreams of hearing from a client: 'As far as money is concerned, there need be no restriction.'[25]

In the event, Bernini's designs for the Louvre were never implemented: French architects, who were wildly jealous at being supplanted by a foreigner, did everything in their power to undermine him, while Colbert, who always favoured a home-grown design for such an important national monument, used the Italian's presence simply to bring them into line with his own personal vision of a state-controlled architecture by reminding them that they were not indispensable. Aside from a few minor commissions, the only tangible product of Bernini's stay in France was a heroic marble portrait bust of the King which he completed – in a flood of tears at the beauty of his creation – on 5 October 1665, two weeks before he returned to Rome.

But, that summer, all this lay in the future. Wren's encounter with Bernini took place some time in early or mid August, either at the Hôtel de Frontenac in the precincts of the Louvre, where the Italian lodged for the first nine weeks of his stay, or at the Palais Mazarin, a few hundred metres north. Bernini and his party had been forced to leave the Louvre on 8 August to make room for members of the court who were taking up residence there when the King arrived from St Germain later that week. The opulence of Cardinal Mazarin's old apartments pleased him, although he swiftly showed a monumental lack of diplomacy that was making him dangerous enemies at the French court. Already he had declared that the infant Dauphin was too fat, told the King that his luxuriously appointed apartments in the Louvre were like those of a woman, and praised Louis' taste in architecture as remarkably good – considering he had never been to Italy. Now he immediately announced that the prized Veronese which hung in his rooms was only a copy.

Some time before 24 August, when Oldenburg relayed the news to Robert Boyle, Justel wrote to him that 'we took [Wren] to the house of that great architect, Chevalier Bernini', although exactly who 'we' were isn't clear.[26] Wren himself recalled some weeks later that 'Mons Abbé Charles introduced me to the Acquaintance of Bernini'.[27] Abbé Charles is usually identified as the papal nuncio, Monsignor Carlo Roberti de' Vittori, on the grounds that although he was not an Abbé, his name was Carlo and he had regular access to the artist. In fact it was almost certainly Charles de Bryas, a Carmelite virtuoso and collector of optical instruments. Huygens, who met him in 1660, called him 'the best man and the most open I ever met'; he was a friend of Auzout and Petit, and as 'Abbé Charles' his name appears frequently as a member of the group that met at Thévenot's house in the mid-1660s.

It would be nice to picture Wren and Bernini discoursing quietly and earnestly together on art and architecture – in Latin, of course – amid the opulent surroundings of the apartment at the Palais Mazarin. The young English professor with the quizzical smile and the deepening enthusiasm for architecture is deferential and eager to learn. For his part, Bernini can afford to be generous; more than thirty years Wren's senior, and acknowledged all over Europe as the greatest living architect, he enjoys the praise, the evident respect, of this youthful acolyte. But his sharp eyes – like those of an eagle, according to contemporaries – discern something more, a passion like his own, an intuitive understanding of what he is trying to do with the Louvre. As he shows Wren his precious drawings for the east range, the courtyard, the new façades with which he proposes to envelop the existing palace, the younger man makes a hesitant suggestion: the pavilions that flank the south façade, facing the Seine . . . if they were the same size, wouldn't this add to the grandeur and symmetry of the whole composition? The Chevalier looks at Wren with a new respect, and immediately calls for pencils and paper.

It didn't happen. In fact, Bernini can hardly have noticed Wren's presence. Since his arrival in Paris he had become used to being paraded (like a travelling elephant, he said) before an endless stream of curious onlookers. They crowded into his rooms to watch him at work on the bust of Louis, making helpful suggestions about the eyes, the hair, the angle of the nose; and during the sittings, when the King was of course actually present, declaiming in loud voices that the Chevalier was hardly doing justice to His Majesty's heroic features. Courtiers plagued him with requests to go and look at their latest building projects, or to provide them with designs for staircases and cascades and altarpieces. Government officials came to discuss the logistics of the new works at the Louvre. Unless they were important, and often even if they were, Bernini regarded their presence as a tiresome intrusion. When Wren and his friends – Justel, the Abbé Charles, perhaps with Auzout and Petit – trooped into the great man's apartment, they were just a few more new faces among many, with neither the aristocratic status to command Bernini's attention nor the artistic distinction to command his respect.

As for the idea of Wren actually daring to comment on the Louvre drawings in Bernini's presence, two examples should suffice to show what happened when anyone did criticize his work. Claude Perrault's brother, Charles, had the temerity to ask why the two pavilions on the south façade of Bernini's Louvre were of unequal size. He was told: 'It is not for the likes of you, Monsieur Perrault, to make objections of this kind . . . You are not worthy to brush the dust off my shoes.'[28] And when, in October, Colbert dared to question the siting of the proposed royal chapel at the new palace, Bernini called him 'a real bugger' and promptly left Paris, never to return. The Italian did not respond well to criticism.

If we want to speculate – and why not? – the historic meeting probably went something like this. The party presented themselves at the Palais Mazarin, where they were led through to Bernini's lodgings. The palace impressed Wren: he wrote later with approval of its 'masculine furniture', the fine hangings and mosaics, the 'great and noble Collection of Antique Statues and Bustos' and 'excellent Pictures of the great Masters' (the Veronese copy notwithstanding).[29] When he reached the architect's chamber, he would have found not only Bernini, but other members of his entourage, who were generally hanging around in the apartments: they included the three servants he had brought with him from Rome, and also his young son Paolo, who was busy carving a marble relief of Christ as a present for Louis' hapless queen, Maria Theresa; his major-domo, Cosimo Scarlatti; and his two assistants, Mattia de Rossi and Giulio Cartari. Various French officials and household servants would also have been present, although unfortunately Paul Fréart de Chantelou, the interpreter and aide appointed by the King to liaise between Bernini and the French, was not likely to have been among them. In an immensely detailed journal which documents virtually every incident and conversation of Bernini's stay, Chantelou makes no mention of Wren, which suggests that he was absent during their meeting – or of course, that he thought it too trivial to mention.

Wren had little or no Italian, and Bernini was generally reluctant or unable to speak Latin. So conversation must have been stilted, to say the least. Nevertheless, after introductions had been made and respects paid, the visitors were shown both Bernini's preliminary sketches for the bust of the King and the unfinished bust itself. Wren also had a tantalizingly brief glimpse of the Italian's drawings for the Louvre, as he recalled a few weeks later in a letter home:

> Bernini's Designs of the Louvre I would have given my Skin for, but the old reserv'd Italian gave me but a few Minutes View; it was five little Designs in Paper, for which he hath received as many thousand Pistoles; I had only time to copy it in my Fancy and Memory . . .[30]

With that, the audience was over, and the group trooped out again.

In some ways, the impact on Wren of this brief personal encounter with Bernini was minimal. What he learned about monumental architecture and the Baroque from its greatest living exponent – and he learned a great deal – was derived from the engravings and published designs which he acquired in Paris and later, or through that peculiar process of osmosis whereby a great artist's work is absorbed into the cultural mainstream, finding an expression in the work of all those who follow. Wren's designs for the Fountain Court at Hampton Court Palace, for instance, which were executed in 1689–94, owe a debt to Bernini, as do his unexecuted plans for rebuilding Whitehall after it was destroyed by fire in 1698. But then so do Thomas Archer's Heythrop in Oxfordshire, and William Talman's south front of Chatsworth, and Nicholas Hawksmoor's work at Greenwich, and even James Gibbs's St Martin-in-the-Fields. None of these lesser men met Bernini. They were operating in the Baroque tradition, and they borrowed from the best.

Yet we can't undervalue the impact of a face-to-face meeting with someone of such awesome intellectual stature. Wren met and talked with any number of talented artists during his long life, and a few great ones. He knew an even greater number of gifted scientists. But with the exception of Isaac Newton, he never, *ever* encountered another genius of the calibre of Bernini. He certainly never met one – Newton included – who commanded so much respect among the kings, princes and intellectual élites of Europe. It is far too simplistic to say that before that meeting Wren was a dilettante who dabbled in architecture, and afterwards he was inspired to devote his life to it. It is also just plain wrong. But to see the personal prestige which was accorded to someone who was, after all, an artisan, a mere builder; to hear, as all Paris heard, of how this man insulted kings and courtiers with apparent impunity, or burst into tears when he completed his bust of the King, or swore at government ministers who failed to share his vision: these things *must* have affected him. If he never succeeded in sharing Bernini's passionate involvement in creation – and this was to be his besetting vice as an architect, a cold, scientific detachment that always held him back from the essentially emotional outpouring which found its expression in the greatest Baroque buildings – he learned from Bernini that architecture was more than just a profession for master-builders or a hobby for gentlemen. It was a vocation, and like any vocation, it required commitment. And – if you were good enough – it promised power and status.

In September Wren took a three-day sightseeing tour into the countryside to the north of Paris. Auzout and the other *savants* were left behind; his companions this time were two Englishmen. Edward Browne (the same Edward Browne who was so disappointed to find that lectures in the medical schools were in French rather than Latin) had met up with Wren while he was finishing his studies in Paris. Henry Compton, the third member of the party, was probably an old friend of Wren's. He was an exact contemporary, and from a similarly Royalist background, although his family had a rather more dramatic war. His father, the Earl of Northampton, had died fighting for the King at Hopton Heath in 1643; his eldest brother had been wounded in the same battle and had fought side by side with Prince Rupert at Lichfield later that year; a second brother had commanded a regiment at Banbury, while a third had died at Bruges, after accompanying Charles II into exile on the Continent. Henry himself had gone up to Queen's College, Oxford in 1649, the year Wren entered Wadham, leaving three years later to tour Europe and, according to rumour, to 'trail the pike' in Flanders with the Duke of York. He swapped soldiering for holy orders after the Restoration, and although he was a keen botanist – his garden at Fulham was later described as being planted with 'a greater variety of curious exotic plants and trees than had at the time been collected in any garden in England' – he devoted most of his time to building a career in the Church, becoming Bishop of London (and hence Wren's employer at St Paul's) in 1675.

The trio's first stop was Chantilly, twenty-six miles north of Paris, where the Abbé Bourdelot was physician to the Prince de Condé – the visit may have been the result of a conversation Wren had had at the Abbé's salon a few weeks before. Both the Prince and Bourdelot were away from home, so the Englishmen contented themselves with touring the grounds, laid out a couple of years previously by the King's gardener, André Le Nôtre. The château had been built at the beginning of the sixteenth century by Pierre Chambiges for the Montmorency family: an equestrian bronze of one of the Montmorencys still stood in front of the house. Edward Browne, however, whose letter home to his father describing the tour is our only source, was more interested in the people than the architecture. He described Chantilly to his father simply as 'old built', and Le Nôtre's gardens and elaborate waterworks as 'neat'; he was much more intrigued by the fact that the three men caught a glimpse of the Prince's heavily pregnant wife being carried round the gardens in a sedan chair.

After Chantilly, the group moved on to Liancourt, designed by Jacques Lemercier and completed in 1637. Here the waterworks were more impressive, 'the water thrown up in pretty shapes, as of a bell turned up or a bell turned downe, out of [a] frog's mouth in a broad thin streame, etc'.[31] From there they went to the Château de Verneuil, a spectacular late sixteenth-century Mannerist fantasy by du Cerceau ('a very neat castel, but furnished with old furniture'). After a night at Senlis, they travelled on to Le Raincy, the most modern of the four châteaux. Begun in the 1640s for the Intendant des Finances, Jacques Bordier, its grounds and waterworks were still unfinished; but the house itself, by the fashionable Le Vau, delighted Browne. Inevitably, it was 'neat' (which seems to have been the young student's best shot at architectural criticism); but more than this, it was 'extremely neat', he said; the chambers were 'excellently well painted'; and Le Vau's central oval vestibule, which made a curved projection on both main façades, was 'one of the best [rooms] I have seen'.

Browne took his cue from Wren, who also admired Le Vau's work at Le Raincy. The younger man told his father that the house 'pleased Dr Wren very much'. Elsewhere on the tour, though, we find the professor pontificating in a rather unattractive manner. He didn't think much of du Cerceau's Verneuil, with its grotesques and its deliberate flouting of classical rules, and announced to his companions (quite wrongly) that the same architect had been responsible for the Louvre, 'there being the same faults in one as in the other'. When Browne asked him which was the greatest work in Paris, Wren said it was the Quays along the Seine, because they had been built 'with so vast expense and such great quantity of materialls, that [they] exceeded all manner of ways the building of the two greatest pyramids of Egypt'. This was an engineer speaking, the same Wren who had been so excited by the structural problems involved in roofing the Sheldonian. But what is revealing here is not that Wren was ready with opinions on architecture – after all, half the fun in sightseeing is making ill-considered pronouncements – but that Edward Browne (and, presumably, Henry Compton, who unfortunately figures hardly at all in Browne's narrative) so obviously deferred to them and took such care to pass them on to his father. As a well-known and respected virtuoso, Wren's opinions on buildings mattered, even though his only completed work was the chapel at Pembroke – which, incidentally, was consecrated on 21 September, just about the time that Wren, Browne and Compton were making their round of private châteaux.

The tourists returned to Paris after their visit to Le Raincy, and the only other incident of note was a fleeting glimpse of the King and his mistress, Louise de la Vallière, who passed them on the road. (She was 'habited very prettily, in a hat and feathers'.) We learn much more of Wren's responses to the current state of French architecture in a long and important letter, written towards the end of 1665 and published in *Parentalia*. His correspondent is unidentified – *Parentalia* says only that the letter was written to the 'particular Friend' who had recommended him to the Earl of St Albans – but the emphasis he places on the business of building suggests the recipient was someone with a professional interest in the practice of architecture, adding some weight to the theory that it was Sir John Denham. On the other hand, it could have been a fellow member of the Royal Society, which was currently obsessed with cataloguing manufactures and trades. (Indeed, Wren mentions that 'my business now is to pry into Trades and Arts', and says that he is currently working on some 'Observations on the present state of Architecture, Arts, and Manufactures in France'.)[32] After opening with the announcement that 'I have busied myself in surveying the most esteem'd Fabricks of Paris, and the Country round', he launches into a lengthy account of the way in which Colbert is running the works at the Louvre, which he has been in the habit of visiting daily:

> No less than a thousand Hands are constantly employ'd in the Works; some in laying mighty Foundations, some in raising the Stories, Columns, Entablements, etc with vast Stones, by great and useful Engines; others in Carving, Inlaying of Marbles, Plaistering, Painting, Gilding etc. Which altogether make a School of Architecture, the best probably, at this Day in Europe . . . An Academy of Painters, Sculptors, Architects, and the chief Artificers of the Louvre, meet every first and last Saturday of the Month. Mons Colbert, Surintendant, comes to the Works of the Louvre, every Wednesday, and, if Business hinders not, Thursday. The Workmen are paid every Sunday duly.

Wren must be referring here to the broader activities of the office of the King's Buildings; otherwise the picture he paints of the Louvre as a hive of creative activity is slightly puzzling. Although the site was cleared so that the foundation stone of Bernini's new palace could be laid by the King on Saturday 17 October 1665, very little else was done that year – or the next, come to that. It wasn't until 1667, when Colbert finally rejected Bernini's designs and turned to Louis Le Vau, Charles Le Brun and Claude Perrault for an alternative, that work on the new palace at the eastern end of the complex eventually began in earnest. But Wren's concern for organizational structures is typical both of the Royal Society's current preoccupations and of his own natural bent for administration and bureaucracy, which would make him such a successful Surveyor-General of the King's Works. *How* a thing worked – whether that thing was a spleen or a comet, a palace or a government department – was as important to him as the end product, and, ultimately, this essentially scientific curiosity set him apart from his contemporary virtuoso-architects, who were content to leave the details of structural engineering to masons and joiners and the running of a large-scale building project to contractors.

Wren mentions visiting nineteen hôtels, châteaux and royal palaces during his stay, including the four seen on his tour with Browne and Compton a month or so earlier. In Paris itself, he didn't think much of Le Vau's Collège des Quatres Nations on the left bank of the Seine – a grandiose Baroque conception intended under the terms of Cardinal Mazarin's will to house sixty young nobles from France's newly acquired provinces of Artois, Alsace, Piedmont and Roussillon. Although he admits that it is usually admired, his verdict is that 'the Artist hath purposely set it ill-favouredly, that he might shew his Wit in struggling with an inconvenient Situation'. (The Collège, now the Institut de France, occupies a roughly triangular site across from the Louvre, and on the same axis; Le Vau meant it to form part of his grand design for the remodelling of the palace.) Outside Paris, Wren says,'the King's Houses I could not miss', and he lists the obvious royal palaces of the previous century like Fontainebleau, which had 'a stately Wilderness and Vastness suitable to the Desert it stands in', and the 'antique Mass' of St Germain. He also comments on more recent private houses such as Mansart's Château de Maisons, which dated from the 1640s, and Le Vau's Vaux-le-Vicomte, the exquisite château thirty miles south-east of the capital built for Louis XIV's finance minister Nicholas Fouquet, with formal avenues and vistas by André Le Nôtre and airy, elegant interiors painted with allegorical scenes by Charles Le Brun. Both Maisons and Vaux, he says, were 'incomparable'.

Wren went twice during the summer and autumn of 1665 to Versailles, then still a minor château rather than the majestic absolutist homage to the Sun King it became in the 1670s. Forty years earlier, Louis XIV's father had built Versailles as a hunting lodge in the forests fifteen miles west of Paris. But by the time Louis took personal control of government on the death of Mazarin in 1661, the lodge had been neglected for several decades, and he decided to renovate it as somewhere away from the capital where he could take Louise de la Vallière. (Much to the exasperation of Colbert, incidentally, who wanted the King to concentrate on the Louvre and said how concerned he was that 'the greatest and most virtuous of kings should be measured by the scale of Versailles'. He needn't have worried.) The building consisted of three modest red-brick ranges with stone dressings and slate roofs, grouped around a central courtyard, with little square pavilions at the corners; Louis added gilded balconies to the roof, built a new, self-contained kitchen block and an orangery, and commanded Le Nôtre to extend the gardens in a series of huge formal parterres.

Le Nôtre's grounds didn't merit a mention from Wren, and the house itself singularly failed to impress: 'The Palace, of if you please, the Cabinet of Versailles call'd me twice to view it: the Mixtures of Brick, Stone, blue Tile and Gold make it look like a rich Livery. Not an Inch within but is crowded with little Curiosities of Ornaments.'[33] Fair enough. But Wren goes on to place the blame for Versailles' failings firmly on the ladies of Louis' court:

> The Women, as they make here the Language and Fashions, and meddle with Politicks and Philosophy, so they sway also in Architecture. Works of Filgrand, and little Knacks are in great Vogue: but Building certainly ought to have the Attribute of eternal, and therefore the only Thing uncapable of new Fashions.[34]

This oft-quoted passage raises three issues: Wren's chauvinism, his misogyny and his conception of architectural style. Only the last is significant. If he thought the French foppish and effeminate, he was doing no more than express the opinions of generations of insular and xenophobic Little Englanders. If the power wielded by women at the French court disturbed him, what else can we expect from a slightly prissy bachelor-don, accustomed to the exclusively male environment of Oxford and raised in a tradition which ruthlessly excluded women from all areas of cultural and academic life? But when the man who steered England towards a new fashion in architecture says that building should be 'uncapable of new Fashions', we need to ask if his remarks were simply ill-considered, or whether they reveal something fundamental about his ideas.

Wren rarely made ill-considered remarks. In an undated rough draft that was written some years after the Paris trip, he expanded on the ideas provoked by his experience of Versailles:

An Architect ought to be jealous of Novelties, in which Fancy blinds the Judgement; and to think his Judges, as well those that are to live five Centuries after him, as those of his own Time. That which is commendable now for Novelty, will not be a new Invention to Posterity, when his Works are often imitated, and when it is unknown which was the Original; but the Glory of that which is good of itself is eternal.[35]

Architecture depends upon three principles, he went on to say – beauty, firmness (i.e., structural integrity) and convenience, which roughly translates as a building's functionality. Beauty is divided into two categories, natural and customary. Customary beauty, which is akin to fashion and hence transient, is to be avoided. Natural beauty, on the other hand, has its basis in mathematical truths. It derives from geometry, resides in uniformity and proportion, and is therefore not susceptible to change. Squares and circles are the most beautiful of all geometrical figures; then parallelograms and ovals. Straight lines are better than curves (and this from the designer of St Paul's!); 'an Object elevated in the Middle is more beautiful than depressed'; verticals are more pleasing than sloping surfaces, which is why Gothic buttresses are 'all ill favoured'. Although 'cones and multangular Prisms want neither Beauty or Firmness', they are not sanctioned by antiquity.

In this, Wren the mathematician was in agreement with Bernini the artist, who said that 'the most perfect forms are the circle, square, hexagon, octagon, etc.'[36] And like all of his contemporaries, the 'old reserv'd Italian' held up antiquity as the paradigm of architecture: 'There are a thousand faults in St Peter's, and none in the Pantheon.' Again, Wren was in accord with this. The expression of the timeless geometry which is the essence of great architecture was to be found in the columns and entablatures of the classical orders, he said. With their set pro-portions and established decorative schemes, they were 'not only Roman and Greek, but Phoenician, Hebrew, and Assyrian; therefore being founded upon the Experience of all Ages, promoted by the vast Treasures of all the great Monarchs, and Skill of the greatest Artists and Geometricians'. Therein lies the difference between ephemeral fashion and permanence. 'Architecture aims at Eternity; and therefore the only Thing uncapable of Modes and Fashions in its Principals, the Orders.'[37]

To us, the free and dynamic monumental forms of Wren's best work seem a world away from antiquity, from Renaissance interpretations of antiquity, even from Jonesian interpretations of the Renaissance; they belong wholly and completely to the end of the seventeenth century. But not to Wren. As his aesthetic began to take shape, he saw himself not as a pioneer of English Baroque – a Spanish word meaning 'mis-shapen pearl', and originally used in art and architecture to denote a bastardization of pure classicism – but as a natural descendant of Vitruvius and the ancients. The fussy details of Versailles in the 1660s, the gilded balustrades and curiosities of ornaments and little knacks, were wrong because they had no precedent in the classical canon, just as the Sheldonian was right because it was sanctioned by the past, in the shape of the Theatre of Marcellus.

The benefits Wren gained from his visit to France were considerable. They range from the experience of a more sophisticated architectural milieu than he knew in England, and the chance to exchange ideas in a less sophisticated, but still rewarding, scientific milieu, to the quantities of books and engravings he brought home with him – 'almost all France in paper'.[38] And in his baggage he also brought back the germ of an idea which would bear spectacular fruit later in the year, making a greater impact on English architecture than all his drawings and pictures. The domed churches of Lemercier and Mansart that he saw during his strolls around the capital – the Sorbonne, the Oratoire, Sainte-Marie de la Visitation, Val-de-Grâce – came as a revelation. There was nothing like them in England. In fact there were no domed churches at all in England. Like the roof of the Sheldonian, the idea of a dome presented Wren with just the sort of challenge he loved, in which a pure geo-metrical simplicity – sanctioned, of course, by antiquity – was combined with enormous structural complexity. And within three months of his return from France he was at work on a proposal for his most ambitious project to date – a dome for St Paul's Cathedral.

8

A Well-Projected Design

*O*ur knowledge of Wren's movements during the last three or four months of his stay in Paris is sketchy. Although in his *Parentalia* letter he talked of returning home at Christmas in company with Lord Berkeley (the FRS who had offered a refuge from the plague to Hooke, Wilkins and Petty the previous August), he decided against it for some reason, and stayed on in France until late February 1666. He continued to spend time with Auzout and Justel; in January, when the latter wrote to Oldenburg to say that he was seeing Wren 'practically every day', he mentioned how he had recently taken him to see the shop of Guillaume Ménard, a well-known optical instrument maker whose collection of telescopes and microscopes was acknowledged to be 'worthy of the praise of lovers of the curious'.[1] On 16 January Louis XIV declared war on England. It was a half-hearted affair forced on the French King by an alliance with the Dutch, who had been at war with England since the winter of 1663/4; Anglo-French hostilities were largely confined to the West Indies. But it may have interrupted Wren's plans.

In any case, he was back in England by the beginning of March. He had some kind words about Adrien Auzout and the other French virtuosi who had entertained him; and books for Oldenburg, including Pierre Petit's observations on the comet sighted in December 1664 and spring 1665, and the latest *Journaux des Scavans* – which, as Oldenburg pointed out with a certain complacent relish, contained little of interest except for material cribbed from the Royal Society's own *Philosophical Transactions*.

Wren had been away from home for nearly eight months. His return coincided with the news that the plague was finally beginning to subside. The bills of mortality showed that the weekly death-toll was down to fifty-six by the end of January, and forty-two by the end of February – although as Lord Brouncker was quick to point out to Pepys, new cases were still appearing in outlying parishes. Nevertheless, life was gradually returning to normal in the capital, and on 21 February Brouncker, Oldenburg and the other members of the Council met to resolve that regular meetings of the Royal Society should resume. A summons was sent out and three weeks later, on Wednesday 14 March, the group gathered at Gresham College for the first time since the end of the previous June.

Not surprisingly, there was plenty of news – much of it from abroad. Oldenburg presented the Society with the copy of Petit's *Dissertation sur la nature des comètes* that Wren had brought home with him; Robert Hooke was deputed to read it and give an account of its contents. The Secretary also showed a couple of silkworm cocoons which had been sent over from Virginia, 'of an extraordinary bigness, equalling almost a hen's egg', while John Wilkins produced some seeds from Bermuda. A report had arrived from Florence that 'a person with an engine for destroying ships' was on his way to England, and that the Society would be allowed to examine the invention.

When Brouncker asked for news of activities during the break, there was the usual evidence of members' wide-ranging interests – and the usual blend of fervour and prevarication. Hooke described some experiments he had carried out to compare the weights of bodies below and above ground, and Sir Robert Moray gave a long and detailed account of trials he had made with lead ore from a Welsh mine. But his enthusiasm was cut short when Brouncker pointedly asked for a progress report on the history of masonry that Moray was supposed to be writing. 'It was yet imperfect,' he said; but not to be fobbed off, the President pressed him to submit it to the Society's scrutiny as it was.

Dr Timothy Clarke fared little better. The Physician in Ordinary to the Royal Household had been injecting various substances into the veins of animals – an extension of the experiment that Wren had carried out at Oxford in the 1650s, although as happened so often with Wren's experiments, Clarke failed to acknowledge this. When Brouncker reminded him of his promise to produce a paper on his work, Clarke blustered, saying he had not neglected it, and intended to finish it as soon as he possibly could. He never did.

Others had been more active. Wilkins and Hooke reported on 'the business of the chariots' that Hooke had initiated the previous year: a sprung one-horse carriage he had described in May 1665 had been designed and built (presumably during their stay at Lord Berkeley's house at Epsom); and Wilkins had actually travelled in it. There were still some teething problems, however, and Wren and Hooke were asked to see what they could do to iron these out.

It was business as usual at Gresham. There were worries about money: when the Council had met in February, the main item on the agenda was the backlog of unpaid subscriptions, and in March the members agreed that if the Society had to break up again for any length of time, the paid assistant should be laid off. The usual techniques of bullying and wheedling were brought to bear to persuade reluctant members to fulfil their research commitments. And the usual rivalries were present. When Clarke prevaricated over his failure to produce an account of injection, Moray piped up that Robert Boyle was trying to transfuse blood from one animal to another. Clarke said he had tried it, and it couldn't be done. Moray said that according to Boyle, it could.

But Wren was still fired by his experiences in France. When the Society met again the following Wednesday, his response to a request to hear what he and Hooke had done about the new carriage design was simply to say that he 'had given Mr Hooke the descriptions of those, which they had in France'.[2] And while he continued to play a reasonably active part in the Society's affairs throughout the spring and summer of 1666, his mind was clearly elsewhere. On 4 April, Auzout wrote a plaintive little note to Oldenburg, begging to be remembered to Wren, and pleading for some drawings of the 1665 comet by Hooke that Wren had promised but that Auzout had still not received. Four months later, when Oldenburg asked John Wallis to give Hevelius's book on the two recent comets to Wren at Oxford with a request for comments, Wallis responded by saying that, 'I doubt he will scarce be persuaded to make observations. For I find him no way propense to it.'[3] The enthusiasm of the previous April, when Wren had risen early each day to take sightings of the comet through the morning mist, implored Moray and Hooke for their own observations, and exclaimed excitedly that he had lighted upon 'the trew Hypothesis' to explain the comet's motion, had vanished.

The truth was that Paris had focused Wren's mind not on comets or carriages, but on architecture. By the time he reappeared in England, Pembroke Chapel, virtually completed before he left for France, had been consecrated; and work on Gilbert Sheldon's Theatre continued to progress satisfactorily. But he was looking for something more. His horizons and ambitions had been immeasurably widened, not only by his visits to Vaux-le-Vicomte and Versailles, the Louvre and the Sorbonne, but also by his meeting with Bernini and his discussions with Auzout. And as he sat in his Oxford rooms, poring over the engravings he had collected on his trip, Wren must have dreamed of an opportunity to put his new knowledge to use, a chance to create an English Sorbonne. That opportunity came within weeks of his return.

In the spring of 1666, St Paul's Cathedral was giving the authorities serious cause for concern – as, indeed, it had for some years. The building had been steadily falling to pieces for decades, but ill-use during the Commonwealth had made it imperative that something should be done to stabilize the largely medieval structure. When Parliamentarian troops marched into London on the eve of Charles I's trial, they and their horses were quartered in the cathedral; the stained glass was smashed and most of the woodwork was stripped out for firewood. During the 1650s, the great scaffolding masts which had been erected before the war to support the crumbling south transept were sold off and removed, causing the roof to collapse. The pillars of the Corinthian portico which Inigo Jones had added to the west end of the building in the 1630s were 'most barbarously spoiled, and in some places cut through even almost to the middle of them' when the portico was converted into a row of shops. And a large part of St Paul's Churchyard was sold off to speculators, who built ramshackle houses right up against the cathedral walls.

Several half-hearted attempts to put matters right had been made during the early 1660s, and we have already seen that Wren may have been involved in some advisory capacity. But nothing seems to have come of it. The Dean and Chapter simply walled off the choir from the ruinous main body of the building, and did their best to carry on as normal.

Then in 1663 Charles II set up a Royal Commission with a brief to look at ways of 'repairing and upholding that magnificent structure, and restoring the same . . . unto the ancient beauty and glory of it, which hath so much suffered by the iniquity of the late times'.[4] As Bishop of London, Wren's Oxford patron Gilbert Sheldon was one of the Commissioners; so too, in his capacity as Surveyor-General, was Sir John Denham. Denham's assistants, John Webb – still hoping that the Surveyorship would one day be his – and Master Mason Edward Marshall found that a wide range of general repairs were needed, such as replacing stolen lead 'else the roofs in a short time will rot and perish'.[5] But the most pressing problem was the tower over the crossing, which had been in rather a precarious state ever since it had lost its wooden steeple in a lightning strike in 1561. The whole tower would have to be taken down to pavement level and rebuilt.

Many of the houses that had been erected in St Paul's Churchyard were pulled down in preparation for the repairs, but work progressed unbearably slowly. Sheldon became Archbishop of Canterbury soon after the Commission was formed, and his successor as Bishop of London, Humphrey Henchman, was a tired old man who lacked the necessary drive. The Dean, Richard Barwick, was already ailing when the Commission started meeting; he died in 1664. And Denham, who had never been particularly interested in the project, bowed out in dramatic fashion early in 1666, after suffering a nervous breakdown when his nineteen-year-old wife became the Duke of York's mistress. But the greatest impediments were first the sheer scale of the enterprise, which was much larger and more costly than the cathedral authorities had hoped; and second, as spring turned to summer in 1665 with hardly anything to show for two years of planning and discussion, the plague.

Barwick's successor as Dean was William Sancroft. Like Christopher Wren's father and uncle, Sancroft had suffered under the Commonwealth, being ejected from his fellowship of Emmanuel College, Cambridge in 1651 and finally going into exile in Holland in 1657. A shrewd and ambitious man, he had risen rapidly at the Restoration, becoming King's Chaplain in 1661, Master of Emmanuel in 1662, Dean of York in February 1664 and, ten months later, Dean of St Paul's. His route to ecclesiastical power would eventually (in 1678) culminate in the Archbishopric of Canterbury. But in the spring of 1666 he had been ensconced in the Deanery in St Paul's Churchyard for eighteen months, during which time he had seen nothing done to repair his cathedral, save for some rough patching and clearing of rubble. Determined to have some progress, he looked for new designs and new ideas from three men – Hugh May, Sir Roger Pratt and Dr Christopher Wren.

Both May and Pratt were obvious choices to advise on a new building enterprise. Like Sir John Denham, Hugh May, who had worked as an agent on various clandestine operations for the Duke of Buckingham during the Commonwealth, had been rewarded for his loyalty at the Restoration with a post in the King's Works. But, unlike Denham, he actually showed some aptitude for architecture. More than aptitude, in fact – in 1666 his recent works included Cornbury House, Oxfordshire, for the Earl of Clarendon, and a town house in Piccadilly for Lord Berkeley. That April he had just received a royal warrant to act as temporary Surveyor of the Works during Denham's illness and, barring Webb's intervention, he looked set to take the post permanently when the ailing Sir John died.

Sir Roger Pratt was even more distinguished. After training as a lawyer, he had spent much of the 1640s travelling in Europe, both to escape the war and to 'give myself some convenient education'. A companion of Evelyn's in Rome, he studied law in Padua, and took an active interest in Italian building design. As a result, he was one of the few men in England with first-hand experience of 'the best authors of Architecture'. And on his return to England after the death of Charles I, he put his knowledge to good use by designing a new house for his cousin at Coleshill in Berkshire – an elegant and compact double-pile that became the model for a whole generation of smaller gentry houses during the Restoration. At the point when he was approached for his ideas on the future of St Paul's, he had just designed a new mansion for the Earl of Clarendon next door to May's Berkeley House, a building that Evelyn described as 'the best contrived, the most usefull, gracefull and magnificent house in England'. Although it was still unfinished, its popularity and its prominent position made Pratt one of the most sought-after authorities on modern architecture. A further point worth noting is that as Lord Chancellor, Clarendon was a member of the Commission. Notwithstanding their reputations as architects, his interest alone would have been quite enough to ensure that his two protégés should be involved.[6]

With the Sheldonian half built, and Pembroke Chapel the only other major architectural work to his name, Wren was something of a surprise. Perhaps Sheldon himself had suggested that he be approached, or Wren's uncle Matthew. Or perhaps John Evelyn or cousin Matthew had put in a good word for him with the King, or Clarendon.

Hugh May's ideas for St Paul's have not survived. Pratt's report, on the other hand, is quite detailed, if conservative. Well aware of the costs involved, he advised that the building should be propped up with scaffolding while 'a most particular and mature examination' of its structure took place. Repairs to Inigo Jones's portico should be a high priority, both for political reasons, since it would 'much illustrate ye Memory of ye Royal Founder' (i.e., the King's father); and because 'being ye most spacious & exposed part of ye Building [it] will most strongly excite ye Charity of ye people'.[7]

Wren's own survey could not have been more different. His covering letter to Sancroft, written from Oxford at the beginning of May, demonstrates how eager he was to work on St Paul's. It also shows that the apparently mild and easy-going professor was more than capable of making some sly digs at a colleague's expense in order to get his own way.

When he is next in Stamford, he says, he will do as Sancroft asks and call at the recently ruined Fotheringay Castle to see whether there is any lead or iron that can be reused for the repairs. Then, after making a plea for a 'trewe latine' style of building for the cathedral, 'which the lawyers say they cannot afford' – a reference to Pratt's legal training – he does his level best to persuade the Dean that accepting Pratt's proposals would end in disaster:

> Take one consideration; How [he] that gives you a well-projected Designe, opens his heart to you, and tells you all at first, It is lyable to censure, and the calculation of Everyman that understands it, you know the worst; he that goeth about a great irregular various peece of work without designe engages himself into an expense unknowne to you and himself to, and the worse way undertaken for thrift proves often more expencefull than the better, and remains an Eyesore at last . . .[8]

The 'well-projected Designe' that Wren put forward to the Commission – and followed up with detailed drawings three months later – was presented as both sound common sense and as a persuasive appeal to contemporary taste. After first acknowledging that the cathedral is 'a pile as much for ornament as use', he dismissed the original building as being structurally and aesthetically flawed. The work was 'both ill designed and ill built from the beginning': the weight of the roof had forced the walls outwards, the rubble infill which formed the core of the piers was not strong enough, and the central tower leaned at an alarming angle due to the subsidence of one of its supporting pillars.

His solution was a complete remodelling, and it would be 'as easy to perform it after a good Roman manner as to follow the Gothick rudeness of the old design'. The nave and transepts should be re-cased in a classical style, with semicircular arcades below an arched gallery. But Wren's most significant innovation was replacing the old tower with a double-shell dome, supported by four huge arches and topped by a lantern. This would give 'incomparable more Grace in ye remote Aspect yn it is possible for ye Lean Shaft of a Steeple to afford', and provide a 'very proper place for a Vast Auditory' by opening out the crossing to the full width of the side aisles. Wren suggested that this dome should be built up around the remains of the crossing-tower and the tower taken down afterwards. His reasons for this show the mixture of sensitivity towards the popular imagination and practical good sense that would characterize the whole of his architectural career. The tower should be retained until the last moment, partly because 'ye expectations of persons is to be kept up (for many unbelievers would bewail the loss of the old Paul's Steeple & despond if they did not see a hopefull successor rise in its stead)'; and partly because it would save a fortune in scaffolding poles.[9]

Not surprisingly, Wren's ideas about St Paul's show the influence of his Paris trip. The dome can be traced back to Lemercier's Sorbonne, while the scheme for re-casing the interior was based on the church of St Paul-St Louis. Indeed, he reminded the Commission of his experience as a traveller in foreign parts with his closing remarks, which were meant to reassure them that his scheme would be nowhere near as expensive as they might think, while at the same time appeal to their patriotic pride:

> Having the opportunity of seeing several structures (of greater expense than this) while they were in rising, conducted by the best artists, French and Italian, and having daily conference with them and observing the engines and methods, [the proposer] hath promoted this geometrical part of architecture yet farther.[10]

France and Italy may be leading the world in architecture, but England can do even better.

Pratt was unimpressed. In fact, he was furious. 'If all incongruities must be reformed,' he wrote in a second report to the Commission, 'what pillars, and arches, to be pulled down! What new ones to be erected! What scaffolds, and engines!' And in a gibe that was clearly intended to remind the Commissioners of Wren's lack of experience in architectural matters, he invoked the name of Inigo Jones himself: 'Mr Jones (who wanted no abilities in the art he professed) caused [the tower] to be exactly scaffolded: to no purpose if he intended not rather a reparation than total abolition of it?'

On the surface, at least, Wren was quite sanguine in the face of such an attack. Early in August, when he told Sancroft that his promised drawings would soon be with him, he mentioned that even if his designs were rejected, 'I shall not repent the great satisfaction and pleasure I have taken in the contrivance, which equals that of poetry or compositions in music'.[11] A shade disingenuous, perhaps. But in spite of his eagerness to clothe London's greatest cathedral in a classical garb, it is clear that he saw St Paul's primarily as a problem to be solved; as so often with his work in other spheres, the joy lay as much in the solving as in the application of the solution.

On Wednesday 22 August Wren was back in London, possibly to deliver his plans in person, and attending the weekly meeting of the Royal Society at Gresham College. A characteristically wide-ranging discussion began with Sir Robert Moray's announcement that he had recently been sent some stag's tears from Warwickshire and that they were like ear wax, with a strong smell, 'but not unpleasant'. (Deer were popularly supposed to weep; their 'tears' are actually oily secretions from the lachrymal gland.) Sir Theodore de Vaux, the King's physician, read a paper on a fur robe said to be the skin of a Tartarian boramez, a legendary plant-animal shaped like a lamb with a golden 'fleece'; the robe was apparently kept in the Bodleian, and Wren was asked to take a look at it when he returned to Oxford.

Members' attention then turned to the subject of ants, chiefly because Moray happened to say that the King had asked how it was that an ant's eggs could be bigger than the ant itself. Wren noted that in Wiltshire it was usual to use ants as a form of organic pesticide, introducing them into wheat to kill mites and even putting them on trees which were infected by worms.

But Wren's mind was on bigger things than mites. By submitting his plans for St Paul's he had precipitated something of a crisis, and five days later, on 27 August, he was called to a site meeting at the cathedral. Several of the Commissioners were there, including Bishop Henchman; so too were Pratt, May and Sancroft, the Master Mason Edward Marshall, and John Evelyn, who had just been chosen as a surveyor of the repairs by the Earl of Clarendon.

The meeting was heated from the outset. Pratt maintained that the outward bulge in the walls was deliberate, and had been designed to enhance the perspective view down the church. Thomas Chicheley, Master of the Ordnance and a member of the Commission, agreed with him. Wren said this was ridiculous (as indeed it was), and Evelyn agreed with *him*. Then the party moved down towards the crossing beneath the disputed tower, and, once more, Pratt and Chicheley sided together, maintaining that it could be patched up. At this point Wren and Evelyn pushed hard for Wren's dome – 'a form of church-building not as yet known in England, but of wonderful grace'.[12] They offered to produce Wren's plans together with an estimate, and a passionate argument broke out, which was only settled when the group agreed to nominate a committee of masons to examine the state of the crossing foundations. Finally, Commissioners and architects retired to Sancroft's Deanery for a little refreshment, although one imagines the atmosphere was tense, to say the least.

It is hard to know whether Wren would have prevailed in his scheme for St Paul's. He had the support of Evelyn and Dean Sancroft, and possibly also of Hugh May. Pratt, on the other hand, could count on his patron, the Earl of Clarendon – and in the summer of 1666, Clarendon was one of the most powerful men in England. As things turned out, the question was settled not by the great and the good, but by an ordinary baker named Thomas Farryner.

The Fire of London started in Thomas Farryner's bakery on Pudding Lane, a narrow street just a few yards from the head of London Bridge, in the early hours of Sunday 2 September. A house-fire was nothing unusual among the tightly packed timber-framed buildings of London; the baker and his wife and son escaped over the rooftops, and neighbours turned out to extinguish the blaze with whatever came to hand – water, earth, milk, sand and urine. The Lord Mayor, Sir Thomas Bludworth, arrived on the scene at three o'clock: he took one look at the fire and went back to bed, saying, 'Pish! a woman might piss it out.'[13] But strong easterly wind fanned the flames, carrying sparks from the burning timbers of Farryner's house across to some hay which was piled in the courtyard of the Star Inn opposite. From there the fire spread to Thames Street, where the warehouses were full of tar, pitch, sugar, brandy and oil, and the nearby wharves were heaped with timber, hay and coal. By Monday night panic was spreading along with the fire, which by now had destroyed Thomas Gresham's Royal Exchange and was raging along Cheapside. The sky was lit up for miles around – in Oxford, Anthony Wood saw the moon turn red – and the Thames was covered with barges and lighters filled with household goods as people took to the river in an effort to escape. The roads leading out of the City were clogged with carts and wagons; and the open fields of Highgate, Islington and Moorfields were turned into seas of rags and canvas, as tens of thousands of refugees set up camp in makeshift shelters.

On Tuesday the fire travelled inexorably north and west, moving from home to home, jumping alleyways and streets, confounding the haphazard and uncoordinated attempts to halt it, and even feeding on them – in the general chaos, the timbers of houses which had been pulled down to make fire-lanes were left in heaps where they lay, so much more fuel for the flames. Those flames reached the old Guildhall, which hours after they passed still glowed 'like a palace of gold, or a great building of burnished brass'.[14] They reached Newgate and spread past the City boundary at Ludgate, and on up Fleet Street towards the Temple and Whitehall. And they reached St Paul's, which was piled high with stock that the booksellers of the Churchyard had just placed there for safe keeping. Sparks caught the scaffolding around the cathedral's tower; they spread to the wooden boards which had been used to protect the old roof; and as the burning timbers fell on to the heaps of books, St Paul's went up in flames, and streams of molten lead ran down the surrounding streets.

It was a scene from hell. 'The Lord is making *London like a fiery oven in the time of his anger*, and in his wrath doth devour and swallow up our habitations'.[15] Women and children ran up and down, screaming for someone to do something. Looters robbed people in the narrow alleyways and ransacked the ruined houses. There were rumours that the fire had been started deliberately by the French, the Dutch, the Papists; and gangs roamed the streets, savagely beating anyone who looked or sounded like a foreigner. Pigeons which Londoners kept for food wheeled frantically round and round their lofts until the heat singed their wings and they fluttered down to their deaths. Across the river on Bankside, Samuel Pepys stood and wept for the city.

King Charles initially left the City authorities to arrange their own fire-fighting measures. But on Monday, when it became clear that Lord Mayor Bludworth wasn't up to the task, he stepped in and placed his brother James in direct charge. The Duke of York organized a string of stations in a great arc round the fire, each supervised by a courtier aided by three justices, thirty soldiers, the parish constables and a hundred civilians. Charles and James personally oversaw the demolition of whole streets of houses, riding among the workmen, urging them on and occasionally dismounting to take up a shovel or a bucket. And over the next couple of days, with help from seamen called in from the dockyards, they managed to create a series of fire-breaks which finally slowed the westward spread of the flames. The wind died on Tuesday night, and although sporadic outbreaks of fire continued until Thursday, by nightfall on Wednesday 5 September, the worst was over.

But the damage was immense. Evelyn compared the blackened, smouldering ruins to the fall of Troy or Armageddon, and the plume of smoke that rose above the city to the destruction of Sodom. Contemporaries shared his sense of having witnessed a cataclysm of biblical proportions:

> I believe there was never any such desolation by fire since the destruction of Jerusalem, nor will be till the last and general con-flagration. Had your lordship [Lord Conway] been at Kensington you would have thought – for five days together, for so long the fire lasted – it had been Doomsday, and that the heavens themselves had been on fire; and the fearful cries and howlings of undone people did much increase the resemblance.[16]

In just five days, around 200,000 Londoners had been made homeless, and 13,200 buildings had been destroyed. Fire damage stretched from Fleet Street and Bridewell in the west right across to the Tower of London, which was only saved after Charles went there by water to supervise the demolition of adjoining houses and thus prevent a catastrophic explosion in the powder magazine at the White Tower. It reached from the river up to Cripplegate in a great bow, 'a bow which had God's *arrow* in it with a flaming point . . . a bow which had fire in it, which signified God's anger, and his intention to destroy *London*'.[17] Wren's old mentor, John Wilkins, who was by now the vicar of St Lawrence Jewry across from the Guildhall, lost his church, his vicarage, his library and his manuscripts. Only the north-eastern sections within the old City's walls were saved; they included Gresham, which was quickly commandeered, first by the Lord Mayor and the City authorities, and then by merchants from the charred Royal Exchange. An area of some 436 acres was in ruins, including St Paul's, the Exchange, the Guildhall, the Custom House, the halls of 44 of the City Companies and 86 parish churches.

The human casualties are harder to estimate. In the ensuing confusion, no bills of mortality were published for the week of the fire, but its slow spread kept the death-toll relatively low. Here and there, we get a heart-rending glimpse of the unlucky ones. William Taswell, a Westminster schoolboy, went souvenir-hunting in the smoking ruins of St Paul's; as he stuffed pieces of melted bell-metal in his pockets, he stumbled over the body of an old woman 'who fled here for safety, imagining the flames would not have reached her there; her clothes were burned, and every limb reduced to a coal'.[18] No doubt there were many who shared that old woman's fate – and many more, according to some accounts, who fell victim to muggers, and whose bodies were carried into the vaults among the ruins and left to rot. Evelyn was stunned by the sight of people wandering around the ruins in a state of shock, 'like men in some dismal desert, or rather in some greate City laid waste by a cruel enemy; to which was added the stench that came from some poore creatures' bodies'.[19]

Every cloud has a silver lining, even when that cloud recalls God's destruction of the cities of the plain. As the sky turned red over Oxford, Wren saw the Fire of London as a God-given opportunity that eclipsed his wildest dreams of a dome for St Paul's. With the embers still glowing, he went to inspect the ruins, and promptly set to work on his most ambitious architectural work to date. This was a design, not merely for a new cathedral, but for an entirely new capital city. He presented it personally to the King on 11 September – without first showing it to the Royal Society, much to Oldenburg's chagrin. The Secretary remonstrated with Wren when he saw the scheme a few days later: 'such a modell, contrived by him, and reviewed and approved by ye R Society, or a Committee thereoff, before it had come to the view of his Majesty, would have given the Society a name, and made it popular, and availed not a litle to silence those, who aske continually, What have they done?' Wren's response was curt and to the point: he wanted to get his design in first, before anybody else had the chance to distract the King's attention, and thus 'could not possibly consult the Society about it'.[20]

He was right to move fast. The chance to design a capital city didn't come along very often, and others were quick to lobby for their own versions of a new Jerusalem. John Evelyn had been pushing for improvements since 1659, when he wrote that 'there is nothing more deformed, and unlike, than the prospect of [the City] at a distance, and its *asymmetrie* within the Walls':[21] on 13 September, two days after Wren submitted his plan to the King, Evelyn was in the Queen's bedchamber at Whitehall, showing his own scheme to Charles, Catherine of Braganza and the Duke of York. Six days after that Robert Hooke presented *his* plan to the Royal Society. It was passed on to the aldermen of the Common Council (London's governing body), who were already considering yet another scheme which had been submitted by Peter Mills, a former City Bricklayer with a long and distinguished pedigree as an architect who had worked as City Surveyor. They preferred Hooke's ideas and noted their 'good Acceptance & Approbacion of the Same'.[22] There were at least two more proposals that we know of (and probably many more that have been lost – 'Every body brings in his idea,' said Evelyn rather ruefully[23]). One was submitted by Richard Newcourt, a surveyor whose knowledge of the pre-Fire layout of the London streets stemmed from a detailed map of the capital made eight years previously. The other was the work of a Captain Valentine Knight, who was promptly arrested for being tactless enough to suggest that his scheme offered 'considerable advantages to his Majesty's revenue . . . if his Majesty would draw a benefit to himself from so public a calamity to his people'.[24]

Although Peter Mills was the only one with a pedigree as a professional builder, all we know of his plan for the city is that the Lord Mayor and the Common Council liked Hooke's better. The other extant proposals* show the fervour with which the post-war generation was coming to embrace Renaissance ideals of symmetry and order. All five made use of a checkerboard layout, turning London into a grid interspersed with open piazzas. Hooke would have had the City's main streets 'lie in an exact strait Line, and all the other cross Streets turning out of them at right Angles';[25] Valentine Knight wanted to create a sea of identical rectangular plots; and Newcourt, whose ideas were the most extreme of all, argued for a regular 8 × 8 grid containing 55 blocks, each with a parish church at its centre, grouped around open squares. Evelyn's original plans (he revised them several times) were rather more sophisticated. Overlaying his basic grid was a series of radiating vistas, dominated by a dead-straight avenue which entered the City from Temple Bar in the west and ran its entire length before leaving through an exit point in the east, diplomatically named Charlesgate 'in honour of our illustrious Monarch'. This main thoroughfare was to be punctuated at intervals by open piazzas and various architectural high-lights, including a new residence for the Lord Mayor, and St Paul's Cathedral, which was also to serve as the focus for two more avenues. One headed north-east to a new Guildhall, modelled after Jacob van Campen's Town Hall in Amsterdam (1647–55), before leaving the City at Bishopsgate; the other went south-east to a semicircular open piazza

---

*Four sets of drawings survive: Wren's, Evelyn's (in three different engraved versions), Newcourt's and Knight's. Hooke's proposal is known only from a brief account of it in the biography which Richard Waller prefixed to his *Posthumous Works of Robert Hooke* (1705).

at the head of London Bridge. Both were linked by further radial streets to a square containing the church of St Dunstan in the East, making a sort of kite-shaped lozenge superimposed on the basic grid pattern of streets. The Royal Exchange would be re-sited on the Thames, and Evelyn provided for an imposing new river frontage with all the old wharves and warehouses removed. The gates into the City would be rebuilt as triumphal arches, 'adorned with Statues, Relievos, and apposite Inscriptions, as Prefaces to the rest within, and should therefore by no means be obstructed by sheds, and ugly shops, or houses adhering to them'.[26]

Evelyn's ambitions for London owed a great deal to the time he had spent in Rome in 1644–5, when he saw at first hand what was then Europe's most famous piece of urban planning – the network of avenues, churches and classical monuments which had been laid out in the 1580s by Pope Sixtus V and his architect, Domenico Fontana. Wren's plan also acknowledged a debt to the Rome of Sixtus V and Fontana, although he only knew of it through books, engravings and conversations with more well-travelled friends such as Evelyn. Striking similarities between the two schemes show that they must have discussed their dreams of an ideal London either before the Fire brought those dreams a dramatic step closer to realization, or when they were both working on them in the second week of September. They both proposed that the area between Temple Bar and the Fleet should be given over to a piazza which would form the intersection of eight streets radiating out on the points of the compass. They both enclosed the buildings which fronted on to this piazza within an octagon of connecting streets. They both made the entrance to the northern end of London Bridge a focal point of their plan, and created a semicircular piazza as a grand introduction to it. They both sent main thoroughfares in from the east to converge at St Paul's. (Wren, who was still determined to get his own way over the cathedral, depicted it with a circular domed choir at the east end.) A passing reference in the explanatory discourse that Evelyn submitted along with his plan confirms some sort of collaboration, and suggests that he adopted some of Wren's ideas. He implies that the two men discussed their respective schemes on or immediately before 11 September, and says that the 'street from St Pauls may be divaricated like a Pythagorean Y, as the most accurately ingenious Dr Wren has designed it, and I willingly follow in my second thoughts'.[27]

Significant differences remain between the two schemes, however, and they show that while Evelyn was a gifted amateur with a cosmopolitan knowledge of European urban planning, Wren added flair and a more deeply thought-out sense of how a modern city should function. So Evelyn placed his new Exchange on the Thames a few hundred yards upstream from London Bridge, arguing that this was 'where the traffic, and business is most vigorous', but in reality conceiving it as no more than a visual element in his reconstructed quayside. Wren kept his Exchange on the site of Thomas Gresham's original building; but he gave it a massive double portico, set it in the centre of a magnificent piazza at the intersection of ten streets and avenues, and encircled it with the City's major commercial buildings – premises for the Excise Office, the Mint, the Post Office, banks, goldsmiths and 'ensurances'. This new commercial district, a tremendously imposing focus for the heart of a major trading nation, was linked directly to the Custom House, which was also left on its existing site between London Bridge and the Tower; to the bridge itself; to St Paul's Cathedral; to all the main routes into the City; and to Wren's new quayside, which was much more straight and regular than Evelyn's, forming a 'Grand Terrace' which was lined with the halls of the major City Companies. His roads were also much wider, both for greater convenience and safety, and to exploit the long, straight vistas to the full.★ And, as one might expect, he also made a much more effective show of St Paul's. Whereas Evelyn's main thoroughfares diverged *behind* the east end of the cathedral, as if their parting were something to be ashamed of, Wren split them in front of its entrance portico, creating a triangular piazza which would have been a spectacular termination to the vista from Fleet Street and Whitehall.

The overall effect of Wren's plan was to divide the new London into zones which were functionally independent but visually and physically connected, to bring the labyrinthine medieval metropolis into the seventeenth century. God was given His due and His cathedral continued to preside over the City. But Wren proposed that St Paul's be slightly reduced in size and the number of churches drop from eighty-six to nineteen, to take account of shifting population patterns which over the centuries had led to some parishes having tiny congregations while others were vast. The real pride of place went to the Exchange

★*Parentalia* later claimed that Wren planned his streets to be of 'three Magnitudes': the main thoroughfares were to be at least ninety feet wide, secondary streets sixty feet and lanes thirty feet. Judging from Wren's original scale drawing (now at All Souls, Oxford), this was something of an exaggeration.

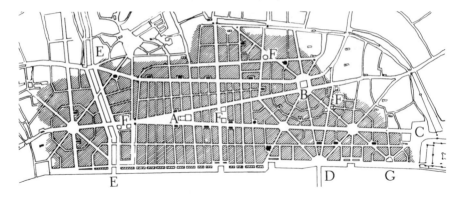

Figure 1. Wren's scheme for London. (A) St Paul's Cathedral. (B) Royal Exchange.
(C) Tower of London. (D) London Bridge. (E) River Fleet. (F) Markets.
(G) Custom House. Churches are solid black.

piazza with its radial vistas and its surrounding complex of commercial
buildings. The absolutist ideology underlying the planning of Sixtine
Rome, which Louis XIV and André Le Nôtre were currently putting to
such good use in the laying out of Versailles, was here called into service
to pay homage to mercantilism. Trade was to be the new religion.

For six weeks the future shape of London hung in the balance. The City
authorities were initially in favour of an entirely new ground-plan for
the burnt area, having suggested the idea themselves on 8 September.
(This may have been what led Wren to produce his scheme: if so, he
worked with astonishing speed.) On 11 September the King commissioned Wenceslaus Hollar and Francis Sandford to make a street
survey, and two days later a royal proclamation was issued, setting out
Charles's intentions. There was to be a new quay, the streets were to be
widened, all rebuilding was to be carried out in brick or stone – and no
citizen was to lose by the changes. But still no decision was taken about
more far-reaching improvements and, as the enormity of the disaster
sank in, so too did the practical implications of rebuilding.

The most pressing problem was to establish the owners and tenants of
more than 13,000 destroyed and fire-damaged properties, and the size
and extent of those properties. Yet there were no land registries, no
official records of ownership. On 22 September the City ordered that
over the next fortnight all occupiers should turn up at special booths set
up in the different wards, each bringing 'a perfect Survey of the Ground

whereon his House, Shop or Warehouse stood, with their Appurtenances, and his Right and Term therein: and that all others who have any Right or Inheritance, Lease, or otherwise to the same, do likewise bring . . . their respective Claimes'.[28] This was a nice idea, but it was doomed to failure. The streets were filled with rubble, making a 'perfect Survey' an impossible task. The population was scattered around the suburbs in rented accommodation, or staying with relatives in distant towns, or still camping out in the surrounding fields. The clerk for St Bride Fleet Street set down the names of 1100 occupiers, but fewer than 100 actually came forward. His experience is probably typical.

Yet speed was vital. The Commons debated the future of London on 27 and 28 September, and came to the conclusion that

> if some speedy way of rebuilding the City was not agreed upon that the City would be in danger never to be built, for if the citizens found a difficulty in it, and that things were not speedily provided for, the merchants and wealthiest of the citizens would alter the course of their life and trade and remove themselves and estates into other countries and so the City would remain miserable for ever.[29]

At the same time, Parliament couldn't agree on the advisability of an entirely new plan. For every MP who spoke for it, another argued that it would be better simply to reconstruct the old City, while a third faction pushed for the compromise implied in Charles's proclamation of 13 September – a proper Thameside quay and wider streets. In the end, they decided that it really wasn't their problem, and left the whole matter to the King's Privy Council and the City while they moved on to more pressing matters, namely the raising of funds to prosecute the war with the Dutch. On 2 October Oldenburg reported to Boyle that 'this very day there is a meeting of some of his Majties Councill and others of ye Nobility, with the leading men of the Citty, to conferre about this great work and to try, whether they can bring it to some issue, before the people, yt inhabited London, doe scatter into other parts'.[30] At this meeting, or shortly after it, Charles announced the appointment of three 'Commissioners for Rebuilding' who would coordinate the survey of interests and come up with detailed proposals in collaboration with a similar group nominated by the City. The King's Commissioners were the same three men that Dean Sancroft had brought in to advise on repairs to St Paul's earlier in the year – Roger Pratt, Hugh May and Christopher Wren. On 4 October the City matched them with its own triumvirate: the architectural tyro Robert Hooke, who had clearly impressed the authorities with his scheme; Peter Mills, who hadn't, but who had an established track record in the City as a surveyor; and Edward Jerman, a former City Carpenter who was, like Mills, 'an experienced man in building'.[31]

With their different backgrounds, the six made up a well-qualified group. Mills and Jerman were both professionals from the London building trades. Pratt was one of the country's most respected gentleman-architects. May, still acting up as Surveyor-General of the Works, was a senior government official. (Denham had recently demonstrated his unfitness to return to work after his breakdown in a spectacular manner, by going to see the King and announcing he was the Holy Ghost.) Hooke and Wren were both leading academics with a declared interest in the future shape of London and, in Wren's case, a rising reputation in architecture – on paper, at least. However, the Commissioners'★ job was to advise the Privy Council and the City and to move the building work forward, not necessarily to design a new capital. Wren obtained leave of absence from Oxford, and, within the week, the Commissioners announced to the Rebuilding Committee of the Privy Council, which sat on Tuesdays to hear their progress, that they were agreed on the width of streets. The new quay should be one hundred feet wide, they said, and major thoroughfares seventy feet. After that, however, things grew more vague. 'Some other Streets [to be] fifty feet and others forty two; The least Streets thirty feet or twenty five; Alleys, if any, sixteen feet'.[32] The reason for the vagueness seems to have been a disagreement between the Commissioners on the feasibility of a detailed survey and hence over whether rebuilding was to follow the existing pre-Fire street-plan or not. Pratt argued that a decision on this had to be their next step. It was essential that they make up their minds 'whether streets shall be laied out in the places where they formerly were, or in such other as shall bee demonstrated to be more for the beauty and conveniencie of the citty, beeing that no man can tell how to offer any acceptable designe till this bee determined, nor any one to build till that design be agreed upon.'[33] One can sense here some of the old antagonism between Pratt and Wren who had, at least as far as *he* was concerned, already made an 'acceptable designe'. And that

---

★Strictly speaking, only Wren, Pratt and May were 'Commissioners'; the City referred to its nominees as 'Surveyors'. In practice the distinction was between their respective allegiances rather than their roles, and it seems easier to call all six Commissioners.

antagonism wasn't so old, either – it was only seven weeks since the two men had nearly come to blows in St Paul's, over just this issue of making do or making new.

The problem hinged on the survey of occupiers and interests which the City had tried and failed to institute a fortnight earlier. Without it, the redistribution of property and the forced relocations that a new plan would involve were impossible, unless the King went back on the promise he had made in the 13 September proclamation that no one 'in any degree [shall] be debarred from receiving the reasonable benefit of what ought to accrue to him'.[34] And that was simply not an option. No matter how enviously Charles II might look across the Channel at the absolute power wielded by Louis XIV, whenever the King of England was tempted to suggest that '*L'état c'est moi*', his father's headless ghost was at his shoulder to remind him of the consequences.

So the Commissioners did their best to carry out the necessary survey. They tried to hire contractors, but found that the rates of pay they offered – one shilling per house with the site cleared by the occupier – weren't enough, and they had to raise them, first to eighteen pence, and then to half a crown. Even then, occupiers were slow to remove fire debris: landlords and tenants argued over whose responsibility it was, and neither would come up with the contractor's fee. The survey never was completed, although attempts continued in a desultory fashion until the end of the year. But long before that – by 17 October, to be precise – any hopes that Wren may have had for his new London seem already to have gone by the board. On that date Wren, Pratt and the other Commissioners met with representatives of the Rebuilding Committees of the Privy Council and the Common Council, and proposed a scaled-down compromise for the capital. Most of the original streets would remain. The hundred-foot quay would become an eighty-foot quay; the seventy-foot thoroughfares were to shrink to somewhere between fifty-five and forty feet. There were still traces here and there of Wren's grand design, in references to a fifty-foot-wide avenue from Fleet Street to the Tower, for example, or to the route from the Guildhall into Cheapside, sixty feet wide with a piazza. But expedience and pragmatism had won out over Wren's ideal city.

As autumn turned to a hard winter, bringing to a halt any thoughts of commencing building work before the following year, the Commission continued to deliberate the architectural character of the new London. At the end of November, for instance, Hugh May told Pepys that 'the design of building the City does go on apace', and from the way May described it, Pepys thought it would be 'mighty handsome and to the satisfaction of the people'.[35] When a Bill for the Rebuilding of the City of London finally came before Parliament on 8 February 1667, it certainly contained plenty of good ideas. The exteriors of all buildings were indeed to be made of brick or stone, and no jetties or oriel windows were allowed to project out beyond 'the ancient foundation line'. Twelve streets were to be enlarged, including Fleet Street, Thames Street and the lane leading from the east end of St Paul's into Cheapside; and regulations laid down the thickness of walls and the heights of each storey. But the grid-patterns and grand avenues, the *ronds-points* and terminations to vistas, the architectural reorientation of the City as a modern mercantile capital, had all gone – and the vision went with them. In the event, the only element of Wren's scheme to be implemented was the canalizing of the Fleet, which had also been part of Evelyn's proposal. It would be another 130 years before Wren's ideas were given concrete expression, and then it was 3000 miles away on the banks of the Potomac, when Thomas Jefferson and Pierre Charles L'Enfant borrowed heavily from his engraved plans in laying out the United States' new Federal City, later renamed Washington.

In the meantime, Wren's London soon passed into legend as the most beautiful capital England never had, the greatest architectural might-have-been in the nation's history. If it hadn't been for bureaucratic incompetence and a failure of governmental nerve, the argument went, it would have been 'the Wonder of the World', as one of the Georgian metropolis's critics lamented in the 1730s.[36] In 1750 *Parentalia* asserted, with a cheery disregard for the facts, that eighty-four years previously Wren had been appointed '*Surveyor-general* and *principal Architect* for rebuilding *the whole City* [*Parentalia*'s emphasis]'; that he was commanded by the King to make an exact survey of the remains; and that he personally traced over 'with great Trouble and Hazard, the great Plain of Ashes and Ruins' before producing an eminently practical scheme which would transform the city. The only thing that prevented him from carrying through the project was 'the obstinate Averseness of great part of the Citizens to alter their old Properties, and to recede from building their Houses again on the old Ground and Foundations; as also, the Distrust in many, and Unwillingness to give up their Properties, tho' for a time only, into the Hands of publick Trustees'. Because of this obstinacy and 'distrust' the opportunity to make London 'the most magnificent, as well as commodious for Health and Trade of any upon Earth was lost'.[37]

Modern historians of urban planning have tended to take a contrary view, suggesting that Wren's London never could have been built, that it was never seriously considered and that it was, in any case, no more than a dreamscape hastily put together by an inexperienced amateur, which failed to take into account the financial and social implications of a wholesale remodelling. 'Divorced from circumstances, a new plan may seem simple, Wren's magnificent: to contemporaries, anxious examination showed that both were Utopian.'[38]

The truth lies somewhere in between. That Wren's plan was a brilliant and sophisticated reinterpretation of London has already been argued. None of the others came close. It was quite literally streets ahead of the efforts of Newcourt, Knight and, from the little we know about it, Hooke. Only Evelyn, who had been preoccupied with the future of the city on and off for the past seven years, approached the grandeur and refinement shown by Wren; and even his ideas seem rigid and lifeless in comparison with Wren's dynamism and variety, his insistence that the form of the city should follow its function. As for the contemporary reaction, we know that King Charles was enthusiastic. He personally produced the plan before his Privy Council and 'manifested much approbation of it'.[39] We know that the scheme was still under serious consideration at the end of September 1666, when a faction in Parliament was arguing for 'a quite new Model, according to Dr Wren's draught'.[40] But Parliament felt the decision was up to the King and the City authorities. Charles, who must have winced when the Church called for a general day of fasting on 10 October 1666, telling congregations across the nation to acknowledge that the Fire was the result of their 'prodigious ingratitude, burning lusts, dissolute Court, profane and abominable lives', had done his best by appointing Wren one of his 'Commissioners for Rebuilding', but it would have been politically disastrous for him to override the City's wishes. The Lord Mayor and the City, who would have borne the brunt of the immensely complex legal wrangling that Wren's scheme involved, began by calling for a new plan and ended by wanting simply to hang out a 'Business as usual' sign as quickly as possible. Once it became clear that dramatic improvements would take time, they veered towards the path of least resistance. Even so, if the Commissioners had made an argument for a radically redesigned capital to be constructed with a minimum of delay, and if King and Parliament had given their backing, the City would have considered it. As for the traumatized and bewildered population upon whom *Parentalia* heaps the blame for the failure of the plan, they were busy setting up wooden shacks in the ruins of their homes and queuing for navy biscuit at the temporary food markets set up in the wake of the Fire. Their wishes counted least of all.

The Commission held the key. But the six men who made up the Commission had conflicting views and conflicting interests. Hooke, who in other circumstances would have been a steadfast ally, was presumably keen to promote his own scheme, and in any case, with his complete lack of architectural experience, his voice can have counted for little. Hugh May is an unknown quantity, but Mills and Jerman both had a professional interest in seeing the work begin as soon as possible – they had clients waiting in the wings. As soon as the rebuilding started, for example, Mills – who was sixty-eight in 1666 and who died four years later – contracted for parts of Christ's Hospital and some of the warehouses on Thames Street which had been destroyed during the Fire; while between 1667 and his own death the following year Edward Jerman designed a new Royal Exchange, repaired the Barber-Surgeons' Hall, and rebuilt the Drapers' Hall, the Fishmongers' Hall, the Goldsmiths' Hall, the Mercers' Hall, the Wax Chandlers' Hall and the Weavers' Hall. Roger Pratt, who was essentially much more con-servative than Wren – and much more experienced – had a low opinion of the younger man's architectural flights of fancy, and disagreed with him on principle; and Pratt was the moving force behind the Commissioners' deliberations. The idea that a 34-year-old astronomer who had designed two buildings (and completed just one, the relatively unprestigious Pembroke Chapel) and who had tried to shout down Pratt's common-sense proposals for St Paul's with his own hopelessly impractical design, born of a few months wandering round Paris – the idea that this jumped-up novice should be allowed to redesign *London* was ridiculous.

'I am exceeding glad the King hath commissioned you (no question in the first place) with Mr May & Dr Renne,' Pratt's cousin Edward had written to him at the end of October (he had obviously been confident that Pratt would head up the Commission). 'They will get more secrets of your art brought from Rome, & so from Athens, then you from them. If you have a hand in repairing St Pauls, the most Royall peice in Christendom, it will be a Jacobs ladder to carry you to heaven beyond all profit & honour in this world.'[41] In fact, although he didn't know it at the time, 'the best Architect in Europe' – also his cousin's estimation, although no doubt Pratt agreed – was soon destined to leave the national scene. The arrival of a Dutch fleet in the Medway in June 1667 precipitated the dramatic fall of his chief patron, the Lord Chancellor, who was held responsible for the mismanagement of the war. The day after the news of the Dutch incursion reached London, a mob was cutting down the trees outside Clarendon House, hurling rocks through the windows and painting a gibbet on the gate. Clarendon's disgrace, impeachment and subsequent exile caused Pratt to retire discreetly from public life, and he spent the rest of his days improving the Norfolk estate he had inherited that April from his admiring cousin Edward.

His departure came too late for a new London. But the way was now open for Wren to climb the Jacob's ladder of St Paul's.

9

Something of a Better Mould

*S*t Paul's was devastated by the Fire. Inigo Jones's blackened portico still stood, along with sections of the western end of the nave. But the outward slant of the walls that Wren had pointed out in August 1666 was now so pronounced that it was a miracle they remained upright. The base of the crossing-tower seemed fairly sound, but a pillar had collapsed in the nave and the stone roof of the choir had caved in, bringing down the north wall and breaking open the vaults of St Faith's, the parish church in the cathedral's crypt. Mummified corpses, their tombs smashed by falling debris, were salvaged and propped up in the Convocation House yard for the amusement of sightseers – as if they had risen from their graves and, like their live brethren, had mistaken the smoke and flames for the Day of Judgement.*

Dean Sancroft's first priority was to bring St Paul's back into use as quickly as possible, and the best way to do this, he believed, was to make do and mend. Indeed, it seemed the only way. The act passed by Parliament in February 1667 to finance the rebuilding and improvement of the capital allowed for the imposition of a ten-year tax of one shilling per chaldron† on all coal that came into the Port of London. But the

---

*Aubrey recalled that the broken tombs provided at least one virtuoso with an opportunity for scientific experiment. A small hole was made in the coffin of John Colet, an early sixteenth-century Dean of St Paul's, and Edmund Wylde, a Fellow of the Royal Society, actually drank some of the liquid he found inside: ''Twas of a kind of insipid tast, something of an Ironish tast.' When Wylde poked Colet's corpse with a stick it felt like 'boyld Brawne' (*Brief Lives*, 70).

†A measure of volume equivalent to just over one Imperial ton.

money, which the authorities hoped would amount to £15,000 a year, was earmarked for street-widening, buying the land needed for a new Thameside quay, and for 'the building and makeing such Prisons within the . . . Citty as shall be necessary for the safe custody and Imprisonment of Felons and other Malefactors'.[1] There was no funding for London's public buildings, let alone its ruined churches or its cathedral. Nor would there be anything to spare. Quite the opposite, in fact: the purchase of land needed for the quay would have swallowed up the entire £150,000.

Wren saw his chance slipping away. When Sancroft looked to him for advice – neither Roger Pratt nor Hugh May played any further part in the proceedings – he pleaded with the Dean, saying that if the authorities were to make a start on repairing the battered cathedral, which 'now appears like some antique ruin of 2000 years standing', they would have to carry on piecemeal until nothing was left of the old building. And, he might have added, until nothing was left of his own ambitions to design a new cathedral for London. Reluctantly, he conceded that part of the west end of the nave was in a fit state to be roofed over and turned into a temporary choir for services. (The other obvious option, stabilizing the old choir and making use of that, he discounted: apart from the fact that it wouldn't be big enough to hold a congregation, the Dean and Chapter's route to divine service would lead them through the remnants of the west end. This, Wren said with a wry smile, would make such a dismal procession through the ruins that 'the very passage will be a pennance'.)[2] Three or four thousand pounds and a building campaign lasting no more than the summer should see the work complete. But he continued to push Sancroft to think in terms of temporary repairs and a more permanent solution for the future:

I hope whatever you doe of this nature is but in order to something of a better mould. For though I despair this age should erect any more such huge piles, yet I believe the reputation of Paules and the compassion men have for its ruines may at least produce some neate fabrick, wch shall recompence in Art and beauty what it wants in bulke, as well as wee see every day such thinges don by the begging fryers of particular convents. I am ready to serve you to the utmost of my power in contriving either the designe or (what is harder) the method of begging.[3]

The eagerness shows through, both in the side-swipe at Catholicism and in the promise to help with the fund-raising. However, Sancroft took Wren's advice on bringing the nave back into use for services, although not before asking for a second opinion on the structural integrity of the west end from masons and carpenters at the Office of Works. The project moved slowly, but at a meeting with the Earl of Manchester in his Lord Chamberlain's lodgings at Whitehall in January 1668, Sancroft, Gilbert Sheldon (in his capacity as Archbishop of Canterbury), the Bishops of Winchester and Ely and others agreed to set up a commission with the aim of restoring St Paul's 'to its religious use, with the least expense of tyme and treasure', by following Wren's recommendations and creating a choir and auditory 'in the body of the Church between the West end and the second pillars above the little North and South dores'.[4] The lean-to sheds and temporary shops which had sprung up in St Paul's Churchyard were swept away, and with the coming of spring scaffolding went up and the work began – only to halt abruptly a few weeks later. In the middle of April a piece of masonry fell from a nave wall on to the vaulting of one of the side aisles, leaving it in such a precarious state that the workmen evacuated the site immediately. The next night one of the pillars collapsed, bringing scaffolding and walling crashing to the ground. Worse than this, it revealed that Inigo Jones's heavy stone cladding wasn't properly tied in to the medieval walls, and that it threatened to come down at any time. Work was suspended, and Sancroft wrote an anguished appeal to Wren in Oxford, earnestly desiring his assistance with all possible speed: 'What we are to do next is the present Deliberation, in which you are so absolutely and indispensably necessary to us, that we can do nothing, resolve on nothing, without you.'[5]

This urgency was certainly flattering, although there was sense behind it – during a recent visit to London, Wren had been to see the repair work in progress, and had predicted just such a disaster. Now Sancroft said that Archbishop Sheldon himself commanded his presence at St Paul's – and asked that he bring his old designs along with him.

Wren wrote back by return: he would be in London just as soon as he had made sure the Sheldonian could continue without him. In the meantime, Sancroft should certainly halt all work on the site, and must surely agree that it was time to take the step that he had been pushing for since the fire and 'set your thoughts upon a new fabrick upon new foundations, artificiall durable and beautifull, but less massive'. True, the times were scarcely propitious for a large-scale building enterprise, but in a year or so, when labour and materials weren't at such a premium, things would be easier. And – almost as an afterthought – 'if you had a good designe . . . it might encline benefactors'.[6]

Wren was as good as his word, coming up to London the following week and carrying out a survey of the damage. The report he produced at the end of May hit just the right tone. There was a carefully worded apology: after all, it was he who had suggested the ill-fated repairs to the west end of the cathedral in the first place, and one senses that Sancroft might well have pointed this out to him as they walked the site together. But it combined self-justification with the gentlest reminder that if there was any blame, the Dean had to take his share: 'I cannot beleeve that any sober man who weighes the motives wee went upon will condemne us . . . noe man that viewed the worke had less confidence in the firmnesse of the old then I had . . .'[7] There was indeed no point in continuing with any repairs, in spite of what 'some workemen that would be in employment' might say to the contrary. The crossing-tower threatened to collapse at any moment, and the heat of the fire had left gaping cracks in the buttresses of the choir, so that they could no longer bear the weight of a roof.

In a final masterstroke, Wren resisted the temptation to fire off any proposals for a new building, arguing that there was no point until he had some idea of the budget. St Paul's was almost within his grasp – and he knew it.

Over the next five weeks Sancroft, Sheldon and Henchman deliberated over what to do next, while Wren sat back in Oxford and waited. In any case, he had several other building projects to occupy his mind. Both the Sheldonian and Ralph Bathurst's new range at Trinity College were nearing completion, while work was just beginning on a chapel and master's gallery he had designed for Emmanuel College, Cambridge, an idea which had first been mooted in 1663 by the then Master – none other than William Sancroft.

Even after he left Cambridge, Sancroft donated money towards the new chapel, £600 in all, out of a total cost of £3972, and kept a keen eye on progress through to its consecration in 1677 and beyond – ten years later he donated the altarpiece. Obviously, the Dean's links with Wren extended beyond his cathedral. It would be nice to know exactly how and when Wren was given the commission. A wooden model of the chapel was sent to Emmanuel for inspection in September 1667, so the design was more or less complete by then; and from this point on Wren seems to have avoided visiting the site, in spite of repeated pleas for help and advice from the dons, which were relayed via Sancroft. (In the course of one of those pleas the Master, John Breton, pointed out to Sancroft that Wren's presence would be 'a great reputation (besides other advantages) to the whole work', suggesting that his renown as an architect was already quite considerable by February 1668, when Breton wrote this letter.)[8] But did Sancroft's relationship with Wren begin much earlier, with an invitation to design the chapel at Cambridge in 1663 or 1664, perhaps as a result of the latter's work for his uncle at Pembroke? Was this the real reason why Wren was included in the commission to advise on the repair of Old St Paul's in the months before the Great Fire of 1666?

We don't know. What we can say is that the Emmanuel chapel is a much more ambitious effort than Pembroke's. Whereas the earlier building is a straightforward single block, at Emmanuel Wren opted for a tripartite arrangement, consisting of a tall three-bay centrepiece flanked by two lower five-bay wings, with the whole composition tied together visually by an open arcade running the full width of the building. The basic idea owes something to the chapel range at Peterhouse which Matthew Wren had begun when he was Master there back in the 1620s; but in place of Matthew's picturesque Tudor-Gothic interspersed with half-understood classical ornament, his nephew gave Emmanuel an uncompromisingly classical façade. This is dominated – *totally* dominated – by the centrepiece, which breaks outwards and upwards in a giant Corinthian order topped with a pediment, broken to take a great clock, behind which is a square block that carries a round cupola. The two flanking wings have separate roofs, giving a decidedly French feel to the whole affair – which is hardly surprising, if Wren designed the chapel soon after his return from France. If there is a certain naïveté to the thing, an overconfident handling of classical decoration and an absence of restraint or due proportion, we shouldn't be too hard on the architect. His immaturity is more than offset by his sheer excitement in the joy of making; and with the passage of time, the building's faults have become virtues, so that, as Kerry Downes so tellingly puts it, the chapel range at Emmanuel is one of those buildings 'which seem jewel-like or model-like because their vocabulary is larger in scale than their actual dimensions'.[9]

The Emmanuel chapel was important to Sancroft – and given the circumstances, its importance to Wren lay not only in designing something good, but in keeping Sancroft happy. However, the project which was really exercising his mind in June 1668, while he waited to hear the news from St Paul's and, no doubt, toyed with various ideas for the sort of cathedral he would build given half a chance, was a new college for the Royal Society.

When its regular meeting rooms at Gresham were commandeered by the authorities in the immediate aftermath of the Fire, the Society had retreated to the lodgings of Walter Pope, Wren's successor as the college's Professor of Astronomy. Then, in January 1667, they took up an offer from Henry Howard, brother of the 5th Duke of Norfolk, to make a temporary home at Arundel House, the sprawling medieval palace which lay between the Strand and the river. Wren, whose work as a 'Commissioner for Rebuilding' kept him in London, socialized with the other members★ and attended the weekly meetings at Arundel House pretty regularly throughout the spring and early summer of 1667.

A measure of his continued (or resumed) commitment to the Society is that, in the previous November, he had agreed to stand once more for election to the Council. And he played an active part in the weekly gatherings. In February 1667, for example, he announced that he had developed a new kind of lamp, 'wherein the oil would not come faster than it is consumed';[10] and in March he described a new level for taking the horizon and presented drawings of curious hailstones which were shaped like marigolds. In April, he was explaining to the assembly how grain-stores worked in Danzig and Russia, and in June he shared his observations of the way in which decapitated flies apparently continued to live for a good while without their heads, in the course of a discussion begun by another Fellow's account of how a cat, with its head and heart removed, had twitched spasmodically when its tail was pulled. Hooke noted that after having taken a puppy's foetus from its mother's womb and dissecting it, he found that its heart was still beating the next morning. Predictably, the meeting ended with a resolution to open the thorax of a dog, blow air into its lungs with a pair of bellows and see how long it lived.†

Wren resumed his professorial duties at Oxford in the autumn of

---

★On 16 February 1667, for instance, he went to Lord Brouncker's house in Covent Garden with Moray, Hooke and Pepys, to hear a concert given by an Italian ensemble, two of whom were eunuchs.

†The *London Gazette* for 8 November 1675 carried the following advertisement: 'Lost on Saturday last, in *New Kings-Street* near *St. James's*, a little black Spaniel, rough hair, white neck. Whoever shall bring the said Dog, or give notice where he is to be found, to the *Angel* in the same street, shall have 20s. reward.' The Duke of York lost a white spaniel in London; so did Prince Rupert (along with two greyhounds and a Yorkshire buckhound). Even the King lost a 'white bitch called Fymm, also a black lurcher with a cut tail called Gypsy'. Where *did* the Royal Society find all those dogs, one wonders?

1667, and inevitably spent less time in London. He duly stood down from the Royal Society's Council at the annual election of officers that November, although he continued to correspond with Neile, Wilkins and Oldenburg, and to put in occasional appearances at Arundel House. He kept up his interest in medicine and anatomy, to judge from a report he sent to Wilkins in February 1668, recounting the strange case of an Oxford boy 'with a consumption of the bones in his head, which bones he pulled out in fragments, whereof some single ones weighed an ounce'.[11] And in the spring of that year, while St Paul's was falling around Sancroft's ears, he produced some drawings for a new college, a permanent Solomon's House for the Royal Society to be built at Arundel House.

The idea of a college had been in the minds of several members – notably Evelyn and Wilkins – for years, and the upheavals caused by the Fire and the move to Arundel House, together with an offer from the Howard family of a permanent site in their grounds leading down to the Thames, encouraged the Society to take it up again at the end of September 1667. Permanent premises would give an air of legitimacy to their proceedings; and legitimacy was something they craved desperately. Charles II had just given them Chelsea College, a half-built academy for the clergy founded by James I and used as a prisoner-of-war camp for Dutch sailors during the Commonwealth; but this was too far away from central London, and was in any case intended 'for all Experiments of Gardning and Agriculture: and by the neighbourhood of the River . . . all Trials that belong to the Water'. A college much closer to the heart of the capital was needed to serve 'for their Meetings, their Laboratories, their Repository, their Library, and the Lodgings for their Curators'.[12] Moreover, the Society was in danger of being upstaged by French rivals: there were rumours that Colbert was about to provide Louis XIV's new Académie des Sciences with an imposing research institute.

In the first week of June 1668 Henry Howard was in Oxford (his sons were going up to Magdalen College), and he summoned Wren to attend him at his lodgings. A summons from the brother of a duke was not something to be taken lightly, and Wren duly went along. Howard was full of ideas for the new college, and asked the don, well-known both for his status in the Royal Society and his architectural interests, what he thought of his designs.

He didn't think much, although he was far too polite to say so. But Howard had heard (probably from Oldenburg or one of the other members of the Society) that Wren had also been playing around with the idea. It excited Wren because, as ever, it presented a unique set of problems to be overcome. How, exactly, could a building combine the functions of assembly hall and research institute, with facilities for just about every conceivable type of scientific experiment? And how could it be accommodated on a site no larger than a hundred feet by forty, which was the plot that Howard was offering? He sketched out his plans, which initially gave Howard a bit of a shock – he hadn't expected anything quite so ambitious. But Wren won him over, and left him to take the sketches back to London, while he gave some thought to a written explanation of their purpose.

The drawings have not survived,[13] but Wren's thinking behind them has.[14] He proposed a building 100 feet by 30 feet and of five storeys, including cellars and attics. The cellars should contain storage space, 'a fair Elaboratory', one or two smithies, and a kitchen. Above this was a housekeeper's room, a repository for curiosities and a library, the books placed in glass cabinets 'after the moderne way'; and on the first floor, a two-storey-high meeting room overlooked by a gallery, which would be 'very usefull in case of Solemnities'. Closets for the curators of experiments completed the accommodation on the second floor, while the attic storey was partitioned into workshops for operators and lodgings for those operators and servants, separated by a narrow gallery which ran the whole length of the building.

Wren's consummate ability to create a building which was perfectly suited for its purpose – already evident in his designs for the Sheldonian – shines through here. The long attic gallery could be used to try out lenses; a flat lead roof above it was perfect for testing telescopes and other optical instruments, and a central cupola could be used as both an observatory and an anatomy theatre. Gaps in the flooring from attic to cellar allowed 'all experiments for hight', such as investigations into barometric pressure, the velocity of falling bodies and the vibration of a pendulum. This last was something which had been exercising the Royal Society for some time, largely because it seemed to hold the key to accurate timekeeping, and thus to the problem of longitude. Four years earlier a delegation including Hooke, Wilkins and Moray had trooped to the top of St Paul's tower and swung a 200-foot line with a 14 lb weight attached – a sight which must have raised a few eyebrows among the booksellers and stationers of St Paul's Churchyard.

Wren's scheme proved too extravagant for the more cautious members of the Society, in spite of his cheery assertion that 'a fair building may easier be carried on by contributions with time, than a sordid one',[15] and his suggestion that once the foundations were laid, half of the college could be built for £2000, with the other half waiting until the necessary funds became available – an echo, no doubt, of his current thinking about the future of St Paul's. Robert Hooke had also drawn up a design, and his more modest proposal was preferred to Wren's when the Society's Council met on 22 June. If Wren was piqued by this rejection, his reaction, like his drawings, has not survived. But in any case, Solomon's House was never built. Although the Council had unanimously agreed the previous November, after 'mature deliberation', that 'it was now a seasonable time for such subscriptions'[16] as would finance the college, such a statement represents a touching triumph of hope over experience at a time when every Londoner's thoughts were turned to rebuilding their devastated city, when materials were as scarce as a unicorn's horn, when the shortage of skilled labour in the capital was so great that even an unregulated influx of craftsmen from the provinces couldn't meet the demand. Although nearly £1300 in subscriptions towards the college were promised – a considerable sum, to be sure, but nowhere near enough, even for Hooke's scheme – it soon became clear that the project wasn't viable. In 1673 the Society returned to Gresham, and nine years later they sold Chelsea back to the Crown.[17]

In the first week of July 1668, Wren finally got the call he had been waiting for. Sancroft wrote to say that Sheldon, Henchman and the Bishop of Oxford had read and re-read his report on St Paul's, and were agreed that there was nothing for it but to build a new cathedral; or, at least, to press ahead with the design of a choir which would be 'a congruous Part of a greater and more magnificent Work to follow'. And without Wren, said the Dean, they could do nothing. He was to come up to London as soon as possible, so that the St Paul's Commissioners could prepare a design to put forward to the King. The only part of Wren's report that they had a problem with was his suggestion that funding must be established before a design was produced: 'The Way their Lordships resolve upon, is to frame a Design, handsome and noble, and suitable to all the Ends of it, and to the Reputation of the City, and the Nation, and to take it for granted, that Money will be had to accomplish it.'[18]

I'd give a lot to see Wren's face as he broke Sancroft's seal and unfolded that sheet of paper. From this moment on he was the de facto architect of St Paul's, and he must have realized it. No cathedral had been built in England since the Middle Ages; no one Englishman had *ever* had the chance to design a cathedral on such a scale and see it through to its completion.

Once all thought of salvaging St Paul's had passed, the next step was to level away the ruins preparatory to staking out the ground. Ideally, everything should have been cleared, from Jones's battered portico to the rubble-strewn east end. But at the time, with the shortages of labour and materials caused by the demand for rebuilding all over the capital in the wake of the Fire, this didn't seem practical. A cautious, step-by-step approach was much more sensible, and so on 25 July 1668 a royal order was given authorizing the demolition of the old choir and tower. In August, the work of clearing the site began in earnest, and by the end of the month Pepys was reporting that the choir would be levelled by Christmas, and a new cathedral started the next year. Little did anyone realize that it would be a full seven years before the foundation stone was laid, or that a further thirty-six years would pass before St Paul's was officially declared to be complete.

Wren made regular visits to assess progress – usually on Saturday mornings – and from 1672 he had his own rather grand suite of rooms in the repaired chapter house (known as the Convocation House), which stood in the old cloisters between the nave and the south transept. The office was fitted out with mantelpieces, a table with drawers and locks, wall hangings, curtains, fire shovel and tongs – even 'a large Map of London to hang over the Chimney' – all paid for by the building fund.[19] But much of the day-to-day work on site was supervised by two salaried officers. The Assistant Surveyor was Edward Woodroffe, who was ten years Wren's senior, an architect in his own right* and a man with six years' experience as Surveyor to the Dean and Chapter of Westminster Abbey. His role was to pass Wren's instructions to the men, to measure the masons' work and keep an account of the stores held in the Churchyard, and to help the Surveyor in negotiating contracts and examining bills. The job of John Tillison, the Paymaster and Clerk of Works, was to make sure that carpenters and labourers, who were on a day-rate, were doing what they were supposed to do. He also received and paid out money for work and materials, checked materials out of the stores and made up the accounts for Wren and

---

*In 1670 Woodroffe designed three houses in Amen Corner for the residentiary canons of St Paul's.

Woodroffe to examine and pass. He had a set of lodgings in the Churchyard, next door to the Surveyor's office.

As a first step in the clearance work, pathways were made through the ruined nave so that the small army of labourers could move to and fro with their handbarrows. Trenches were dug to establish exactly where the old foundations lay, and the debris that had fallen into the vaults of St Faith's was cleared so that the coffins, skulls and bones that had been disturbed could be reinterred with due ceremony. Masons sorted through the stones to find material that could be recycled, and the rubbish was washed and sifted for lead which was melted and cast into pigs and sheets ready for use in the new building. Between October 1668 and September 1675 more than 45,000 loads of rubbish were carted away from the site, much of it to be reused on building new roads around the City. (Londoners were also intent on reusing both the lead and the serviceable building stone, apparently, to judge from the fact that first wooden fences and then a rubble wall were erected around the site to keep out intruders; night-watchmen were engaged to patrol the site, and two bigs mastiffs were kept in Convocation House Yard.)

The process of taking down fire-damaged walls, pillars and the remains of the crossing-tower was difficult and dangerous: Pepys, who wandered along to watch the demolition in its early stages, suffered an attack of vertigo brought on just by the sight of so many huge stones raining down from the tower. And inevitably there were casualties among the workers. Ropes broke. There were sudden falls of masonry. Men slipped from scaffolding, or lost their footing as they clambered around high up among the ruins of the tower with crow-bars and pick-axes, trying to prise away huge chunks of stone. The cathedral account books are full of small private tragedies: burial expenses for William Hepworth, who fell from the east end of the church; surgeon's fees for bleeding Daniel Hill, who slipped and fell from one of the pinnacles; compensation to Ann Pigot, whose husband Thomas died when part of a wall in the north-east angle of the cathedral collapsed, and to Widow Thorrowgood, whose husband was killed when he lost his footing and came crashing down from the top of the tower into a side aisle. Such incidents may not have much historical significance in the greater scheme of things, but let's not forget that they still devastated someone's life. They still made some mother weep when a workmate came banging on the door with the news of an accident at St Paul's, some wife feel sick with fear or disbelief as she ran down to Convocation House Yard to have Tillison or Woodroffe tell her that she was a widow.

★   ★   ★

As the demolition work began, Wren left both Oxford and London behind for his home county of Wiltshire, where he visited an old friend and pondered the future of another cathedral. Seth Ward, his astronomy teacher and predecessor in the Savilian chair, was busy carving out a political career for himself on the bishops' bench. Recently translated to the see of Salisbury after five years at Exeter, his chief pastime in his new diocese was the suppression of dissent and Nonconformity. Gilbert Burnet, a later Bishop of Salisbury, whose *History of My Own Times* provides a gloriously prejudiced picture of the later Stuarts, admired his political acumen but doubted his sincerity, saying rather slightingly that 'to get his former errors to be forgot, [he] went into the high notions of a severe conformity'.[20] When he was not rigorously enforcing the more oppressive measures of the Clarendon Code (which sought to re-establish the position of the Anglican Church after the Restoration), he looked anxiously to the welfare of his medieval cathedral, the visible expression of the Church's power. The Bishop's old pupil was asked down to survey the fabric of the building.

Wren was fast becoming the Church of England's unofficial consultant on architectural matters. In the four or five years since he had first begun to dabble in building, the Dean of St Paul's, the Bishops of Ely, London and now Salisbury, and the Archbishop of Canterbury himself had either commissioned work from him or looked to him for advice. In fact every one of his buildings to date, with the exception of Ralph Bathurst's new range at Trinity, had a strong Anglican connection.

Unlike St Paul's, Salisbury was no ruin in search of an ambitious young designer. Long admired as 'one of the principal ornaments of England',[21] it had been begun by Bishop Poore and the master mason Nicholas of Ely in 1220, after Poore decided to abandon the old cathedral up at Sarum, a mile north, for a more congenial site down in the meadows. The new building was completed before 1300, with the exception of the cathedral's most famous feature – a slender spire which at 404 feet is the tallest in Britain, and which was added in the mid-fourteenth century.

Wren's survey was perceptive and surprisingly fair to Salisbury's medieval builders. As a rule he didn't like the Gothic, which he habitually referred to as 'the Saracen Style', from his belief that it originated with the Arabs rather than the Goths. There was nothing particularly revolutionary in this: back in the 1620s Sir Henry Wotton had heaped scorn on pointed arches which, 'both for the naturall imbecility of the sharpe Angle it selfe, and likewise for their very

Uncomelinesse, ought to bee exiled from judicious eyes, and left to their first inventors, the Gothes or Lumbards, amongst other Reliques of that barbarous Age'.[22] And John Evelyn agreed, relieved that in recent times architecture had been 'newly recovered from its Gotic [sic] barbarity' and bewailing the fact that 'the Goths and Vandals, having demolished the Greek and Roman architecture, introduced in its stead a certain fantastical and licentious manner of building which we have since called modern or Gothic. . . full of fret and lamentable imagery'.[23] *Parentalia* echoes Evelyn's sentiments, speaking contemptuously of Henry VII's Chapel at Westminster with its 'sharp Angles, Jetties, narrow Lights, lame Statues, Lace, and other Cut-work, and Crinkle-crancle'.[24]

Wren was more moderate in his views – Henry VII's Chapel, for instance, was 'a nice embroidered Work'[25] – and while he deplored some later Gothic architecture which 'glut[s] the Eye' with its over-rich ornament and, 'though more elaborated with nice and small workes, yet want[s] the naturall beauty which arises from proportion of the first dimensions',[26] he was much taken with Salisbury. In particular, he was impressed by the fact that the cathedral's designers had shown an almost classical regard for proportion, creating a vault whose height equalled the width of the nave and aisles, making each aisle half the width of the nave and making the lengths of the main transepts and choir transepts equal to the lengths of the nave and choir respectively. He also liked the austere quality of the interior, the restrained use of tracery in the window. 'Our Artist', he told Bishop Ward, 'knew . . . that nothing could add beauty to light, he trusted in a stately and rich Plainnesse'.[27]

All the same, though he admired the visual qualities of the cathedral, his mathematician's eye was quick to condemn structural defects in the design. The low-lying site, praised by the medieval poet Henry of Avranches as a valley filled with lilies, roses, violets and crystal-clear springs of sweet ambrosia, a place which Adam would have preferred to Paradise, was a mistake. The foundations were inadequate for the marshy soil, and the floor was not high enough to prevent it being damaged by floodwaters from the Avon; 'besides it is unhandsome to descend into a place'.[28] But the main problem was the spire. Clambering around in the guts of the tower, Wren concluded (quite rightly) that it had been an afterthought, and that the buttresses, bracing arches and rusting bands of iron employed to transfer the downward pressure of 6400 tons of masonry away from the four 6-foot-square pillars which supported it were inadequate and 'against the Rules of good

Architecture'. Moreover, the spire was bent at the top and also leaning several inches from the perpendicular.

Wren proposed strengthening the timberwork of the tower and containing the spire by means of a 'curbe of iron' made by naval smiths, who were accustomed to forging anchors and other heavy ironwork. He didn't particularly like this latter solution, but it was a 'speedy cure', he said; 'and because the Artist at first hath much trusted to Iron I should advise that this [i.e., the spire] be likewise secured by Iron.'[29] But Seth Ward didn't have the money to act on these recommendations. Mindful of his own status and comforts, he turned his attention instead to the Bishop's Palace in the close, which he had extensively remodelled in 1670–4. Wren maintained his links with Ward and the cathedral, however: he was back visiting Salisbury in 1669, and two years later the joiner Alexander Fort contracted to make new prebends' stalls in the choir and a 'very decent and handsome' seat for the Dean according to Wren's designs. In 1671 Fort also agreed to provide a new bishop's throne for Ward, again according to Wren's 'form and modell'.★

At the end of February 1669 Sir John Denham, recently recovered from his mental breakdown,† was taken ill once again. This time the Surveyor-General's sickness was physical; and although he was only fifty-four, it seemed likely to everyone that he was going to die. According to the terms of his patent, it was up to him to nominate his 'sole lawful and efficient deputy', the man who in all probability would succeed him to the post of Surveyor-General of the King's Works. And apparently there were only two possible candidates.

One was Hugh May, who had already deputized for Denham during his spectacular nervous breakdown in 1666–7, and who had recently been promoted from Paymaster of the Works to Comptroller, the most senior post after the Surveyor, with a salary of £197 14s 2d and responsibility for keeping an eye on the latter's accounting.‡ May had powerful connections: his long-time patron was the Duke of

---

★Wren's furnishings in the choir at Salisbury have all disappeared, swept away in James Wyatt's drastic restoration of 1789. There is no evidence that he was responsible for modernising Ward's Bishop's Palace; the former Cathedral School, completed in 1714 and now known as Wren Hall, is not by him.

†Denham's recovery was hastened by the death of his errant young wife – he was popularly supposed to have fed her poison in a cup of chocolate.

‡Although the move from Paymaster to Comptroller, which took place on 23 June 1668, was certainly a promotion, it wasn't as if May had won the lottery: his salary went up by only £8 11s 4d.

Buckingham, one of Charles II's closest friends and the man who put the B in CABAL. The other contender was John Webb, passed over for the Surveyor's job once, and currently hard at work building a new palace for the King at Greenwich. Roger Pratt, who in other circumstances might also have been in the running, was marginalized by the disgrace of his patron Clarendon.

On 6 March, the ailing Denham nominated Christopher Wren as his deputy. He died two weeks later, and on 29 March Charles II confirmed Wren in the post of Surveyor.

Hugh May was hurt, particularly since it was the Duke of Buckingham who had whispered in Denham's ear that the King wanted Wren rather than the Comptroller for the job. He shared his woe with anyone who would listen, complaining that he had been Buckingham's servant 'in all his wants and dangers, saving him from want of bread by his care and management, and with a promise of having his help in his advancement': now the Duke was 'so ungrateful as to put him by'.[30] He shouldn't perhaps have been so surprised at the harsh treatment: Buckingham was notorious as a rake-hell, a man with 'no principles of religion, virtue, or friendship . . . no steadiness nor conduct'.[31] In any case, he was obviously acting on the King's behalf.

Charles could manage people well when the mood took him, and it was in his interests to keep a talented worker happy. May kept his £197-a-year Comptrollership, and if he was piqued at having to serve under a place-man eleven years his junior, the blow was quickly softened. As soon as the news of Wren's imminent appointment broke, the King awarded him an additional pension of £300 a year as a consolation prize. The next year he was also granted the Surveyorship of the King's Gardens at Whitehall, Hampton Court, St James's and Greenwich, which brought in another £200 a year; and a lucrative sinecure as Clerk of the Recognizances in the Court of Common Pleas and King's Bench. In 1673 he was put in charge of rebuilding work at Windsor Castle, earning fees that amounted to around £500 a year. He might not have got the job he wanted, but he could cry all the way to the bank.

Webb, on the other hand, was beside himself with rage and frustration. He simply could not believe that he, the true heir of Inigo Jones and without doubt the best-qualified architect in the country, had been passed over yet again. He was nearly sixty, and this had been his last realistic chance at royal preferment. What on earth was Charles thinking of? He immediately fired off a petition, but if he was hoping to change the King's mind, he didn't exactly strike the right tone. He

16. The Royal Observatory, Greenwich.
Two telescopes are shown: one on the roof, and a larger instrument on a gantry
in the courtyard.

17. William Sancroft, in 1680
(David Loggan).

18. Gilbert Sheldon, *c.* 1665
(studio of Sir Peter Lely).

19. St Paul's Cathedral: the First Model. 'Wholly different from that of all the Cathedrals of the whole Worlde.'

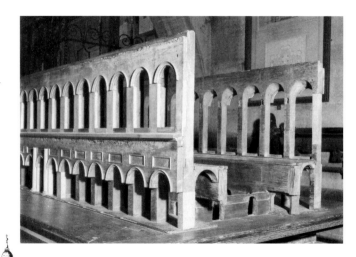

20. St Paul's Cathedral: the Greek Cross Design, shown from the west.

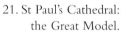

21. St Paul's Cathedral: the Great Model.

(*Left*) 22. St Paul's Cathedral: the Warrant Design.

(*Below*) 23. St Paul's Cathedral: the so-called 'Definitive' Design.

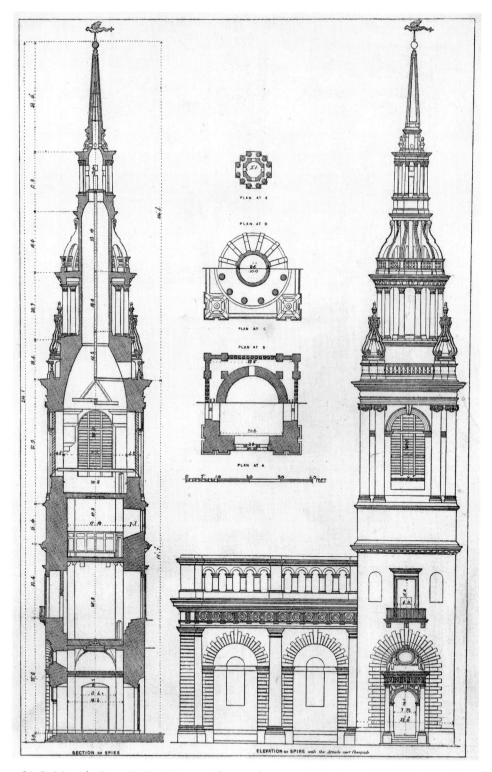

PLAN AT E

PLAN AT D

PLAN AT C

PLAN AT B

PLAN AT A

SECTION OF SPIRE

ELEVATION OF SPIRE *with the Arcade next Cheapside*

24. St Mary-le-Bow (1670–80): part of a set of measured drawings of the City churches made by John Clayton and published in 1848.

25. St Mary Abchurch (1681–6),
with Grinling Gibbons' altarpiece.

26. Almost certainly designed by Robert Hooke,
St Martin Ludgate (1677–86) shows the influence
of contemporary Dutch design.

27. St James Piccadilly
(1676–84) was one of
Wren's favourite churches.
He recalled it in later life
as both 'beautiful and
convenient'.

28. St Stephen Walbrook (1672–80): 'Italy itself can produce no modern Building that can vie with this, in Taste or Proportion.'

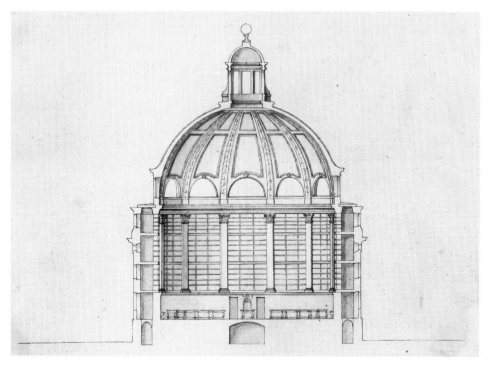

29. Wren's first scheme for the library at Trinity College, Cambridge.

30. Trinity College: the library as executed, seen from Nevile's Court.

31. Wren's design for Charles I's mausoleum, intended to stand at the east end of St George's Chapel, Windsor.

32. The inside elevation of Tom Tower, Christ Church, Oxford.

33. Winchester Palace: a late eighteenth-century engraving showing a conjectural view of the building 'as intended to have been finish'd by Sir Christopher Wren'.

had been promised the Surveyorship, he said, and though he had grudgingly accepted having to work under Denham, who was at least 'a person of honour', there was no way he was going to continue if Wren was in charge. It was 'much beneath him' to serve a man 'who in whatever respects is his inferiour by farr', a man who 'professeth to bee wholy ignorant' of the Office of Works.[32] Charles must reconsider: if he wouldn't give Webb the Surveyorship outright, then couldn't he turn it into a joint post, so that the older man could instruct the younger? And as if questioning the King's judgement in such an uncompromising fashion weren't enough, he also took the opportunity to point out that the Crown owed him money for work done on Greenwich Palace.

This didn't go down well. In fact the King completely ignored Webb's pleading, and the architect retired to Somerset where he died, bitter and disappointed, in 1672.

The post he so conspicuously failed to obtain carried with it a respectable salary of £382 5s 8d, and a rent-free house with its own gardens, coach-house and adjoining office in Scotland Yard, only a hundred yards or so from the King's privy lodgings at Whitehall. There was also another official residence at Hampton Court. But it was the power and the prestige which really appealed to Wren. The Surveyor was the King's architect, responsible for maintaining the fabric of all the royal palaces. Chief among these was Whitehall. (For a plan of the palace, see Figure 5, page 282.) In the 140 years since Henry VIII had seized the medieval palace of the Archbishops of York from the hapless Cardinal Wolsey, it had grown until it covered a huge area, from St James's Park down to the Thames, and from Elizabeth I's bowling green in the south, close to the Houses of Parliament, over to Charing Cross and the labyrinth of lodgings, offices, storerooms and courts piled high with building materials in Scotland Yard itself. This warren of buildings with its battlements and towers dominated the Thames skyline for more than a quarter of a mile. The Street, part of the public road from Westminster to Charing Cross, ran through it, protected by two Tudor gatehouses – the Holbein Gate to the north and the King's Street Gate to the south – both of which carried galleries connecting the two sections of the palace. This road broadened out above the Holbein Gate into the thoroughfare known as Whitehall, running past the west front of Inigo Jones's Banqueting House, Palace Gate – the main entrance to the complex – and Scotland Yard, which lay at its northern end. The area furthest from the Thames, on the western side of the Street and Whitehall, had originally served as Henry VIII's playground, containing a tiltyard, cockpit, bowling alley and four tennis courts, but most of it had since been converted into apartments which were currently assigned to the Duke of Ormonde and the Duke of Monmouth, among others. The tiltyard was built over with quarters for the Horse Guards.

A wall ran along the eastern side of the Street, and behind it lay the Privy Garden, a formal area planted with trees, roses and statuary. The garden was bounded on the east by an assortment of lodgings and galleries leading down to the Thames, where the King and Queen and the Duke and Duchess of York had their apartments; and on the north by an irregular range of offices. Further north again lay the Pebble Court, with the east front of the Banqueting House to the left and the Tudor core of the palace, including the Great Hall and the Chapel Royal, to the right. Then came the kitchens and larders, butteries and pantries, the King's Herb House and Wine Cellar; yet more lodgings, for minor courtiers and household officials; and finally Scotland Yard, with its own Thameside dock for bringing in building materials. Wren's office, house and garden stood in the south-west corner, looking on to Whitehall.

The other royal palaces were Henry VIII's St James's, where Mary Tudor died with 'Calais' lying in her heart, and where both Charles II and the Duke of York had been born; Hampton Court, another of Henry's acquisitions from Cardinal Wolsey; and Webb's half-completed Greenwich.★ Then there were other Crown buildings, both great and small: Somerset House, which had been Henrietta Maria's dower-house and now belonged to Catherine of Braganza; the Palace of Westminster; the Custom House between the Tower and London Bridge, which had burned to the ground during the Fire, and which Denham had begun to rebuild; the Savoy Hospital, founded by Henry VII for charitable purposes but currently used as army barracks, private tenements and a refuge for debtors on the run from the bailiffs; and royal hunting lodges at Newmarket in Suffolk and in the New Forest. The care of all these buildings lay with the Office of Works, along with responsibility for most of the theatricals that went hand in hand with royal occasions. The Works decked out biers and coffins for state funerals in Westminster Abbey, created the necessary settings for coronations, and even fitted up the temporary seating when a peer of the realm stood trial in Westminster Hall.

★Of the other two major royal buildings, Windsor Castle had its own Office of Works, and the Tower of London came under the jurisdiction of the Office of the Ordnance.

This called for a degree of political and administrative competence that went way beyond Wren's previous managerial experience, which up to now had been confined to supervising a couple of one-off building projects. A large body of officials and craftsmen were involved, all of them answerable to the Surveyor. There was the disappointed but rich Comptroller, Hugh May, whose job it was to fix the workmen's rates for a particular job, to check the bills when they came in and make sure they agreed with the rate, and to check contracts so that it was clear from the outset 'in what manner the work is to be done, what scantlings the Timbers shalbee of, what thickness the walls, withall particular circumstances incident to the respective trade, and in what time it is to bee finished'.[33] The Paymaster, Philip Packer, was in charge of the cash and, true to the spirit of his age, managed it so prudently that he was able to build himself a country house on the proceeds. Edward Marshall and Richard Ryder held the offices of Master Mason and Master Carpenter respectively. All of these men (except for Packer) sat on the Board of Works with Wren, and all (again, except for Packer) had official houses near his own in Scotland Yard. Other artisans by royal patent included the Master Joiner, Plasterer, Glazier, Sculptor and Blacksmith, and the Sergeant Painter and Sergeant Plumber, and there were also full-time Clerks of Works for each of the royal buildings.

Most officers of the Works exploited their royal connections and did jobs on the side. When Wren took over the Surveyorship, for instance, Robert Streater was busy completing the ceiling for the Sheldonian, and Hugh May had just finished building Burlington House, Piccadilly, for the 1st Earl of Burlington. Moonlighting was perfectly acceptable – in fact the main reason why official positions in the King's Works were so eagerly sought after was the opportunity they provided for advertising one's skills among the great and the good. In theory the Crown always had first call on a craftsman's time and energy, but in practice official duties often took second place to high-paying private commissions, and a good Surveyor-General had to manage potential conflicts of interest and absentee workers.

The pilfering of materials, both from Scotland Yard and from actual building sites, was another constant problem. So was the payment of wages – there was often no money in the kitty, and both contractors and day-labourers had to make do with 'tickets', or promises to pay. So was the practice of turning a blind eye to royal priorities and prerogatives: one of Wren's first acts as Surveyor was to persuade the Secretary of State for the South, Lord Arlington, to issue an edict banning the movement of stone from the royal quarries at Portland unless he had checked that it was for use on either one of the King's houses or on St Paul's. Then there was constant pressure from important and not so important courtiers who wanted improvements made to their grace-and-favour lodgings. The rule was that essential repairs were the responsibility of the Crown, and hence the Surveyor-General's office; but that non-essential work – the installation of a fashionable new chimneypiece, perhaps, or other cosmetic alterations – was down to the occupant. And unless the King had given his prior approval, that occupant had to pay. In practice, members of the court and other hangers-on were constantly pressing the Surveyor to carry out non-essential work on their own quarters, so much so that Pepys reckoned Hugh May had been lucky to miss the Surveyorship, since it was 'a place that disobliges most people, being not able to do what they desire to their lodgings'.[34] A great deal of tact and diplomacy was required to reject a command from a minor official for anything from a new doorcase to a complete refit without making an enemy of him.

So why did Wren do it? Why did he take on a complex administrative post which went far beyond the business of designing buildings? And how come it was offered to him, rather than May or Webb?

Problems notwithstanding, the 'why' is easily explained by the status, the money, the official residences, the validation of Wren's architectural skills and the fulfilment of his architectural dreams. Anyone with his aspirations and ambitions would be out of his mind to turn down a chance like this. (However, he prudently decided to keep his Oxford chair, paying a deputy to substitute for him; so if the worst came to the worst and he found he didn't like the job, or it didn't like him, he could always go back to academia. He finally resigned the Savilian Professorship in the spring of 1673.) At a deeper level, the Surveyorship offered a wonderful outlet for that drive to impose order on chaos which had led him first into the mathematical sciences, and then to architecture and the Sheldonian, St Paul's, the ambitious plans for a new London. For Wren, buildings were always ideas made real, theories put into practice, public demonstrations of problems solved and obstacles overcome. There were few buildings in England more public than the King's palaces.

At first glance, the question of how an astronomy professor came to be offered the most influential architectural post in the country seems harder to answer, and we'll probably never know the precise sequence of events which led to his appointment. Partly, of course, it was because he knew the right people. King Charles already knew and liked him, but in any case by the spring of 1669 he had built up an impressive network of influential contacts. His reputation among the members of the Royal Society was considerable, and some of those members had the ear of the King. Of the men who had founded the Society after that lecture of Wren's at Gresham back in 1660, Sir Robert Moray was a Privy Councillor, a Commissioner for Scotland and now one of Charles's most trusted courtiers, with coveted lodgings (albeit rather small ones) looking on to the Privy Garden at Whitehall. Sir Paul Neile, one of Wren's most devoted disciples, was another member of the royal household; his own Whitehall apartment stood at the entrance to Scotland Yard, just a few feet from the Surveyor-General's house. And John Evelyn, who thought Wren 'a wonderful genius [and] an incomparable person' was enough of an intimate for the King to feed him a piece of 'that rare fruit call'd the King-pine' (a pineapple) from his own plate at a state banquet.[35] Then there were the connections in the Church, particularly Archbishop Sheldon and Bishop Henchman. Both had good reasons of their own for advancing Wren's cause as an architect, in the shape of St Paul's – and both, interestingly enough, were also Fellows of the Royal Society, although they played no part in its proceedings.

So there was no shortage of friends in high places to plead Wren's case over the heads of less well-connected rivals. But to suggest that influence alone gained him the Surveyor's post is to sell him short. He was already respected at court as the gifted designer of the revolutionary new theatre at Oxford and a more than competent Commissioner for the rebuilding of London. In fact, outside the immediate circle of the Royal Society, Wren was probably better known as an architect than as a mathematical scientist or astronomer. He was also de facto architect to St Paul's. And it no doubt suited Charles that a figure who was already playing a pivotal role in the reconstruction of both the capital and its major landmark should be a man who was publicly endorsed by and politically bound to the Crown.

10

The Honour of the Nation

*T*he Surveyor didn't waste any time launching into his new role. The order regulating the transport of Portland stone went out on 4 May, just over five weeks after Wren had been confirmed in the post; and on 11 May, he was at a meeting of the Treasury, saying that Denham's scheme for the new Custom House on Thames Street simply wouldn't do. This was either a courageous move or a foolish one, depending on your point of view. Charles II had singled out the rebuilding of the Custom House as a priority back in September 1666, and both the Crown and the City were desperate to move their tax-farmers back to the waterfront, for fear that the inconvenience of their temporary accommodation in Mark Lane, several hundred yards back from the river, would lead to a fall in revenues and a decline in the Port of London's international status. But negotiations over who was actually responsible for the rebuilding had dragged on for two and a half years, and it was only in February 1669 that the Treasury had finally been persuaded to grant £6000 towards the project. The Chief Clerk of the King's Works, William Dickinson, who was also at the meeting, clearly thought that his new boss hadn't quite got to grips with the financial realities: any alterations to the agreed scheme would cost money, he said, and that meant further delays.

Wren was given twenty-four hours to produce a detailed proposal of his own. Characteristically, he did; and although his plan has not survived, it obviously impressed the Lords of the Treasury, since on 25 May they agreed to a further grant of £3000 and issued a warrant to build the Custom House 'after Mr Wrenns Modell'.[1]

Finished by the summer of 1671, the Custom House was Wren's first building as Surveyor-General, his first in London, and only his fourth to be completed. It was heavily remodelled in the early eighteenth century (after suffering damage when a nearby house used for storing gun-powder exploded), and then destroyed by fire in the early nineteenth, so its appearance is known to us only from a handful of engravings. They show a grand two-storeyed façade of brick with stone dressings, facing the Thames but set well back from the river across a bustling court scattered with piles of goods. Covered storage and unloading bays were provided in two projecting wings (called 'pavilions' in the building accounts) which were open on the ground floor and supported by arcades of uneasily-spaced Tuscan columns with an Ionic order above. The centre of the main block and the ends of the two pavilions had pedimented temple-fronts, while Wren used segmental pediments to either side of the centrepiece to denote wide carriage-ways into the warehouse which occupied the ground floor. The space above was taken up with a single 'Great Room' where the Commissioners of Customs examined the goods, and there were various offices, including a Searchers' Room, a Secretary's Room and a Treasury Chamber, in the upper parts of the pavilions. The overall effect is vaguely – *very* vaguely – like a mid-century arcaded Dutch weigh-house, and this has led to speculation that Wren may either have spent time in the Netherlands – which he didn't – or have modified and extended a design by Hugh May, who did, when he was in the service of the Duke of Buckingham in the 1650s. It is more likely that Wren took inspiration from printed sources, something he learned to do when he was in Paris and brought back 'almost all France in paper', and continued to practise throughout his career. He wanted to make his mark with his first building as Surveyor, and tinkering with a subordinate's designs was not his way, no matter how far advanced those designs might be.

Encouraged by his worldly success, the prestigious post, the house in Scotland Yard, Wren decided that he needed a wife to go with them. His choice was Faith Coghill, his childhood neighbour from the days when he was growing up at William Holder's Bletchingdon rectory. After a courtship which for all we know may have lasted weeks, months or decades, the couple were married on 7 December 1669 at the Temple Church of St Mary, just off Fleet Street.

Faith is a mystery. No likeness of her survives, although Hooke records going to view her picture 'at Monr Caskades in Leicester fields' in July 1675.[2] She was thirty-three in 1669, rather old for a time when, on average, daughters of squires married at twenty. This may have been due to her family's finances rather than her looks: in 1656 her parents were forced to sell up their 'Greate House' at Bletchingdon and move to a smaller yeoman farmstead, Old House, which stood next door to the church, so perhaps the dowry that a suitor had the right to expect wasn't forthcoming. There seem to have been some family problems, too. Sir Thomas died three years after the move, cutting his oldest son out of his will and leaving his property first to his wife, and then to his two younger sons. (Nevertheless, the oldest boy somehow managed to sidestep the will: he inherited anyway.)

If we know little of Faith's background, we know even less of her relationship with Wren, their courtship, their feelings for each other, whether or not they were happy together. All that survives is a single, rather touching letter from her husband-to-be, which is dated only 14 June with no year given, but which was surely written in the summer of 1669. Faith had accidentally dropped her pocket-watch in some water, and Wren had arranged to have it repaired, presumably through one of his Royal Society contacts. He returned it with a note:

Madam

The Artificer having never before mett with a drowned watch; like an ignorant physician has been soe long about the cure, that he hath made me very unquiet that your commands should be soe long deferred; however, I have sent the watch at last & envie the felicity of it, that it should be soe neer your side & soe often enjoy your Eye, & be consulted by you how your Time shall passe while you employ your hand in your excellent workes. But have a care of it, for I have put such a Spell into it; that every Beating of the Ballance will tell you 'tis the pulse of my Heart, which labours as much to serve you and more trewly than the Watch; for the Watch I beleeve will sometimes lie, and sometimes perhaps be idle & unwilling to goe, having received much injury by being drenched in that briny bath, that I dispair it should ever be a trew servant to you more: But as for me (unless you drown me too in my teares) you may be confident I shall never cease to be

Your most affectionate humble servant
Chr Wren

I have put the watch in a Box that it might take no harme, & wrapt it about with a little Leather, & that it might not jog, I was faine to fill up the corners with either a few shavings or wast paper.[3]

The courtly and elegant style, the elaborate metaphors, the formal mode of address, are all representative of the age. Analogies drawn from medicine – 'like an ignorant physician' – feature elsewhere in Wren's writings: in his correspondence with Dean Sancroft over St Paul's, for example, he justified the attempt to keep up the west end of the old cathedral as 'the rationall attempt of a Physician in a desperate disease', the true causes of which could only be known 'by the anatomist after the dissolution'.[4] And the practical, commonsensical postscript that comes as something of an anti-climax after all the high-flown sentiment is typical of the man.

Yet the tenderness which underlies the convoluted conceit of the beating watch, the gentle passion – a contradiction in terms, I know, but I can't think how else to characterize it – reassure me as much as they must have charmed and reassured Faith Coghill. The couple would be married for less than six years before Faith's death from smallpox in September 1675, still only in her thirties. The public face of Wren during those years is that of a man who was above all businesslike, hard, totally preoccupied with his own schemes and ambitions. But the chance survival of that solitary letter reminds us of a more human side to him; reminds us, again, that we should be wary of jumping to conclusions about a private life based on the evidence of a public persona. I do hope they were happy together.

However else Wren spent the first months of his marriage, a significant part of his time was employed in producing designs for St Paul's. His initial scheme, usually known as the First Model, was an innovative attempt to meet the brief set out by the cathedral authorities, and quite unlike any building the Anglican Church had ever seen. Our knowledge of it is sketchy, coming as it does from a detail drawing, a fragment of a wooden model and a hurried and critical eye-witness description by Pratt. It consisted of a rectangular block about 70 feet wide and 180 feet long, with no transepts and nothing to distinguish nave from choir. This was joined at its west end to a domed vestibule – throughout its long and convoluted design stages, a dome was the one feature that Wren insisted on including – with entrance porticos to the north, south and west.

Bishop Matthew must have turned in his Laudian grave. The new cathedral would have been small – about the same length as Bristol or St David's, and tiny in comparison with Winchester, York, Ely or Salisbury. The notion of a single auditory was strange, and in no way in keeping with contemporary liturgical practice which, in cathedrals at least, still demanded some symbolic and architectural degree of separation between clergy and congregation; it only makes sense if we remember Sancroft's request for 'the design of a Quire, at least, as may be a congruous Part of a greater and more magnificent Work to follow', and think of the First Model as a first step to something much grander.

What made the First Model even weirder was Wren's decision to turn the conventional choir of a cathedral inside out. The vaulted aisles one would expect to find on the north and south sides of a medieval English cathedral became two exterior Ionic colonnades, exposed to the elements but supporting above them interior galleries lit by round-arched windows interspersed with Corinthian pilasters. The view from the domed vestibule to the east end thus opened out in a T-section. The interior widened as the eye rose upwards, an inversion of the usual Gothic arrangement with its sense of tapering closure. At divine service Sancroft and his fellow clergy would have taken an unusually narrow processional route from the vestibule, where they would gather, to the high altar; the broad space above them became a metaphor for the heavens.

This was a daring experiment, which is sometimes justified as an attempt to cast the money-lenders out of the temple by giving the hawkers, vendors and playing children who used to hang around in the nave of Old St Paul's some shelter outside the sacred precincts of the building proper.[5] But one can't help feeling that Wren was playing around with structural possibilities. Never one to be bound by tradition, he wanted to try something different, something new.

The First Model design was completed in the winter of 1669/70, and the wooden model itself, made by the joiner William Cleere, was taken to the Palace of Whitehall for the King's inspection. It remained there for two years before being returned to St Paul's and set up in Wren's office in the Convocation House, where anyone who hadn't had the chance to view it at Whitehall might examine it.

Roger Pratt was one of those who saw the First Model on its return – and he hated it. No surprises there. In July 1673 he spent fifteen minutes taking a 'shorte and confused vewe' of both Wren's drawings and Cleere's model. But that was enough for him to decide that the fenestration was clumsy and inadequate, the placing of the dome over the west end 'most causelessly and ungracefully' shortened the nave, the decision to turn the two side aisles into external loggias was pointless, and the absence of transepts was perverse, making the building 'wholly different from that of all the Cathedrals of the whole Worlde . . . all others besides, in the form of a Cross either more or lesse'.[6]

Pratt, once the leading light of English architecture, no longer counted for much among London's decision-makers: he had *never* counted for much, as far as Wren was concerned. He was out of touch with the latest news – so out of touch, in fact, that he failed to realize the First Model had already been discarded. Events had overtaken Wren's design almost as soon as it was presented for the King's inspection. On 1 May 1670, a second Rebuilding Act came into effect, trebling the coal tax to three shillings per chaldron and extending it for an additional ten years, until September 1687. Most important of all, half the tax was to go on rebuilding the City's churches, with a quarter of that sum – 4½d per chaldron – earmarked specifically for St Paul's.

As we shall see, this was still nothing like enough. By the time the three-shilling duty was wound up and the accounts closed in March 1688, the cathedral had received £88,489; the eventual cost of the building work, excluding fittings, furnishings and clearing the site, was more than eight times that amount. At a massive £722,779, it came to twice the cost of all the fifty-six new City churches put together.

But the welcome news of the increased coal dues had been enough to make Sancroft and the cathedral authorities think again. As it was, the First Model was a compromise, and Pratt was not the only critic. Although *Parentalia* claimed that it was praised 'by Persons of good Understanding', others shared Pratt's view that it was too unconventional, too much of a departure from the traditional Gothic cathedral that the English were accustomed to. And, to quote *Parentalia* again, others 'observed it was not stately enough, and contended, that for the Honour of the Nation, and City of London, it ought not to be exceeded in Magnificence, by any Church in Europe'.[7]

So during 1671 Wren got down to work for a second time – a third, in fact, if we include his pre-Fire designs. He was still determined to create a cathedral which broke with medieval tradition and stated its allegiance to the Renaissance and 'the best Stile of the Greek and Roman architecture';[8] but if it was big enough and grand enough, he hoped it would confound his conservative critics while earning the support of the cognoscenti.

He sketched out ideas which he showed to friends – including, one imagines, Hooke and Evelyn. A selection of the best were presented to King Charles for his approval, and the design that the King liked best, and that Wren duly worked up into a more detailed scheme over the winter of 1671/2, was quite simply a marvel. Totally alien to these shores, it was much more sophisticated, both visually and structurally, than anything Wren had produced to date. Indeed, at the end of his life he thought it the best thing he did in his entire career. He was right.

The building was quite unlike anything seen in Britain before. A round central space more than 120 feet in diameter had four stubby arms of equal length projecting out to north, south, east and west. The sloping sides of the octagon thus formed were concave, so that in plan the cathedral looked like a Greek cross. And, inevitably, the central space was crowned with a monumental dome, supported on a ring of eight pillars. The basic conception owes a lot to the Bourbon Chapel that Colbert and François Mansart planned for Saint-Denis in the early 1660s, although there the arms were also domed, and the spaces between them filled with small chapels; it was never built, but the design was almost certainly being discussed in the circles in which Wren moved during his stay in Paris. He may also have seen a study by Inigo Jones for a cathedral which has a number of affinities with the Greek Cross design: the central domed space; the way in which the building is raised on a continuous high plinth; and the use of a Corinthian order for everything, including the pedimented entrance and the pilasters which punctuate the fenestration. Other borrowings can be traced back to Bramante's centralized plan for St Peter's, Rome, and Michelangelo's proposals for a high, ribbed dome to crown it.

But the Greek Cross design is much more than an amalgam of borrowings, the sort of book-learned architectural dabbling that any educated English gentlemen might engage in in the later seventeenth century. It shows Wren growing in confidence, becoming a master of spatial awareness, using his knowledge of geometry and the possibilities inherent in a given structure to create something much greater than the sum of its parts. In fact it is hard to think of the Greek Cross design as a collection of parts: structurally and aesthetically it forms an indivisible whole.

The Surveyor-General was paid £100 for his drawings early in 1672. But progress was still slow. War with the Dutch broke out again that March, giving Charles II matters of greater moment than new cathedrals to think about. And, inevitably, the coal dues were affected by the outbreak of hostilities. The share allotted to St Paul's fell proportionately, from £4496 in 1671 to £3295 the following year, and £3048 the year after that.

Nearly six years had passed since the Fire; and there was still no prospect of beginning the building work. Far from it, in fact: the workers were finding the task of clearing the site more and more difficult. Steadfastly refusing to yield to pick-axes and hammers, the immensely thick walls and pillars were subjected to pounding with hand-held rams – but to little effect. The four pillars of the crossing-tower, each of them fourteen feet across, were particularly stubborn; and with work almost at a standstill, Wren eventually hit on the idea of blowing them up with gunpowder. Early in 1672 he brought in a gunner from the Tower of London and, together, the two men ordered the labourers to dig a trench beside the north-west pillar and hack out a recess some two feet square at foundation level. A deal box filled with eighteen pounds of gunpowder and fitted with a long fuse was slipped into the recess; the trench was filled in with stone and mortar; and a train of powder laid along the ground from the projecting fuse to a spot a safe distance away. Then the train was lit.

The inhabitants of St Paul's Churchyard thought that there had been an earthquake. The whole north-west angle of the tower, along with two arches that rested on it and parts of the adjoining aisles – some 3000 tons of masonry, according to one estimate – lifted 'somewhat leisurely' about nine inches into the air, and then fell with a gigantic, muted thump.[9] A single match had managed to achieve in a matter of seconds something which would have taken the workforce of nearly seventy labourers months, if not years.

Wren was delighted, and decided to extend his experiment to blow up the north-east and south-west angles of the tower. But this time things didn't go quite so smoothly. According to *Parentalia*, the Surveyor was out of town on the King's business when the next explosion was scheduled to take place, leaving Edward Woodroffe to supervise the operation – and to determine the amount of gunpowder to pack into the breach. Woodroffe over-estimated, as a group of women sitting in the upstairs room of a nearby bookseller's found out in a spectacular fashion: a large chunk of masonry flew across the Churchyard, came straight through their balcony door and landed at their feet. A joiner was promptly packed off to repair the damage, but the local population was in fear of its life. Representations were made to Dean Sancroft, and Wren was told in no uncertain terms that there were to be no more explosions.

Undaunted, he turned to a demolition device which was at once both traditional and novel. The battering-ram has a long history, dating back to Ezekiel and the Siege of Jerusalem. The Greeks used it; the Romans perfected it; and there are stories of rams as long as 180 feet, with heads weighing 1.5 tons, being used in ancient siege warfare. The ram Wren designed for St Paul's was rather more modest, although it was still pretty damn big, measuring forty feet in length with a reinforced iron spike at the business end, and needing thirty men to swing it from a frame consisting of two triangular gantries. But it did the trick, although not so dramatically as the gunner's mines – it took two days of constant pounding to demolish a wall (and cracked at least one skull, when a rope suspending the ram broke and crushed a man's head beneath the mast). But Wren the classicist found a particular satisfaction in resurrecting an engine 'of so great Service to the Ancients'.[10]

With clearance work still progressing, the King finally approved the Greek Cross design, and over the winter of 1672/3 Wren worked on the details, extending the western arm of the cross to accommodate a library vestibule beneath a second, much smaller dome, adding an imposing entrance portico and creating burial vaults with separate access, 'that the Pavement above might be preserved'.[11] (The disturbance of stone paving in churches and cathedrals to allow the interment of local dignitaries was a constant source of annoyance in the seventeenth century, and often led to subsidence and dangerously uneven flooring.) On 12 November 1673 a warrant announced the appointment of a Royal Commission for the Rebuilding of the Cathedral Church of St Paul, as impressive a collection of the great and the good as you could wish for. The Church of England was represented by Dean Sancroft and three residentiary canons of the Chapter of St Paul's, Sheldon as Archbishop of Canterbury, the Archbishop of York and a bevy of bishops – Henchman for London, plus the Bishops of Winchester, Oxford, Ely and Rochester. The Lord Chancellor, the Earl of Shaftesbury, was there for the Crown, along with the Lord Treasurer, Thomas, Lord Clifford, the two Secretaries of State, Lord Arlington and Henry Coventry – and of course the Surveyor-General of the King's Works. The City had the Lord Mayor, the City Chamberlain, the Recorder of London and various aldermen. And in addition, there was an awesomely long list of privy councillors, judges, officers of the royal household and other worthies. Anticipating that few of these important figures would actually turn up for meetings to discuss the building of the cathedral, the warrant laid down a quorum of six, provided that either Dean Sancroft or Bishop Henchman was present.

The Commission was empowered to dismantle what was left of Old St Paul's, to engage all the craftsmen necessary for the new cathedral, and to issue a nationwide appeal for contributions to the building fund. The King himself promised £1000 a year towards the project (although he never actually paid it); and optimistically trusted 'that the piety and charity of our good subjects will eminently appear by their frequent and liberal contributions to so honourable and pious a design'.[12]

By the terms of the warrant, Wren was finally appointed as official architect to St Paul's, with Charles stating his preference for the modified Greek Cross design, better known to posterity as the Great Model:

> We have caused several designs . . . to be prepared by Dr Christopher Wren, Surveyor General of all our Works and Buildings, which we have seen and one of which we do more especially approve and have commanded a model thereof to be made after so large and exact a manner that it may remain as a perpetual and unchangeable rule and direction for the conduct of the whole work.[13]

At last, nearly seven and a half years after the Fire, Wren's revolutionary new cathedral was about to be built. And at five o'clock in the morning of Friday 14 November, two days after the warrant was issued, the King summoned him suddenly to his candle-lit chamber at Whitehall. Later that day Robert Hooke sat down in his own lodgings at Gresham College and wrote a terse little entry in his diary: 'Dr Wren knighted and gone to Oxford.'[14]

The knighthood was a satisfying and well-earned acknowledgement of the part Wren had played and continued to play in the rebuilding of London. And he lost no time in finding out how his new rank might help him in the public arena. Only a few days earlier the Attorney-General, Sir Heneage Finch, had been appointed Lord Keeper of the Great Seal, leaving his Oxford University constituency in need of a new MP. Wren had harboured ambitions to enter Parliament for some time – in the spring of 1667 he stood for Cambridge University, losing by just six votes – and his swift departure for Oxford within hours of the early morning audience with the King was apparently in order to get his campaign under way as quickly as possible. He moved so fast that one wonders if Charles himself didn't suggest the idea to him.

On the face of it, Sir Christopher's candidacy had everything going for it: royal patronage, a distinguished academic and architectural record at Oxford, the support of several college heads. But as he lobbied his friends and acquaintances, Wren didn't reckon with the more worldly tactics of his rival for the seat. Thomas Thynne, 'a person now much against the King's interest in Parliament',[15] was Finch's son-in-law. More importantly, he had deep pockets and a thorough understanding of what it took to win an election; and for a week or more in the lead-up to the ballot he plied voters with an impressive supply of free food and drink. As Anthony Wood reported with regret, Wren 'was not so expert this way';[16] and when it came to election day on 16 January 1674, Thynne took the seat by 203 votes to 125.

Wren had much better luck with another bid for fame which also seems to have been prompted by the knighthood. According to his son, in around 1673 he commissioned a marble bust of himself. Given the timing, it is hard not to see this as a celebration of his new status.[17]

The bust, by Edward Pierce, is the earliest of several likenesses made of the Surveyor during his lifetime. Sir Godfrey Kneller's three-quarter-length portrait, for example, which was painted in 1711, shows a stiff, slightly apprehensive figure with ruddy cheeks, a prominent beaked nose and a peruke of curls perched high on his head and flowing down over his shoulders. He wears a plain white cravat and a velvet jacket decorated with gold braid and buttons; and his right hand, which holds a pair of compasses in long, artist's fingers, rests on a table draped with the plan of St Paul's. Adopting a low viewpoint which effectively disguises his subject's low stature, Kneller shows us a successful courtier, proud of his architectural achievements yet becomingly modest, even slightly uneasy with the whole business of having his picture painted.

Another likeness, now hanging in the Sheldonian Theatre, was the work of no fewer than three artists. Begun by Antonio Verrio and finished after his death in 1707 by Kneller and Sir James Thornhill, it shares striking similarities with the portrait painted by Kneller alone – the same high wig, the same white cravat, even the same velvet and gold jacket (which suggests either that Wren was inordinately fond of it or that one painting drew heavily on the other). But the face itself is much younger and bland, almost expressionless. Wren is surrounded by emblems of his interests and accomplishments. He sits in the midst of books and drawing instruments, holding another plan of St Paul's in his left hand, and with his right he points to a large celestial globe – at once both architect and astronomer. A telescope and *that* lunar globe lie at his feet, along with an engraving of the Sheldonian Theatre, while the background is dominated by a view across the Thames to a London skyline in which St Paul's and the City churches figure prominently.

Both portraits are revealing in their way. But in both, Wren contrives to keep his distance – and this is revealing in itself, of course. He invites us to admire him, to show respect for what he has done with his life – the buildings, the discoveries. But we have no sense of him as a witty companion or a friend. We don't know him as a human being, we don't have any inkling of what goes on behind those dark eyes.

The marble bust, now in the Ashmolean Museum, Oxford, is in a different league. Edward Pierce was highly regarded in his day as a sculptor and decorative carver and, as we shall see, he also ran a successful business as a mason-contractor. Until he fell out with Wren over money matters in the 1680s, his team was employed at St Paul's and four of the City churches. His other portraits, the best of which are busts of John Milton and Oliver Cromwell, are competent enough; but he excelled himself with the newly knighted Surveyor, inviting comparison with Bernini's famous sculpture of Louis XIV at Versailles (which Wren saw in its unfinished state in Paris), and producing a piece of work which has been hailed as the finest English sculpture of the seventeenth century. His sitter's shoulders are wrapped in loose drapery and his natural flowing curls, much more appealing than a high-perched wig, fall down nonchalantly over them. Wren's head is turned slightly to one side as he gazes off into the distance – not, this time, through any reluctance to engage with us, but because he sees things that we do not see, he understands more than we can ever hope to understand. Yet the bust shows no trace of hauteur or intellectual arrogance. There is wit and kindness in the hooded eyes and wry humour in the slightly rueful smile. This is the face of a man you would give a great deal to know.

At St Paul's, attention during the spring and summer of 1674 was focused on the model which Charles II's warrant had ordered 'as a perpetual and unchangeable rule and direction for the conduct of the whole work'. This was a massive undertaking, as monumental in its own way as the cathedral itself. Wren had decided it should be built to a scale of one inch to one-and-a-half feet, making it six yards long and big enough for a man to walk through without stooping. From the point when Wren and Edward Woodroffe began work in the Convocation House 'drawing the Lines of ye Designe of the church upon ye Table there, for ye Joyner's Directions'[18] in September 1673 – two months before the royal warrant was issued and the Rebuilding Commission set up – every care was taken to create as accurate and detailed a replica of the finished work as it was possible to conceive. A team of joiners put in over 2230 man-hours on the model, which eventually cost more than £600. The great dome was plastered by the King's Master Plasterer, John Grove; and the floor beneath was constructed so it could be lowered by lines on brass pulleys, enabling visitors to stand inside and admire the design. The carver Richard Cleere made 907 ornaments, including 78 pilasters for the exterior (at 3s 9d a piece), festoons and cartouches, cherubims' heads and a figure of St Paul; and Robert Streater, the Sergeant Painter, painted the walls a stone colour inside and out, coloured the roof to simulate lead and gilded the detailing.

Already in February 1674, when Hooke walked through the bare bones of the model at the Convocation House, it was an impressive sight. As it neared completion that summer, protected from the sun by calico curtains hung specially for the purpose, Wren must have grown more and more excited. He started to stake out the ground at the east end of the site, and looked forward to the following season when work could finally begin on laying the cathedral's foundations. By October the Great Model, one of the wonders of the capital and an awesome token of what was to come, was finished.

The Commissioners decided they didn't like it.

You'd think it was a little late for anyone to be having second thoughts about the project. But as far as the Commission was concerned, they were first thoughts. The Great Model design may have been passed by the King, Archbishop Sheldon and Dean Sancroft – but that was months before the Commission was set up. Although its remit was for building the cathedral 'according to the design and model'[19] previously agreed, after a settling-in period several of its members were now starting to flex their muscles and question the wisdom of a centralized plan. Chief among them were the three residentiaries. Edward Layfield, Francis Turner and Edward Stillingfleet saw the new cathedral in a different light from the lay members of the Commission: to them, St Paul's was a working building rather than a monument, and use came before aesthetics. How long would it take to complete the new cathedral? When could services begin? Wasn't the whole idea rather foreign, rather Popish, rather too unconventional – especially at a time when continuing tradition played such a vital role in re-establishing church unity?

They had a point. The Great Model design was uncompromisingly modern, for England, at least; and the cultural references it made towards the High Renaissance inevitably invited comparison with Catholic Europe. It marked a decisive, even unsettling break from the comfortable Gothic-cake-with-classical-icing with which the clergy were familar. Nor was it particularly practical. Most cathedral services didn't play to packed houses: they were taken by one or two clergy and watched by tiny congregations of worshippers, or often by no worshippers at all. By creating a huge circular choir Wren allowed form to overwhelm function, ignoring the compartmentalization which was necessary if the space was to adapt to different needs at different times.

Most important of all, the body of the church would have to be finished and the dome raised and roofed before it could be brought into use. Even if money had been no object, that was likely to take a decade or more. With the project depending almost entirely on a fluctuating trickle of coal tax revenues, most of the Commissioners would be dead before the first service was held in the new St Paul's. At least with a conventional arrangement of choir, crossing and nave, the cathedral could be built in easy stages as funds became available, and if the choir was tackled first, the daily round of worship could begin again as soon as it was roofed.

The residentiaries had supporters among the bishops on the Commission, and they got their way. Sancroft admired Wren as an architect, but he was a practical man, and he didn't want to come into conflict with the Chapter. He was in any case swayed by the promise of a speedy resumption of cathedral life. Sheldon and Henchman were likewise reluctant to do battle with the Chapter which, in spite of the Commission, was legally in control of all matters to do with the fabric of the building. The financial arguments carried weight with the City; and Charles was too much of a pragmatist to engage in a bothersome and needless confrontation.

Wren cried when he heard the news. It was the biggest setback of his career. The Great Model design was terribly dear to him, the finest thing he had ever produced and the classical jewel at the heart of a London emerging transformed from the crude Gothic ashes of the Middle Ages. In fact he never got over the blow: even as an old man, when the new St Paul's was being hailed as 'Glory of London, Glory of the Isle!/Best of the best! Double superlative!',[20] he would still talk to his son of how he 'set a higher Value on this Design, than any he had made before or since'.[21] As it was, he begged Charles to intercede, to negotiate, to command; and for the only time in their lives, the King and his Surveyor fell out with each other; the London building trades gossiped in the coffee-houses about how the royal architect was in 'disfavour' at court.[22] But Charles and the Commissioners were adamant. The Great Model wouldn't do.

His next reaction was anger. There was no question of his being replaced, but he had to come up with yet another design for the cathedral – something much closer to his pre-Fire scheme – and he had to come up with it fast. Fine. He would give the authorities what they wanted, a traditional plan with some Jonesian dressings as a half-hearted concession to modernity – just like the cathedral they had lost in the Fire, in fact. But he would make no more models, no more presentation drawings. Such devices 'did but lose Time, and subjected his Business many Times, to incompetent Judges'.[23]

In the spring of 1675 he offered the Commission a new scheme, as conventional as anything they could imagine, as practical as anything they could hope for, as breathtaking in its ugliness as the Great Model was beautiful. It consisted of a three-bay choir with an apse at the east end, a crossing with transepts and a five-bay nave with a single-storey Jonesian portico tacked on at the west to form an entrance. Spiky finials capped pilaster strips which looked more like buttresses, and the transepts terminated in two-storey porticos which, like the west front, recalled Jones's work of the 1630s. Strangest of all was the treatment of the crossing, which lurched upwards into a squat flattened dome, then into a tall drum topped with a smaller dome, and finally ended in a stepped wooden spire, as if it couldn't make up its mind what it wanted to be. In the words of *Parentalia*, it was an effort 'to reconcile, as near as possible, the Gothick to a better Manner of Architecture'.[24]

The Chapter loved it. The Commission loved it. The King was less enthusiastic. A new warrant was issued at Whitehall on 14 May 1675 approving the design 'as well because We found it very artificial, proper, and useful; as because it was so ordered that it might be built and finished by Parts',[25] and ordering that work should begin immediately on the east end. But Charles privately told Wren that he was at liberty to make 'variations, rather ornamental, than essential, as from Time to Time he should see proper'; and that the management of the whole project was left in his hands.[26] The drawings were returned to the architect, with the warrant attached.

So was Wren ever seriously committed to this ungainly, ultra-conservative St Paul's? Of course he was. It is sometimes said that he designed a bad building in a fit of pique after the rejection of the Great

Model, or that the Warrant design was no more than a stop-gap measure to keep Chapter and Commission quiet while he went his own way in secret. But the first theory fails to take account of his long-held personal ambitions for St Paul's, the huge prestige involved in being the architect of London's cathedral. The building mattered to him. He was neither the first nor the last architect to come up with an imaginative scheme which simply served to show his clients what they didn't want and made them think a little harder about what they *did* want. The Warrant design was a natural and perceptive response to this more restrictive brief; if it seems to hark back to a Jonesian, pre-Commonwealth golden age, then it works, since that is just what it was meant to do. As he wrote around this time, 'Whatever a man's sentiments are upon mature deliberation it will still be necessary for him in a conspicuous Work to preserve his Undertaking from general censure, and to aim to accommodate his Designs to the Gust of the Age he lives in, though it appears to him less rational.'[27]

The second notion, that Wren knew from the outset he would alter the Warrant design out of all recognition in the course of construction, at least has hindsight to recommend it, since this is exactly what he did. But it assumes an unrealistic degree of premeditation. Wren may have had private assurances from the King about the extent to which he would be allowed to modify the Warrant design drawings; but those assurances didn't count for much, since Charles had already demonstrated over the Great Model that he couldn't be relied on in a showdown with the Church.

Nevertheless, during the summer of 1675 Wren did begin to rework the Warrant design, with the ink scarcely dry on the warrant. He retained the traditional cathedral plan. (And this was the key to his success – the truth was that the Chapter didn't really care what the new St Paul's looked like, so long as it conformed to conventional ideas about the Anglican liturgy and could be brought into use as quickly as possible.) But that was about it: his view of what constituted 'variations, rather ornamental, than essential' was an exceptionally liberal one. So he did away with the more obvious Jonesian borrowings: the west end now had a much more restrained two-storey portico of paired columns (six pairs on the lower storey and four above), set between cylindrical twin towers which were based on Bramante's Tempietto di San Pietro in Montorio. The entrances to the north and south transepts became single-storey semicircular porches of six columns, a device borrowed from Pietro da Cortona's Santa Maria della Pace in Rome, with a

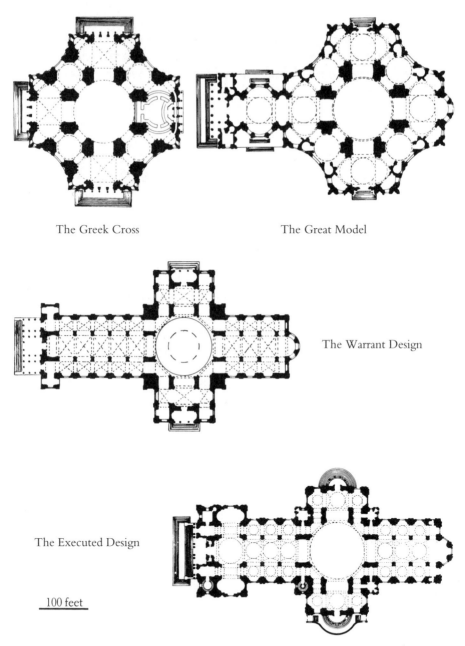

The Greek Cross   The Great Model

The Warrant Design

The Executed Design

100 feet

Figure 2. Four stages in the design of St Paul's Cathedral.

window in the storey above, and a plain pediment above that. He jettisoned the bizarre and indecisive arrangement over the crossing in favour of a single dome. Ribbed and topped with a lantern, this rested on a drum divided into sixteen bays by projecting buttresses with coupled pilasters; it was an obvious borrowing from Michelangelo's scheme for St Peter's, Rome.

He also tightened the whole composition to balance the massive scale of the dome. The nave was shortened to three bays by the introduction of two oval rooms at the west end with a circular vestibule between them, so that its proportions corresponded more closely to those of the choir. The north-west oval contained a morning prayer chapel, where the clergy could read the daily office; its counterpart on the south-west housed the Bishop's consistory court. Most dramatically of all, Wren dispensed with the Warrant design's conventional set-back clerestory, deciding instead to raise screen walls above the side aisles. This decision served several purposes at once. It concealed a system of flying buttresses which supported the upper walls of the nave and choir; and in the process it unified the entire exterior, transforming it into a two-storeyed block on a single plane. Wren may also have thought that the screen walls would serve a useful structural function, increasing the load on the lower walls and thus helping to counteract the outward thrust on the side-aisle vaults – a point he made in a different context over forty years later, when he suggested that the weight of a central tower at Westminster Abbey would prevent the piers in the crossing below from moving outwards. He was right in principle, but wrong at St Paul's: recent studies suggest the screen walls make little or no difference to the structural integrity of the side aisles.[28]

So out went the plain pilaster strips, and in came a basic decorative unit of coupled pilasters on both storeys; with a round-headed window below and a blank pedimented window with a niche above. (He was initially undecided about whether or not to adopt a Corinthian order for both storeys: in the end, he went for Corinthian for the lower order and Composite for the upper.) With variations, this unit was continued right round the building.

This so-called Definitive design – although in truth it was far from definitive – was stronger, more confident, more innovative and more modern than the Warrant. It was what the Warrant tried to be, in fact: an attempt to bring the Gothic into line with a 'better Manner of Architecture' by retaining a conventional cathedral plan and bringing every element of it up to date.

It is a testament to Wren's dogged determination that the Definitive design was his sixth attempt to build a new St Paul's.★ It had been preceded by the pre-Fire design which he and Roger Pratt had nearly come to blows over in August 1666; the inside-out First Model; the Greek Cross and its cherished and much-lamented successor, the Great Model; and the compromises of the Warrant. After nine years, St Paul's was still a long way from its final incarnation: Wren would continue to develop his vision of the cathedral as it grew, refining his ideas over and over again during the next three-and-a-half decades. But it was finally taking shape. On 21 June 1675, with no fanfares, no public ceremony or celebrations, master mason Thomas Strong laid the first foundation stone. He then handed the trowel to master carpenter John Longland, who laid the second. St Paul's was begun.

One day while Wren was laying out the site, he called over a labourer and asked him to look through the heaps of rubble for a flat stone to use as a marker. The man came back with a fragment from a grave-stone, with nothing left of the inscription except for a single word, *Resurgam* – 'I will rise again'.

★The seventh, if one includes the Penultimate design identified by Sir John Summerson (*Burlington Magazine*, CIII [1961], 83–9) as an intermediate stage between the Warrant and the Definitive.

II

Our Reformed Religion

he design of St Paul's was such a tortuous and heart-breaking business for Wren, and the end-product itself such an icon, that we could be forgiven for thinking it dominated his whole life during the early 1670s. Not so. There was never, ever, a time when a single project absorbed him to the exclusion of everything else. He wasn't made that way.

Let's go back to the spring of 1670. Wren was still only thirty-seven, and it seemed as though nothing could go wrong for him. While his academic career was effectively on hold, he still kept his Oxford chair as Savilian Professor of Astronomy, paying a substitute, Edward Bernard, to do his teaching for him. He and Faith had been married for less than six months, and were settled in Scotland Yard with their own coach and a respectably large establishment. Like that drowned watch he envied with such metaphysical longing during their courtship, he presumably enjoyed her eye, and the way in which he was 'consulted by you how your Time shall passe while you employ your hand in your excellent workes'.

And in spite of Webb's complaints to the King that Wren was 'wholy ignorant' of the Office of Works, the Surveyor-Generalship was going well. He was settling into the job, and there were plenty of opportunities in the pipeline for him to prove Webb wrong. Besides the ordinary, day-to-day administration involved in the maintenance of the royal palaces – a task that Wren took to like a duck to water – several bigger projects were in the offing. The 3rd Earl of Suffolk had just sold Audley End in Essex, one of the grandest houses in the kingdom, to the Crown for £50,000, although Charles hadn't paid for it yet. (He never did.) There were plans afoot to create a spectacular new set of lodgings for the Duke and Duchess of York at Hampton Court; and Charles was also toying with a scheme for the wholesale remodelling of his main palace at Whitehall, right on Wren's doorstep. And of course there was St Paul's. The First Model design had been finished and submitted for the King's inspection that March and, as far as he knew, it was only a question of raising the necessary funds before work started on the huge vaulted auditory. You would think he had plenty to keep him busy. But you'd be wrong. In May 1670 he took on the most complex and demanding job of his entire career – the rebuilding of the London churches.

If St Paul's is Wren's greatest memorial, the City of London churches come a close second. And they share the same mythical status, defining the landscape of the capital in the eighteenth and nineteenth centuries, rising phoenix-like from the ashes of the Blitz in the twentieth. They have bizarrely comical names – St Benet Fink, St Vedast-alias-Foster, St Olave Jewry, St Dionis Backchurch – and equally bizarre histories. St James Garlickhythe, which had a miraculous escape in 1941 when a high-explosive bomb fell through the roof and failed to detonate, was almost destroyed fifty years later when a passing crane toppled over into the south transept; St Christopher-le-Stocks was demolished in 1782–4, after the Governor of the nearby Bank of England argued that its tower could be used by insurgents to direct an assault on the Bank; St Mary Aldermanbury, which was firebombed in December 1940, was dismantled in 1965 and re-erected in Fulton, Missouri, where it still stands today. But although over the last three hundred years so many of the churches have been demolished, bombed, or bastardized – only twenty-three of the original fifty-six★ survive intact, and the majority of these have been drastically altered – most writers on London's heritage would still agree with Francis Bumpus (even if they flinch at his imperialism), when he declared in 1923 that, 'What are styled "The City Churches" have, as everybody knows, one especial value to Londoners, and indeed to all Englishmen – let me say to all English-speaking people throughout the globe. They are Wren's churches.'[1]

Except that they are not.

At least, not in the same way that St Paul's is Wren's cathedral. For

---

★There were actually fifty-one churches rebuilt within the City boundaries. Five others, outside the walls but put up as part of the same post-Fire building programme, are usually included in discussions of Wren's City churches. They are: St Anne Soho; St Bride Fleet Street; St Clement Danes; St James Piccadilly; and St Thomas the Apostle, Southwark.

forty-seven years, from 1670 to 1717, Wren acted as Chief Surveyor to the Commission set up to rebuild the City churches after the Fire. But of the fifty-six new churches only half a dozen can definitely be attributed to his personal designs. True, they are the pick of the crop – masterpieces like the domed St Stephen Walbrook, and high-status commissions such as the church for the fashionable new parish of St James Piccadilly. Some of the others may be by him, and him alone; but a number were certainly designed by Robert Hooke, who worked as Wren's assistant until shortly before his death in 1703; while others were almost certainly the result of collaboration between the two old friends. Others still could conceivably have been the work of the third member of the team, Edward Woodroffe, or John Oliver, the glazier and City surveyor who succeeded to Woodroffe's post after his early death in 1675. Several of the later towers and steeples were designed by two of Wren's protégés, Nicholas Hawksmoor, who replaced Hooke, and William Dickinson,* who took over from Oliver. Even those churches undoubtedly designed by Wren himself were sometimes finished by other hands: the steeple of St Clement Danes, for instance, was by James Gibbs; that of St James Piccadilly was possibly by the master carpenter Edward Wilcox. One or two churches which were rebuilt soon after the Fire were entirely unconnected with the main building programme, and were the work of local masons and other craftsmen.

So to claim, as most writers on Wren used to claim,[2] that he single-handedly designed all, or even most, of the City churches, is simply wrong. He didn't. Yet taken as a whole, as a single body of work, they do have an undeniable coherence, a sense of style and, despite their occasional oddities and lapses of taste, a particular idiosyncratic beauty which delights enthusiasts and drives the purists to distraction and disdain. They show Wren as director, administrator and architect; as a magisterial intellect whose influence was felt by everybody who worked with and for him. And we shouldn't forget his real achievement: the manager may be a less glamorous figure than the creative artist, but his successful management of the largest church-building programme the nation had seen since the Middle Ages was little short of miraculous.

---

*This William Dickinson, who trained with Wren at the Office of Works in the late 1680s and went on to be a measuring clerk at St Paul's and Deputy Surveyor to Westminster Abbey, should not be confused with the William Dickinson whose sole contribution to architecture was to act as Chief Clerk to the Works for more than forty years, from 1660 until his death in 1702. He is generally assumed to have been the latter's son, although there is no evidence of this.

In the summer of 1666, the City worshipped in 109 churches. The Fire destroyed or badly damaged eighty-six of them. And, even in the days immediately following the disaster, it was obvious to everybody – except the proud and shell-shocked parishioners who had lost their ancient places of worship – that there was no point in replacing every single one. The Fire offered an opportunity to respond to changing demographics which, in spite of the fact that the vast majority of the population went to church at least once every Sunday (and were liable to a fine of one shilling if they didn't), meant that by the 1660s some congregations could be numbered in thousands while others could be counted on the fingers of two hands. In his own plans for rebuilding the capital, Evelyn was quick to point out that London's parochial churches 'may well be reduced to a moiety, for 'tis prodigiously true, that there are some parishes no less than two hundred times larger than others'.[3] In his own post-Fire design Wren envisaged that nineteen churches could meet the spiritual needs of the City.

The first Rebuilding Act of 1667, which attempted to get the reconstruction of London under way, was more liberal. It proclaimed that the eighty-six fire-damaged churches would be reduced to thirty-nine, with Gilbert Sheldon, as Archbishop of Canterbury, and Humphrey Henchman, the Bishop of London, deciding which parishes should go and which should stay. Even so, the proposal was greeted with predictable cries of outrage and rumours of corruption and vested interest. Within weeks of the announcement, Pepys was told that 'those few churches that are to be new built are plainly not chosen with regard to the convenience of the City . . . all of them are either in the gift of the Lord Archbishop or Bishop of London or Lord Chancellor or gift of the City. Thus all things, even to the building of churches, are done in this world!'[4]

The Church and the City authorities might still have got away with their plans: the blatant pursuit of vested interests was not exactly unusual in Restoration England. But the idea that the Fire should be used to further personal or institutional ambitions at the expense of suffering London was unacceptable to a population which already thought that their city's destruction was an act of divine vengeance for their godless ways. The proposal to abolish so many churches was 'to add humane Rage against those places where the Divine displeasure hath left us hope of making them agayne fit for his service'.[5] So Crown, City and Church relented. In the second Rebuilding Act of 1670, the figure of thirty-nine was raised to fifty-one, with every pre-Fire parish retaining its own identity and, where it shared a church with a neighbour, simply contributing an agreed proportion towards the upkeep of the building. The money for building the new churches was to come from the coal tax, fifty per cent of which was to be devoted to London's churches and St Paul's Cathedral. The responsibility for providing pews, pulpits, bells and other fittings lay with the parishes themselves.

If only life were that simple. As it turned out, the joined parishes squabbled over what proportion each should pay, over who would sit where in the new church, over burial rights and organists' stipends. When they did manage to bury their differences along with their parishioners, it was only to unite against a common enemy. They were jealous when the designs for churches of neighbouring parishes were grander than theirs, angry with Wren when the construction of those neighbouring churches took priority over their own, suspicious that their builders weren't working fast enough. Some parishes had influence and powerful friends among the City authorities, which they used ruthlessly to further their claims at the expense of others. In one or two cases, parishes were not really all that bothered whether they had a new church or not.

The three Commissioners appointed under the new act were the Archbishop of Canterbury, the Bishop of London and the Lord Mayor, and their first decision was to name Wren to take charge of the whole project. In May 1670 they announced that he was 'to direct and order the dimensions, formes and Modells of the said Churches', to negotiate with contractors and craftsmen, and to control the payment of the considerable sums of money which would be involved in such a huge building scheme.[6] The following month Robert Hooke and Edward Woodroffe were appointed to assist him, and the task before the three men was defined more precisely. They were authorized to begin work on a first wave of fifteen churches chosen by the Commissioners, and to

> take an account of the extent of the parishes, the sites of the churches, the state and conditions of the ruins and accordingly prepare fit models and draughts to be presented for his Majesty's approbation and also estimate proper to inform us what share and proportion of the money out of the imposition upon coals may be requisite to allow for the fabric of each church.[7]

Work had already started on repairing or rebuilding five of the fifteen – it was, after all, nearly four years since the Fire – and the vestry committees were looking for coal money to complete them, so Wren and his assistants were also empowered to call for contracts and balance sheets in order to decide how much more needed to be spent.★

Within weeks it became obvious that this plan of action, commendably straightforward though it seemed in theory, wasn't going to work. The coal dues were much too slow in coming in; and when some parishioners whose church (St Edmund the King) had been omitted from the list offered to advance money if it could be included, Wren and the Commissioners hit on a completely new idea. Parish vestries were asked to do some fund-raising of their own: for every £500 they lent, the Commission would allocate £1500 from the coal tax towards the rebuilding of their church, and priority would be determined by the order in which the vestries deposited their loans in the Chamber of London. In the meantime, ten simple wooden 'tabernacles' were to be erected as temporary places of worship. This figure eventually rose to twenty-seven, an indication of how progress continued to be impeded by lack of funds – as was the fact that in the summer of 1671 the Commissioners refused to accept any more deposits, ordering 'that no more churches be begun, until a competent number of those that are in hand be finished and paid off'.[8] The following year they were forced to create a second category, allowing those parishes which had the resources to go ahead with their building work without any help from the coal dues, on the understanding that they would be reimbursed as and when more money became available. By 1674, eighteen churches were under way. At the height of the building activity, in 1684, that figure had risen to twenty-six.

Wren was central to this massive building programme. Never mind the actual design-work (which actually occupied very little of his time); it was Wren, and not the three Commissioners, who argued with masons and fended off influential and importunate parishioners, who juggled with schedules and explained to irate contractors that they would have to wait for their money. It was Wren who approved the

---

★The fifteen churches were: Christchurch Newgate; St Anne and St Agnes; St Augustine Old Change; St Benet Gracechurch; St Bride Fleet Street; St Christopher-le-Stocks; St Lawrence Jewry; St Magnus the Martyr; St Mary-at-Hill; St Mary-le-Bow; St Michael Cornhill; St Michael Queenhythe; St Olave Jewry; St Sepulchre; and St Vedast-alias-Foster. Rebuilding had already begun at St Christopher-le-Stocks, St Magnus the Martyr, St Michael Cornhill, St Sepulchre and St Vedast-alias-Foster. When this list was discarded in favour of the system of £500 deposits, work at five churches had advanced far enough for it to be allowed to continue: they were St Christopher-le-Stocks, St Mary-le-Bow, St Michael Cornhill, St Sepulchre and St Vedast.

work and made the decisions, drafting warrants for Archbishop, Bishop and Mayor to sign.

Twice a week, on Thursday and Saturday mornings, he met with Hooke, who came over to Scotland Yard or the office in St Paul's, where they went through the business of the week, usually with Woodroffe or, after his death, John Oliver. The three men examined and signed off the craftsmen's accounts as they came in, and discussed the progress of individual churches with those craftsmen. Sometimes Wren also saw petitioners: in January 1679 there was an angry confrontation with the widow of mason-contractor Joshua Marshall, who turned up at Scotland Yard demanding that the Commission should settle her husband's outstanding account. But widow or not, the Surveyor-General didn't take well to being hectored by a woman: he sent her away empty-handed, leaving even the loyal Hooke shocked and surprised at his brusque attitude.

Wren also received deputations of parish worthies at Scotland Yard, pushing him to provide more funds for their own churches, urging him to instruct the workers to get a move on with the building, offering him 'presents' to make sure that *their* church was given priority. Bribery was the accepted way of doing business – any kind of official business – in Restoration England. On two separate occasions in 1671, for example, the churchwardens of St Nicholas Cole Abbey, who were lobbying hard to prevent the site of their church being given to the Lutheran community, meticulously recorded in their accounts payments of sixpence for half a pint of canary wine to one of Wren's servants, while other parishes presented his clerks with gifts ranging from a princely six guineas 'for encouraging the forwarding of the building of the church' from St Mary Abchurch, to a measly 10s 9d given by St Michael Wood Street after the rector, Dr Martyn, suggested that this might help to speed repairs and alterations to St Michael's church tower.

Wren was not himself averse to accepting bribes, and he really did quite well out of the system. There is no record of the official salary he received from the Commission, but between June 1670 and the end of 1675 the accounts show that he was paid nearly £1600, which averages out at just over £290 a year, in addition to the £382 5s 8d he received from the Crown for the Surveyor-Generalship, the £100 p.a. as Surveyor to St Paul's (rising to £200 when rebuilding began in 1675) and, until he resigned in 1673, his professor's salary at Oxford. There was also the dowry he presumably received from the Coghills on his marriage to Faith and various perks, travelling expenses and ex gratia payments. In 1670, for instance, he was awarded one hundred guineas for his work on the First Model design of St Paul's. The City, which didn't pay him a regular salary for his work as a commissioner for rebuilding the capital, twice sent him presents of a hundred guineas in gold. And in March 1676 Hooke noted that his friend had let 'his house' – probably the Surveyor's second official residence at Hampton Court – for one year, at an annual rent of £32.[9]

It was a sad change in family circumstances which led Wren to let the house, and not merely a desire to make a little extra money on the side. He and Faith had had two children. Gilbert, who was named for Archbishop Sheldon, was born on 14 October 1672 and baptized at St Martin-in-the-Fields twelve days later. (A Dr Bradford assured the new father that his next child would also be a boy, 'this being born in the increase of the Moon' – he obviously didn't know Wren's views on astrology).[10] But Gilbert was sickly – on one occasion, Hooke went round to Scotland Yard to find him 'in convulsion fitts' – and he died suddenly when he was seventeen months old.[11] A second son, Christopher junior, was born in February 1675 (so Dr Bradford was right).

That summer Faith was taken ill. When Hooke arrived for his regular Saturday meeting on 28 August, his friend told him that she had been suffering from smallpox for the past five days. She struggled with the disease for another week before dying on the night of 3 September. Faith was buried the following night next to Gilbert, in the chancel of St Martin-in-the-Fields. Three days afterwards Wren was sitting up with Hooke, discussing a model of Solomon's Temple which a Dutch rabbi had recently brought to London. Who is to say if this shows him as a cold-hearted brute or a grieving husband desperately looking for distraction?

Nor can I find out how he ran his household as a widower with a baby son. Lady Coghill – either his mother-in-law or his sister-in-law – arrived at Scotland Yard within days of Faith's death. Perhaps she took the child back to Oxfordshire with her: if she did, he was in London again by October 1676, when Hooke, in a tender gesture which belies his generally grumpy image, sent him a hobby horse.★

In any case, Wren could well afford to employ a nurse for young

★The night before (20 October), Wren had celebrated his forty-fourth birthday by throwing a party at the Palgrave's Head near Temple Bar. 'He paid all,' Hooke noted: so perhaps the hobby horse was by way of a thank-you present.

Christopher. By 1676 his official salaries, together with the rent from the Hampton Court house, amounted to something just over £900, with free accommodation at Scotland Yard – and this at a time when a loaf of bread cost 1d, a leg of beef cost 6d, and a general maid's annual wages were around £3 plus board, lodging and clothing. (Robert Hooke paid £4 to Nell, his maid at Gresham College – but, as we have seen, she provided him with services above and beyond the call of duty). He was a wealthy man – perhaps not in the same league as the courtiers and City merchants he was dealing with on a day-to-day basis, but well able to maintain a position in society which was appropriate for a knight of the realm.

And on top of the official income there were the presents – lots and lots of presents. Gifts for services rendered and inducements for favours yet to come tend to lurk in the twilight world of the black economy. Neither the donor nor the recipient is particularly keen to record the transaction, so they go unregistered, and posterity is usually left to guess at the going rate for a bribe. There are occasional references in Hooke's diaries which give hints about the way business was done. In 1674, for instance, when the master bricklayer John Fitch was bidding for the bricklaying contract at St Paul's, Hooke escorted him to the 'Dutch House in Green Street', where Fitch bought some china to present to Lady Wren.[12] (Although Faith got the china, Fitch didn't get the job, which may say something about the efficacy of bribery in seventeenth-century London; although as a consolation prize he was given the contract for St Anne and St Agnes three years later.) But it is the careful record-keeping demanded of the City's churchwardens and vestry committees which gives the greatest insight into Wren's business ethics. If those ethics were no worse than any other public official of the time, they were certainly no better.

Gifts, meticulously recorded in vestry minutes and churchwardens' accounts, were sometimes given as straightforward thank-you presents when construction neared completion, sometimes to speed up the building work. Often they performed both functions. In April 1673, for example, the vestry of St Mary Aldermanbury agreed that 'having considered the kindness of Dr Xtopher Wren and Mr Robert Hooke in expediting the building of the church, and that they may be encouraged to assist in the perfecting of that work, it is now ordered that the parish by the churchwardens do present Dr Xtopher Wren with twenty guineas, and Mr Robert Hooke with six guineas'. (In the event, Hooke's share of the loot was raised to ten guineas.[13])

Such gifts were of three types: hospitality, payments in kind and cash. So at the beginning of March 1673, when St Stephen Walbrook wanted to show its gratitude to Wren for providing them with a design for their new church, the parish paid nine guineas for a dinner at the Swan tavern in Old Fish Street, where they entertained Wren and Hooke. ('Eat with great stomack,' Hooke noted in his diary.) At the same dinner, 'ye Survaer Gennerall' was presented with 'a gratuety to his Lady to incuridg and hasting ye rebuilding ye church twenty ginnes'. No doubt it was sheer coincidence that only a few days previously the vestry had agreed to be bound by Wren's decision in a property dispute they were having with one of their neighbours. And in 1675–6, when St Michael Bassishaw was looking for a £500 grant out of coal revenues towards rebuilding, the parish paid out £9 19s for two dinners in Old Fish Street 'when we met Sir Christopher Wren about the church'. The Swan was obviously a favourite venue for corporate entertainment.[14]

Payments in kind included a piece of plate worth a considerable £21 15s, sent to Wren's home by the parishioners of St Benet Fink in 1672, and gifts of wine: St Martin Ludgate, St Stephen Walbrook and St Magnus the Martyr each sent Wren a hogshead of wine – around fifty gallons – at various times in the late 1670s and early 1680s (claret, in the last two cases); while St Clement Eastcheap, where the parish was pressing the Commissioners to give them a bigger church, could only manage a third of a hogshead.

But money was the real currency of persuasion. When the vestry committee of St Antholin Budge Row wanted to thank Wren and Oliver for their help with the new church, and to 'engage their assistance and advice till it be completed',[15] they voted twenty guineas – twelve to Wren, five to Oliver and two to Wren's clerk. (What happened to the other guinea? one wonders.) St Mary Abchurch, St Mary-le-Bow and, as we have seen, St Mary Aldermanbury and St Stephen Walbrook, all gave twenty guineas apiece. St Clement Eastcheap gave seven, in addition to the third of a hogshead; St Peter Cornhill gave £10 after Wren procured them a tabernacle; and poor St Matthew Friday Street and its sister parish St Peter Cheap could only manage the rather odd sum of £3 8s between them. Cheap by name and cheap by nature.

Occasionally, churchwardens tried a stick instead of a carrot. When St Michael Cornhill found itself out of pocket to the tune of £252 13s 4d, the vestry ordered its churchwardens to 'apply themselves to Sir Christopher, and earnestly press him to pay the said money, and, if he further delayeth, to apply themselves to the Lords Commissioners'. With what result, I don't know. St Lawrence Jewry was slow to learn the rules of the game. In 1677 representatives waited on Wren twice to complain about the slow progress of the building work; it wasn't until 1679, when they voted a hefty thirty guineas 'in thankful acknowledgement of his past favour to this parish, and to make requests for effecting things still to be done', that the church was completed.[16]

Just one more example from vestry minutes before we leave these murky waters for the clean air of architectural design. It shows a refreshingly human side to Wren the super-efficient administrator. St Dionis Backchurch was finished in 1674, all bar the tower and steeple. Four years later a committee waited on the Commissioners to beg for an order to complete the building. Their timing was bad: at the end of 1677, in an attempt to direct scarce funds towards the construction of usable places of worship, the Commission (which in this case almost certainly meant Wren) had decreed that all unfinished towers 'for the present remain to the height of the churches' – that is, they should be boarded over and left until there was money to finish them. After applying a lot of pressure (but no presents), the committee persuaded Wren to obtain the Bishop of London's signature on the order, and told him that if he handed it over, they were sure they could get the Lord Mayor to countersign it. He stalled. And stalled. And finally explained why he couldn't give them the order. He had lost it.

So what about the churches themselves? That drops us right back in the minefield of speculation over attributions and authorship. Of the fifty-six designs, there is enough documentary and stylistic evidence to suggest that six are definitely by Wren: St Mary-le-Bow (1670–80); St Bride Fleet Street (1671–8); St Stephen Walbrook (1672–80); St James Piccadilly (1676–84); St Clement Danes (1679–85); and St Andrew Holborn (1684–6). As we might expect, they are the pick of the bunch, with an average building cost of nearly £12,000 apiece – twice that of the other fifty.[17] Four of them are to the west of St Paul's, in the more fashionable parts of London; none are in the east, and only St Mary-le-Bow and St Stephen Walbrook are in the central section of the City. Gilbert Sheldon had a special interest in the former, since it was the historic seat of the archbishops' court of ecclesiastical appeal and the chief of thirteen City churches which belonged to the diocese of Canterbury rather than London; while the patron of the living of St Stephen's when work began was Sir Robert Hanson, Lord Mayor of London in 1672/3 and hence one of the three Commissioners for rebuilding the churches. Most of the churches generally reckoned to be by Hooke, on the other hand, are in the north and east of the City, not too far from his lodgings at Gresham, and they tend to be the smaller, lower-status commissions.[18]

It would be handy if we could extrapolate from this pattern, in which Wren undertook the grander churches, the churches closer to Scotland Yard and/or the churches where powerful patrons insisted on having the Surveyor's personal attention, to establish his authorship of other churches where the situation is less clear-cut. If only things were that simple. But St Martin Ludgate (1677–86) is right on the western boundary of the City; and it is undoubtedly the work of Hooke. At a total cost of £13,741 17s 10¾d, Christchurch Newgate (1677–87), a few hundred yards from St Paul's, was the fourth most expensive church; but drawings for an unexecuted design in Hooke's hand suggest that he was closely involved in the design process, even if he wasn't solely responsible for the finished building. And Wren, rather than Hooke, seems to have been involved in the design of St Augustine Old Change (1680–4), a small and relatively cheap church – no doubt because it was on the doorstep of St Paul's.

The drawings don't help much. None at all survive for some of the churches. Of those that do, most are the work of draftsmen in Wren's office. Only two sets, for St Stephen Walbrook and the east end of St Magnus the Martyr, are in Wren's own hand. Rather more are by Hooke, although this doesn't necessarily mean that the designs were all his own work, or, when they were, that they were always accepted. He made a site plan for St Mary-le-Bow, one of Wren's churches, for example, and produced an unexecuted scheme for the tower and steeple of St James Piccadilly, a building which Wren himself described not only as 'beautiful and convenient', but as 'the cheapest of any Form I could invent'.[19] Wren was in complete charge of the church-building pro-gramme, with Hooke contributing designs for his approval: a Hooke drawing of the street façade of St Edmund the King (1670–4) is endorsed with the Surveyor-General's initials neatly written into the pediment, and an inscription in another hand confirming that it was done 'With His M^{ties} Approbation'.[20] (In the early days of the Commission all designs were supposed to be passed by the King, a requirement which soon fell by the wayside.) No doubt Hooke sometimes modified and resubmitted his schemes after the two men had discussed them.

The one clear thought that can be salvaged from all this is that Wren personally designed some of the City churches, although we don't know how many. Hooke designed some of the others – again, we can't say how many. And the two men collaborated to varying extents on a third group, which we can't identify with any certainty.

So what did they look like? In three cases – St Alban Wood Street, St Mary Aldermary and St Sepulchre – the parish set its face against modernity and insisted on a building which harked back to a comfortable and familiar pre-Fire Gothic, leading Wren to talk years later of 'some few Examples (where I was oblig'd to deviate from a better Style) which appears not ungraceful, but ornamental to the East part of the City'.[21] But the vast majority were of that 'better Style' – classical in spirit and in detail, although the need to work with existing and often awkward sites, and to utilize medieval foundations – much cheaper than starting from scratch – meant that in a surprising number of cases all thoughts of symmetry went out of the window, making balanced façades and ninety-degree angles something of a rarity.

In 1670, the only English precedent for a classical parish church was Inigo Jones's St Paul's Covent Garden, an uncompromising temple of a building consecrated in 1638. According to Horace Walpole, the 4th Earl of Bedford, who developed Covent Garden, told Jones that he wasn't prepared to spend a huge amount on the church; in fact he didn't want it to cost much more than a barn. In that case, said the architect, the Earl would have the handsomest barn in England. So it was: a great aisle-less rectangle, with no screen to separate nave and chancel, and defined entirely from the Covent Garden Piazza by its massive Tuscan portico.

Such powerful simplicity wasn't to Wren's taste at this stage in his architectural career. Even if it had been, the crowded irregular sites bequeathed by the Fire militated against it, and the conservative tastes of the vestry committees required buildings more readily identifiable as places of worship.

But what exactly *were* the requirements for a place of worship? This was what Wren had to decide. In the 1670s, an evolving and slightly uncertain Anglican liturgy tended to steer a middle way between High Church ritual and Low Church simplicity. The need was for an architectural vocabulary which emphasized the importance of the pulpit – and hence the sermon, the teaching function of the clergy and the role of the church building as an auditorium – without neglecting the altar as a mystical symbol of sacrifice and redemption. The Laudian battle for the sanctity of the east end of a church, with an altar properly railed in and placed against the east wall, was largely won by the end of the seventeenth century; but it was won with none of the stridency which had characterized the efforts of Dean Wren and Bishop Matthew. As one commentator wrote in 1710, 'Since the Restoration, no positive determination therein being made . . . the dispute has very happily died; and the tables have been generally set altar-wise, and railed in, without any opposition thereto; the generality of all parishioners esteeming it a very decent situation, they coming of themselves to a good liking of it, which they could not be brought to, by the too rigid methods which were heretofore used.'[22] At the same time, the Puritanism of the Commonwealth had given parishioners a taste for a more inclusive form of worship which the Restoration Church ignored at its peril.★ This involved a partnership between minister and congregation, with the minister as guide and instructor rather than intermediary. There was no place for the old division between the inner sanctum of the chancel and the nave, just as there was no place for a liturgy in which worshippers looked on passively as their priest celebrated a mystical rite. Moreover, as the Catholic Church already knew and even the Laudian old guard finally came to realize, placing the altar at the east end of a traditional narrow chancel meant that whenever the priest stood before it, the members of the congregation who were sitting in the aisles of the nave couldn't even *see* him. An inclusive box-like space served the needs of High and Low Church alike.

We can get an insight into Wren's own thinking on the connection between form and function from a memorandum he wrote forty years after he began work on the City churches. In 1708, when he was seventy-six, he was appointed a Commissioner for building 'Fifty new additional Parish Churches in the Cities of London and Westminster'[23] and as a result he set out, as he said, 'to communicate briefly my sentiments [on church-building], after long Experience'.

By and large they are an old man's sentiments, querulous and carping. Contractors were crooked; brickmakers didn't know how to make good bricks these days. Churchwardens neglected the fabric of the building in their care: they 'set up their Names, but neglect to preserve the Roof over their Heads'. Preachers had lost the art of oratory. They allowed their voices to fall away at the end of a sentence, 'an insufferable Fault in the Pronunciation of some of our otherwise excellent Preachers;

★Old habits died hard, however. At one time, statues of Moses and Aaron at the east end of All Hallows the Great on Thames Street were threatened with removal after the congregation fell into the habit of genuflecting before them whenever they entered the church.

which School-masters might correct in the young, as a vicious Pronunciation'. But there is also some sound common sense. Burials in churches were a bad thing, not only because they were unhealthy, but because the upheaval and subsequent settling disturbed the paving and caused pews to lean away from the upright. Nor was there any need to worry overmuch if ritual east didn't correspond with the point on the compass; an architect should work with his site, rather than against it.

The most interesting passage in the memorandum comes in a discussion of the appropriate size for a new church. Though each of the fifty churches would have to serve a congregation of up to 8000 adults, Wren argued strongly that none should hold more than 2000:

> In our reformed Religion, it should seem vain to make a Parish-Church larger, than that all who are present can both hear and see. The Romanists, indeed, may build larger Churches, it is enough if they hear the Murmur of the Mass, and see the Elevation of the Host, but ours are to be fitted for Auditories. I can hardly think it practicable to make a single Room so capacious, with Pews and Galleries, as to hold above 2000 Persons, and all to hear the Service, and both to hear distinctly, and see the Preacher.

Scholars have often seen in this passage a Protestant emphasis on the pulpit rather than the altar, the sermon rather than the Eucharist. That would be an odd position for the son of one distinguished Laudian cleric and the nephew of another to adopt. It reflects the spirit of the times, in which Anglicanism feared both Catholic ritual and Nonconformist dogma, while taking what it needed from both. Including the congregation in worship without actually empowering it was a central premise of High Church liturgy.

The idea of the regular, rectangular auditory dominates the City churches, even when the buildings themselves are neither regular nor rectangular. The structurally separate chancel makes an appearance in only fifteen instances, often consisting, as at St Mary-le-Bow and St James Piccadilly, of no more than a slight recess, a half-hearted nod to tradition. The position of the altar still needed ceremonial emphasis, of course – these were Anglican churches, not Nonconformists' meeting houses – and this was usually achieved by the introduction of a carved reredos, a backdrop to the stage-set of holiness. Although most of these sumptuous altarpieces have been destroyed or tampered with, a good example by Grinling Gibbons, in place by 1684 and restored in 1947–54 after bomb-damage, survives at St James Piccadilly. But the best, again by Gibbons and again restored after the Second World War, is at St Mary Abchurch (1686). Described by Edward Hatton in 1708 as 'the most magnificent Piece of carved Work I have thus far met with', it consists, as Hatton went on to say, of

> 4 Columns, their Entablature, and spacious open Pediment of the Corinthian Order; on which last is the letter R within a Garter supported by 2 Cherubims . . . Over the Columns are 4 lamps on Acroters. Enrichments, in great variety, of spacious Festoons of Fruit, Leaves, Palm-branches, and a Pelican feeding her Young, all curiously carved in Relievo.[24]

We need to bear in mind, though, that while Wren and Hooke may have hoped to see their work adorned with something like, say, Grinling Gibbons' reredos at St Mary Abchurch, hoping was all they did. Their brief didn't extend to furnishings or fittings, and their job was done when the structure was complete and the building contractors' bills had been examined and passed.

John Evelyn's story of how he discovered Gibbons is well known. Early in 1671 he came across the young man in a 'poore solitary thatched house, in a field' near Sayes Court, his Deptford home, and was bowled over by Gibbons' carving of Tintoretto's *Crucifixion*. When Wren and Pepys came to dine with him a few weeks later, he dragged them off to see it, and later brought carving and carver up to Whitehall, where one of Catherine of Braganza's French attendants dissuaded her from buying the work, 'which she understood no more than an asse or a monkey'. However, 'His Majesty's Surveyor, Mr Wren, faithfully promis'd me to employ him'.[25]

It is worth noting, then, that the Surveyor didn't exactly rush to fulfil his promise. True, in 1678 Gibbons designed the monument in Wren's abortive Mausoleum for Charles I in Westminster Abbey. But St James Piccadilly, where he also carved the font, was the first Wren building he actually decorated, some thirteen years after Evelyn brought him to the Surveyor's notice. This and St Mary Abchurch were the only City churches he worked on;[26] and both commissions are just as likely to have come directly from the parishes as from Wren's recommendation. It wasn't until well after Gibbons had established himself, with his work for Hugh May at Windsor Castle in the early 1680s, that Wren started to take a serious interest in him: the decoration of James II's Catholic

Chapel and Mary of Modena's lodgings at Whitehall (1685–7) was the first time the two men worked closely together. Even after that, when the architect was in a position to commission high-profile stone-carving, he was just as likely to ignore Gibbons, as he did with the east pediment at Hampton Court (1694), which he gave to Caius Gabriel Cibber, and the west pediment of St Paul's (1706), which went to Francis Bird.

Wren preferred to rely on his own stable of craftsmen. Not surprisingly, a number came from Scotland Yard. Officials of the Works were men he knew and could depend on, something which was particularly important when the church-building programme was in its early stages and he was still quite new to the job. And of course, they were keen for a slice of the pie. Most of them got something: Maurice Emmett, the Master Bricklayer, was awarded contracts for two churches; the Sergeant Plumber, Charles Atherton, did the leadwork on five; and the Master Carpenter, Matthew Banckes, twelve. The Sergeant Painter, Robert Streater, and his son (who succeeded him in 1679) painted thirteen of the churches; the Master Plasterers John Grove senior and junior and their partner Henry Doogood managed an impressive total of forty-three contracts, worth an equally impressive £8060. Joshua Marshall, who had stepped into his father's post as Master Mason of the Works in 1673, built just six of the City churches before his death in 1678, including St Bride Fleet Street and St Mary Aldermanbury. But they were big contracts, worth well over £19,000.

The Works couldn't hope to supply all the skilled labour needed for such a huge rebuilding programme. At one time or another more than 170 different firms were employed on the construction of the churches, ranging from big outfits of mason-contractors with dozens of workers, down to the otherwise unknown Mary Grimes, who was paid £9 for painting St Michael Bassishaw in 1679.

Some of these craftsmen were Londoners and long-standing members of their respective Companies. Thomas Cartwright the elder, who built four churches including St Mary-le-Bow, was Warden of the Masons' Company in 1671, and Master in 1673. He was obviously held in high regard by the City, since between 1667 and 1673 he was involved in rebuilding four of the Company Halls: the Weavers', the Haberdashers', the Tallow Chandlers' and the Mercers'. The mason-sculptor Edward Pierce, who carved the magnificent marble bust of Wren in 1673, is another example. Actually a member of the Painter-Stainers' Company (he started his career as a decorative painter), Pierce worked on the

Guildhall, the Coopers' Hall and the Grocers' Hall, as well as making statues of various kings and queens for the Fishmongers' Company, the Skinners' and the Goldsmiths'. On his own account and in partnership with John Shorthose and William Stanton (both of whom also ran established pre-Fire firms), he contracted for four of the City churches: St Clement Danes, St Andrew Holborn, St Matthew Friday Street and St Lawrence Jewry.

Wren also made extensive use of outsiders who had been lured to London in the wake of the Fire by the prospect of work – and by a clause in the 1667 Rebuilding Act which said that all artificers, labourers and workmen employed on the rebuilding of the capital were to enjoy the same rights and privileges as freemen. When the City authorities realized to their horror that 25% of the population had failed to return after the Fire, they relaxed the regulations still further, allowing anyone who moved into a new house to be admitted as a freeman. This meant that provided their Company accepted them – and pressure was brought to bear on the Companies to do just that – a small fee would assure a provincial craftsman of a good living in the capital. John Fitch, the bricklayer who tried to bribe Wren with some china for Faith, took up the offer. So did the mason Thomas Wise, whose family was involved in running the royal quarries on the Isle of Portland, and the Burford quarry-owners Thomas Strong and Christopher Kempster. Wise, who eventually succeeded Joshua Marshall as Master Mason of the Works, obtained contracts to build three of the City churches. Thomas Strong had worked for Wren on the Sheldonian and the new quadrangle at Trinity College; after the Fire he left his home in the Cotswolds and 'took up masons with him to London to work with him, to serve the City in what they wanted in his way of trade, and continued there in that employment many years till most of the houses and halls were built'.[27] He also won contracts for three churches, including the important St Stephen Walbrook. Kempster contracted for the masonry at St James Garlickhythe, St Mary Abchurch and, with Strong's firm, St Stephen Walbrook. 'I can rely upon him,' said Wren.[28]

Most of these men, both native Londoners and post-Fire newcomers, were employed by Wren on other buildings besides the City churches, including the royal palaces and his Oxford and Cambridge designs. Chief among them, though, was St Paul's. Pierce, Wise, Strong and Kempster were all major contractors: it was Strong who laid the foundation stone of the Cathedral in June 1675; and his brother Edward, who took over the firm after Thomas's death in 1681, helped Wren's son to put the final stone in place in 1708. In fact, of the thirteen teams of masons who worked on St Paul's, ten had contracts for one or more of the churches (and the other three were almost certainly involved as apprentices or assistants).[29] The names of the same master craftsmen are constantly cropping up both at St Paul's and in the building accounts of the churches: carpenters John Longland, Israel Knowles and Thomas Woodstock; bricklayers Thomas Warren and John Bridges; joiners Charles Hopson and Roger Davis, to name just a few.

Wren tended to treat the larger, more important churches – such as St Bride Fleet Street, St James Piccadilly and St Clement Danes – as basilicas: the familiar medieval arrangement of nave and aisles could be translated readily into a classical idiom (which he probably derived from Vitruvius's description of the basilica he designed at Fano)* in which a barrel-vaulted central space was flanked by arcades carried on columns. Round-headed windows filled with clear glass were the norm: as he said to Seth Ward, nothing could add beauty to light.† The columns, which were sometimes raised on high plinths so that their lines wouldn't be spoiled when the box-pews were installed, might also support additional seating for the congregation in the form of galleries, as at St Bride Fleet Street, where they floated rather strangely between the cross-vaulted aisles. There was plenty of room for variation, however. At Christchurch Newgate, the nave was cross-vaulted, the aisles had flat ceilings, and the wood-panelled plinths were raised so high that they supported the galleries as well as the columns. St James Piccadilly had the high plinths combined with barrel-vaults at right angles to the nave; St Clement Danes, cross-vaulted aisles and a semicircular east end, broken by a smaller semicircular apse. There were Tuscan coupled columns (St Bride), single Corinthian (St James Piccadilly and St Clement Danes), Ionic (St James Garlickhythe). In fact the overriding impression, even among this relatively small group of basilicas, is of a refusal to work to a formula, a rage to try out different forms, different structural techniques, different decorative combinations. The rebuilding of the City churches was an opportunity for experiment. And Wren exulted in it.

---

*In 1676 Wren paid £3 for a copy of Vitruvius 'for the use of the office' (Margaret Whinney, *Wren* [Thames & Hudson, 1971], 52). At his death, he personally owned a 1684 edition of Claude Perrault's translation. The fact that he was acquainted with Vitruvius when he was designing St Bride in 1670–1 suggests he owned, or at least had access to, Daniele Barbaro's 1556 Latin edition.
†He was right. The nineteenth- and twentieth-century stained glass which is such a feature of many of the surviving City churches is beautiful, but inappropriate.

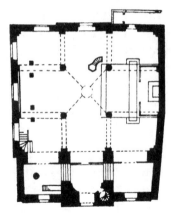

St Martin Ludgate

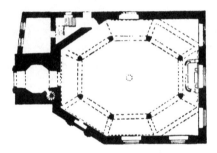

St Antholin Budge Row

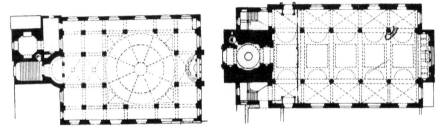

St Stephen Walbrook

St Bride Fleet Street

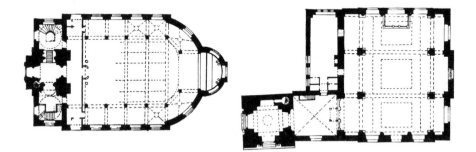

St Clement Danes

St Mary-le-Bow

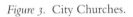

Figure 3. City Churches.

The same feeling comes across when one looks at the smaller churches, where there is a bewildering variety of shapes, from the simple aisle-less rectangle of St Benet Gracechurch to the hexagonal coffin of St Olave Jewry and the flattened decagon of St Benet Fink. Robert Hooke seems to have been particularly interested in the cross contained within a square, in which four high vaults run in from the outer walls to meet in the centre. The idea first appeared in Jacob van Campen's Nieuwe Kerk in Haarlem (1645–9), and was found in various guises in Holland. Hooke was keen on Dutch architecture: although there is no evidence of his ever having visited the Low Countries, he made a drawing of the Nieuwe Kerk, and listened avidly to the mason Abraham Storey's accounts of recent ecclesiastical architecture in Amsterdam. St Anne and St Agnes, St Martin Ludgate and St Mary-at-Hill all borrow van Campen's cross-in-a-square form, and all can reasonably be attributed to Hooke.

Wren was naturally interested in such centralized plans, especially in the early 1670s, when he was still absorbed in the Greek Cross and Great Model designs for St Paul's. Seven of the City churches have (or had) central domes: St Mary-at-Hill; St Benet Fink; St Stephen Walbrook; St Swithin London Stone; St Antholin Budge Row; St Mary Abchurch; and St Mildred Bread Street.

The pick of the bunch is St Stephen Walbrook. The foundation stones were laid on 17 December 1672 by the now knighted Sir Thomas Chicheley, Master of the Ordnance, whose ancestors had built the previous church in the fifteenth century; Sir John Robinson, Lieutenant of the Tower; and Sir Robert Hanson, the current Lord Mayor of London and a member of the Grocers' Company, which held the living. By February 1677 the churchwardens were busy touring other recently completed churches to find out 'which is the best to take patterns by in order to the pewing of the Church';[30] and the building was more or less complete (except for the tower and steeple) in May 1679, when the vestry voted to present 'Sir Christopher's Lady' with ten pieces of gold and to hold a celebratory dinner at the Bull's Head on Cheapside. Wren was invited, along with the principal craftsmen employed on the building. They included Thomas Strong and Christopher Kempster, who had the contract for the masonry; carpenter John Longland; joiner Roger Davis, Thomas Creecher, who made the altarpiece, pulpit and communion table; William Davis, who painted the Lord's Prayer, Creed and Commandments and '2,200 of gold roses . . . at 16 shilling per hundred';[31] and Stephen Colledge, who did the pews and wainscot on one side of the church while Roger Davis did the other. (Colledge was soon to meet an untimely end. Known as the 'Protestant Joiner', he was much given to mouthing off about how the Protestants would force Charles to pass the Bill of Exclusion, which was intended to prevent the Catholic Duke of York from succeeding. Unfortunately for him, he said it once too often, and was accused – quite falsely – of plotting to assassinate the King. He was executed in August 1681.)

St Stephen is a regular rectangle about ninety feet long by sixty-eight feet wide, with an undistinguished exterior that gives no hint of the complexities which lie within. Wren turned the rectangle into a square, by making a little nave of the westernmost bay, and set up the cross-in-a-square plan by providing vaulted nave, chancel and transepts. These vaults run into arches which, together with four others in the angles of the square, support the dome floating above the central space. The eight equal arches – an echo of the Greek Cross design, which Wren must have been working on almost contemporaneously with St Stephen Walbrook – are in turn supported on eight Corinthian columns. Further columns to the north-west, north-east, south-west and south-east complete the impression of not only a cross-in-a-square, but also a circle-in-a-square.

The excitement comes from this ambiguity, the alternative readings of the space. These are not so obvious today, when the first thing to strike you is Henry Moore's circular altar, a huge block of travertine marble fifteen feet across, which was installed in 1972 and sits directly beneath Wren's dome, faced on all sides by modern bench-pews. The impression now is very unEnglish, very Vatican II. All the liturgical emphasis is concentrated on the space beneath the dome: there is no sense of ritual east, and Thomas Creecher's altarpiece stands ignored, like some redundant relic of the past. To understand the church as it was in the seventeenth century, we need to remove the Moore altar and the benches, and replace them with high box-pews arranged in the usual manner. The central aisle was clear, giving a view through from the entrance at the west end to the altar and, at first sight, implying a conventional box with nave and aisles. It was only as you advanced further into the body of the church that the dome opened up, the relevance of the columns became obvious and the ambiguities declared themselves, so that you were left wondering exactly what the dominant geometry was – circle, square, octagon, oblong, cross?

The sense of unresolved tension was maintained by the fenestration – round-headed windows, oval windows, circular windows – and even the furnishings. Beneath his altarpiece, for example, Creecher placed an unusual semi-elliptical communion table within a similarly shaped rail; and these found their counterpart in the curving lines of an apse-like entrance at the west end. Although we know the Surveyor had no official role in fitting out the City churches, it is very hard not to see his hand in Creecher's work. And in spite of the twentieth-century rearrangements, we can still see why the more discerning Georgian connoisseurs thought Walbrook to be 'the Master-piece of the celebrated Sir Christopher Wren', and why one commentator was moved to declare that, 'Italy itself can produce no modern Building that can vie with this, in Taste or Proportion. There is not a Beauty which the Plan would admit of, that is not to be found here in its greatest perfection; and Foreigners very justly call our Judgment in question for understanding its Graces no better, and allowing it no higher a Degree of Fame.'[32]

As a rule, the exteriors of the City churches are plain. 'For enriching the outward Walls . . .' Wren wrote, 'Plainness and Duration ought principally, if not wholly, to be studied.' In principle, he liked to see a portico, 'both for Beauty and Convenience' – although here he was disappointed, since none of the churches was given one – and also 'handsome Spires, or Lanterns, rising in good Proportion above the neighbouring Houses'.[33] Even so, towers and steeples were a luxury – and an expensive one at that, sometimes amounting to more than half the cost of a church. Hence the temporary embargo in 1677, when he felt that precious coal money, which could be helping to provide churches for parishes which didn't have them, was being needlessly diverted towards embellishing those which could already function as places of worship.

The City's vestries didn't agree. To them, towers and steeples weren't optional extras: they were inextricably bound up with the idea of what a church should be. They were functional, accommodating the bells which called the faithful to prayer and marked their passing. They were status symbols: each parish vied with its neighbour to have a bigger, better, more visible expression of its importance. But more than this, they represented continuity and tradition. Before the Fire, the spires of the City churches had dominated the skyline, proclaiming the piety of the population. It was unthinkable that they shouldn't rise again above a capital which had been reduced to ashes precisely because of its godlessness.

On a practical note, while all the lead-covered timber steeples had gone, eleven of the towers had survived relatively unscathed. There was no point in going to the expense of replacing them with something new: they could simply be repaired. And so they were, although in several cases structural defects which had been overlooked or ignored by the vestries and their contractors would become apparent in later years. The towers of St Christopher-le-Stocks, St Mary Aldermary, St Mary Woolnoth, St Michael Cornhill and St Sepulchre had all been patched up by their parishes before the Commission began its work. All had to be repaired or completely rebuilt in the early eighteenth century.

The perils of this make-do-and-mend approach, and the difficulties Wren faced in coping with the well-meaning efforts of the vestries, are well illustrated by the story of St Mary-le-Bow. A year or two before the Commission was established, the parish paid for work to begin on restoring the tower of the church, said to derive its name from the pre-Fire steeple, a distinctive arrangement of 'bows' or flying buttresses which carried a short central lantern.[34] The church itself was one of the first group of fifteen to be rebuilt under the auspices of the Commission, and construction began on the main body of the building in the summer of 1670. By the following winter, it was becoming obvious to Wren that the old tower was not quite as sound as the vestry had imagined. Cracks began to appear in the stonework, and then to widen. He tried to patch them up, and in April an anchor-smith was paid for iron cramps and braces; but in May 1671 the Commission reported that 'new discovery is made that the foundations are naught, and the Core of the Wall so Crushed and weakened that in all judicious men's Opinons, who have viewed it of late, the Tower will be very dangerous'.[35] Wren decided to take it down and start all over again on a new site on Cheapside, a few yards south-west of the old tower.[36]

There were no precedents from the ancient world to show how he should set about this. Vitruvius's sketchy account of the octagonal first-century BC Tower of the Winds in Athens, which had 'a conical shaped piece of marble' for a spire and a weather-vane in the form of a bronze triton,[37] came closest; but the pure, aspirational verticality of the traditional church steeple was unequivocally a Gothic creation, and Wren's problem once again was how to reconcile it to 'a better Manner of Architecture'. There was nothing in either England or France to turn to for inspiration; he may have known, through engravings and printed texts, some of the Italian Renaissance's various attempts to produce classical equivalents;[38] and he certainly knew – because he owned a drawing of it – of at least one piece of Netherlandish Baroque. This was the tower and steeple of the Jesuit church of St Charles Borromeo in Antwerp, designed around 1620 by Pieter Huyssens, probably with help from Rubens. Quotations from St Charles Borromeo, which had a square belfry leading to an octagonal cupola, a smaller lantern and finally a little spire capped with a ball and cross, crop up in several of the City steeples. That of St Magnus the Martyr is a near copy; it was probably designed by Hooke, although it wasn't constructed until after his death.[39]

An early drawing for the tower and steeple of St Mary-le-Bow, made by Edward Woodroffe but presumably to Wren's design, shows a passing resemblance to the Antwerp church. But the Surveyor went on to develop a fresher, more dynamic treatment for the steeple. For the entrance, a niche set in a rusticated surround, he turned to France, borrowing from François Mansart's doorway to the Hôtel de Conti in Paris but adding a Doric doorway. The upper storey of the tower is quite plain, with Ionic pilasters and louvred, round-headed openings to the belfry. Then the fun really begins. The four corners of the tower are decorated with scrollwork and urns, the equivalent of the four lanterns which stood on the parapet of the pre-Fire tower. Between them there is a small, circular, colonnaded 'temple', the dome of which consists of twelve brackets or flying buttresses. They support a second little temple – this time square in plan – which finally leads to an obelisk, topped with a ball and, 225 feet above the street, a weather-vane in the shape of a dragon. (Edward Pierce was paid £4 for carving a wooden model 'for ye Vane of Copper upon ye top of ye Steeple', and also for 'cutting a relive in board to be profered up to discerne the right bignesse'.)[40] There are playful, deliberate quotes from the earlier steeple in the four urns and the twelve 'bows'; in another context and another age, one would call such self-referential devices Post-Modern. The tiered composition, certainly the most successful and striking of all the City's steeples, is neither Gothic nor classical, just Wren at his very best, breaking fresh ground in his quest for visual effect. As one eighteenth-century critic wrote, it is not 'to be reduced to any settled Laws of Beauty; without doubt, if we consider it only as a Part of some other Building, it can be esteemed no other than a delightful Absurdity: But . . . [it is] as perfect as human Imagination can contrive or execute'.[41] Indeed it is.

The steeple of St Mary-le-Bow was finished in 1680, one of the first to rise above the rooftops of the rebuilt capital. Like the building of the City churches themselves, the steeple-building programme was a long and convoluted process – longer and more convoluted, in fact, since, despite the complaints of the vestries, it was given a much lower priority, with original designs from Wren's office being modified or discarded by the time money was finally available to put them into execution. The business was still continuing when the Commission was finally wound up in 1717: St Anne Soho had to wait until the following year for its spire; James Gibbs's magnificent steeple to St Clement Danes went up the year after that. Altogether, around a third of the churches had to wait until the early years of the eighteenth century for their steeples; another third didn't get them at all. Yet in spite of, or because of, this lengthy gestation period, the sheer variety of ways in which Wren and his team responded to their task is astounding. Every steeple, every tower, was distinctive, innovative, different from its neighbours. There were simple lead-covered bell-cages; complex clusters of columns; miniature temples and plain towers with pierced parapets; urns and obelisks and ogees and domed lanterns.

'I have given several Examples in the City of different Forms [of spire],' Wren later wrote, with his usual modesty.[42] It would be fairer to say that the collaboration he masterminded for close on fifty years redefined the London skyline, just as it reshaped the capital's idea of how a modern place of worship should function. That it *was* a collaboration in no way detracts from the fact that a mastermind was behind it.

12

The Most Essential Part
of Architecture

Sir Christopher Wren
Said, 'I am going to dine with some men.
If anybody calls
Say I am designing St Paul's.'[1]

*T*here's more than a germ of truth to E. C. Bentley's
clerihew. Wren certainly didn't devote all – or even most – of
his time to clambering over scaffolding at site meetings, or
sitting hunched over a drawing board designing St Paul's, or any other
building, come to that. Working life in the seventeenth century was a
relatively civilized business for a government official in his position. One
was judged by results, insofar as one was judged at all; how you spent
your time was entirely up to you.

Robert Hooke was the Surveyor's constant companion and closest
friend throughout the 1670s and beyond. His diaries are the chief source
for our knowledge of Wren's movements in this period, and the *only*
source to tell us much about his day-to-day life. For example, we know
from Hooke that the two men often ate together at Wren's house: 'Past
Kemsters bills at Scotland Yard. dind with Sir Ch Wren on beans and
Bacon' is a typical entry.[2] They also dined out together: in August 1677,
for instance, they went to visit Robert Boyle's sister, Lady Ranelagh, in
Pall Mall (Hooke ate too many grapes and had diarrhoea when he got
home); and that November they were in illustrious company at the Earl
of Danby's lodgings, where fellow dinner guests included Prince
Rupert, the Earl of Bath 'and other learned men'.[3] They sometimes
went to the theatre together – on one occasion they saw Thomas

Shadwell's operatic version of *The Tempest* - and they made expeditions to view the occasional curiosity. 'To Dog wonder with Sir Ch Wren, spent 1sh', was Hooke's enigmatic note in November 1676.[4]

But on a typical day the diminutive figure of the King's Surveyor could be found, not in his Scotland Yard office or seeking out strange meetings with sideshow freaks, but sitting contentedly in one of the hundreds of coffee-houses which had sprung up around Westminster and the City over the past twenty years. He was a regular at Garaway's in Change Alley, Cornhill, which claimed to have been the first to have 'publicly sold tea in leaf and drink' back in 1657; at Jonathan's, also in Change Alley; and at Child's in St Paul's Churchyard, which was a popular spot with Greshamites and members of the Royal Society, and handy for business meetings with cathedral contractors. In such noisy but congenial settings, he could sit with friends and for a penny or two take a dish of thick black coffee. Or perhaps he might take some chocolate, which was reckoned to be particularly good for the stomach – although since it was usually boiled up with claret, thickened with egg yolks and sweetened, it's a wonder that anyone managed to keep it down.

Wren's favourite haunt was Man's Coffee House, 'an old-fashion'd room like that of a Cathedral Tenement'.[5] Standing at the end of a dark alley off Charing Cross and just round the corner from Wren's house in Scotland Yard, Man's was the place to be. Its proximity to Whitehall meant that all sorts of courtiers gathered there to discuss affairs of state in hushed whispers, to plot their next moves in private rooms at the back of the house, to pass on titbits of news and court intrigue to favoured hangers-on and snub the hordes of petitioners who flocked around them. At any time of the day men of fashion could be found, 'walking Backwards and Forwards with their Hats in their Hands, not daring to convert 'em to their intended Use, lest it should put the Foretop of their wigs to some disorder'.[6] Pipe-smoking, a habit Wren sometimes indulged in, was frowned upon, so habitués took snuff instead. According to one customer, 'the clashing of their snuff-box lids, in opening and shutting, made more noise than their tongues [and] sounded as terrible . . . as the melancholy Tick of so many Death-watch beetles'.[7]

Man's isn't the sort of milieu in which we would expect to find the ascetic, austere Surveyor-General. Nor were Jonathan's and Garaway's, come to that – all three houses were reckoned to be among the most notorious hotbeds of Popery and sedition in the whole of London. But they were also the accepted places to do business. Bankers and stock-jobbers met at Jonathan's and Garaway's; doctors and clergymen congregated at Child's. And because of its closeness to Scotland Yard – and the presence of the Surveyor-General – the building trades mixed in with the fops and wits who paraded up and down at Man's. Wren often sat there for hours with Hooke and Oliver, talking over the progress of the City churches, going through the accounts, sometimes just listening while Hooke poured out his thoughts on anything from 'philosophical spring scales' and a 'new way of sayling by slope sayles' to Hagia Sophia and the Alexandrian Bible of Tecla. Friends and colleagues would drift in and out; contractors would arrive to discuss a particular job, or negotiate a decent rate. As the day wore on, the two men would go for a walk in St James's Park, or separate and move on, to another coffee-house and another meeting.

For the first six months of 1676 Wren's Saturday nights were taken up with a 'New Philosophicall Clubb' that he and Hooke founded that January. It was intended as a forum for the discussion of natural philosophy and mechanics and the select membership was drawn from existing Royal Society members, including William Holder, Abraham Hill and Sir Jonas Moore, the Surveyor-General of the Ordnance and the man who had gone to Tangier in Wren's stead back in the early 1660s.[8] The group met each week at Wren's house, and in marked contrast to their host's open approach to scientific debate, they resolved at the outset 'not to speak of any thing that was then reveald . . . to any one nor to declare that we had such a meeting at all'.[9]

The first meeting, on 1 January, was a lively affair. Wren and Hooke discussed the latter's theory, set out in the *Micrographia*, that light was a series of pulses or waves, with Hooke arguing that Newton had stolen his idea in a paper he had recently sent to the Society.* (Perhaps this was one reason for the secrecy surrounding the Saturday Club.) They also talked of the geography of the moon, which was still one of Wren's abiding interests. Hooke declared that it was possible to see water there; 'Sir Christopher affirmd noe water nor River nor cloudes'.[10] William Winde dropped in just as the discussion was moving on to earthly waters, and the possibility of travelling across swamps on rafts of hurdles; he told the company about the snow-boots he had seen in Holland in the 1650s, which were equipped with teeth to grip the ice.

---

*Newton cheerfully admitted as much. It was in the course of their correspondence on the matter that he famously wrote of how, 'if I have seen farther, it is by standing on the shoulders of giants'.

And so the evening wore on, with the talk moving from chemical combustion to stage effects – 'Sir Christopher [told] of the way of thunder by a ball falling in Archimedes screw sett upright about 12 foot high' – to ballistics, luminous fish slime and maggots in decaying flesh. The party broke up at nine and everyone went off to Child's, where they found Aubrey and carried on chatting for another two hours. When Hooke finally got back to Gresham College, it was so late that he found the gates locked.

With around half a dozen regulars, the Saturday Club flourished for several months. But by the late spring interest was tailing off. Wren, Hooke, Holder and Aubrey met on 20 May – 'Discourse nothing worth,' wrote Hooke – after which things ground to a halt. The reason for the club's demise was to be found, oddly enough, on the London stage. That month the Duke of York's Company put on a new play by Thomas Shadwell at Dorset Gardens, Fleet Street. *The Virtuoso* was a witty, well-informed and wonderfully vicious attack on experimental philosophy in general and the Royal Society in particular. Its eponymous hero, Sir Nicholas Gimcrack, was 'the finest speculative Gentleman in the whole World':[11] and his experiments bore a marked resemblance to many of those described in Thomas Sprat's *History of the Royal Society*, Hooke's *Micrographia* and the pages of the Society's *Philosophical Transactions*. Gimcrack spends his time in weighing air, in examining flies, maggots and cheese-mites through his microscope, in transfusing blood from one dog to another and in one case from a sheep to a madman: 'The Patient, from being Maniacal or raging Mad, became wholly Ovine, or Sheepish; he bleated perpetually, and chew'd the Cud: He had Wool growing on him in great Quantities, and a Northamptonshire Sheep's Tail did soon emerge or arise from his Anus . . .'[12] He reads his Geneva Bible by the light given off from a putrescent leg of pork, has managed to cut an animal's windpipe and keep it alive by blowing air into its lungs with a pair of bellows; and is preparing to publish a lunar atlas. Through the telescopes set up in his garden, he can see 'all the mountainous parts, and valleys, and seas, and lakes in [the moon]; nay, the larger sort of animals, as elephants and camels; but public buildings and ships very easily. They have great guns and have the use of gunpowder. At land they fight with elephants and castles. I have seen 'em.'[13]

There had been attacks on the Royal Society before, from conservatives who clung doggedly to their Aristotle and Galen, from theologians who mistrusted the new philosophy's emphasis on empirical observation, from scholars who were exasperated with the apparent pointlessness of the Society's experiments. 'I think the reading of Histories,' wrote one commentator in 1669, '. . . will much more become them than attending on furnaces, or raking into the entrails of men or beasts to find somewhat which it may be will never make them much wiser when they know it nor ever prove of any great use'.[14] And only two years before Shadwell's play appeared, Sir William Petty had pointed out that the Society 'has been censured (though without much cause) for spending too much time in matters not directly tending to profit and palpable Advantages (as the weighing of Air and the like) . . . We have been also complained of for producing nothing New.'[15]

But popular ridicule was more damaging than the dry arguments of scholars, particularly when it was well researched. (*The Virtuoso* repeats whole passages from the *Philosophical Transactions* and Hooke's *Micrographia* almost word for word.) Sprat had early on articulated the danger posed by the men of wit:

We ought to have a great dread of the power of these terrible men: I confess I believe that New Philosophy need not (like Caesar) fear the pale or the melancholy as much as the humorous and the merry: For they perhaps by making it ridiculous because it is new . . . may do it more injury than all the arguments of our severe and frowning and dogmatical adversaries.[16]

Sir Nicholas Gimcrack proved Sprat's point with a vengeance. Wren must have winced at the references to the selenography: only a few months before he had been sitting round a table at Scotland Yard and earnestly debating the existence of water on the moon. Hooke, who along with Robert Boyle was the butt of most of Shadwell's jokes, was mortified. He steeled himself to visit the Dorset Gardens playhouse one Friday night at the beginning of June. 'People almost pointed,' he wrote in his diary that night. 'Damned Doggs.'[17] Interest in the Saturday Club waned dramatically, and by the first Saturday in July Wren and Hooke were left alone at Scotland Yard, glumly discussing the play.[18]

While the first wave of City churches was going up, the two friends were also at work on another project connected with the Fire. The first Rebuilding Act had stipulated that 'the better to preserve the memory of this dreadful visitation', a column or pillar of brass or stone should be put up on or near the site of Farryner's bakery.[19] A shortage of materials and more pressing priorities meant that nothing happened until early in 1671, when the City approved Wren's wooden model. It was another six years before the 202-foot-high Monument on Fish Street Hill (the height is equal to the distance from Farryner's house), was finished at a cost of £13,450 11s 9d, taken from the coal dues; and another two years before the inscription was in place commemorating – with a brazen disregard for the truth – the fact that 'London rises again . . . three short years complete that which was considered the work of an age'.

The mason-contractor for the 'Fish Street Piller' was Joshua Marshall, whose bill came to £11,300 for a difficult job: the column is 15 feet in diameter and hollow, with 311 steps leading up to an observation deck. The carving on the pedestal, one of the most underrated pieces of allegorical sculpture in London, is by Caius Cibber. It depicts a distraught female figure, symbolizing the capital, being gently raised up by Time and reminded that through Industry she can achieve Peace and Plenty once more. King Charles and the Duke of York look on in Roman dress, surrounded by Science, Architecture, Liberty, Justice and Fortitude. As to who designed the Monument, John Evelyn was certainly under the impression that it was Wren's work. Aubrey was just as convinced it was by Hooke. No doubt it was another collaboration, perhaps dictated by political considerations: Hooke was the City's chief representative on the team of surveyors who were managing the rebuilding of the capital; Wren was the King's. The surviving drawings – some by Edward Woodroffe, others by Hooke – show that several alternatives were put forward before the executed scheme, a fluted Doric column, was finally agreed. The rejected designs included a plain obelisk, and a column garnished with tongues of fire, which was drawn by Hooke and endorsed by Wren 'With His M[ties] Approbation'. There was also a great deal of discussion about the most appropriate ornament to crown the Monument. Wren's first idea, and the one used on the wooden model, was a phoenix rising from the ashes. But by 1675, when the column was nearing completion, he changed his mind. It would be too costly, he told the City authorities; no one on the ground would be able to recognize it for what it was; and it would be dangerous, since 'by reason of the sayle, the spread winges will carry in the winde'.[20] His preferred choice was a fifteen-foot-high statue of either King Charles, the founder of the reborn capital, or a sword-wielding female personification of London triumphant. This, he said, 'would undoubtedly bee the noblest finishing that can be found Answerable to soe goodly a worke, in all men's judgments'.[21] The King favoured a simple copper-gilt ball with flames sprouting from its top; and, since it could be cast for £350 (one-third the price of the statue), Wren reluctantly acknowledged that it would do. But the City, perhaps anxious to assert its independence, rejected both the statue and the ball; and when Hooke came before the Lands Committee on 22 September with a proposal for a flaming gilt-bronze urn, they accepted it. There were no hard feelings: the two friends were happily drinking chocolate and smoking tobacco together at Garaway's a few days later. Mind you, Hooke paid the bill.

Meanwhile, Wren was working – alone, this time – on two other highly specialized buildings, both of which harked back in their different ways to his career as an astronomy professor.

The first was the Royal Observatory at Greenwich. In 1675, when the accurate measurement of the movements of the stars still seemed the most obvious solution to the problem of longitude, Charles II resolved to build an observatory 'in order to the finding out of the longitude of places for perfecting navigation and astronomy'.[22] The moving force behind the decision was Sir Jonas Moore. That summer Moore had taken the young astronomer John Flamsteed under his wing, giving him lodgings and a makeshift observatory at his house in the Tower of London and encouraging him in his plan to make a reliable catalogue of the positions of the fixed stars. It was through his influence that the King agreed to finance a more permanent structure and to appoint Flamsteed as the first Astronomer Royal.

Wren's credentials for designing the observatory were obvious; although even if they hadn't been, it was the King's building and he was the King's architect. The word 'observatory' is a little misleading, however: in the seventeenth century, serious observations of the stars were invariably carried out in the open air, using immensely long telescopes suspended from vertical poles. All that was really needed was a walled court and secure and weatherproof storage for the instruments. But as Wren said a few years later, the building served two further purposes. It was 'for the Observator's habitation' – Flamsteed and his assistant were to live there – and it was 'a little for Pompe'.[23] When Charles II and his courtiers came to view the moon, or to peer at the rings of Saturn and the moons of Jupiter, they needed to be entertained in something more than a shed.

After some deliberation Wren decided against Sir Jonas Moore's preferred site in Hyde Park (thereby ensuring that the world would never talk of Hyde Park Mean Time) in favour of a medieval tower on a hilltop in Greenwich Park, which overlooked the Queen's House and the half-built Greenwich Palace. The old tower was demolished, leaving only the foundations, and above them he created a compact two-storey building with turrets, free-standing pavilions, and a large court – the business end of the observatory – to the rear. The King laid the first stone on 10 August and work progressed swiftly, so that Flamsteed could move in that Christmas. The budget was £500, and Wren managed to keep the costs down to just over £520 – something of an achievement for him – by using bricks brought down from Tilbury Fort and wood, iron and lead recycled from a demolished gatehouse at the Tower of London. (Some of the 'stone' dressings are actually made of wood, suggesting that economy was a significant factor in the construction.) Although the King paid Flamsteed £100 a year, he neglected to provide his Astronomer Royal with any instruments, which were supplied by the Royal Society and Sir Jonas, 'with the Advice and Assistance of Sir Christopher'.[24]

Although the Royal Observatory marks a handy if somewhat misleading conflation of Wren's two careers, its role in his developing architectural style and in the history of British architecture is unimportant. The same can't be said for the other unusually specialized building he designed in the mid-1670s. The library at Trinity College, Cambridge was the brainchild of Isaac Barrow, Master of Trinity from 1673 until his untimely death in 1677 at the age of only forty-six, and Vice-Chancellor of the University from 1675 to 1676. According to the lawyer-architect Roger North, Barrow was keen for Cambridge to build a theatre to match Oxford's Sheldonian, and for the same reason, 'it being a profanation and a scandal that the speeches should be had in the university church, and that also be deformed with scaffold and defiled with rude crowds and outcries'.[25] He put the idea before a council of the college heads, arguing that the more 'magnificent and stately' the building, the easier it would be to solicit contributions towards the cost. But they quailed at the prospect and, to quote North again,

> Dr Barrow was piqued at this pusillanimity, and declared that he would go straight to his college and lay out the foundations of a building to enlarge his back court and close it with a stately library, which should be more magnificent and costly than what he had proposed to them, and doubted not but upon the interest of his

college in a short time to bring it to perfection ... That very afternoon he, with his gardeners and servants, staked out the foundation upon which the building now stands.[26]

The story is a little more complicated than that. The building Barrow actually proposed was a combination of theatre and new university library, and he got as far as asking for a design from Wren, whom he knew well by reputation, and probably in person.[27] In the 1660s the two men had moved in the same scientific and academic circles. Both were protégés of John Wilkins; both were mathematicians and Fellows of the Royal Society, although Barrow rarely if ever attended its meetings; and both put in time at Gresham, where Barrow held the chair of geometry from 1662 to 1663. (Wilkins recommended him for the post on the death of Laurence Rooke: his inaugural address contained a glowing tribute to Wren.) When Dr Barrow stormed out of his meeting, determined to show his pusillanimous colleagues what a single college could accomplish in the way of magnificent and stately architecture, it was natural for him to turn once more to Wren.

The Surveyor was ready to oblige. As he said years later, 'Nothing is more acceptable to me than to promote what in me lies any public Ornament, and more especially in the Universities, where I find something of a public spirit to be yet alive'.[28] It wasn't entirely due to his own public-spiritedness that he undertook the commission. There was the kudos – he was only human, and by the time it was finished Trinity Library would turn out to be the largest building put up by the university since King's College Chapel. There was the considerable engineering challenge of creating a structure which would bear the massive weight of thousands of books. And there was perhaps also an element of fortuitous timing. In 1674 Michael Honeywood, the Dean of Lincoln Cathedral, had paid for a new library in the cloisters at Lincoln. The contract stipulated it should be built 'according to Sir Christopher Wren's directions and Mr Tompson's modell',[29] implying that while Wren's Office was involved in some way, the actual design was Tompson's (probably the London mason John Tompson). The project may have whetted his appetite, setting him thinking about what exactly was involved in building a classical library; so that when Barrow approached him the following year, he was more than ready to use the opportunity to work out ideas which had been bubbling away for months.

The first of those ideas was ingenious, but impractical. The site for the new library was at the west end of Trinity's three-sided Nevile's Court, and the obvious solution was to complete the quadrangle with a fourth range. But obvious solutions rarely appealed to Wren, and initially he proposed a centralized domed space, derived ultimately from Palladio's Villa Rotunda, which was to stand in glorious isolation, linked to the existing buildings by low curving screen walls topped with iron railings. An Ionic portico faced into the quad, and the bookshelves were arranged around the walls in three tiers, broken by Corinthian pilasters. Seating for those consulting the books was underneath these tiers, and there were no galleries: access to the shelves was via narrow corridors built into the thickness of the walls, which would have been badly lit and dangerous – there is nothing in the design to show how the students seated below were to be protected from the occasional falling book. And in order for anyone wandering round the circular corridors to find a given book, the spines would have to have faced the outer walls: to modern eyes, at least, this would have given a very odd look to the domed, book-lined interior.

The rotunda was dropped; perhaps it was a little too *outré* for Barrow and the Fellows. But pencil sketches on a surviving site plan[30] suggest that Wren was simultaneously experimenting with this scheme and a more orthodox rectangular range, set to the west of the existing quad; in the event, it was the rectangular range which won out, with the north and south wings of Nevile's Court extended to meet it. This second design was much bigger and grander. The library proper was at first-floor level – the usual practice in Oxford and Cambridge colleges at the time – and consisted of a single gallery thirteen bays long, with high, round-headed windows on both sides to let in the maximum amount of light. The bookcases filled the lower walls and projected out to form a total of twenty-two study areas, or 'cells' as Wren called them, each with its own window, reading desk and stand. (The four end bays had no desks: they were slightly longer than the others, the result, as Wren pointed out to Barrow, of having to bring windows and doors 'to answer to the old building'.) Access was to be via staircases in small domed pavilions to the north and south. Only the northern pavilion was actually built; a more ceremonial ascent to the south side was proposed – an open, curving double flight of stairs – but in the end the college settled on an iron balcony. The gallery was supported on an open arcade facing east into the court, with a plain ashlar wall to the west and a single row of columns running down the long axis between the two to take the strain of the forty-foot span. 'I have chosen middle pillars . . . rather than a middle wall,' he said, 'as being the same expense, more graceful, and according to the manner of the ancients who made double walkes (with three rowes of pillars, or two rowes and a wall), about the forum.'[31] The Nevile's Court façade was particularly richly treated, with a Doric order for the arcade and Ionic three-quarter columns above. It was unbroken and the central three bays were marked simply by four statues perched on the balustrade, 'according to ancient example'; he rejected the notion of a grand frontispiece 'because in this case I find any thing else impertinent, the Entrances being endwise'.

Jacopo Sansovino's Library of St Mark's in Venice (begun 1537), then already famous throughout Europe and revered by Palladio as 'the richest and most ornate building that has been put up, perhaps since the time of the ancients', is the obvious source for Wren's design – but not necessarily the right one. It owes more to the First Model for St Paul's, where he had used the device of a Doric colonnade supporting a gallery lit by round-headed windows with, in that case, Corinthian pilasters. This feature of the First Model derived from the Theatre of Marcellus; so did Sansovino's building. Thus it would perhaps be fairer to say that Trinity Library and the Library of St Mark's shared a common ancestry. A source rather closer to home was John Webb's pioneering library and repository for the Royal College of Physicians in Amen Court (1651–3), again built over an arched loggia. It was destroyed in the Great Fire but, as Professor Colvin has pointed out,[32] Amen Court was close enough to Bishopsgate for both Wren and Barrow to have been familiar with Webb's building during their time at Gresham. It is also worth recalling that Wren almost certainly had an even closer acquaintance with the College through his old mentor Charles Scarburgh, who was a lecturer there while the two men were removing canine spleens in the 1650s.

Work started on Trinity Library in February 1676 under the general supervision of the Cambridge mason Robert Grumbold; the roof was leaded in 1680, but the finishing touches ran on into the 1690s. Wren, who waived his fee, visited Cambridge in October 1676, accompanied by William Holder, and Grumbold made at least eight trips to Scotland Yard between 1676 and 1685. When in November of the latter year it became clear that the floor wouldn't support the weight of the projecting bookcases, even with Wren's line of 'middle pillars' to reduce the span, the Surveyor sent the Office of Works' Master Carpenter, Matthew Banckes, to see what could be done. The 'modell' which arrived from London the following month[33] presumably showed the joiners how to rectify the problem, which was solved by a combination of cantilevers under the floor and iron bars, which were bolted at one end to the wall and at the other to girders running the length of the library beneath the bookcases.

One of the most interesting features of the library's building history is the care and attention Wren lavished on both the design and its execution. In the specification which he sent to Barrow along with the drawings,[34] he said that the windows were deliberately made large enough and wide enough to take stone mullions, with the glass pointed in, 'which after all inventions is the only durable way in our climate for a public building, where care must be had that snowe drive not in'. The central area of the library should be paved in marble, 'which would much consult the quiet of the place'; while the cells must be floored in wainscot, 'for the cleanesse of the bookes from dust'. He even designed the reading desks and stands and, I imagine, the bookcases – although the drawings for these, dated 1686, are in Nicholas Hawksmoor's hand. (Hawksmoor had started in Wren's office as a domestic clerk in around 1679 when he was eighteen. He lived in Wren's house in the 1680s and, after an informal apprenticeship which involved witnessing contracts on the Surveyor's behalf, copying drawings, acting as a measuring clerk and even buying stationery and transcribing accounts, his aptitude for architecture led Wren to appoint him Clerk of the Works at Kensington Palace in 1689, and to put him forward as his assistant at St Paul's two years later.)

This attention extended to the building work itself. Wren promised to give a careful estimate of costs, and to scale up details of the design so that the workmen had no room to develop them in their own way, even though this was the usual practice in the seventeenth century. Where there were elements which might pose problems for the mason, 'I shall direct him in a firme manner of executing the designe'. Barrow was to keep the original drawings safe and not to allow the workmen to take them on site and ruin them. And if he thought Wren was being over-scrupulous, 'you must pardon us, the Architects are as great pedants as Critics or Heralds'.

Most Restoration architects were neither scrupulous nor pedantic, in fact. They were happy for craftsmen to interpret their ideas and to modify them, often quite radically, in execution. That was the way things were done, because that was the way things had always been done. Wren's professionalism, his holistic approach to design and, most significantly, his need to control every stage of the process, were something new in British architecture. And the library itself shows a new maturity in his own work. We might regret the loss of the rotunda, but it belongs to the first stage of his architectural career: a stage in which unorthodoxy could easily overpower fitness for purpose; a stage in which he exhilarated in the act of creation and gloried in the opportunities to demonstrate his classical scholarship and to innovate. The calm simplicity of Trinity Library as executed, its tacit acknowledgement that less is more, mark a turning point. With Trinity, Wren came of age.

Seventeen months after Faith's death, Wren married for a second time. The wedding took place on Saturday 24 February 1677 in the Chapel Royal at Whitehall, which he was in the process of refurbishing for the King. The bride, and a mother for the motherless Christopher junior, was Jane Fitzwilliam.

Jane's father, the second Lord Fitzwilliam of Lifford in the Irish peerage, had estates in Northamptonshire and lodgings in the Savoy, where he died in 1659. Her mother, Catherine, who followed him to the grave twelve years later, came from a City background – she was the daughter and heiress of one London merchant and, when she married Fitzwilliam, the widow of another.

But the woman herself is a complete mystery, as she seems to have been to Wren's intimates. Certainly Hooke, who saw him socially and professionally two or three times a week in the months leading up to the happy day, either didn't know or couldn't remember Jane's name when he came to record the event in his diary – a fact which hardly suggests it was constantly on his friend's lips. He didn't meet the new Lady Wren until six weeks later, after the couple had settled into the Scotland Yard house, where their life quickly assumed a comfortable and familiar pattern. They entertained: Hooke often dined with them, talking to Jane of subjects as varied as the Koran and the celebrated follies of the annual Bartholomew Fair, where there were stiltwalkers, sideshows with tigers at twopence a time, an elephant which could wave flags with its trunk and shoot a gun, and, more intriguing than all of that, a child who did 'strange tricks'.[35] And they procreated. Their first child, a daughter named for her mother, was born eight months and thirteen days after the wedding, on 9 November. A son, William, followed in June 1679; his godparents were John Evelyn, Viscountess Newport (wife of Charles II's Treasurer of the Household) and a relative of Jane by marriage, Sir William Fermor of Easton Neston, in her home county of Northamptonshire.

The two children had very different futures. Jane stayed by her father's side and never married; she grew up to be bright, musically gifted and a tower of strength. 'Poor Billy', as Wren called him, also remained at home – not out of filial devotion, but because he was mentally handicapped. We can only wonder at the emotional impact his presence in the household had on the brilliant, impatient, tightly controlled Surveyor, a man for whom intellectual prowess meant everything.

And there was no wife to share his worries. In the middle of September 1680, Jane was taken ill. She seemed to recover, but three weeks later, on Monday 6 October, she died. On the Wednesday, Wren buried her in the chancel of St Martin-in-the-Fields, next to Faith and Gilbert.

A widower for a second time, with three children under the age of six, the obvious step for a man in Wren's position was to find another wife as quickly as possible. But he didn't. For whatever reason – grief, pride, apathy, an angry determination not to rely on anything as transient as an emotional relationship – he turned his back on marriage for ever, and remained a widower until his own death forty-three years later.

Indirectly, it was another death which led Wren to renew his interest in the Royal Society, which had taken second place to his architecture for some years now. Speechless and senseless, Henry Oldenburg breathed his last at the beginning of September 1677. For a decade and a half the Royal Society's Secretary had done as much as anyone, and more than most, to promote and maintain the organization, publishing research findings at more-or-less regular intervals in the *Philosophical Transactions*, championing the claims of individual Fellows and ensuring, through his astonishingly wide correspondence with figures of the stature of Hevelius, Huygens, Auzout, Leibniz and Leeuwenhoek, that the gatherings at Gresham College were recognized as a major force by the European scientific community at large. After a swift and rather unseemly visit to Oldenburg's grieving widow to 'demand, receive, or take order for securing . . . all such goods, books, and writings belonging to the Society',[36] the Society was plunged into a bout of vicious political dogfighting. This first took the form of a struggle for the vacant Secretaryship between Hooke, who stepped into the place temporarily, and the physician and botanist Nehemiah Grew; and then developed into a battle royal between those of the 21-man Council who thought Oldenburg's death heralded a change of leadership, and the supporters of Viscount Brouncker, who had held an iron grip on the Presidency ever since the first royal charter of 1662.

Brouncker still had his friends among the old guard on the Council, but they were in a minority. Hooke, who admittedly wasn't on the Council (hence his anxiety about the Secretaryship), thought him 'a busybody' and 'a dog'. Pepys, who was, called him 'a rotten-hearted, false man as any else I know'.[37] He hadn't shown his face at either a regular weekly gathering at Gresham or a meeting of the Council for months, and even among those who didn't dislike the President personally, there was a sense of disquiet that autumn. Memories of Sir Nicholas Gimcrack and the scoffers still rankled.

Wren belonged to the anti-Brouncker faction. On Wednesday 10 October, after an afternoon spent plotting with Fellows and Council members in a coffee-house, Robert Hooke called round to see him with a proposition. If it came to an election, would he stand against Brouncker? Wren said yes.

At a Council meeting the following week (which the President attended, presumably having got wind of the conspiracy), there was a huge row: the lawyer Sir John Hoskins insisted on calling for a ballot on election day, and Brouncker flew into a great passion and walked out. Over the next three weeks, Hooke lobbied tirelessly for his friend. He plotted with him over dishes of chocolate at Jonathan's and Child's, although the incurably earnest pair couldn't focus on politics for too long, and their conversation had a habit of straying into territory which was at once more exotic and, I suspect, more comfortable – the precise shape of Lars Porsenna's tomb, flying, cats, falling sickness and 'the curious gardener of Amsterdam'.[38] Hooke also did his best to strengthen Hoskins' determination to insist on a ballot, and went to see Council member Daniel Whistler who, after he had promised to examine Mrs Whistler's 'viviparous onions', reassured him that he was resolved 'never to see Royal Society if Brouncker President'.[39] Mindful of the ballot, Hooke even went to the trouble of canvassing support from Fellows who usually played little or no part in the Society's proceedings.[40]

As befitted a presidential candidate, Wren remained aloof from all this, leaving the work to his campaign manager. To be sure, he had other things to occupy his mind, not least the fact that his wife Jane was heavily pregnant. By a quirk of fate, the news of the death of Wren's patron, Gilbert Sheldon, arrived the day their daughter was born. In a move which surprised everyone, but which must have delighted the architect almost as much as the birth of his daughter, the King appointed

William Sancroft his successor as Archbishop of Canterbury, and Wren immediately wrote to congratulate him, rejoicing for the Church of England and St Paul's that 'his Majestie hath made so wise and exact a choyce for the service both of them and himselfe'.[41] Residentiary Edward Stillingfleet moved into the Deanery.

In spite of all Hooke's hard work, Wren couldn't enlist the necessary support at the Society. The rest of the anti-Brouncker faction seems to have thought that he lacked the necessary political clout and, with only a fortnight to go to the anniversary elections, some frantic cloak-and-dagger negotiations took place before they set out to catch an altogether bigger fish. Five days after Jane's birth (on the fourth anniversary of Wren's knighthood, as it happened), a deputation of ten Fellows, including Hooke, Wren, William Holder, John Evelyn and John Aubrey, went round to the home of Sir Joseph Williamson, Charles II's principal Secretary of State, to 'bid [him] about accepting the presidentship'.[42]

Variously described by contemporaries as cold and formal, severe to his servants, mean with his huge fortune and prone to making passes at his King's mistresses, Sir Joseph had been elected to the Society in 1662 and had served on the Council for the past three years, without making much of an impact. A career politician, his interests leaned towards genealogy and music (Evelyn reckoned him an expert performer at '*Jeu de Goblets*') rather than the mathematical or physical sciences; but his position at the heart of government meant a great deal more than scientific achievement. He was a consummately clever choice.

Sir Joseph entertained the deputation well, and accepted the dissident Fellows' offer. For his part, Wren gave way with a good grace. He could hardly do anything else. Although when poor Hooke visited him the following Saturday and begged him to intercede with Williamson over the vacant Secretary's place, he showed one of those bursts of petulance to which he was prone when crossed, and told his friend to his face that he wasn't the man for the job. In the event, Brouncker stood down and the election went through without a hitch on 30 November – four days later Williamson threw a celebration party for his supporters – and Hooke and Nehemiah Grew were appointed joint Secretaries to the Society. Brouncker kept his seat on the Council, but disappeared from the scene, angry and hurt. Wren was elected to the Council – his sixth stint since the charter of 1662 – and his disappointment at losing the Presidency was tempered by Williamson's shrewd decision to make him Vice-President.

Williamson turned out to be quite a good thing for the Royal Society, and a conscientious President. But affairs of state meant that he was sometimes unable to attend the regular weekly meetings, and he was a conspicuous absentee at the less regular but arguably more important meetings of the Council. In his absence, Wren often took the chair: during the three years of Williamson's Presidency, he officiated at 11 out of 24 Council meetings and 12 of the 108 full gatherings of the Society. That's not a bad record, and it stimulated a renewal of his interest in experimental philosophy after a period of relative inactivity in the earlier 1670s, when he was working hard to make a success of the Surveyor-General's post. His contributions to the discussions at Gresham were characteristically wide-ranging, taking in everything from monstrous births (on one occasion both he and Aubrey asserted that they had personally seen the offspring of a union between a tomcat and a rabbit) to his opinion on the composition of china-ink, how to cure a wasp-sting by raising a blister and how to desalinate seawater by letting it stand, by straining it through 'the pores of sea-plants' or by freezing it.[43]

Astronomy seems to have taken a back seat. Apart from a passing reference by Hooke to a discussion at Williamson's house on the 'Vibrative motion of comet[s]',[44] there is nothing to show that Wren was engaged in what he called 'the Trade . . . I was once well acquainted with'.[45] What did fire his interest, however, was the nature of air and theories of respiration which, a century before Priestley, Scheele and Lavoisier discovered oxygen, were being debated by the scientific community right across Europe. Clearly air – or something *in* the air – was necessary to life: Boyle's early experiments with his vacuum pump had shown that conclusively, while in 1664 Hooke had vivisected a dog and, using a pair of bellows and a pipe inserted into its trachea, 'was able to preserve [it] alive as long as I could desire, after I had wholly opened the thorax, and cut off all the ribs, and opened the belly'. The suffering he caused the animal was so terrible that he resolved never to repeat the experiment.[46]

The question was, just *how* did air sustain life? Was the true use of respiration 'to discharge the fumes of the blood', as Hooke once proposed, echoing traditional Galenic physiology, which talked in the same context of 'sooty impurities' in the blood? Or, as Wren and others suspected, rather than getting rid of impurities, did it *add* something to the blood? Recent speculation revolved around the notion that some kind of vital nitrous component was taken in by the lungs during respiration. In 1621 the Dutch inventor Cornelius Drebbel had demon-strated what may have been the world's first submarine before James I, who witnessed the astonishing spectacle of twelve oarsmen rowing a vessel underwater from Westminster to Greenwich. Drebbel refused to disclose how he had kept the air in the submarine pure; but Boyle, who interviewed his son-in-law nearly forty years later, discovered that at intervals the Dutchman had unstopped a flask containing something variously described as saltpetre or a mysterious nitrous liquor, thus restoring 'to the troubled Air such a proportion of Vitall parts, as would make it again, fit for respiration'.[47]

Wren probably became interested in air and respiration when he was associating with Boyle and John Wilkins in the 1650s: it is no coincidence that Wilkins discussed the difficulty of providing breathable air in submarines in his 1648 *Mathematical Magick*. It was perhaps in relation to Wren's collaboration with Wilkins in Oxford that in 1663 he reminded Brouncker of how he had devised an engine or vessel 'for cooling and percolating the Aire' and filtering out 'the fuliginous Vapours and Moisture, it was infected wth in Expiration'.[48] His description of this breathing apparatus is lost, although it was known to both Sprat and *Parentalia*. In the same letter he went on to say that merely cooling exhaled air and filtering out the impurities wouldn't be enough to render it recyclable: 'nitrous Fumes' would also have to be added to replace those lost during respiration. 'Ways may possibly be found to supply that too, by placing some benign Chymical Spirits, that by fumeing may infect the Air within the Vessel.'

In January 1678, at the first meeting Wren chaired that year, Hooke affirmed the existence of the ether as a vehicle in which the 'exhalations or vapours' which make up the atmosphere are dissolved in the same way that salt or sugar are dissolved in water. Wren was quick to take issue, doubting whether there was any such thing as 'that aether, which Mr Hooke had hypothetically supposed', and saying rather pointedly that he would be glad to see some experiment which demonstrated its existence.[49] The phrase 'hypothetically supposed' was a red rag to an experimental philosopher, and Wren's remarks upset Hooke. Perhaps there was still some ill-feeling between the two friends over the Presidency and the Secretaryship, although, for some reason, Sancroft's appointment was another point of difference between them – in sharp contrast to Wren, Hooke was 'not overjoyd' when he heard the news.[50] Anyway, he retorted that he could come up with hundreds of experiments, that in fact he had a whole catalogue of experiments waiting in the wings; and that any day now he was going to carry them out.

The pair soon made up, and a few weeks later they were sitting in a coffee-house talking over Wren's theories of respiration and muscular motion, which he had passed on to Boyle.[51] The theories seem to have been related. Wren believed that the expansion and contraction of muscles 'might proceed from a fermentative motion arising from the mixture of two heterogeneous fluids'[52] – a chemical reaction which produced a violent gaseous expansion, in other words, like the explosion of gunpowder – and it may be that he saw the 'nitrous fumes' which were a constituent of air as an essential ingredient in that reaction.

At a Royal Society meeting that April, with Wren again in the chair, members wondered how it was that some creatures – including coral-divers in the Aegean – could hold their breath underwater for long periods. Descartes' assertion that the heart of the otter retained the *foramen ovale* (the opening in the interatrial septum of the foetus which allows blood to bypass the lungs, and which closes after birth) was raised, and Wren flatly denied it, saying that he had 'dissected and examined an otter for that purpose' and found no such opening to exist.[53] Implying that marine animals had other physical mechanisms to help them hold their breath underwater, he also commented that the seal in St James's Park, a member of the royal collection of rare waterfowl and other exotica, had a way of blocking up its nostrils so that it could sink to the bottom of its pool and lie there for long periods at a time.* Hooke was evidently intrigued by this line of enquiry: some time later he bought a porpoise for 7s 6d and dissected it, although the spot he chose for the operation, Garaway's coffee-house, must have raised more than a few eyebrows.

Judged from the point of view of Wren's career, the most interesting thing about the exchanges to which he contributed at Gresham in the period 1678–80 is also the most obvious – that he retained an active and informed interest in science long after he had made the switch from professional scientist to professional architect. We have no way of dating the experimental work he refers to at this time – he had a long memory and a good one, and the dissection of the otter, for example, may well have taken place back in the 1650s, when he was more deeply involved in anatomical research. In those days he was working at the cutting edge of the new science; now architecture was the great experiment.

*St James's Park held quite a menagerie. As well as the seal, there were goats, antelopes and other assorted deer, Arabian sheep, an elk, a pelican (an ancestor of the present collection?) donated by the Russian ambassador, a stork, an albino raven and two cranes, one of which had a wooden leg.

Inevitably, the contributions he made to scientific debate, both in private conversations with Hooke and in his more public pronouncements at Society meetings and the short-lived Saturday Club, tended either to draw heavily on the work he had carried out as a young man or to take the form of intelligent – and sometimes positively combative – queries, comments and criticisms of sloppy thinking.

Around this time, Wren was working on a systematic discourse on architecture, covering the origins of beauty, the history of building from earliest times, and the principals of statics and structure – 'the geometrical, which is the most essential Part of Architecture'.[54] Typically, he never finished it; the original manuscripts are lost, and what survives is far from systematic. There are four fragmentary and incomplete essays, which were printed in *Parentalia* as 'Tracts on Architecture'. (And I really do mean incomplete: Tract II, for example, ends in the middle of a sentence.) A fifth Tract, also incomplete, was copied out by Christopher Wren junior some time before 1736. It was placed in the Wren family's own copy of *Parentalia*, which contains a number of manuscripts that for one reason or another Wren's son decided not to include in the published text.[56]

None of the Tracts can be dated with any precision, and Wren probably returned to them several times in the course of his life. However, both from internal evidence and from the fact that he was discussing their subject-matter in detail with Hooke from 1675 onwards, we can deduce that he was working on sections of the Tracts, at least, during the second half of the decade.[55]

One of the things which occupied Wren's interest was the hypothetical reconstruction of iconic classical monuments. Most of Tract IV and parts of Tract V are taken up with discussions of the Temple of Diana at Ephesus, the Basilica of Constantine and the Temple of Mars Ultor in Rome, the Mausoleum of Halicarnassus and the tomb of the Etruscan king, Porsenna, at Clusium. But for the beginnings of architecture, Wren went right back to Old Testament scripture. Drawing on Genesis and the commentaries of the first-century AD Jewish historian Josephus, he described how Cain built 'the first City Enos, and enclos'd it with Walls and Ramparts', before discussing Noah's Ark as 'the first Peece of Naval Architecture' and the Tower of Babel, 'the first Peece of Civil Architecture'. The pyramids, he thought, were an early example of a job-creation programme. His reasoning for this was simple: 'I cannot think any Monarch however Despotick could effect such things meerly for Glory; I guess there were reasons of State for it.'[57]

Part of his purpose was to trace a continuous line between the earliest known buildings and the paradigm of classical civilization, which could be followed through to the Renaissance and 'those who first laboured in the Restoration of Architecture, about three Centuries ago'.[58] The classical orders, he wrote, were not only Greek and Roman, but Phoenician, Hebrew and Assyrian. The Doric, generally reckoned to be the first of the Greek orders, had developed from the Tyrian (i.e., Phoenician). The Tyrians were quite possibly 'the Imitators of the Babylonians, and They of the Egyptians', while the ultimate origin of the orders lay, as Vitruvius had said, in the tree-trunks and rough timbers used to construct the earliest temples and 'publick Places of Meeting'.[59] He also postulated a network of connections: Solomon, for example, discovered the Tyrian order when he built his legendary temple, through making use of builders sent by King Hiram of Tyre. Most interesting of all is his suggestion that our ideas of architecture – even classical architecture – are culturally informed. Modern authors, he claims, have tried to reduce the orders to a set of rules which are 'too strict and pedantick'; they fail to realize that 'they are but the Modes and Fashions of those Ages wherein they were used'.[60] This was a marked departure from accepted theory. Serlio, for example, defined architectural error as 'breaking the rules of Vitruvius', and held that 'unless reason tells us to the contrary, we must always follow the teaching of Vitruvius as an infallible rule and guide'.[61]

For all their fragmentary nature, the Tracts show an enquiring, commonsensical attitude to both architecture and history, a healthy refusal to accept received ideas at face value. Wren dismisses the notion so beloved of Renaissance theorists, that since man is the measure of all things, the cylindrical shape of a classical column reflects the human torso – a column looks nothing like a torso. The origins of the column obviously lie with the trunks of trees: 'This I think the more natural Comparison, than that to the Body of a Man, in which there is little Resemblance of a cylindrical Body.'[62] If Samson was able to bring down the Philistine temple of Dagon by taking 'hold of the two middle pillars upon which the house stood, and on which it was borne up' (Judges, 16:29), then we can deduce something about its structure. Wren hypothesizes an oval amphitheatre, 'where a vast Roof of Cedar-beams resting round upon the Walls, centered all upon one short Architrave, that united two Cedar Pillars in the Middle . . . Now, if Sampson, by his miraculous Strength pressing upon one of these Pillars, moved it from its Basis, the whole Roof must of necessity fall.'[63]

As the phrase 'miraculous Strength' suggests, Wren was in no way attempting to debunk the stories of the Old Testament. As far as he was concerned, they were history, incontrovertible fact, and he wanted to provide them with a rational basis. In his discussion of the Ark in Tract V, for instance, he points out that although God was said to have instructed Noah to make a single window in the Ark one cubit high (that is, about the length of a forearm), 'one small Window was not sufficient to emit the Breath of all the Animals; It had certainly many other Windows as well for Light as Air'. And although Genesis makes no mention of them, there also must have been stairs, since the Ark was several storeys high; a pump; and great cisterns to hold fresh water for drinking, and as a suitable habitat for waterfowl and insects. And 'some Greens must grow in Tubs, the only food of Tortoises'.[64]

The second point to emerge from the aphorisms and theories which make up the Tracts is Wren's remarkable awareness of the psychological and symbolic impact of architecture. Discussing the sacrificial grove as the progenitor of the colonnade, he notes that 'a Grove was necessary not only to shade the Devout, but, from the Darkness of the Place, to strike some Terror and Recollection in their Approachers'.[65] He also shows how readily he could read a building as metaphor. Thus, the Basilica of Constantine, which was known in Wren's day as the Temple of Peace, not only functions as a religious structure, it perfectly expresses the *idea* of peace through its architecture:

No Language, no Poetry can so describe Peace, and the Effects of it in Men's Minds, as the Design of this Temple naturally paints it, without any Affectation of the Allegory. It is easy of Access, and open, carries a humble Front, but embraces wide, is luminous and pleasant, and content with an internal Greatness, despises an invidious Appearance of all that Height it might otherwise justly boast of, but rather fortifying itself on every Side, rests secure on a square and ample Basis.[66]

This ability to perceive and interpret the symbolic qualities of architecture was unusual for the time. It shows itself several times in the Tracts, most memorably in the opening lines of Tract I, in which Wren states that 'Architecture has its political Use. . . it establishes a Nation'.[67] However, it was an idea which would gain currency during the later seventeenth and early eighteenth centuries, coming back to haunt Wren in old age. And it finally destroyed him.

13

The Trade I Was Once Well Acquainted With

*D*uring the early months of 1678, while he was arguing with Hooke over ether and muscular action, and still pondering the precise shape of Porsenna's tomb, Wren was also focusing on an important royal project – a grand mausoleum for the King's father. Although the almost hysterical fervour with which Charles the Martyr had been worshipped by Royalists had abated with time, he was still a potent symbol. The anniversary of his execution, 30 January, was a national day of mourning, 'a Day of Trouble, of Rebuke, and Blasphemy', in the opening words of a sermon given by the royal chaplain, 'distinguished in the Annals of our Nation, and the Calendar of our Church, by the sad Sufferings of an excellent Prince, who fell a Sacrifice to the Rage of his Rebellious Subjects'.[1] In case anyone failed to appreciate the enormity of what the regicides had done, the lesson appointed in the 1662 prayer book for that day was Luke's account of Christ's Passion.

Naturally, Charles II took a lively interest in his father's cult. Any reinforcement of the notion of divine kingship in the popular imagination was all to the good as far as he was concerned; it is no coincidence that on his triumphant return to England in 1660 he immediately reinstituted his father's habit of touching as a cure for scrofula, 'the King's Evil'. The demand for this was so great (there were several cases of people being crushed to death in the rush to be 'stroked') that within weeks of the Restoration it was made a ticket-only affair. Even so, in the course of his reign Charles II was reckoned to have touched nearly 100,000 people – around one in fifty of the entire population. Either England was a particularly scrofulous nation, or sufferers kept coming back for more treatment.

Charles I had been buried at dead of night in Henry VIII's vault in the choir of St George's Chapel at Windsor Castle, 'his Head lying over against the eleventh Stall on the Sovereign's Side', as Echard's *History of England* rather unfortunately put it.[2] There were few mourners and no funeral service – the Parliamentarian garrison commander forbade it. Ceremonial reinterment in a suitably splendid tomb would be more than an act of filial piety – it would also serve as a useful piece of public relations in praise of the monarchy and, as Thomas Sprat said, give 'a Resurrection to his Memory, by designing magnificent Rites to his sacred Ashes'.[3]

Wren's old friend spoke those words in the course of an anniversary sermon before the Commons at St Margaret's, Westminster, on 30 January 1678. The previous day Parliament had voted the colossal sum of £70,000 'for a solemn Funeral of his late Majesty . . . and to erect a Monument for the said Prince of glorious Memory'.[4] As usual, the Surveyor-General went to work immediately. Two days after the vote, he was enthusiastically talking through his ideas with Hooke at their regular Saturday meeting at Scotland Yard; and the following Saturday he had a draft design to show.

The site chosen for the mausoleum was at the east end of St George's Chapel, where Cardinal Wolsey had begun a monument to himself. The little Tudor-Gothic Tomb House, as it was called, was duly commandeered by Henry VIII for his own use, but remained unfinished at his death. It had been in a ruinous state since April 1646, when it was stripped of its copper-gilt statues and other furnishings by a disapproving Parliament.* Wren chose to sweep it all away and replace it with a domed rotunda some 70 feet in diameter, set in a shallow dry moat and towering up well over 120 feet from the base of its plinth to the 10-foot-high statue of Fame, 'of gilt Brass, on the Summit of the Lantern'.[5] The lower storey of rusticated ashlar was broken by twenty Corinthian half-columns, topped with figures of gods and goddesses who encircled and protected the raised and ribbed dome; and beneath the royal arms a brass door opened into the marble interior. There the Martyr-King stood – or floated, rather, supported on an upturned shield by four larger-than-life Virtues who, in Grinling Gibbons' design, crushed beneath their feet four squirming allegorical figures representing Rebellion, Heresy, Hypocrisy and Envy.[6]

---

*The marble sarcophagus that Wolsey imported from Italy to hold his bones ended up in the crypt of St Paul's. It is occupied by Lord Nelson.

By now Wren was becoming expert in the theatrical grand gesture. The designs for the Windsor mausoleum show a confident recycling of Renaissance ideas. Like the west towers of the Definitive design for St Paul's, the rotunda clearly owes something to Bramante's Tempietto di San Pietro, which commemorates the spot in Rome where St Peter was crucified – a cultural resonance which Wren's contemporaries would no doubt have relished. But whereas Bramante was reinterpreting ancient Roman forms, Wren, whether he realized it or not, was reinterpreting the Renaissance, creating a building which was much more than a homage to antiquity, or a memorial to a dead king, or an appropriate setting for Gibbons' glorious group of statues. The monumental scale, the drama and movement of the dome and the promise it held that something or someone larger than life lay within, did not simply glorify death: they *overcame* it, offering an immortality which the building's sad, flawed, arrogant occupant, whose last word on the scaffold was 'Remember', would have found entirely appropriate.

Wren reckoned the cost of immortality at £43,663 2s, including £8200 to Gibbons for the monument and £17,477 for the interior decoration. But without even seeing the designs, Parliament had second thoughts and the bill granting Charles II his £70,000 failed. Like so many of Wren's schemes, the mausoleum became another one of British history's unrealized pieces of paper architecture.

But his architecture wasn't all on paper. In the spring of 1678 twenty-one of the London churches were in various stages of completion, ranging from the small St Benet Paul's Wharf in Upper Thames Street, where construction was just beginning (probably to Hooke's designs), to the prestigious St Stephen Walbrook, which was in the process of being glazed. Work on the library at Trinity resumed after the usual winter break, in spite of a shortage of cash; and at St Paul's, Joshua Marshall's men were raising the walls of the north and south transepts, while labourers were ramming down the stonework of the old nave preparatory to digging the foundations of the new one. The 'Fish Street Piller' was finished, except for the Latin inscriptions which were to go on three panels of the pedestal. (Cibber's sculpture fills the fourth.) Rather oddly, the City authorities had left it up to Wren and Hooke between them to find a suitable author, and they deliberated long and hard on this – Wren came up with a passable effort of his own, but this was evidently judged not to be dramatic enough – before turning to the 'learned schole-master of St Paul's School', Dr Thomas Gale.[7] Gale seems to have collaborated closely with the two men[8] before producing a commendably straightforward account of the Fire and the rebuilding.★

In the spring of 1681 John Fell, who was by now Bishop of Oxford as well as Dean of Christ Church, approached the Surveyor with a proposal. He wanted to add a tower to the gatehouse of his college, which had been begun by Wolsey back in the 1520s but never finished. And he wanted Wren to provide the design.

The commission was a tricky one. A piece of modern – i.e., classical – architecture was obviously the preferred choice, but a classical tower would look very odd indeed hovering over the ogee-capped turrets of Wolsey's Tudor-Gothic work. So, as Wren told Fell in a letter accompanying his drawings, 'I resolved it ought to be Gothick to agree with the Founder's Worke', quickly going on to qualify this by saying that 'I have not continued soe busy as he began.'[9] His idea was to carry up the first stage of the gatehouse on a square plan, which would then turn into an octagon with little ogee domes in the angles, topped with a much larger ogee dome surrounded by a crown of crocketted pinnacles. The tower would be a stripped-down reinterpretation of Tudor-Gothic, less busy in that it relied for effect less on decorative elements than on simple geometrical forms – square, octagon and ogee. It evoked Christ Church's ancestry without ever degenerating into pastiche.

The building history of Tom Tower is a good example of the problems that can arise with mail-order design. It also shows us a Wren supremely confident of his own talents, at a stage in his architectural career where he was no longer prepared to put up with a meddling client who didn't know the business, even when that client was as distinguished as the Bishop of Oxford. From the outset, he didn't think that local craftsmen were up to the job: 'I cannot boast of Oxford Artists,' he told Fell at the end of May, 'though they have a good opinion of themselves.' He recommended the mason Christopher Kempster, who had recently finished St Stephen Walbrook and was currently working

---

★Too straightforward for the City authorities who, caught up in the anti-Catholic hysteria caused by the Popish Plot, ordered an additional sentence declaring that 'Popish frenzy, which wrought such horrors, is not yet quenched.' They also commissioned a further plaque – this time in English – which announced that 'Here by permission of heaven, hell broke loose upon this Protestant city from the malicious hearts of barbarous Papists.' James II quite naturally took exception to these sentiments and ordered their removal, only for William III to reinstate them. They remained until 1830 when, in the wake of the Catholic Emancipation Act, the City finally reconsidered and allowed their obliteration.

on St Mary Abchurch. He was, in Wren's opinion, 'a very able Man, modest, honest and Treatable', and as his Burford quarry was less than twenty miles away, 'you will have the stone from him at first hand'.[10] Fell was agreeable, but he was in a hurry. When he returned the drawings to Scotland Yard for copying a week or two later (they were the only set), he let slip that his own men had already started work on the foundations. The news sent Wren into a rage which he barely managed to conceal. The workmen had no idea of what they were doing, he said; they just didn't have the experience or the ability to lay adequate foundations in a situation where a new structure was going to be bonded in to the old and where, therefore, any settling of the ground would cause the new to break away. No matter what they said, there were bound to be 'inexcusable flawes and cracks and weakenesse' and, unless they started again from scratch according to his instructions, the architect was 'out of all hope that this designe will succeed'.[11]

Suitably chastened, Fell handed over the direction of the project to Wren and Kempster, after some further awkwardness when the Bishop's masons drew up an inaccurate ground-plan and provoked another impatient outburst. ('I fear Your Workmen if they cannot give me a Groundplot will hardly follow one that's given.')[12] Things quietened down that summer, only for more problems to surface at the end of the year. Fell decided an observatory at the top of the tower would encourage sponsors, but if he thought the former professor of astronomy would congratulate him on his commitment to science, he had another think coming. An observatory meant a balustraded flat roof for the telescope with no pinnacles and no ogee cap. It would wreck the Gothic quality Wren was aiming for and, without the spires and 'pyramidal formes', would end up as the 'unhandsome medley' that he had been at pains to avoid. If this was the outcome, what on earth was the point of opting for Gothic rather than 'the better formes of architecture' in the first place?[13]

Wren went on to tell Fell that the exercise was pointless in any case, since there was no real need to site an observatory in a tower. In an interesting passage, he set out the requirements for star-gazing as he saw them:

First a large Murall Quadrant fixt to a wall trewly built in the meridian, and this is best in an open Court or Garden, 2ndly a pole to rayse large Telescopes and manage them, and the like place is properest for this also. 3rdly A Quadrant to take distances fixt to a Foot soe as it may turne to all sort of plains, this having Telescope sights & as many nice Joynts & Screwes must be housed for its better preservation [i.e., it needed to be protected from the weather], but the best house will be a little house of boardes about 12 foot square & 7 foot high & noe other roofe but what may be taken quite off when the Instrument is used, as you draw off the sliding lid of a box, or upon hinges as you open the Cover of a Trunke, & this will be as well don in a Garden as the top of a Tower, for wee valewe noe observations made neer the Horizon.[14]

Bludgeoned with science and superior knowledge, Fell backed down, and the observatory disappeared from view.

While this anguished correspondence was passing to and fro between Scotland Yard and Oxford, Wren had finally arrived at the Presidency of the Royal Society, albeit by rather a roundabout route. Sir Joseph Williamson lost his post as Secretary of State in February 1679. The immediate cause was anti-Catholic fervour in the wake of the Popish Plot. Williamson dared to speak against the motion to exclude the Duke of York from the King's presence and councils, arguing that it would drive the heir to the throne into the arms of the French and the Catholics. As a result the Commons, whose notions of liberty didn't encompass dissent, had him committed to the Tower. Within hours, Charles stepped in to order his release, but his position was untenable and he was removed from office. (The underlying reason for his fall was the fact that he had just married the wealthy widow of his friend, Lord Ibrackan – Lady Catherine had been earmarked for the son of the Lord Treasurer, the Earl of Danby, who didn't take kindly to being thwarted.) Either he lost interest in the Royal Society, or the Royal Society lost interest in him, and at the anniversary elections in November 1680 the neurasthenic Robert Boyle was elected in his stead.

Despite his delicate health, Boyle was a good choice. He was wealthy and well connected, a renowned scientist and a man whose commitment to the ideas of the Society was beyond question. Everyone thought he would make a good president: Evelyn reckoned he 'indeede ought to have ben the very first; but neither his infirmitie nor his modestie could now any longer excuse him.'[15] But Evelyn was wrong. Boyle was a deeply committed Protestant and, like many Protestants of the time, he had what he described as 'a great (and perhaps peculiar) tenderness in point of oaths'.[16] (This aversion to oath-taking had its origins in Matthew 5:34–7, where, in the Sermon on the Mount, Christ says, 'Swear not at all . . . But let your communication be, Yea, yea; Nay, nay:

for whatsoever is more than these cometh of evil.') He initially seems to have thought he could simply ignore the requirement laid down by the Test Act of 1673, whereby all office-holders had to swear allegiance to the monarch as head of the Church of England and repudiate the Catholic doctrine of transubstantiation. But after taking legal advice, he decided he didn't dare presume himself to be 'unconcerned in an act of parliament to whose breach such heavy penalties are annexed'.[17] So on 18 December, after much heart-searching and wrestling with his conscience, he wrote to inform the Society that he was declining the honour after all. This left a rather embarrassing vacuum. After some hurried negotiations it was filled by Wren, who was sworn in as President at a Council meeting on 12 January 1681.

Throughout his two-year Presidency, Wren showed himself to be just what he was: an intelligent speaker and a brilliant administrator. Keen to make his mark, his first act was to call for the setting-up of anatomical, agricultural and cosmographical committees, 'to register all things, that should be remarkable'.[18] After some debate – William Croone objected that an anatomical committee would tread on the toes of the Royal College of Physicians – all three were agreed, and the Council left it to him to consider who was best fitted to sit on them. At full meetings of the Society he was always ready with an observation, on comets, or meteorology or optics; he was still a master of 'the Trade . . . I was once well acquainted with'. But his interests ranged as wide as ever. In January 1682, for example, he treated members to a lecture on the practice of Chinese doctors who were, he said, 'extremely curious about feeling the pulse of the patient, examining the beating thereof, not only in the wrist, but in divers other parts of the body, by which they pretended to make great discoveries of the disease'.[19] On another occasion he gave a long and colourful account of the flora and fauna of Hudson Bay.* The North American moose, he said, had a neck that was so short it couldn't reach its food without kneeling. The natives of Hudson Bay lived to 130 or 140 years 'without the use of spectacles' and when they grew too old to hunt, they 'give themselves up to their eldest sons to be strangled'. After hunting, they slept in deep holes in the snow, but before settling down for the night they would

---

*He must have garnered the information during committee meetings of the Hudson's Bay Company, which he had joined in 1679. During the years 1679 to 1683 he attended 154 of the Company's meetings, acting as Deputy Governor on several occasions and eventually holding £1200 of stock (Bryan Little, *Sir Christopher Wren* [Robert Hale, 1975], 109, 124, 133–4).

trail the guts of what they have killed in hunting in the day round their cabins at a pretty good distance; and having so done, they leave them as bait to divert the bears from falling on them; for upon scenting the entrails, the bears proceed no farther, but follow the [trail] of the guts till they find and eat them; after which they lose their sense of smelling, and are not sensible of so good a booty so near at hand, but depart satisfied.[20]

Wren's most important contribution, though, was administrative rather than scientific. When he took over the Presidency from Williamson, the Royal Society was in the grip of a financial crisis. Money was always needed to pay for equipment and experiments, for postage costs incurred in keeping up a correspondence with foreign scientists, for the amanuensis and the salaries of the Society's employees. (As Curator of Experiments, for example, Robert Hooke received £30 a year.) Virtually all of the cash had to come from the contributions of members, each of whom was expected to pay £2 admission money on election, and a subscription of one shilling a week thereafter.[21] There were plenty of exceptions to this rule: foreign members; some country members; celebrities like Prince Rupert and the Duke of York, and august clerics such as Humphrey Henchman and Gilbert Sheldon, whose presence on the printed lists was reckoned to enhance the honour of the Society; some Oxford and Cambridge dons, whose membership also helped to legitimize its work; and the professors at Gresham College, who were exempted as a courtesy to the institution which hosted the Society's meetings. Several Fellows, including Wren, William Holder and John Wallis, were allowed a 50 per cent discount – Wren's dispensation dated from the end of 1662, when it was clear that his chair at Oxford was preventing him from playing a full part in the weekly meetings at Gresham. Even so, with a total membership which had hovered around 200 since the late 1660s, and stood at 220 by the end of Wren's first year in office, this still left a small but steady income which should have gone some way towards salaries and expenses.

But only if members were conscientious and paid their dues. An alarmingly high proportion of them weren't, and didn't. Some defaulted as they lost interest in the work of the Society: the men of fashion who had joined in the early 1660s when experimental philosophy was the thing of the moment; country squires whose commitments at home prevented them from visiting the capital. Others, however, were active members who just never seemed to get round to putting their hands in their pockets. Wren, ironically, had been one of the worst offenders, having paid nothing between 1661, when he left Gresham College, and 1674, when he stumped up his arrears. Although he occasionally fell behind in his payments by a year or two, he kept more or less up to date from then on.[22]

Every now and then steps were taken to try to bring some semblance of order to the Society's financial affairs. Back in 1666, four Fellows, including Wren's mentor Charles Scarburgh and his predecessor at the King's Works, Sir John Denham, were actually expelled for failing to stump up their subscriptions. The expulsion of such high-profile characters was probably deliberate, and intended as an example to the others; but it had little effect, and by 1672 the Society was owed £1818 7s in arrears – almost 700 years' worth of individual subscriptions, in fact. There was another purge in 1675, after an unsuccessful attempt to persuade every member to sign a legally binding bond (drawn up by the Attorney-General, no less) which guaranteed payment. Only around sixty or so complied, and a further dozen members were excluded – although the criteria for exclusion seem rather murky, since the arrears of a large number of active, well-connected or aristocratic members were conveniently overlooked.

Financial management and bureaucratic efficiency had never been among the Royal Society's strengths. Wren, on the other hand, was accustomed to handling substantial budgets and running a large government department; such things were an integral part of his working life. At a Council meeting in December 1681 he asked that the Society's statutes concerning the payment of subscriptions and the ejection of erring members should be transcribed for discussion. The following January the Treasurer, Abraham Hill, read out a list – an uncomfortably long list – of Fellows who were either heavily in arrears or hadn't paid at all; and Wren invited a committee consisting of Hill, the Vice-President, Sir John Hoskins, and the two Secretaries, Robert Hooke and the courtier Francis Aston, to convene at his house every Monday evening, in order to discuss how to recover the money owing.

The immediate result of this was a call for active members to cajole, threaten and plead with defaulters of their acquaintance, and it brought some comic replies. The Oxford divine Benjamin Woodroffe and the courtier Alexander Stanhope sent back word that they had resigned from the Society years before. Sir Nicholas Steward, another courtier, who had played no part in the Society's proceedings since he joined in 1667, and who was told he owed eleven years' subscription money, announced that Hill's arithmetic was at fault: he simply refused to believe he owed so much. Sir William Petty said his wife would pay, and the gentleman-architect William Winde decided that an appeal to a fellow architect was in order, declaring that he would speak to Wren personally about the matter. Ralph Bathurst, Wren's old friend from Trinity College, Oxford, sent £10 and a promise that he would leave something in his will; while the cleric Daniel Milles refused point-blank to pay a penny, and Thomas Sheridan, a friend of the Duke of York, optimistically suggested that he would come up with £10 if he could continue a Fellow and be exempted from all future fees.

Most pathetic of all was the aged poet and politician Edmund Waller, the amiable but unprincipled author of such verses as 'Panegyric to My Lord Protector' and 'Upon His Majesty's Happy Return'. Waller, who had joined the Royal Society only seven weeks after it was founded, but who had paid nothing since 1663, sent back a sad little message pleading that,

> the plague happening some time after the Society was established, and he being perpetually in Parliament had never been able to attend the Society, either to serve them, or to receive any advantage thereby; that he was now of a great age [he was nearly seventy-two], had lost half his fortune for the king, and having a great charge of children, hoped, that he should be considered as others, who had not been able to wait on them as well as he; and he humbly took leave to consider how he might be able to serve them.[23]

Wren was having none of this. A Fellow was packed off to see how much he could get out of Waller (which turned out to be nothing). Defaulting members who had signed the bond in 1675 were threatened with legal action, while letters were written to others hinting darkly at expulsion and dishonour. The Council also decided to change the rules. From now on, whenever anyone was elected to the Society, their proposer must take them straight round to Hill so they could pay their admission money, and the Treasurer was to be provided with a blank book of bonds for them to sign on the spot. More radically, at the beginning of August 1682 Wren tabled a draft statute, to the effect that no one could stand for the Council at the anniversary elections if they were in arrears at Michaelmas, 29 September. Their names would therefore be left off the printed lists of members which were circulated in November.

The measure was characteristic of Wren's dealings with people. Like the avenues which would have cut ruthlessly through property and lives if his plans for London had gone ahead, the new statute was a straightforward and apparently simple solution to the problem: if you don't pay, you don't play. In reality, it was neither simple nor straightforward: unless there was a stampede of repentant debtors over the next seven weeks – something which seemed most unlikely, given the Council's earlier attempt to extract cash from recalcitrant Fellows – well over one hundred Fellows, around half the membership, would disappear from the Society's lists at a stroke. The President's intention, to get rid of the dead wood and at the same time send a clear message to waverers, was a laudable one. But the idea proved too much for the rest of the Council, several of whom had been none too punctual with their own subscriptions. They jibbed at the prospect of having to face friends, acquaintances, colleagues and patrons who had had their names removed so peremptorily. So after some discussion Wren's proposal was shelved as 'not fit at present to be made a statute' and, instead, the Council adopted the more pragmatic approach of targeting people who didn't really matter very much. All the same, the expulsion hit-list which was drawn up as a compromise contained twenty-three names, including a viscount and six earls.*

Under Wren's aegis and, I imagine, at his instigation, the Council did pass one new statute in August, ordering that from now on it must consider prospective candidates, deciding 'whether the person is known to be so qualified, as in probability to be useful to the society', before that person could be put up for election.[24] It seems that in the past members had been reluctant to vote against a candidate, even if they knew nothing of him. They assumed that his proposer's word was good enough; and this had led to some inappropriate types getting into the club. The statute had the desired effect: new elections declined dramatically, from twenty-five in 1681 to nine the following year, and seven the year after that.[25] When Wren gave up the Presidency in November 1682, to be replaced by Sir John Hoskins, he left the membership of the Royal Society in a far better state than he had found it.

---

*There was obviously a degree of agonizing over these names. One, for instance, was Robert Boyle's nephew, the Earl of Ranelagh; the words 'consult Mr Boyle' appear next to his name on the list. In the event, several Fellows marked for expulsion survived, although Ranelagh was not one of them (Michael Hunter, *The Royal Society and its Fellows 1660–1700* [British Society for the History of Science, 1982], 99). There was a second, rather larger round of expulsions in 1685, when Samuel Pepys was President.

Apart from membership difficulties, the other big problem during Wren's Presidency was the forlorn and increasingly dilapidated Chelsea College. Nearly fifteen years had passed since the Society had been given the college, but the Fellows had made no progress in building their new, permanent home. As with the scheme for a purpose-built research institute in the grounds of Arundel House, plans to put Charles II's grant to good use had foundered on the rocks of financial reality during the 1670s. Still, there was a substantial brick building (albeit unfinished) on the thirty-acre site, surrounded by open fields and looking out across the meadows towards the Thames. It was 4 storeys high and 130 feet long, with a hall, 2 parlours, 12 good-sized sets of lodgings and a long gallery. There were detached kitchens and stables, walled gardens and a scattering of wooden huts, the legacy of the period in the 1650s when it had functioned as a prisoner-of-war camp.

But the college was in poor repair, and the Royal Society lacked both the will and the money to do much about it. From time to time one or other of the members raised the subject at Council meetings, only to be fobbed off with promises of swift action which came to nothing. In December 1672, for example, Sir Paul Neile remonstrated with his fellow Council members over 'the strange neglect of Chelsea-college, and the reproaches thence falling on the Society';[26] everyone agreed that something must be done, and Moray, Croone and Neile were deputed to consult with Wren, as Surveyor-General, about letting out the college on a repairing lease. Nothing happened.

The Council still didn't give up all hope of actually making use of the college. In October 1674, Hooke and Sir Jonas Moore went down to assess Chelsea's suitability as a site for an observatory. The plan was to find a market-gardener who would take a lease on the place, while allowing the Society to make horticultural experiments and build the projected observatory in the grounds. In fact, Sir Jonas, who had done rather well for himself since taking up the job-offer in Tangier that Wren turned down back in 1661, promised up to £200 towards the building costs. Flamsteed, who also looked over the site, actually preferred it to Greenwich – not for the clear skies, but because it was nearer to court – but again nothing happened. In a move which suggests that they were growing quite desperate, Brouncker and three well-connected members of the Council – Moore, Samuel Pepys and the statesman Sir Robert Southwell – agreed to tell Prince Rupert that their 'strange neglect' of Chelsea was all his fault. He had put up a glassworks next door to the college and this, apparently, was the only reason the

Society hadn't been able to let it. In the circumstances, perhaps he might care to put the whole estate to some use, 'and to consider the Society for it'?[27]

Rupert's reaction didn't reach the Society's minute-books. But he was obviously unimpressed, since the saga continued with scheme after scheme falling by the wayside, either because prospective tenants wouldn't stump up the rent the Society demanded, or because they wouldn't submit to its strict conditions of use. In November 1677 Robert Hooke heard from Boyle that Chelsea College was 'being carried away by poor people';[28] and the following May Hooke lobbied hard for a project of his own for Chelsea, but neither his diaries nor the Society's records shed any light on exactly what it was he intended. That same month, the roof fell in, and in June the Council resolved to remove the tiles and timber of the college and keep them safe nearby, as a guard against pilfering.

When Wren took up the Presidency in January 1681, the Council was in the middle of talks with yet another prospective lessee – a Mr Rossington, who was negotiating to take a 61-year lease on the college and 6 acres at a rent of £30 a year. This was £5 less than the Society wanted, but the Council was minded to accept the offer if Rossington would agree to spend £2000 on putting the buildings into reasonable repair within two years. However, by this stage long neglect of the property had thrown up some tiresome legal difficulties. In March, Wren and the rest of the Council heard that gravel pits had been dug in the grounds without permission, while a neighbour had enclosed a strip of land which the Society thought belonged to the college, blocking off a right of way and causing locals to complain. Wren went down to Chelsea to discuss the situation with local farmers, while the Society's lawyer, Joseph Lane, was asked for an opinion on the legality of demolishing the buildings still standing and selling off the materials. In the meantime, the Council decided to secure the site by paying 'some person in the country to mound the ground before the college with a very sufficient mound and ditch of earth, and a plain gate and post'.[29]

That summer, Rossington dropped his offer to £20 a year, pre-sumably because he had heard of the ongoing boundary dispute. This was too much – or rather, too little – and he was told to forget it, while Wren and a deputation from the Council trooped down to Chelsea for a difficult discussion with Lord Cheyne, the neighbour whose enclosure of the disputed field was giving them such a headache, and who was steadfastly maintaining that the land belonged to him. The results of this meeting aren't recorded. But when the Council convened again in October after the summer recess, Wren produced something of a *coup de théâtre*. He calmly announced that he had recently had talks with Sir Stephen Fox, one of the Lords Commissioners of the Treasury. And the upshot of those talks was that King Charles wanted to buy back Chelsea College.

You can hear the sigh of relief go up around the table. No more difficult discussions with Lord Cheyne. No more worries about illicit gravel pits, or awkward interviews with prospective tenants. Best of all, no more embarrassment over a royal gift which the Society had so publicly failed to put to good use. The Council desired their President to get £1500 if he could, and on no account to go lower than £1400. But when he came back to them in January 1682 and announced that, subject to their approval, he had sold the college for £1300, no one voiced any complaints. I should think they cheered.

Although Wren didn't mention the fact to his fellow Council members (or if he did, no record survives in the minutes), he was well aware of why the King wanted Chelsea College. Three weeks before Wren announced that negotiations were in hand with Fox, John Evelyn had dined with the Treasury Commissioner, who confided in him that Charles wanted to build 'an Hospital or Infirmary for Souldiers there, in which he desired my assistance as one of the Council of the Royal Society'.[30] Evelyn knew how desperate the Society was to unload its royal gift, and apparently suggested that Fox should write to Wren straight away, outlining the King's offer; in the meantime he would approach the President informally.

The problem of what to do with military veterans returning home to a land unfit for heroes was nothing new. During Elizabeth's reign disabled soldiers were exempted from the vagrancy laws and licensed to beg on the streets, and the 1593 Statute for Maimed Soldiers levied parish rates, which were administered by county treasurers. In theory, they could award pensions of up to £10 a year to soldiers injured in the Queen's service, and £20 for officers. In practice, the county authorities were reluctant to part with the money, and lame, disfigured and sometimes aggressive ex-soldiers soliciting alms were a common sight on the streets of London and other major cities throughout the first half of the seventeenth century, prompting Francis Quarles to write that:

Our God and soldiers we alike adore,
When at the brink of ruin, not before;
After deliverance both alike requited,
Our God forgotten and our soldiers slighted.

The situation was of course much worse during and after the Civil War. In 1644 the four London hospitals, St Bartholomew's, Bridewell, St Thomas's and Bethlehem, were exempted from taxes on account of the 'great numbers of sick, wounded, and other soldiers [that] have for the time of twenty months past been constantly kept in the said hospitals, at very great and extraordinary charges'.[31] Parliament also designated two specialist military hospitals in London – at the Savoy and Ely House, Matthew Wren's commandeered episcopal palace in Holborn – and periodically voted funds for disabled troops, widows and orphans, which were administered by four 'treasurers for maimed soldiers'. The money was never enough – in May 1650, for instance, the treasurers threatened to resign if more was not forthcoming, saying that they were constantly besieged by angry and desperate veterans: 'Some threaten us that though they be hanged at our doors or shot to death, they will try whether we be pistol proof or no.'[32] At the Restoration the military hospitals were closed, military pensions were halted, and the pensioners (some 2250 of them) were given 12 weeks' pay and told to look for further relief to their local justice of the peace or overseers of the poor.

At its peak Charles II's army numbered 19,000 officers and men. But little attention was paid to the plight of disabled soldiers, and the complaints about poor treatment which surfaced from time to time have a familiar ring to them. Explaining why recruitment during the Dutch War of 1664–7 was slow, one anonymous writer told the King that, 'saie the people, be a souldier, noe, we have prsedents [precedents] daily in the streets, we will fight no more, for when the wars is over we are slited like dogs'.[33] Attempts were made to ensure that soldiers crippled during the Dutch Wars should have priority in various charitable institutions and almshouses; and from about 1676 money was set aside from the annual Army estimates to provide pensions for eighty-five retired officers and disabled soldiers.

By this time, voices were being raised in support of a more permanent solution. Sir James Turner, in his *Pallas Armata: Military Essayes of the Ancient Grecian, Roman, and Modern Art of War*, wrote hopefully that it would 'much redound' to the honour and fame of princes 'to build some

Hospitals, and endue them with some small Revenue, in which those Commanders who are lame, old, and poor, might get a morsel of Bread; which would be an exceeding great relief to those distressed Gentlemen, and much encourage younger people to engage in a fresh War'.[34] And in 1677 the Earl of Orrery, one of the century's great soldier-statesmen (and the unlikely older brother of the decidedly unsoldierly Robert Boyle) lamented how few hospitals were available to maimed or superannuated soldiers: 'Yet were all of them for that use yet the plaster would be much too narrow for the sore; and would be rather a sign of the thing than the thing itself.'[35]

It was not just a matter of compassion, or even army morale: national pride was at stake. In 1670 Louis XIV had shown his concern for the welfare of his own considerable army by founding the Hôtel des Invalides in Paris, and this vast arcaded building, designed by Libéral Bruant to house every one of the Sun King's indigent or incapacitated veterans – 5000 men in all – was currently the talk of European military circles. The Duke of Monmouth, who visited Les Invalides in 1672 and again in 1677, even went so far as to ask Louis' Minister of War, the Marquis de Louvois, for the plans to be sent over for the King's consideration. If the French could look after their own, why couldn't we?

The answer came back that 'we' could, although the first military hospital in the British Isles wasn't to be built in Chelsea – or even in England. Nor was it to be designed by Wren. In 1679, after pressure from the Earl of Granard and successive Lord Lieutenants of Ireland, the King agreed to a levy of 6d in the pound on Irish military pay to finance an almshouse for soldiers who 'by reason of Age, Wounds, or other Infirmities, since their first coming into Our Army, are grown unfit to be any longer continued in Our Service'.[36] The design for the Royal Hospital at Kilmainham, County Dublin, was provided by William Robinson, Engineer and Surveyor-General of the Fortifications and Buildings in Ireland. And a good job he made of it, too, producing a closed arcaded courtyard plan along the lines of Les Invalides, with accommodation for 300 soldiers – and, in the process, Ireland's first classical building. In fact Kilmainham was so impressive that while it was still half-built the authorities of Trinity College, Dublin suggested to the Duke of Ormonde, then Lord Lieutenant, that it might be a good idea to do a swap. The old soldiers could take the spartan and old-fashioned buildings on College Green in the heart of Dublin, since 'the Hospital would make a magnificent college and being out of town would be free from those mischiefs that now attend it'.[37]

The sequence of events leading up to the building of the Royal Hospital at Chelsea is easy enough to piece together. Kilmainham's foundation stone was laid on 29 April 1680; and the following year the Earl of Longford, who was closely involved with the Irish project, came over to England and had three audiences with the King on 2, 3 and 6 September. It was eight days after the last of these meetings that Sir Stephen Fox broached the subject of using Chelsea as a 'Hospital or Infirmary for Souldiers', and three weeks after that that Wren broke the news to his delighted Council. He must have realized even then that, as the King's architect, he was the obvious choice to design the hospital. 'Great Monarchs are ambitious to leave great Monuments behind them', as he wrote in another context;[38] and this was emphatically a royal project. As Charles said so proudly when it was nearing completion, 'Fox and Hee [i.e., the King] had done that great worke without the help of the Treasury, who indeed never gave the least contenance towards it.'[39] Fox's share of the 'great worke' was actually rather larger than the King's. He paid the Royal Society for the site out of his own pocket and, while Charles donated £6787 4s 2½d towards the building costs, he voluntarily gave up £10,000, a 'commission' on military pay which was due to him as Paymaster General of the Army.

The brief was drawn up by Fox and John Evelyn, whose interest in the problem of military pensioners dated back to the Dutch Wars when he was a Commissioner for the Sick, Wounded and Prisoners of War. In January 1682, the two men fixed on accommodation for 422 men 'as in a colledge or monasterie', with lodgings for a governor, chaplain, steward, housekeeper, surgeon, cook, butler, gardener and porter. Ever the optimist, Evelyn pressed for a library, too, 'since some souldiers might possibly be studious when they were at leisure to recollect'.[40] We don't know for sure when Wren was formally (or even informally) asked to come up with a design for the Hospital; but we can assume it was soon after this meeting. Mindful of his mortality, the King was eager to push things forward. On 16 February, only eight days after the Royal Society conveyed the site to the Crown, he went down to Chelsea to lay the foundation stone; and at the end of May a deputation consisting of Fox, Wren and Evelyn waited on Archbishop Sancroft, taking with them 'the plot and designe of the College to be built at Chelsey, to have the Abp's approbation'.[41] The plan was passed and that summer Narcissus Luttrell reported that the old college had been pulled down, 'and preparations are there making for the goeing on with the building the Hospitall for poor maimed souldiers'.[42]

As Evelyn and Fox realized, the requirements of a military rest-home weren't far removed from those of a college or monastery: a dining hall and a chapel to meet the inmates' bodily and spiritual needs; and simple wards or cells for them to sleep in. The obvious model, and the one adopted by Bruant and Robinson, was the cloistered quadrangle. Wren was familiar with Les Invalides – he possessed a 'large Port Folio containing finished Drawings of the Hôtel des Invalides at Paris'[43] – but he opted for a less conventional plan consisting of three ranges grouped around an open court (known as Figure Court after Grinling Gibbons' rather stubby statue of Charles II in Roman dress which stands in the centre). The focal point of the central range was a Doric portico leading into an octagonal vestibule, with the Great Hall to the left, and the Chapel to the right.

The hall must have had a positively medieval feel to it; there was a black and white marble dais, and the only heating came from an open hearth in the middle of the floor, with a louvre in the ceiling to let out the smoke. To complete the picture of Merrye Englande the pensioners, who sat at sixteen long benches, were supplied with two pewter plates each and a pewter pot, while their beer was served from five-gallon leather jacks. The barrel-vaulted chapel, on the other hand, was opulently decorated with marble flooring, ornamental plasterwork and a magnificent reredos by William Emmett, Carver of the King's Works.*

By way of contrast, the wards for the pensioners were spartan, with floors of scrubbed oak and simple wainscoted cubicles. Inmates were housed in the two wings, each of which held two back-to-back galleries on four floors (one of which was a dormered attic), making sixteen in all. Each gallery contained twenty-six single cubicles, and each cubicle contained a bed, a rush-bottomed chair, a built-in table and a wooden chest mounted on castors.

The hospital managed to be stark and imposing at the same time. Austere brick walls were relieved by Portland stone dressings, and incident and variety were provided by the addition of further porticos in the centre of each wing, and pavilions at the four corners of the building, which were to house the kitchens, the infirmary and laundry, and lodgings for the governor and officers. The vestibule was crowned

---

*Several members of Wren's team at the Works were involved in building the hospital, including Master Bricklayer Maurice Emmett (William Emmett's brother); Master Carpenter Matthew Banckes; Sergeant Painter Robert Streater; and Sergeant Plumber Charles Atherton.

with a cupola and lantern rising to a height of 100 feet: at one stage Wren wanted to recycle one of Inigo Jones's towers from the west end of St Paul's, but the cathedral commissioners jibbed at the idea of putting consecrated stones to secular use, and even though he offered to swap the tower for a like weight in Portland stone, they turned him down.[44]

Long before it officially opened for business, the hospital was enlarged by the addition of two flanking quadrangles, Infirmary Court and Light Horse Court. This was agreed early in the reign of James II, who doubled the size of the standing army and hence increased both the demand for places and the revenue to finance them, which was tied into military pay. By the time it finally opened in March 1692, Chelsea had grown into a tremendous undertaking far beyond anything Fox and Evelyn might have imagined when they had mapped out the idea ten years previously. With an 800-foot-long façade and elaborate formal gardens and canals by the gardeners George London and Henry Wise, the whole project ended up costing well over £156,000, and earned the architect a hefty fee of £1000 'for his great Care and Paines in Directing and Overseeing the Building'.[45]

Of all Wren's mature work, the Royal Hospital has caused the most unease and attracted some of the strongest criticism. On a practical level, the wisdom of putting old and disabled men in four-storey buildings might be questioned, although in Wren's defence one can point to the savings in materials (and he did his best to minimize the inconvenience, by specifying wide treads and low risers to the staircases). And if one can't help smiling at the seventeenth century's sense of priorities – the pensioners' lavatories consisted of just four brass pails on each floor, for example, yet over the door of each cubicle Robert Streater was commissioned to paint its number enriched with 'folidge ornamentation at 5s p piece' – that was hardly the fault of the architect. The grandiose conception of what was only a rest-home for old soldiers, also provoked comment: in 1708 the author of *A New View of London* noted that Chelsea 'would be taken by strangers rather for the Palace of a Prince than a habitation for Pensioners'.[46] But any criticism of Wren's redefinition of an almshouse would be misplaced. The scale is monumental rather than human because the hospital was much more than just a place where old soldiers could go to die. It was a public statement of the King's gratitude and beneficence, a home fit for heroes. If fitness for purpose is the criterion by which architecture should be judged, then Chelsea passes with flying colours.

More problematic is the tension between the regimented rows of identical windows which light the wards and the palatial decorative features – particularly the three-bay Doric porticos which form the entrances to the two ward-blocks – that Wren used to relieve the monotony. There are four of these porticos, all in Portland stone. The two which face each other across Figure Court stand almost flush to the brick walls, while their counterparts, which look out into Infirmary Court and Light Horse Court, project prominently, because they were meant to house the brass buckets and Portland stone sinks which were supplied with water from tanks in the roof. Their mere presence was enough to send one nineteenth-century critic into a rage of righteous indignation: 'Style there is none. The Grecian forms of pediments and Doric pillars are united with the flat brick wall and high slated roofs, and bare windows of the commonest mode of house-building.'[47] But they are not so much inappropriate as downright odd. On the ground floor and the first floor, windows in the porticos carry through the fenestration of the wings; but on the second floor they are squashed to about two-thirds the height of all the other windows by the Doric frieze, which Wren decided to keep low in order to maintain a continuous line between the pediment and the cornice to either side. This gives the impression of an attic storey below the 'real' attic of third-storey dormers in the wards themselves. Of itself, this isn't so awful. But then he introduced a full-height window in the central bay of each portico, rearing up through the frieze and breaking it in half.

The effect is really very peculiar, a grunt of surprise in stone which disturbs the eye and unsettles the mind. If Wren had tried it with the Sheldonian, or Pembroke Chapel, we might dismiss it as an unfortunate slip by an amateur who was still finding his way in architecture. But by the 1680s he knew far too much about classical architecture for his bizarre treatment of the Chelsea porticos to have been an accident. He knew the rules. And he broke them quite deliberately, simply to provide this grunt of surprise and add visual emphasis to each façade. The purists hate that, and either excuse it as an unfortunate lapse or use it to point to his lack of confidence in handling a classical idiom. But the purists are wrong. Chelsea suggests an overweening confidence. To me, it suggests that Wren had reached a point where he felt he could break rules with impunity – or rather, that he could make rules instead of following them.

Laying the foundation stone of the Royal Hospital seems to have given Charles II a taste for new buildings. Since the late 1660s the King had been in the habit of relaxing each autumn at Newmarket, where he spent his mornings hawking, his afternoons either cock-fighting or watching foot-races and horse-races, and his evenings watching rustic plays put on by very ordinary Bartholomew Fair comedians. His seat was an unpretentious building on the High Street put up in 1668–71 – by the gentleman-architect William Samwell rather than the Office of Works, perhaps because Sir John Denham was having one of his turns when it was first mooted.* He enjoyed both the Suffolk countryside and the chance to mix with his people, but for some reason, in September 1682 he went instead to Winchester, the ancient capital of England. So taken with the place was he that he decided to build himself another hunting lodge on the site of the ruined medieval castle just outside the city walls, and 'to render Winchester the seat of his Autumnal field diversions for the future'.[48] Wren was ordered down to look over the site twice in October, taking with him his measuring clerk John Scarborough; but either at this point, or very soon thereafter, the hunting lodge transformed itself into something much, much bigger: a summer residence for the entire court, in fact. The King wanted a new royal palace to vie with Versailles, which the whole of Europe had been talking about since Louis XIV had formally declared it the seat of French government the previous May. The Sun King knew – because Colbert had told him – that nothing spoke so eloquently of the grandeur and cleverness of princes than buildings. And just as Chelsea was conceived in a spirit of competition with Les Invalides, Winchester Palace was to be Charles II's Versailles.

A palace was in an entirely different league from a hospital for old and decrepit soldiers (Narcissus Luttrell's words, not mine),[49] or a university library, or even a cathedral. The chance to design a major royal residence was the crowning achievement to which any royal architect naturally aspired. No new royal palace had been seen in England for nearly 150 years, not since Henry VIII's fabled Nonsuch. Charles had toyed with rebuilding Whitehall, as had his father, but he had abandoned the idea as tactless in the wake of the Great Fire. For a time, he had focused his attention on 'building his Palace of Greenewich & quite demolishing the old';[50] but although the Tudor buildings were

---

*At one time Wren was credited with the design of the King's House at Newmarket. The attribution gave rise to an apocryphal anecdote in which Charles, who was over six feet tall, complained about the low ceilings. Wren – who wasn't – replied that 'they were high enough', at which the King crouched down until he was on a level with his Surveyor and strutted around saying, 'Ay, Ay, Sir Christopher, I think they are high enough.' (Noble's *Biographical History of England* [1806], 327.)

taken down in 1662 and work began to the designs of John Webb, money ran short and the palace was abandoned ten years later with only one range anywhere near completed. The nearest the King had come to a new residence was the wholesale remodelling of the state apartments at Windsor Castle, begun in 1675 by Hugh May, who had recently acquired the Comptrollership of the Windsor Office of Works to add to his position as Comptroller of the King's Works. But with the paint still wet on Antonio Verrio's sumptuous allegorical ceilings, and the gilders still at work on the Grinling Gibbons carvings, Charles decided he preferred the air at Winchester to Windsor.

Wren's design aligned the palace on an east–west axis, with the intention (never carried out) of creating a broad avenue through the city which terminated at the west door of Winchester Cathedral, about a quarter of a mile away. As with Chelsea, the architect opted for red brick with stone dressings and a main block which extended around three sides of an open court.

There were projections, with small internal courtyards behind them, in the angles made by the wings and the central range, a device Wren borrowed from Versailles, which he had seen – and disliked – during his visit to France in the mid-1660s. This central range was colonnaded, with a portico placed on top of the rusticated colonnade to emphasize the *piano nobile*, a low balustraded roof and a shallow, rather French-looking dome capped with a further balustrade and a little cupola from which – on a very clear day indeed – King Charles might catch a glimpse of the sea and the fleet at Spithead, twenty miles away.

There was no entrance hall as such: the dome covered a staircase hall rising the full height of the building, with the King's side of the palace to the left, or south, and the Queen's side to the right. Charles and Catherine of Braganza had their own chapels – an Anglican one for him, and a Catholic one for her – and there were three further sets of state apartments, for the Duke of York, his Duchess, and the King's mistress, the Duchess of Portsmouth. The ground floor was given over to lodgings for secretaries, ladies-in-waiting and other personal servants, while the top floor, above the rooms of state, contained sixty rooms 'for accommodation of the Family'.[51] The ground fell steeply below the courtyard, and Wren decided to terrace it and create a second court with lodgings for courtiers and other members of the household, so that when viewed along the avenue from the cathedral, the palace proper would have seemed to hover above the buildings in the lower court, presenting a series of receding planes which climaxed theatrically in the dome and cupola.

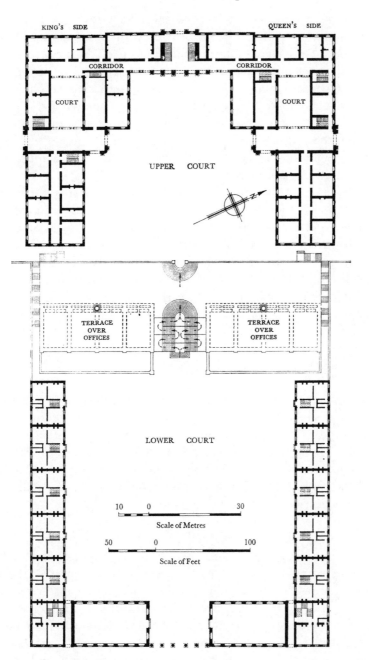

Figure 4. Winchester Palace.

Given the speed with which Wren always responded to a new commission, it is safe to assume that he drew up his initial designs at the end of 1682. They were soon modified, but since Winchester was never finished, it is not clear how significantly. A late eighteenth-century view showing the palace 'as intended to have been finish'd by Sir Christopher Wren' and claiming to be 'copied from a coloured drawing, made by the architect himself', shows some important differences from Wren's own elevation: the central portico uses a giant order, for instance, rising up the full height of the façade; the dome is raised on a much more prominent drum; and there are cupolas to both wings.

Whatever the truth, it is clear that Charles was passionate about Winchester. He took his entire court down to see the foundations in September 1683, when he stayed for a month; the Earl of Sunderland reported that he was 'growing fonder of his building and the country every day'.[52] He was there again for a few days in June 1684, and again for a full month in September. Obsessed with intimations of his own mortality, although still only in his early fifties, he was desperate to see the palace finished, and pushed Wren hard to move things along as quickly as possible. Roger North recalled how in the early days of the scheme the Surveyor was summoned to appear before the King and the Lords Commissioners of the Treasury:

> [Charles] pressed him to say how soon it might be done. He answered in two years. The King urged him to say if it might possibly be done in one year. Yes, said the Surveyor General, but not so well, nor without great confusion, charge and inconvenience, and however diligent they were, he feared disappointments would happen. Well, said the King, if it be possible to be done in one year, I will have it so, for a year is a great deal in my life.[53]

Wren's misgivings were brushed aside, and any qualms he had about rushing the greatest project of his life were softened when he was awarded a salary of £500 a year plus expenses to supervise the construction. And Charles certainly got his way. Joiners made a series of models; and 'very fine' they were too, according to the traveller and diarist Celia Fiennes, who saw one of them in 1696.[54] Two London brickmakers arrived in Winchester in January 1683, where they immediately set about digging the brickearth for two million bricks in a local farmer's field. (By the end of the following year, they had contracted to produce a total of seven million.) Two of Wren's established stable of masons, Christopher Kempster and Edward Strong, agreed in March that they would have the foundations laid and the cellars raised by September, using the 'old Ashler of the Castle' wherever possible. The Portland quarries delivered stone for the cornices, columns and capitals that summer, and the usual winter break in building operations was cut short, with the raising of the walls beginning on 2 January 1684. There were now five gangs of masons at work: Kempster and Strong were joined by Samuel Fulkes and Thomas Wise, John Tompson, and William Byrd. Byrd was an Oxford mason, who had executed the stone-carving on the Sheldonian. The others were London men who had contracted for the City churches and who would at one time or another work on St Paul's. The team was completed by Master Bricklayer of the Works Maurice Emmett, who promised to employ at least thirty-two bricklayers and sixteen labourers and agreed, like the masons, to have the job finished by the end of July.

In the autumn, the carpenters and plumbers moved in. Over the winter of 1684/5 the palace was roofed, floors were laid and doorcases installed, and two plasterers, John Grove junior from the Office of Works and Henry Doogood, another regular from the City churches, contracted for the plasterwork. Plans were in hand to start on the buildings of the lower court, and Wren had a scheme to create a thirty-foot-high cascade in the gardens. At the beginning of February King Charles announced that, 'I shall be most happy this week, for my building will be covered with lead.'[55]

Five days later he was dead.

14

Free Conversation

*C*harles II's successor was a dour character. James II was markedly lacking in the charisma and political acumen which had enabled his brother to manage his kingdom so effectively for twenty-five years. 'Dismal Jimmy', as he was none too affectionately known, was diligent and dull where Charles had been indolent and witty. He was honest and straightforward to the point of naïvety, a pathologically earnest Roman Catholic who was overwhelmed with guilt and self-loathing whenever he failed to live up to his religious principles, which was often; Charles once joked that James deliberately took only ugly women for his mistresses in order to mortify himself.★ Not surprisingly, the easy-going and cheerfully debauched life that courtiers had grown accustomed to at Whitehall came to an abrupt end on his accession to the throne. On 11 February, Evelyn noted that 'the face of the whole Court was exceedingly chang'd to a more solemn and moral behaviour; the new King affecting neither prophanenesse nor buffoonery'.[1]

The change was no doubt to Wren's taste: he never had been much of an enthusiast for either 'prophanenesse' or 'buffoonery'. If James's Catholicism was rather less acceptable to a staunch Anglican like him, at least the King was open about his religion; and the propitiatory noises he made to the Privy Council on the day of his brother's death, when he promised he would govern according to the laws of the kingdom and

---

★Catherine Sedley, who became James's mistress in 1681, was at a loss to understand his devotion to her: 'It cannot be my beauty, for I have none; and it cannot be my wit for he has not enough to know that I have any' (quoted in Maurice Ashley, *James II* [J. M. Dent & Sons, 1977], 94).

'always take care to defend and support' the Church of England, went a long way towards allaying fears when his speech was printed and circulated.

One of James's first acts was to summon a new Parliament, which he needed to vote him the revenues enjoyed by his brother. But he didn't need a Parliament inclined to question his authority and, due to carefully managed elections and some deft gerrymandering, the MPs who met on 19 May were the most slavishly Royalist bunch that Westminster had seen for nearly a century. Wren was one of them.

There were no political parties as such in the seventeenth century, merely loose groupings, unpredictable tendencies and unreliable alliances. The words 'whig' and 'tory' were just coming into common parlance, and their origins as terms of abuse – the former meant a Scottish carter, the latter an Irish outlaw – had not yet been forgotten. If they were now being used to refer vaguely to those who opposed the divine right of kings, and those who upheld it, they certainly did not denote coherent political ideologies. Insofar as these existed at all, they were based on self-interest. The court faction tended to consist of London-based placemen like Wren – men who went into Parliament to serve the Crown without question. The country 'party' was anti-metropolitan, loyal to local interests and generally more independent-minded.

Wren was a court tory. His upbringing was tory, in that it had conditioned him to believe that kingship was sacred. And he inclined towards the court, if only because his career depended on royal patronage. In the 1685 Parliament he sat for Plympton St Maurice in Devon, a tiny borough which had previously been represented by the lawyer Sir George Treby. As a well-known anti-Catholic who had helped to draft the unsuccessful bill to exclude James from the succession, Treby's political credentials were a little tarnished, and the electorate, which was packed with loyal tories, had no difficulty in choosing the King's Surveyor-General.* Treby later complained about sharp practice to the Commons' Committee of Privileges, but to no avail.

Wren was a conscientious MP, and he took naturally to the everyday business of politics. From 22 May, when King James first addressed the two Houses, until Westminster adjourned at the beginning of July, he

---

*One of those loyal tories was the prominent Cornish landowner Sir Nicholas Slanning, who had been an FRS until Wren expelled him for non-payment of fees in the 1682 purge. He obviously bore no grudges.

sat on no fewer than eleven parliamentary committees. Some, such as those which examined a proposed tax on new buildings and a bill setting up the new parish of St James Piccadilly, fell within his sphere of professional expertise. Others did not. He was involved, for example, in a committee to report on a bill against the import of tallow candles, another on maintaining the prices of wool and corn, and another on the regulation of hackney coaches. He also voted along with the rest of the Commons in favour of the Bill of Attainder against the Duke of Monmouth. Monmouth, Charles II's bastard but staunchly Protestant son, had fled England in 1683, after the Rye House Plot against his Catholic uncle failed. In June 1685 he landed in Dorset, declaring himself the legitimate heir of the dead King and thus the rightful monarch of England, and accusing James of everything from starting the Fire of London to murdering his brother. The rebellion failed; Monmouth was captured and condemned to death. Did Wren feel any qualms when Monmouth went to his awful end on Tower Hill that July? (The executioner hacked at his neck five times, and eventually had to use his knife.) I shouldn't think so. His memories of the Civil War were too vivid, and no doubt he shared John Evelyn's conviction that Monmouth's rebellion 'must needs have caus'd universal disorder, cruelty, injustice, rapine, sacrilege, and confusion, an unavoidable civil war and misery without end'.[2]

The parliamentary committee closest to his heart was one which met on 22 June to consider the future of the coal dues. Under the optimistic terms of the 1670 Act these were due to run until September 1687, by which time the City would be rebuilt, its new churches would be packed with grateful worshippers and the noble pile of St Paul's would have risen, triumphant, from the ashes. By and large, the City authorities had fulfilled their part of the bargain, and had in fact been raiding their share of the dues for years to pay for general public improvements, such as new wharves and landing stairs, street-widening schemes and modernized markets. The churches, which by the end of 1684 had received well over £240,000 from the coal tax, had rather further to go. Building work at twenty of them was finished. Many of the remaining thirty-six were usable, although they were still in need of towers and steeples. Construction was only just beginning at four, and it hadn't even started at one, All Hallows Lombard Street.[3]

Not surprisingly, the biggest building project of all was the furthest away from completion. It was ten years almost to the day since Thomas Strong and John Longland had laid the first stones at the east end of the cathedral. In that time, the choir and the north and south transepts had been taken up to the top of the lower order, a height of some fifty feet. The eight piers which would eventually support the dome over the central crossing had reached a similar height, and masons were building the walls of the nave and carving 'the great Capitells of the Pilasters both for the Inside & the Outside'.[4]

This was pretty fair progress, especially since the building fund was desperately short of cash, and there were problems with the supply of stone from the royal quarries on the Isle of Portland. Still, Dean Stillingfleet could be forgiven for wondering how much longer it would be before his new choir would actually be ready for divine service. As the warrant of 1675 had noted, the cathedral was 'so ordered that it might be built and finished by Parts', but from very early on Wren had made a decision not to focus all his resources on the east end, fearing that if he did – and the choir was finished and ready for use – then the momentum would fade away, funds would dry up, and he might be dead and forgotten before anyone in authority had the spirit to complete the building. Hence the crossing-piers, the north and south porticos, the nave, the inexorable drive westwards. There were sound technical reasons for this approach, as well. Wren appreciated, for example, that if all the piers were not started more or less simultaneously, they might not settle equally, with potentially disastrous consequences when the time came for them to support their colossal load. And he no doubt argued that by establishing a rolling programme of construction, he could roof the eastern sections and press ahead with fitting out the interior while the western walls were still going up. This would cut costs and, by allowing for year-round construction, reduce to a minimum the delays caused by the traditional winter break. Perhaps Stillingfleet even believed him.

There had been a high turnover of staff in the past ten years. Fatal accidents, of course, were to be expected: 'Paid the charges of the Coroners Enquiry of the death of Patrick Pratt a Laborer killed by a fall in ye Church' is a typical entry in the accounts.[5] But labourers could be replaced; changes in senior personnel were more disruptive. Thomas Strong and Joshua Marshall, the two mason-contractors who had begun the foundations of the choir in the summer of 1675, were both dead. Marshall died in 1678, with no one to succeed him but his widow, Katherine – the same Widow Marshall whose peremptory treatment at Wren's hands had so shocked Robert Hooke. Although she continued the firm for a time, the Surveyor wasn't inclined to employ her, and new tenders went out.

Marshall had run a big operation. In an industry where firms had to wait years and sometimes even decades for payment, no single contractor had the capital to step into his shoes, and three separate masons took his place. One was Thomas Wise, his successor as Master Mason at the Office of Works. Another was Edward Pierce, who had carved the bust commemorating Wren's knighthood. The third was Jasper Latham, who like Pierce was also a sculptor: his best-known work is a monument to Gilbert Sheldon in Croydon parish church. Wren would later have cause to regret employing him.[6] All three had already proved themselves by carrying out contracts for Wren on the City churches, although Wise's position at the Works meant that in his case proof was hardly needed. In 1681 Thomas Strong died, aged only forty-nine; his business, however, was taken over without a break by Edward, his younger brother.

There were new faces, too, among the salaried staff at St Paul's. Edward Woodroffe had died in November 1675; the post of Assistant Surveyor, and the £100 a year that went with it, passed to John Oliver. Ten years later the death of John Tillison left a vacancy for a Clerk of Works and Paymaster. It was filled by a none-too-scrupulous character named Lawrence Spencer, who acted as Clerk to the Commissioners and also received £100 a year. Acknowledging how much the building project had grown in complexity since the early days, the Commission dispensed with the Labourer in Trust, who for 20d a day had helped the Clerk of Works to keep a check on the hundreds of day-workers, and created a new £50-a-year post of Clerk of the Cheque. Three times a day – at six in the morning, one in the afternoon and six in the evening – Thomas Russell had to call a register of all the labourers, carpenters and bricklayers who were on day-rates, to make sure they were actually there. In between times he acted as a general site foreman, 'constantly going from place to place in the work to keep those men to their business'.[7] A fourth officer arrived in 1691, after Wren applied to the Commissioners for permission to employ 'a Servant in drawing Designes for ye Works and other necessary business of this Church, when his health or their Majesties service may hinder him'.[8] His name was Nicholas Hawksmoor.

There would be more changes over the next few years. At the end of 1685 Thomas Wise died: his work was taken over by his son Thomas junior, in partnership with Thomas Hill. (And his post as Master Mason of the King's Works went to John Oliver. Wren looked after his own.) Around the same time, Edward Pierce and Jasper Latham put in bids for the west end of the cathedral.

Much to their annoyance, they were unsuccessful, and the contracts eventually went to two new masons, John Tompson and Samuel Fulkes. Tompson got the work because the Lord Mayor, who sat on the St Paul's Commission, personally recommended him, although he had already built the south front of Winchester Palace and obtained six City church contracts from Wren. Fulkes, who had also been at Winchester, had eight, plus the additional recommendation of having been a foreman for the Strong brothers at St Paul's.

At the beginning of September 1687 a newsletter told Londoners of the arrival of Tompson and Fulkes: 'Two new masons are added to the work of St Paul's with a commission to Sir Christopher Wren to see the work go on with all expedition possible, the Act which gave the Coal Money commencing Michelmass next, so that a few years will now perfect the edifice.'[9] The overoptimistic tone suggests just how little the general population appreciated the scale of the enterprise, but the essential details are accurate. The parliamentary committee which met on 22 June 1685 to consider the future of the coal tax had, with some ardent advocacy from the Member for Plympton, agreed to extend the eighteen pence per chaldron which the churches received until 1700. (The City of London's share, also eighteen pence, was stopped.) Better than that, they readjusted the dues to take account of the fact that St Paul's was in greater need. The 1670 act had given 1s 1½d to the City churches and only 4½d to the cathedral, a 75%:25% split. For thirteen years from September 1687, St Paul's was to receive 80% of the coal money. The bill passed its third reading three days later, and Wren responded by trebling expenditure in a renewed effort to move the building work forward.

For all the Surveyor's loyalty to the Crown, the new regime had an immediate and unwelcome impact on his hopes for Winchester Palace. Within days of Charles II's death, James summoned Wren and asked him what was needed 'to make tight and preserve from damage the buildings at Winchester and to work up all the materials that lie ready there'.[10] The project was halted, and although that spring Wren came up with an estimate and a scaled-down design for completing the palace, by September the word was that 'his Majesty did not seeme to encourage the finishing it'.[11] Unused timber was sold off in 1687 to raise money for the workmen's wages; the windows were boarded up in April 1688; and Winchester Palace was abandoned to the care of two labourers and a watchdog.

And that was the end of that. 'It's never like to be finished now,' wrote a wistful Celia Fiennes, when she toured the shell in the mid-1690s.[12] She was quite right. Wren's hopes were raised twice: once in 1694, when William III took him to Winchester 'to survey the house there, in order to goe on with building that which was begun by King Charles the 2d';[13] and again in the summer of 1705, when Queen Anne ordered her 72-year-old Surveyor down to Hampshire to 'view the buildings there which the Queen has a mind to finish'.[14] But neither sovereign was prepared to pay out the £18,000 which Wren reckoned was needed to complete the palace. For most of the eighteenth century the Office of Works continued to keep it watertight and in good repair, while various schemes to pull it down and sell off the materials, or to turn it into a permanent prisoner-of-war camp, came to nothing (although it was used to house French and Spanish prisoners during both the Seven Years' War and the War of Independence). Winchester Palace was finally handed over to the military in 1796, and served as a barracks until it was destroyed by fire in 1894.

One reason for James's lack of interest in Winchester was that his own architectural ambitions lay elsewhere – on Wren's own doorstep, in fact. Within weeks of coming to the throne, dismal Jimmy had resolved to make his mark on the Palace of Whitehall by modernizing a section on the north side of the Privy Garden, running from Holbein Gate down past the south end of the Banqueting House. This range had once been the most important in the palace, containing Henry VIII's own lodgings. Now it was an irregular agglomeration of offices and courtiers' apartments. The Treasury Chambers were here, along with King Charles's bathroom and one of three laboratories he had installed in the palace. The Council Chamber stood behind it, projecting out into Pebble Court.

James wanted a new Council Chamber, on more or less the same site as the old. He wanted new rooms for his officials and new lodgings for his Italian Queen, Mary of Modena. But most of all he wanted a new chapel, designed expressly for Catholic worship – a magnificent public protestation of his faith.

During the reign of his brother, James had been forced to hear mass privately. But within weeks of Charles's death, with 'the Romanists swarming at Court with greater confidence than had ever ben seene in England since the Reformation', services became public affairs, and a new pulpit was set up in his 'Popish Oratorie'.[15] The obvious next step was the refurbishment of the existing Chapel Royal, but with anti-Catholic feeling on the increase and tracts appearing on the London streets attacking 'Dissenters, Papists, and Fanatics',[16] this would have been a step too far for James, who at this early stage in his reign was anxious not to alienate a deeply suspicious court and country. A second chapel at Whitehall was a compromise (even so, James initially put the word about that it was intended for his wife), while its position, next to Holbein Gate and fronting on to the Street, was enough of a public statement to satisfy the King's missionary fervour.

Notwithstanding any personal qualms Wren may have had, he was a servant of the Crown. On 15 May 1685 he submitted his estimate of £14,325 to his new employer.[17] It included

> the whole South side of the privy Garden [a slip of the pen – he meant the north side], the ground story 11 foot high, the Second Story 19, containing the Gallery & the Queens apartment, & the Chapell the highth of both stories. The ground story to be fitted with deale wanscote into lodgings & offices for the Treasury, Secretaries, Ld Chamberlain & others. The 2nd story & galleries to be finished [in the same manner] as the Kings new Lodgings, and the Chapell decently adorned.[18]

The demolition of the old range began three days later. Furniture was stored in the Banqueting House; timbers and tiles were stacked in the Privy Garden for reuse; Portland-stone window surrounds and other carved work on the old buildings were carefully dismantled and lowered down on tackles. An army of labourers started to dig new foundations in June; by August, carpenters were setting up work benches for the stone-carvers 'to enrich the Cornice of the outside of the new Building';[19] and by the following February the chapel was roofed and joiners were at work in the Council Chamber and the Queen's apartment. The first service was held in the chapel on Christmas Day 1686.

The exteriors were quite plain. As at Chelsea and Winchester, Wren opted for red brick with stone dressings as a cheap, fast alternative to stone. The main range facing the Privy Garden had a central doorway and was lit by three tiers of windows plus a row of dormers in the attic; the Council Chamber, which projected out at right angles to it, was also dormered and raised on a rusticated arcade. A 'Great Staircase' connected the range to the south end of the Banqueting House. Some of the interiors were quite lavishly decorated. The ceilings of the

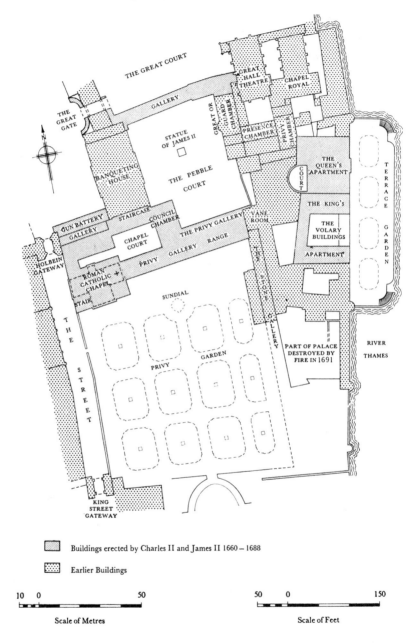

Figure 5. The Palace of Whitehall, *c.* 1695.

Queen's bedchamber and closet were painted by Antonio Verrio, and new furniture for her apartment included a suite of blue and gold velvet chairs and stools for her withdrawing room, musk velvet hangings for her closet, and flowered velvet chairs for her eating room. Her bedchamber was particularly grand, with a marble chimneypiece carved by Grinling Gibbons and gilded with burnished gold. (Evelyn, when he saw it in January 1687, declared it to be 'incomparable'.[20]) Expectations were high, and the Queen's crimson velvet bed, with hangings said to have cost £3000, didn't come up to scratch first time round. On 4 December 1686 an order was given that 'the feathers [were] to be made larger and the bedding altered with a new satten quilt and bolster and a downe bed with 4 blankets, one of them to be covered with satten'. The same order also required an eight-foot-high screen 'to stand about the bed . . . to keep off the Dogs'.[21]

Wren wasn't an interior decorator, of course, and his part in the creation of the new range was confined to the design and supervision of the building and fittings. In September 1686, for example, he was asked to fit the wainscot in Mary of Modena's new withdrawing chamber to take the 14ft 3in hangings intended for the room. But the high point of the work was the Catholic chapel, and here his role was crucial.

The site was an awkward one, since the Privy Garden range which determined the east-west alignment of the chapel wasn't quite at right angles to the Street, which determined the position of its west façade. But after his experience with the City churches, a problem of this sort held no fears. He created a not-quite-square vestibule at the western end, with a screen of columns supporting the gallery which held the royal pew. Lodgings for the priest were above this gallery, on the second floor. The asymmetry of the space was effectively disguised by the screen. Apart from the irregular west wall, the chapel consisted of a straightforward rectangular box, with a vestry to the south, and a first-floor gallery to the north which allowed the King and Queen to arrive in their pew via the Privy Garden range without having to enter the body of the chapel. This arrangement didn't last long, however. In April 1687 Wren received a warrant to 'enlarge His Majesty's New Chapell Royall into the Privy Garden in Whitehall'.[22] The enlargement involved building a side-chapel, staircase and new vestry on to the south side, and creating a gallery over the side-chapel to take an organ which alone cost £1100.

The chapel must have been stunning. Over 10,000 leaves of gold were used on the ceilings; the doors were cedar-grained and picked out in gold. The pulpit, which was also gilded, was carved by Grinling Gibbons; and there were Persian carpets on the floor and crimson damask curtains edged with gold and silver for the organ loft. The King and Queen sat beneath a canopy of crimson velvet embroidered with gold and silver and festooned with wooden putti, again carved by Gibbons. Even the strings to draw the curtains were of silver.

But even in the midst of all this sybaritic and wonderfully unspiritual splendour, one feature dominated the chapel. Designed by Wren and carved by Grinling Gibbons and his partner, Arnold Quellin, the massive altarpiece – nearly 40 feet high and around 25 feet wide – filled the entire east end. There were life-size statues of St Peter and St Paul, flanked by Faith and Charity, with angels on the upper storey and a huge framed painting of the Annunciation, perhaps by Verrio, who also painted the Assumption of the Virgin in the vault of the ceiling.

Evelyn, who witnessed the celebration of mass in the new chapel when it was opened to the public on 29 December 1686, was awed by its grandeur and appalled by its purpose. After sneering at the waving of censers and the antics of the Jesuits, and grumbling about their 'divers cringes' and the 'world of mysterious ceremony', he wrote that 'I could not have believ'd I should ever have seene such things in the King of England's Palace, after it had pleas'd God to enlighten this Nation.' But all his Anglican antipathy towards Rome couldn't suppress his admiration for Wren's building:

> Nothing can be finer than the magnificent marble work and archi-tecture at the end, where are four statues, representing St John, St Peter, St Paul, and the Church [he mistook the iconography of the altarpiece], in white marble, the work of Mr Gibbons, with all the carving and pillars of exquisite art and greate cost. The altarpiece is the Salutation, the volto in fresca, the Assumption of the Blessed Virgin according to their tradition, with our Bl Saviour, and a world of figures, painted by Verrio. The throne where the King and Queene sit is very glorious, in a closet above, just opposite the altar.[23]

Wren carried out one further commission for James II at Whitehall. In February 1688 he was given a warrant to rebuild Mary of Modena's old lodgings facing the Thames 'according to the Draught and designe you have shewed unto the King and Queen's Majesties, which they have approved off'.[24] The work, which eventually involved not only a new block for the Queen, but also a formal terrace garden projecting about seventy feet into the river, wasn't completed until 1693. By that time James II had lost his throne, Mary of Modena had fled Whitehall disguised as an Italian laundress, and no one had any use for Wren's Catholic chapel. Queen Mary gave the organ to St James Piccadilly. King William sent Gibbons' pulpit to the Danish Church in Wellclose Square, and had the altarpiece dismantled and taken to Hampton Court, where it stayed until 1706, when Queen Anne gave it to Westminster Abbey. By that time the Chapel itself had been burned to the ground in the fire which engulfed Whitehall in 1698. The figures of Faith, Hope, St Peter and St Paul now stand in the garden of Westminster School, weathered beyond recognition; but the other parts of the legendary altarpiece (or some of them, anyway) survive in the unlikely setting of the parish church – St Andrew's – at Burnham-on-Sea, a dreary seaside town on the Bristol Channel with no redeeming features save this. In the 1820s Westminster Abbey had decided the altarpiece wasn't appropriate, and the Bishop of Rochester, who also happened to be vicar of St Andrew's Burnham, carried it off to Somerset.

Glorious though it was, the theatrical, rather Continental Baroque of the Whitehall chapel represents a marked departure from Wren's usual style. But though the nation looked askance at its gilded Popery, he saw only the thing itself – one more architectural problem looking for one more solution.

Wren's favourite sister Susan, the 'vertuose wife'[25] of William Holder, died on 30 June 1688 at the age of sixty-one. She was buried in the still-uncompleted crypt of St Paul's, and from this point on we hear no more about the Surveyor's sisters. Two were certainly already gone. Elizabeth died of consumption back in 1649, when she was only sixteen. Anne married a canon of Ely Cathedral, Henry Brounsell, and died in 1668 after a long illness. She was thirty-four. Nothing is known of the lives of Mary, Katherine and Rachel. Perhaps Susan was the last.

The day of her death had a significance for the future course of English history which far outweighed any private grief. James II's determination to give equal rights to Roman Catholics had been growing steadily over the past three years, setting him on a collision course with the Anglican establishment. Henry Compton, Wren's old friend and travelling companion on the trip to France, was now Bishop of London, having succeeded Humphrey Henchman in 1675. However, Compton had been suspended in August 1686, after he refused to discipline one of his clergy, Dr John Sharpe, for a sermon arguing that

Protestants should resist the arguments of Catholics. Then in May 1688 the King issued his second Declaration of Indulgence suspending the penal laws against Catholics and Nonconformists, and ordered the bishops to distribute the declaration and to ensure it was read out in every church in the kingdom. Seven bishops, including Archbishop Sancroft, protested; and at ten o'clock on the night of 18 May six of them went to Whitehall, where they presented James with a petition which asked him to withdraw the order.* The King reacted by flying into a rage and calling them rebels. When their petition was printed and circulated around London, and the declaration went unread in all but a handful of churches, he had the seven thrown in the Tower and prosecuted for seditious libel.

The move was massively unpopular, particularly in London: 'violent courses were every moment expected', said Evelyn;[26] huge crowds of people gathered on their knees at Tower Wharf to pray for the bishops' safe deliverance; and the word was that the Protestant nobility were poised to come to the aid of the clergy.

The bishops' trial was held at the Court of King's Bench in Westminster Hall on 29 June and, after a night of suspense, the jury brought in its verdict the next morning – not guilty. As Susan died, bells were rung all over the City, bonfires were lit and the streets were thronged with cheering crowds. And that night, while Wren and Holder mourned their loss, Henry Compton and six prominent nobles signed a letter inviting the Protestant William of Orange, James's own son-in-law, to invade England and save the nation from Popery.

Dissatisfaction with James's blunderingly autocratic attempts to enforce religious toleration had been simmering ever since Bishop Compton's suspension, an event which in itself had caused all sorts of problems for Wren. In January 1686 the King had been pleased to renew the Commission for rebuilding St Paul's – his enemies said he was eager to see the Cathedral finished so that he could hand it over to the Catholics – but with Compton's removal from office that August, the regular gatherings of the Commission, which were supposed to take place in the Chapter House at 3 p.m. on the first Thursday of each month, simply stopped. The management of the project was left in the hands of a standing committee. After the events of June 1688, meetings of this committee also ceased abruptly.

---

*Sancroft, who had already been barred from the King's presence, stayed behind at Lambeth, although he signed his name to the petition.

Likewise, Compton's suspension also seems to have brought to a halt the meetings of the Commission for rebuilding the City churches, leaving Wren to carry on the work as best he could. Small wonder that he told Billy's godfather, Sir William Fermor, that, 'Wee are ... uncertain wch way the next wind may tosse us. Wee are afrayd of being absent from our charge, & therfore watch [like] those who travell in suspected places.'[27]

William Fermor's seat at Easton Neston in Northamptonshire is one of a number of country houses attributed to Wren. The list is − or rather was − a long one, including work at Tring Manor, Hertfordshire; Winslow Hall, Buckinghamshire; Longleat House, Wiltshire; Arbury Hall, Warwickshire; Thoresby Hall, Nottinghamshire; Fawley Court, Buckinghamshire; Belton House, Lincolnshire; and Newby Hall, Yorkshire.*

Country-house design was a normal part of architectural practice, even for public officials. The Comptrollers who served under Wren during his forty-nine years as Surveyor − Hugh May, William Talman and John Vanbrugh − are arguably the three greatest names in late Stuart domestic architecture. To take just a few examples, May's Cassiobury Park in Hertfordshire (*c.* 1677–80; demolished), Talman's work on the south and east fronts of Chatsworth (1687–96) and Vanbrugh's Castle Howard (1700–26) and Blenheim Palace (1705–25) rank among the finest country houses of this or any other period. Even Robert Hooke produced designs for three or four country houses in the 1670s and 1680s − and one important London mansion, Montagu House in Bloomsbury, which he built for Ralph Montagu in 1675–9.

But Wren was essentially a *public* architect. He rarely had either the time or the inclination to work for private patrons, an attitude which set him apart from his contemporaries in general and his colleagues at the Office of Works in particular. The country houses credited to him at one time or another fall into three groups. With Fawley, Belton and Newby, there is no evidence at all for the attribution beyond the fact that the houses look good and were built around the right time − the Grinling Gibbons syndrome, in other words, which early in the twentieth century gave Gibbons the credit for any piece of decent Stuart wood-carving that couldn't be assigned to anyone else. The second

---

*There is also one town mansion, Marlborough House in St James's.

group consists of houses where there is some evidence for his involvement, but where that involvement didn't amount to much. At Longleat,
he designed a doorcase, which was taken down in 1705 and re-erected
at Warminster School two years later. At Arbury he designed another
doorcase; but although his client, Richard Newdigate, presented him
with a pair of silver candlesticks worth £11 9s, it wasn't executed.
Thoresby, which was remodelled in 1685–7 for the 4th Earl of Kingston,
is a mystery. The accounts show a payment of five guineas to 'Sr
Christopher Wren's man' in 1686, and there is a related drawing among
the Wren papers at All Souls, implying that the Office of Works was
involved in some way.[28] But exactly what way is impossible to tell. The
house was badly damaged by fire as soon as it was finished – it was
remodelled again *c.* 1690, almost certainly by William Talman, and
altered out of all recognition in the eighteenth century.

This leaves Tring Manor, Winslow Hall and Easton Neston. The case
for including Tring in the dwindling canon of Wren houses is convincing. It was built, probably in the 1680s, for Henry Guy, who was
then Secretary to the Treasury and thus in a good position to ask Wren
for help. Wren is known to have visited the house in 1687.[29] An
illustration in a county history of 1700 shows an attractive but conventional building of two storeys raised on a half basement, with a
hipped roof, pediment and dormer windows; the engraving is dedicated
to Guy by John Oliver, who was Wren's Assistant Surveyor at St Paul's
and the Master Mason at the Works.[30] But the most telling evidence is
that Roger North, who knew both Tring and Wren, stated categorically
that the house 'is new, of Sir Chr Wren's invention'.[31] As he described
it, a central entrance porch with two rooms and backstairs to either side
led into a sort of cross-passage with a gallery above it. A screen to the
left opened on to the two-storeyed great hall – an arrangement
reminiscent of the medieval country house – while the great staircase
stood to the right. The passage led on through to a third range of rooms,
chief of which was a withdrawing room or great parlour ('I remember
not well which'). North was particularly intrigued by Wren's treatment
of the central section: the hall was decorated with giant pilasters except
at the lower end, where a double order screened the cross-passage and
the gallery above. Wren took the ceiling of the gallery right up through
the attic storey, covering it with a shallow internal dome. This 'looks
well underneath [i.e., from the hall],' said North, 'but above, is a
monster.'[32]

Tring was 'I thinck the onely intire house [Sir Christopher] hath done'.[33] But North was writing in about 1698, and that doesn't help us with Winslow Hall. Winslow was built in 1699–1702 for another Secretary to the Treasury, William Lowndes. The building accounts have survived, and they show without doubt that the Office of Works was involved. Three of the craftsmen employed were from Wren's office, and the Surveyor himself checked through the bills and amended them as necessary: there are a number of entries stating that such-and-such a sum has been 'Abated out of this bill by Judgmt of Sr Christ Wren Survr Genll of his Mats Works', or 'Abated on this bill by Sir Chr Wren's Judgmt'.[34] This isn't to say that he necessarily provided the design, of course, and stylistically, Winslow is hardly at the cutting edge of Baroque architecture. A double-pile dolls' house of a building with hipped roof, slightly projecting pedimented centre and four tall panelled chimneystacks, it could easily have been built in the 1660s by Pratt, May or William Winde. But it wasn't. And there is an austere restraint about it that fits well with Wren's character.

So Tring belongs in the canon, and we can give Winslow the benefit of the doubt. But the arguments for and against Easton Neston are frankly too close to call. The main block of this splendid house seems to date from the later 1690s, soon after Sir William Fermor acquired a title and a rich third wife; the two wings (only one of which survives) may be ten years or so earlier. On the plus side there is the fact that Fermor was a relation by marriage and a godfather to Wren's son William: with the nation's leading architect in the family it would be rather odd *not* to turn to him for advice. In 1708 it was said that the 'noble staires' were by 'Sir Christopher Renn and Mr Hawkesmoore';[35] and a county history written before 1724 states that the wings were by Wren and the main block by Hawksmoor, who 'hath very much departed from the first design'.[36] In its final form the main block certainly *is* the work of Hawksmoor, who later wrote of it as one of his 'owne children'.[37] But as Kerry Downes has pointed out, he also described the wings as 'good for nothing'; and the fanatically loyal Hawksmoor never, *ever* spoke so dismissively about the work of the man who made him an architect. As far as we can tell, it looks as if Wren provided Fermor with a design for the house early on and handed the project over to his assistant, who went on to modify it so radically that he made it his own. As to who built the wings, both men at different times spoke of them as though they were by someone else entirely.

After four months of uncertainty William of Orange landed near

Torquay on 5 November 1688 – an auspicious date for one whose avowed intention was to deliver the nation from Papism. His banners announced that he was here in the cause of 'Religion and Liberty'. James rushed down to rally his troops, who were encamped on Salisbury Plain. But, deserted by his closest followers and plagued by nosebleeds, he just as swiftly rushed back to Whitehall, only to find that Bishop Compton had buckled on his sword and taken the King's younger daughter Anne off to Nottingham, which had been occupied for William by the Earl of Devonshire. 'God help me!' he exclaimed. 'Even my children have forsaken me.' He packed Mary of Modena and the infant Prince of Wales off to France and, after an unsuccessful effort to negotiate with his son-in-law, who was steadily advancing on the capital, he decided all was lost and attempted to join them, disguised in a black wig and an odd pair of boots. But his boat was boarded in the Channel by some English fishermen, who stole his valuables and stripped the poor man of his breeches 'even to the discovery of his nudity' in their search for hidden treasure, before he was sent back to London.[38] By now there were riots in the streets, with mobs looting the houses of prominent Catholics and burning the library of the Spanish ambassador. The Royal Society postponed its anniversary elections 'by reason of the public commotions'. 'It looks like a Revolution,' wrote Evelyn.[39]

So it was. James was finally allowed to leave Whitehall by barge at eleven o'clock on the morning of 18 December, accompanied by two boatloads of Dutch guards. William arrived at St James's Palace five hours later, and on Christmas Day the exiled King landed at Ambleteuse near Calais. He never saw England again.

With James gone, William of Orange's popularity began to wane a little. John Sharpe, whose anti-Catholic preaching had led to Bishop Compton's suspension two years previously, now gave a sermon arguing that the deposing of monarchs was a Popish practice – he obviously liked to live on the edge. Archbishop Sancroft was appalled that his actions had indirectly led to the ousting of a king; he refused to pay his respects to William, saying he had a cold, and he subsequently refused to take the oath of allegiance. He was suspended in August 1689, and deprived of his office the following February. This heralded an elaborate game of musical chairs at St Paul's. Dean Stillingfleet, recommended to the King as 'the learnedest man of the age in all respects',[40] was made Bishop of Worcester; and the Dean of Canterbury, John Tillotson, took his place. This was only a prelude to the offer of Sancroft's archbishopric.

Tillotson resisted for two years, both out of respect for Sancroft – who flatly refused to leave Lambeth Palace – and because he thought Henry Compton wanted the job. He eventually succumbed to pressure from both William and Mary. Poor old Sancroft, without whose vision Wren would never have had the chance to design his new cathedral, finally left Lambeth in 1691, after being served with a writ for trespass. Tillotson moved in, and St Paul's was presented with another new Dean. Unfortunately, William Sherlock possessed none of Sancroft's principles, and none of Stillingfleet's scholarship. He initially sided with the Archbishop and the nonjurors, then changed his mind; around the same time he published a theologically suspect discussion of the Trinity, leading the coffee-house wits to say it was no surprise that the Dean could swear allegiance to more than one king, when he was willing to swear to more than one God. Perhaps the best that can be said for him is that he was content to leave St Paul's to one architect.

Wren's own reaction to the Glorious Revolution was to resume his political career, which had been suspended since November 1685 when James II prorogued Parliament. (After five further prorogations, the King finally dissolved Parliament in July 1687.) He stood as a court candidate for New Windsor in the elections to the Convention Parliament, which was called in January 1689 to decide who should have the crown. And he was returned. But, unfortunately for his political aspirations, there was some question in New Windsor about exactly who was entitled to vote – the mayor, the bailiffs and a small group of burgesses, or a larger number of townsfolk. The two groups returned different Members of Parliament, and after an appeal to the Committee of Privileges, Wren's election was ruled to be void. He tried for the same seat in the election of 1690, with precisely the same result – an apparent victory overturned on appeal. In the meantime, however, Parliament had, after a great deal of agonizing, decided that William and his wife Mary, James's daughter, should rule jointly. Mary arrived in England to join her husband on 12 February 1689, and the next day she and William were formally offered the Crown in the Banqueting House at Whitehall.

Whatever the couple thought about the throne of England – and they both seem to have had mixed feelings about it – Whitehall itself was not to their taste. As monarchs go, they were rather private people, and neither of them took very well to the pomp and public scrutiny that accompanied their every move when they were there. 'I still love Holland,' wrote the Queen, 'and I shall always remember the tranquillity I enjoyed there and that I shall never find here.'[41] For his part,

William recoiled from public displays of kingship. He refused point-blank to touch for the King's Evil and to wash paupers' feet on Maundy Thursday and, partly because his English was poor, he did his best to ignore the courtiers and nobles who clustered round him. Gilbert Burnet remembered how 'he was shut up all day long, and his silence, when he admitted any to an audience, distasted them as much as if they had been denied it'.[42] He was also a chronic asthmatic, and the smoky, polluted air of the city exacerbated his condition. When Mary came over from Holland she found him coughing blood, and within days the couple had left the capital in search of relative privacy and clean country air. They quickly found it at Hampton Court Palace.

Hampton Court possessed few of the qualities that the later seventeenth century admired in a royal palace. Like Whitehall, it was a vast, rambling collection of courtyards and lodgings and, in spite of various piecemeal alterations and additions, its architectural character remained much the same as it had been at Henry VIII's death more than 140 years earlier. A battlemented and turreted gatehouse to the west led (as it still does today) into an outer courtyard, then known as the Green Court. From here another gate gave access to what in the 1680s was called the Fountain Court, the north side of which was filled with Henry VIII's Great Hall, with a warren of kitchens and domestic offices behind it. At the eastern end of the complex a third courtyard, the Cloister Court, was devoted to the state apartments.*

The palace had been kept in a relatively good condition throughout the seventeenth century. Oliver Cromwell was fond of the place, using it as his principal country residence from 1653 until his death in 1658;[43] and it was repaired and given a new coat of paint in 1662 when Charles II decided to honeymoon there with Catherine of Braganza. The honeymoon was not a wild success, largely because the King spent most of it alternately cajoling and bullying his buck-toothed bride into accepting his mistress, Lady Castlemaine, as a Gentlewoman of the Bedchamber.[44] (The Queen's reaction on first being introduced to Lady Castlemaine was to burst into tears, have a nosebleed and collapse in a dead faint at her feet.) For the rest of his reign Charles and Catherine spent little time at the Palace – perhaps because it held such embarrassing and awkward memories for both of them. But he did order some major

---

*All three major courtyards have changed their names since William and Mary's time: the Green Court is now the Base Court; the Fountain Court is known as the Clock Court; and the Cloister Court, which was called the Quadrangle Court when Wren rebuilt it, has become the Fountain Court. I have used the old names throughout.

works. Between 1668 and 1674 the mason Joshua Marshall created a long canal – the Long Water – aligned on the east front of the state apartments in the Cloister Court, for example. And in 1669–70 plans were drawn up for a new set of lodgings for the Duke and Duchess of York overlooking the Tudor chapel, and apartments for Charles in the south-east corner of the Cloister Court. Both were completed by 1676. As the King's recently appointed Surveyor-General, Wren was presumably responsible for the building work; little survives of the Yorks' apartments, and nothing at all of the King's block, which was demolished thirteen years later to make way for William and Mary's own apartments.

The King and Queen went down to Hampton Court on 23 February 1689, ten days after accepting the Crown. They immediately decided to modernize it and make it their principal residence. Wren was at the palace by 25 February, presumably to wait on them and hear their plans for rebuilding. On 2 March, the newsletters were reporting that 'the bed of state is removed . . . to Hampton Court', and that 'Sir Christopher Wren hath received orders to beautify and add some new building to that fabric.'[45]

So the Surveyor had managed once again to weather the change of monarch without incident, although he must have had some anxious moments during the winter of 1688/9, when the talk was all of the King's mistrust of the English in general and the tories in particular. It wouldn't have come as any surprise if William had imported one of his own architects to fill the post of Surveyor-General, or used it to help repay his debt to the whigs who had invited him over to rescue nation and religion. But Wren's track record, his quiet professionalism, his refusal to involve himself in court intrigue and political manoeuvres, meant that he held on to the Works: the Letters Patent granting him the office of Surveyor were dated 27 September 1689. There is no reason to read anything into the seven-month delay – James II had been on the throne for nearly a year before he got round to formally confirming Wren in his post.

Wren's first scheme for Hampton Court must have been worked up in March and April of 1689. It was characteristically ambitious, involving the demolition of the whole complex, with the exception of the Tudor Great Hall. This was to be given a sweeping double stair and turned into the centrepiece of a new Great Court, flanked by blocks containing offices and barracks and opening northward towards a tree-lined avenue stretching across Bushey Park. The main entrance to the palace was

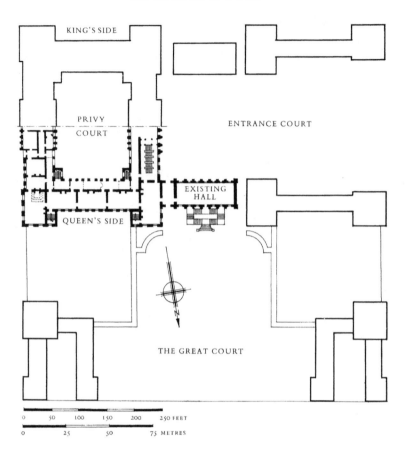

KING'S SIDE

PRIVY
COURT

ENTRANCE COURT

EXISTING
HALL

QUEEN'S SIDE

THE GREAT COURT

| 0 | 50 | 100 | 150 | 200 | 250 FEET |

| 0 | 25 | 50 | 75 METRES |

Figure 6. Wren's project for a new palace at Hampton Court.

south of the hall, another vast open court aligned this time on an east–west axis. Visitors approached from the west, passing first between long ranges of offices and then between the Great Hall and an answering block to the south – before coming face-to-face with what Wren called the Grand Front. This was an elaborate and very French-looking range with a projecting central section that was given a giant order, an attic storey adorned with statues and a dome which hovered serenely over a curious concave drum. Behind it lay the Privy Court, a large closed quadrangle containing the state apartments, with Queen Mary's to the north and King William's to the south. The pedimented frontispiece overlooking the canal, if a little less lively than the Grand Front, was none the less stately and impressive; and the four corners of the Privy

Court were treated as big pavilions, also with attic storeys but this time topped with balustrades and urns. The lower sections between pavilions and frontispieces appeared, from the outside at least, to be little more than linking corridors.

The first floor of the Grand Front, marked in the centre with the royal arms and an equestrian statue of the King, was largely given over to William's Council Chamber. Beneath it were three openings, described on Wren's drawing as '3 Thorow visto into ye Park the midlmost looking downe ye Canall'.[46] There were three similar openings in the central section of the east range facing across the Home Park, so that as one approached the Grand Front one could see right through it, across the Privy Court and down the full length of the Long Water.

This emphasis on establishing axial vistas is one of the most prominent features of the design. Wren also played with the idea of opening up the north–south axis, so that from the Great Hall one could look southwards across the Entrance Court to a long formal garden leading down to the Thames: architecture and landscape would thus have been integrated even more closely. But the other aspect which comes across strongly from the surviving drawings is the scheme's vitality and variety, the sense of movement provided by the different heights and the advancing and receding planes. The inspiration came from France: there are references to Bernini's unexecuted designs for the Louvre, the drawings which the young astronomer had yearned to copy twenty-four years earlier; references also to Versailles, to Mansart and Le Vau. But the interpretation was uniquely his own, and it shows him at the height of his powers, confident in the handling of ever-more complex combinations of masses and spaces, looking for – and finding – just the right balance between stately formality and excitement.

Unfortunately, both for Wren and for us, it was all too much for the King and Queen. The cost would have been enormous. But much more important was the fact that the new palace would have taken far too long to build, and William and Mary were both desperately eager to complete Hampton Court as quickly as possible. They couldn't stand Whitehall, didn't even consider living at St James's Palace – which was turned into apartments for close advisers and senior courtiers – and showed no interest in Windsor Castle. When, by the beginning of June 1689, it became clear that the practicalities of government called for a winter residence within striking distance of Whitehall, they paid £14,000 for the Earl of Nottingham's house and estate at Kensington, ordering Wren to enlarge it as quickly and cheaply as possible. They moved into the new Kensington Palace on Christmas Eve, although work there continued for several years more. ('Your closet as yet smells of paint, for which I will ask pardon when I see you,' Mary wrote to her husband the following summer.[47]) But Hampton Court was to be their palace and, while they realized that building a palace took a little longer than making modest alterations to a suburban villa, they weren't prepared to start again from scratch.

So over the spring of 1689 Wren was made to reduce his scheme, until by June, when building work began in earnest, it had come down to little more than a set of state apartments on the site of the old Cloister Court. The Tudor palace survived more or less intact to the west and north, complete with Cardinal Wolsey's Great Gatehouse, Henry VIII's Great Hall and the labyrinth of kitchens and offices beyond it. The Grand Front with its dome was given up, along with the remodelling of the hall as the focal point towards Bushey Park. The imposing axial vistas went, since neither of the existing Tudor courtyards lined up with the Cloister Court, which was now called the Quadrangle Court. And the reduction in scale meant that the grand corner pavilions were left as little more than memories.

Armed with the knowledge of what might have been, it is easy to see Wren's work at Hampton Court as static, too much of a compromise, ever so slightly dull. But taken on its own terms, it is a delight. The walls are of bright red brick with stone dressings: anything more extravagant was ruled out because stone from the royal quarries at Portland was in short supply (shipments were continually at risk from French privateers in the Channel) and was, in any case, desperately needed for St Paul's. But there is something stately and restful about the combination, as there is about the quiet horizontal emphasis to the façades, achieved by unbroken balustraded rooflines and serried ranks of windows. The latter follow a strict pattern on both the south front, where the King's apartments overlooked the Privy Garden leading down to the river, and the east, where the Queen's lodgings faced on to the Long Water and the Home Park. They were round-headed on the ground floor, flat-headed on the *piano nobile*, bull's-eyes above, and square on the attic storey.

The basic pattern is repeated with variations on the inner façades of the Quadrangle Court. The ground-floor openings become a low colonnade; the *piano nobile* is emphasized by pediments over every window; and the bull's-eyes, some of which are false to disguise the high, coved ceilings of the principal floor, are given carved surrounds of lions' skins – an allusion to William's image of himself as Hercules, pitting his strength against Louis XIV, the Nemean lion of France. (The conceit also appears in the pediment on the east front, where Cibber carved a group showing Hercules triumphing over Envy; and again in the bull's-eye windows on the south side of the court, which are not windows at all, but grisailles by Laguerre depicting the Labours of Hercules.)

Here and there one finds Wren's characteristic touches of ingenuity. When the Grand Front fell by the wayside, for example, the ceremonial staircase to the King's apartments had to be squeezed into the south-east corner of the middle courtyard, opposite the Great Hall. To disguise the asymmetry while at the same time marking the transition to a 'better style' of architecture, he created a colonnade of coupled Ionic columns which fills the south side of the court. Because the King's asthma made it difficult for him to climb long flights of stairs, he also positioned the *piano nobile* rather lower than one might expect (and, incidentally, placed William's private apartment on the ground floor). But he successfully disguised the fact by filling in the upper parts of the colonnade in the Quadrangle Court and recessing the resulting segments, so that from the outside the floor level seems rather higher than it really is.

Demolition work began in the Cloister Court in April 1689, and joiners moved in to take out the wainscot in the old state apartments. Foundations were being dug by June, and the roof timbers of the south front, where the King's apartment was to be, were already in place by the end of October. The extensions to Kensington Palace were roofed and leaded by the same date. If Wren had misgivings about working at such a pace, those misgivings were soon justified. At the beginning of November part of the new building at Kensington collapsed suddenly, killing several workmen and injuring others: it was said that the foundations had been laid over a vault, which gave way under the weight. This was bad enough. But five weeks later the central section of roof over the south range at Hampton Court collapsed. The fall brought down some walling, and it killed two carpenters and hurt eleven others.

People began to talk. Accidents caused by falling masonry, broken hoists or a careless slip of the foot were to be expected, but new walls and new roofs were supposed to stay in place. Mary promptly blamed herself for being too impatient: the incidents 'shewed me plainly the hand of God was in it, and I was truly humbled'.[48] But there was one person at least who would much, much rather blame her Surveyor.

Wren found it hard to make enemies. Everybody, from kings and princes to the copyists and draftsmen in his office, liked and admired his obvious ability, his natural reticence, his sheer enthusiasm for whatever project happened to fire his imagination at the time. These qualities were rare in the seventeenth century, and very few public figures were so consistently and affectionately praised by contemporaries. Sightseers made a point of visiting St Paul's on Saturdays – because that was when he was usually on site – and they always found him ready to discuss the progress of the building work. If his answers to their questions were brief and to the point, as they often were, he still had the knack of sending them away happy. Even Robert Hooke, who was more prone than most to imagined insults and paranoid suspicions, only quarrelled with him twice during their long friendship: once at St Paul's in 1674, when either Wren or Faith made some chance remark which made him rush back to Gresham to confide to his diary that he had been 'slighted';[49] and again in 1677 when the two men fell out over Hooke's bid for the Secretaryship of the Royal Society. On both occasions the estrangement lasted a matter of days.

The exception to the rule, ironically enough, was Wren's right-hand man at the Office of Works. William Talman had been appointed to the Comptrollership of the Works in June 1689, after a five-year period in which the post lay vacant following Hugh May's death. Already highly regarded as an architect in whig circles – he was currently remodelling Chatsworth in Derbyshire for William Cavendish, the 4th Earl (later the 1st Duke) of Devonshire, who had played a leading role in the Glorious Revolution – he had a powerful patron in Hans Willem Bentinck, Earl of Portland, William's most trusted adviser. The month after Talman moved into Scotland Yard, Portland was appointed Superintendant of the Royal Gardens, with the garden designer George London as his deputy and his 49-year-old protégé as Comptroller. This gave Talman tremendous influence at Hampton Court, where he and London eventually managed to spend £85,000 on the greatest formal layout ever seen in England.

What Talman really wanted was to build the palace. He was a fine architect, but he had a bad attitude, a mean, thin mouth and a high opinion of his own worth. Within months of his arrival at the Works, he had become convinced that the Surveyorship should be his, and when the fatal accident at Hampton Court occurred, he jumped at the chance of damaging Wren's reputation.

The incident at Kensington was shrugged off as just one of those things, but the Hampton Court disaster, coming so soon after it, was taken much more seriously. Work on the palace was immediately halted, amidst fears for the structural integrity of the whole building. Wren was troubled, not only about the deaths and injuries, which were commonplace enough in the Stuart construction industry, but because of the implications for the whole project – and for his reputation as an architect. He confided his worries to Hooke, and there were hurried consultations with his measuring clerk John Scarborough and his brother-in-law William Holder. Those worries were borne out at the end of December, when he was told that 'the King is of the opinion ye Building is in a bad condition'.[50] The Commissioners of the Treasury demanded reports on the incident from both Wren and Talman; they were duly read to the King at Kensington on 10 January, but although Wren appeared in person to plead his case, there was obviously a conflict between the two accounts, since William decided that work could only resume after Talman had also been heard. The two men were summoned to appear before the Treasury Commissioners three days later.

The hearing took place on Monday 13 January 1690 in the new Treasury Chambers at Whitehall, part of the Privy Garden range which Wren had built for dismal Jimmy. The Surveyor already knew the four Commissioners seated across the table from him: they were his paymasters, the men who authorized all works on the King's buildings. Lord Delamere, Sir Henry Capel and Richard Hampden had only recently been appointed, but the fourth member of the Board, Lord Godolphin, had been at the Treasury on and off for the past eleven years. He had a terse, laconic manner, but he was honest and intelligent, and known as one who 'despatched business with great method'.[51] Wren could rely on him to be fair; but Godolphin's loyalties lay entirely with the King. There would be no favours.

As the Surveyor's second-in-command, Talman was naturally expected to support his boss. That didn't happen. Instead, he brought in evidence from Edward Pierce and Jasper Latham. Neither man had forgiven Wren for failing to award them the contracts for the west end of St Paul's three years previously, and both were currently in dispute with him over rates of pay at the cathedral.[52] They asserted that the new work at Hampton Court was structurally unsound, and an acrimonious exchange followed.

When Latham's evidence was read out, Wren said he was mad. The work was perfectly sound: in fact, two days before the hearing it 'had stood new tryal in a hurrycane', which had blown down trees and houses and killed a number of people. Talman flatly contradicted him. Latham wasn't mad, and the only reason the new range hadn't blown down was because it was sheltered by the Tudor buildings. Matthew Banckes, Master Carpenter of the Works, stood by the Surveyor and pointed out that of the twenty-four piers on the south front 'next the Garden', just four stones showed any sign of stress, and this was only in the form of hairline cracks: 'The building every day it stands is stronger and grows lighter.'[53] Talman, who was obviously in a combative mood, flatly contradicted *him*: every single one of the piers was cracked, he said – and the cracks were so big you could poke a finger into them.

Tension mounted. John Oliver, whose reputation as Master Mason was also on the line, said none of the experts Talman had brought to the site to examine the work were capable of understanding masonry of such high quality. Talman responded that they were good enough for Wren to have employed them in the past. And the masonry wasn't up to much. The piers were all hollow and cramped with iron to hold them together.

Wren lost his temper at this. 'What was done for greater caution ought not to be maliciously interpreted.'

'Pray let six be chosen by me,' said Talman, 'and six by you to judge in this matter.'

'I'll put it on this,' replied Wren. 'A man cannot put his finger in the cracks.'

That was because they had been stopped up, said his Comptroller.

Godolphin and the other Commissioners were exasperated by the unedifying row played out in front of them. These exchanges were getting them nowhere. After observing that the two men weren't likely to agree on anything – 'one part will say one thing th' other another' – they seized with some relief on the issue of the cracked piers. Here at least was a matter of fact rather than opinion. Wren, Talman, Banckes and Oliver were dismissed from the room, and the Commission decided to appoint a committee of three 'indifferent [i.e., unbiased] persons' to go down to Hampton Court and examine the cracks. With William breathing down their necks, there was no time to lose: the committee had just forty-eight hours to read the relevant documents, survey the suspect work and report their findings.[54]

Their report is lost. Hooke had an account of it from Wren ten days after the hearing,[55] but he gives no indication of its contents. The Commission obviously decided in the Surveyor's favour, since building recommenced shortly afterwards, although at a slightly more cautious rate than before. What Wren and Talman said to each other as they stalked out of the Treasury Chambers and crossed over to their respective houses in Scotland Yard can only be imagined.

The Surveyor got his own back on Jasper Latham a few weeks later, when he had him suspended from St Paul's 'untill he shall have agreed to ye measurements and prices of his Work allready done, and adjusted all Accounts'.[56] Latham was dismissed in June and his share of the work given to his own foreman, Nathaniel Rawlins. Pierce hung on for a while; then he too left St Paul's.

The King doesn't seem to have thought any the less of Wren as a result of the affair. He publicly praised the design of the new state apartments at Hampton Court, saying that 'for good Proportion, State, and Convenience, jointly, [they] were not paralleled by any Palace in Europe'; and at the same time he took the blame on himself for what contemporaries saw as their most obvious defect – the lowness of the cloisters in the Quadrangle Court – which were, he announced, executed 'according to his express Orders'.[57]

Although relations with William remained good, Wren was much closer to Mary – closer, perhaps, than to any of the other five monarchs he served. Thirty years his junior, her earnest nature and quick intelligence struck an immediate chord with him, after twenty years of dealing with one sovereign who was charmingly irresponsible and another who had 'no vivacity of thought, invention, or expression'.[58] She was, moreover, something of a rarity: a cultured woman whose knowledge of the arts *and* the sciences was reckoned 'much superior to any of her Sex, in that, or (it may be) any former Age'.[59] And she was unhappy. Mary worshipped her husband, and hated the fact that he spent every summer abroad campaigning against Louis XIV. William was also devoted to her, in his own way. But since his own way included keeping a mistress, contracting male friendships so intimate that they were the talk of the court, *and* being generally uninterested in sex, their relationship was inevitably quite complicated. Although in theory they ruled jointly, Mary was a good Protestant, asking only that William 'would obey the command of "Husbands love your wives" as she should do that "Wives be obedient to your husbands in all things"'.[60] The nobles and policy-makers at court soon realized that she had little political influence, with the result that they ignored her. And she was unpopular with her subjects: having been advised not to show her distress at taking the Crown from her own father, she overdid it and 'came into Whitehall laughing and jolly, as to a wedding'.[61] She soon stopped laughing.

Lonely, neglected, 'censured of all, respected by none',[62] the Queen threw herself into the new works at Kensington Palace and Hampton Court, and she and Wren spent a great deal of time together in 'free Conversation', discussing not only architecture, but also 'other Branches of Mathematicks, and useful Learning'.[63] She moved back to Whitehall in the summer of 1690, while the remodelling of Kensington continued and while William, who refused point-blank to live there, was in Ireland subduing the armies of her father and Louis XIV. So her Surveyor was close at hand. They went over the drawings for Hampton Court again and again, while she made suggestions – her judgement, says *Parentalia*, 'was exquisite'[64] – and pushed him to hurry along the workmen. He in turn explained why things were not progressing more quickly: 'want of money and Portland Stone, are the hindrances,' she reported to her husband.[65] She would walk over to Kensington from Whitehall, and no doubt Wren often went with her, calming her impatience to see the palace habitable again and explaining why, as she told William, 'the outside of ye house is ye fideling work wch takes up more time than one can imagin'.[66]

It was to the Queen that Wren addressed a humble petition in July 1691. His salary from the Surveyorship was £383 19s 6d, an increase of £1 13s 10d from the 1660s. As we have already seen, this was far from his only source of income. There was the Commission for rebuilding the City churches, St Paul's, and also Windsor Castle, where he had stepped into the Comptrollership of Works after Hugh May's death in 1684. He was a comparatively wealthy man: in 1685 he had been in a position to lend the government £1000 (at seven per cent interest per annum); and in the same year he and Sir Stephen Fox bought Hungerford Market, off the Strand. Three years later he was involved in a serious piece of property speculation when, with a character named George Jackson, he paid £4400 for the site of Bridgewater House near Aldersgate, which had burned down in 1687.* But underfunding (and overspending) at the Office of Works had meant that he hadn't received either salary or expenses for nearly five years, and now seemed a good time to ask for his money. As he told the Queen, he had

---

*Ten of Wren's acquaintances in the building industry bought plots, including Nicholas Hawksmoor, the masons Edward Strong and Samuel Fulkes, and the carver William Emmett (Guildhall Library MS 2461). Wren had already produced a scheme for houses on the site for the Earl of Bridgewater in 1673, but nothing came of it.

spent great part of his Life in the Service of the Crown faithfully & labouriously, and not Served himselfe, but caused all Salleries to himselfe or Officers to be payed in Strikt Course [i.e., in rotation] as the Artificers are pay'd without any Anticipation: by wch means as he hath kept up a Credit in the Office, soe he hath Endangered the Ruine of his poor Family, there being an Arreare of Sallery justly due by Patent to the petitioner upon the Ordinary Account of two Thousand and Ten pounds and not Reckoning his Extraordinary Service in many great workes for which all his predecessors were wont to have particular and liberall Allowances.[67]

The petition (which was supported by William Talman, incidentally) seems to have worked, since no more was heard about the arrears.

Queen Mary was a frequent visitor to Hampton Court: it took just two hours to travel down from Whitehall, and she sometimes went there and back in a morning. In April 1689 a temporary set of lodgings was installed for her next to the Great Hall, while Wren built a riverside pavilion (or more accurately, he converted an existing Tudor watergate) where she could rest and watch the building work. The Water Gallery, as it was known, lasted only ten years: it was ready for the Queen's use at the end of 1690 and demolished in 1700. No pictures of it survive, but to judge from contemporary accounts it was an engaging little plaything, all turrets and sash windows. There was a bath-house, a dairy and a grotto-cum-boathouse on the ground floor, and above them the Queen's apartment, including her bedchamber, closets, a balconied gallery and a 'great room next the Thames'.[68] The interiors, which may have been designed by the Huguenot Daniel Marot rather than Wren, were fitted out with japanned and mirrored panelling and marble chimneypieces, and filled with the blue and white delftware and Chinese porcelain she loved so much. The gallery was hung with a series of full-length portraits of ladies of the court which she commissioned from Sir Godfrey Kneller. The 'Hampton Court Beauties', which were moved to the King's private dining room at the palace when the Water Gallery was pulled down, proved to be another public relations disaster for the hapless Mary, for just the reason predicted by a gentlewoman who warned her against the idea: 'Madam, if the King was to ask for the portraits of all the wits in his court, would not the rest think he called them fools?'[69]

15

Virtues and Accomplishments

he Water Gallery was the closest Queen Mary came to living in her new palace. On 20 December 1694, she woke at Kensington with a headache, pains in her back and a slight fever. Smallpox was rife in London that winter and, sensing that something serious was wrong, she spent the next night alone in her closet, putting her personal papers in order and burning those she didn't want anyone to see. Two days later she broke out in a rash and her doctors confirmed her fears. She did indeed have smallpox.

William, whose parents had both died of the disease, went to pieces. This aloof, tightly controlled character ranted and raved and wept and fell into fainting fits. There was no hope for the Queen, he said; he was now going to be 'the miserablest creature upon earth'.[1] He insisted on sleeping on a campbed in his wife's bedchamber, where the sound of his asthmatic wheezing and constant crying in the night only made matters worse. For her part, Mary was quite stoical. When Thomas Tenison (Tillotson's successor as Archbishop of Canterbury)[2] gently explained on Christmas night that her physicians had given up hope, she received the news calmly, showing 'no fear nor disorder'. The only time she became upset was when she took communion for the last time, on 27 December, and fretted that she wouldn't be able to swallow the bread. She died at one o'clock the following morning, aged just thirty-two.

The last service Wren performed for his Queen was to design the funeral carriage which carried her to Westminster Abbey through streets draped with black cloth, and the catafalque on which she lay in state – an elaborate affair, based on his hypothetical reconstruction of the Tomb of Porsenna. There would be no more opportunities for 'free

Conversation' about mathematics and architecture; no more comfortable discussions about the progress of Hampton Court in the congenial setting of the Water Gallery.

If Mary's death was a personal blow to Wren, it also had frustrating implications for his career, as he was about to find out. The extent of William's distress amazed and worried the court. Racked with guilt over his infidelities and the frequent occasions on which he had treated his wife in as offhand a manner as he treated his subjects, he became depressed and reclusive, bursting into tears at the slightest provocation and spending long periods shut up with Tenison in secret prayer. He dumped his mistress (a case of shutting the stable door after the horse had bolted, if ever there was one), and vowed that from now on he would be an exact and exemplary Christian. His advisers were worried, and began to whisper that if he didn't pull himself together, he was surely going to follow Mary to the grave.

By the early spring of 1695, the King was finding other ways of coping with his grief – drinking through the night with his Dutch confidants at Kensington and going hunting at Windsor or Richmond. But he couldn't face the idea of Hampton Court without his wife. The shell of Wren's new court was finished, with Cibber's Triumph of Hercules in place over the east front; and a start had been made on fitting out Mary's apartment. And that was where the work stopped. The history of Winchester Palace was repeating itself.

Mary had unwittingly left Wren a rather spectacular consolation prize, however: a scheme to turn Greenwich Palace into a hospital for 'lodging and entertaining . . . disabled Seamen with their necessary Attendants'.[3]

The future of Greenwich had been hanging in the air ever since Wren arrived at the Works. Like most of the royal residences, it was a mixture of ancient and relatively modern. Most of the palace proper, which lay on the south bank of the Thames, dated back to the sixteenth century; but the jewel in its crown was the Queen's House, the 'curious devise'[4] which Inigo Jones had begun for Anne of Denmark in 1616 and completed for Henrietta Maria some twenty years later. Conceived as both a retreat for the Queen and a link between the gardens and the park beyond – the house spanned the public road from Deptford to Woolwich which separated the two – its classicism marked a new departure in English architecture, a rejection of Jacobean flamboyance in favour of a style which was, in Jones's own words, 'sollid, proporsionable according to the rulles, masculine and unaffected'.[5]

Soon after his marriage to Catherine of Braganza, Charles II resolved to pull down the Tudor palace and replace it with an entirely new design by John Webb: this consisted of a king's block and a queen's block facing each other across an open court which looked down to the Thames, with an enlarged Queen's House closing the vista to the south.[6] But by 1669 royal revenue was in short supply, and building operations ground to a halt with only the shell of the King Charles Block to show for six years' work. Wren's hopes of completing the palace were raised four years later, when a £10,000 warrant was issued for finishing the king's block and 'laying the foundations of another part';[7] but nothing came of it, and the Office of Works was left to do little more than maintain another boarded-up monument to Charles's palace-building ambitions.

In 1687 James II toyed with giving Greenwich to Trinity House, the corporation founded in the early sixteenth century to manage the interests of seamen and shipping. He thought it might 'be fitted for the service of impotent Sea Commanders'.[8] The idea of a naval hospital to match Chelsea's facilities for invalid-soldiers surfaced again in 1692, when English and Dutch ships inflicted a crushing defeat on the French in a six-day battle off the Normandy coast at Cape La Hogue, and sick and wounded seamen were housed in the King Charles Block. Wren inspected the empty, half-built palace with Navy Commissioners the following January, with a view to converting it; and in October 1694 the scheme finally began to take shape, when William and Mary granted the site to trustees. Mary was particularly enthusiastic: Hawksmoor, who was working in Wren's office at the time, later recalled that the Queen was 'ever solicitous for the Prosecution of the Design', and that she 'press'd earnestly to pursue the great Work'.[9]

Because the King Charles Block and the land around it had been given away by the Crown, the project wasn't the responsibility of the Office of Works. Nevertheless, Wren was the obvious choice of architect. He already had experience in designing the military hospital at Chelsea, which had formally opened its doors in March 1692; and Mary respected his work at Hampton Court and knew that he would listen sympathetically to her suggestions.

As it turned out, those suggestions stretched Wren's sympathy somewhat. His initial scheme, which was probably drawn up before William and Mary granted the site,[10] was a masterpiece. He retained Webb's King Charles Block as the western side of an open court, with a replica answering it to the east. The court continued beyond these ranges; but it narrowed, with two further blocks set a little way forward of the first two. Steps led up to another court which terminated in a semicircular colonnade, the centrepiece of which was an enormous pedimented portico. In an arrangement which recalled the view from the Seine of Le Vau's Collège des Quatres Nations, this portico formed the entrance to a high domed vestibule. A hall and a chapel stood to either side.

Chelsea may have been grand; but the Greenwich scheme is closer in spirit to Winchester.★ Seeing the succession of courtyards culminating in the grand climax of portico and dome, no one who didn't know its purpose would have dreamed they were looking at a home for worn-out seamen. It was a palace.

This was just what Mary wanted. Keen to outdo her uncle in the public display of her philanthropy, she had a 'fixt Intention for Magnificence', and urged Wren 'to build the Fabrick with great Magnificence and Order'.[11] But there was a problem. The central range with its dome and portico blocked the vista from the Queen's House's down towards the river – and that was something she wouldn't countenance. In fact when she and William granted Greenwich to the hospital, they held on to a strip of land 115 feet wide between the Queen's House and the Thames, which prevented it from being built upon and secured both the vista and, more importantly, the royal couple's access to the house from the river. But retaining the view meant that the grand parade through the new complex must terminate in a distant sight of Jones's Palladian villa – a beautiful building certainly, but as Wren understood rather better than the Queen, hopelessly out of scale with the rest of the hospital. 'The Architect ought, above all Things, to be well skilled in Perspective,' he wrote in Tract I: 'Regard [must] be had to the Distance of the Eye in the principal Stations.'[12]

Mary was adamant. So Wren's next thought was simply to sidestep the problem by repositioning the entire hospital on a site several hundred feet to the east. The Queen would have her route down to the river; he would have his grand termination. Of course, this meant abandoning the King Charles Block. And that wouldn't do, either: 'Her Majesty received the Proposal of pulling down that Wing, with as much Indignation as her excellent good Temper would suffer her, order'd it

---

★According to Hawksmoor, at one stage there was a proposal to use Winchester instead of Greenwich for the naval hospital (*Remarks on the Founding and Carrying on the Buildings of the Royal Hospital at Greenwich*, 1728).

should remain, and the other Side of the Royal Court made answerable to it, in a proper Time.'[13]

Mary wasn't being perverse. It was simply that she had different priorities from her Surveyor, whose concern for pure visual impact was becoming a passion. Against this, she pointed out that the block was 'both beautiful and durable' – why not make use of it? There was also perhaps an element of respect for the past: the destruction of a work by Webb, who was seen as a direct link with Inigo Jones and the pre-lapsarian days of Charles I, wasn't a thing to be undertaken lightly. And the 'Esplanades, Walks, Vistas, Plantations, and Lines' of Greenwich Park, laid out in the 1660s, had been conceived as part and parcel of Webb's scheme. They needed the King Charles Block and its counterpart.[14]

Rather wearily, I imagine, Wren went back to his drawing-table. He was used to disappointment; but the familiar pattern of grand design, rejection and compromise can't have grown any easier with repetition. His third scheme sought to make the best of the limitations. The King Charles Block and its unbuilt companion framed the view from the river, after which there were two further ranges, projecting forward slightly as in the original design. Each consisted of six pavilions containing wards for the inmates, which were set at right angles to the main axis and linked together by a Doric colonnade. At the point where the court narrowed, Wren created a seventh pair of pavilions, a hall and a chapel. Both carried domes which faced each other and relieved the natural visual emphasis on the distant Queen's House. He also took the colonnades right up to meet the Queen's House – a distance of some 350 feet – so that Jones's villa would be drawn into the whole composition instead of being left in glorious isolation.

Even now, there were more compromises to be made. The garden of the Queen's House, which extended northwards for several hundred feet, wasn't included in the grant. So the long colonnades connecting the complex to the Queen's House were cut back and the seven pairs of pavilions were reduced to four, then to three, and were eventually arranged around flanking open courtyards instead of all being set at right angles. The domed hall and chapel ranges remained as wings to these courts.

On 20 February 1695, eight weeks after Mary's death, a Royal Commission was formed to oversee the construction of the hospital. The Commission met for the first time in early May, at the Guildhall. John Evelyn was appointed Treasurer. Wren, who gave his services for nothing, was Surveyor. The project was to be funded by subscription and, as usual, this meant that progress would be limited by the rate at which the money came in. The first step was to convert the King Charles Block and build a subsidiary base block to the west of it; the foundation stone was laid by Wren and Evelyn on 30 June 1696, at exactly 5 p.m. (The time was determined precisely by John Flamsteed, who brought his instruments over from the Observatory for the purpose.) The hospital's subsequent building history is complicated, and as it progressed, Wren had less and less to do with the actual design. The replica of the King Charles range, now known as Queen Anne's Block, was begun in 1699; the two groups of wards, King William's Block and Queen Mary's Block, were begun in 1698 and 1699 respectively. By this time Nicholas Hawksmoor was Clerk of Works, and parts of the complex were perhaps designed by him.[15] James Thornhill's stunning allegorical murals in the Painted Hall, one of the glories of the English Baroque, weren't completed until 1717, the year after Wren resigned as Surveyor to the hospital and fourteen years after he had stopped attending regular board meetings. Other parts weren't completed until the middle of the eighteenth century, long after his death.

Still, the basic design of Greenwich belongs to Wren, and Wren alone. We can't escape its obvious flaw: the two domes of the hall and chapel face each other across an avenue which effectively leads nowhere, like 'two cats looking at each other in the absence of a king', as John Summerson puts it.[16] But that wasn't the Surveyor's fault. Given the scale of the problem he was presented with – and the problem was ultimately one of scale – the fact that he managed to create a coherent composition of any sort was remarkable enough. But he did much more than that. Viewed from across the Thames, the receding planes of the hospital which so artfully frame the Queen's House make up one of the most memorable scenes in the entire history of English architecture. Even in his sixties, Wren showed no sign that his powers were diminishing.

The public perception of his reputation was eloquently summed up by John Evelyn in 1697. During a visit to St Paul's, Evelyn was flattered to hear from some of the workmen that they had been making use of his translation of Fréart's *Parallèle*. The second edition included a glowing dedication to his old friend, declaring

the great Esteem I have ever had of Your Virtues and Accomplishments, not only in the Art of Building, but thro' all the learned Cycle of the most Usefull Knowledge and Abstruser Sciences, as well as of

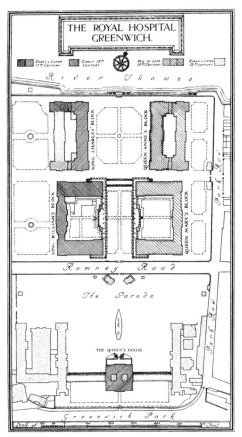

Figure 7. Greenwich Hospital.

the most Polite and Shining: All which is so Justly to be allow'd You, that You need no Panegyric, or other History to Eternise them, than the greatest City of the Universe, which You have Rebuilt and Beautified, and are still improving . . . if the whole Art of Building were lost, it might be Recover'd and found again in St Paul's, the Historical Pillar, and those other Monuments of Your Happy Talent and extraordinary Genius.[17]

Wren didn't share Evelyn's high opinion of his abilities. As the century drew to a close he was beginning to experience an uncharacteristic crisis of confidence, fuelled by a sense that his own life was coming to an end. Perhaps it seemed as though it was time to die: of the men who had sat together in Laurence Rooke's Gresham lodgings in 1660, and decided to found a 'Colledge for the Promoting of Physico-Mathematicall Experimentall Learning', only he and Abraham Hill were left. John Wilkins, whose careful guidance at Wadham had done so much to foster Wren's early scientific interests, had died a terrible death back in 1672, after a urinary blockage probably caused by an enlarged prostate. He was followed to the grave a year later by Sir Robert Moray, who suddenly 'choked with flegme in indeavouring to vomit'.[18] Sir Charles Scarburgh (Wren's old mentor had been knighted in 1669) had performed the post-mortem – now he too was dead, after a 'gentle and easy decay' denied to Moray.[19]

Lord Brouncker had gone in 1684, lamented no doubt by his family but not, presumably, by the Royal Society which had ousted him so unceremoniously. Sir Paul Neile, to the end one of Wren's most devoted admirers, had followed him two years later; then William Petty, William Balle, with whom Neile and Wren had observed Saturn back in the 1650s, and Robert Boyle, all in the space of six years. Seth Ward went in January 1689; he had struggled with senile dementia for some time, and by the end his 'melancholy Distemper and decay of Memory' was so great he could neither recognize his friends nor grasp that James II had been deposed.[20] Hooke, Wren's closest friend, was still going strong. So were Sprat and Evelyn. (The three men would survive into the eighteenth century, but the Surveyor was destined to outlive them all.) On 24 January 1698 William Holder died. The brother-in-law who had given him 'his first Instructions in Geometrie and Arithmetique'[21] nearly six decades before was buried next to his wife Susan in the crypt of St Paul's.

The deaths of so many friends weighed heavy with Wren. And in his own home, although Jane, the daughter that he doted on, was still keeping house for him, both young Christopher and the mentally handicapped William were giving cause for concern. In March 1698 he wrote to Christopher, then on a tour of France with Edward Strong junior, son of the chief mason-contractor at St Paul's. The two youngsters were thinking of moving on to Rome and Naples; and the prospect of a difficult Alpine crossing, roving bands of ex-mercenaries and 'abominable lodgings' filled the old man with alarm and added to his feelings of depression:

You would have it to say hereafter that you have seen Rome, Naples & other fine places; a hundred others can say as much & more; calculate whither this be worth the expence and hazard as to any advantage at youre returne. I sent you to France at a time of businesse and wher you might make your obsevations of the world & find acquaintance who might hereafter be usefull to you in the future concernes of your Life: if this be your ayme I willingly let you proceed, provided you will soon returne, for these reasons, the little I have to leave you is unfortunately involved in trouble, & your presence would be a comfort to me, to assist me, not only for my sake, but your own, that you might understand your affaires, before it please God to take me from you ... I doe not say all this out of parsimony, for what you spend will be out of what will in short time be your owne ...[22]

The nature of the money troubles referred to in the letter isn't clear. In 1694 he had brought a lawsuit laying claim to the Coghills' old home, the 'Greate House' at Bletchingdon, saying that the late Earl of Anglesey, who bought the estate in 1666, had mortgaged it to him. The claim was eventually thrown out of court as a plain lie – a verdict which doesn't sit well with our impression of Wren who, while he moved with ease in a corrupt construction industry that turned a blind eye to bribes and backhanders, was hardly a crook or a conman. Perhaps his failure to reclaim the Anglesey loan had made him anxious about his finances. Anyway, in case the querulous you'll-miss-me-when-I'm-gone tone wasn't enough to bring young Christopher running, his father added a poignant – and manipulative – little postscript about the boy's brother. 'Poor Billy,' he said, 'continues in his indisposition, and I fear is lost to me and the world, to my great discomfort and your future trouble.'

At St Paul's, things had been going pretty well since the arrival of the extra coal money voted by James II's Parliament. Annual expenditure, which had averaged around £11,600 between 1675 and 1687, doubled to nearly £23,500 over the next eleven years.[23] But income wasn't enough to cover expenditure: in 1692, for instance, the Commission reckoned the cathedral was nearly £23,000 in debt, and sometimes the only way to pay the long-suffering workmen was to take out loans against future coal dues. But Wren had made significant progress. By the autumn of 1694 the choir was roofed and leaded; its stonework was finished, inside and out; and paving was ordered. The Surveyor decided the time had come to strike the scaffolding and begin the work of fitting and decorating the interior; and a timber partition was put up to divide it from the rest of the building and keep it safe from frost, rain and builders' dust. (The joiner Charles Hopson later put in a bill for fitting it with '3 paire of Glass Dores'.[24]) John Evelyn, who went along to take a look at what nearly twenty years of building work had achieved, was impressed, describing the choir as 'a piece of Architecture without reproach' – although he did in fact reproach the architect for his exterior treatment of the apse which terminated the east end. Wren emphasized its ritual significance by introducing columns rather than pilasters to the upper storey – a device which, since the columns rested on the pilasters of the lower storey, left the conservative Evelyn with an uneasy feeling that the rules had been broken.[25]

Work continued on the masonry at the west end, but there was pressure to bring the choir into use. According to a contemporary broadsheet, at one stage Wren wanted a 'free and airy Prospect of the whole length of the church'.[26] If he did, he either had second thoughts or was overruled by the Dean and Chapter; and in 1695 Jean Tijou was commissioned to produce a choir-screen 'of curious Iron-work'. This would eventually be crowned with an organ designed by the German Bernard Schmidt, the famous Father Smith who was organ-maker to the Crown and organist at St Margaret's Westminster. 'Eventually', because although Schmidt had agreed to produce the instrument ready and tuned by March 1696, and Wren had had a special workshop set up for him just to the west of the north choir aisle, he was slow to fulfil his contract, complaining that there were problems fitting the organ into the case which Gibbons had designed for it. Some of those problems were of his own making. In February 1699 his workshop caught fire – the flames were only just prevented from spreading to the timber screen separating the crossing from the choir.* In 1700 he was still working on the organ, and the wits were asking 'Whether the cupola or the organ at St Paul's will be first finished?'[27] It was a close-run thing – the organ wasn't completed until 1702, and Schmidt's widow was still petitioning for a final payment five years later.

But organ or no, Dean Sherlock and Bishop Compton were determined that the choir should be ready as soon as possible. By the summer of 1697 things were at fever pitch. Scaffolding went up again, this time for the painters, and sail-cloth was draped over the carved stonework for protection. Two rows of wooden stalls, elaborately decorated by Grinling Gibbons, were put in place facing each other in

---

*Shaken by the narrow escape, Wren enforced a series of fire-prevention measures, ranging from moving the joiners' glue-pots clear of the sheds to banning all smoking in the workplace (St Paul's Minute Book, 1 March 1699, in *WS* XVI, 95).

the traditional manner, with galleries over them and seats for Bishop Compton and the Lord Mayor in the centre of each. Compton's canopied ceremonial throne, decorated (also by Gibbons) with 'Cherubs Heads, ffestoones & Mitre', stood by the altar, at the eastern end of the southern range of stalls. Seats for the Dean and Archdeacon were at the west end of the choir, facing east. Crimson velvet was bought for the cushions, along with 200 pounds of swans' down and 309 pounds of feathers to fill them.

At one stage Wren proposed a free-standing reredos for the altar, but the idea was dropped, or at least postponed, and it wasn't resurrected in his lifetime.[28] Instead, the apse itself was made to form the backdrop to a relatively simple communion table. This was separated from the choir by three shallow steps, a further step and a low altar-rail – features which would have gladdened the heart of Bishop Matthew. The altar-rail was marbled, as were the upper walls of the apse, 'being first twice soaked with Oyle, then Primed and Painted with fflake White & Vained'.[29] The lower sections were hung with crimson flowered velvet and Genoese damask; the four fluted pilasters were heightened in ultramarine and veined in gold; and the communion table was draped in Holland damask and set on a Persian carpet.

Whereas Wren left the fitting-out of the City churches to others, at St Paul's he involved himself closely in the decorative scheme for the interior. This had always been part of the plan, ever since Charles II's original Commission had referred to 'rebuilding, new erecting, finishing, and adorning the said Cathedral'.[30] Wren had presented his design 'for ye Inside of the Choire' to a general meeting of the Commissioners on 1 May 1694, and a model of the stalls to the Commission's Building Committee the following October.[31] The details had then been worked out with or by Gibbons and the other craftsmen, but always subject to his approval. Here and there the fittings showed characteristically inventive touches which hark back to the ingenious devices that had engaged his attention when he was at Oxford and Gresham. Gibbons' organ case, for example, was provided with a complicated arrangement of sliding sash windows to protect Father Smith's pipes from the dust and grime of what was still, after all, a building site. The pulpit was on wheels, so that it could be moved out of the way when not in use; and extra tiers of retractable seating, running on lignum vitae rollers, were fitted to the front panelling of both ranges of stalls.

In the autumn of 1697 King William's sister-in-law and heir apparent,

Princess Anne, paid a semi-official visit to see how the work was progressing. No details of the event have survived, but it isn't stretching the bounds of credulity to suppose that Wren was deputed to show her round. All we do know is that everyone (except the Princess, presumably) went round to the local tavern for a drink afterwards. Then on Thursday 2 December, exactly thirty-one years and three months after the spark in Farryner's bakery had set the heavens themselves on fire, St Paul's opened for business. The occasion was a grand one, a service of national thanksgiving to celebrate the Peace of Ryswick which had just ended nine bitter years of war with France. The King was due to attend but, never at ease with public ceremony, he cried off at the last minute. Even so, the choir was filled with clergy, government officials and City worthies, while the people packed into the Churchyard and the streets around, anxious for a glimpse of celebrity. The King's Organist, Dr John Blow, composed an anthem specially for the occasion (Father Smith's organ had temporarily been brought into action); and the Lord Mayor and aldermen listened while Henry Compton preached a sermon on the text of Psalm 122, verse 1: 'I was glad when they said unto me, Let us go into the house of the LORD.'

'For there are set thrones of judgment,' the psalmist goes on to say. The following Sunday divine service was performed in the cathedral for the first time since the Fire, and the general public had a chance to explore the half-finished building. The nave was still unroofed and shrouded in scaffolding. There were no western towers; and there was still no dome. But there was enough in the finished and newly decorated choir to give Londoners a taste of what St Paul's might become.

Reactions were mixed. Many people were excited at the grandest piece of modern architecture they had ever seen, and they responded with unrestrained enthusiasm. The lawyer-poet James Wright probably spoke for the majority when he wrote that 'Without, within, below, above, the eye/Is fill'd with equal wonder and delight'.[32] But not everyone agreed. In Wren's advanced circle, the idea that Gothic architecture was crude and barbarous might be a cultural commonplace; but the conservative resistance to change shown by the clergy of St Paul's back in the early 1670s was still shared by large numbers of ordinary people. There was an air of Popery about the gilded capitals, the heavy arches and opulent carving. They were unfamiliar, un-English and, for those who remembered, quite unlike the old St Paul's. A broadsheet, directed at Wren and his 'Happy Invention of a Pulpit on Wheels', declared that

> This little structure (excellent Sir Kit)
> Holds forth to us that you bestow'd more wit
> In building it than on all Paul's beside

and in a dig at Dean Sherlock's elastic principles, predicted the pulpit would 'truckle to and fro 'twixt cause and cause,/Just as the strongest pull of interest draws'.[33]

The more discerning were uneasy about Wren's breaks with classical tradition, as Evelyn had been three years earlier. Roger North took the architect to task over his failure to use a giant order on the façade, and criticized the way the entablature broke out over each pair of pilasters and then returned, instead of being continuous. Wren's response was pragmatic, showing both the difficulties that beset the work and the ability to compromise which characterized his entire career:

> They could not have materialls to make good single Columnes [North recalled], nor to project the entabletures so farr as to range strait over the heads of the columnes, but were force't in the one to double the orders, and in the other to double both columnes and the orders, and in both to break the entablements without, which shift Sir Christopher Wren informed me of . . .[34]

The shortage of large stones was one of the reasons why Wren discarded an idea he had been toying with in the late 1680s and early 1690s. A number of surviving drawings (none, however, in his own hand) show that as the masonry-work at the west end neared completion, he thought of treating the main portico as a single monumental object, using a giant Composite order. But the weight of the resulting massive pediment would have been immense, and the large stones required for the supporting columns weren't available. So he opted for the double order which he had originally shown in the Definitive design.[35]

Wren had no time to sort through his reviews, or to dwell for long on the public reception given to his cathedral. He was preoccupied with problems involving the quarries on Portland. Ensuring a regular supply of Portland stone for the cathedral had been a worry from the beginning; but in February 1696 a section of the cliff overhanging the south pier on the Isle had suddenly collapsed into the sea, bringing down a large section of the roadway with it. The 'dismal destruction of the wayes, cranes, and peers'[36] that resulted effectively stopped any stone from being shipped out by sea, and hauling it overland, along Chesil Beach and then 140-odd miles to London, was quite out of the question. Once current supplies were exhausted, there would be no more until a new road and pier were constructed.

As soon as they heard the news, the Commissioners authorized Wren to send a team down to Portland to assess the damage. Within weeks, Bishop Compton, Dean Sherlock and the Surveyor heard a report from the high-powered group of specialists Wren had despatched, including master masons Edward Strong and Samuel Fulkes, master carpenter John Longland and the measuring clerk John Scarborough. The south pier and the way down to it from the quarries were damaged beyond repair; if it was too expensive to tear down what remained and start again, it seemed that the best option lay in restoring a jetty on the north side of the island, long disused and blocked by shingle.

For the next twelve months or so the quarrymen tried to do just that, but it soon became obvious exactly why the north pier had fallen into disuse: as soon as the shingle was cleared, the implacable waves heaped more in its place. Fierce winds halted the work during the autumn and winter of 1696/7, and by the following spring the sea had undone all the previous season's efforts. To add insult to injury, the Portland agent, Thomas Gilbert, reported that because he couldn't employ his quarrymen they had taken to working the royal quarries themselves and selling the stone privately to a stone merchant in nearby Weymouth. Wren lost patience. That May, he hired a carriage and went down to Portland to see the situation for himself, taking Strong and Nicholas Hawksmoor with him. Once he arrived, he saw that the repair of the north pier was hopeless. Gilbert tried to convince him that the only solution was to build an entirely new wharf close by Henry VIII's old coastal fortress, with a new road to it from the quarry. But making the new route – nearly two miles of it, uphill and across a rough common – would be prohibitively expensive. Wren reckoned it at £1350, without even taking into account the costs of transporting the stone the extra distance. His favoured options were either to reroute the old south road and pier away from the cliff-fall, or to repair the crane and pier and resort to a time-honoured method of delivering the stone to the vicinity of the wharf, by having the quarrymen topple it over the cliff. The locals were none too keen on this idea – and Wren was honest enough to say so when he returned to London after his twelve-day excursion. But he estimated that repairing the south pier and its lifting gear would cost £500, while remaking the road down to the beach entailed further delays and another £400. In the comfort of Lambeth Palace, the Commissioners met and decided it was a question of simple economics. They went for the short, swift and dangerous route down, and by the middle of 1698 Portland stone was again being delivered to St Paul's.

This wasn't the end of Wren's troubles with the Portland quarrymen. Realizing that smaller stones couldn't be tipped over the cliff without their shattering into a thousand pieces, he agreed in January 1699 that Thomas Gilbert should make a new road down, wide enough for two mule-carts to pass, at a cost of £500. This Gilbert did, only for the quarrymen to decide they weren't going to work for him any more: he and his partner, Ezekiel Russell, were cheating them out of what was rightfully theirs, they claimed. They could eliminate the middlemen and provide St Paul's with stone at a cheaper price. In any case, as far as they were concerned the landslide had invalidated Charles II's original grant to St Paul's of exclusive rights to Portland stone.

The dispute dragged on into the reign of Queen Anne, and ended with Gilbert's dismissal, a protracted legal action over the Portland quarrymen's ancient rights and privileges, and one of Wren's testiest letters, in which he all too clearly shows his exasperation with the way the quarrymen were trying to exploit their monopoly:

> Though 'tis in your power to be as ungrateful as you will, yet you must not think that your insolence will always be borne with, and though you will not be sensible of the advantage you receive by the present working of the quarries yet, if they were taken from you, I believe you might find the want of them in very little time; and you may be sure that care will be taken both to maintain the Queen's right and that such only will be employed in the quarries as will work regularly and quietly, and submit to proper and reasonable directions, which I leave you to consider of.[37]

The labour dispute was never really solved; or to be more accurate, it eventually solved itself as St Paul's neared completion and the desperate need for Portland stone diminished. But back in the spring of 1698, when Wren was mourning his losses and still lacking confidence, there were other problems. One was the attitude of Parliament, which criticized him for the slow progress of the project and jibbed at the prospect of providing further funding by extending the coal tax past 1700, when it was due to run out. In February 1697 he had reckoned that more than £178,000 was still needed to complete the cathedral, with another £25,000 for the City churches. Archbishop Tenison and the rest of the Commissioners thought that this was pushing their luck, especially with a Parliament that was not particularly disposed to look favourably on the scheme. They opted to lobby for a twelve-year extension of the coal tax at one shilling per chaldron, a proposal which Parliament agreed to in March 1697, although not without strings. The tax was now to run for another sixteen years rather than twelve, until 1716, which was a good thing. But out of every shilling, twopence was to go towards repairing Westminster Abbey, and another twopence or more to the City churches and St Thomas's Hospital in Southwark, which had also put in a bid for coal dues to repair its premises. This meant slowing down the work to take account of the reduced income, and an eventual shortfall of more than £7000.

And there was a very personal slap in the face for Wren. Rumours had been flying for some time that he was in no hurry to finish St Paul's, because when he did his £200 a year would cease – along with the backhanders and bribes which the tradesmen were popularly supposed to be supplying. Parliament heeded the gossip, adding a rider to the bill to the effect that from now on half of his salary would be held back until the cathedral was completed, to encourage him to finish it 'with the utmost Diligence and Expedition'.[38] He wasn't working hard enough to finish St Paul's, in other words. The delay was his fault.

The Commission met to discuss the implications of the bill on 23 March, and again a week later. Wren was there, as he always was; so were Archbishop Tenison, Bishop Compton and Dean Sherlock. The choir was nearing completion and, as the architect saw it, they had two choices: to finish off the west end of the cathedral, and hope that in time more funds would be made available to build the dome; or to press ahead with the dome and trust to fortune for the nave and the west front. For Wren, that was no choice at all. Opting for the nave, he argued, would be more expensive, and would leave the building with an odd appearance, 'like two fabricks with a round open Court between them'. If, on the other hand, the dome were finished, it 'would be so remarkable an ornament to this mighty City, which is yet inferior in Publick Buildings to many Cities of less note and wealth, that all persons natives or foreigners will be extreamly satisfied; neither will any repine at the charge of completing the whole Work, when they see the noblest most difficult and most expensive parts brought to a desireable effect.'[39]

The Commissioners didn't take much persuading. They resolved that 'the work of the Dome be now set upon and carried on as fast as conveniently may be'; and then moved on to more important matters – the patterns and prices of velvet and fringes for the altar, pulpit and cushions in the choir, and the problem of keeping out children who played around the site 'and do many times harm to the building'.[40] No mention was made of the slight Parliament had dished out to Wren. No expression of support was minuted.

The architect felt the hurt keenly. Armed with his cut of the coal dues, his old Oxford friend Thomas Sprat, now Bishop of Rochester and Dean of Westminster Abbey, stepped in the following year to offer him the job of Surveyor to the Abbey and an annual salary which, at £100, was intended not only to make good his temporary financial loss, but also to be a gesture of solidarity. Wren took the post and – in public, at least – kept his opinions about the parliamentary committee that had insulted him to himself. In 1700, however, he put in a claim for all the 'Large Imperiall Paper, Pencills, Letters & Postage' he had used since 1675.[41] The amount came to £200, exactly the arrears of salary that had been stopped to date. Sheer coincidence, of course.

There were also other fears, more awful to contemplate than recalcitrant quarrymen or a spiteful Parliament. Over the past couple of years it had begun to dawn on him that he might have made a terrible mistake over the design of his new cathedral. Back in the 1670s, when construction work began, he had specified that the eight massive piers in the crossing which were necessary to support the dome of St Paul's should rest on similar piers down in the crypt. The latter were slightly larger than those above but, like them, they consisted of rubble cores held together with mortar and cased in stone. This was standard building practice and was, in any case, dictated by sound economics: there was plenty of rubble on site, whereas Portland stone was costly and, even in the 1670s, in relatively short supply. But because they were smaller, each of the main piers rested on the rubble core of the pier below, rather than on its casing; and, as they grew, the tremendous pressure they exerted began to have a potentially catastrophic effect. By the mid-1690s the crypt piers were showing signs of bursting. Cracks were appearing in the stonework. Mortar was being pushed out through the joints. It was too late to do much about it. And the dome wasn't in place yet.

All in all, Wren was not having a great time. And to cap this, on 4 January 1698 the Palace of Whitehall burned to the ground.

The fire started in the royal lodgings overlooking the Terrace Garden and the Thames, and spread until it consumed virtually the whole of the palace proper – the old Great Hall and the Chapel Royal where Wren had been married to Jane Fitzwilliam, the Catholic Chapel and Privy Gallery he designed for James II, Mary of Modena's apartments, the Council Chamber. 'Nothing but walls and ruins left,' wrote Evelyn.[42] That wasn't quite true. As the blaze raged through the Privy Gallery and crept up the Great Staircase which linked it to Inigo Jones's Banqueting House, a bricklayer named Henry Evans rushed into Wren's house at Scotland Yard to break the news. The Surveyor told Evans to gather up the books and papers in his closet while he went across to see what was happening. One glance was enough, and within seconds he was back in the house 'in a great consternation'. 'We are undone!' he yelled: the precious Banqueting House was in danger. 'For God's sake let all things alone here', he told Evans, 'and try to save that fabric.' Evans swiftly organized a team of bricklayers to block up a window on the south side of the building so the flames couldn't burst in and, largely due to his efforts, the scene of Charles I's execution and one of the most hallowed shrines in Stuart iconography was saved.★ The rest of the palace was a blackened shell.

A catastrophe for Crown and nation can be an opportunity for an architect, a truth that Wren knew better than most. Even though King William had never liked Whitehall, his first thought was to rebuild, and within six weeks his Surveyor had measured the site and presented him with two alternative designs for a new palace.

The centrepiece of the first was an entrance portico with a giant order, facing east across a huge open courtyard to the river and flanked by the Banqueting House to the south and a replica of it to the north. Long colonnaded wings with lodgings for the household enclosed the court, and extended back beyond the Banqueting House range to join a much larger block which looked out on St James's Park and contained the state apartments. A central east–west hall and grand staircase linked

---

★This incident had an aftermath which doesn't reflect too well on Wren. In 1714 Evans, who had been given £5 as a reward for his efforts during the fire, petitioned for a job with the Works, citing his prompt action in stopping up the window of the Banqueting House. Wren responded that his behaviour and performance as a bricklayer 'gave little satisfaction' (he had been employed on several of the City churches back in the 1680s), and that all Evans had done was to act on Wren's direct orders during the crisis. Evans flatly contradicted this. From the moment he left Sir Christopher's house, he said, armed only with instructions 'in General Termes' to preserve the building, he hadn't set eyes on him for two days, and then Wren only showed up to thank him after others had informed the King of his heroic efforts. The Surveyor reluctantly backed down and admitted that Evans's 'Courage & diligence' had saved the day. Evans still didn't get his job at the Works (*WS* XVIII, 165–7).

the state apartments to the entrance block, creating two smaller square courts between them. The palace would have been spectacular, particularly when seen from the river across the spacious main court, but it was hardly original: the scheme was a modification of one proposed by John Webb in the early 1660s, right down to the doubled Banqueting House (in Webb's plans the replica served as a Chapel Royal), the open vista down to the Thames, the two square courts behind it and the state apartments to the west. Wren certainly knew of Webb's drawings: in fact he seems to have played around with a similar idea himself as far back as 1664 when, capitalizing on Charles II's delighted reception of his lunar globe, he apparently collaborated with the King over a scheme 'for the future building of White-hall' which involved a two-tier portico and twin Banqueting Houses.[43] The new design may perhaps have been a hasty reworking of this.

The second plan was altogether more innovative and altogether grander, reflecting Wren's increasing interest in architecture on a monumental scale. Inigo Jones's building was retained, of course – doing away with it was unthinkable – and now it was given added prominence by being made the centrepiece of the whole composition. The imposing court towards the river was also kept, with the two wings terminating in pedimented façades, each as wide as the Banqueting House itself. Below the state apartments, which still overlooked St James's Park, he envisaged an elaborate formal garden leading down to the canal laid out for Charles II back in 1660–2; and since this Long Water ran off to the left at a slight angle from the Banqueting House, he designed a second, much shorter canal to balance it. Visually, the major problem was to keep the Banqueting House as the central focus for the whole palace complex without letting it be dwarfed by the monumental scale of the surrounding buildings. His solution – not a happy one, it has to be said – was to emphasize it by adding circular domed towers to either side, and slapping a giant unpedimented portico on to the three centre bays.

But he was thinking of much more than just a royal residence. To the south of the palace, and aligned on the north-south axis of the Banqueting House, he created a long gallery which joined the royal complex to a new Parliament House. This in turn looked over to Westminster Hall and the Abbey, and the whole composition was enclosed by walls to create a government compound, with Church, Parliament and Crown joined architecturally, just as they were joined politically, culturally and symbolically.

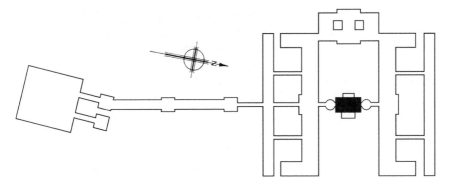

Figure 8. Block plan of the Palace of Whitehall scheme. The Banqueting House is in the centre of the complex, with the new Parliament House to the south, linked to the palace by a long gallery.

The new Whitehall would have been magnificent, arguably the greatest palace England had ever seen. But like Winchester and the grand project for Hampton Court, it was never built. By the beginning of March 1698, William had changed his mind, saying that rebuilding would have to wait until Parliament voted money for it, which it never did. Wren was allowed only to design a single-storey council chamber and five sets of lodgings (for courtiers displaced by the fire), which were tacked onto the southern end of the Banqueting House.

King William, meanwhile, continued to live mostly at Kensington, although the following year he finally decided to put his widowerhood behind him and have his state apartment at Hampton Court fitted up. As Surveyor-General, Wren put in an estimate for £6800 – only for William Talman to undercut him by £1300. In May 1699 the King 'appointed Mr Talman to have the care and overseeing of this work' – another blow to Wren's self-esteem and, given the relations between him and his Comptroller, a hard one to bear.[44] The previous year Talman had resumed his vendetta against the Surveyor, accusing him of nepotism over the appointment as Clerk of the Works at Hampton Court of John Ball, the grandson of Bishop Matthew. Now, flushed with his success, he deliberately flouted Wren's authority again, by going behind his back and ordering the Portland quarries to supply 500 tons of stone for use in the gardens at Hampton Court – and this at just the time when his boss was trying desperately to solve the labour disputes on the Island and ensure the resumption of regular supplies for St Paul's. The news of Talman's high-handed action reached Wren at the beginning of October, and made him so angry that he called a special meeting of the St Paul's Commissioners to acquaint them with the facts. However, reluctant to provoke an out-and-out confrontation with the Comptroller, who still had powerful whig friends at court, he authorized the shipments. Archbishop Tenison agreed to write to the Earl of Portland about the matter – although it is hard to see exactly what this was meant to achieve, since not only was Portland Talman's patron, but he had also recently resigned all his offices at court, including that of Superintendant of the Royal Gardens, after being replaced in William's affections by the young and exceptionally pretty Earl of Albermarle.* Talman, in the meantime, continued his offensive by petitioning the Treasury for the Comptrollership of the Works at Windsor, a post which Wren had held since Hugh May's death in 1684. He was unsuccessful.

The daily routine at Scotland Yard continued much as it had for the past thirty years.[45] The four officers who made up the Board of Works – the Surveyor, the Comptroller, the Master Mason and the Master Carpenter – met together in Wren's office for an hour at eight each morning to go over the business of the day. The local Clerks of the Works and master artisans were required to 'give their attendance at the same hours, if not otherwise employ'd'. At the ringing of a bell in the yard, labourers gathered for their orders: they weren't allowed to leave until a second bell was rung, and if they took more than thirty minutes for breakfast, they lost half a day's pay – and a full day's pay for a second offence. When workmen presented themselves for payment, Paymaster Thomas Lloyd might ask them to bring along a witness who could testify to their identity; and even then, if the Exchequer had been slow in supplying Lloyd with ready cash (something which occurred pretty frequently), they had to be content with an IOU, known in the trade as a 'ticket'. One of the most common abuses of the system seems to have been the officers' habit of buying up workers' tickets at a discount of up to 15 per cent and then using their position to jump the queue and press for early payment.

Building in the seventeenth century was carried out by day, by great or by measure. Each had its own advantages and drawbacks. As the phrase implies, day-work involved direct employment by the day. It was

---

*Perhaps a shade disingenuously, King William found the court gossip about his close relationship with Albermarle irritating and incomprehensible: 'It seems to me very extraordinary that it should be impossible to have esteem and regard for a young man without it being criminal.'

generally viewed with suspicion: Pratt was not alone in believing that 'if workmen be employed by the day, they will make but small haste to finish the building'.[46] But most unskilled labour was hired on this casual basis and, when the occasion seemed to demand it, so were skilled artisans and their teams. When Wren began the delicate task of completing the dome of St Paul's, for example, he insisted that master carpenter Richard Jenings should work by the day, since the operation required so much care and precision. The architect didn't want his workers to rush the job, as they might have done if Jenings had contracted to work by measure or by great. Just how successful the strategy was is debatable: by the early 1700s the phrase 'as lazily as a Paul's labourer up a ladder with a hod of mortar' was doing the rounds of the satirical broadsheets; and the monthly *London Spy* published a cruel (though no doubt pretty accurate) account of a visit to the site, where in a corner of the Churchyard the author met with a group of stone-cutters and sawyers 'so very hard at work that, I protest, notwithstanding the vehemency of their labour and the temperateness of the season, instead of using their handkerchiefs to wipe the sweat off their faces, they were most of them blowing their nails'. After being sarcastically reminded by his companion that this was work not to be hurried, since it was 'carried on at a national charge', he went inside to see 'ten men in a corner very busy about two men's work, taking as much care that everyone should have his due proportion of the labour as so many thieves in making an exact division of their booty'.[47]

The day-rate would be established beforehand, and in the case of a craftsman-contractor like Jenings, paid directly to him. How much of it he handed over to his workers was entirely his own affair – although, as we shall see, a contractor's practice of taking a hefty cut of his men's wages could lead to ill-feeling and dissent.

On the face of it, work by the great, in which a contractor undertook to do the job for a fixed price, was the simplest system to administer. Talman seems to have acted as sole undertaker when he snatched the finishing of Hampton Court in 1699: he would then subcontract to joiners, plasterers, carvers and so on, negotiating the keenest possible price in order to maximize his profit. If the work went over budget, that was the undertaker's problem. But seventeenth-century architects tended to be just as wary of work by the great as they were of day-rates. Care had to be taken to arrive at a realistic price at the outset and to ensure high standards throughout, since contractors often under-quoted in order to get the job and, as Wren warned John Fell while they were discussing Tom Tower, 'when they begin to find it, they shuffle and slight the work to save themselves'.[48]

Work by measure was Wren's favoured method of employing builders. It involved agreeing a rate by the foot or the yard, and using a skilled measurer to check the extent and quality of the work at intervals. A few examples from the Hampton Court accounts can serve to show the general principle. In October 1691 John Grove junior, Master Plasterer at the Works since the death of his father fifteen years previously, was paid 'for 1215 yrds ⅓ lath plaster on the ceilings of the Gallery, Withdrawing Room, Ante Room, Presence, back stair roome and the cloyster ceiling finished with Kidd's hair for painting at 20 [pence] per yard'. The previous year Robert Streater junior (who had also inherited his position as Sergeant Painter from his father – jobs at the King's Works tended to run in families), was paid for graining 223 yards of wainscot a 'walnutt tree colour' at 6d a yard, and marbling a further 114 yards at 1s 6d a yard. And mason Thomas Hill received £56 15s 5¼d for 681ft 3in 'of attic cornice' – in other words, he was paid at the rate of 1s 8d per foot, with Wren's measuring clerk, John Scarborough, obviously being a stickler for accuracy down to the nearest inch.[49] Where measuring wasn't practical, craftsmen worked at a piece-rate, as when (still at Hampton Court) Tijou was paid £40 apiece 'for making two Iron Vanes with movements to show the points of the winds within and without, having eight supporters of Iron finely wrought in scrowle worke and bands to each supporter'.[50] Work by day and by measure were often mixed. On one occasion at Hampton Court Hill's masons, oddly enough (it was a job for the carpenters) were employed on a day-rate to make scaffolding. More prosaically, there is an entry in the November 1689 palace accounts 'for 45 Carpenters each halfe a day to shovell and turne of and sweepe away the snow'.[51]

In theory, at least, the Board of Works met once a month for a formal meeting to go over the accounts, again at eight in the morning. Books and bills were brought in by the nine Clerks of the Works: for Audley End; the Queen's House at Greenwich; Hampton Court; Kensington; Newmarket; Somerset House; the Tower of London (where, although the Ordnance was responsible for the fortifications, the Office of Works generally looked after the living accommodation and carried out minor repairs); Whitehall, Westminster and St James's (a single post); and Winchester Palace. The Clerks would wait downstairs while William Dickinson, the Chief Clerk or 'Clerk Ingrosser', went through their books and called out each entry for Talman as Comptroller to check it against the bills. If any discrepancies were found, the culprit was called up and asked to explain the errors. Otherwise, the books were passed by Wren and the other officers and locked away in a cupboard, to be brought out at six-monthly intervals, signed by all four officers and submitted for audit.

There was a fair amount of administrative work for Wren to carry out. Simply keeping track of the Works was in itself a gargantuan task. Apart from the accounts and a ledger in which contracts were entered, the only ongoing records of project management were entries of current business which were written in a day-book at Scotland Yard and crossed out when the work was done. When each book was full, it was apparently thrown away – none seems to have survived. But the Surveyor also had to arbitrate over disputed bills, 'abating' (i.e., reducing) them when he thought the builders were overcharging. He had to attend on King, courtiers and Treasury officials, and respond to petitions from craftsmen who were owed money and others of the King's subjects who complained that royal building work had infringed their rights or impinged on their property. In the spring of 1698, for example, he was called upon to sort out a rather awkward problem that had arisen over Sayes Court, the house of John Evelyn. His old friend had let his Deptford house for three months to Tsar Peter of Russia, then in England to learn about shipbuilding (and the state of the English theatre, judging from the amount of time he spent with the actress Letitia Cross). Peter and his 'right nasty' retinue trashed the place, causing damage to the cost of £150 to the house and gardens. Evelyn looked to the Crown for compensation and Wren, in his capacity as Surveyor-General, went down at the beginning of June to investigate. Evelyn duly received his money.

An awesome array of tasks like this, necessary but hardly glamorous, constantly claimed the Surveyor's attention, so that one sometimes wonders how he found the time to design anything. In 1695, for instance, he was asked to provide an estimate for refurbishing the Beauchamp Tower and the Bloody Tower so that they were fit to receive prisoners of state. 'If by that expression it be intended they should be wainscotted and made fitt for hangings and furniture,' he warned, 'it may cost £200 or much more.' On other occasions he had to meet a group of 'french Comedians' to receive their instructions over alterations to the theatre at Windsor Castle, and examine the feed-bills of 'their Majesties Fowle keeper and Pond keeper in St James Parke'. The Treasury asked him for an estimate of the cost of sweeping the street outside the Palace of Whitehall, and another for double-sashing the windows of the House of Commons to keep out the draughts: a cheaper alternative, Wren said, was for Members to keep the existing windows closed. King William needed to know whether the enclosure of part of the Horse Guards' stables had caused any inconvenience. It hadn't: 'the Dungyard as now allowed is confessed by the officers to be more convenient for the Guards than the former . . . and is large enough to hold more Dung than there can be at one time.' When William was campaigning in Ireland, he slept in a prefabricated camphouse designed by Wren. And when he died in March 1702, it was Wren who had to decide if the bill of £329 10s for his coffin ('with a strong chest to hold the bowells') was reasonable.[52]

We tend to regard architects, especially architects of Wren's stature and with Wren's vision, in the same way that the nineteenth century regarded poets and painters – as lonely, driven prophets whose acts of creation are a solitary vice. Buildings aren't built that way, nor have they ever been. Not only did Wren spend little of his life at the Works on design – his days were usually filled with answering correspondence, attending committee meetings and ambling from one coffee-house to another – but the actual design process was essentially a collaborative one, often involving a team of creative and not-so-creative assistants.

This inevitably raises questions of attribution. Drawings were generally unsigned, and while some of those which came out of the office in Scotland Yard were undoubtedly by his own hand – his penmanship is clearly identifiable – others were the work of his clerks and draftsmen. Sometimes these men acted as simple copyists: they would fix a plan, elevation or detail drawing to a table or board, lay several sheets of thin paper over it and prick through with a stylus at the junctions of lines before removing the top sheets, one by one, and joining up the dots in their own particular style.[53] But to complicate matters further, Wren's assistants worked up details under his supervision, and sometimes actually undertook the design of particular features.* Nicholas Hawksmoor is the most famous instance of this.

Hawksmoor emerged in the early years of the eighteenth century as a leading figure in the Office of Works, and as one of the greatest architects England has ever produced. The extent of his creative input into Wren's office during the 1680s and 1690s is impossible to establish with any certainty, but I suspect it has been over-estimated. Wren

---

*As did the craftsmen themselves, of course.

taught him, encouraged him, gave him work and advanced his career as an architect. Doubtless he asked for the young man's ideas on various architectural problems and, particularly when he was a recent widower and Hawksmoor was a member of his household and eager to learn, they must have talked through his plans and ambitions – for Charles II's great palace at Winchester, for Hampton Court, for St Paul's. But they remained *his* plans. It is significant that when the younger man was taken on at St Paul's in 1691, and Lawrence Spencer wrote down his duties as 'assisting the Surveyor in drawing designs', Wren had the entry amended to '*copying* [my italics] designs'.[54] Whatever Wren owed to Hawksmoor in these years, it was nothing compared to the debt Hawksmoor owed him.

16

The Poor Old Man

On 20 October 1702 Wren was seventy – a more than respectable age, when the average life expectancy at birth was only around thirty-two years. He had already outlived most of his contemporaries. Ten weeks later he had outlived his precious daughter Jane.

There are no clues as to what happened to Jane or whether she had an easy death, only that the 25-year-old died on 29 December. Her monument in the crypt of St Paul's was carved by Francis Bird, a sculptor with a growing reputation who had studied in Flanders and Rome, and whom Wren would later employ at the cathedral.[1] This isn't among his best work. Stiff and stylized, it shows Jane as St Cecilia, patron saint of musicians, seated at her organ and surrounded by putti: the inscription remembers her as affectionate, kind, and skilled in music and the arts. Wren must have felt her loss – and not only because, even in an age inured to early death, a child predeceasing a parent seemed against the natural order of things. She was his companion, the mistress of his household, his favourite child.*

Three weeks before Jane's death, Christopher junior, who was definitely not a favourite child, buckled down and entered the family firm. His father's influence had secured his appointment as Chief Clerk to the Works, although the life of a civil servant didn't hold much appeal: he continued to travel abroad and three years later, when he was

---

*She was also his collaborator, according to a nineteenth-century legend that credits her with designing the steeple of St Mary-le-Bow. Since she was only three when it went up, she must have been quite a prodigy.

thirty, he was harbouring romantic notions of taking up soldiering as a career. But he had second thoughts – much to the relief of his father, who told him, 'I am very well satisfied you have layd aside your designe for the Army; which I thinke had not been safe or pertinent, at least not soe much as Bookes & Conversation with ye Learned.'[2] When it came to choosing between a life of action and the life of the mind, there was no contest.

Wren still had a bureaucratic workload that would have crushed a man half his age. This was joined to a nagging sense of self-doubt, a handicapped child whose condition was worsening and a Parliament whose only response to his *magnum opus* was 'could do better'. He might have been forgiven for loosening his hold on some, at least, of his string of official positions – at the Works, St Paul's, the Commission for rebuilding the City churches, Greenwich Hospital, Windsor Castle and Westminster Abbey.

In retrospect, perhaps he should have done just that. While he kept a tight hold on his offices, he was beginning to lose his grip on their day-to-day management. The mutterings about the slow progress of St Paul's were damaging enough, but in 1704 a specific complaint was made directly to Lord Treasurer Godolphin about Wren's conduct of the Works. The complainant was John Vanbrugh.

Like Wren, Vanbrugh didn't turn to architecture until he was in his thirties, although his early career was rather more colourful than the Surveyor's. Born in 1664, he went into the wine trade briefly before spending a fifteen-month stint at Surat, north of Bombay, as a factor for the East India Company. On his return in 1686 he took up soldiering with the Earl of Huntingdon's regiment. There followed a period as a hostage in various French gaols (including a spell in the Bastille); a captaincy in the marines; and celebrity in London as the author of such comedies as *The Relapse, or Virtue in Danger* (1696) and *The Provok'd Wife* (1697). In 1699, as Swift famously wrote a few years later, 'Van's genius, without thought or lecture,/Is hugely turn'd to architecture'. His first project, the 3rd Earl of Carlisle's Castle Howard in Yorkshire (1700–26), was undertaken in collaboration with Hawksmoor and at the expense of Talman, who had already begun to design the new house and who never forgave either Vanbrugh or Carlisle. He soon had a much greater cause for resentment. For a brief period between November 1701 and May 1702 Carlisle replaced Lord Godolphin at the Treasury. William III died in March 1702; and with Talman's royal patron out of the way, Carlisle saw an opportunity to reward his ex-architect for his insolence and his current architect for his service. Talman's patent as Comptroller of the Works was not renewed. The post went instead to Vanbrugh.[3]

Wren was already acquainted with his new Comptroller. When, in the previous year, Vanbrugh had been given permission to build himself a house on the site of the Vice-Chamberlain's lodgings at Whitehall, the two men had become neighbours. The Surveyor had been uneasy about the grant, telling the Treasury that 'it may be a precedent for more of this nature'[4] – in which case his hopes of building a new palace would be dashed for ever. His concerns were duly noted, but work on Goose Pie House, as the building became known (after Swift's satirical reference to it in his 'Vanbrug's House' as 'A Thing resembling a Goose Py'), went ahead anyway.* After he obtained the Comptrollership, Vanbrugh let out his official Scotland Yard residence, preferring to remain in Goose Pie House. He was a much more attractive character than Talman, witty, urbane, at ease in noble company and generous in his praise of others – all the things that Talman was not, in fact. Wren must have viewed the prospect of working with him with some relief after years of watching his back and fending off Talman's periodic attempts to undermine his authority and oust him from office.

Vanbrugh spent two years settling into the job and learning the ropes. But by 1704 he was unhappy with the way the Office was being run and, in particular, with the 'shamefull abuse' whereby craftsmen–contractors, right up to the Master Mason and Master Carpenter, were allowed to undertake private contracts for royal work while simultaneously receiving salaries from the Crown. They were, in effect, tendering for building jobs and then accepting their own tenders. There was nothing new in this: one of the main attractions of a senior post in the Works had always been the opportunity it offered for obtaining lucrative government contracts. But Vanbrugh believed (mistakenly, as it happens) that the practice had been forbidden back in the early years of Charles II's reign. He was also motivated by the fact that one of the regular culprits, the current Master Mason Benjamin Jackson, was a close associate of Talman's. Vanbrugh despised Jackson, who had taken over John Oliver's job at the Office of Works on the latter's death in 1701. He reckoned him to be 'so Villainous a Fellow and so Scandalous

---

*Swift wasn't the only satirist to poke fun at Vanbrugh's Whitehall residence. The anonymous author of a funny and spiteful attack on his sexuality, declared that 'even the Building's by itself betray'd,/Itself confesseth for what use 'twas made./It self's the Emblem of your Darling Sin./No other way but only Backwards in' ('A True Character of the Prince of Wales's Poet, with a Description of the new erected Folly at White-Hall', 1701).

in every part of his Character; and that in the unanimous opinion of all Sorts of People he is known to; that he is indeed a disgrace to the Queen's Service and to everybody that is oblig'd to be concern'd with him'.[5] We don't know what Jackson thought of Vanbrugh, but we can guess. The monthly Board meetings in Scotland Yard must have been rather tense affairs.

As was proper, Vanbrugh went to Wren with his concerns and Wren promised to do something. Nothing happened. The Comptroller went back again and again, each time with the same result, until at last he lost patience with the old man and complained directly to Godolphin, who had been reinstalled at the Treasury soon after the accession of Queen Anne. Godolphin promptly wrote an official letter to the Board of Works, stating in no uncertain terms that its officers were not to undertake royal contracts.

This was just what Vanbrugh wanted. Jackson was currently carrying out a contract at Kensington Palace. He had already put in a bill for over £2000 for unspecified works in the gardens. Now he and his men were employed on an orangery for Queen Anne designed ostensibly by Wren, but more likely the work of Hawksmoor and (perhaps) Vanbrugh. The Comptroller went back to Wren once more, this time armed with Godolphin's order, and demanded that 'there might immediately be another mason got to work at Kensington upon the New Greenhouse'.[6] He didn't care who it was, just so long as it wasn't Jackson.

Wren didn't want any fuss. Privately, he could see nothing wrong with a system which had served him and the Works pretty well for more than thirty years. But Godolphin's letter meant he had no choice except to act, and he duly suggested another mason, Thomas Hill, who had worked for him before at Kensington, and also at Hampton Court, Whitehall and St Paul's. Vanbrugh summoned Hill to Scotland Yard and explained the job; Hill agreed to start right away. When he didn't turn up for work, the Comptroller asked around for the reason, to be told Hill was too scared: either Jackson or one of his men had been making thinly veiled threats 'of what should befall him if he durst meddle with the Master Mason's business'.[7] Hill sent word that he wouldn't take the contract after all.

Wren's reaction to this news didn't inspire Vanbrugh with confidence. He made a joke of the whole business, saying that Hill was 'a piece of an Astrologer, and would Venture upon nothing till he had consulted the Starrs, which probably he had not found favourably enclin'd upon this Occasion and therefore had refus'd the Work'. Never mind that it was Jackson who was making the predictions, or that one of his own Officers on the Board was intimidating Crown contractors for his own gain and getting away with it. Vanbrugh, fired in equal measure by reforming zeal and a loathing for Jackson, wouldn't let the matter drop. He was about to leave for Castle Howard, but while he was away perhaps Wren would employ someone who was a little less superstitious? Wren said of course he would – only for Vanbrugh to find on his return that Jackson's men were back at work at Kensington. Now they were working for a mason named Palmer. And Palmer, as the foreman on site readily admitted, was simply a cover. He was Jackson's deputy.

Vanbrugh was outraged, and stormed off to Scotland Yard to acquaint Wren with the shameful abuses which were going on under his nose. This time there were no jokes – just an embarrassed admission. The Surveyor already knew that Jackson was sending in bills in Palmer's name. What? said Vanbrugh. Had he forgotten Godolphin's commands, and all the conversations they had had on the subject? Not at all, Wren answered. 'But Jackson would not be quiet without he let him do the Work.'[8]

The whole sorry episode ended with Vanbrugh blowing the whistle on Wren's conduct. He wrote another letter of complaint to the Lord Treasurer, setting out the precise sequence of events. 'This Story is so very improbable I'm afraid y'r Lordship will scarce give me credit for it,' he wrote. 'Yet it is a plain and literal truth in every Article.'[9] He was quick to deny that Wren was working the system for his own profit; there was no question of that. It was simply that after thirty-five years in the job, the Surveyor was no longer able to control a government department with an annual expenditure of some £30,000–£40,000. Leonard Gammon, the influential Clerk of the Works at Whitehall, Westminster and St James's Palace, was a drunk, a 'dos'd sott' who would pass any bill put before him; Jackson was a crook; and he and the other tradesmen at the Works – 'those Fellows', Vanbrugh called them – were running rings round Wren.

Godolphin summoned both Wren and Jackson to a meeting of the Treasury Commissioners. The Master Mason flatly denied everything, while all Wren could say was that the business ought to have been dealt with by the Board of Works rather than the Treasury. He carefully sidestepped the fact that he was being called to answer Vanbrugh's charges precisely *because* the Board had so signally failed to deal with them. The upshot was that in 1705 new orders were issued, stating that from henceforth no Officer of the Works could carry out a contract for any Crown building operation, 'or have any advantage directly or indirectly by it'.[10] Wren remained Surveyor, and Jackson kept his post as Master Mason, although he disappeared from the Kensington Palace accounts. Around the same time an otherwise unknown mason, John Smoote or Smoute, began to put in bills for work done at Kensington and St James's. Call it coincidence, but at the beginning of the eighteenth century 'smout' was slang for a proxy worker.

Vanbrugh's criticisms weren't motivated by malice – or if they were, the malice was directed at Jackson rather than Wren. Nor was he trying to have the old man dismissed so that he could take his place. He liked and respected him: years later, when Wren's failure to manage the Works finally led to a major shake-up of its organization, he was actually offered the Surveyorship, but 'refus'd it,' he said, 'out of Tenderness for Sr Chr: Wren'.[11] But doubts about the Surveyor's abilities began to mount. When Queen Anne granted the royal park of Woodstock to the Duke of Marlborough, a reward for his victory over the French at the Bavarian village of Blenheim in August 1704, it was Vanbrugh who was chosen to design Marlborough's palatial mansion. Wren's part in the project was confined to providing an estimate for the building work. He was expected at Woodstock in the summer of 1705 but, according to the Duchess of Marlborough, he never arrived, making 'an excuse for not being able to attend it from his old age and the distance it was from London'.[12] The estimate was for between £90,000 and £100,000. (It excluded work in the gardens and park – wisely, considering he hadn't seen the site.) This was far too low, although we needn't take that as a sign of senility: even in his prime, he often underestimated the cost of a major building project. Three years later the Queen gave the Marlboroughs a further grant of land, just across from St James's Palace, for a new town house. This time Wren *was* asked for a design, perhaps because the Duchess thought he would be easier to manage than Vanbrugh, with whom relations over Blenheim were rather fraught.

Marlborough House was a single two-storey block of eleven bays in bright-red Dutch brick, with a half-basement, a low-pitched balustraded roof and prominent quoins. It was one of Wren's last works, and he was assisted for the first and only time by Christopher junior. Wren went on to credit Christopher junior with the entire design – in an apparent attempt to ensure that when he finally did retire, his successor as Surveyor would be his son rather than Vanbrugh, who was the obvious choice. As a contemporary wrote in about 1711, the year the house was finished, Vanbrugh would now be hard put 'to get the better of the little old man and his son'.[13] But things didn't go smoothly. A rumour went round town that Wren had taken bribes from contractors; it was taken sufficiently seriously for the tradesmen to publish a joint denial, condemning it as 'a false, malicious, and scandalous report' and solemnly declaring that 'neither the Surveyor, nor his agents, nor any persons for them, or belonging to them, ever had or received, or are to have or receive, directly or indirectly, from any of us, any gratuity, reward, allowance, or advantage whatsoever'.[14] Whether or not this put a halt to the whispering campaign – and as we shall see, it probably didn't – the fact was that the Duchess herself was unhappy with Wren's conduct of the work. She had no quarrel with the design – 'The poor old man undertook this business very readily and as everybody says the house is a very good one' – but once again, the problem was his inability to manage the contractors. 'I began to find that this man from his age was imposed upon by the workmen and that the prices for all things were much too high for ready money and sure pay, upon which I took the finishing part upon myself.'[15]

The Duchess is not an impartial source: as Vanbrugh found to his cost, she had little time for architects, especially when they were spending her money, and was firmly of the opinion that they 'have very high flights, but they must be kept down'.[16] But the claims of inefficiency, high prices and bad management at the Works were gaining momentum with every year that passed. The architect Thomas Archer was voicing widely-held concerns when he complained that 'the frauds and abuses are so great that by the price of work set by the Queen's servants the whole nation . . . is a great sufferer'.[17]

For all the rumours, Wren was still intellectually active. When Thomas Sprat died in 1713, Francis Atterbury, his successor as Bishop of Rochester and Dean of Westminster, asked Wren for an account of his work on the Abbey during the fifteen years since Sprat had appointed him Surveyor; and, as he wasn't going to be around for ever, what his thoughts were for carrying on the work in the future. His response, which gives no hint of failing mental powers, was a detailed building history going right back to the legend that a temple of Apollo on the site was destroyed in an earthquake in the second century AD. ('I cannot readily agree', he wrote.[18]) He outlined the repairs he had already carried out, which mainly consisted of stabilizing the walls of the nave and south transept where they joined the cloister, and replacing decayed stonework on the south side of the Abbey; and ended with proposals for a new central tower and spire, additions to the still-unfinished west front, and a remodelling of the north transept. (Only the work on the transept porch was actually carried out, *c.* 1722.) He makes some mistakes in his chronology, but they are hardly outrageous: the examples he cites of Saxon work are all Norman Romanesque, for instance – a common misconception at the time – and he attributes the Henry III Chapter House to his son, Edward I. Much more interesting is the fact that his report is grounded in a keen historical perspective, focusing on *how* and *why* particular elements of the building are as they are before recommending changes.

The report also shows Wren's characteristically pragmatic approach to the Gothic, confirmed by his years on the Commission for rebuilding the City churches. His design for a new central tower was, he told Atterbury, 'still in the Gothick Form, and of a Style with the rest of the Structure, which I would strictly adhere to, throughout the whole Intention: to deviate from the old Form, would be to run into a disagreeable Mixture, which no Person of a good Taste could relish'.[19] One remembers Tom Tower, which was 'Gothick to agree with the Founder's Worke'. He wanted crocketing on the new spire, and for the most practical of reasons: medieval masons had employed it not primarily as a decorative device, he said, but so that workmen could climb up the projections to carry out minor repairs without the need for scaffolding. This seemed like a good idea, so his own spire would also have crockets.

The old Surveyor also kept up his interest in the Royal Society. Although his attendances at meetings were now sporadic, he had served on its Council six times during the 1690s, and continued to do so on and off during the early 1700s.* So did Christopher junior, who was elected a Fellow in 1693 when he was still only eighteen (although he wasn't admitted until November 1698, after he got home from his continental travels with the younger Edward Strong). In February 1704, the Society was at a loss as to how to make use of the lenses for a 123-foot telescope donated twelve years earlier, without the tube, by Constantijn Huygens, Christiaan Huygens' brother. Wren came up with the novel idea of

---

*It is interesting that several of the major players at St Paul's in the early 1690s were Royal Society members. Edward Stillingfleet was elected in 1688, although he was never admitted; John Tillotson had been a member since 1672, when he was proposed by Seth Ward; and William Stanley, one of the residentiaries who was on the Rebuilding Commission, served on the Council with Wren three times in the 1690s.

installing them in the south-west staircase of St Paul's. Sweeping the skies was obviously out of the question, but the resulting zenith telescope would be valuable in measuring stellar parallax. The scheme eventually had to be abandoned because the staircase wasn't high enough to take the lenses.[20]

At that same February meeting the issue of new premises was raised yet again. Hooke had died the previous March, and now that Gresham College's last important link with the Royal Society was severed, the trustees decided they wanted the Society out, and asked for their keys back. The new President, Isaac Newton, stalled for time while the Society pondered what to do. In fact he stalled for an impressive seven years before announcing in September 1710 that suitable premises had been found in Crane Court, just off Fleet Street.

Over the next two years Wren's advice was sought over the repair and conversion of Crane Court. It is not always easy to see how directly he was involved, since Christopher junior acted as a go-between and, presumably with his father's blessing, was inclined to talk up his own role in organizing the work. For example, he told Hans Sloane, the Society's Secretary, that 'I have given directions to [par]ticular Workmen, Persons I know well and trust, to take an Exact Survey of all necessary repairs of ye House'.[21] These workmen were in fact all employed by Wren at the time, and not at the Works, where Christopher junior was still Chief Clerk, but at St Paul's and Westminster Abbey. They included Edward Strong, the master smith Thomas Robinson, and Richard Jenings, who had taken over as master carpenter at St Paul's when John Longland died at the end of 1706.[22] However, what does seem clear is that when the Society decided it needed an additional building in the grounds to hold its collections, Sir Christopher Wren provided the design. In March 1711 his son told Sloane that, 'By my father's direction a Modell is made of the room for ye Repository of ye Royal-Society in Crane Court, wch may give ye Gentlemen a better idea, than the designe on paper: It will be very light, very commodious, and the cheapest building that can be contrived.'[23] The repository, put up by Richard Jenings and the bricklayer Thomas Hughes in 1711–12, was indeed cheap and cheerful, a two-storey block about forty feet long by twenty-three feet broad, with dormers and a gallery at first-floor level. Here the interested visitor could examine the Society's eclectic collection of antiquities and rarities, ranging from the skin of a rhinoceros and the skull of a tiger, to armadillos and crocodiles, an Indian canoe and 'The Tail of an Indian Cow, whose Hair is about a yard and quarter long'.[24] There is something peculiarly appropriate in the fact that what was almost certainly the last building Wren designed was for the Society he had helped to found at Gresham more than fifty years before.

No matter what the Duchess of Marlborough might say, and Vanbrugh might think, the 'poor old man' was not suffering from a failing intellect. At worst, he was getting tired, not so able and not so willing to juggle all the demands on his time. He needed to think about his priorities. And in the first decade of the eighteenth century his one big priority was St Paul's.

In 1700 Londoners were still waiting – perhaps not with bated breath, but at least with a modicum of interest – for the scaffolding to be struck and their new cathedral to be revealed in all its glory at last. The only clear picture they had of the finished building came from the published engravings of the Warrant design, with its Jonesian-revival west front and its curious combination of dome and stepped spire. Anyone who had eyes could see the design had evolved considerably since 1675. The completed east end bore no relation to the Warrant engravings. Nor did the north and south transepts, which now boasted carved pediments by Gibbons and Cibber. Gibbons produced a rather pedestrian version of the King's arms. Cibber had toyed with something similar for the south transept,[25] and a painted board was actually put in place to try out the effect. It didn't work, and Wren opted for a more fitting alternative which depicted that recurring motif of post-Fire London – a phoenix eighteen feet long and nine feet high, with an inscription taken from the fragment of gravestone he had come across decades earlier, the single word: *Resurgam*.[26]

While the original design of the cathedral had obviously been modified, people still expected a conventional treatment for the crossing-tower. The *London Spy* looked forward to seeing a 300-foot-high spire, 'whose towering pinnacle will stand with such stupendous loftiness above Bow steeple dragon, or the Monument's flaming urn, that it will appear to the rest of the holy temples like a cedar of Lebanon among so many shrubs, or a Goliath looking over the shoulders of so many Davids'.[27] The Commissioners knew different, of course. Wren deliberately played his cards close to his chest after the Great Model disaster, determined to keep the design safe from 'incompetent Judges'. But the idea which is sometimes mooted, that successive archbishops, bishops and deans were kept in the dark about the shape of the cathedral until Wren unveiled it with a flourish, like a cheap conjurer at

Bartholomew Fair, is frankly ridiculous. For one thing, it presumes that in the midst of all the deliberations over contracts and coal dues and staff appointments no one ever thought to ask what the object of desire would look like – and anyone who has ever sat on a fund-raising committee will know how absurd *that* notion is.

In January 1700 the Building Committee asked the Surveyor to bring the designs 'of the whole ffabrick' so that they could check them, and he obliged two weeks later; the Commissioners 'were well pleased, and Ordered him to carry them back again'.[28] We don't know for sure what these drawings, over which Tenison, Compton, Dean Sherlock and the others pored so enthusiastically, showed, but we have a pretty good idea. To drum up funds for the building work, in 1702 and 1703 the Commission published engravings of the cathedral, including a plan and north prospect by Johannes Kip (best known for the bird's-eye perspectives of country houses he made in partnership with Leonard Knyff) and a view of the west front by Samuel Gribelin. It seems fair to assume that these views followed the designs 'of the whole ffabrick' that Wren presented to the Committee. Indeed, it is likely that the request to see the drawings and the publication of the engravings were connected.

The engravings show that as far as the body of the cathedral was concerned, Wren hadn't departed far from the Definitive design of 1675. The double order of doubled pilasters, with large round-headed windows below and pediments above, was still the unifying decorative feature. Of course the Commissioners knew that already, since the choir and transepts were finished, or as good as. Above the roofline, they could see that Wren still intended to crown the two west towers with simple, circular *tempietti*, although the towers themselves were now to be taller than originally intended: an extra storey with a broken-based segmental pediment had been inserted between the upper order and the *tempietti*, to take two huge clocks. (The north-west tower actually housed the bells.) His plans for the dome had undergone more radical changes since the 1670s. The most obvious were, firstly, that it was now slightly flatter than in the Definitive design, with two tiers of pierced openings rather than three; and, secondly, that the Michelangelesque treatment of the drum with its pilastered buttresses had been discarded in favour of a 32-bay colonnade or peristyle, with a somewhat solid attic storey above that, lit by eight large windows in carved surrounds. Every fourth bay was solid, an ingenious touch which varied the visual rhythm of the colonnade and, more importantly, served as a buttress to help control the thrust of the dome above.

But Wren was still not happy with either the dome or the towers. Even while the views by Kip and Gribelin were being distributed among the great and the good, he was re-thinking both. The dome, in particular, had been the feature which fascinated him most ever since, in the days before the Great Fire, he had promised Dean Sancroft that it would offer 'incomparable more Grace in ye remote Aspect yn it is possible for ye Lean Shaft of a Steeple to afford'. And no wonder: for someone who revelled in finding ingenious solutions to complex problems, a dome was an opportunity sent from heaven.

A dome is an extraordinarily difficult thing to build. The scale has to be right; and when the building it crowns is 515 feet long from the west portico to the apse, that means it has to be big. The mathematics have to be right. A dome is a much greater load than the lean shaft of a steeple, and exerts thrust all round its perimeter – the flatter the dome, the greater the thrust. A more complicated structural system is needed to transfer this outward pressure to the ground, and vertical supports must be strong enough to cope with the result. The relationship between exterior and interior experience has to be right, too: what looks grand and monumental from the outside may seem far too large from the inside. Conversely, an appropriate interior space may not be large enough to function as an imposing landmark. Each of these issues – scale, structural integrity and exterior/interior relationship – affects the other two, and all three are inextricably bound up with the aesthetic appeal.

Wren struggled to come up with a satisfactory combination of answers for most of his architectural career. In the Pre-Fire design, he proposed a melon-shaped dome over a high 24-bay drum about 100 feet in diameter (roughly the dimension of the finished drum, as it happens), topped with a 100-foot-high lantern-cum-spire. Even at Old St Paul's, Wren had envisaged his dome to be London's landmark; but he realized at this early stage that there had to be a difference between internal space and silhouette, and he designed an inner hemispherical dome which ended forty feet or so below the apex of the outer shell. It was built of masonry, while the outer skin and the spire were timber and lead to reduce both the thrust and the load on the supporting piers.

By the Definitive design, Wren was considering masonry for both inner and outer skins. But that shouldn't be taken to imply that he had arrived at a form which truly satisfied him: there are a number of dome-studies made from 1675 right up to the turn of the century (most are impossible to date with any accuracy) which show him experimenting with a range of different ideas, from a drum raised on a concave octagonal platform to a lantern topped with a simple obelisk.[29] But with each new building season, the options narrowed. Four teams of masons were working on the dome: Edward Strong's men took the north-west quarter; Thomas Wise junior and Thomas Hill the south-west; and Christopher Kempster and his partner Ephraim Beauchamp the south-east. Jasper Latham's ex-foreman and successor, Nathaniel Rawlins, took the north-east quarter. By the summer of 1700 they had reached the level of 'ye Outside Pedestal Cornice which is under ye Collumns of ye Collonade without'[30] – the foot of the peristyle, in other words – and the next summer John Longland and Richard Jenings were raising gibbets to set the columns in the south-east quarter of the colonnade.

Wren's final scheme for the dome, which he was working on while the printer was running off copies of the authorized engravings, was more restful and, in its cool simplicity, more monumental than the version shown in Gribelin's west prospect of 1703. He completely revised the heavy attic storey of the drum above the colonnade, lightening it by the introduction of thirty-two pilasters interspersed with rectangular windows. The dome consisted of a smooth, elegant arrangement of converging ribs. The columns of the peristyle, the pilasters of the attic and the upward curve of the ribs combined to give a vertical emphasis which united the entire structure, lifting it and drawing the eye inexorably upward to the 88-foot-high lantern which crowned the cathedral, its glinting gilt ball and cross seeming to pull light down from the heavens and absorb its power.

The undoubted visual appeal of this executed design hides more than it reveals. As Wren had realized back in the 1660s, if the interior space was to convey a sense of lofty repose while the exterior towered over the City in the manner expected of a cathedral spire, he needed to use a double skin to make the inner dome quite considerably lower than the outer. And there is indeed a difference of some sixty-four feet in height between the brickwork inner shell and the outer, which consists of lead sheathing over a timber frame. The lead and timber couldn't support anything too bulky, and the obvious choice would have been to build the lantern of timber as well. But that would be too flimsy, too insignificant. So he plumped for an idea he had been toying with since he first worked up the Definitive design, and decided to build a third skin, a cone which was inserted between the inner and outer dome. Made of thin brickwork, this was a relatively light structure which anchored the outer shell and served as a base for the massive stone lantern, which in turn helped to stabilize the cone by pressing down upon it.

It is worth stating the obvious here, if only because the obvious can too easily be overlooked. Eighteenth-century Britain had nothing – *nothing* - to rival the dome of St Paul's. The lantern alone weighs some 850 tons. The entire structure – inner and outer domes, central cone, drum, piers and supports down to foundation level – has been reckoned at 67,270 tons. That is over 1200 tons more than the displacement of the fully-laden *Titanic*. It is a masterpiece of structural engineering, and one can't help but look for connections between Wren's background in the mathematical sciences and the mechanics which underpin it. They are hard to find. Various writers have tried to show that Wren derived the shapes of one or more of the three shells from the idea of the catenary arch – that is, by inverting the form created by hanging a chain from two points, so that the tensions caused by gravity are converted into compression. Wren certainly knew of Robert Hooke's experiments with catenary arches in the early 1670s, which resulted in Hooke's conviction that 'the true Mathematical and Mechanichal form of all manner of Arches for Building' could be found in the following formula: 'As it hangs in a continuous flexible form, so it will stand contiguously rigid when inverted.'[31] And in June 1675, when Wren was working on the Definitive design for the cathedral, Hooke went round to Scotland Yard to find he was 'making up of my principle about arches and alterd his module by it'.[32] But no one has managed to show conclusively that the domes of St Paul's are actually based on the catenary arch.*

Rather than making use of theoretical mechanics, as we might have expected, Wren relied heavily on basic geometry and contemporary building practice. I would give a lot to hear his on-site conversations with mason-contractors like Edward Strong and Christopher Kempster – men raised in the building trades, whose experience must surely have played an unknown and unacknowledged part in the Herculean task of moving from paper design to implementation.

More striking is Wren's pragmatic approach to the design process. Evelyn felt qualms over his friend's ability to flout the principles of classical orthodoxy in 1694, when he noted how columns had been

---

*Another of Hooke's ideas did find a place in the new cathedral. In 1693 he noted that Wren 'approved Shell lime: vide Pauls' (*Diary*, 16 June). Ten years later Hawksmoor was paid to experiment with this lime, which was made of pounded cockle shells, and plasterer Henry Doogood used it extensively on the vaults and arches.

placed over pilasters on the exterior of the apse; Roger North was unhappy about the double order. But the feature which seems most unsettling today is the treatment of the eight crossing-arches which support the dome. In the Warrant design, the aisles were exactly half the width of the nave and the eight piers that carried the arches were equally spaced; which would have made them of equal heights. But in the Definitive design Wren increased the thickness of the outer walls, thus reducing the width of the side aisles, so that where the aisles met the transepts the spaces between the piers were also reduced. In other words, he found that the diagonals of the octagon formed by the piers were slightly shorter than the other four sides.

This was a tricky problem. If the spaces between the diagonal pairs of piers were shorter, then the arches they carried would be lower. Wren's solution was to have four semicircular arches at the cardinal points as intended, and four lower elliptical arches between them. To maintain the impression of consistency he placed a second, semicircular arch above each elliptical arch and inserted vaulting behind it. This vaulting transferred some of the thrust exerted by the massive weight of the dome above to four bastions in the angles of the crossing. It was an ingenious response, but the lack of uniformity in the treatment of the crossing broke all the rules, and it still arouses *angst* among the critics.[33]

The Surveyor rarely allowed prejudice or principle – classical or otherwise – to stand in the way of a solution. He criticized 'the affectation in the Gothic way of making weight seem to rest upon Nothing', and then went to astonishing lengths to give the impression that the great lantern was perched on top of a lead dome which couldn't support it.[34] He told Francis Atterbury that flying buttresses 'are the first Things that occasion the ruin of Cathedrals, being so much exposed to the Air and Weather'; but he still used them to support the nave of St Paul's.[35] At Salisbury, he deplored the medieval habit of 'tying walls together with Iron, instead of making them of that substance and forme, that they shall naturally poyse themselves upon their butment'; such a practice was 'against the Rules of good Architecture'.[36] But the bursting piers in the crypt of St Paul's (which were still waiting to be repaired) focused his mind on the need to put structural integrity above the rules of good architecture. He commissioned the three smiths, Jean Tijou, Thomas Robinson and Thomas Coalburne, to produce tons of iron chains, cramps, ties, bolts and screws. The west portico was chained in place; wrought-iron ties were used to span the eight main piers under the dome; and a great chain or girdle was set into the base of the brickwork cone, sheathed in lead and with links ten feet long.

Succeeding generations, accustomed to having heroes who could do no wrong, have found it hard to deal with some of these transgressions. The most serious was the extensive use of both buried and exposed ironwork which, as it corroded, caused considerable problems. One of the more endearing stories of St Paul's describes how Wren was forced to put the great chain in place even though he knew it was unnecessary, because others feared for the cone's stability. To prove his point, he is supposed to have sawed through one of the iron links, concealing his act of sabotage with the lead sheathing. The anachronistic idea that the mathematical genius must necessarily have been a master of structural engineering is a potent element in his legend.

As the dome developed into a simpler, purer shape – albeit a simplicity and purity which disguised a vastly complicated structural system – Wren's thinking about the west towers moved in the opposite direction. By 1705, when Fulkes and William Kempster,* the two mason-contractors working on the west end of the cathedral, had raised the towers to the level of the roofline and were coming close to finishing the portico, he had decided on a complete revision of the elegant Bramantesque *tempietti* which had been a feature of the design from 1675 right up to the publication of the authorized engravings in 1702 and 1703. The broken-based pediments on the clock stage in Gribelin's west prospect turned into continuous horizontal cornices which break upward like eyebrows over the circular clock-faces in the south-west tower and the openings for the bells in the north-west. Above them, Wren placed what is perhaps his most exuberant and wholeheartedly Baroque composition. Clusters of coupled columns advance and recede, producing sharp and ever-changing contrasts of light and shade beneath a complicated upper storey with brackets and urns and, finally, an ogee cap topped with a gilt pineapple. The whole effect is dynamic, exciting, a perfect counterpart to the cool repose of the dome.

As Wren was working out the last vitally important details of the cathedral in 1701–4, work on site slowed down. This was partly because of the problems over the supply of stone from the royal quarries on Portland and partly, no doubt, because he was still trying to decide on

---

*William Kempster was Christopher's brother, and had worked as John Tompson's foreman on the west end until 1700, when Tompson died and he took over the contract.

the final form of the dome and towers. He now had a new Assistant Surveyor: old John Oliver died in November 1701, and his place was taken by Thomas Bateman, a family connection of Wren's. Unlike Oliver, who had come up through the building trades, Bateman was primarily an administrator, but Wren had every faith in him. He had already secured him, in 1696, the post of Clerk of the Works at Winchester Palace – something of a sinecure, since the only works going on there involved the most basic maintenance – and in 1700 Bateman had been appointed Collector and Receiver of the Coal Dues. As far as we know, he played no part in the design of the cathedral. Help in that direction – the making of working drawings, for example – came from Hawksmoor and William Dickinson, the young surveyor who had been working as measuring clerk at St Paul's since the mid-1690s.

Another reason for the delay was money. At the February 1700 meeting when Wren brought in his designs, the Committee cut back the number of day-labourers employed on the site to twelve, called in Strong and the other mason-contractors and asked them to work on credit, and dropped the interest rate it was offering on loans against the coal money from six per cent down to five per cent.* In a number of cases the debts owed to contractors were commuted to loans. (By 1702 the Strongs were receiving quarterly interest (at five per cent) on £3800, and Samuel Fulkes on £1000; the accounts show that Wren had himself lent £1900 to the project, and even Hawksmoor had chipped in with £500.) The Commission geared itself up to plead with Parliament for an increase in the coal dues and the 69-year-old Wren, keen to influence events from the inside, successfully stood as an MP in the court interest for a second time, after his failures in 1689 and 1690. In the general election of December 1701 he was returned as the member for Melcombe Regis in Dorset.

Parliament didn't get round to debating the coal tax. William's unexpected death the following March brought the session to an abrupt close and also, as it happened, ended the Surveyor's unspectacular career in the Commons: he didn't stand again. But the tory majority that controlled Queen Anne's first Parliament proved a good friend to St

---

*In between their periodic panic attacks over money, the Commissioners were quite creative in their use of building funds. Various payments to cleaning-women for sweeping the choir, and rat-catchers for keeping it clear of vermin, could conceivably be justified on the grounds that the building works had contributed to the problems. But – to take just one example – £80 to the Sub-Dean for copying out anthems for the singing-boys was stretching things a little (*WS* XV, 55).

Paul's, voting two shillings per chaldron to be devoted exclusively to the finishing of the cathedral for the last eight years of the life of the tax – i.e., from 1708 until 1716. This didn't solve all the financial problems at a stroke. But it did mean the Commission would find it much easier to borrow more money against the dues.

The building work didn't really begin to gather momentum again until the building season of 1705; but now the last great push was on. That summer Samuel Fulkes was carving the Composite columns for the upper order of the west portico, and Longland and Jenings were putting up templates for the bricklayers on the dome. In 1706 those bricklayers were building up the cone, and Francis Bird was executing his spectacular sculpture in the west pediment, 'in length 64 foot and in height 17 foot, being the history of St Paul's Conversion, and containing 8 Large Figures, 6 whereof on horseback, and severall of them 2½ ft imbost'.[37] By the following February, the four contractors working on the stonework of the dome had reached the top of the attic wall, 'wch intirely finishes the same';[38] and in May Edward Strong's men were cutting holes in the masonry of the attic for Jenings' carpenters to fit the timber framing which supported the outer dome.

Working in all weathers, the plumbers laid the lead sheets on the dome during the spring of 1708: tarred cloths were supplied to protect them from the sun and the rain. The final stone was set in place on top of the lantern by Christopher Wren junior on 26 October, six days after his father's seventy-sixth birthday. Edward Strong, whose brother Thomas had laid the foundation stone more than thirty-three years earlier, was there to witness the ceremony, along with his own son and other 'Free and Accepted Masons'.[39] The architect, by now too old and frail to make the difficult climb, remained on the ground more than 360 feet below.

But he didn't need to be there. It was enough just to know that it was happening. The decades of struggle, the tears and the compromises and the sniping criticisms, had all been worth it. He had done it. For the first time in English history, a single architect had built a cathedral.

17

My Great Work

*A*s the screens and scaffolding came down around St Paul's in the winter of 1708/9, all London marvelled at Wren's achievement. Crowds of sightseers flocked through the streets to wonder at the dome. The more adventurous among them made the precipitous climb up to the lantern, where they could look out over the City and Westminster and across the Thames to Southwark and the open spaces of St George's Fields and Newington. (They paid for the privilege, incidentally; the pennies collected 'at the Stairfoot dore' went into a fund for the benefit of the workmen.)[1] The cathedral was eulogized in verse. Its cupola was 'a diadem that crowns not Paul's alone/But the whole Island, plac'd on her head-town'; its architect was a national hero:

> How will the much-admiring Artists then
> Applaud the Builder? yielding all the Fame
> Of former Masters to the greater *Wren*,
> That rais'd, and finish'd this Majestick Frame.[2]

But while London applauded, the Rebuilding Commission did not. William Sherlock had died in 1707, and his place at the Deanery and hence on the Commission was given to Henry Godolphin, younger brother to the Lord Treasurer. Dr Godolphin was familiar with the building work, having been a prebendary of St Paul's since 1683: he had watched as his predecessors, Stillingfleet, Tillotson and Sherlock, had been content to leave questions of design in the hands of their architect. Now, however, the completion of the cathedral was in sight. There was still plenty to do: walls to be built and railings put up in the Churchyard, some plastering and glazing, internal painting and other decoration. A statue of Queen Anne, made from marble which she had personally donated, remained to be finished and set up outside the west door; bells had to be cast and hung; statues for the three pediments, carved panels and other external ornaments were still wanting. But the time had come for the clergy to reclaim ownership of the project. And by 'the clergy', the Dean meant himself.

As it happened, Godolphin was absent when Wren first discovered that his position as arbiter of taste at St Paul's was in jeopardy. One Saturday in April 1708 the Surveyor went along to a meeting of the Building Committee at Lambeth Palace. Besides Archbishop Tenison, he found four other Commissioners present, including William Stanley – the residentiary canon and Archdeacon of London who had recently become Dean of St Asaph – and two other residentiaries, John Younger and Francis Hare.[3] All three were loyal to the Dean, as one might expect. Dr Hare, who as Chaplain-General to the Duke of Marlborough's army was almost as powerfully placed as Godolphin himself, was particularly staunch in his support; and like Godolphin, he was convinced that control of the project belonged with the Chapter rather than the Surveyor.

One of the matters discussed was the decoration of the interior of the dome. Wren had toyed with the idea of figurative painting back in the 1670s, but he now meant to cover it in mosaic, 'which strikes the Eye of the Beholder with a most magnificent and splendid Appearance'.[4] The Committee begged to differ. It was too expensive, too time-consuming. They ordered instead 'that the inside of the Dome, or Cupola, be painted & that Sir Chr Wren do procure Designs, & proposals for the same to be laid before the Commissioners'.[5] This decision, which certainly had Godolphin's backing even if it didn't actually originate with him, came as quite a shock. Wren reacted by doing nothing about the order until the following spring, perhaps hoping that in the general euphoria surrounding the completion of the lantern he would be able to talk the Dean and Chapter round to his own way of thinking.

He didn't succeed, and his next thought was that if the dome had to be painted, then it should be given 'ornaments of architecture' in the form of coffering, with the mouldings picked out in gold.[6] After some discussion, Godolphin and the other clergy on the Commission said no. They didn't want ornaments of architecture. They wanted scenes from the Acts of the Apostles, and scenes from the Acts of the Apostles were what they were going to have. Five artists were invited to submit designs – Pierre Berchet, Giovanni Battista Catinat, Louis Cheron, Giovanni Antonio Pellegrini and James Thornhill. The choice was narrowed down to Thornhill and Pellegrini, both of whom were asked to paint miniature versions of their schemes on little cupolas provided for the purpose. For the time being, the matter rested there.

In the meantime, the power struggle between Dean and Surveyor was turning nasty. At a Committee meeting in March 1709 – the same meeting at which the decision was taken, against Wren's wishes, to paint the dome with figures – two master smiths were asked to provide estimates for a railing to enclose the new building. One was Thomas Robinson, who had a forge in Fetter Lane and had already successfully carried out several contracts for ironwork around the cathedral, including the supply of the great chain which encircled the brick cone of the dome; the other was a certain Richard Jones. Wren's preference was for wrought-iron and Robinson; Godolphin's was for cast-iron and Jones. It was eventually put to a vote, Wren was outnumbered, and the job went to Jones.

Exactly why the Dean was so determined to employ Jones is a mystery: he was a dubious character with a conviction for manslaughter (he had killed a man during an anti-Catholic demonstration) and a brand on his hand to prove it. There was also something odd about his business dealings. He was tied up with a Sussex ironfounder, Peter Gott; and Gott's son, a tax-gatherer, was currently in trouble with the Exchequer for gathering land tax and spending it. For reasons that aren't clear, Jones agreed to hand £6000 of the £11,000 he received for the cathedral contract straight over to the Tax Commissioners to pay Gott junior's debts. Conspiracy theorists can make what they like of that, but I'm sure Godolphin's real motive for choosing Jones was that Wren didn't want him. The affair was an opportunity to demonstrate just who was really in charge at St Paul's.

The 'poor old man's' reaction was angry and unexpected. He refused point-blank either to draw up Jones's contract or to attend any more meetings of the Commission. This left the Dean in a quandary. He had no authority to replace Wren, even if he wanted to; but he still needed an architect to supervise the completion of the cathedral. Nor was he immune to public opinion: in the words of a contemporary pamphleteer, the Jones affair 'made a great Noise in Town and Country; and it was thought strange by most People, that after Sr Chr had compleated so noble a Fabrick with universal Applause, the Direction of so small a Circumstance as a Fence to encompass it, should be peremptorily and obstinately denied him'.[7] Godolphin had no intention of compromising, however – quite the opposite, in fact. In 1710, in a move calculated to undermine his Surveyor's authority and cast doubt on his ability to manage, he personally launched an attack on Wren's trusted master carpenter, accusing Richard Jenings before the Building Committee of cheating his workmen, stealing building materials and deliberately defrauding the Commission. According to Jenings, the immediate causes of this fresh assault were his support for Wren over the issue of the fence, which angered the Dean and Chapter; and his refusal to pay a premium on payments for work done, which made an enemy out of Lawrence Spencer, the influential and pro-Godolphin Clerk of Works and Paymaster at St Paul's.

Perhaps the only edifying aspect of the controversy is the light it sheds on the early eighteenth-century construction industry. Among other things, Jenings was accused of underpaying his carpenters and sawyers by between 20 per cent and 40 per cent of the agreed daily rate (which was 2s 6d), and pocketing the difference; of employing workmen who were too old or crippled to do the job; and of spiriting away quantities of timber, boards, ropes, nails and other materials for his own use. The Commissioners also charged that 'several of the said Under-workmen after they had answered their Call at St Paul's, were sent to Work by him at other Churches and Places.⋆ And that some of the Workmen of the Church were employed within the Church to make Models for other Churches, Presses, Windowcases &c of the Church's Materials'.[8] Jenings argued that the bargains he struck with his workers were his own affair, and entirely separate from the bargain made between him and the Commissioners; he had agreed daily rates with individual carpenters and stuck to them, and if he profited from the deal, this was no more than accepted custom and practice in the building trade. In a touching but not altogether convincing display of compassion, he also admitted that he was indeed employing some men who had grown old or been injured in the building of the cathedral; but that 'I thought it too cruel,

---

⋆As well as working on St Paul's, between 1706 and 1717 Jenings won carpentry contracts at no fewer than twelve of the City churches, mostly in connection with the construction of their towers and steeples. The churches were All Hallows the Great, St Christopher-le-Stocks, St Edmund the King, St James Garlickhythe, St Margaret Pattens, St Mary Woolnoth, St Michael Bassishaw, St Michael Crooked Lane, St Michael Paternoster Royal, St Sepulchre, St Stephen Walbrook and St Vedast-alias-Foster.

and inhuman, to dismiss them out of that Work, wherein their Age and Hurts had come upon them.'[9]

As regards the more serious charges of embezzlement and fraud, Jenings had answers, backed up in most cases by affidavits. Under-carpenters who turned up at Paul's Churchyard before going off to work on other jobs were only there because they knew they would find their master at the site; if they inadvertently answered to their names at one of the hours of call, when Richard Marples, the Clerk of the Cheque, ticked off workers who were present in his call book, then either they or Jenings himself always pointed out the error. Any materials that he removed from the site were 'useless at St Paul's', and Jenings made sure they were set against his bills. Whenever shutters, sashes and presses were made in Paul's Churchyard for use elsewhere, he paid for both materials and labour.

This stretched the bounds of credibility a little. But Jenings and Thomas Bateman, who as Assistant Surveyor acted as Wren's proxy in the affair, also took a few retaliatory swipes at the enemy. Several of the under-carpenters submitted sworn statements that they had carried to Paul's Wharf 'a great quantity of Wood by Order of Mr Spencer, Clerk of the Works . . . which the Deponents have been informed was for the use of the said Mr Spencer at his Lodgings at Chelsea'.[10] Details of Richard Jones's criminal past were also raked up, including the manslaughter conviction and the fact that he was indicted at the Old Bailey in 1711 for altering an official voucher for payment for supplying the Ordnance with one hundred mortars. The full debenture was for £250, but it was endorsed with a note to the effect that Jones had received £100 on account: it was this endorsement that he scratched out. (He got off, although it is hard to see why, since his defence was that he couldn't sell the debenture with the endorsement still on it.)★

Jenings was dismissed from his post as master carpenter at St Paul's in April 1711, and Godolphin tried his level best to have him prosecuted. In the end the Attorney-General, Sir Edward Northey, decided that there was little likelihood of a conviction, but his conclusions hardly amounted to a glowing testimonial for either Jenings or Wren. The Surveyor was criticized for poor judgement in letting Jenings hire his own under-carpenters and agree their wages privately with them. And

---

★Around the time of Jones's trial there was also gossip that he had been 'dismiss'd the Ordnance' for selling three of its guns to an East India captain. It isn't clear whether this was a separate transgression or simply a case of Chinese whispers (Thomas Bateman to Sir William Trumbull, 1 May 1711, *WS* XVI, 179).

as for the master carpenter himself, Northey was pretty sure he was guilty, although the reasons he produced weren't the sort to stand up in court: 'From the Opinion I have of Workmen in general, I cannot doubt but that there have been great Frauds committed by them in the great Work of Rebuilding of the Cathedral.'[11]

Wren supported Jenings throughout, testifying before the Commission to his honesty and diligence, praising his high standards of workmanship and, much to Godolphin's annoyance, employing him on the new Chapter House in Paul's Churchyard. The ironwork contract went to Thomas Robinson, who was also appointed Chief Smith at the Office of Works in Scotland Yard – Wren looked after his friends. But he had troubles of his own. On 25 January 1711, the Dean sent word requiring the Surveyor 'or some sufficient deputy' to look at examples of Jones's work and give an opinion. He did; it wasn't favourable; and the Committee ignored it. Moreover, he was also ordered to 'satisfye the Committee, why a Contract with Mr Jones is not made'.[12] This peremptory treatment was the last straw. He decided it was time to take the offensive, and the same day he sat down and wrote an angry letter to Archbishop Tenison and Bishop Compton, demanding the half of his salary, by now amounting to £1325, which had been set aside in 1697 pending the completion of St Paul's:

> I think nothing can be said now to remain unperfected, but the Iron-fence round the Church, and painting the Cupola; the direction of which is taken out of my Hands; and therefore I hope that I am neither answerable for them, nor that the said suspending Clause can, or ought to affect me any further on that Account. As for Painting the Cupola; Your Lordships know it has been long under Consideration, that I have no Power left me concerning it, and that it is not resolved in what manner to do it, or whether at all. And as for the Iron-fence; it is so remarkable and so fresh in Memory, by whose Influence and Importunity it was wrested from me, and the doing it carrying in a way that I may venture to say will ever be condemned.[13]

Tenison had done his best to remain aloof from the infighting on the Commission, although in practice the effect of this had been to give Godolphin and his faction free rein. Compton, by now old and infirm and plagued by gout and gallstones, was firmly allied to the Dean, in spite of a friendship with Wren which dated back over half a century. He 'moves with Jones's Junta', as Thomas Bateman put it.[14] Archbishop and Bishop responded promptly to Wren's act of brinksmanship by consulting Sir Edward Northey as soon as they received the letter. The Attorney-General, who was also on the Commission, seems to have been a decent, fair-minded sort of man. He replied that, while it seemed harsh, the 1697 Act of Parliament had stipulated quite clearly that the Surveyor shouldn't have his backpay until six months after the cathedral was finished. And since it wasn't finished, he couldn't be paid.

Wren's next move was to petition Parliament, asking for his money and complaining that his attempts to complete the cathedral 'are wholly over-ruled and frustrated'.[15] And as accusations started to fly in all directions, he submitted evidence before a committee of the House of Commons, again asking for his arrears and, in the process, giving a verdict on Jones's fence which laid bare the extent of his bitterness and hurt:

> I have no reason at all to alter my own opinion, though a great deal to confirm me in it, from the part of the fence put up, which is far from being performed workmanlike, and I cannot but think it altogether absurd, and the price extravagant . . . But I own myself obliged to the dean and chapter for clearing me from having a hand in it, and I promise I will never envy the credit they may get by it.[16]

This time he was successful: the Commons agreed that to all intents and purposes the cathedral was finished, and that he should receive his arrears on or before Christmas Day 1711. But money wasn't really what he wanted, and he wasn't finished with Godolphin yet. Trading on his status at the Office of Works, on 3 February 1711 he complained directly to Queen Anne about the treatment of her Surveyor. Emphasizing an incident that had happened a couple of days previously, when the Commision had barred him from employing Tijou to make a railing for Anne's statue, he protested at the 'arbitrary proceedings of some of the Commissioners', mentioning the Dean and Dr Hare by name and hinting darkly at their lack of taste and scruples. ''Tis well known,' he told the Queen, 'what sort of Person and Way they are inclined to.' He begged to be allowed to finish the cathedral 'in such manner, and after such Designs as shall be approved by her Majesty, or such Persons as her Majesty shall think fit to appoint'.[17] In other words, dissolve the Commission and let me get on with the job.

This raised the stakes considerably. What had started as a petty squabble between a stubborn old man and an ambitious cleric over some iron railings had grown until it involved the Attorney-General, the Archbishop of Canterbury, the House of Commons and finally the Queen herself. Politically, the appeal to Anne was a very astute move, giving us a good idea of just how Wren had managed to hang on to power for more than forty years. St Paul's was dear to her heart (unlike Archbishop Tenison, whose whiggish principles and slow manner got on her nerves); and by focusing on the trouble over the statue – which was, after all, a royal gift – Wren made his opponents seem churlish and disrespectful. And, as he was well aware, the previous August the Queen had dismissed the Dean's brother from office, leaving Dr Godolphin in a vulnerable position at court. The Surveyor-General, on the other hand, had access to Anne and a political track record calculated to appeal to the tory ministry which had come to power following the Earl of Godolphin's fall from grace.

The petition was passed back to the Dean for comment, arriving at the Chapter House on a Monday afternoon at the end of April. As it happened, the Commissioners were meeting that day. They were right in the middle of a discussion about Jenings' replacement, and were just about to choose John James, who was not only a carpenter, but also an architect and surveyor who had been trying unsuccessfully to obtain a job in the Office of Works for some time. His salary was to be £200, exactly equal to Wren's. Jenings wasn't the only one who was being replaced by James.

Godolphin, Compton and the other Commissioners were rattled when Wren's letter was read out to them. The thinly veiled request for a new Commission was unexpected; and, for the first time, they were put on the defensive. They immediately forgot all about John James (although he was formally appointed at their next meeting), and set about organizing their response. It was to be drafted by Godolphin and the Deans of St Asaph and Sarum and presented for signature five days later. When the meeting broke up, the workmen in Paul's Churchyard stood and watched as the frail Bishop Compton was helped to his coach, shaking their heads in disbelief as they saw who had the honour of conducting him through the crowds of sightseers. It was Richard Jones.

The Commission's response to Wren's charges was to adopt a tone of injured innocence. His slur on the characters of the Dean and Chapter was 'a very malicious and unjust Reflection, they never having had any Inclination or Designs, but for the Honour of her Majesty, and the Benefit of this Church'. But they couldn't resist some malicious reflections of their own. The Surveyor obviously had his own secret motives for objecting to Jones's work in fencing round the cathedral; what they were, it was up to others to judge. The only reason he hadn't been allowed to press ahead with railing the Queen's statue was that whenever he was left to his own devices, his 'Performances . . . have proved very faulty'. If the completion of the work had been delayed, then that was the fault of the Surveyor and his band of corrupt workmen, who hoped to gain by it. When it came to exposing the frauds and abuses which had been carried on at St Paul's (and here the charges against Jenings were brought out, along with a request for his criminal prosecution), it was the Commissioners who took the lead, and the Surveyor who tried to hinder them. As for trying to call a new Commission, how dare he impugn the character of those who served on the old one – the Archbishops of Canterbury and York, several bishops, the Lord Mayor of London, the Attorney-General, the Solicitor General, the Advocate General, the Dean and Chapter of the cathedral and others, 'whose known Honour, Justice and Integrity should have kept Sir Christopher from making any Reflection upon them'.[18]

This bickering couldn't go on. All through the summer and early autumn of 1711, Queen Anne and her Lord Treasurer, the Earl of Oxford, deliberated on what to do, while the rumours flew, the work virtually ground to a halt, and scandalous advertisements ridiculing the Commissioners were posted on the cathedral doors almost daily. John James seems to have been forgotten, since no one bothered to pay him his salary. Then, at the end of October, Wren got his way. The Commission was dissolved.

It was a Pyrrhic victory, and only a temporary defeat for Godolphin. Dean and Surveyor both kept their places on the new Commission, as did Tenison and Compton; the other eleven members were government officials with no real interest in St Paul's. True, there were signs of compromise: Jenings continued to work on the Chapter House and Tijou's railing went up around the statue of Queen Anne; the question of how to decorate the interior of the dome was tactfully postponed, and Jones was allowed to press on with the iron fence which had caused so much grief. But the scars left by two years of infighting refused to heal, and the truce – if it was a truce – was uneasy. Francis Hare, who along with the other residentiaries had been left off the new Commission, published *Frauds and Abuses at St Paul's* in April 1712, which insinuated, implied, and occasionally stated quite baldly that Wren was guilty of at best gross incompetence and, at worst, embezzlement and corruption. Jenings and Thomas Bateman responded the following year with *Fact against Scandal . . . in vindication of Mr Richard Jenings, Carpenter. . .* It seems pretty clear from the contents of these pamphlets that Godolphin and Wren both gave their backing to their respective champions – while neither would stoop to a public exchange of insults, they had no objections to others doing their dirty work for them. The war of words dragged on throughout 1713 with the publication of *A Continuation of Frauds and Abuses at St Paul's* and *The Second Part of Fact against Scandal,* before it finally petered out.

The death of Queen Anne in August 1714 and the accession of George I meant yet another Commission, which convened for the first time in the Chapter House on 25 June 1715. This time Godolphin had the upper hand, and his vengeance was swift. Bateman was accused of malpractice and his place as Assistant Surveyor at the cathedral was given to John James. Lawrence Spencer who, if *Fact against Scandal* is to be believed, had happily altered the minutes of Committee meetings to suit the needs of the Dean, was rewarded by being confirmed in his post as Clerk and Paymaster. Poor Richard Marples, the Clerk of the Cheque, whose only crime was to have sworn to Jenings' probity, was reappointed for four days before Godolphin made a complaint against him and had him suspended. Jones was given another contract, making the casements for the windows in the dome; and James Thornhill was chosen to paint that dome, with scenes from the life of St Paul.*

Wren was completely marginalized, and although he was named as Chief Surveyor on the 1715 Commission, it was clear from the beginning that John James was the architect in charge. A typical entry in the Commission's minute-book says it all:

[19 July 1715] Ordered. That Mr James, Assistant Surveyor, doe consider of proper wayes of glazing & repairing the Lanthorne upon the great Dome, and securing the same. That he wait on Sir Chr Wren for his Opinion therein, if he can get it, and if he cannot, to give his own Opinion with an Estimate of the Charge thereof to the Commissioners at their next Meeting.[19]

'If he can get it.' Getting Wren's opinion on anything to do with St Paul's was difficult. After attending two of the first meetings of the

---

*Apparently, when the ailing Tenison – he died at the end of 1715 – was asked for his opinion on the decoration of the dome, he replied that he didn't know much about art, but he thought the artist should be a Protestant and an Englishman. Of the five painters who were originally invited to submit designs, only Thornhill fitted the bill.

Commission (on 28 June and 2 July 1715) he simply walked away. Old, tired and outflanked, he never again set foot in his cathedral in any official capacity. From time to time either James or Isaac Newton (who had been a member of the St Paul's Commission for some years) would walk over to Scotland Yard to ask what he thought about some detail or another. But he knew it was only a courtesy. His views didn't matter any more.

Wren's last contribution came in October 1717. It concerned a balustrade that the Commission had decided to set up around the roof of the cathedral, even though it was no part of Wren's design. At one point Godolphin wanted something in cast-iron (by Jones, of course). This grotesque idea was eventually dropped, and the Surveyor was grudgingly asked what he thought about a stone balustrade. If he hadn't replied within a fortnight, then the work would go ahead. He did reply, and although he was now eighty-five, he had lost none of his wit or sense. 'Persons of little skill in architecture,' he wrote, 'did expect, I believe, to see something they had been used to in Gothic structures; and ladies think nothing well without edging.' But they were wrong. A continuous balustrade was structurally unsound — it was likely to blow down in a high wind — and would in any case be contrary to the principles of architecture. It would 'break into the harmony of the whole machine' — an intriguing image, which says a lot about Wren's conception of the cathedral. He had convinced himself that he had followed the best Greek and Roman architecture (and perhaps, in his own way, he had) — all that was needed to finish off the building were statues on the pediments. 'And if I glory, it is in the singular mercy of God, who has enabled me to begin and finish my great work so conformable to the ancient model.'[20] The statues, which were carved by Francis Bird, eventually went up. But by this stage no one was paying much attention to the harmony of the whole machine, and after James and Newton pressured Wren into giving his assent to the balustrade, that went up, too.

Godolphin's coup at St Paul's followed hard on the heels of a major shake-up at the Office of Works in Scotland Yard. For most of Queen Anne's reign the Treasury had been growing impatient with Wren's management of affairs at Scotland Yard, particularly the way in which he persisted in carrying out work without any authorization from the Lord Treasurer. He had always done this. If the Sovereign or a senior courtier personally demanded repairs or modifications to their lodgings, it was much less complicated to press on and deal with the consequences later; and whenever the Treasury called on him to explain the Works' exorbitant charges – as it often did – he would apologize, or claim that the Queen had given him a verbal command, or simply say that orders had been carried out without Treasury warrants because they were 'indispensably necessary for accommodating the persons concerned'.[21] The Board of Works kept no official minutes – the day-books at Scotland Yard certainly weren't for the Treasury's eyes – and this must have made his life much easier.

Things came to a head at the beginning of 1714. Vanbrugh had just been sacked as Comptroller over an unrelated matter (a letter in which he indiscreetly attacked the Queen's ministers had found its way to the government);* the Works had run up a colossal and unauthorized debt of nearly £80,000; and the Auditor had announced that he refused to pass the last five years' accounts. Wren was ordered to come up with a strategy for reducing costs, which he did at the beginning of March; but his remarks on 'such Alterations and Additions as occur to me on the present general Model' haven't survived.[22] They seem to have been heeded, since the Treasury told the Surveyor and the other officers on the Board to expect new regulations to run from 25 March 1714.

The regulations, whatever they were, didn't materialize. But plans for reform were resurrected by Lord Halifax and the whig ministry which came to power on the accession of George I that summer. Vanbrugh was restored to favour† and, in January 1715, to the Comptrollership. He was also invited to put in his own ideas for reorganizing the Works. These formed the basis for some sweeping changes which came into force in April. The new Board of Works was to consist of five Commissioners – the Surveyor-General, the Comptroller, the Paymaster, and the Surveyor-Generals of Crown Lands, and Woods and Forests – and two Secretaries to the Treasury, whose purpose, no doubt, was to keep a check on unauthorized expenditure (although in practice they never attended meetings). For the same reason, minutes of the proceedings were to be kept from now on by a new Secretary to the Board; the job went to Hawksmoor.

---

*Talman petitioned to get his old job back, but Vanbrugh was not replaced, because the Treasury was already considering a major reorganization of the Works in which the Comptrollership was to be abolished and the Master Mason and Master Carpenter replaced on the Board by two Assistant Surveyors (H. M. Colvin, *History of the King's Works* V [HMSO, 1976], 49-50). Queen Anne's death seems to have put a stop to this idea.

†'The first knight that King George made is one Vanbrugh, a silly Fellow, who is the Architect of Woodstock' (Thomas Hearne, *Diary*, September 1714).

Other changes took place during the following months. The separate Office of Works at Windsor, where Wren had been Comptroller for nearly twenty-eight years, was abolished in August and its responsibilities taken over by Scotland Yard. And to mark the start of the new regime, nearly all of the Clerks were replaced. Those who lost their jobs included Thomas Bateman, Bishop Matthew's grandson John Ball, Christopher Wren junior and William Dickinson the younger. (Poor Dickinson had enjoyed the post of Clerk of Works at the palaces of Whitehall, Westminster and St James's for less than two years; he was replaced by Nicholas Hawksmoor.) But by far the most remarkable feature of the reforms was that Wren himself was allowed to remain in office. True, his authority was dramatically curtailed: 'Alltho' I had the honour to be first nam'd with the old title of Surveyor,' he recalled a few years later, 'yet in acting I had no power to over-rule, or give a casting-vote.'[23] Overall control of the department was now vested in the Commission; this was obviously one of the main reasons for the reforms. But why didn't the new administration just dismiss him? At almost eighty-three it was clearly time for him to go; there were serious doubts about his competence; and his political allegiances lay with the outgoing dynasty.

We shall probably never know the reasoning behind Lord Halifax's decision to renew Wren's patent, or the extent to which the old Surveyor was personally involved in planning the future of the Office of Works. It seems likely that Vanbrugh was instrumental in keeping him on, and his remark, already quoted, about how he refused the Surveyorship 'out of Tenderness for Sr Chr: Wren' probably refers to his own discussions with Halifax in the winter of 1714/15. It seemed unnecessarily cruel to turf out of office a man he had worked with for more than ten years. As it was, Wren was certain to die quite soon, and there was no other contender for the post except him. At forty-one, he was relatively young. He could afford to bide his time.

The other question, of course, is why Wren didn't seize the opportunity to retire gracefully. He had already made preparations against the day, persuading the Crown to grant him a fifty-year lease on his official residence at Hampton Court and, in 1713, laying out £19,000 for a country estate. Wroxall Priory in Warwickshire was bought for Christopher junior, with the intention of setting him up as a member of the landed gentry; and his father must have imagined the time when he could relax with his family in the pleasant surroundings of the rather beautiful Elizabethan mansion.[24] But the habit of power was hard to break. He had walked with kings for too long, and now he found it impossible to believe that they could manage without him. He couldn't see that the reforms of 1715 were an attempt to bring much-needed financial order to the Works: as far as he was concerned, they represented a personal favour from George I. 'In regard of my great age, He was pleas'd of his Royal Clemency to ease me of the burden of the business of that Office, by appointing other worthy Gentlemen with me in Commission.'[25]

He did begin to slow down. When a new Commission for Chelsea Hospital was appointed in 1715, he was not included; and in the summer of 1716 he resigned his Surveyorship of Greenwich Hospital in favour of Vanbrugh – perhaps as part of a deal done with the latter over the Office of Works. The Commission for Rebuilding the City Churches, which had been given a new lease of life when the coal tax was renewed for sixteen years back in 1700, was drawing to a close, half a century after the Great Fire. However, with the single exception of St Thomas the Apostle in Southwark, which was a late addition to the building programme, all of the new churches had been fit for use since the turn of the century. Since then it had been a matter only of adding towers and steeples; and for years now, Wren had been content to leave the construction of these, and often the actual design, to the successors to Hooke and Oliver, William Dickinson and Nicholas Hawksmoor, both of whom had trained in his office. A lack of documentary evidence means that Wren's precise involvement in this last phase is even less clear than his role in the initial collaboration with Hooke. But he could rest easy in the knowledge that London's skyline had been created in an image which, if it wasn't entirely his own invention, was at least his own intention – no small achievement.

The City Churches Commission was finally wound up in 1717, the year after the coal dues ran out. But Wren kept on the Surveyorship of Westminster Abbey and, if he steered clear of the Chapter House at St Paul's, he was remarkably diligent in his attendances at meetings of the King's Works, putting in an appearance at all but 43 of the 204 Board meetings which were held between May 1715 and April 1718. Vanbrugh, who later claimed that 'I (in effect) presided at the Board of Works', missed thirty-two.[26]

For three years, life at Scotland Yard had flowed along quite smoothly. It looked for all the world as though Wren would die happy in office and Vanbrugh, who used some pretty deft accounting to show how the reforms were benefiting the Treasury, would step effortlessly into his shoes. Neither man reckoned on William Benson.

Like Pietro Torrigiano, who has gone down in history as the man who broke Michelangelo's nose, Benson is remembered today for ousting Wren from the Surveyorship. And with more justification. Torrigiano was a sculptor of genius; Benson was a crook with the management skills of a sheep and the moral rectitude of a tax-gatherer. The son of a Bristol iron-merchant, he was an architectural dilettante and an ardent Palladian – not that we should hold either of those things against him – who first came to the notice of George I in 1716, when he designed a water-work for the King's gardens at Herrenhausen in Hanover. This and his support for the whigs meant that soon the talk was of how, 'it is very well known that Mr B [is] a favourite of the Germans'.[27] He looked for advancement, and in 1717 he was promised the reversion of a lucrative sinecure, the Auditorship of the Imprests, as and when one of the two incumbent Auditors died. While he waited, he hit on the idea of taking over the King's Works. With more influential friends at court than the old Surveyor, he succeeded: Wren's patent was revoked on 26 April 1718, after forty-nine years in office.

This was hard. But there was nothing to be done, and Wren received the news stoically. He duly cleared out his house in Scotland Yard and 'betook himself to a Country Retirement' at Hampton Court,[28] where he sought refuge in the study of scripture. He was, *Parentalia* records, 'chearful in solitude, and as well pleased to die in the Shade as in the Light'.[29]

But Benson wasn't finished with him yet. He persuaded the Treasury to turn back the clock to 1715 and abolish Lord Halifax's reform of the Works, leaving him with all the powers Wren had once enjoyed. Then he sacked Hawksmoor, giving his posts as Secretary to the Board and Clerk of the Works at Whitehall, Westminster and St James's to his own brother. He gave the Clerkship of the Works at Winchester to the Mayor of Shaftesbury, where he happened to be seeking re-election as an MP; and he did his level best to have Vanbrugh removed from the Comptrollership. One of the 'dark Stroaks in the King's Closet', as Vanbrugh put it,[30] was to accuse the ex-Surveyor and the other Officers of gross mismanagement, a charge which the Treasury took seriously – seriously enough to demand an answer from Wren. Bruised, battered and bewildered at this ignominious end to his career, he replied:

> Notwithstanding the Pretentions of the Present Surveyor's Manage-
> ment to be better then that of the late Commissioners, or Theirs to
> be better then what preceeded, yet I am perswaded, upon an impartial

view of Matters . . . there will be no just grounds for the censuring former Managements; and as I am Dismiss'd, haveing worn out (by God's mercy) a long Life in the Royal service, and haveing made some Figure in the World, I hope it will be allow'd me to Die in Peace.[31]

Benson's attempt to discredit Wren and the others failed, and no more was heard of the charges. The remainder of his term as Surveyor, which has rightly been described as 'beyond question the most disastrous episode in the whole history of the royal works',[32] was mercifully short. Having bullied and alienated Vanbrugh and the other officers of the Board (the Paymaster, Charles Dartiquenave, was 'scar'd out of his Witts'),[33] he brought the Works to a virtual standstill. No business was done and the regular monthly meetings fell by the wayside, while Benson devised an ingenious plan to contract out the maintenance of the royal palaces for an annual fee of £12,000. Ostensibly the contractors were to be the Master Mason, Master Carpenter and Master Bricklayer, but in reality they would have been frontmen for Benson himself. 'They were told,' wrote Vanbrugh in a letter of complaint to the Treasury, '. . . that they should have each of them sallaries of about 200£ per Ann: Each, for the use of their Names, wch was either for Bribes or Hush money.'[34] And emulating Wren's dream of a new Parliament House, the Surveyor concocted an ingenious scheme to rebuild the Houses of Parliament in collaboration with his new Deputy, the Scottish architect Colen Campbell; not content to leave anything to chance, they announced to the Lords that their Chamber was about to collapse. The stonework was not fit to bear any weight, the wall plates were quite rotten and the roof in such a dangerous condition that even with props there was no guarantee that it wouldn't fall down. Their Lordships had better evacuate the premises without delay.

This was Benson's undoing. The Lords were unconvinced and called for a second opinion from Benjamin Jackson, who had no love for his new employer. He promptly blew the whistle and exposed the claims as a pack of lies. Benson was dismissed in July 1719, having, as Hawksmoor said, 'got more in one year (for confusing the King's Works) than Sr Chris Wren did in 40 years for his honest endeavours'.[35]

We don't know how Wren reacted to the news of his successor's spectacular fall from grace; no doubt it helped to put some cheer into his 'chearful solitude' at Hampton Court. But the damage had been done, and at eighty-six there was of course no question of his returning to the

Works. It wasn't simply a matter of his age, either; times were changing. Benson may have been the immediate cause of his dismissal, but for some years before this the cognoscenti had been murmuring against the Baroque and its leading exponent. In 1712 the Earl of Shaftesbury, in his famous letter to Lord Somers *Concerning the Art, or Science of Design,* had explicitly condemned Wren: 'Thro' several reigns we have patiently seen the noblest publick Buildings perish (if I may say so) under the Hand of one single Court-Architect; who, if he had been able to profit by Experience, wou'd long since, at our expence, have prov'd the greatest Master in the World. But I question whether our Patience is like to hold much longer.'[36] Shaftesbury wanted a new national style which was more in tune with the constitutional freedoms the whigs had wrested from the Stuarts back in 1688, a style which wasn't tainted by its associations with the absolutist tyrannies of the past. He didn't define it; but Benson, Campbell and their friends did. The works of 'the renowned Palladio' and his English disciple 'the Famous Inigo Jones' showed the way ahead. After Palladio, wrote Campbell, 'the great Manner and exquisite Taste of Building is lost'.[37]

This is not the place to discuss either the eighteenth-century Palladian revival or the merits of its exponents' passion for the Rule of Taste, their more earnest response to antiquity and the anti-Stuart ideological programme that underpinned that response. But it is worth bearing in mind that Palladianism's early landmarks were all built, or at least begun, in Wren's lifetime: William Benson's own Wilbury House, Wiltshire (1710), designed 'in the Stile of Inigo Jones';[38] Campbell's Wanstead House in Essex (1713–20) and his Stourhead (1721–4, also in Wiltshire), designed for Benson's brother-in-law, the banker Henry Hoare. The same is true for the initial salvos in the Palladian attack on Wren and the Baroque. The first volume of Campbell's *Vitruvius Britannicus* (1715) praised the buildings of Wren's generation, mentioning by name the Surveyor, his son (who was credited there with the design of Marlborough House), Vanbrugh, Hawksmoor and Talman. But the praise was hollow: Campbell poured scorn on the Baroque, dismissing the works of Bernini and Fontana as 'affected and licentious' and censured Baroque architecture as 'Parts . . . without Proportion, Solids without their true Bearing, Heaps of Material without Strength, excessive Ornaments without Grace'.[39] Giacomo Leoni's edition of Palladio's *Quattro Libri d'Architettura* appeared the following year, with a frontispiece by Sebastiano Ricci showing Father Time unveiling a bust of Palladio, while Britannia, accompanied by two putti bearing the royal arms, looks on. The message was clear: it was for England and George I to reveal Palladio's glories, thus rescuing English architecture from the dire straits into which it had been led by Wren and his contemporaries. It is significant that Benson's successor as Surveyor-General in 1719 was not Vanbrugh (much to his chagrin) but a well-known Palladian named Thomas Hewett.

By the mid-1720s Palladianism had a stranglehold on building in England. With the paint scarcely dry on Thornhill's murals, St Paul's was already being criticized for being 'too heavy ... and too gross'[40] – by which was meant too Baroque. Lord Burlington, obeying Pope's injunction to 'make falling Arts your care'[41] and restore Palladio and Jones to their rightful place as the only masters, was now the acknowledged arbiter of taste. (When the new portico of St Paul's was unveiled Burlington was overcome by the thought of Jones's west front and exclaimed, 'When the Jews saw the second temple, they wept.') It was generally recognized that in England 'the reigning taste is Palladio's style of building and a man is heretick that should talk of Michel Angelo or any other modern architect'.[42]

But by the mid-1720s Wren was dead.

Death came quietly in the end, as a friend. Wren was unable to do much in his last years: Christopher junior, who was already compiling *Parentalia*, said that 'Time had enfeebled his limbs', but that his mind stayed clear and in spite of everything he remained free from 'all Moroseness in Behaviour or Aspect'.[43] That isn't quite true. Hurt by his unceremonious ejection from the Works, baffled by a new architectural milieu which placed no value on his life's work, he couldn't keep back a creeping sense of failure and regret. It was all Charles II's fault, he used to tell his son, and anyone else who would listen. By offering him the Surveyorship back in 1669, the King had lured him away from his scientific studies and obliged him 'to spend all his time in Rubbish'.[44] Now he wished he had been a physician instead of an architect. Then he would have made some real money.

So the disillusioned doctor who never was sat brooding in his house at Hampton Court. He studied his Bible, seeking comfort in religion and rebuilding Old Testament monuments in the safety of his own mind. He went over his old work in astronomy and mathematics, determined to find the answer to the problem of longitude which had evaded him since the 1650s, and dreaming of the £20,000 prize that would be his if he succeeded. Every now and then he travelled up from

Hampton Court to stay at a house he had leased in St James's Street and, according to a touching nineteenth-century legend, he paid unofficial visits to St Paul's, where he checked on the progress of 'my great work'.

On one of his trips to London he caught a cold, and over the next few days he became increasingly ill and confused. On 25 February 1723 a servant went into his room to wake him from his afternoon nap, and couldn't. That was all.

18

An Ornament to the Age

As dusk fell on the evening of Tuesday 5 March 1723, Sir Christopher Wren's funeral cortège left the house in St James's Street. Preceded by a cavalcade and followed by a train of fifteen coaches carrying friends, relatives and 'many persons of honour and distinction', the hearse made its way eastwards. 'With great funeral State and Solemnity',[1] the cortège travelled along the Strand and Fleet Street, through the medieval Ludgate, until it arrived at last before St Paul's Cathedral. There, in the south-east corner of the crypt, the body of the nation's greatest architect joined his daughter Jane, his sister Susan Holder and her husband William. A simple stone was inscribed with an equally simple message:

> Here lieth
> Sir Christopher Wren Knight
> The Builder of this Cathedral
> Church of St Paul, &c
> Who dyed
> In the year of Our Lord
> MDCCXXIII.
> And of his age XCI.

Dean Godolphin at least had the decency to waive the burial fees.

Wren's name was still a household word, and the London news-sheets mourned the passing of 'the most famous Architect in all Europe', 'a great Mathematician and the best Architect of his Time'.[2] But there was no denying that his reputation had taken some knocks over the past ten years or so, and as the Palladians continued to deride his heavy buildings and lightweight classical scholarship, others came forward to plead his cause. Daniel Defoe, in the second volume of his *Tour through the Whole Island of Great Britain* (1725), heaped praise on Hampton Court and the hospitals at Greenwich (still unfinished) and Chelsea. In Oxford, the Sheldonian was 'in its grandeur and magnificence, infinitely superior to any thing in the world of its kind'.[3] If St Paul's and the City churches seemed solid and plain in comparison with the cathedrals and churches of Catholic Europe, that was a positive virtue: they showed a 'true Protestant plainness'.[4] This perception of Wren's architecture as somehow morally superior to the European mainstream, the pinnacle of an English Renaissance untainted by Popish practices, would eventually come to figure large in discussions of his work.

His greatest champion, understandably, was his son. Christopher junior was sole heir and executor of Wren's estate. (The will, drawn up in 1713, directed him to take particular care that poor Billy was looked after until his death.)* Christopher junior had already started collaborating with his father on catalogues 'of all the Works of Sr: Chr: Wren that could be discoverd, under the distant Heads and Branches of Mathematicks and Architecture' in 1719.[5] Five years later, with a view to illustrating these catalogues – and commemorating his father's achievements – he commissioned a series of engravings of subjects including the Monument, the plan for rebuilding the City, the Great Model design for St Paul's, and a curious pyramid emblazoned with sixty-four medallions, each inscribed with the name of one of Wren's buildings.[6] He also wrote a second, more laudatory memorial for the tomb, praising Wren's work for the public good and including what has become one of the most famous epitaphs of all time: *Lector Si Monumentum Requiris Circumspice* [Reader, if you seek his monument, look around].

The catalogues, to which Christopher would return again and again right up until his death in 1747, were eventually published (without the original set of engravings) by his own son Stephen in 1750 under the title of *Parentalia: or Memoirs of the Family of the Wrens*. As well as making substantial claims for Wren's work in anatomy and the mathematical sciences and providing the first detailed account of his buildings, Christopher went to considerable lengths to defend his father's memory

---

*John Ward, who was in regular contact with Christopher junior when he was writing his *Lives of the Professors of Gresham College* (1740), said that William Wren died unmarried on 15 March 1738.

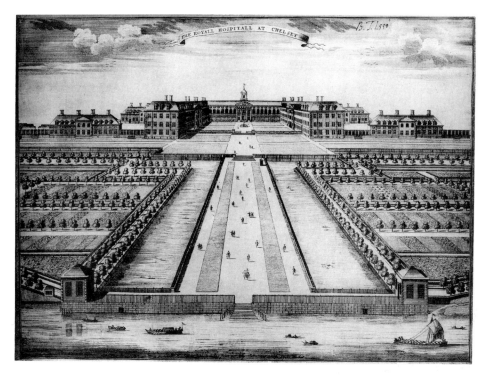

34. The Royal Hospital, Chelsea.

35. The Palace of Whitehall from the Thames, *c.* 1695.
Inigo Jones's Banqueting House stands at the left of the picture, at right angles to the Privy Gallery range. Scotland Yard, where Wren had his official residence as Surveyor of the Royal Works, is at the extreme right, between the river and the street.

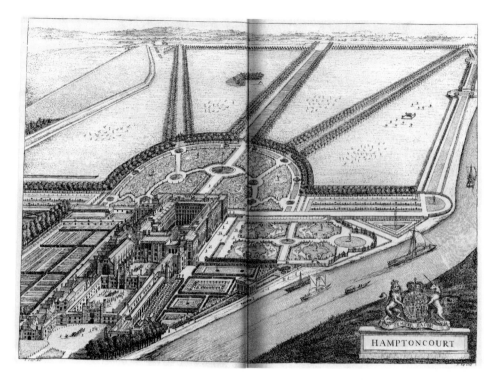

HAMPTONCOURT

36. A bird's-eye view of
Hampton Court Palace,
c. 1712. Wren's Fountain
Court looks out onto
the vast semicircular
parterre.

37. Hampton Court
Palace: the centre of
the south front.

38. Wren's first scheme for the Royal Hospital for Seamen at Greenwich. John Webb's King Charles II Block of 1664–9 is on the right.

39. Tring Manor, Hertfordshire – 'of Sir Chr Wren's invention', according to Roger North. The engraving, which dates from 1700, is by John Oliver.

40. Samuel Gribelin's 1702 engraving of St Paul's.
Wren had not yet decided on the final form of either the dome or the two west towers.

(*Facing page*) 41. The west front of St Paul's Cathedral.

42. The interior of St Paul's in the eighteenth century, looking north-west across the dome space.

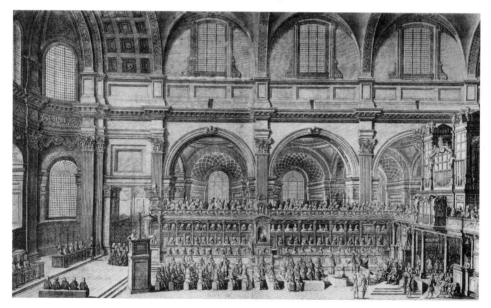

43. St Paul's Cathedral: the choir on 31 December 1706, during a service of thanksgiving attended by Queen Anne and both Houses of Parliament.

FACING PAGE
(*Above*) 44. St Paul's Cathedral, looking towards the choir.
(*Below*) 45. St Paul's during the Blitz – 'the parish church of the British Empire'.

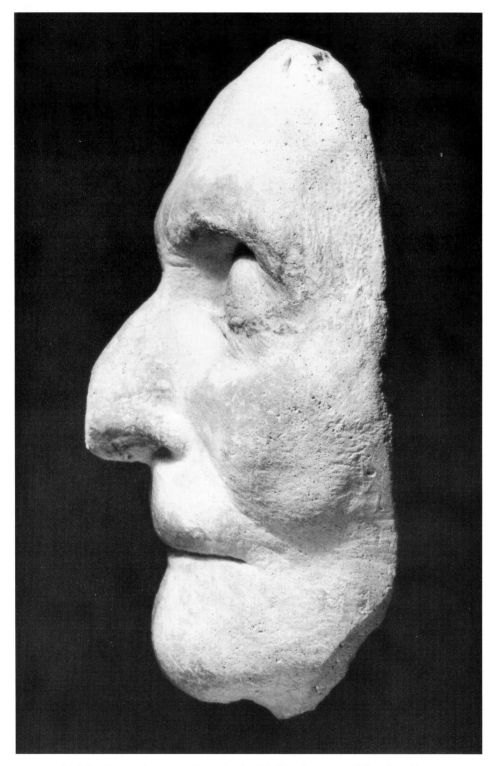

46. 'Haveing made some Figure in the World, I hope it will be allow'd me to Die in Peace': the death mask of Sir Christopher Wren.

against the critics. Mindful of the persistent rumours about corruption, he emphasized that Wren had always preferred 'the publick Service to any private Ends';[7] and claimed that he had invariably rejected the chance to take 'any private Advantage of his own, by the Acquest of Wealth, of which he had always a great Contempt'.[8] Objections to particular features of the design of St Paul's continued to be voiced throughout the 1720s and 1730s, and Christopher answered them all with a mixture of practical common sense and appeals to ancient authority. There was no grand piazza to form a stately approach to the cathedral, as there is at St Peter's, Rome, for example, because there was no money to buy up the adjoining property. There were no window-openings in the outer dome (as, again, there are at St Peter's) because they weren't needed: Wren sunk light wells around the lantern, 'so that he only ribb'd the outward Cupola, which he thought less Gothick, than to stick it full of such little Lights in three Stories . . . which could not without Difficulty be mended, and if neglected would soon damage the Timbers'.[9] Those who said it was unorthodox to double the columns of the west portico should look to the Basilica of Constantine. And if anyone thought it improper 'to incorporate great and small Pillars together; as is done in the Aisles at St Paul's, let him consider the Basilica of the Colonia Julia, at Fanum; which is the only Piece Vitruvius owns himself to be the Author of'.[10]

The fact that Christopher took such pains to answer criticism is revealing in itself. Wren's scientific achievements were beyond dispute: John Ward, in his *Lives of the Professors of Gresham College*, was merely reflecting contemporary opinion when he wrote a glowing appreciation of a man whose invention was so fertile, his discoveries so numerous and useful, 'that he will always be esteemed a benefactor to mankind, and an ornament to the age, in which he lived'.[11] Mathematics and astronomy had a limited popular appeal; but architecture is the most public of the arts, and where Wren's architecture was concerned, the critics had their knives out. There was no place for his flexible approach to classical convention in the strict Palladianism of Burlington and his followers. Inigo Jones was the only respectable seventeenth-century architect, and

> That true politeness we can only call,
> Which looks like Jones's fabric at Whitehall;
> Where just proportion we with pleasure see,
> Though built by rule, yet from all stiffness free.[12]

Polite mid-eighteenth century taste veered sharply away from the monumental splendours of St Paul's and Hampton Court, as it did from the works of Wren's contemporaries. Vanbrugh's houses were universally condemned for their weight and clumsiness; Talman's Chatsworth possessed 'few of those architectural beauties which are now so conspicuous in more modern structures'.[13] The churches of Wren and Hawksmoor had too much pride, and not enough holiness:

> One might expect a sanctity of style
> August and manly in an holy pile,
> And think an architect extremely odd,
> To build a playhouse for the church of God;
> Yet half our churches, such the mode that reigns,
> Are Roman theatres, or Grecian fanes;
> Where broad-arch'd windows to the eye convey
> The keen diffusion of too strong a day;
> Where, in the luxury of wanton pride,
> Corinthian columns languish side by side,
> Clos'd by an altar exquisitely fine,
> Loose and lascivious as a Cyprian shrine.[14]

There were dissenting voices: in 1749 the architect and pioneering town planner John Gwynn published *A Plan for Rebuilding the City of London after the Great Fire in 1666, designed by that Great Architect Sir Christopher Wren;*[15] and four years later Hogarth praised St Paul's in his *Analysis of Beauty*, calling Wren the Prince of Architects. But they were voices in the wilderness. To the generation of neo-classicists which made its appearance in the 1750s and 1760s, Wren's buildings seemed even clumsier than they had to the Burlingtonians. A spate of scholarly archaeological publications – Robert Wood's *Ruins of Palmyra* and *Ruins of Balbec*, Stuart and Revett's *Antiquities of Athens*, Robert Adam's *Ruins of the Palace of the Emperor Diocletian at Spalatro in Dalmatia* – took them back beyond Palladio, to the ancient world itself. This process of rediscovery gave them yet more rules to follow – and showed them more rules which Wren had broken.

Towards the end of the century the slow rehabilitation of the English Baroque began, with a 1786 lecture to students at the Royal Academy by Joshua Reynolds, who applauded Vanbrugh for his exuberant display of imagination at Blenheim Palace and Castle Howard. A little later the Picturesque writer Uvedale Price admired the way he had brought together 'in one building [Blenheim] the beauty and magnificence of Grecian architecture, the picturesqueness of the Gothic, and the massive grandeur of a castle'.[16] But Wren's cool, essentially intellectual style possessed none of Vanbrugh's melodrama and brio. Reynolds was relieved that his plan for London never came to anything: the result would have been 'rather unpleasing; the uniformity might have produced weariness, and a slight degree of disgust'.[17]

The Surveyor's ghost was held in limbo between a medieval past and a neo-classical present, his architecture neither picturesque enough for the antiquarians nor scholarly enough for the moderns. 'Why not, when rebuilding in London, follow such a model?' asked a medievally inclined tourist, confronted with the thirteenth-century splendours of Lincoln Cathedral in 1791: 'How superior to a lumbering Grecian St Paul's.'[18]

At the very end of the eighteenth century, however, when even the classicists were beginning to tire of dull good manners and 'Adametic' elegance, there were signs that Wren had served his time in purgatory. Dublin's new Custom House on the Liffey (1781–91), by the London-born James Gandon, has a dome which is obviously influenced by Greenwich Hospital, daring to combine Wren motifs with a more orthodox Palladianism in a way that would never have occurred to Gandon's more staid contemporaries. The same architect's Four Courts (1786–1802, also in Dublin) shows a similar debt to Wren: its colonnaded drum evokes memories of St Paul's, although the low dome which crowns it owes more to French neo-classicism; and the façade is loosely based on the lower parts of the west front of the cathedral.[19]

Attractive though they were, Gandon's borrowings from the Baroque had little impact over in England. But in the first half of the nineteenth century Wren found two more influential champions much closer to home. The first was James Elmes, an indifferent architect who combined the Surveyorship of the Port of London with a career as a lecturer and architectural writer. While still in his twenties Elmes developed what was, for the time, an unusual interest in Wren's work. He catalogued drawings and acquired manuscripts; and in 1823 he published the first detailed biography of the architect, to mark the centenary of his death. Pulling together *Parentalia*'s motley collection of documents and observations into a continuous narrative, its full title was *Memoirs of the Life and Works of Sir Chr Wren, with a View of the Progress of Architecture in England, from the Reign of Charles I to the End of the Seventeenth Century* – a brave statement in itself, since, when it was published, very few people thought English architecture *had* progressed from the age of Inigo Jones to that of Wren. The *Memoirs* was full of mistakes and misattributions; but 'that incorrigibly inaccurate old gossip', as the editors of the Wren Society volumes affectionately called him,[20] did his hero an important service, legitimizing the study of his work and presenting him as the only seventeenth-century architect whose buildings were on a par with those of Jones.★

Wren's other advocate was Charles Robert Cockerell. One of the nineteenth century's most remarkable architects, Cockerell succeeded his father Samuel Pepys Cockerell (who was named for the diarist, his great-great-uncle) as Surveyor to St Paul's in 1819. Perhaps it was the close acquaintance with Wren's greatest building that taught him respect for the unfashionable end of the seventeenth century. Whatever the reason, he had little time for the great names of the eighteenth – James Paine's buildings showed 'a certain baldness & vacancy', and Adam 'was not an artist of any force nor of very sound judgement'[21] – but he developed a passionate attachment to the English Baroque in general and Wren in particular. 'The Scheme of an architectural combination will be comprehended by very few who do not study the subject with intelligence', he wrote in 1826. 'It is the first excellence, to which proportion & Taste are secondary. In this order of merit Sir C Wren stood higher than any, either the Italians or the moderns.'[22] And he kept this high opinion throughout his life. 'Nothing in Paris can compare with Greenwich,' he said in a Royal Academy lecture in 1856: St Paul's was 'without a rival in beauty, unity and variety', St Stephen Walbrook a 'bubble of unexampled lightness which has stood more than 150 years and not yet blown away'.[23]

Cockerell's reverence for Wren influenced his own designs. The interior of St George's Hall, Liverpool, which he completed in 1851–4 after the early death of the original architect, Harvey Lonsdale Elmes (son of James), is a stunning exercise in Wrennian reinterpretation. And when he was given the commission to build a new St Bartholomew-by-the-Exchange in the City, after Wren's church was demolished in 1841 as part of a road-widening scheme, he personally insisted on re-using not only the pews, organ, altarpiece and pulpit, but also the very stones. The west front of the new church (which was itself demolished in 1902) echoed Wren's original: as the architect said at the time, 'We will just

---

★The centenary was presumably also the reason why Wren's bust was chosen to represent Architecture on the pediment of the Academy of Arts in Carlisle in 1823. His unlikely companions were the painter Benjamin West and the sculptor Francis Chantrey. The artist was Paul Nixson of Carlisle.

follow Sir Chr Wren and reproduce the old church as near as we can in its architectural character'.[24]

Cockerell's greatest homage, however, was not a building but a water-colour. *A Tribute to the Memory of Sir Christopher Wren* (1838) was a wonderful capriccio in which he brought fifty-eight of Wren's most famous works together into a single, magical landscape.[25] The Sheldonian rubs shoulders with the library at Trinity; the Monument towers over Greenwich Observatory and Chelsea Hospital; and, almost lost in the clouds, the majestic dome of St Paul's looks down on Winchester Palace and thirty-three of the City churches. The *Tribute*, which was engraved and distributed widely in the 1840s, concentrated the minds of early Victorians on Wren's monumental contribution to English architecture as nothing had before. It dared the establishment to deny that Wren was one of the most gifted architects in the nation's history.

By and large, the establishment agreed with Cockerell. St Paul's was now vying with Westminster Abbey as a shrine to national heroes, and steadily filling up with enormous monuments of varying quality to famous (and not-so-famous) military and naval figures: Nelson was buried there in 1806, for instance, and the Duke of Wellington in 1852 (13,000 people attended his funeral). In an increasingly imperialistic age, the panoply of state funerals and statuary contributed to the cathedral's absorption into British culture and, by association, it enhanced its creator's reputation. Lord Macaulay reckoned that in architecture, 'our country could boast of one truly great man, Christopher Wren', and declared that, 'Even the superb Louis [XIV] has left to posterity no work which can bear a comparison with St Paul's.'[26] Nor was the reappraisal confined to the cathedral: Cockerell's *Tribute* so inspired John Clayton, an eighteen-year-old pupil of his at the Royal Academy, that he spent ten years making measured drawings of all Wren's City churches; the results were published, with a dedication to Cockerell, in 1848. And in a quintessentially Victorian aphorism, Thomas Carlyle decided that Chelsea Hospital was obviously built by a gentleman – the highest praise imaginable.

Just when it seemed that Wren's rehabilitation was complete, however, the Gothic Revival, with its passion for moral architecture and misty medievalism, began to fight back. Wren's 'dishonesty' in concealing the true structure of St Paul's – the screen walls hiding the buttresses, the sham outer dome – was anathema to the Gothicists. *The Ecclesiologist*, a campaigning architectural journal which was read by many High Church Gothicists with more reverence than the Gospels, suggested it would have been better to burn the old fittings from St Bartholomew-by-the-Exchange, and declared Cockerell's new church to be 'disgraceful to the age and city in which it is built'.[27] The mad, fanatical prophet of Gothicism, A. W. N. Pugin, who had borrowed the idea of Cockerell's *Tribute* for his own impression of the contrast between pagan classicism and what he believed to be the true pointed Christian style of architecture, dismissed English Baroque as degenerate and announced that 'when Protestantism did anything of itself, it was ten times worse than their [Roman Catholic] extravagances, since it embodied the same wretched pagan ideas, without either the scale or richness of the foreign architecture of the same period . . . St Paul's Cathedral, London, and many other buildings of the same class, are utter departures from Catholic architecture, and meagre imitations of Italian paganism.'[28] Taking his cue from Pugin, John Ruskin also wanted to turn the clock back to the Middle Ages – not on religious grounds, but because the Gothic represented a pastoral utopia before the factory system and the division of labour had dehumanized the worker and corrupted public taste. Like Pugin, he deplored the English Renaissance (the entire Renaissance, in fact) as a regrettable lapse after the sublime purity of the Gothic. Although he grudgingly allowed Wren to be an artist of 'real intellect and imagination',[29] that was as far as it went: he criticized the rustication at St Paul's – 'the expedient of architects who do not know how to fill up blank spaces' – and described the carved garlands and panels on the exterior as 'an ugly excrescence . . . It makes the rest of the architecture look poverty-stricken, instead of sublime.'[30]

Ironically, it was Ruskin, with his idealization of the pre-industrial past, who indirectly brought about the 'Wrenaissance'. Later Victorian architects, especially the young avant-garde, shared Ruskin's disdain for modern design, but not his conviction that Gothic was the only pre-industrial style worth emulating. The Queen Anne Movement of the 1870s and '80s, with its penchant for soft red brick and white-painted woodwork, looked for inspiration first towards the artisan-builders of the late seventeenth and early eighteenth centuries; then to the hipped roofs and dormer windows of houses such as Roger Pratt's Coleshill and Hugh May's Eltham Lodge (coining in the process the misleading phrase 'a Wren-style house', which still persists to this day); and finally to Hampton Court, Greenwich, Chelsea and Wren himself.

Interest began to stir with the appearance of A. H. Mackmurdo's *Wren's City Churches* (1883), which offered Queen Anne architects a fresh and exciting design vocabulary. Then in 1897 Reginald Blomfield published his *History of Renaissance Architecture in England*, full of praise for 'the most English of all English architects', in whose work he found 'a singularly direct and unaffected method of expression, free from pedantry and foolishness, and, above all, pre-eminently English in its sober power'.[31] Country houses began to appear which borrowed heavily and very freely from Wren. Blomfield's own Moundsmere in Hampshire (1908–9), which harks back to Hampton Court, and Stansted Park, Sussex (1900, by his cousin, Arthur Blomfield) are two notable examples, but there are plenty more. One can see elements of the so-called Wren style in Richard Norman Shaw's Bryanston, Dorset (1889–94). Edwin Lutyens played with neo-Wren at Great Maytham, Rolvenden (1909), and the Salutation, Sandwich (1911), among others. So did Ernest George: his redbrick Ardenrun Place, Surrey (1906–9), for the racing driver Woolf Barnato, was a splendid reinterpretation of domestic English Baroque, complete with dressings of Portland stone, hipped roofs, dormers and a cupola.

Truth to tell, most of the buildings that make up the Edwardian Wrenaissance have little to do with Wren. What the Wrenaissance did, however, was to confirm its namesake's status in the public imagination as *the* quintessential English architect. Now he was praised for breaking the rules, just as he was praised for his solid walls and heavy piers. A slavish adherence to theory was for foreigners who didn't know any better; so were extravagant flights of fancy. Blomfield's assessment of him as the archetype of good honest practicality, 'free from pedantry and foolishness' recurs throughout the writings of early twentieth-century critics. 'One is inclined to think that it is as well, on the whole, that Wren did not go to Italy,' said one; St Paul's 'is prodigiously English', wrote another.[32] J. A. Gotch talked of Wren's 'splendid common-sense', and applauded his cavalier attitude to classical precedent. Referring to Palladian rules of art, he claimed that 'Wren was too powerful a genius, too much occupied in solving constructional problems, to become their slave. He was too busy surmounting real architectural difficulties to occupy his time in half-hearted attempts to translate Italian villas into terms of English mansions.'[33]

The downside of this adulation was the myth-making that accompanied it. Visitors came to pay homage in the room where Wren died at Hampton Court, even though he didn't die there. They came to stand silent before his tomb in St Paul's, and listened in awe as they heard that his was the first grave to be sunk in the cathedral, which it wasn't. And as the legends grew, so did the list of his works, until it seemed that he was responsible for every decent building put up in the later seventeenth century. All Saints Northampton became a Wren church, and the town's Sessions House became a Wren sessions house; both are now thought to be the work of two local surveyors, Henry Bell and Edward Edwards. Bromley College in Kent (architect: Richard Ryder) was given to Wren; so were Morden College, Blackheath, and Rochester Guildhall. The Great Gateway leading from the Temple into Fleet Street was credited to him, although it is now known to have been by Roger North. Then there were the country houses mentioned in Chapter 14 – Arbury and Newby, Belton, Fawley Court and a string of others.★

If Wren was connected with a building, however remotely, it was slotted into the rapidly expanding canon. As early as 1724, Americans were claiming the College of William and Mary in Virginia (put up by the Reverend James Blair in 1695-9) as an original Wren design. Despite the fact that it has burned down and been rebuilt three times since, it is now known as 'the Wren Building', and acclaimed as the oldest college building in the United States. In the 1690s the Surveyor produced a scheme for the church of St Mary's Warwick; it wasn't executed (the church was built to the designs of Sir William Wilson) but that was enough to make St Mary's a Wren church. He approved a design for Lord Ashburnham's family pew at Ampthill in Bedfordshire; it duly became a Wren pew. The Market House in Abingdon was built by one of his masons, Christopher Kempster; almshouses and a church at Farley in Wiltshire were put up for Sir Stephen Fox, who financed the building of Chelsea Hospital; St Mary's Ingestre in Staffordshire was built for Walter Chetwynd, who belonged to the Royal Society at the same time as Wren. They all joined the list.

The deification of 'the most English of all English architects' reached a peak with the bicentenary of his death, in 1923. *The Times* described how the weekend of 24-5 February was marked 'by tributes to the memory of the great architect and by pilgrimages to places which stand as monuments of his genius'.[34] The commemoration service at St Paul's, which took place on Monday 26 February, was a particularly grand affair, attended by the Bishop of London, the Lord Mayor and Sheriffs

---

★The cult occasionally produced some strange and welcome side-effects. At the end of the nineteenth century, for example, the 3rd Earl Brownlow restored Belton House, which had been remodelled by James Wyatt, to its late seventeenth-century glory in the mistaken belief that his family home had been designed by Wren.

and a bevy of establishment figures. The order of service included Psalm 122, from which Bishop Compton had taken his text at the consecration of the choir back in 1697: 'I was glad when they said unto me, Let us go into the house of the LORD.' The Dean took his text for the occasion from Haggai, 2:9: 'The glory of this latter house shall be greater than of the former, saith the LORD of hosts.' After the service was over, a deputation went down into the crypt, where a wreath was laid on Wren's tomb by the President of the Royal Institute of British Architects, Paul Waterhouse, on behalf of the architects of Britain and 'in reverent homage to that great man's name and memory and in profound admiration for his mighty works'; French architects presented a palm in honour of the '*grande artiste, grand citoyen, grand patriote*'; and a second wreath was laid on behalf of the Architectural League of New York, with a card declaring that Wren's work 'marked so distinct a step in world architecture, and to so large a degree influenced the Colonial architecture of America'.[35]

Yet another wreath was laid before Kneller's painting in the National Portrait Gallery. A pilgrimage of thanksgiving was organized by clergy at some of the surviving City churches; they started from St Lawrence Jewry complete with choirs, vestments and banners, and spent an afternoon processing from one church to another. The young Aldous Huxley celebrated with an eccentric essay in which, besides taking an entertaining side-swipe at the Arts and Crafts movement and 'the nauseous affectation of "sham peasantry"' in architecture, he reinvented Wren as a character from *The Forsyte Saga*:

> a great gentleman: one who valued dignity and restraint and who, respecting himself, respected also humanity; one who desired that men and women should live with the dignity, even the grandeur, befitting their proud human title; one who despised meanness and oddity as much as vulgar ostentation; one who admired reason and order, who distrusted all extravagance and excess. A gentleman, the finished product of an old and ordered civilisation.[36]

And a special exhibition at the RIBA's headquarters proudly displayed, like the relics of a medieval saint, the love-letter to Faith Coghill, 'a fine embroidered waistcoat which [Wren] presumably wore on great occasions', and a boxwood bas-relief of the architect by Grinling Gibbons.[37] (The relief may not have been by Gibbons. It may not even have depicted Wren.)

True, some of the paeans of praise were qualified. In his memorial sermon, the Dean of St Paul's defined Wren's attributes as an architect as rationality, completion and sober dignity, saying that these qualities appealed to his age – 'a sane and sensible age with not much poetry about it'.[38] Mervyn Macartney, the Cathedral Surveyor, entertained the audience at a commemoration banquet thrown by the RIBA with an account of the structural flaws in the dome. And in a ramble round Hampton Court organized by the RIBA and the London Society, the Director of the Office of Works, Sir Frank Baines, dwelt at unnecessary length on the fact that Wren had 'demolished much of the incomparable Tudor work, including the magnificent state apartments of Henry VIII'.[39] But in general the bicentenary was a national celebration. Never had an English architect been accorded such an honour. In fact, with the single exception of Shakespeare, I'm hard put to think of *any* figure from English history who has ever received such an awesome display of reverence and gratitude.

The bicentenary celebrations had several results. One – the whole *raison d'être* for the revels, as far as the authorities were concerned – was a much-needed boost to a St Paul's repair fund which had been set up in 1913, when it became obvious that the cathedral was growing unstable. At one stage a 'Dangerous Structure' notice was served on the building: the dome was found to be six inches wider from north to south than from east to west, with a slight break at each end; and it was tilting towards the south-west. By 1930 a total of £400,000 had been raised and spent on strengthening the eight piers supporting the dome and the four bastions in the angles of the crossing, and on reinforcing the dome with new alloy steel bars and chains.

A second offshoot was the formation in March 1923 of the Wren Society, the aim of which was 'the elucidation of the career and achievements of the great architect, by searching out and publishing original drawings, documents and facts of proved authenticity'.[40] It has become fashionable over the last thirty years or so to talk rather patronizingly of the Society's efforts, especially that reference to 'proved authenticity'. And to be sure, in the twenty volumes of letters, building accounts and plates which went out to subscribers each year up to 1943, the editors often let their enthusiasm for their subject get the better of their scholarship. (They also decided to abandon an original plan to cover Wren's career as a scientist.) But the Wren Society volumes still represent a truly remarkable achievement. Subscribers included not only prominent architects such as Lutyens, Aston Webb and Albert

Richardson, but institutions across the globe from California to Copenhagen, Yale and Princeton to Berlin, Sydney and South Africa; and if the Society made mistakes and misattributions, credit is due to it for its role in turning Wren into an internationally famous figure.

A third consequence of the bicentenary was a heightened appreciation of the City churches – those that were left, anyway. Eighteen had already been demolished. As we've seen, the first to go was St Christopher-le-Stocks, pulled down in 1782–4 in the wake of the Gordon Riots, after the Governor of the Bank of England persuaded Parliament that insurrectionists might use it to launch an assault on the Bank. Over the next sixty years, road-widening and improvement schemes accounted for St Michael Crooked Lane (1831), St Bartholomew-by-the-Exchange (1841) and St Benet Fink (1846). But the biggest threat came from within. The Anglican authorities had been struggling with the problem of a declining residential population in the City of London ever since the nineteenth century; and the 1860 Union of Benefices Act, which gave the Church powers to amalgamate parishes and demolish redundant buildings, paved the way for thirteen more casualties between 1867 (St Benet Gracechurch) and 1904 (St George Botolph Lane). St Mary Magdalen Old Fish Street, which was damaged by fire in 1886, was also pulled down, even though it was insured and reparable.[41]

Various steps were taken to extend the work of demolition. The Phillimore Commission of 1919 proposed the destruction of a further nineteen churches, but in the face of opposition from the Corporation of the City of London, the Royal Academy, the RIBA, the National Trust and the Victoria and Albert Museum, the scheme was dropped. It was, however, resurrected in a slightly different form in November 1924, when the Church of England's Assembly voted by an overwhelming majority for a new Union of Benefices and Disposal of Churches (Metropolis) Measure. If the Measure had been passed by Parliament, it would have allowed for the demolition of any City church and the sale of its site; it provoked an uproar. Blomfield wrote a long letter to *The Times,* complaining that 'these buildings are a priceless legacy of the past which it is our duty to preserve for posterity'.[42] The same day *The Times* took up the fight in a leader which questioned the Anglican hierarchy's right to treat 'Church buildings, especially when they happen to be famous and beautiful, as its own property'.[43] Others rallied to the cause. The demolition of the City churches would be 'a double sacrilege', said one writer. 'They are consecrated not only to our religious sympathies, but to our national pride.'[44] After widespread protests, Parliament rejected the Measure. But in 1939 the earlier Act of 1860 was invoked to destroy one more church, All Hallows Lombard Street.[45]

German bombers did even more damage than the Church of England. Twenty-two of Wren's churches were devastated during the Second World War. Nine were hit on a single night. But if anything, the Blitz only served to strengthen Wren's hold on the public imagination. The image of a miraculously preserved St Paul's, swathed in smoke and surrounded by ruins and rubble, became a potent symbol of defiance and salvation. Bloody but unbowed, it was a sign that God was on the country's side; and that Wren's masterpiece, 'the parish church of the British Empire',[46] had been singled out for divine favour.★

Thirteen of the damaged churches were restored after the war. Even so, only twenty-three – fewer than half of the original fifty-six – are still standing today. But the post-war generation's respect for Wren, and the welcome imposition of statutory controls on historic buildings, has meant that whether or not they still serve viable congregations, it has become inconceivable that buildings of the stature of St Stephen Walbrook, St James Piccadilly and St Mary-le-Bow should be bulldozed and forgotten. The survivors are all now Grade I listed, and while suggestions for alternative uses still surface from time to time, their future seems reasonably secure.

But it was the cathedral, by now inextricably bound up in the national consciousness, which kept Wren's memory green in the second half of the twentieth century. When in 1951 George VI launched the Festival of Britain as a 'corporate re-affirmation of faith in the nation's future',[47] he launched it at St Paul's. When Charles, Prince of Wales and Lady Diana Spencer made their ill-fated match thirty years later, millions of people across the globe watched the fairy-tale unfold at St Paul's. And when in 1987 Prince Charles gave his famous Mansion House speech attacking modern architecture, Wren's cathedral was the springboard for his vision of the City:

> I would like to see a roofscape that gives the impression that St Paul's is floating above it like a great ship on the sea. I would also like to see

★The cathedral was actually hit several times. We can attribute the fact that it suffered no serious damage to the astonishing bravery and quick thinking of the staff, but its survival was indeed little short of a miracle.

the kinds of materials Wren might have used – soft red brick and stone dressings perhaps, and the ornament and detail of classical architecture, but on a scale humble enough not to compete with the monumentality of St Paul's.[48]

Any assessment of Wren's contribution to cultural history has to contend with this iconic status. Expressing admiration for St Paul's or the library at Trinity or Greenwich Hospital is rather like saying that Shakespeare wrote some good plays. Nearly three hundred years after his death, he is without question the most famous architect in Britain – the only British architect that most people have heard of, in fact.

Judged by his own standards, on the other hand, this ambitious, austere and ultimately unknowable man's career was a failure. His contributions to astronomy and the mathematical sciences – the solid base on which his reputation rested for half of his life – are remembered dimly, if at all. The pioneering experiments in anatomy, the lunar globe, the pivotal role he played in the early Royal Society, are little more than footnotes in the history of science. He never did find a solution to the problem of longitude. The schemes that mattered most to him – a new capital, the Great Model, new palaces at Winchester, Hampton Court and Whitehall – all foundered on the rocks of reality. Even at St Paul's, fate and Dean Godolphin ensured that at the last minute he managed to snatch defeat from the jaws of victory.

But if failure means Hampton Court and St Paul's, the wonder of Trinity College Library and the bubble of unexampled lightness that is St Stephen Walbrook, then perhaps we need more failures in the world. Wren once told Roger North that 'there was that distinction in Nature, of gracefull and ugly; and that it must be so to all creatures that had vision'.[49] He was wrong – not because such an intuitive conception of beauty is outmoded, but because he didn't realize that some people have more vision than others. No one, either then or now, has ever possessed as much vision as Christopher Wren. As a mathematician and astronomer, as a founder of the Royal Society, he changed the course of scientific history. As an architect, he changed the face of England and the course of architectural history. To have changed the world is no small thing. If you seek his monument, look around.

Notes

Introduction

1. *The Diary of John Evelyn*, ed. William Bray (Simpkin, Marshall, Hamilton, Kent & Co., n.d.), 11 July 1654; William Oughtred, *Clavis mathematicae denvo limata . . .* (1652), preface.

Chapter 1

1. Anthony Wood to John Aubrey, in *Aubrey's Brief Lives*, ed. Oliver Lawson-Dick (Mandarin, 1992), lix.
2. MS note by Dean Wren in a copy of Helwing's *Theatrum Historicum* (1618), now in the National Library of Wales.
3. Christopher Wren (ed.), *Parentalia: or, Memoirs of the Family of the Wrens* (1750), 46.
4. Robert Skinner, *A sermon preached before the king at Whitehall* (1634), 21–2.
5. William Laud, *Works* VI, eds. J. Bliss & W. Scott (1847–60), 57.
6. Bodleian Tanner MS 68, fo. 221 r.
7. Quoted in Kenneth Fincham, 'Episcopal Government, 1603–1640', in Kenneth Fincham (ed.), *The Early Stuart Church, 1603–1642* (Macmillan, 1993), 85.
8. Fulke Robarts, *Gods holy house and service* (1639), 41.
9. Jones Waylen, 'Christopher Wren of East Knoyle, DD', *Wiltshire Archaeological Society* III (1857), 117–18.
10. Articles of impeachment, quoted in *Parentalia*, 13–14.
11. Clarendon's *History of the Rebellion in England*, in Christopher Hill, *The Century of Revolution 1603–1714* (Routledge, 1993), 104.

12. Deposition of George Styles of Knoyle, in Waylen, *Wiltshire Archaeological Society* 3, 116.
13. Quoted in *ibid.*, 118.
14. Deposition of John Niffen, 22 July 1646, in Lena Milman, *Sir Christopher Wren* (Duckworth, 1908), 16.
15. 'Parliamentary Church Surveys in Wiltshire 1649–50', *Wiltshire Archaeological Society* 40, in *A Guide to East Knoyle Church* (1996), 9.
16. *Brief Lives*, 161.
17. *ibid.*

Chapter 2

1. *Parentalia*, 346.
2. Quoted in Lena Milman, *Sir Christopher Wren* (Duckworth, 1908), 10.
3. Translated in John Lindsey, *Wren: His Work and Times* (Rich & Cowan, 1951), 42.
4. *Parentalia*, 346.
5. B[ritish] M[useum] Add 6209, fo. 209, in J. A. Bennett, *The Mathematical Science of Christopher Wren* (C[ambridge] U[niversity] P[ress], 1982), 14; *Parentalia*, 185.
6. *Parentalia*, 146.
7. *ibid.*, 142.
8. Henry Peacham, *The Compleat Gentleman* (2nd edn., 1634), 104–5.
9. Evelyn, *Diary*, 1 March 1644.
10. Francis Bacon, *The Advancement of Learning* (1605), Book 1, V, 11.
11. *ibid.*
12. *Compleat Gentleman* (1st edn., 1634), dedication.
13. *Brief Lives*, 160–1.
14. *Parentalia*, 181. Aubrey, on the other hand, suggested it was Wren's father who first instructed him in arithmetic.
15. *Brief Lives*, 160.
16. For example, *see* J. A. Bennett, *Mathematical Science of Wren*, 15.
17. William Holder, *A Discourse concerning Time . . .* (1694), 14.
18. *Brief Lives*, 161; *Parentalia*, 184.
19. Thomas Fale, *Horologiographia: The art of Dialling* (1593), title-page.
20. *The Diary of Samuel Pepys*, ed. Henry B. Wheatley (G. Bell & Sons, 1920), 3 June 1663.
21. *Parentalia*, 182.
22. *Brief Lives*, 129.
23. *ibid.*

24. Quoted in J. J. Keevil, 'Sir Charles Scarburgh', *Annals of Science* 8 (June 1952), 117.
25. *Parentalia*, 186.
26. *ibid.*, 185.
27. Walter Pope, *The Life of Seth, Lord Bishop of Salisbury* (1697; Luttrell Society reprint, 1961), 20–1.
28. C. J. Scriba, 'The Autobiography of John Wallis', *N[otes and] R[ecords of the] R[oyal] S[ociety]* 25 (1970), 40.
29. *ibid.*
30. Francis Bacon, *Novum Organum* Book I (1620), 19.
31. All described in Alexander Ross, *Arcana microcosmi* (1651).
32. Bacon, *Novum Organum*, Argument.
33. Evelyn, *Diary*, 10 March 1695.
34. *Parentalia*, 185.
35. William Oughtred, *Clavis mathematicae denvo limata . . .* (1652), preface.
36. Anthony Wood, *Fasti Oxonienses* II, ed. Philip Bliss (1815–20), 100.
37. John Allibond, trans. in Milman, *Wren*, 27.
38. Pope, *Life of Seth*, 29.
39. *ibid.*
40. *Parentalia*, 183.
41. *ibid.*
42. *Oxford University Statutes*, trans. G. R. M. Ward (1845–51), IX 3 4.
43. 'Statutes of the Savilian Professorships', *Oxford University Statutes* I, 273–7.
44. *ibid.*, 273–4.
45. *Parentalia*, 200.
46. *ibid.*, 195.
47. *ibid.*
48. Quoted in Kenneth Dewhurst, *Thomas Willis as a Physician* (William Andrews Clark Memorial Library, 1964), 4.
49. *ibid.*

Chapter 3

1. John Ward, *Diary* X [1663–5], fo. 56 v.
2. Quoted in Charles Webster, 'The Helmontian George Thomson and William Harvey: the Revival and Application of Splenectomy to Physiological Research', *Medical History* 15 (1971), 159.
3. BM MS Add 25071, fos. 92–3. The precise date of Wren's first injection experiments isn't altogether clear. Timothy Clarke, in a

letter published in the Royal Society's *Philosophical Transactions* (18 May 1668), gives the date as 1656; and J. A. Bennett ('A Study of *Parentalia . . .*', *Annals of Science* 30 [June 1973], 145) argues from other internal evidence in the Petty letter that this is correct. However, Wren refers in the same letter to a new theory of the rotation of Saturn; his hypothesis regarding Saturn's rings wasn't formulated until December 1657. It wasn't until 1658 that Samuel Hartlib, who was usually pretty quick to find out the latest news from the scientific community in Oxford, noted 'A new anatomy experimented at Oxford to open veines and to spout medicins in'.

4. *Parentalia*, 229–30.

5. Pepys, *Diary*, 16 May 1664.

6. Letter from Johan Major of Hamburg to Henry Oldenburg, 13 December 1664, in A. R. Hall & M. B. Hall, *The Correspondence of Henry Oldenburg* II (University of Wisconsin Press, 1966), 336.

7. Quoted in A. R. Hall, *The Scientific Revolution 1500–1800* (Longmans, Green & Co., 1954), 153–4.

8. Walter Charleton, *The Immortality of the Human Soul Demonstrated by the Light of Nature* (1657), 50.

9. 'A Catalogue of New Theories, Inventions, Experiments, and Mechanick Improvements, exhibited by Mr Wren . . .' in *Parentalia*, 198–9.

10. As they had been during the Royalist occupation of Oxford. In 1646 Scarburgh obtained his MD, which theoretically required fourteen years of medical study, after a couple years, because the Chancellor felt sorry for his having been deprived of his Cambridge fellowship and 'spoiled of his library at the beginning of these troubles' (in J. J. Keevil, 'Sir Charles Scarburgh', *Annals of Science* 8 [June 1972], 115).

11. Anthony Wood, *The History and Antiquities of the University of Oxford*, ed. John Gutch (1792–6), quoted by Robert G. Frank jr, 'Medicine', in Nicholas Tyacke (ed.), *The History of the University of Oxford: Seventeenth-Century Oxford* (Clarendon Press, 1997), 543.

12. William Petty to Hartlib, 1649, in G. H. Turnbull, 'Samuel Hartlib's Influence on the Early History of the Royal Society', *N[otes and] R[ecords of the] R[oyal] S[ociety]* 10 (1953), 120–1.

13. *ibid.*

14. John Wallis to Hartlib, in Turnbull, *NRRS* 10, 111.

15. Letter from Seth Ward to Sir Justinian Isham, 27 February 1652, in

H. W. Robinson, 'An Unpublished Letter of Dr Seth Ward Relating to the Early Meetings of the Oxford Philosophical Society', *NRRS* 7 (1949), 69.

16. Evelyn, *Diary*, 8 May 1656.
17. *ibid.*, 10 February 1656.
18. Hartlib, after 7 November 1653, in Turnbull, *NRRS* 10, 114.
19. Evelyn, *Diary*, 13 July 1654.
20. John Wilkins, *Mathematical Magick* (1648), in *The Mathematical and Philosophical Works* (1708), 167.
21. John Wilkins, *Works* II (2nd edn., 1802), 194.
22. *Parentalia*, 215.
23. Wren to unidentified correspondent (perhaps John Wilkins), in *Parentalia*, 215.
24. BM MS Add 25071, fo. 42, in J. A. Bennett, 'A Study of *Parentalia*, with two unpublished letters of Sir Christopher Wren', *Annals of Science* 30 (June 1973), 144.
25. *Parentalia*, 216, 215.
26. Hartlib to Robert Boyle, 8 May 1654, in Thomas Birch (ed.), *The Works of the Honourable Robert Boyle* VI (1772), 88.
27. *Parentalia*, 216.
28. Balthazar de Monconys, *Journal des voyages . . .* II (1665–6), 53.
29. *Brief Lives*, 191.
30. Derek T. Whiteside, 'Wren the Mathematician', *NRRS* 15 (1960), 107. Whiteside is referring specifically to Wren's 'lack of concentration on mathematical studies'.
31. Galileo Galilei, *Sidereus Nuncius*, trans. E. S. Carlo (1880), 10.
32. *ibid.*, 42–3.
33. Quoted in David W. Waters, *The Art of Navigation in England in Elizabethan and Early Stuart Times* (Hollis & Carter, 1958), 299.
34. Wren, *De Corpore Saturni . . .*, English translation in Albert Van Helden, 'Christopher Wren's *De Corpore Saturni*', *NRRS* 23 (1968), 219; Oldenburg to Hartlib, 12 July 1659, Hall & Hall, *Correspondence* I, 277.
35. Hartlib Papers, in Turnbull, *NRRS* 10, 116.
36. Quoted in R. Grant, *History of Physical Astronomy* (1852), 524.
37. Wilkins, *Works* (1708 edn.), 114–15.
38. Wren to Hartlib, Hartlib Papers, in Turnbull, *NRRS* 10, 114.
39. BM MS Add 25071, fos. 92–3.
40. Letter from Wren to Lord Brouncker, 30 July 1663, Royal Society MS EL W 3, 3; *Parentalia*, 198.

41. BM MS Add 25071, fos. 92–3; Thomas Sprat, *The History of the Royal Society of London* (1667), in *Parentalia*, 209.

Chapter 4

1. *See* note 14, Chapter 3.
2. John Wallis to Samuel Hartlib, in G. H. Turnbull, 'Samuel Hartlib's Influence on the Early History of the Royal Society', *N[otes and] R[ecords of the] R[oyal] S[ociety]* 10 (1953), 114, fn 69.
3. Douglas McKie, 'The Origins and Foundation of the Royal Society of London', *NRRS* 15 (1960), 4.
4. *Brief Lives*, 39.
5. *ibid.*, 116.
6. Quoted in Charles Webster, *The Great Instauration: Science, Medicine and Reform 1626–1660* (Duckworth, 1975), 52.
7. John Ward, *The Lives of the Professors of Gresham College* (1740), 241.
8. *ibid.*, 143.
9. Sheffield University Library, Hartlib Papers XLVII 18. Petty's proposals are reprinted as Appendix VII in Webster, *Great Instauration*, 548–51, from which these excerpts are taken.
10. *See* W. S. C. Copeman, 'Dr Jonathan Goddard, FRS (1617–75)', *NRRS* 15 (1960).
11. Ward, *Lives*, 23.
12. T. Carlyle (ed.), *The Letters and Speeches of Oliver Cromwell* II (Methuen, 1904), 493.
13. *Parentalia*, 200. All quotations from Wren's address come from the English draft of the speech, preserved in *Parentalia*. The Latin version which he actually delivered is reprinted as an appendix to Ward's *Lives of the Professors of Gresham College*.
14. John Wilkins, *A Discourse concerning a new Planet, tending to prove that 'tis probable our Earth is one of the Planets* (1640), in E. J. Bowen & Harold Hartley, 'The Right Reverend John Wilkins, FRS', *NRRS* 15 (1960), 53; Seth Ward, *Vindiciae Academiarum* (1654), 29.
15. Quoted in Nathaniel Carpenter, *Geography Delineated Forth in Two Books* I (1625), 145.
16. Robert South, *Discourses on Various Subjects and Occasions* (1827 edn.), 323.
17. *See Philosophia naturalis* (1681), a compendium of lectures by Wolferd Senguerd, Professor of Philosophy at Leyden.
18. Samuel Foster, 'Of the Planetary Instruments', *Miscellanies of Mr Samuel Foster* (1659), 25.

19. In John Wallis's *Tractatus de cycloide* (1659).

20. Derek T. Whiteside, 'Before the *Principia*: The Maturing of Newton's Thoughts on Dynamical Astronomy', *Journal for the History of Astronomy* 1 (1970), 8; J. A. Bennett, *The Mathematical Science of Christopher Wren* (CUP, 1982), 60.

21. Quoted in Patrick Moore & Garry Hunt, *The Atlas of the Solar System* (Chancellor Press, 1997), 316.

22. Galileo to Cesi, August 1616, in Albert Van Helden, 'Christopher Wren's *De Corpore Saturni*', *NRRS* 23 (1968), 214.

23. Ideas which were proposed by, among others, Giovanni Battista Hodierna; Hevelius; Honoré Fabri; and Gilles de Roberval.

24. John Wallis, *Defence of the Royal Society* (1678).

25. Wren, *De Corpore Saturni*, in Van Helden, *NRRS* 23, 221.

26. *ibid.*, 225.

27. Letter to Sir Paul Neile, 1 October 1661, in C. A. Ronan & Sir Harold Hartley, 'Sir Paul Neile FRS (1613–1686)', *NRRS* 15 (1960), 163.

28. Thomas Birch, *The History of the Royal Society of London* I (1756), 43.

29. Wren to Neile, 1 October 1661 in Ronan & Hartley, *NRRS* 15, 163.

30. John Evelyn, *Fumifugium* (1661), in Liza Picard, *Restoration London* (Weidenfeld & Nicolson, 1997), 6.

31. BM Birch MS 4279, fo. 273.

32. Both quotes from Bryant Lillywhite, *London Coffee Houses* (George Allen & Unwin, 1963).

33. *Parentalia*, 33–4.

34. Evelyn, *Diary*, 11 October 1659.

35. *Parentalia*, 254.

36. *ibid.*

37. Conversation reported by Wood to Hartlib, 23 March 1661, in Turnbull, *NRRS* 10, 121, 95n.

Chapter 5

1. D. C. Martin, 'Sir Robert Moray, FRS', *N[otes and] R[ecords of the] R[oyal] S[ociety]* 15 (1960), 244.

2. Royal Society Journal Book, memo 28 November 1660.

3. The list also included Boyle and Wren, implying perhaps that these two men left before the end of the meeting.

4. Francis Bacon, *The New Atlantis* (1627).

5. William Bray (ed.), *The Diary and Correspondence of John Evelyn* III (1852), 92.

6. Thomas Birch, *The History of the Royal Society of London* I (1756), 4–5.

7. *ibid.*, 7.

8. *ibid.*, 405–7.

9. *ibid.*, 289.

10. *ibid.*, 290.

11. *Parentalia*, 30; Bishop Wren's visitation articles for the diocese of Ely, 1662, in G. W. O. Addleshaw & Frederick Etchells, *The Architectural Setting of Anglican Worship* (Faber & Faber, 1948), 162n.

12. Quoted in Charles Saumarez Smith, 'Wren and Sheldon', *Oxford Art Journal* 6 (1983), 46.

13. Anthony Wood, *Athenae Oxonienses* (1691), in R. H. Syfret, 'Some Early Critics of the Royal Society', *NRRS* 8 (1951), 29.

14. Birch, *Royal Society* I, 218, 234.

15. *Parentalia*, 210–11.

16. Oldenburg to Huygens, 7 September 1661, in Hall & Hall, *Correspondence* I, 422.

17. Birch, *Royal Society* I, 468–9.

18. Oldenburg to Hevelius, 13 November 1664, in Hall & Hall, *Correspondence* II, 307.

19. Samuel Sorbière, *A Voyage to England . . . done into English from the French Original* (1709), 36.

20. *ibid.*, 37.

21. Thomas Sprat, *Observations on Mons de Sorbière's Voyage into England, written to Dr Wren, Professor of Astronomy in Oxford* (1708 edn.), 164–5.

22. Robert Hooke, *Micrographia* (1665), preface.

23. W. Feindel (ed.), *The Anatomy of the Brain and Nerves* II (McGill University Press, 1965), preface.

24. Thomas Sprat, *The History of the Royal Society of London* (1667), 311.

25. *ibid.*, 317–8.

26. Sir John Summerson, *Sir Christopher Wren* (Collins, 1965 edn.), 59.

27. *Parentalia*, 259.

28. H. W. Robinson & Walter Adams (eds.), *The Diary of Robert Hooke 1672–1680* (Taylor & Francis, 1935), 28 October 1672.

29. *ibid.*, 16 January 1677.

30. Harrington, in Syfret, *NRRS* 8, 52; Pepys, *Diary*, 1 February 1664; Evelyn, *Sylva* (1664), in Syfret, 46; Sprat, in Syfret, 42–4.

31. *Parentalia*, 221.
32. *ibid.*, 224.
33. Birch, *Royal Society* I, 300.
34. John Ward, *The Lives of the Professors of Gresham College* (1740), viii; *see* note 44, Chapter 2.
35. 'Errors in the Arte of Navigation commonly practized', in Thomas Digges, *A Prognostication everlastinge . . . Published by Leonard Digges Gentleman. Lately corrected and augmented by Thomas Digges, his sonne* (1576).
36. 'The Ballad of Gresham College', quoted in full in Dorothy Stimson, *Scientists and Amateurs* (Sigma Books, 1949), 57–63.
37. *Parentalia*, 206.
38. BM MS Add 25071, fo. 89, in J. A. Bennett, *The Mathematical Science of Christopher Wren* (CUP, 1982), 48.
39. BM MS Add 25071, fo. 115, in Bennett, *Mathematical Science of Wren*, 48. The cipher was decoded in the nineteenth century after Sir David Brewster found a copy by Edmund Halley among Newton's papers.
40 Birch, *Royal Society* I, 76. Sir Robert Moray picked up the idea and mentioned the use of graphite in pumps at a meeting on 31 December 1662, but nothing seems to have come of it.
41. Sprat, *History of the Royal Society*, 317.
42. *Parentalia*, 206.
43. BM MS Add 25071, fos. 92–3; *Parentalia*, 240.
44. Quoted in Bennett, *Mathematical Science of Wren*, 53.

Chapter 6

1. *Parentalia*, 260, where the letter is wrongly dated 1663 – Baylie had resigned the previous summer.
2. The only major royal buildings which didn't come under the aegis of the Surveyor-General were Windsor Castle, which had its own local Office of Works; and the Tower of London, which was the responsibility of the Office of the Ordnance.
3. *Parentalia*, 260n.
4. *ibid.*, 198.
5. H. M. Colvin, *A Biographical Dictionary of British Architects 1600–1840* (John Murray, 1978), 871.
6. Osler MS 7612, 65.
7. R. T. Gunther (ed.), *The Architecture of Sir Roger Pratt* (OUP, 1928), 289, 60.

8. Anon., *Essay on the Usefulness of Mathematical Learning, in a Letter from a Gentleman in the City to his friend in Oxford* (1700), in Rudolph Wittkower, *Palladio and English Palladianism* (Thames & Hudson, 1983), 99–100.

9. *Parentalia*, 52.

10. Draft memorandum in Wren's hand, reproduced in Peter Meadows, 'Sir Christopher Wren and Pembroke Chapel', *Georgian Group Journal* (1994), 55–7.

11. *Parentalia*, 34.

12. Sir John Summerson, *Sir Christopher Wren* (Collins, 1953), 48; Margaret Whinney, *Wren* (Thames & Hudson, 1971), 23; H. M. Colvin, *The Sheldonian Theatre and the Divinity School* (OUP, 1981), 7; Timothy Mowl & Brian Earnshaw, *Architecture Without Kings: the Rise of Puritan Classicism Under Cromwell* (Manchester University Press, 1995), 192.

13. Oldenburg to Evelyn, 16 April 1663, in Hall & Hall, *Correspondence* II, 44-5.

14. Birch, *Royal Society* I, 230; letter from Abraham Hill to John Brookes, 19 May 1663, in Charles Saumarez Smith, 'Wren and Sheldon', *Oxford Art Journal* 6 (1983), 46.

15. *Parentalia*, 335.

16. Evelyn, *Diary*, 7 November 1644.

17. Samuel Sorbière, *A Voyage to England . . . done into English from the French Original* (1709), 39.

18. Robert Plot, *The Natural History of Oxfordshire* (1677), quoted in *Parentalia*, 335.

19. *Parentalia*, 337.

20. Pepys, *Diary*, 1 February 1669.

21. Plot, *Natural History of Oxfordshire* (1677), in Colvin, *Sheldonian Theatre*, 15.

22. Robert Whitehall, in Marilyn Yurdan, *The Sheldonian Theatre* (n.d.), 6.

23. Wren to Bathurst, 22 June 1665, in Arthur T. Bolton & H. Duncan Hendry (eds.), *[The] W[ren] S[ociety]* V, (OUP, 1923–43), 14.

24. Evelyn, *Diary*, 9 July 1669.

25. Quoted in Saumarez Smith, *Oxford Art Journal* 6, 48.

26. Hooke to Boyle, in Thomas Birch (ed.), *The Works of the Honourable Robert Boyle* V (1772), 513, quoted in Birch, *Royal Society* I, 508.

27. John Gadbury, *De cometis: or, A Discourse of the Natures and Effects of*

Comets (1665), frontispiece. Gadbury was paraphrasing Guillaume de Salluste Sieur du Bartas.

28. Marcus Manilius, *Astronomica*, trans. G. R. Goold (Harvard University Press, 1977), in Sara Scechner Genuth, *Comets, Popular Culture and the Birth of Modern Cosmology* (Princeton University Press, 1997), 23.

29. *A Blazing Starre* (1642).

30. *Parentalia*, 200.

31. *ibid.*, 223.

32. Birch, *Royal Society* I, 123.

33. *Brief Lives*, 165.

34. Wren to Moray, 11 April 1665, Royal Society MS EL W 3, 5, in J. A. Bennett, *The Mathematical Science of Christopher Wren* (CUP, 1982), 67.

35. Wren to Hooke, 20 April 1665, Royal Society MS EL W 3, 6, in *ibid.*

36. *Parentalia*, 220.

Chapter 7

1. *Newes*, 5 January 1665, in Walter G. Bell, *The Great Plague in London in 1665* (John Lane, 1924), 1.

2. George Thomson, *Loimotomia, or the Pest Anatomized* (1666), 66.

3. 'The Plague of London AD 1665', in Bell, *Great Plague*, 350, 340.

4. Oldenburg to Hevelius, 3 August 1665, in Hall & Hall, *Correspondence* II, 452.

5. Evelyn, *Diary*, 4 August 1665.

6. Evelyn to Wren, 4 April 1665, in *W[ren] S[ociety]* XIII, 40.

7. *Parentalia*, 261.

8. Anon., *A New Journey to France, with an exact description of the sea coast from London to Calais* (1715), 24 December 1643.

9. John Lough (ed.), *Locke's Travels in France 1675–1679* (CUP, 1953), 280, 279.

10. Peter Heylyn, *A full relation of two journeys: the one into the Main-Land of France; the other into some of the adjacent Islands* (1656), 69; Evelyn, *Diary* II (1852 edn.), 24 December 1643.

11. James Howell, *Epistolae Ho-Ellianae, Familiar Letters, domestic and forren . . .* (1645), Sect. I, 27.

12. Richard Ferrier, *The Journal of Major Richard Ferrier MP, while travelling in France in the year 1687* (Camden Miscellany, New Series 53, 1895), 24; Heylyn, *Two Journeys*, 70.

13. Evelyn to Wren, 4 April 1665, in *WS* XIII, 40.

14. Quoted in H. Brown, *Scientific Organisations in Seventeenth-Century France* (Williams & Wilkins, 1934), 137.

15. Justel to Oldenburg, 14 January 1666, in Hall & Hall, *Correspondence* III, 12.

16. Adrien Auzout, *Mémoires* VII, 28.

17. Martin Lister, *A journey to Paris in the year 1698* (1699 edn.), 102, 30.

18. Edward Browne, *A Journal of a Visit to Paris in the year 1664*, ed. G. Keynes (John Murray, 1923), 4.

19. Donald Crawford (ed.), *Journals of Sir John Lauder, Lord Fountainhall, with his Observations on Public Affairs and other Memoranda, 1665–1676* (Edinburgh University Press, 1900), 127–8.

20. Samuel Sorbière, Permanent Secretary to the Montmor Academy, in Brown, *Scientific Organisations*, 126.

21. Quoted in *ibid.*, 146.

22. Auzout to Oldenburg, 1 July 1665, in Hall & Hall, *Correspondence* II, 429 [Paris, 11 July NS].

23. Quoted in Brown, *Scientific Organisations*, 234.

24. Wren to Bathurst, 22 June 1665, in *WS* V, 14.

25. Quoted in Cecil Gould, *Bernini in France* (Weidenfeld & Nicolson, 1981), 33–4.

26. Oldenburg to Boyle (quoting a letter from Justel), 24 August 1665, in Hall & Hall, *Correspondence* II, 480.

27. *Parentalia*, 261.

28. Gould, *Bernini in France*, 105.

29. *Parentalia*, 261.

30. *ibid.*, 262.

31. Edward Browne to Sir Thomas Browne, in Margaret Whinney, 'Sir Christopher Wren's Visit to Paris', *Gazette des Beaux-Arts* 51 (1958), 233.

32. *Parentalia*, 262. The projected *Observations* never appeared.

33. *ibid.*, 261.

34. *ibid.*

35. Tract I, *Parentalia*, 352.

36. Gould, *Bernini in France*, 37.

37. Tract I, *Parentalia*, 351–2.

38. *Parentalia*, 262.

Chapter 8

1. Justel to Oldenburg, 14 January 1666, in Hall & Hall, *Correspondence* III, 12.
2. Birch, *Royal Society* II, 74.
3. Wallis to Oldenburg, 9 August 1666, in Hall & Hall, *Correspondence* III, 204.
4. *WS* XIII, 13.
5. *ibid.*, 14.
6. R. T. Gunther (ed.), *The Architecture of Sir Roger Pratt* (OUP, 1928), 60; Evelyn, in H. M. Colvin, *A Biographical Dictionary of British Architects 1600–1840* (John Murray, 1978), 658.
7. Bodleian Tanner MS 145, 109, in *WS* XIII, 15.
8. *WS* XIII, 44.
9. 'Proposals To ye Right Honble ye Commissioners for ye Reparation of St Paul's Cathedral', Bodleian Tanner MS 145, 110–12, in *WS* XIII, 17.
10. *Parentalia*, 277.
11. Bodleian Tanner MS 145, 117, in *WS* XIII, 45.
12. Evelyn, *Diary*, 27 August 1666.
13. James Malcolm, *Londinium Redivivum* IV (1807), 73.
14. Thomas Vincent, *God's Terrible Voice in the City* (1722), 76.
15. *ibid.*, 62.
16. Letter to Lord Conway, in Walter Besant, *London in the Time of the Stuarts* (A. & C. Black, 1903), 263.
17. Vincent, *God's Terrible Voice*, 70.
18. Dean Milman's *Annals of St Paul's*, in Walter Besant, *London*, 268.
19. Evelyn, *Diary*, 7 September 1666.
20. Oldenburg to Boyle, 18 September 1666, in Hall & Hall, *Correspondence* III, 230–1.
21. John Evelyn, *A Character of England* (1659), in E. S. de Beer's introduction to Evelyn's *London Revived: Consideration for its Rebuilding in 1666* (Clarendon Press, 1938), 5.
22. Journals of the Court of Common Council XLVI, fo. 121.
23. Evelyn to Sir Samuel Tuke, 27 September 1666, in *Diary*, 397n.
24. *London Gazette*, 29 September 1666.
25. Richard Waller, *The Posthumous Works of Robert Hooke* (1705), xiii.
26. Evelyn, *London Revived*, ed. de Beer, 50–1.
27. *ibid.*, 45–6.
28. *London Gazette*, 20–4 September 1666.
29. John Milward, *Diary*, ed. C. Robbins (CUP, 1938), 8–9.

30. Oldenburg to Boyle, 2 October 1666, in Hall & Hall, *Correspondence* III, 238.

31. Pratt's opinion of Jerman is quoted in H. M. Colvin, *Biographical Dictionary of British Architects*, 459.

32. From Pratt's notes on the Commission's proceedings, in R. T. Gunther, *The Architecture of Sir Roger Pratt* (OUP, 1928), 12.

33. *ibid.*, 13.

34. T. F. Reddaway, *The Rebuilding of London after the Great Fire* (Jonathan Cape, 1940), 50.

35. Pepys, *Diary*, 25 November 1666.

36. Benjamin Ralph, *A Critical Review of the publick buildings, statues and ornaments in and about London and Westminster, etc.* (1734), 2.

37. *Parentalia*, 263, 269.

38. Reddaway, *Rebuilding of London*, 312.

39. Oldenburg to Boyle, 18 September 1666, in Hall & Hall, *Correspondence* III, 230–1.

40. Oldenburg to Boyle, 2 October 1666, in *ibid.*, 238.

41. Gunther, *Architecture of Sir Roger Pratt*, 11.

Chapter 9

1. First Rebuilding Act, in T. F. Reddaway, *The Rebuilding of London after the Great Fire* (Jonathan Cape, 1940), 182.

2. Bodleian Tanner MS 145, 129; reprinted in *WS* XIII, 20–1.

3. Bodleian Tanner MS 145, 127, reprinted in *ibid.*, 45–6.

4. Quoted in *WS* XIII, 22–3.

5. Sancroft to Wren, 25 April 1668, in *Parentalia*, 278.

6. Bodleian Tanner MS 145, 144.

7. *ibid.*, 145.

8. Breton to Sancroft, 19 February 1668, in *WS* V, 29–30.

9. Kerry Downes, *The Architecture of Wren* (Redhedge, 1988), 45.

10. Birch, *Royal Society* II, 164.

11. *ibid.*, 250.

12. Thomas Sprat, *The History of the Royal Society of London* (1667), 434.

13. An elevation reproduced from BM Sloane 5238, 66, in *WS* 5, plate XXVII, and often cited as Wren's scheme for the college, is now thought to be a design for a private house. It is probably also by Robert Hooke.

14. In a letter to Oldenburg dated 7 June 1668, in Royal Society MS EL W 3, 7.

15. *ibid.*

16. Birch, *Royal Society* II, 205.

17. For a detailed account of the long and complicated history of the Royal Society's plans for a college at Arundel House, *see* 'A "College" for the Royal Society: the Abortive Plan of 1667–8', in Michael Hunter, *Establishing the New Science* (Boydell, 1989), 156–84.

18. Sancroft to Wren, 2 July 1668, in *Parentalia*, 279.

19. St Paul's Building Accounts, July–September 1672, in *WS* XVI, 199.

20. Gilbert Burnet, *The History of My Own Times* I (1833 edn.), 350–1.

21. Guy Miége, *The New State of England* (1691), 244.

22. Sir Henry Wotton, *The Elements of Architecture* (1624), 51.

23. Evelyn, *Diary*, 6 November 1644; 'Account of Architects and Architecture' appended to Evelyn's *A Parallel of the Antient Architecture with the Modern* (1707 edn.), 9.

24. *Parentalia*, 308.

25. *ibid.*, 299.

26. Report on Salisbury Cathedral, 31 August 1668, Salisbury Cathedral Library MS 192, fo. 3 v. Wren's report is partially reprinted in *Parentalia*, 304–6; and reprinted in full in Lydia M. Soo, *Wren's 'Tracts' on Architecture and Other Writings* (CUP, 1998), 61–78. I have used Soo's version here.

27. *Parentalia*, 63.

28. Report on Salisbury Cathedral, 31 August 1668, Salisbury Cathedral Library MS 192, fo. 4, in Soo, *Wren's 'Tracts'*, 67.

29. Report on Salisbury Cathedral . . . MS 192, fo. 4 v., in *ibid.*; Report on Salisbury Cathedral . . . MS 192, fo. 7, in *ibid.*, 73.

30. Pepys, *Diary*, 21 March 1669.

31. Burnet, *History* I, 183.

32. *WS* XVIII, 156.

33. PRO Shaftesbury Papers 30/24/7/601, quoted in H. M. Colvin (ed.), *The History of the King's Works* V (HMSO, 1976), 11.

34. Pepys, *Diary*, 21 March 1669.

35. Evelyn, *Diary*, 5 May 1681; *ibid.*, 19 August 1668. Evelyn was impressed by the royal favour, but not by the pineapple's flavour.

Chapter 10

1. Treasury Minutes, 25 May 1669, in T. F. Reddaway, 'The London Custom House 1666–1740', *London Topographical Record* XXI (1958), 11.

2. Hooke, *Diary*, 27 July 1675.
3. Reprinted in *WS* XIX, 152–3.
4. Bodleian Tanner MS 145, 145, quoted in *WS* XIII, 47.
5. *See*, for example, Jane Lang, *Rebuilding St Paul's* (OUP, 1956), 46; and Margaret Whinney, *Wren* (Thames & Hudson, 1971), 84.
6. R. T. Gunther (ed.), *The Architecture of Sir Roger Pratt* (OUP, 1928), 213.
7. *Parentalia*, 282.
8. *ibid.*
9. *ibid.*, 284.
10. *ibid.*, 285.
11. *ibid.*, 282.
12. *WS* XIII, 29.
13. *ibid.*, 27.
14. Hooke, *Diary*, 14 November 1673.
15. Quoted in Bryan Little, *Sir Christopher Wren* (Robert Hale, 1975), 89.
16. Anthony Wood, *Life and Times*, ed. Clark, *Oxford Historical Society* XXI (1892), 279.
17. 'The marble Bust of my Father in the picture Gallery at Oxford was the Performance of Edward Pierce, about the Year 1673' (BM Add MS 6209, 220).
18. John Tillison to William Sancroft, 22 September 1673, in *WS* XIII, 51.
19. *WS* XIII, 28.
20. James Wright, *Phoenix Paulina* (1709), in Lang, *St Paul's*, 242.
21. *Parentalia*, 282.
22. Hooke, *Diary*, 3 October 1674.
23. *Parentalia*, 283.
24. *ibid.*, 282.
25. *WS* XIII, 31.
26. *Parentalia*, 283.
27. Tract V, 'Discourse on Architecture', 'Heirloom' copy of *Parentalia*; reprinted in Lydia M. Soo, *Wren's 'Tracts' on Architecture and Other Writings* (CUP, 1998), 188. (*See* note 55, Chapter 12.)
28. For Wren's comments on the crossing-piers at Westminster Abbey, see *Parentalia*, 300–1. The most interesting modern discussion of the mechanics of St Paul's (and the Sheldonian) is in Harold Dorn & Robert Mark, 'The Architecture of Christopher Wren', *Scientific American* 245 (July 1981), 126–38.

Chapter 11

1. T. Francis Bumpus, *Ancient London Churches* (T. Werner Laurie, 1923), 256.

2. Among the more eminent sources, one might include John Summerson – 'It is very nearly certain that Wren originated the design of every church' (*Sir Christopher Wren* [Collins, 1965], 83) – and Margaret Whinney – 'It is likely that in all cases Wren was responsible for the plan, and in many cases for much more . . . (*Wren* [Thames & Hudson, 1971], 45). The case for Hooke as the architect of many of the churches is convincingly argued in Paul Jeffery's excellent *The City Churches of Sir Christopher Wren* (Hambledon Press, 1996), on which I have drawn heavily for parts of this chapter.

3. John Evelyn, *London Revived . . .*, ed. E. S. de Beer (OUP, 1938), 38.

4. Pepys, *Diary*, 5 April 1667.

5. Bodleian Tanner MS 142, fo. 118.

6. Guildhall Library MS 25540/1, fo. 1, 17 May 1670.

7. Guildhall Library MS 25540 fo. 3, 13 June 1670.

8. Guildhall Library MS 25540, 6 September 1671, in Paul Jeffery, *The City Churches of Sir Christopher Wren* (Hambledon Press, 1996), 47.

9. *The Diary of Robert Hooke 1672–80*, eds. Henry W. Robinson & Walter Adams (Taylor & Francis, 1935), 18 March 1676.

10. *ibid.*, 15 October 1672.

11. *ibid.*, 15 September 1673.

12. Fitch (1642–1706) was a protégé of Hooke's, working for the latter on Bethlehem Hospital (1675–6), Royal College of Physicians, Warwick Lane (1674–8) and Montagu House, Bloomsbury (1675–9).

13. Vestry Minutes 1610–1763, in *WS* XIX, 36.

14. St Stephen Walbrook churchwardens' accounts, in *WS* IX, 114; Hooke, *Diary*, 4 March 1673; St Michael Bassishaw churchwarden's accounts 1617–1716, in *WS* XIX, 41.

15. *WS* XIX, 6.

16. *ibid.*, 25.

17. Building costs taken from Jeffery, *City Churches*, *passim*, but especially 356–7. Valuable though these figures are, they should be treated with caution, as Jeffery points out. The total sum of building costs, which is £362,793 7s 10d, excludes the cost of St Anne Soho, for which no accounts survive, and omits private

donations, some of which were fairly hefty and many of which went unrecorded. It includes the cost of towers and steeples, often the result of later building campaigns to the designs of other architects (the steeple of St Clement Danes is by James Gibbs, for example, and the upper stages of the tower of St Andrew Holborn was probably by Hawksmoor). In two cases – All Hallows Bread Street and St Andrew Holborn – it includes a sum for furnishings. That said, the figures still seem to me to be revealing, in that they show Wren concentrating on the biggest commissions, and leaving many of the smaller ones to Hooke.

18. For example: St Bartholomew-by-the-Exchange (£5077 1s 1d), St Peter Cornhill (£5647 8s 2d); and St Anne and St Agnes (£2348 0s 10d).

19. *Parentalia*, 320.

20. *WS* IX, plate 15.

21. *WS* XI, 20. The medieval character of St Sepulchre wasn't really his fault. The conservative restoration of the church began around 1668, two years before the Commission started work.

22. William Nicholls, *A Commentary on the Book of Common Prayer* (1710), in G. W. O. Addleshaw & Frederick Etchells, *The Architectural Setting of Anglican Worship* (Faber & Faber, 1948), 155.

23. *Parentalia*, 318.

24. Edward Hatton, *A New View of London* (1708), reprinted in *WS* X, 30.

25. Evelyn, *Diary*, 18 January, 19 February, 1 March 1671.

26. The font at St Margaret Lothbury is traditionally attributed to Gibbons; there is no documentary evidence to support the claim. The pulpit at St Benet Paul's Wharf is also sometimes said to be his. It isn't.

27. Robert Clutterbuck, *History and Antiquities of the County of Hertford* I (1815–27), 167.

28. Wren to John Fell, 26 May 1681, in *WS* V, 18.

29. They were Edward Pierce; Joshua Marshall; Christopher Kempster; Thomas Strong; Thomas Wise senior; Edward Strong senior; Edward Strong junior; Samuel Fulkes; Jasper Latham and John Tompson. We can probably also include the three other main contractors at St Paul's in this list, even though they weren't awarded individual contracts for the City churches. Thomas Wise junior was apprenticed to his father in the 1670s; William Kempster

worked as *his* father's assistant; and the last member of this distinguished baker's dozen, Nathaniel Rawlins, had originally worked for the Strong family.

30. 7 February 1676/7, Vestry Minutes 1648–99, in *WS* X, 112.

31. *WS* X, 122.

32. Benjamin Ralph, *A Critical Review of the publick buildings, statues and ornaments in and about London and Westminster, etc.* (1734), 12.

33. *Parentalia*, 319.

34. A less picturesque explanation is that the bows referred to the arches of the Norman crypt.

35. Quoted in Jeffery, *City Churches*, 280.

36. It was while digging the foundations for the new tower that he came across the remains of a Roman causeway about eighteen feet below the surface of the street. 'Underneath this Causeway lay the natural Clay, over which that Part of the City stands, and which descends at least forty Feet lower. He concluded then to lay the Foundation of the Tower upon the very Roman Causeway, as most proper to bear what he had design'd, a weighty and lofty structure' (*Parentalia*, 265).

37. Vitruvius, *The Ten Books of Architecture*, trans. Morris Hicky Morgan (Dover, 1960), 26.

38. The passage in Alberti's *De re aedificatoria* (1485) where he proposes a stack of little rotundas, progressively decreasing in diameter, is often cited in this context, as are the twin towers of Sangallo's model for St Peter's, Rome, which was engraved in the 1540s.

39. *See* Jeffery, *City Churches*, 131–2.

40. *WS* X, 73.

41. *Publick Buildings in London*, 13.

42. *Parentalia*, 319.

Chapter 12

1. E. C. Bentley, *Biography for Beginners* (T. Werner Laurie, 1905).

2. Hooke, *Diary*, 4 July 1678.

3. *ibid.*, 27 November 1677.

4. *ibid.*, 18 November 1676.

5. Ned Ward, *The London Spy: The Vanities and Vices of the Town Exposed to View* (1703), in Aytoun Ellis, *The Penny Universities: a History of the Coffee-Houses* (Secker & Warburg, 1956), 73.

6. Ward, *London Spy*, in *ibid.*, 74.

7. Ward, *London Spy*, in *ibid.*

8. Moore had been elected to the Royal Society in December 1674.

9. Hooke, *Diary*, 1 January 1676.

10. *ibid.*

11. Thomas Shadwell, *The Virtuoso*, eds. Marjorie Hope Nicolson & David Stuart Rodes (University of Nebraska Press, 1966), I, i, 267–8.

12. *ibid.*, II, ii, 190–4.

13. *ibid.*, V, ii, 82–8.

14. Meric Casaubon, *Letter to P du Moulin* (1669), in R. H. Syfret, 'Some Early Critics of the Royal Society', *N[otes and] R[ecords of the] R[oyal] S[ociety]* 8 (1951), 40.

15. Quoted in *ibid.*, 45.

16. Sprat, *History*, in R. H. Syfret, 'Some Early Critics of the Royal Society', *NRRS* 8 (1951), 43–4.

17. Hooke, *Diary*, 2 June 1676.

18. *ibid.*, 1 July 1676. Hooke sat down the next afternoon and decided to found a new club for 'chemistry, anatomy, Astronomy and opticks, mathematics and mechanicks'. It met a few times that summer, usually at Wren's house, before it too petered out.

19. 19 Charles II, 3 29.

20. Report to City Lands Committee, 28 July 1675, reprinted (from a transcript) in *WS* V, 47.

21. *ibid.*

22. Royal Warrant, 22 June 1675, in *WS* XIX, 113.

23. Wren to John Fell, 3 December 1681, in *WS* V, 21.

24. *Parentalia*, 334.

25. Roger North, *The Lives of the Norths* II, ed. A. Jessop (1890), 326.

26. *ibid.*

27. Wren's designs are reproduced in *WS* V, plates XIII and XIV.

28. 31 March 1697, in *WS* XIX, 103. Wren was writing to the Master of St John's, Cambridge, in connection with a design for a new bridge.

29. *WS* XVII, 76–7.

30. *See WS* V, plate XV.

31. Undated and unsigned letter, almost certainly written in 1675, reprinted in *WS* V, 32–34.

32. H. M. Colvin, 'The Building', in David McKitterick (ed.), *The Making of the Wren Library* (CUP, 1995), 34. Webb's drawings for the College are reproduced as plate 20.

33. Extraordinary expenditure, 7 December 1685, in *WS* V, 42.

34. Undated but presumably written in 1675, in *WS* V, 32–34.

35. For the varied attractions at Bartholomew Fair, see Hooke, *Diary*, 25 August 1677, 1 September 1679, 31 August 1680.

36. Council meeting, 13 September 1677, in Birch, *Royal Society* III, 42.

37. Hooke, *Diary*, 6 March 1676, 29 April 1675; Pepys, *Diary*, 29 January 1667.

38. Hooke, *Diary*: for Porsenna's tomb, *see* 4, 17, 18 and 20 October 1677; for flying, *see* 24 October 1677; for cats, falling sickness and the curious gardener, *see* 31 October 1677.

39. Hooke, *Diary*, 19 October 1677 and 8 November 1677.

40. As, for example, when he spoke to 'Sir P Whitchcot [Sir Paul Whichcote, FRS, a Cambridgeshire gentleman then up in London] for Sir Ch Wren, President, he agreed' (*Diary*, 25 October 1677).

41. Wren to Sancroft, 30 December 1677, in Bodleian Tanner MS 40, 123.

42. Hooke, *Diary*, 14 November 1677.

43. Birch, *Royal Society* III, 413.

44. Hooke, *Diary*, 23 March 1678.

45. Letter to John Fell, 3 December 1681, in *WS* V, 21.

46. Hooke to Boyle, 10 November 1664, in Margaret 'Espinasse, *Robert Hooke* (Heinemann, 1956), 52. In spite of his marked reluctance, Hooke was prevailed on to reproduce this early attempt at artificial respiration before the Royal Society three years later, after Fellows with medical backgrounds failed to do so.

47. Robert Boyle, *New Experiments Physco-Mechanicall, Touching the spring of the Air, and its effects* (1660).

48. *Parentalia*, 226.

49. Royal Society meeting, 10 January 1678, in Birch, *Royal Society* III, 373.

50. Hooke, *Diary*, 30 December 1677.

51. And which Boyle had kept, much to Wren's annoyance. 'He told me of his paper Mr Boyle had not returnd him, about the fabric of the muscle, advised me to perfect things and shew them the King . . .' (Hooke, *Diary*, 17 December 1677).

52. Birch, *Royal Society* III, 403.

53. *ibid.*, 402.

54. Tract II, *Parentalia*, 356.

55. All five tracts are reprinted as pp. 153–95 of Lydia M. Soo, *Wren's 'Tracts' on Architecture and Other Writings* (CUP, 1998), which is also far and away the most detailed and interesting account of them to date. Christopher junior's transcript of Tract V must date to before 1736, since it contains a sketch of the Mausoleum of Halicarnassus by Hawksmoor, who died in that year.

56. The evidence for dating the Tracts to the later 1670s is circumstantial, but compelling. For example: there is a reference to 'the great Pillar of London' (i.e., the Monument) in Tract III (*Parentalia*, 359); on four occasions in October 1677 Wren discussed with Hooke the appearance of Porsenna's Tomb, which he reconstructed in Tract V; in September 1675 the two men talked of Solomon's Temple, which appears in Tracts IV and V. Wren also mentions a model of the Sepulchre at Jerusalem, which was shown to the Royal Society in March 1677.

57. Tract V, 1–3, reprinted in Soo, *Wren's 'Tracts'*, 188–90. A new edition of the *Works* of Josephus, 'revised and amended, according to the excellent French translation of Monsieur Arnauld d'Andilly', was published in 1676; Hooke mentions seeing a copy that April (*Diary*, 12 April 1676).

58. Tract III, *Parentalia*, 354; Tract I, *Parentalia*, 353.

59. Tract V, 7, reprinted in Soo, *Wren's 'Tracts'*, 191; Tract I, *Parentalia*, 353.

60. Tract II, *Parentalia*, 353.

61. Sebastiano Serlio, *Tutte l'Opere d'Architettura et Prospettiva* (1611 edn.), Book III, Chapter 4.

62. Tract I, *Parentalia*, 353.

63. Tract IV, *Parentalia*, 359–60.

64. Tract V, 2, reprinted in Soo, *Wren's 'Tracts'*, 189.

65. Tract II, *Parentalia*, 355.

66. Tract IV, *Parentalia*, 363.

67. Tract I, *Parentalia*, 351.

Chapter 13

1. Francis Atterbury, 'On the Martyrdom of King Charles I' (early 18th century), reprinted in C. H. Sisson (ed.), *The English Sermon 1650–1750*, (Carcanet Press, 1976), 245.

2. Laurence Echard, *History of England* II, 649, in *Parentalia*, 332.

3. Thomas Sprat, sermon preached before the Commons on 30 January 1678, in *Parentalia*, 331.

4. Echard, *History* III, 441; in *Parentalia*, 331.
5. *Parentalia*, 332.
6. While the basic conception for the statuary group remained the same, Gibbons produced two alternative schemes – one in brass, the other in marble.
7. Evelyn, *Diary*, 29 January 1683.
8. *See*, for example, Hooke, *Diary*, 5, 13 and 17 October 1677.
9. Wren to Fell, 26 May 1681, in *WS* V, 17.
10. Wren to Fell, 26 May 1681, in *ibid.*, 18.
11. Wren to Fell, 11 June 1681, in *ibid.*, 18.
12. Wren to Fell, 25 June 1681, in *ibid.*, 20.
13. Wren to Fell, 3 December 1681, in *ibid.*, 21.
14. Wren to Fell, 3 December 1681, in *ibid.*, 21.
15. Evelyn, *Diary*, 30 November 1680.
16. Boyle to Hooke, 18 December 1680, in Sir Henry Lyons, *The Royal Society 1660–1940* (CUP, 1944), 91.
17. *ibid.*
18. Birch, *Royal Society* IV, 65.
19. *ibid.*, 120.
20. *ibid.*, 92.
21. The original admission fee of 10s was raised to 20s in February 1661, and 40s in September 1662. Peers were expected to pay £5.
22. Michael Hunter, *The Royal Society and its Fellows 1660–1700* (British Society for the History of Science, 1982), 162–3. I am indebted to Hunter's important study of the workings of the Royal Society for much of what follows.
23. Birch, *Royal Society* IV, 130.
24. *ibid.*, 158.
25. Hunter, *Royal Society*, 111.
26. Birch, *Royal Society* III, 70.
27. *ibid.*, 161.
28. Hooke, *Diary*, 13 November 1667.
29. Birch, *Royal Society* IV, 75.
30. Evelyn, *Diary*, 14 September 1681.
31. Husbands, *Ordinances* II, 587, in C. H. Firth, *Cromwell's Army* (Greenhill, 1992), 260.
32. *Report on the Duke of Portland's MSS* I, 568.
33. Quoted in C. G. T. Dean, *The Royal Hospital Chelsea* (Hutchinson, 1950), 19–20.
34. Sir James Turner, *Pallas Armata: Military Essayes of the Ancient*

Grecian, Roman, and Modern Art of War, Written in the years 1670 and 1671 (1683), 352.

35. Roger Boyle, Earl of Orrery, *A Treatise of the Art of War: Dedicated to the King's Most Excellent Majesty* (1677), 53.

36. Quoted in Edward McParland, 'The Royal Hospital Kilmainham, Co. Dublin' (reprint from *Country Life*, 9 May 1985), 2.

37. Sir Francis Brewster to the Duke of Ormonde, August 1682, in *ibid.*, 3.

38. Tract IV, *Parentalia*, 360.

39. Earl of Ilchester's MSS, in *WS* XIX, 65.

40. Evelyn, *Diary*, 27 January 1682.

41. *ibid.*, 25 May 1682.

42. Narcissus Luttrell, *A Briefe Historical Relation of State Affairs from 1678 to 1714*, in *WS* XIX, 65.

43. *WS* XX, 79. Professor Downes suggests that these drawings may be the set that the Duke of Monmouth requested from the Marquis de Louvois in 1677 (Downes, *The Architecture of Wren* [Redhedge, 1988], 126, 181n).

44. St Paul's Minute Book, 17 February 1687, in *WS* XVI, 56.

45. Treasury Warrant, 4 June 1693, PRO 1/1467/7.

46. Edward Hatton, *A New View of London* (1708), 737.

47. *The Penny Magazine* (1844), in Dean, *Royal Hospital*, 45. The jibe about the windows was well placed, but Wren wasn't to blame: his original transoms were replaced with sashes in the eighteenth century.

48. Evelyn, *Diary*, 23 September 1683.

49. Luttrell, *State Affairs*, in *WS* XIX, 69.

50. Evelyn, *Diary*, 24 January 1662.

51. *WS* VII, 19.

52. Earl of Sunderland to Sir Leoline Jenkins, in *Calendar of State Papers Domestic 1683* II, 352.

53. Roger North, *The Lives of the Norths* II, ed. A. Jessop (1890), 207, in H. M. Colvin (ed.), *The History of the King's Works* V (HMSO, 1976), 23.

54. John Hillaby (ed.), *The Journeys of Celia Fiennes* (Macdonald & Co. 1983), 64. All trace of the model or models has disappeared. Hooke recorded that he 'Saw module of Winchester house at Sr Christoph Wrens' on 24 April 1693 (*Diary*); and one model was at Kensington Palace in November 1697, when joiners were paid to make a case for it (Colvin [ed.], *King's Works* V, 309).

55. W. E. Buckley (ed.), *Memoirs of Thomas, Earl of Ailesbury* I (1890), 23, in Colvin (ed.), *King's Works* V, 310.

Chapter 14

1. Evelyn, *Diary*, 11 February 1685.
2. *ibid.*, 15 July 1685.
3. To be accurate, two churches were not yet begun – All Hallows Lombard Street and St Thomas the Apostle in Southwark. But the latter was something of an afterthought: it wasn't included in the original building programme and only came under its auspices in 1697, when £3000 out of the coal fund was granted for the replacement of the old (and unsafe) church. There is no evidence that either Wren or Hooke was involved in the design.
4. St Paul's Contract Book, 14 April 1681, in *WS* XVI, 20.
5. St Paul's Building Accounts, June 1680, in *WS* XIII, 130. The going rate of compensation to widows varied considerably, from 40s to £10. By the early 1700s, the Commission's responsibility towards the deceased workman extended to paying for a coffin, a shroud, and even the 'laborers that carryed him to the grave' (St Paul's Building Accounts, October 1701, in *WS* XV, 79).
6. In the autumn of 1677 Latham had caused some sort of problem. Hooke records six separate occasions between the end of October and the middle of December when he was at Scotland Yard to talk with Wren about the mason. Wren proposed an 'expedient about Latham', but Hooke doesn't give any indication of what the difficulty was or how it was solved. The following September, when the news broke that Latham was to get one of the St Paul's contracts, William Slayer (another master mason) 'huffed at Sir Chr Wren about Latham' (Hooke, *Diary*, 3 September 1678).
7. Harleian MS 4941.
8. St Paul's Minute Book, 5 March 1691, in *WS* XVI, 67.
9. Downshire MS I, Pt 1 (1924), 261.
10. *Calendar of Treasury Books* VIII, 133, in H. M. Colvin (ed.), *The History of the King's Works* V (HMSO, 1976), 311.
11. Evelyn, *Diary*, 16 September 1685.
12. John Hillaby (ed.), *The Journeys of Celia Fiennes* (Macdonald & Co, 1983), 64.
13. Narcissus Luttrell, *A Brief Historical Relation of State Affairs from September 1678 to April 1714* III (1857), 280.

14. Abel Boyer, *History of the Reign of Queen Anne* IV: *1703–13*, 178–80, in Colvin (ed.), *King's Works* V, 312.

15. Evelyn, *Diary*, 5 March 1685.

16. *ibid.*, 22 February 1685.

17. This included £1020 allowed for reusing existing materials (Colvin [ed.], *King's Works* V, 287–8). As usual, the final cost greatly exceeded Wren's estimate, ending up at £35,343 12s 3½d.

18. Bodleian MS Clarendon 6, fo. 301, in Colvin (ed.), *King's Works* V, 287.

19. Works accounts, in *WS* VII, 94.

20. Evelyn, *Diary*, 24 January 1687.

21. Quoted in *WS* VII, 133.

22. 10 April 1687, in *WS* VII, 134.

23. Evelyn, *Diary*, 29 December 1686. Impressed though Evelyn was, it seems that Verrio, who was notoriously unreliable, still hadn't finished work on the chapel when it opened. In a report dated 30 December 1686 (i.e., the day after Evelyn saw it), Wren noted that Verrio demanded full payment of £1250, going on to say that, 'I suppose when ye rest of ye ceilings & ye walls are finished as they ought to be, it may fully deserve it. What is done I valew at £800' (Court Orders 1686, in *WS* XVIII, 64).

24. 16 February 1688, in *WS* VII, 134. Evidence of the difficult course Wren had to steer in remodelling the royal palaces is given later in the same warrant, when he is ordered to 'give notice to such persons who are to remove out of theire Lodgeings, that they do not take away chimneypieces, wainscott, or partitions, which are in theire respective lodgings'.

25. *Brief Lives*, 161.

26. Evelyn, *Diary*, 25 May 1688.

27. Wren to Sir William Fermor, 14 May 1687, in *WS* XII, 23.

28. H. M. Colvin, *A Biographical Dictionary of British Architects 1600–1840* (John Murray, 1978), 804–5.

29. Letter from Wren to Fermor, 14 May 1687, in *WS* XII, 23.

30. Sir Herbert Chauncey, *History of Hertfordshire* (1700), 593, reproduced in *WS* XIX, plate LXXIII.

31. H. M. Colvin & John Newman (eds.), *Of Building: Roger North's Writings on Architecture* (Clarendon Press, 1981), 62.

32. *ibid.*, 74.

33. '. . . except Winchester, which is left in a deplorable state', *ibid.*, 73.

34. The craftsmen were Master Carpenter Matthew Banckes; the Purveyor of the Works, Charles Hopson (who in 1706 also became Master Joiner); and Matthew Roberts, who was master plumber at Windsor Castle. The measuring clerk was John Churchill, who succeeded Matthew Banckes as Master Carpenter in 1706. Some of the building materials came from Scotland Yard (and others from St Paul's Churchyard); and when the job was finished, Lowndes gave the workmen in Scotland Yard £1 1s 6d for a drink. Extracts from the building accounts are reprinted in *WS* XVII, 54–75.

35. The architect John Lumley in a letter to Lord Lumley, quoted in Pearl Finch, *A History of Burley-on-the-Hill, Rutland* I (J. Bale, Sons & Danielsson, 1901), 110.

36. John Bridges, *History of Northants* I (1791), 289. Bridges died in 1724; his *History* was published from his notes.

37. Quoted in Kerry Downes, *Hawksmoor* (Thames & Hudson, 1970), 34.

38. *Historical Manuscripts Commission Dartmouth*, 236.

39. Evelyn, *Diary*, 29 November, 2 December 1688.

40. *Dictionary of National Biography*.

41. Quoted in John Miller, *The Life and Times of William and Mary* (Weidenfeld & Nicolson, 1974), 121.

42. Quoted in *ibid*.

43. Mrs Cromwell seems to have grown attached to the furniture. After her husband's death she attempted to claim most of the contents of the palace as part of his personal estate, and was later found to have stored large quantities in a fruiterer's warehouse.

44. *See*, for example, Evelyn's first impressions of Catherine: 'Her teeth wronging her mouth by sticking a little too far out; for the rest lovely enough' (*Diary*, 30 May 1662).

45. Newsletter of 2 March 1689, in Colvin (ed.), *King's Works* V, 155.

46. The drawing and its legend are reproduced in *WS* IV, plate XI (top).

47. Quoted in Sir John Dalrymple, *Memoirs of Great Britain and Ireland* II (1773), 150.

48. Sir John Dalrymple, *Memoirs of Great Britain and Ireland* (1771–88), in *WS* VII, 135.

49. Hooke, *Diary*, 15 August 1674.

50. St Paul's Minute Book, 30 December 1689, in *WS* IV, 72.

51. Gilbert Burnet, *The History of My Own Times* II (OUP, 1833), 245.

The Earl of Monmouth, who was the fifth Treasury Commissioner, was absent from the hearing.

52. *See* St Paul's Minute Book, 19 June 1689, 11 and 23 December 1689 (*WS* XVI, 63–5). Talman also called evidence from a third mason, referred to only as 'Tompson'. This was presumably John Tompson, who worked for Wren on Winchester Palace, St Paul's and half a dozen of the City churches. The two men seem to have got on perfectly amicably, except for a brief spat when Wren refused to pay a £22 bill of Tompson's for work at St Dionis Backchurch in 1676. I can find no other reason why he chose to testify against the Surveyor – perhaps he just saw Talman as the coming man.

53. This and the following exchanges come from a Treasury Minute Book, reproduced in *WS* IV, 73.

54. The 'indifferent persons' were the mathematician and inventor Sir Samuel Morland; Philip Ryley, Surveyor-General of Woods and Forests South of the Trent; and master bricklayer John Fitch, who had just completed some work for the Ordnance at the Tower of London. Presumably the Commissioners didn't know that Fitch had also been employed by Wren as both a bricklayer and a main contractor on several of the City churches.

55. Hooke, *Diary*, 23 January 1690.

56. St Paul's Minute Book, 13 March 1690, in *WS* XVI, 65.

57. *Parentalia*, 326–7.

58. Burnet, *History* IV, 539.

59. *Parentalia*, 326.

60. Quoted in Miller, *William and Mary*, 82.

61. Evelyn, *Diary*, 21 February 1689.

62. Quoted in Miller, *William and Mary*, 121.

63. *Parentalia*, 326.

64. *ibid.*

65. Mary to William, 22 July 1690, in *WS* VII, 136.

66. Mary to William, 5 August 1690, in *ibid.*

67. Reproduced in *WS* XVIII, 168.

68. Quoted in Colvin (ed.), *King's Works* V, 157.

69. Horace Walpole, *Anecdotes of Painting* (1765–71), in Ernest Law, *The History of Hampton Court Palace* III (1891), 30.

Chapter 15

1. Gilbert Burnet, *The History of My Own Times* IV (OUP, 1833), 247.
2. Strictly speaking, Thomas Tenison was not yet Archbishop of Canterbury. John Tillotson died in November 1694 – he had a stroke while attending divine service at Whitehall – and Tenison, who was the Bishop of Lincoln, was nominated as his successor on 8 December. He was elected on 15 January 1695, and enthroned that May.
3. 29 April 1696, reproduced in *WS* VI, plate I.
4. 'The Queen . . . is building somewhat at Greenwich wch must be finished this summer, yt is saide to be some curious devise of Inigo Jones, and will cost above 4000 li' (John Chamberlain to Sir Dudley Carleton, 21 June 1617, *State Papers* 14/92, 70).
5. Quoted in John Summerson, *Architecture in Britain 1530–1830* (Penguin, 1977), 118.
6. Webb produced several schemes for Greenwich. His earliest designs, prepared around 1661, envisaged a much grander palace with a central section (domed, in one proposal) connecting the two ranges and thus blocking off the view of the Queen's House.
7. *Calendar of State Papers Domestic, 1673*, 358, in H. M. Colvin (ed.), *The History of the King's Works* V (HMSO, 1976), 150.
8. Narcissus Luttrell, *A Brief Historical Relation of State Affairs from September 1678 to April 1714* III (1857), 21.
9. Nicholas Hawksmoor, *Remarks on the Founding and Carrying on the Buildings of the Royal Hospital at Greenwich* (1728), in *WS* VI, 19.
10. Since it doesn't fit within the boundaries of the site as granted – as Kerry Downes has pointed out in *The Architecture of Wren* (Redhedge, 1988), 109.
11. Hawksmoor, *Remarks*, in *WS* VI, 20, 19.
12. *Parentalia*, 352.
13. Hawksmoor, *Remarks*, *WS* VI, 20.
14. *ibid.*
15. I.e., the base block of the Queen Anne Court and the west range of the King William Block. See Downes, *Wren*, 110.
16. Summerson, *Architecture 1530 to 1830*, 296.
17. Dedication to 'An Account of Architects and Architecture', in John Evelyn, *A Parallel of the Antient Architecture with the Modern* (1707 edn.). The dedication is dated 21 February 1697.
18. Hooke, *Diary*, 4 July 1673.

19. J. J. Keevil, 'Sir Charles Scarburgh', *Annals of Science* 8 (June 1952), 120.

20. Walter Pope, *The Life of Seth, Lord Bishop of Salisbury* (1697; Luttrell Society reprint, 1961), 192.

21. *See* note 13, Chapter 2.

22. Heirloom copy of *Parentalia*, reprinted in *WS* XIX, 119.

23. Summary of annual expenditure on St Paul's 1675–1710, *WS* XIII, 10.

24. St Paul's Building Accounts, July–September 1697, in *WS* XV, 33.

25. Evelyn, *Diary*, 5 October 1694.

26. Anon., *Questions about St Paul's Organ*, BM 816 m 9(93).

27. *ibid.*

28. There is some confusion over Wren's intentions for the high altar. A pencil drawing in the Bute Collection (Bute 19), which dates from some time before May 1694, clearly shows one half of the reredos, a free-standing screen placed about ten feet forward of the east end. *Parentalia*, on the other hand, assures us that Wren wanted a canopy 'of four Pillars wreathed, of the richest Greek Marbles, supporting a Canopy hemispherical, with proper Decorations of Architecture and Sculpture' (292). The description corresponds roughly with a surviving model for a reredos with four Solomonic columns and a segmental canopy (*WS* XIII, plate XXVII [left]); but it is the origin of a persistent story that what he *really* wanted was a baldacchino to rival Bernini's work for St Peter's, Rome. To complicate matters further, *WS* XIII reproduces a design, possibly by Hawksmoor, for an equestrian monument to King William, and mislabels it as the altar canopy (plates XXXI, XXXII).

29. St Paul's Building Accounts, October–December 1697, in *WS* XV, 36.

30. Royal Commission, 12 November 1673, in *WS* XIII, 28.

31. St Paul's Minute Book, 1 May, 19 October 1694, in *WS* XVI, 76, 78.

32. James Wright, *The Choire* (1697).

33. W. Sparrow Simpson (ed.), *Documents Illustrating the History of St Paul's Cathedral* (Camden Society, 1880), 156–7.

34. BM MS Add 32540, fos. 42v–43, in H. M. Colvin & John Newman (eds.), *Of Building: Roger North's Writings on Architecture* (Clarendon Press, 1981), 22.

35. *See ibid.*, xvii–xviii, 16n.

36. St Paul's Minute Book, 11 February 1696, in *WS* XVI, 79.

37. John Hutchins, *The History and Antiquities of the County of Dorset* II, (1774), 818, in Jane Lang, *Rebuilding St Paul's* (OUP, 1956) 204.

38. *Parentalia*, 343.

39. Wren, 'Considerations about the Works of St Paul's, what is next to be taken in hand this yeare 1697', in *WS* XVI, 85.

40. St Paul's Minute Book, 23 March 1697, in *WS* XVI, 82.

41. St Paul's Building Accounts, July–September 1700, in *WS* XV, 63.

42. Evelyn, *Diary*, 2 January 1698. (Evelyn was writing up his diary infrequently and retrospectively by this time, hence the apparent discrepancy in the dates.)

43. The notion that Wren was designing a royal palace at this early date, when Pembroke Hall Chapel and the Sheldonian Theatre were scarcely off the drawing board, is an intriguing one. The evidence centres on a surprisingly sophisticated elevation in the All Souls collection of a two-storey portico attached to one end of the Banqueting House. This seems to be related both to a model façade made by the Works in the first half of 1665, and to an entry in Evelyn's diary for 27 October 1664 in which he describes how the King personally drew a 'plot' of a new Palace of Whitehall during an audience in the Privy Gallery. Wren's authorship of the drawing is discussed by Kerry Downes in 'Wren and Whitehall in 1664', *Burlington Magazine* CXIII (1971), 89–92.

44. *Calendar of Treasury Books* XIV, 80, in Colvin (ed.), *King's Works* V, 164.

45. The account of the daily routine of the Works draws heavily on Colvin (ed.) *King's Works* V, 11–15, 21, which in turn is based largely on two documents: an agreement drawn up by the Officers of the Works after a conference at Scotland Yard on 27 March 1663 (BM Loan 29/217, fos. 635–6); and 'Severall proposalls humbly offered for regulating the Office of his Majesties Works', written by an anonymous author (possibly the Comptroller, Francis Wethered) in July 1667 (PRO Shaftesbury Papers 30/24/7/601).

46. R. T. Gunther (ed.), *The Architecture of Sir Roger Pratt* (OUP, 1928), 87.

47. Ned Ward, *The London Spy: The Vanities and Vices of the Town Exposed to View*, ed. Arthur L. Hayward, (Cassell, 1927), 45, 78.

48. Wren to John Fell, 25 June 1681, in *WS* V, 20.

49. *WS* IV, 50, 47, 51.

50. *ibid.*, 48.

51. *ibid.*, 41.

52. Wren to the Committee of Council for the Affairs of Ireland, 17 April 1695, in *WS* XVIII, 118; warrant from the Lord Chamberlain, the Earl of Musgrave, August 1688, *Works* 6/1, fo. 38 v.; Wren to Treasury Commissioners, 13 August 1690, in *WS* XVIII, 72; *WS* XVIII, 66; *WS* XVIII, 101; Wren to the King, 14 November 1693, in *WS* XVIII, 102; Luttrell, *Relation* II, 12; *WS* IV, 64.

53. An unexecuted pen-and-pencil study for a transept entrance to St Paul's (Bute 2, reproduced in Kerry Downes, *Sir Christopher Wren: the Design of St Paul's Cathedral* [Trefoil Publications, 1988], 54) is covered with prick-marks which show that it was accidentally left under a plan of the Great Model design that was being pricked for transfer. A stylus was also used to score a scale grid on a plan of Wren's first proposal for Hampton Court (All Souls Collection, II 1 16) in order to make it easier to scale up the elevations.

54. Lang, *Rebuilding St Paul's*, 154.

Chapter 16

1. By a quirk of fate, Bird had already designed monuments for two other characters who figured in Wren's life: Richard Busby, his old headmaster at Westminster; and the dramatist Thomas Shadwell, whose *Virtuoso* had made the Royal Society the laughing-stock of London. Both are in Westminster Abbey. Later Bird monuments in the Abbey include those to the Earl of Godolphin (1712) and Thomas Sprat (1713).

2. Wren to Christopher Wren junior, 11 October 1705, in *WS* XIX, 120.

3. Jonathan Swift, 'The History of Vanbrug's House' (1706); Vanbrugh was actually appointed on 18 May, twelve days after Godolphin had returned to the Treasury in Carlisle's stead; but it seems clear that the move to oust Talman had been set in train weeks or even months earlier.

4. The correspondence is reprinted in *WS* IV, 74–5.

5. Vanbrugh to Godolphin, 9 November 1704, in Geoffrey Webb (ed.), *The Works of John Vanbrugh* IV (Nonesuch Press, 1928), 13.

6. *ibid.*

7. *ibid.*

8. *ibid.*

9. *ibid.*

10. *Works* 6/368/3.

11. Webb (ed.), *Vanbrugh* IV, 123.

12. Quoted in Kerry Downes, *Sir John Vanbrugh* (Sidgwick & Jackson, 1987), 299.

13. Arthur Maynwaring to the Duchess of Marlborough, Blenheim Archives E 20(2), in H. M. Colvin (ed.), *The History of the King's Works* V (HMSO, 1976), 37.

14. *The Post Boy*, 27 December 1712. Eight of the ten signatories were from the Works (Marlborough House was a private job, so the 1705 Orders did not apply). They were: Master Carpenter John Churchill; Master Gardener Henry Wise; Master Glazier John Ireland; Sergeant Painter Thomas Highmore; Master Bricklayer Richard Stacey; Master Plasterer David Lance; Master Joiner John Hopson; and Sergeant Plumber Joseph Roberts. Only the masonry contracts went outside the Office, to Edward Strong junior and Henry Banckes rather than Benjamin Jackson.

15. Quoted in David Green, *Blenheim Palace* (Country Life, 1951), 106.

16. Quoted in Downes, *Vanbrugh*, 199.

17. BM Portland Deposit, Harley Papers XLVI, fos. 637–42, in Colvin (ed.), *King's Works* V, 48. Archer was writing in 1713.

18. *Parentalia*, 296.

19. *ibid.*, 302.

20. J. A. Bennett, *The Mathematical Science of Christopher Wren* (CUP, 1982), 42. Wren and Hooke had mooted the idea of using the Monument as a telescope back in the 1670s. According to James Hodgson, a kinsman of Wren who worked with Flamsteed at the Royal Observatory, this was why it was hollow (*see* Bennett, *Mathematical Science*).

21. BM Sloane 4042, fo. 179, in J. A. Bennett, 'Wren's Last Building?', *N[otes and] R[ecords of the] R[oyal] S[ociety]* 27 (1972–3), 110. Bennett's article deals in detail with the history of Wren's involvement with Crane Court.

22. Besides Strong, Robinson and Jenings, the list of workmen at Crane Court included bricklayer Thomas Hughes; glazier Matthew Jarman; plumber Joseph Roberts; painter Joseph Thompson; joiner John Tufnell; and plasterer Chrystom Wilkins. Their work was measured by William Dickinson the younger, who was the measuring clerk at St Paul's and (from February 1711) Wren's Deputy Surveyor at Westminster. To be strictly accurate, when the repair work was carried out over the winter of 1710/11, Joseph Roberts *was* at the Works, having been appointed as

Sergeant Plumber in October 1710; and Wren junior worked with him and Strong at Marlborough House. But I think the main point, that this was Wren senior's team, still holds.

23. BM Sloane 4042, fos. 262–3, in Bennett, *NRRS* 27, 111.

24. *British Curiosities of Nature and Art* (1713), 44. The collection also contained a large glass urn, thought to be Roman, which Wren presented in 1678. The best account of the Royal Society's collection in the seventeenth and early eighteenth centuries is Michael Hunter's 'Between Cabinet of Curiosities and Research Collection: the History of the Royal Society's "Repository"', in Michael Hunter, *Establishing the New Science* (Boydell, 1989), 123–155.

25. 'For a Model of a Relieve with 2 Figures & Emblems for ye sd Front' (St Paul's Building Accounts, January–March 1699, *WS* XV, 50).

26. In 1705 the phoenix figured again in St Paul's building history, in unusual circumstances. A ship of that name carrying stone from Portland was captured by a French privateer in the Channel, and sold with its cargo to a Rotterdam merchant. The captain, Henry Perry, bought it back the following year and duly delivered his load as if nothing had happened. *Resurgam*, indeed.

27. Ned Ward, *The London Spy: The Vanities and Vices of the Town Exposed to View*, ed. Arthur L. Hayward (Cassell, 1927), 81.

28. St Paul's Minute Book, 19 January and 1 February 1700, in *WS* XVI, 97, 98.

29. Kerry Downes suggests the obelisk was probably Hawksmoor's idea (*Sir Christopher Wren: the Design of St Paul's Cathedral* [Trefoil Publications, 1988], 155).

30. St Paul's Building Accounts, July–September 1700, in *WS* XV, 63.

31. The 'formula' was inserted as an anagram at the end of Hooke's *A Description of Helioscopes, And some other Instruments* (1676). For the most recent discussion of Wren's use of the catenary arch in the construction of St Paul's, see Lisa Jardine, *Ingenious Pursuits* (Little, Brown, 1999), 72–6.

32. Hooke, *Diary*, 5 June 1675.

33. E.g., 'a little uncomfortable' (Margaret Whinney, *Wren* [Thames & Hudson, 1971], 125); 'aesthetically not wholly successful' (Nikolaus Pevsner & Bridget Cherry, *London* I [Buildings of England series, Penguin, 1973 edn.], 132).

34. Bodleian MS 907, fo. 17v.

35. Report on Westminster Abbey, *Parentalia*, 298. Ironically, the flying buttresses were unnecessary – or, at least, their job could have been done equally well by solid piers. See Harold Dorn & Robert Mark, 'The Architecture of Christopher Wren', *Scientific American* 245 (July 1981), 133.

36. Report on Salisbury Cathedral, 31 August 1668, Salisbury Cathedral Library MS 192, fo. 4 v., in Lydia M. Soo, *Wren's 'Tracts' on Architecture and Other Writings* (CUP, 1998), 67.

37. St Paul's Building Accounts, December 1706, in *WS* XV, 146.

38. St Paul's Building Accounts, February 1707, in *ibid.*, 148.

39. *Parentalia*, 293.

Chapter 17

1. St Paul's Minute Book, 14 April 1711, in *WS* XVI, 114.

2. James Wright, *Phoenix Paulina, a Poem on the new Fabrick of St Paul's Cathedral* (1709).

3. The fourth was Sir John Cooke.

4. *Parentalia*, 292.

5. St Paul's Minute Book, 21 April 1708, in *WS* XVI, 106. The minutes actually relate to another meeting, held at Bishop Compton's palace in Fulham. Its sole purpose seems to have been to ratify decisions taken at Lambeth the previous Saturday.

6. *WS* XVI, 174.

7. *Fact against Scandal, or a Collection of Testimonials, Affidavits, and other Authentick Proofs in vindication of Mr Richard Jenings, Carpenter . . .* (1713), in *WS* XVI, 149.

8. Report of the Attorney-General, 25 January 1712, in *Fact against Scandal*, in *WS* XVI, 159.

9. Jenings' testimony before a Committee of the Commissioners, 20 September 1710, in *Fact against Scandal*, in *WS* XVI, 151.

10. Affidavits of George Guest, Edward Ayres, Thomas Ealman, John Stanford and John Wilkins, in *Fact Against Scandal*, in *WS* XVI, 161.

11. Report of the Attorney-General, 25 January 1712, in *Fact against Scandal*, in *WS* XVI, 162.

12. St Paul's Minute Book, 25 January 1711, *WS* XVI, 110.

13. Wren to the Archbishop of Canterbury and Bishop of London, 25 January 1711, in *WS* XVI, 154–5.

14. Thomas Bateman to Sir William Trumbull, 4 May 1711, Downshire MS, in *WS* XVI, 180.

15. Wren, February 1711, in *An Answer to a Pamphlet entitled Frauds and Abuses at St Paul's . . .* (1713), in *WS* XVI, 155.

16. Wren, 12 March 1711, *Portland Papers* X, 133.

17. The Most Humble Petition and Representation of Sir Chr Wren, 3 February 1711, in *Frauds and Abuses at St Paul's* (1712), 24–5, in *WS* XVI, 156.

18. Commissioners' reply to the Petition and Representation of Sir Christopher Wren, 5 May 1711, in *Frauds and Abuses*, 28–32, in *WS* XVI, 157–8.

19. St Paul's Minute Book, 19 July 1715, in *WS* XVI, 117.

20. Wren, 28 October 1717, in James Elmes, *Memoirs of the Life and Works of Sir Christopher Wren* (1823), 508.

21. *Works* 6/5, fo. 242, 19 November 1713.

22. Treasury Board Papers 173, fo. 100, in H. M. Colvin (ed.), *The History of the King's Works* V (HMSO, 1976), 50.

23. Treasury Board Papers 220, fo. 216, in *ibid.*, 52.

24. Christopher decamped to Wroxall after he lost his post at the Works in 1716; the previous year he had married the widow who sold the estate to his father. There are memorials to three Christopher Wrens in the local church.

25. Treasury Board Papers 220, fo. 216, in Colvin (ed.), *King's Works* V, 52.

26. Quoted in Lawrence Whistler, *The Imagination of Vanbrugh and his Fellow Artists* (Batsford, 1954), 244.

27. *Memoirs of John Ker of Kersland* II (1726), 111.

28. *Parentalia*, 344.

29. *ibid.*

30. Geoffrey Webb (ed.), *The Works of Sir John Vanbrugh* IV (Nonesuch Press, 1928), 109.

31. Treasury Board Papers 220, fo. 216, in Colvin (ed.), *King's Works* V, 52.

32. Colvin (ed.), *King's Works* V, 65.

33. Webb (ed.), *Works of Vanbrugh* IV, 109.

34. Treasury Board Papers 216, fo. 82 v. (March 1719), in Kerry Downes, *Sir John Vanbrugh* (Sidgwick & Jackson, 1987), 390.

35. Quoted in H. M. Colvin, *A Biographical Dictionary of British Architects 1600–1840* (John Murray, 1978), 109. For a full account of Benson's disastrous Surveyorship, see Colvin (ed.), *King's Works* V, 57–65. Benson went mad in later life, and Colvin suggests he was already of unsound mind in 1718. This is a charitable view.

36. *A Letter Concerning the Art, or Science of Design*, in Benjamin Rand (ed.), *Second Characters or the Language of Forms* (CUP, 1914), 21. Although Shaftesbury's letter was not printed until 1732, it was being circulated in London soon after it was written.

37. Colen Campbell, *Vitruvius Britannicus* I (1715), introduction, 1.

38. Wilbury was actually based on John Webb's Amesbury House, Wiltshire (*c.* 1660), which was thought at the time to be by Jones. It isn't clear if Benson was his own architect, although Campbell wrote that the house was 'invented and built by himself [i.e. Benson] in the Stile of Inigo Jones, who, by this excellent Choice, discovers the Politeness of his Taste' (*Vitruvius Britannicus* I, 5).

39. Campbell, *Vitruvius Britannicus* I, introduction, 2.

40. Daniel Defoe, *A Tour through the Whole Island of Great Britain* II (1724–6), Letter V.

41. Alexander Pope, Epistle to Richard Boyle, Earl of Burlington, 'Of the Use of Riches'.

42. Quoted in James Lees-Milne, *English Country Houses: Baroque* (Country Life, 1970), 30.

43. *Parentalia*, 346.

44. MS copy of *Parentalia*, BM MS Add 25071, fo. 38 v.

Chapter 18

1. *Weekly Journal or British Gazetteer* 2491 (9 March 1723).

2. *ibid.*; *Weekly Journal* 227 (2 March 1723).

3. Daniel Defoe, *A Tour through England and Wales* II (J. M. Dent, 2 vols., n.d., verbatim reprint of the 1st edn. excluding the *Tour through Scotland*), 25.

4. Defoe, *Tour through England and Wales* I, 331, 333.

5. Note at the beginning of the All Souls draft of *Parentalia* (All Souls MS 313), in J. A. Bennett, 'A study of *Parentalia*, with two unpublished letters of Sir Christopher Wren', *Annals of Science* 30 (June 1973), 132.

6. The prints were engraved by Henry Hulsbergh. The pyramid (reprinted as *WS* XVII, plate XIX) is titled 'A Catalogue of the Churches of the City of London, Royal Palaces, Hospitals, and Public Edifices, Built by Sir Christopher Wren Kt Surveyor General of the Royal Works during Fifty Years'.

7. *Parentalia*, 344.

8. *ibid.*, 328.

9. *ibid.*, 291.

10. *ibid.*, 290.

11. John Ward, *The Lives of the Professors of Gresham College* (1740), 106. Christopher supplied Ward with material for his biography of Wren: *see* Bennett, *Annals of Science* 30 (June 1973).

12. James Forrester, *The Polite Philosopher, or, An Essay on that Art which makes a Man happy in himself, and agreeable to others* (1734).

13. William Bray, *Tour Through Some of the Midland Counties, into Derbyshire and Yorkshire . . . performed in 1777*, in *The British Tourist* II, ed. William Mavor (1800 edn.), 318.

14. James Cawthorn, *Of Taste* (1756), quoted in B. Sprague Allen, *Tides in English Taste* I (Harvard University Press, 1937), 111.

15. In 1755 Gwynn also issued an engraving of St Paul's, 'decorated according to the original intention of Sir Christopher Wren'.

16. Uvedale Price, *Essays on the Picturesque* II (1810 edn.), 212.

17. Joshua Reynolds, 'Discourse XIII', *Literary Works* II (1819 edn.), 138.

18. C. Bruyn Andrews (ed.), *The Torrington Diaries* II (Methuen, 1970), 345.

19. *See* John Summerson, *Architecture in Britain 1530–1830* (Penguin, 1977), 445–7.

20. *WS* VIII, 16.

21. C. R. Cockerell, *Diary*, March 1823, July 1821, in David Watkin, *The Life and Work of C. R. Cockerell* (Zwemmer, 1974), 60.

22. Cockerell, *Diary*, 29 March 1826, in *ibid.*, 62.

23. C. R. Cockerell, *Royal Academy Lecture Notes, 1841–56* (Library of the Royal Academy of Arts), in *ibid.*, 121.

24. J. E. Goodchild, *Reminiscences of My Twenty-Six Years' Association with C. R. Cockerell, Esq.* (MS), in *ibid.*, 234.

25. Cockerell included eight buildings which are now very definitely outside the canon, such as Buckingham House (by William Winde) and Hawksmoor's west towers at Westminster Abbey. Nobody's perfect.

26. Thomas Babington Macaulay, *The History of England from the Accession of James II* (1849–61), Chapter 3.

27. *The Ecclesiologist* VIII (1847), 54.

28. A. W. N. Pugin, *Contrasts* (1841 edn.), 57.

29. John Ruskin, *The Stones of Venice* I (1851–3), i, 38.

30. Ruskin, *Stones of Venice* I, v, 7; John Ruskin, *The Seven Lamps of Architecture* (Everyman, 1940), 115.

31. Reginald Blomfield, *A Short History of Renaissance Architecture in*

England 1500–1800 (George Bell, abridged edition, 1900), 302, 142.

32. T. Francis Bumpus, *Ancient London Churches* (T. Werner Laurie, 1923), 262; Lawrence Weaver, quoted in Stanley B. Hamilton, 'The Place of Sir Christopher Wren in the History of Structural Engineering', *Newcomen Society Transactions* 14 (1933–4), 41.

33. J. A. Gotch, *The Growth of the English House* (Batsford, 1909), 232, 237–8.

34. *The Times*, 26 February 1923.

35. *ibid.*, 27 February 1923.

36. Aldous Huxley, 'Sir Christopher Wren', *On the Margin* (Chatto & Windus, 1923).

37. *The Times*, 26 February 1923. Other exhibits included Wren's compasses and measuring staff and a piece of stone quarried at Portland for the building of St Paul's, showing his quarry mark. 'His white flowered waistcoat with its beautiful embroideries, very long for a small man's wear, tells something of his fine taste.'

38. *ibid.*, 27 February 1923.

39. *ibid.*, 26 February 1923.

40. *WS* XIX, 270. The idea originated with the historian Ernest Law, who suggested that rather than producing a conventionally hagiographic memorial volume of tributes, it would be better to celebrate the bicentenary by publishing a selection of Wren's drawings, so that students could see for themselves what all the fuss was about. Mervyn Macartney and Sidney Alexander, the cathedral treasurer and the moving force behind the repair fund appeal, took up the challenge, and a committee was formed on 7 March 1923.

41. *See* Paul Jeffery, *The City Churches of Sir Christopher Wren* (Hambledon Press, 1996), 295. Chapter 13 of Jeffery's book contains the best overview of the recent history of the churches, along with some concerns about their future prospects.

42. *The Times*, 21 November 1924. As in 1860, the proposals weren't confined to Wren's churches, but it was their fate which primarily concerned Blomfield and his contemporaries.

43. *ibid.*

44. Bumpus, *London Churches*, 258.

45. Its furnishings and fittings were removed to the new church of All Hallows Twickenham, as was its tower.

46. *Cathedrals* (Great Western Railway, 1925), 8, quoting a sermon given during the First World War by Canon Alexander.

47. Festival of Britain *Exhibition of Science* guide-catalogue, (HMSO, 1951), 4.

48. Speech given by HRH the Prince of Wales at the Annual Dinner of the Corporation of London Planning and Communication Committee, Mansion House, 1 December 1987.

49. H. M. Colvin & John Newman (eds.), *Of Building: Roger North's Writings on Architecture* (Clarendon Press, 1981), 10.

Bibliography

WREN STUDIES

Beard, G. *The Work of Christopher Wren* (Bartholomew, 1982)

Bennett, J. A. *The Mathematical Science of Christopher Wren* (CUP, 1982)

Bennett, J. A. 'A Study of *Parentalia*, with two unpublished letters of Sir Christopher Wren', *Annals of Science* XXX (1973), 129–47

Bennett, J. A. 'Wren's Last Building?', *Notes and Records of the Royal Society* XXVII (1972–3), 107–18

Biswas, A. K. 'The Automatic Rain-Gauge of Sir Christopher Wren, FRS', *Notes and Records of the Royal Society* XXII (1967), 94–104

Bolton, A. T. & Hendry, H. D. (eds.) *The Wren Society* (OUP, 1923–43)

Dorn, H. & Mark, R. 'The Architecture of Christopher Wren', *Scientific American* 245 (July 1981), 126–38

Downes, K. *The Architecture of Wren* (Redhedge, 1988)

Downes, K. *Sir Christopher Wren: the Design of St Paul's Cathedral* (Trefoil Publications, 1988)

Downes, K. 'Wren and Whitehall in 1664', *Burlington Magazine* CXIII (1971), 89–92

Elmes, J. *Memoirs of the Life and Works of Sir Christopher Wren* (1823)

Fuerst, V. *The Architecture of Sir Christopher Wren* (Lund Humphries, 1956)

Gibson, W. C. 'The Medical Interests of Christopher Wren', *Some Aspects of Seventeenth-Century Medicine & Science* (William Andrews Clark Memorial Library, 1969), 23–41

Hamilton, S. B. 'The Place of Sir Christopher Wren in the History of Structural Engineering', *Newcomen Society Transactions* XIV (1933–4), 27–42

Huxley, A. 'Sir Christopher Wren', *On the Margin* (Chatto & Windus, 1923)

Jarvis, J. *Christopher Wren's Cotswold Masons* (Thornhill Press, 1980)

Jeffery, P. *The City Churches of Sir Christopher Wren* (Hambledon Press, 1996)

Jones, H. W. 'Sir Christopher Wren and Natural Philosophy: with a checklist of his scientific activities', *Notes and Records of the Royal Society* XIII (1958), 19–37

Lindsey, J. *Wren: His Work and Times* (Rich & Cowan, 1951)

Little, B. *Sir Christopher Wren* (Robert Hale, 1975)

Meadows, P. 'Sir Christopher Wren and Pembroke Chapel', *Georgian Group Journal* (1994), 55–7

Milman, L. *Sir Christopher Wren* (Duckworth, 1908)

Sekler, E. F. *Wren and his Place in European Architecture* (Faber & Faber, 1956)

Smith, C. S. 'Wren and Sheldon', *Oxford Art Journal* VI (1983), 45–50

Soo, L. M. *Wren's 'Tracts' on Architecture and Other Writings* (CUP, 1998)

Summerson, J. 'The Penultimate Design for St Paul's', *Burlington Magazine* CIII (1961), 83–9

Summerson, J. *Sir Christopher Wren* (Collins, 1953)

Van Helden, A. 'Christopher Wren's *De Corpore Saturni*', *Notes and Records of the Royal Society* XXIII (1968), 213–29

Webb, G. *Wren* (Duckworth, 1937)

Whinney, M. 'Sir Christopher Wren's visit to Paris', *Gazette des Beaux-Arts* LI (1958), 229–42

Whinney, M. *Wren* (Thames & Hudson, 1971)

Whiteside, D. T. 'Wren the Mathematician', *Notes and Records of the Royal Society* XV (1960), 107–11

Wren, C. (ed.) *Parentalia: or, Memoirs of the Family of the Wrens* (1750)

PRIMARY SOURCES

Anon. *An Answer to a Pamphlet entitled Frauds and Abuses at St Paul's . . .* (1713)

Anon. *Fact against Scandal, or a Collection of Testimonials, Affidavits, and other Authentick Proofs in vindication of Mr Richard Jenings, Carpenter . . .* (1713)

Anon. *Frauds and Abuses at St Paul's* (1712)

Anon. *A New Journey to France, with an exact description of the sea coast from London to Calais* (1715)

Andrews, C. B. (ed.) *The Torrington Diaries* (Methuen reprint, 1970)

Aubin, R. A. (ed.) *London in Flames, London in Glory: Poems on the Fire and Rebuilding of London, 1666–1709* (Rutgers University Press, 1943)

Bacon, F. *The Advancement of Learning* (1605)

Bacon, F. *The New Atlantis* (1627)

Birch, T. *The History of the Royal Society of London* (1756–7)

Birch, T. (ed.) *The Works of the Honourable Robert Boyle* (1772)

Boyle, R., Earl of Orrery *A Treatise of the Art of War: Dedicated to the King's Most Excellent Majesty* (1677)

Bridges, J. *The History and Antiquities of Northamptonshire* (1791)

Browne, E. *A Journal of a Visit to Paris in the year 1664*, ed. G. Keynes (John Murray, 1923)

Burnet, G. *The History of My Own Times* (1833 edn.)

Campbell, C. *Vitruvius Britannicus, or the British Architect* (1717–25)

Carpenter, N. *Geography Delineated Forth in Two Bookes* (1625)

Charleton, W. *The Immortality of the Human Soul Demonstrated by the Light of Nature* (1657)

Chauncey, H. *History of Hertfordshire* (1700)

Clutterbuck, R. *History and Antiquities of the County of Hertford* (1815–27)

Colvin, H. M. & Newman, J. (eds.) *Of Building: Roger North's Writings on Architecture* (Clarendon Press, 1981)

Cooper, A. A., 3rd Earl of Shaftesbury *Second Characters: or, the Language of Forms*, ed. Benjamin Rand (CUP, 1914)

Crawford, D. (ed.) *Journals of Sir John Lauder, Lord Fountainhall, with his Observations on Public Affairs and other memoranda, 1665–1676* (Edinburgh University Press, 1900)

Dalrymple, J. *Memoirs of Great Britain and Ireland* (1771–88)

Defoe, D. *A Tour through England and Wales* (J. M. Dent, n.d.)

Digges, T. *A Prognostication everlastinge . . . Published by Leonard Digges Gentleman. Lately corrected and augmented by Thomas Digges, his sonne* (1576)

Evelyn, J. *The Diary of John Evelyn*, ed. William Bray (Simpkin, Marshall, Hamilton, Kent & Co., n.d.)

Evelyn, J. *London Revived: Consideration for its Rebuilding in 1666*, ed. E. S. De Beer (Clarendon Press, 1938)

Evelyn, J. *A Parallel of the Antient Architecture with the Modern* (1707 edn.)

Ferrier, R. *The Journal of Major Richard Ferrier MP, while travelling in France in the year 1687* (Camden Miscellany, N.S. 53, IX, 1895)

Forrester, J. *The Polite Philosopher, or, An Essay on that Art which makes a Man happy in himself, and agreeable to others* (1734)

Foster, S. 'Of the Planetary Instruments', *Miscellanies of Mr Samuel Foster* (1659)

Gadbury, J. *De cometis: or, A Discourse of the Natures and Effects of Comets* (1665)

Gunther, R. T. (ed.) *The Architecture of Sir Roger Pratt* (OUP, 1928)

Gunther, R. T. (ed.) 'Robert Hooke's Diary, 1688 to 1693', *Early Science in Oxford* X (1935)

Hall, A. R. & Hall, M. B. *The Correspondence of Henry Oldenburg* (University of Wisconsin Press/Taylor & Francis, 1965–86)

Hatton, E. *A New View of London* (1708)

Hawksmoor, N. *Remarks on the Founding and Carrying on the Buildings of the Royal Hospital at Greenwich* (1728)

Heylyn, P. *A full relation of two journeys: the one into the Main-Land of France; the other into some of the adjacent Islands* (1656)

Hillaby, J. (ed.) *The Journeys of Celia Fiennes* (Macdonald & Co., 1983)

Holder, W. *A discourse concerning time . . .* (1694)

Hooke, R. *Micrographia* (1665)

Howell, J. *Epistolae Ho-Ellianae, Familiar Letters, domestic and forren . . .* (1645)

Hutchins, J. *The History and Antiquities of the County of Dorset* (1774)

Jessop, A. (ed.) *The Lives of the Norths* (1890)

Lawson-Dick, O. (ed.) *Aubrey's Brief Lives* (Mandarin, 1992)

Lister, M. *A Journey to Paris in the Year 1698* (1699 edn.)

Lough, J. (ed.) *Locke's Travels in France, 1675–1679* (CUP, 1953)

Luttrell, N. *A Brief Historical Relation of State Affairs from September 1678 to April 1714* (OUP, 1857)

Malcolm, J. *Londinium Redivivum* (1807)

Marcus Manilius *Astronomica*, trans. G. R. Goold (Harvard University Press, 1977)

Miége, G. *The New State of England* (1691)

Milman, H. H. *Annals of St. Paul's Cathedral* (1869)

Milward, J. *Diary*, ed. C. Robbins (CUP, 1938)

de Monconys, B. *Journal des voyages . . .* (1665–6)

Morgan, M. H. (ed.) *Vitruvius: The Ten Books of Architecture* (Dover, 1960)

Oughtred, W. *Clavis mathematicae denvo limata . . .* (1652)

Peacham, H. *The Compleat Gentleman* (1634 edn.)

Pepys, S. *The Diary of Samuel Pepys*, ed. Henry B. Wheatley (G. Bell & Sons, 1920)

Plot, R. *The Natural History of Oxfordshire* (1677)

Pope, W. *The Life of Seth, Lord Bishop of Salisbury* (1697; Luttrell Society reprint, 1961)

Price, U. *Essays on the Picturesque* (1810 edn.)

Pugin, A. W. N. *Contrasts* (1841 edn.)

Ralph, B. *A Critical Review of the publick buildings, statues and ornaments in and about London and Westminster, etc.* (1734)

Reynolds, J. *Literary Works* (1819 edn.)

Robarts, F. *Gods holy house and service* (1639)

Robinson, H. W. 'An unpublished letter of Dr Seth Ward relating to the early meetings of the Oxford Philosophical Society', *Notes and Records of the Royal Society* VII (1949), 68–70

Robinson, H. W. & Adams, W. (eds.) *The Diary of Robert Hooke 1672–1680* (Taylor & Francis, 1935)

Ross, A. *Arcana microcosmi* (1651)

Ruskin, J. *The Seven Lamps of Architecture* (Everyman, 1940 edn.)

Ruskin, J. *The Stones of Venice* (1851–3)

Shadwell, T. *The Virtuoso*, ed. M. H. Nicolson & D. S. Rodes (University of Nebraska Press, 1966)

Simpson, W. S. (ed.) *Documents Illustrating the History of St Paul's Cathedral* (1880)

Sisson, H. (ed.) *The English Sermon 1650–1750* (Carcanet Press, 1976)

Skinner, R. *A sermon preached before the king at Whitehall* (1634)

Sorbière, S. *A Voyage to England . . . done into English from the French Original* (1709)

South, R. *Discourses on Various Subjects and Occasions* (1827)

Sprat, T. *The History of the Royal Society of London* (1667)

Sprat, T. *Observations on Mons de Sorbière's Voyage into England, written to Dr Wren, Professor of Astronomy in Oxford* (1708 edn.)

Thomson, G. *Loimotomia, or the Pest Anatomized* (1666)

Turner, J. *Pallas Armata: Military Essayes of the Ancient Grecian, Roman, and Modern Art of War, Written in the years 1670 and 1671* (1683)

Vincent, T. *God's Terrible Voice in the City* (1667)

Waller, R. (ed.) *The Posthumous Works of Robert Hooke* (1705)

Wallis, J. *Defence of the Royal Society* (1678)

Ward, E. *The London Spy: The Vanities and Vices of the Town Exposed to View*, ed. Arthur L. Hayward (Cassell, 1927)

Ward, G. R. M. (trans.) *Oxford University Statutes* (1845–51)

Ward, J. *The Lives of the Professors of Gresham College* (1740)

Ward, S. *Vindiciae Academiarum* (1654)

Webb, G. (ed.) *The Works of John Vanbrugh* (Nonesuch Press, 1928)

Wilkins, J. *The Mathematical and Philosophical Works* (1708)

Willis, T. *The Anatomy of the Brain and Nerves*, ed. W. Feindel (McGill University Press, 1965)

Wood, A. *Fasti Oxonienses*, ed. Philip Bliss (1815–20)

Wood, A. *The History and Antiquities of the University of Oxford*, ed. John Gutch (1792–6)

Wood, A. *Life and Times* (OUP, 1961)

Wotton, H. *The Elements of Architecture* (1624)

SECONDARY SOURCES

Addleshaw, G. W. O. & Etchells, F. *The Architectural Setting of Anglican Worship* (Faber & Faber, 1948)

Allen, B. S. *Tides in English Taste* (Harvard University Press, 1937)

Allen, P. 'Scientific Studies in the English Universities of the Seventeenth Century', *Journal of the History of Ideas* X (1949), 219–53

Andrade, E. N. da C. 'Robert Hooke, FRS (1635–1703)', *Notes and Records of the Royal Society* XV (1960), 137–45

Bell, W. G. *The Great Plague in London in 1665* (John Lane, 1924)

Bennett, J. A. 'A Note on Theories of Respiration and Muscular Action in England *c*. 1660', *Medical History* XX (1970), 59–69

Besant, W. *London in the Time of the Stuarts* (A. & C. Black, 1903)

Blomfield, R. *A Short History of Renaissance Architecture in England 1500–1800* (George Bell, 1900)

Bowen, E. J. & Hartley, H. 'The Right Reverend John Wilkins, FRS', *Notes and Records of the Royal Society* XV (1960), 47-56

Brown, H. *Scientific Organisations in Seventeenth-Century France* (Williams & Wilkins, 1934)

Bumpus, T. F. *Ancient London Churches* (T. Werner Laurie, 1923)

Cathedrals (Great Western Railway, 1925)

Claydon, A. *A Guide to East Knoyle Church* (East Knoyle Parochial Church Council, 1996)

Colvin, H. M. *A Biographical Dictionary of British Architects 1600–1840* (John Murray, 1978)

Colvin, H. M. (ed.) *The History of the King's Works* V (HMSO, 1976)

Colvin, H. M. *The Sheldonian Theatre and the Divinity School* (OUP, 1981)

Copeman, W. S. C. 'Dr Jonathan Goddard, FRS (1617–1675)', *Notes and Records of the Royal Society* XV (1960), 69–77

Dean, C. G. T. *The Royal Hospital Chelsea* (Hutchinson, 1950)

Dewhurst, K. *Thomas Willis as a Physician* (William Andrews Clark Memorial Library, 1964)

Downes, K. *Hawksmoor* (Thames & Hudson, 1970)

Downes, K. *Sir John Vanbrugh* (Sidgwick & Jackson, 1987)

Ellis, A. *The Penny Universities: a History of the Coffee-Houses* (Secker & Warburg, 1956)

'Espinasse, M. *Robert Hooke* (Heinemann, 1956)

Fellows, R. A. *Sir Reginald Blomfield: An Edwardian Architect* (Zwemmer, 1985)

Finch, P. *A History of Burley-on-the-Hill, Rutland* (J. Bale, Sons & Danielsson, 1901)

Fincham, K. (ed.) *The Early Stuart Church, 1603–1642* (Macmillan, 1993)

Firth, C. H. *Cromwell's Army* (Greenhill, 1992)

Frank, R. G. 'Institutional Structure and Scientific Activity in the Early Royal Society', *Proceedings of the XIVth International Congress of the History of Science* (1974), 82–101

Genuth, S. S. *Comets, Popular Culture and the Birth of Modern Cosmology* (Princeton University Press, 1997)

Gotch, J. A. *The Growth of the English House* (Batsford, 1909)

Gould, C. *Bernini in France* (Weidenfeld & Nicolson, 1981)

Green, D. *Blenheim Palace* (Country Life, 1951)

Hall, A. R. *The Scientific Revolution 1500–1800* (Longmans, Green & Co., 1954)

Houghton, W. E. 'The English Virtuoso in the Seventeenth Century', *Journal of the History of Ideas* III–IV (1942), 51–73, 190–219

Hunter, M. *Establishing the New Science* (Boydell Press, 1989)

Hunter, M. *The Royal Society and its Fellows 1660–1700* (British Society for the History of Science, 1982)

Hunter, M. *Science and Society in Restoration England* (CUP, 1981)

Hunter, M. *Science and the Shape of Orthodoxy: Intellectual Change in Late Seventeenth-Century Britain* (Boydell Press, 1995)

Impey, O. & MacGregor, A. *The Origins of Museums: The Cabinet of Curiosities in Sixteenth- and Seventeenth-Century Europe* (Clarendon Press, 1985)

Jardine, L. *Ingenious Pursuits* (Little, Brown, 1999)

Keevil, J. J. 'Sir Charles Scarburgh', *Annals of Science* VIII (1952), 113–21

Lang, J. *Rebuilding St Paul's* (OUP, 1956)

Law, E. *The History of Hampton Court Palace* (1891)

Lees-Milne, J. *English Country Houses: Baroque* (Country Life, 1970)

Lillywhite, B. *London Coffee Houses* (George Allen & Unwin, 1963)

Lloyd, C. 'Shadwell and the Virtuosi', *Publications of the Modern Language Association of America* XLIV (1929), 472–94

Lough, J. (ed.) *France Observed in the Seventeenth Century by British Travellers* (Oriel Press, 1984)

Lyons, H. *The Royal Society 1660–1940* (CUP, 1944)

Martin, D. C. 'Sir Robert Moray, FRS', *Notes and Records of the Royal Society* XV (1960), 239-50

Macaulay, T. B. *The History of England from the Accession of James II* (1849-61)

McKie, D. 'The Origins and Foundation of the Royal Society of London', *Notes and Records of the Royal Society* XV (1960), 1–37

McKitterick, D. (ed.) *The Making of the Wren Library* (CUP, 1995)

McParland, E. *The Royal Hospital Kilmainham, Co. Dublin* (offprint from *Country Life*, 9 May 1985)

Middleton, W. E. K. *The History of the Barometer* (John Hopkins Press, 1964)

Miller, J. *The Life and Times of William and Mary* (Weidenfeld & Nicolson, 1974)

Moore, P. & Hunt, G. *The Atlas of the Solar System* (Chancellor Press, 1997)

Mowl, T. & Earnshaw, B. *Architecture Without Kings: the Rise of Puritan Classicism under Cromwell* (Manchester University Press, 1995)

Mulligan, L. & Mulligan, G. 'Reconstructing Restoration Science: Styles of Leadership and Social Composition of the Early Royal Society', *Social Studies of Science* XI (1981), 327–64

Picard, L. *Restoration London* (Weidenfeld & Nicolson, 1997)

Reddaway, T. F. 'The London Custom House 1666–1740', *London Topographical Record* XXI (1958)

Reddaway, T. F. *The Rebuilding of London after the Great Fire* (Jonathan Cape, 1940)

Ronan, C. A. & Hartley, H. 'Sir Paul Neile FRS (1613–1686)', *Notes and Records of the Royal Society* XV (1960), 159–65

Scriba, C. J. 'The Autobiography of John Wallis', *Notes and Records of the Royal Society* XXV (1970)

Stimson, D. *Scientists and Amateurs* (Sigma, 1949)

Summerson, J. *Architecture in Britain 1530–1830* (Penguin, 1977)

Syfret, R. H. 'Some Early Critics of the Royal Society', *Notes and Records of the Royal Society* VIII (1951), 20–64

Turnbull, G. H. 'Samuel Hartlib's Influence on the Early History of the Royal Society', *Notes and Records of the Royal Society* X (1953), 101–30

Turner, A. J. 'Mathematical Instruments and the Education of Gentlemen', *Annals of Science* XXX (1973), 51–88

Tyacke, N. (ed.) *The History of the University of Oxford* IV: *Seventeenth-Century Oxford* (Clarendon Press, 1997)

Waters, D. W. *The Art of Navigation in England in Elizabethan and Early Stuart Times* (Hollis & Carter, 1958)

Watkin, D. *The Life and Work of C. R. Cockerell* (Zwemmer, 1974)

Waylen, J. 'Christopher Wren of East Knoyle, DD', *Wiltshire Archaeological Society* III (1857)

Webster, C. *The Great Instauration: Science, Medicine and Reform 1626–1660* (Duckworth, 1975)

Webster, C. 'The Helmontian George Thomson and William Harvey: the Revival and Application of Splenectomy to Physiological Research', *Medical History* XV (1971), 154–67

Whistler, L. *The Imagination of Vanbrugh and his Fellow Artists* (Batsford, 1954)

Whiteside, D. T. 'Before the *Principia*: the maturing of Newton's thoughts on dynamical astronomy', *Journal for the History of Astronomy* I (1970), 5–19

Wittkower, R. *Palladio and English Palladianism* (Thames & Hudson, 1983)

Index